Web Mining:
Applications
and Techniques

Anthony Scime
State University of New York College at Brockport, USA

IDEA GROUP PUBLISHING
Hershey • London • Melbourne • Singapore

Acquisitions Editor:	Mehdi Khosrow-Pour
Senior Managing Editor:	Jan Travers
Managing Editor:	Amanda Appicello
Development Editor:	Michele Rossi
Copy Editor:	Ingrid Widitz
Typesetter:	Jennifer Wetzel
Cover Design:	Lisa Tosheff
Printed at:	Yurchak Printing Inc.

Published in the United States of America by
> Idea Group Publishing (an imprint of Idea Group Inc.)
> 701 E. Chocolate Avenue, Suite 200
> Hershey PA 17033
> Tel: 717-533-8845
> Fax: 717-533-8661
> E-mail: cust@idea-group.com
> Web site: http://www.idea-group.com

and in the United Kingdom by
> Idea Group Publishing (an imprint of Idea Group Inc.)
> 3 Henrietta Street
> Covent Garden
> London WC2E 8LU
> Tel: 44 20 7240 0856
> Fax: 44 20 7379 3313
> Web site: http://www.eurospan.co.uk

Library of Congress Cataloging-in-Publication Data

Web mining : applications and techniques / Anthony Scime, Editor.
    p. cm.
 ISBN 1-59140-414-2 -- ISBN 1-59140-415-0 (ppb) -- ISBN 1-59140-416-9 (ebook)
1. Data mining. 2. Web databases. I. Scime, Anthony.
QA76.76.E95W43 2004
006.3'12--dc22
                                    2004003756

British Cataloguing in Publication Data
A Cataloguing in Publication record for this book is available from the British Library.

All work contributed to this book is new, previously-unpublished material. The views expressed in this book are those of the authors, but not necessarily of the publisher.

Web Mining:
Applications and Techniques

Table of Contents

Section I: Introduction

> *Gilbert W. Laware, Purdue University, USA*

> *Penelope Markellou, University of Patras, Greece and Research Academic*
> *Computer Technology Institute, Greece*
> *Maria Rigou, University of Patras, Greece and Research Academic*
> *Computer Technology Institute, Greece*
> *Spiros Sirmakessis, University of Patras, Greece and Research Academic*
> *Computer Technology Institute, Greece*

Section II: Content Mining

> *Fan Wu, National Chung-Cheng University, Taiwan*
> *Ching-Chi Hsu, Institute for Information Industry, Taiwan*

> *Roberto Navigli, University of Rome "La Sapienza", Italy*

> *Xiannong Meng, Bucknell University, USA*
> *Zhixiang Chen, The University of Texas - Pan American, USA*

Section V: Conclusion

Preface

Web mining is moving the World Wide Web toward a more useful environment in which users can quickly and easily find the information they need. It includes the discovery and analysis of data, documents, and multimedia from the World Wide Web. Web mining uses document content, hyperlink structure, and usage statistics to assist users in meeting their information needs.

The Web itself and search engines contain relationship information about documents. Web mining is the discovery of these relationships and is accomplished within three sometimes overlapping areas. Content mining is first. Search engines define content by keywords. Finding contents' keywords and finding the relationship between a Web page's content and a user's query content is content mining. Hyperlinks provide information about other documents on the Web thought to be important to another document. These links add depth to the document, providing the multi-dimensionality that characterizes the Web. Mining this link structure is the second area of Web mining. Finally, there is a relationship to other documents on the Web that are identified by previous searches. These relationships are recorded in logs of searches and accesses. Mining these logs is the third area of Web mining.

Understanding the user is also an important part of Web mining. Analysis of the user's previous sessions, preferred display of information, and expressed preferences may influence the Web pages returned in response to a query.

Web mining is interdisciplinary in nature, spanning across such fields as information retrieval, natural language processing, information extraction, machine learning, database, data mining, data warehousing, user interface design, and visualization. Techniques for mining the Web have practical application in m-commerce, e-commerce, e-government, e-learning, distance learning, organizational learning, virtual organizations, knowledge management, and digital libraries.

BOOK OBJECTIVE

This book aims to provide a record of current research and practical applications in Web searching. This includes techniques that will improve the utilization of the Web by the design of Websites, as well as the design and application of search agents. This book presents this research and related applications in a manner that encourages additional work toward improving the reduction of information overflow that is so common today in Web search results.

AUDIENCE

Researchers and students in the fields of information and knowledge creation, storage, dissemination, and retrieval in various disciplines will find this book a starting point for new research. Developers and managers of Web technologies involved with content development, storage, and retrieval will be able to use this book to advance the state of the art in Web utilization.

ORGANIZATION OF THE BOOK

In any Web search effort the user wants information. To find information the search engine must be able to understand the intent of the user and the intent of the Web page author. Chapter I, "Metadata Management: A Requirement for Web Warehousing and Knowledge Management" by Gilbert Laware, brings into focus why Web mining is important and what is important to Web mining.

Understanding the user's intent leads to personalization of search. Personalization can influence user search results, and through collaboration, the results of others. Personalization spans the divisions of Web mining. Chapter II, "Mining for Web Personalization" by Penelope Markellou, Maria Rigou, and Spiros Sirmakessis, provides an introduction to this important area. Other chapters discussing personalization issues are Chapters III, V, XI, XIII, XIV, XVII, XVIII, and XIX.

In keeping with the three primary areas of Web mining the remaining chapters are organized in sections on content, structure, and usage.

Section II presents content mining. Content mining extracts and compares concepts from the content of Web pages and queries. Information retrieval techniques are applied to unstructured, semi-structured, and structured Web pages to find and rank pages in accordance with the user's information need.

In Chapter III, "Using Context Information to Build a Topic-Specific Crawling System," Fan Wu and Ching-Chi Hsu discuss several important criteria to measure the relevancy of Web pages to a given topic. This includes rank ordering the pages based on a relevancy context graph.

This is followed by "Ontology Learning from a Domain Web Corpus" from Roberto Navigli (Chapter IV), which describes a methodology for learning domain ontologies from a specialized Web corpus. This methodology extracts a terminology, provides a semantic interpretation of relevant terms, and populates the domain ontology automatically.

Chapter V, "MARS: Multiplicative Adaptive Refinement Web Search" by Xiannong Meng and Zhixiang Chen, applies a new multiplicative adaptive algorithm for user preference retrieval to Web searches. This algorithm uses a multiplicative query expansion strategy to adaptively improve and reformulate the query vector to learn the user's information preference.

Chapter VI, Neil C. Rowe's "Exploiting Captions for Web Data Mining," presents an indirect approach to indexing multimedia objects on Web pages by using captions.

This novel approach is useful because text is much easier for search engines to understand than multimedia, and captions often express the document's key points.

"Towards a Danger Theory Inspired Artificial Immune System for Web Mining" by Andrew Secker, Alex A. Freitas, and Jon Timmis is Chapter VII. As part of a larger project to construct a dynamic Web content mining system, the Artificial Immune System for E-mail Classification (AISEC) is described in detail.

Chapter VIII, "XML Semantics" by Yasser Kotb, Katsuhiko Gondow and Takuya Katayama, introduces a novel technique to add semantics to XML documents by attaching semantic information to the XML element tag attributes. This approach is based on the same concept used by attribute grammars in attaching and checking static semantics of programming languages.

Existing classifiers built on flat files or databases are infeasible for classifying large data sets due to the necessity for multiple passes over the original data. "Classification on Top of Data Cube" by Lixin Fu, Chapter IX, gives a new approach for classification by designing three new classifiers on top of a data cube for both transactional and analytical purposes.

Structure mining, Section III, is concerned with the discovery of information through the analysis of Web page in and out links. This type of analysis can establish the authority of a Web page, help in page categorization, and assist in personalization.

In Chapter X, "Data Cleansing and Validation for Multiple Site Link Structure Analysis," Mike Thelwall provides a range of techniques for cleansing and validating link data for use in Web structure mining. He uses multiple site link structure analysis to mine patterns from themed collections of Websites.

Mohamed Salah Hamdi's "Extracting and Customizing Information Using Multi-Agents," Chapter XI, discusses the challenge of complex environments and the information overload problem. To cope with such environments and problems, he customizes the retrieval system using a multi-agent paradigm.

The Web is a graph that needs to be navigated. Chapter XII, "Web Graph Clustering for Displays and Navigation of Cyberspace" by Xiaodi Huang and Wei Lai, presents a new approach to clustering graphs, and applies it to Web graph display and navigation. The approach takes advantage of the linkage patterns of graphs, and utilizes an affinity function in conjunction with k-nearest neighbor.

Section IV on usage mining applies data mining and other techniques to discover patterns in Web logs. This is useful when defining collaboration between users and refining user personal preferences.

Web usage mining has been used effectively as an approach to automatic personalization and as a way to overcome deficiencies of traditional approaches such as collaborative filtering. Chapter XIII, "Integrating Semantic Knowledge with Web Usage Mining for Personalization" by Honghua Dai and Bamshad Mobasher, discusses the issues and requirements for successful integration of semantic knowledge from different sources, including the content and the structure of Websites. Presented is a general framework for fully integrating domain ontologies with Web usage mining and personalization processes using preprocessing and pattern discovery.

Search engine logs not only keep navigation information, but also the queries made by users. In particular, queries to a search engine follow a power-law distribution, which is far from uniform. Queries and user clicks can be used to improve the search engine user interface, index performance, and results ranking. Ricardo Baeza-Yates in Chapter XIV, "Web Usage Mining in Search Engines," presents these issues.

Efficient mining of frequent traversal path patterns, that is, large reference sequences of maximal forward references from very large Web logs, is a fundamental problem in Web mining. Chapter XV, "Efficient Web Mining for Traversal Path Patterns" by Zhixiang Chen, Richard H. Fowler, Ada Wai-Chee Fu, and Chunyue Wang, discusses two new algorithms to solve this problem.

"Analysis of Document Viewing Patterns of Web Search Engine Users," Chapter XVI by Bernard J. Jansen and Amanda Spink, discusses viewing patterns of Web results pages and Web pages by search engine users. This chapter presents the advantages of using traditional transaction log analysis in identifying these patterns.

Chapter XVII, "A Java Technology Based Distributed Software Architecture for Web Usage Mining" by Juan M. Hernansáez, Juan A. Botía, and Antonio F.G. Skarmeta reviews a technique of each of the Web usage mining approaches: clustering, association rules, and sequential patterns. These techniques are integrated into the learning architecture, METALA.

In Chapter XVIII, "Web Usage Mining: Algorithms and Results," Yew-Kwong Woon, Wee-Keong Ng, and Ee-Peng Lim focus on mining Web access logs, analyzing algorithms for preprocessing and extracting knowledge from such logs, and proposing techniques to mine the logs in a holistic manner.

We conclude the book with one chapter in Section V, a summary of Web mining and personalization and their application in another part of the Internet. Chapter XIX, "The Scent of a Newsgroup: Providing Personalized Access to Usenet Sites through Web Mining," by Giuseppe Manco, Riccardo Ortale, and Andrea Tagarelli discusses the application of Web mining techniques to the problem of providing personalized access to Usenet services. It focuses on the analysis of the three main areas of Web mining techniques: content mining, in which particular emphasis is posed to topic discovery and maintenance; structure mining, in which the structure of Usenet news is studied by exploiting structure mining techniques; and usage mining, in which techniques for tracking and profiling users' behavior are devised by analyzing access logs. The chapter ends with an overview of personalization techniques, and the description of a specific personalization method to the case of Usenet access.

Acknowledgments

Completion of this book is due to the contributions of many people. I first thank the authors for their research and resulting chapters. Also, I am most grateful to the reviewers. Each chapter underwent a blind review by three referees, and their comments and suggestions led to chapter selection and improvement. Special thanks go to the staff at Idea Group Publishing, especially to Mehdi Khosrow-Pour, Jan Travers, Michele Rossi, Amanda Appicello, and Jennifer Sundstrom. Finally, I thank my wife and sons for their love and support during this project.

Anthony Scime
Editor
February 2004

SECTION I

INTRODUCTION

Chapter I

Metadata Management:
A Requirement for
Web Warehousing and
Knowledge Management

Gilbert W. Laware
Purdue University, USA

ABSTRACT

This chapter introduces the need for the World Wide Web to provide a standard mechanism so individuals can readily obtain data, reports, research and knowledge about any topic posted to it. Individuals have been frustrated by this process since they are not able to access relevant data and current information. Much of the reason for this lies with metadata, the data about the data that are used in support of Web content. These metadata are non-existent, ill-defined, erroneously labeled, or, if well-defined, continue to be marked by other disparate metadata. With the ever-increasing demand for Web-enabled data mining, warehousing and management of knowledge, an organization has to address the multiple facets of process, standards, technology, data mining, and warehousing management. This requires approaches to provide an integrated interchange of quality metadata that enables individuals to access Web content with the most relevant, contemporary data, information, and knowledge that are both content-rich and practical for decision-making situations.

INTRODUCTION

Today, many of us use computers and the World Wide Web to communicate. We enter a Website name or address (www.informationbydesign.biz, www.ibm.com, www.tech.purdue.edu) into a browser on our desktop computer, where a unique numerical number replaces the words representing the Website name or address. It is analogous to a telephone number. We then are connected immediately to another computer assigned a numerical address somewhere on the World Wide Web. This allows us to access any document (Web page) on that computer. The Internet is capable of connecting us with any computer anywhere in the world. This computer sends the Web page we have requested from its Internet address to our desktop computer, where it is displayed using our browser. In most cases, the returned Web page is written in English and we are able to understand its content. But, if the Web page is written in another language, we would need an interpreter to understand its content. In a telephone analogy — if a person who responds to our telephone call speaks another language, then what is said may not have any meaning to the caller. If the information that describes the currency, content, and location of the Web page or telephone number is erroneous, it is of little value.

Now, in a different way, let's consider the reason why it is difficult for computer systems to communicate and to share data. First, the data often have been structured differently in one system than in another. This is particularly true with older application systems. Second, the data may not be stored in the same format (i.e., they are in a numerical format rather than in text format). Third, the name for the data may be different, causing a problem in identification or recognition of what they represent between systems. Last, the values of the data stored may be inconsistent between the systems. Technically, the programs in each system can be interconnected if they are designed, defined, and structured logically and physically for that purpose. But, each of the above items has to be evaluated for possible integration and sharing of the data between the systems if that is not the case.

One of the most common problems is that identical data are named differently in different systems. All too often, different names or terms refer to the same data that need to be shared. For example, a human resources system may use the term *employee* or *candidate* to refer to a person. An ordering system may refer to a person or an organization as a *customer*. In a sales system, the term may be *prospect, client, or customer*. Each system may use different terminology — a different language in a sense — to refer to similar or identical data. But if they use the wrong language, again, the systems cannot share the data to provide required information.

The problem can be even worse. Consider terms used in different parts of a business. Accountants use jargon — a technical language — that is difficult for non-accountants to understand. Similar terms used by individuals in engineering, production, sales, or in marketing may have different meanings. Likewise, managers may use another vocabulary. Each speaks a slightly different language and uses the same words in different ways. What is said may have no meaning without a common definition and so they cannot easily share common information. Each organization has its own internal language and jargon that becomes part of the subculture that evolves over time and is a key part of the way individuals communicate. In fact, in some organizations it is a miracle that people manage to communicate meaning at all!

As we saw above, there can be more than one language used in an organization. Metadata, the data about the data, identifies and uses their organization's own language. Where different terms refer to the same thing, a common term is agreed upon by all to use. Then people can communicate clearly. The same is true in the use of systems. Systems and programs intercommunicate when there is understanding and meaning between them. But without a clear definition and without common use of an organization's metadata, information cannot be shared effectively throughout the enterprise.

Previously we discussed how each part of an organization maintains its own version of customer, client, or prospect data. Each defines processes (a series of actions) — and assigns staff (persons) — to add new customers, clients or prospects to their own files and databases. When common details about customers, clients or prospects change, each redundant version of that data also has to be changed, requiring staff to make these changes. But, wait a minute, how about the metadata? They are also a consideration. Both the organizational and technical metadata may be affected and may also be redundant. This is the same rationale for reusable programs! These are all redundant processes that make use of redundant data and metadata. This is enormously expensive in both time and people — all quite unnecessary.

So, as metadata gains prominence, the process of managing metadata becomes critical since it becomes the common language used within an organization for people, systems and programs to communicate precisely. Confusion disappears. Common data are shared. Enormous cost savings can be made since it means that redundant processes (used to keep up-to-date redundant data) are eliminated as redundant data versions are integrated into a common version for all to share.

BACKGROUND

The mission statement of the Data Administration Management Association is to deliver the right data to the right person at the right time. This is a concept that has been around Information Resource Management (IRM) for years (Burk & Horton, Jr., 1988). Data are proclaimed to be an enterprise asset but little management of that asset has occurred. As a result, the world is made up of much disparate data and metadata, resulting in erroneous information being used in decision-making.

From a computing systems perspective, disparate data and metadata have also been around for years. It started with the early development of computing systems. Much of the data about data (their format and structure) was packaged within programming languages and their supporting technology. With the development of database management systems, these same technical metadata were incorporated into the database management system's catalog or dictionary. This content became known as *metadata*. They are needed by all systems.

Metadata is more than just a means for technological implementation. It is much broader in scope. Metadata embraces the fundamental data that are needed to define requirements. It is the information (metadata) that is used to design a product, understand business processes, provide information access, obtain data understanding, outline the rules applying to actions and data, and ultimately, make business decisions. In this context, metadata encompasses many aspects of an organization: its processes, organizational structure, technologies, motivations and, certainly, the format, structure, and context of data required to meet informational needs.

So, What are Metadata?

Let us examine the definition of metadata. This requires us to examine the meaning of data, information, and knowledge. These three terms need to be defined for the purpose of this discussion because of their key role in today's organizational environment.

- *Data.* Discrete facts that are represented in some symbolic way and are recorded in many different formats. By themselves, data may have little meaning or use.
- *Information.* Data being used and interpreted by a person. The data are relevant and have a purpose in influencing or altering a person's decisions or behavior.
- *Knowledge.* Personal or organizational experience, value and insight gained from an applied use of information. It is actionable information that is relevant information available in the right place, time, and context to the person using it in a decision-making situation.

Together, these terms (DIKs) are fundamental to every organization's daily existence. They work closely together to build the foundation for knowledge management (KM) and the use of Web mining.

So, what is metadata and where do they fit? There are definitional differences of metadata among authors (e.g., Devlin, 1997; Inmon, 1992; Kimball, 1998; Loshin, 2001; Marco, 2003; Tannenbaum, 2002). These definitions differ either in basic purpose (administrative, structural or descriptive), depth and richness, or in specificity for a particular situation. As such, *metadata is our knowledge of data that we have interpreted as information in a particular decision-making situation.* Therefore, it is a continuum between data (facts) and knowledge (experience) used in a personal or organizational context.

Where does metadata fit? Without naming, defining, structuring, categorizing, standardizing, and storing both the data and metadata, the utility of Web mining, warehousing and KM is suspect. Why? Because it is the semantic bridging mechanism (requirements and specification for semantic data models) that enables effective information access and exchange to occur both internally and externally for organizations. It requires management.

There is Management

In a sense, management takes action to produce a certain effect. Management is the activity that embodies four major functions: planning, organizing, leading, and controlling. Planning function is the selection and prioritization of goals and the ways to obtain them. Organizing function assigns the responsibilities to individuals to perform work or actions to produce something (product or service). Leading uses influence to effectively motivate individuals to attain the goals desired. In controlling, work activities or actions are monitored and corrected as required to meet stated goals. By focusing on doing the right things, the organization chooses the right goals to be effective, and by doing things right the organization is making the best use of its resources, including data.

Management is the art of getting things done by taking action and using people to achieve the goals of the organization. These goals are clearly communicated to all the individuals who are involved in their implementation by providing the reasons the actions are performed in an organizational context. Peter Drucker made the point of how management has changed with the use of information technology. He states: "So far, for 50 years, Information Technology has centered on DATA — their collection, storage, transmission, and presentation. It has focused on the 'T' in 'IT'. The new information revolutions focus on the 'I'. They ask, 'What is the MEANING of information and its PURPOSE?' And this is leading rapidly to redefining the tasks to be done with the help of information and, with it, to redefining the institutions that do these tasks" (Drucker, 1999, p. 82). The process of making a choice and taking action is a decision.

Management uses business processes that combine information technologies and people in attaining the goals of the organization. As they become more knowledge-based, individuals must take more personal responsibility for contributing to the whole organization by understanding the objectives, the values, the measurements, and the performance required. They must communicate effectively and efficiently with their peers and the other professional knowledge workers with whom they interact. The outcome is that "Every knowledge worker in modern organization is an *executive* [italics added] if, by virtue of his position or knowledge, he is responsible for a contribution that materially affects the capacity of the organization to perform and to obtain results" (Drucker, 1989, p. 44). Drucker (1999a) stated that the most valuable assets of the 21st century company are its knowledge and its knowledge workers. Knowledge workers face interesting challenges to use data, information, and knowledge more effectively and efficiently. The executives and leaders who manage have different organizational perspectives. Each piece of metadata has core elements of a name, meaning, descriptive content, structure and overall context. All of theses elements are essential to create metadata that are universally acceptable.

Each organizational perspective must ensure that effective communication of DIKs occurs. Each dimension provides different management perspectives and implications. People have different skills, talents, and needs. They are organized in a way to achieve some goal in a business process. Each process has a set of business practices that are executed in well-defined steps in accordance with internally or externally accepted rules or conventions. Many of these practices, steps, and tasks are part of organizational systems and in many instances may be automated in computerized software applications. In other cases, the basic tools (i.e., hardware or software) become instrumental parts of our daily work activities. An important implication of this environment is that each individual should have an understanding of the meaning, context, naming, structure, and content of data, information, and knowledge that are represented in each organizational situation.

Figure 1. Organizational Perspectives Cause Different Metadata to be Captured

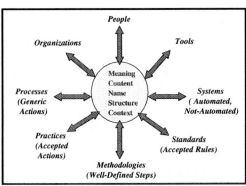

The Purpose of Decision-Making

The purpose of delivering information and knowledge content through the Web is for one critical purpose: to help an individual gather *DIKs* for making a decision. Therefore, one has to question the various assumptions used in decision-making. What business are we in? What should it be? What changes are necessary to get it to the next level? These questions are contextually meaningful for decision-making. They set the stage for determining excellence and the priorities of processes, practices, and methods needed to implement the desired strategy to achieve the goals. Decision-making involves making choices in taking action and is an important ingredient in the overall process. Today's knowledge workers understand their contribution to achieving a result and must concentrate on opportunities that provide a competitive advantage in a systematic, purposeful, and organized manner for the welfare of the overall organization within its environment.

From an organizational perspective, an organization creates capital by combining ideas, materials or both and transforming them into some product(s) or service(s) that are marketed or sold to its customers, as shown in Figure 2.

The organization uses explicit or implicit mission statements, sets objectives, and outlines goals for the benefit of the owners of the organization. It structures itself along the lines of traditional business functions: accounting, finance, development, manufacturing, marketing, sales, and distribution of its final product(s) or services(s).

An assumption that underlies decision-making situations in any organizational environment is that data, information, and knowledge applicable to a particular situation provide a factual representation of the environment used by the decision-maker(s) in assessing the options available. Unfortunately, this premise does not hold true, as evidenced by documented studies about the low quality of data (English, 1999; see also Brackett, 1996, 2000; Loshin, 2001). Inaccurate data can be found in 1-5% of the time while impacting costs from 8-12% of revenue (Redman, 1998). Others have stated that data quality contributed to reducing the GNP by .5% in the year 2000 (Mandel, 1998). Thomas Redman described 15 ideal characteristics for data quality (Redman, 1992) and suggested

Figure 2. Transforming Inputs into Product(s) or Services(s) in an Organization

Organizational Environment

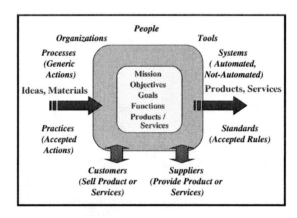

groupings of these attributes into three areas: conceptual (level of detail, view consistency, composition, robustness and flexibility), data value (accuracy, completeness, currency, and value-consistency), and data representation (appropriateness, interpretability, and portability) (Redman, 1996). By substituting the term metadata for data, the same characteristics are applicable in decision-making situations.

A human activity that is part of any leader or managerial role is decision-making. Henry Mintzberg (1971) described the characteristics of decision-making in a managerial role as an entrepreneur, disturbance handler, resource allocator, and negotiator. In each role, the use and quality of data, information, and knowledge are critical to understanding the problem, examining the options, and taking action. We use a decision rule or policy embedded in the world that we perceive from the data, information and knowledge that we have experienced. From a different perspective, Herbert Simon (1957) has best articulated the limits of human decision-making ability in his *principle of bounded rationality,* stating: "The capacity of the human mind for formulating and solving complex problems is very small compared with the size of the problem whose solution is required for objectively rational behavior in the real world or even for a reasonable approximation to such objective rationality" (p. 198). Faced with complexity in the real world and time pressures to make decisions, we fall back to habits, heuristics (rules of thumb), procedures or simple mental models to make a decision. This drives a critical requirement for quality data and information because it is paramount to producing the best possible results under the most stringent of time constraints and the critical need for high quality metadata. It has a tremendous impact on the processes used to collect, analyze, classify, standardize, translate, select, and distribute DIKs in a timely fashion to the organization and its collaborative parties.

With the introduction of the Internet and the World Wide Web, organizational boundaries have been significantly altered. This technology has enabled a global economy to develop in which any organization with its accountants, distributors,

Figure 3. Organizational Electronic Environment Increases Scope of Communications with Internet Technologies

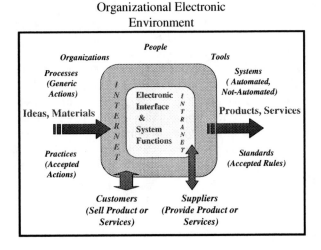

financiers, customers, manufacturers, or suppliers can operate without regard to physical and geographical boundaries. In this environment, the digital transmission of all types of data, information, and knowledge, regardless of their form (numbers, words, graphs, photos, voice, video, etc.) is electronically moved throughout the world, as in Figure 3.

Within an organization, the application of the Internet's protocol (TCP/IP) is called an intranet. This is where an organization maintains proprietary, confidential, or intellectual property-based DIKs. Using both intra/Internet technologies can provide an immediate access to internal and external data, information and knowledge. This makes the management of the metadata critical for the decision-making process since knowledge workers can have access to too much information that may or may not be relevant to the decision-making situation. In cases in which various collaborative partnerships exist between organizations, electronic transactions exist between customers (B2C) and between other privileged organizations (B2B) that can access your *DIKs*. This further emphasizes the need for a mentality within an organization that data, information, and knowledge are an asset.

The Need for Asset Mentality

Realizing that data, information, and knowledge are so critical to an organization's overall success, why have we not seen a more strategic approach to managing DIKs in an organization? Should data and metadata be considered an asset? An asset is defined as "a useful desirable thing or quality" (Braham, 1998, p. 26). An *intangible asset* is something valuable which a company possesses which is not material, such as a good reputation or a patent (Merriam-Webster, 2003). Both definitions describe some factor or circumstance that benefits the possessor (advantage) or is considered a resource (source of information or expertise).

Dow Chemical Corporation in 1993 (Davenport, p. 85) started to manage data and metadata as an intangible asset and turned them into an asset by managing their company's patent database. Dow claims that they saved more than $1 million in patent maintenance fees within the first 18 months. This example also illustrates the concept of intellectual capital (such as documented patents in databases) tied to knowledge available in a managed environment.

Historically, organizations have set up programs, policies, and procedures to support managing data and information as an asset, but for the most part, "information and data are identified assets without an associated management process" (Metcalfe, 1988. p. 19). This is due largely to the diversity of technologies, differing organizational and management directives, incompatibility of data development and their implementations, lack of integrated solutions, and evolutionary standards. Figure 4 shows the implications of missed organizational opportunities from a business perspective since the relationships between business objectives/goals and metadata have to be aligned.

Metadata is a mediator in the *DIKs* environment. A higher degree of alignment between metadata and business objectives/goals results in a more flexible, consistent, integrated, interoperable environment for an organization. The tremendous payoff for Dow Chemical illustrates this point.

Figure 4. Impact of Metadata Alignment with Business Objectives

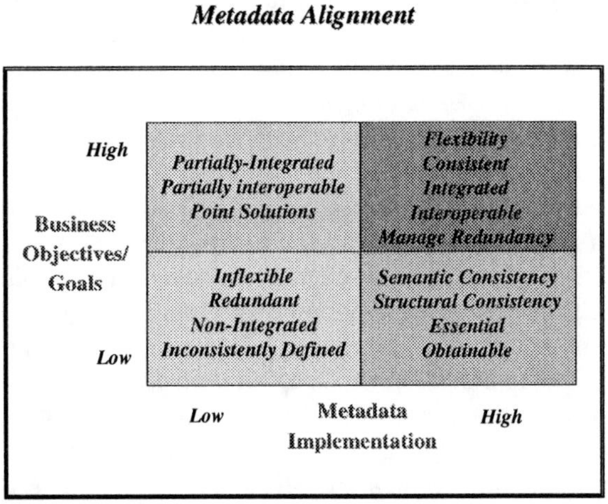

Metadata Alignment

High	*Partially-Integrated* *Partially interoperable* *Point Solutions*	*Flexibility* *Consistent* *Integrated* *Interoperable* *Manage Redundancy*
Business Objectives/ Goals		
Low	*Inflexible* *Redundant* *Non-Integrated* *Inconsistently Defined*	*Semantic Consistency* *Structural Consistency* *Essential* *Obtainable*
	Low	*High*

Metadata
Implementation

Need for Web Warehousing and Knowledge Management

Since data, information, and knowledge are so critical to an organization's overall operational success, Web mining, warehousing and KM are logical extensions of existing operational activities. In the quest for timely, accurate decisions, an essential element is to obtain the best DIKs possible to produce appropriate and effective courses of action.

The concept of Web warehousing originated with the development of data warehousing. W.H. Inmon (1992) defined data warehousing as a "subject-oriented, integrated, non-volatile, time variant collection of data in support of management's decisions" (p. 29). The only difference between data and Web warehousing is that in the latter, the underlying database is the entire World Wide Web. As a readily accessible resource, the Web is a huge data warehouse that contains volatile information that is gathered and extracted into something valuable for use in the organization situation. Using traditional data mining methodologies and techniques (TechReference, 2003), the Web mining is the process of extracting data from the Web and sorting them into identifiable patterns and relationships. Various data techniques of analysis determine:

- *Association.* A pattern exists in which one event is connected to another event
- *Sequence or path analysis.* A pattern exists in which one event leads to another later event
- *Classification.* A totally new pattern exists (develops a new structure)
- *Clustering.* Relates facts previously not known by finding and visually inspecting new groupings of data
- *Forecasting.* Predicting future conditions based on existing patterns in data

Given this sense of what Web mining is and warehousing is, what, then, is knowledge management (KM)?

Like metadata, knowledge management has multiple interpretations (Davenport, 1998; Firestone, 2003; Gates, 1999; Malhotra, 1998; Tiwana, 2001). Firestone (2003) provides a discussion of additional authors' treatment in the context of his definitions.

In this discussion, KM is *the embodiment of all management activities (in the handling, directing, governing, controlling, coordinating, planning, organizing, disseminating of data, metadata, information, and knowledge) in a planned, directed, unified whole for the purpose of producing, maintaining, enhancing, acquiring, and transmitting the enterprise's DIKs assets to meet organizational objectives and goals.* This definition is slightly different from Firestone's in that it encompasses data, metadata, information, and knowledge elements. The rationale for this distinction is the criticality of timely, accurate, quality-based information needed for organizational decision-making. In today's global market, maintaining an organization's knowledge base not only gives a competitive advantage, but is also necessary for its own survival. It is from this perspective that today's implementation of Web mining, warehousing and KM activities have to be closely aligned with management perspectives to ensure its success and the ultimate achievement of their goal.

With this New Environment

Without question, the development of Web technologies has been a great enabler to access data from worldwide sources. The growth of Internet hosted Websites continues to rise exponentially (Figure 5).

The Information and Research Division of InterGOV International indicated that online Web users in 2002 numbered 625 million, with an estimate that there will be 700 million in 2003 (InterGov, 2003). Currently hosted sites provide 3 billion Web pages (Sargent, 2003) with content. The Internet and its infrastructure can deliver a glut of information and data to a user. A million Web pages are added to the World Wide Web each day. If we also consider the volume of Intranet publications that occur each day, which is difficult to estimate, the Internet/intranet is a wonderful resource of useful *DIKs* to anyone accessing the Web.

Figure 5. Internet Hosted Sites Survey — An Historical Profile

Internet Hosted Web Sites

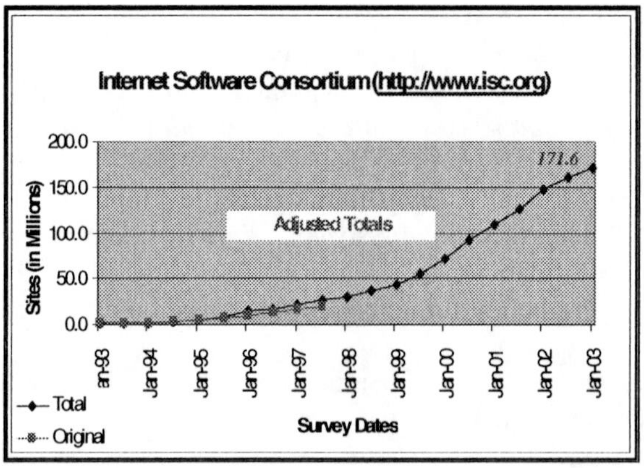

ISSUES, CONTROVERSIES, PROBLEMS

Internet/intranet Web page publications present some interesting issues, concerns and problems.

Ever-Increasing Proliferation of Redundant Data and their Disparate Metadata

Twenty years ago, if you needed certain information, you would drive to an excellent resource library. For example, you might ask the assistance of a highly skilled librarian for information on Peter F. Drucker's conclusions in his book: *Managing for Results.* Perhaps, in a couple of hours, you would receive the required information.

Today, using one of the Internet's most successful search engines, Google, you might formulate a search for information on "Peter Drucker". It returns a result with 99,700 possible Web pages to examine. If you refine your search to "Peter F. Drucker," the search gives 41,400 choices. Again, you might refine your search to "P.F. Drucker," resulting in 950 choices. If you just chose "Drucker," 1,820,000 referenced Web pages are returned. This illustrates the difficulty one has in assessing potential overlaps; currency of the content; material source generated whether from commercial, private, or foreign; or the possibility of mislabeled content. If you were interested in specific information from one of his books, *Managing for Results,* your next search would yield 20,700 possible references. This result allows you to get closer to your objective but still may not be sufficient since you might be interested in his chapter *The Commitment* (7,670 references) or finally, to his conclusion (2,870). The issue is the quality of the metadata that describe accurately the characteristics of the Web page. Even using a refined search process, it would take time and computing resources to get the required information sought. Much of the results from these searches might not contain what you require. This searching technique is illustrated in Figure 6.

Figure 6. Search Technique to Access Details on Managing Results by P.F. Drucker

Searching Techniques

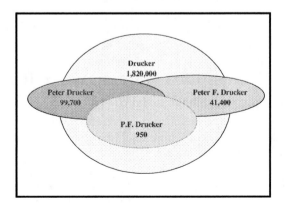

Without standardized metadata, an ever-increasing proliferation of redundant data and their disparate metadata is a key inhibitor to successful data, information, and knowledge integration.

This brings up the next point.

Management of Metadata has not been a Key Part of Data Management Implementations

In a review of the implementation of Information Resource Management (IRM) or Data Administration (DA) organizations and practices, the predecessors of Web warehousing and KM, there is little external evidence that corporations have valued these practices. Very few public success stories have documented the value of data administration or data management in organizations, since these activities are not considered part of the value chain that directly contributes to the profit or bottom line of the organization. Only recently at an Information Quality conference was there a claim by attendees of savings of over one-half (1/2) a billion dollars (English, 2003). The U.S. government, however, through the Clinger-Cohen Act of 1996, has driven governmental organizations to be much more proactive in setting up and adopting IRM-based programs in the public sector.

In an attempt to standardize metadata, a meeting hosted by the Online Computer Library Center, Inc. (OCLC), in Dublin, Ohio set up standards for Web page metadata documentation elements. This is similar to a library's catalog card: title, subject, author, publisher, other agent, data, object type, form, identifier, language, relation and coverage. But this is only an initial step in the evolution of Web standards for metadata delivery. Will these developing standards be successful in the management of metadata and the software tools to manage them?

Software Solutions do not Address the Management of Metadata

Commercialization of software to support various business applications has increased dramatically. But the commercialization of software to assist in developing, cleaning, and relationship standardization of data has not been a key market item or a commercial success. What is the reason? Is it the quality of the software or is it the organization's lack of recognition for the need to manage the metadata? Why should there be thousands of ways to collect personal contact information? Likewise, why have software standards not addressed the uniformity and interchange of data? We are just beginning to see commercialization of this type of software.

Lack of Support to Manage Data and Metadata Inhibits Successful Implementation Efforts

By far, the profit motive drives most commercial organizations to focus on maximizing revenue while minimizing costs. In the service sector, generating a profit requires maximizing the services while minimizing the cost of resources to produce that service. The implication of this heuristic is that anything not directly related to the actual production of the product or service is non-essential. Thus, any resource (data, metadata, etc.) that is consumed in the process that does not directly contribute to the end product or service has little or no added value. This references a mentality that leads to *redundant processes, redundant data and metadata* that actually inhibit long-term solutions.

SOLUTIONS AND RECOMMENDATIONS
Explicit Recognition that Data and Metadata are Assets

Until an accepted norm for evaluating the value of data in the world of accounting and finance is established, the recognition and management of data and metadata will continue to be difficult. Although many engineering practices are accounted for in the manufacturing of a product, the same accounting practices (GAAP, taxes, etc.) have to be applied to data, metadata, information, and knowledge. The concept of intellectual capital has to encompass all activities used in the development of DIKs. This would mean a shift in the management of data and metadata, allowing for the adoption of a framework to manage these assets.

Adaptation of a Framework for Managing Data, Information and Knowledge

Using a Web-enabled metadata data warehouse with an Organization Search Assistant System (Scime, 2000) begins to provide a framework to access current, relevant DIKs and serves as a foundation for expanding enterprise KM. In order to become an effective enterprise resource, these metadata need to be managed with the same vigor and enthusiasm as data. The information glut must be overcome with contextual information and management practices that provide competitive advantage to those who are decisive about its practice. Two essential items have to be addressed from a communication perspective:

*   *Collaboration.* A willingness to share, to cooperate, and to enhance subject DIKs
*   *Communities of Practice.* A sociological grouping of people whose interests and experience complement the KM process

Foremost in the enterprise environment is a concerted effort to ensure that collaborating is rewarded. In a sense, declarative knowledge has much in common with explicit knowledge in that it consists of descriptions of *what* tasks, methods and procedures are used. Procedural knowledge describes *how* to do something, and strategic knowledge is *knowing-when and knowing-why.* Collaboration and communities of practice need all three forms of knowledge. An absence of organizational support, encouragement, and rewards often hinders the development of this practice. This inhibits the successful development of a process and practice, preventing it from becoming one of the basic beliefs of the organization. These values and beliefs need to be an integral part of development that requires declarative, procedural, and strategic knowledge.

Management provides an organization with a unifying framework for operating the organization. Much like Zachman's 1987 article, *Framework for Information Systems Architecture,* management needs a framework for DIKs. His framework contains 36 cells that represent the possible intersections of design perspectives and their aspects, from generic descriptions to specific details, in a consistent manner, as a way to support the organization's information systems requirement (O'Rouke, 2003). In a sense, these aspects provide the variety of perspectives needed to define requirements to implement an organization's need for an information-based solution (i.e., Web mining and KM). This framework requires one to address several key perspectives in answering the *"why, who, when, where, what_and how"* to provide an insight into the motivations, initiatives, and expectations desired from Web mining, warehousing, and **KM** activities. Supporting processes address the following: *knowledge cycle, program and project management, policies and procedures, methods and techniques, controls, and best practices.* This framework is shown in Figure 7.

These processes provide the foundation for identifying, naming, defining, storing, documenting, authorizing, changing, securing, distributing, and deleting DIKs. They become the roadmap to successful implementation. From a different perspective, the underlying metadata supporting this taxonomy help to map the relationships to navigate across the 36 discrete cells of the Zachman Framework. Jeff Angus and Jeetu Patel in their InformationWeek article (1998, March 16) described the key KM processes to be gathering, organizing, refining, and disseminating DIKs. There is a significant need to develop tools and standards to ensure consistent semantic integrity of Web-delivered data to anyone who needs the DIKs.

Figure 7. A Framework for Information Systems Architecture

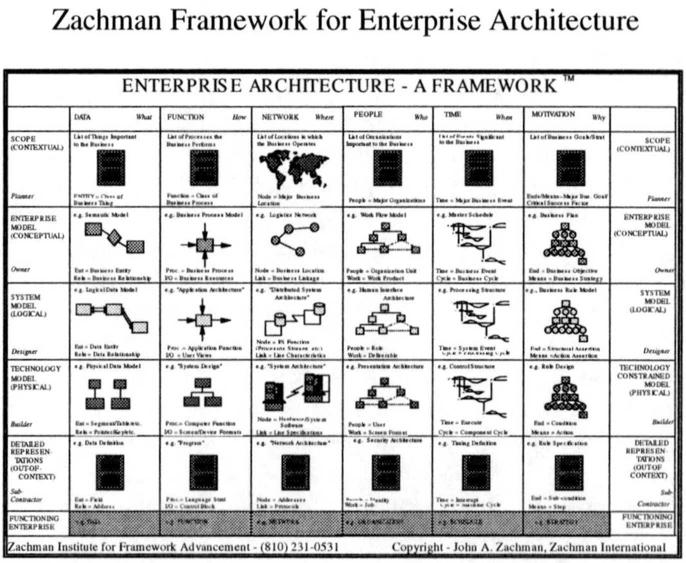

Zachman Framework for Enterprise Architecture

Development of Web-Based Warehouse to House Consistent Data Definitions and Taxonomy to Ensure Semantic Consistency and Effective Communications

In the development of Web mining and warehousing, consistency of terminology becomes increasingly important in decision-making. Figure 8 shows a traditional matrix used to assess one's understanding in determining the current state of knowledge.

From the perspective of one who is accessing DIKs, each grid has different search criteria and different levels of DIKs that constrain the search requirements and impact the tools needed to support that request.

- In the *KK* quadrant, the requestor knows what he or she is looking for and where to get it. No additional investment is required in time or resources.
- In the *KDK* quadrant, the person realizes the DIK exists but does not have a means to access it. In this case, the person would use time and consume resources to determine how to access a DIK that exists.
- In the *DKK* quadrant, the DIKs are available but the person is not knowledgeable of the availability of the DIKs. In this case, the person would spend time and resources to determine if the DIK exists and later to determine how to access it if it does exist.
- In the final quadrant-*DKDK,* a person is totally unaware of the DIKs and any means to access them. In this case, the person may not even spend time and resources to determine if the DIK exists, since he or she is not aware of the possibility.

Consider the searching strategies we use on the Web and you can probably relate to the different scenarios above. How much time do we consume in search of quality information on the Web? Are the metadata critical to success or frustration with the Web's ability to retrieve something about which we are inquiring?

Figure 8. A Knowledge Assessment Map

Knowledge Assessment Map

KK *(Know that you know)*	**KDK** *(Know that you do not know)*
DKK *(Do not know that you know)*	**DKDK** *(Do not know that you do not know)*

Metadata and basic terminology are critical to the access and use of DIKs. It is clear from the prior discussion that without metadata, it would be difficult to move from one grid to another. From that perspective, let's discuss the development of a data warehouse. The team that develops the data warehousing application has to understand all the required data from a business perspective. They must determine the best source of those data from various information systems and must inventory their associated technical (IT) metadata. This provides a profile of the data's current implementations. Design of the target data for implementation is required and becomes the basis for developing the Extraction-Translation-Load (ETL) rules; an automated process is set up to build the data warehouse. In implementing a data warehouse, the metadata that are collected and delivered as a part of this application are a critical part of the delivery of the warehouse for the organization's knowledge workers. The reason knowledge workers and information systems professionals develop a data warehouse together is that neither have the requisite knowledge to build the application independently. The knowledge workers (seekers of knowledge) understand the context of the required information required but do not have the insight and depth to organize it effectively. On the other hand, the information systems analyst has the knowledge of the DIKs and possible classification and structuring of the required DIKs, but does not have the contextual knowledge of its use from inside the organization.

Develop a Measurement to Assess Quality, Timeliness, and Accuracy of Web Content to Start to Minimize the Amount of Disparate Metadata

Given the acceptance of a financial recognition of the economic value of "intellectual capital," the assessment of the quality, timeliness, and accuracy of data, metadata and ultimately, Web content, has to be measured. Redman's grouping of characteristics, conceptual, data value and data representation would be an excellent starting point for measurement. Work currently being done to address data quality by MIT's Total Data Quality Management program is starting to address this issue from different perspectives (see Aerve, 2001; Kahn, 2002; Segev, 2001; Wang, 2003).

Management of Metadata has not been a Key Part of Data Management Implementations

Whenever information systems organizations design something new (i.e., applications, data, functions, systems, networks, or other key artifacts) for operating an organization, models are used. Models are descriptive or mathematical representations supporting a new design. It is significantly better to design models to communicate new requirements than it is to implement solutions without them. Because of the complexity in many of today's organizations, analysts develop various models (business model, business process, etc.) to portray a new design's requirements. In this process, an analyst gathers DIKs to build contextual representations of the new design requirements with his/her associated knowledge workers. The gathering of these DIKs is the metadata necessary to complete the modeling activity. Figure 9 shows one view of models that could be used in the process.

Figure 9. Metamodel of Models — A Structure of Models for Relating Metadata

Meta-Model of Models

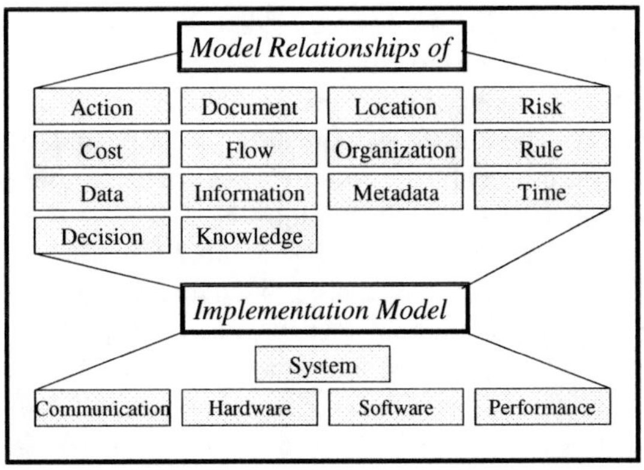

Model Relationships of			
Action	Document	Location	Risk
Cost	Flow	Organization	Rule
Data	Information	Metadata	Time
Decision	Knowledge		

Implementation Model

	System		
Communication	Hardware	Software	Performance

We perform various types of metamodel implementations in the development of information technology-based systems. Typical types of analysis associated with models include: clustering (combine, intersect, select), comparing (similar, different), inferring (seeing relationships between objects), ordering (by grouping or special sequence) and ranking (subjective evaluations) to provide recommendations.

With the implementation of repository (database) systems, we have an opportunity to perform some of the above analysis by modeling different relationships. The example in Figure 10 illustrates a transition in thinking which may require us to re-think the way we have done this process in the past.

Figure 10. Transitional Thinking — A Repository Structure for Relating Metadata

Transition in Thinking

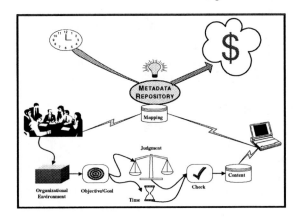

Teaming concepts are critical to operational activities in delivering new ideas, concepts, approaches, and results. Organization dynamics often necessitate internal and external participation in cooperative efforts, so organizational objectives and goals need to be clearly understood by all. This process involves time and judgment in assessing the right content, experience, and knowledge that is applicable to the organization's requirement and operational activity. Supporting DIKs are involved in this process and are checked against the assumptions made and implemented in various systems. To assess the success of the decision, measurements are taken as part of the implementation of the system. Today, the critical factor is the necessity of timely decisions with sufficient return on investments in terms of implementation.

How does Web mining and KM fit into the picture? A central theme is that a metadata repository (database) provides the semantic mechanism and transitions necessary to deliver effective interchange of content appropriate to the operational activities. This is the beginning of the era of ever-increasing demand for automated DIKs. John F. Rockart and James Short (1989, p. 16) describe an increasing spiral of demand for information systems and technology in the business world, stating, *Accessible, well-defined and a transparent network are, therefore, the keys to effective integration in the coming years. Developing these resources, however, is not easy. Excellence at investing in and deploying IT isn't sufficient to achieve superior business performance: companies must also excel at collecting, organizing and maintaining information, and at getting their people to embrace the right behaviors and values for working with information.* In today's environment, it means that Web mining and KM are a large part of building and managing a new type of culture and infrastructure. Thus, organizations and their IT units must develop an architecture, establish standards, communicate the value of the infrastructure, and operate the increasingly complex infrastructure to deliver the content supporting this transition in thinking.

In an unpublished book in the 1990s, Ron Shelby wrote, "Senior management is sponsoring high-visibility initiatives to build common systems and databases to support their organization in the future. Increasingly, information resource management (**IRM**) organizations are asked to architect, integrate, and manage shared-data environments that will support the core of tomorrow's enterprise." In 1999, Shelby was cited in an *InformationWeek* article about data warehouses:

> *"One of the early reasons for data warehousing was to optimize your own business," says Ron Shelby, acting chief technology officer of General Motors Corp. "Sharing data with suppliers is an extension of that. To be more agile, we have to have a supplier base that's equally agile." The automotive giant is starting to use Internet technologies and data-analysis tools so it can share its data warehouse with suppliers and, in effect, treat them like other divisions. (Davis, 1999, June 28)*

Since the 1999 articles, the likes of GM, GE and others have successfully implemented Internet technologies and data mining techniques, with significant dollar savings in supply chain logistics and marketing. For example, GM's Buy Power Website operates in 40 countries and, with other efficiencies, is saving the company $1.5 billion annually, with 9,900 GM suppliers linked in real time to the company (Riftin, 2002). A large part of the success of these implementations is based upon the management of data and metadata, a key proposition stated by Shelby and highlighted by Rockhart and Short.

Development of Software Standards and Measurements to Address Metadata Management Functionality

Given an organizational environment that addresses the objectives/goals, leadership is required to cultivate, motivate, and manage a knowledge and IRM initiative. Metadata, in combination with real-time data, provides immediate information for decision-making purposes in business systems. This is a valuable lesson since using metadata as an active participant in the management and control of this decision support system make the human-system interaction far more valued, flexible, and operationally successful as a knowledge-based information resource.

The premise of this 1986 integrated Business Information and Data (**iBID**) (Shields, 1986) architecture work, as shown in Figure 11, was to deliver a mechanism for a business to develop integrated, flexible, adaptive, and predictive information-based products and services.

This author included *knowledge* as a dimension in the *business environment* since it was an assumed element in the development of this architecture. A key part of this architecture was the collection, resolution, and dissemination of the business rules (Ross, 2003) that the organization currently operates, plans to operate, and analysis of gaps prior to their implementation. This type of simulation and forecasting of current business dynamics (Sherman, 2003) seeks to project the future environment prior to its implementation. This architectural representation provides a clear analogy to today's *operating environment*. Each organization or business environment has business models, business process management, data models, and data semantics. The organization performs a series of actions (broadly categorized as business processes) that effectively utilize data (internal or external) that have been created, updated, or deleted either by a business system (manual/semi-manual) or by an application of an information system. These business systems are networked internally, externally, or some combination of both to locations by some type of communications network.

Figure 11. Management of an Integrated Business Information Architecture

Management & Responsibilities

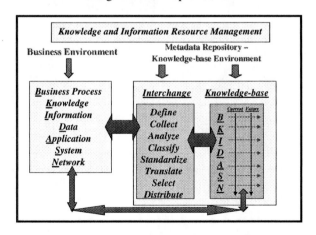

Within the *knowledge base,* two aspects are highlighted: the current (*as-is*) or the future state (*to-be*) across each dimension and is comparable to Zackman's use of interrogatives (who, what, where, when, how, and why) within each dimension. The main purpose is to understand current and future states to ensure transitional planning between the states so that they work. This transition between states is done effectively and efficiently because understanding the many interrelationships avoids errors in implementation.

The *interchange* mechanism enables and facilitates some of the services required (*define, collect, analyze, classify, standardize,_translate, select, distribute*). Each service uses appropriate metadata that require management with a support system or tool in the delivery of repository services. Finally, the bi-direction arrows represent the system capability to access the knowledge-information resource repository from any- where at any time, and for any purpose. Today, our mechanism to accomplish this is the intranet/Internet.

This knowledge base environment cannot be achieved without some critical considerations for the technology components that are required of such an environment. The focal point is the delivery of quality DIKs. Three essential components are required to be integrated, as shown in Figure 12 below.

The catalog/dictionary/thesaurus/repository system component is needed to pro- vide the translation mechanism to bridge to various semantic questions that arise in the implementation of languages. A dictionary also would include relationships to other synonyms to ensure that content would be delivered properly to the requestor. Both logical and physical implementations should be available through the public domain. The semantic engine component provides a series of self-describing programs that hone in on the knowledge worker's descriptive model of context and searching needs. With a type of semantic matching (Rahm, 2003) and profile technique, this component would understand some of the context of the knowledge worker's characteristics to use as a means to extract and mine more meaningful results from the knowledge base. Based upon the overall experience in the knowledge base, it would develop fuzzy-set solutions. The

Figure 12. Technology Requirements for Delivery of KM Environment

Technology Requirements for Delivery

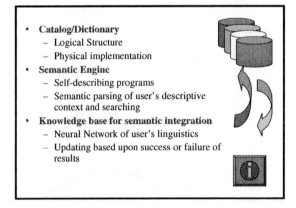

semantic integrity component provides an artificial intelligence engine that dynamically adjusts a neural network of the results achieved from the knowledge worker's inquiries. This would improve the quality of the results from the inquiries based upon the various states from which the person may operate.

FUTURE TRENDS

Increasing Importance for an Organization to Adopt a Framework for Managing Information and Data

Because data and metadata will become an "asset" as part of the KM function, organizational leaders will be faced with competitive situations that will dictate their need for it. With distributed Web warehousing activities, the key role of DIKs is to become a new resource in an organization's environment. A centralized logical approach to develop and manage metadata content databases may be necessary. With centralized logical metadata that is indexed, searched, and processed by tools, it becomes an enabler for organizations to assess and use its knowledge. This IRM metadata repository and knowledge-based environment supports the overall mission and goals of the organization.

The implication of this change is that more robust analytical tools will be required. They will need to support automatic indexing, validation, searching, mapping of casual relationships, adaptive modeling, and fuzzy-set logic technologies to measure the metadata's utility in the context of organizational delivery and adaptation to their environment. Tools in many forms will develop: glossaries, dictionaries, subject taxonomies (generic-to-specific hierarchies), semantic maps (term/definition-to-homonym(s)-synonym(s)), visualization techniques to build relationship maps and new languages to support relationship structures.

This implies that managing metadata, data and information is clearly and explicitly linked to the organization's strategy with a real understanding of its knowledge advantage.

Assessing Organizational Context in a Systematic Approach for Adopting a Knowledge Management Practice

Because data and metadata are essential in the delivery of a robust Web mining and knowledge management solution, a systematic approach is needed to develop the organization's mission and requirements. Basic principles are the foundation for success in providing a systematic approach. They are: (1) to capture, codify, and share both information and knowledge; (2) to focus on the collaborative efforts among people and communities with an emphasis on learning and training; and (3) to prioritize the knowledge and expertise used in the everyday workplace. Remember, in the initial assessment of an organization's needs, one KM best practice may not work in another situation due to organizational culture and context (Glick, 2002). A plan can be put in place using this systematic approach and analysis, specific project goals, requirements, resources, and metrics. The essential design elements of the approach address several areas: content management, the knowledge chain and its dissemination, the infrastructure needs, and its components. In assessing the implementation of the knowledge chain, understanding the organizational context plays a significant part in delivering solutions that emphasize context, interaction and flows, the knowledge base with its content, and the acquisition strategy to be deployed. Knowledge delivery, services, and technology are a key part of the organization's infrastructural practices and culture. The evolution of an organization's knowledge management practice can move from short-term to longer-term projects to full acceptance based upon the success of each knowledge initiative within its proper context. This implies a compelling vision and architecture for your organization's KM mission and goal.

Emerging Standards to Address the Redundancy and Quality of Web-Based Content

The mapping of relationships between different objects in the meta-model of models is starting to play a key role in both organizational and industry standards. The development of various industry-based taxonomies (a class of objects and relationships that exist between them in a generic-to-specific structure) has started. The mapping of synonyms, homonyms, and data with definitional clarity becomes an essential ingredient to the interchange of DIKs. Ontologies (databases that contains the mapped relationships of one object to one or more objects) will be frequently used to provide the capability to infer new facts and observations. Concepts discussed in the InfoMap (Burk, 1988), especially those that focus on measuring cost and the retention practices for DIKs, will be of critical importance to the utility of the metadata knowledge base repository.

Information systems vendors and consultant organizations will support efforts to build these taxonomies and ontologies to provide hardware, software and consulting services that support their use. The implication is that if software products are developed to support these activities, the products may be proprietary in nature.

The American National Standards Institute (ANSI) is one of a number of member bodies that propose U.S. standards be accepted by the International Standards Organization (ISO). Each standards organization is made up of volunteers who develop, assess, and submit a standard for formal approval. There can be competing standards that are developed and some have to be reconciled. Due to the length of time, the level of detail and cost of participating in these standards, delays in the standards process often occur. This delay results in de facto standards being used and implemented prior to full acceptance as a standard. This could impact the development and transitional efforts needed to build robust taxonomies and ontologies. This implies a systematic approach for capturing explicit and implicit knowledge into a well-developed knowledge infrastructure.

Development of Tools and Standards to Assess Semantic Integrity of Web Delivered Pages

The efforts to develop a semantic Web by the W3C group will be key in development of standards. This effort from diverse participants will address a large opportunity to increase the utility of the Web. Various tools (agents) will be generated to assist in the functional services needed by the interchange architecture previously (*define, collect, analyze, classify, standardize, translate, select, distribute*). The most difficult service will be the semantic translation between a Web user's request and utility of the results. Products being developed for natural language, conversational, and parametric searching (Abrams, 2003) will be vital to their successful implementations.

Increasing Use of Intelligent Software to Enable Delivery of New Content to be Delivered into a Knowledge Base Under Users' Metadata Requirements

The efforts supporting the development of DARPA's Agent Markup Language (DAML) and Resource Definition Framework (RDF) are focused on the semantic integration, retrieval and utility of the Web's resources. A key effort is to have a unifying meta-model to store the metadata effectively in its knowledge-base repository for effective and efficient use in the organization. The success of the knowledge-based environment is predicated on linking multiple technologies and practices with critical focus on the quality of the data, information, and maintaining knowledge. This will be one of the biggest organizational challenges!

CONCLUSIONS

To create solutions for today's marketplace needs, the opportunity to build a quality knowledge base depends upon the following:

- The metadata management of DIKs as the major vehicle for the successful implementation of Web mining, warehousing and KM.
- The requirement that organizations adopt new methods/processes, organizational roles, standards and tooling.
- Addressing emerging standards in terms of redundancy and quality of DIKs being delivered through the Web warehousing of content and metadata.

Because of today's global marketplace, a KM system becomes necessary for economic survival. It enables an organization to assess internal and external content via World Wide Web resources and its own internal content-rich knowledgebase. To successfully develop that system, the enterprise has to establish an environment in which the system can succeed. This means integrating many processes and technologies in orchestrating a different environment. A significant hindrance has been the inability to access current, relevant DIKs. Much of the reason lies in the fact that the metadata used in support of the collection of DIKs' knowledge have been limited, or non-existent, ill-defined, erroneously labeled, and disparate. With the ever-increasing demand for Web-enabled mining, the KM environment has to address multiple facets of process, technology, metadata Web mining and warehousing management approaches to provide an integrated content-rich and practical enterprise solution to assist in the delivery of Web warehousing and knowledge management.

REFERENCES

Abrams, C. (2003, March 9). *Metadata management: Crucial for the real-time enterprise*. Paper presented at the Gartner Symposium ITxpo. Retrieved April 16, 2003: *http://symposium.gartner.com/docs/symposium/2003/spr4/documentation/spr4_02b.pdf*.

Allen, T., Harris, W., Madnik, S., & Wang, R. (2003). *An information product approach to total information awareness*. Retrieved May 10, 2003: *http://web.mit.edu/tdqm/www/publications.shtml*.

American National Standards Institute. (2003). Retrieved May 10, 2003: *http://www.ansi.org/*.

Anguss, J., & Patel, J. (1988, March). Knowledge-management cosmology. *Information Week OnLine*. Retrieved May 10, 2003: *http://www.informationweek.com/673/73olkn2.htm*.

Au, W., & Chan, C. (2003, April). Mining fuzzy association rules in a bank-account database. *IEEE Transactions on Fuzzy Systems, 11*(2), 238-248.

Brackett, M. (1996). *The data warehouse challenge: Taming data chaos*. New York: John Wiley.

Brackett, M. (2000). *Data quality resource: Turning bad habits into good practices*. Boston, MA: Addison-Wesley.

Braham, C. (ed.). (1998). *School & office dictionary* (Rev. ed.). New York: Random House.

Burk, C., & Horton, F., Jr. (1988). *InfoMap: A complete guide to discovering corporate information resources*. Englewood Cliffs, NJ: Prentice Hall.

Davenport, T., & Prusak, L. (1998). *Working knowledge: How organizations manage what they know*. Boston, MA: Harvard Business School.

Davis, B. (1999, June 28). Data warehouses open up: Sharing information in your company's data warehouse with suppliers and partners can benefit everyone. *Information Week*. Retrieved May 10, 2003: *http://www.informationweek.com/741/warehouse.htm*.

Devlin, B. (1997). *Data warehousing: From architecture to implementation*. Boston, MA: Addison-Wesley.

Drucker, P.F. (1989). *The new realities*. New York: Harper Business.

Drucker, P.F. (1999a). Knowledge-worker productivity: The biggest challenge. *California Management Review, 41*(2), 79-85.

Drucker, P.F. (1999b). *Management challenges for the 21st century*. New York: Harper Business.

Drucker, P.F. (2000). Knowledge-worker productivity: The biggest challenge. *The knowledge management yearbook 2000-2001*. Woburn, MA: Butterworth-Heinemann.

English, L. (1999). *Improving data warehouse and business information quality*. New York: John Wiley.

English, L. (2003). How to save $576,295,000 through IQ management. *DMReview, 13*(6), 80.

Firestone, J. (2003). *Enterprise information portals and knowledge management* (p. 172). Burlington: Butterworth-Heinemann, an imprint of Elsevier Science.

Gates, B., & Hemingway, C. (1999). *Business @ the speed of thought: Using a digital nervous system*. New York: Warner Books.

Glick, W.H. (2002, April 5). *Configurations of knowledge management practices: Three ideal types.* Paper presented at the meeting of the Third European Conference on Organizational Knowledge, Learning and Capabilities, Athens, Greece.

Gruber, T.R. (1993). *Knowledge Acquisition, 5*(2), 199-220. Retrieved January 31, 2003: *http://www-ksl.stanford.edu/kst/what-is-an-ontology.html.*

Inmon, W. (1992). *Building the data warehouse.* New York: John Wiley.

InterGov International. (2003). Latest Web statistics available from the InterGov International Website [Data File]. Retrieved May 10, 2003: *http://www.intergov.org/public_information/general_information/latest_web_stats.html.*

International Standards Organization. Available: *http://www.iso.ch/iso/en/ISOOnline.openerpage.*

Kahn, B., Strong, D., & Yang, R. (2002). Information quality benchmarks: Product and service performance. *Communications of ACM, 45*(4), 188. Retrieved May 15, 2003: *http://web.mit.edu/tdqm/www/publications.shtml.*

Kimball, R., Reeves, L., Ross, M., & Thornthwaite, W. (1998). *The data warehouse lifecycle toolkit.* New York: John Wiley.

Knowledge Management Network, Brint Institute. Retrieved May 20, 2003: *http://www.kmnetwork.com/.*

Liu, J., & You, J. (2003, April). Smart shopper: An agent-based Web-mining approach to Internet shopping. *IEEE Transactions on Fuzzy Systems, 11*(2), 226-237.

Loshin, D. (2001). *Enterprise knowledge management: The data quality approach.* San Francisco, CA: Morgan Kaufmann.

Malhotra, Y. (2003). World Wide Web virtual library on knowledge management. Retrieved May 15, 2003: *http://www.brint.com.*

Mandel, M., Coy, P., & Judge, P. (1998, March 2). ZAP! How the Year 2000 bug will hurt the economy (It's worse than you think). *Business Week, 3567,* 47.

Marchand, D., Kettinger, W., & Rollins, J. (2000, Summer). Information orientation: People, technology and the bottom line. *Sloan Management Review, 41*(4), 69-80.

Marco, D. (2002). *Building and managing a meta data repository: A full lifecycle guide.* New York: John Wiley.

Merriam-Webster's collegiate on-line dictionary. Retrieved May 10, 2003: *http://www.m-w.com/home.htm.*

Metcalfe, J.T. (1998, December). *Information resource management – Data ownership, organization, roles and responsibilities.* Unpublished IBM Business Systems-Internal Publication. Norwalk, Connecticut, USA.

Mintzberg, H. (1971). Managerial work: Analysis from observation. *Management Science, 18*(2), 97-110.

Online Computer Library Center, Inc. Retrieved May 20, 2003: *http://www.oclc.org/home/.*

O'Rourke, C., Fishman, N., & Selkow, W. (2003). *Enterprise architecture: Using the Zachman framework.* Boston, MA: Thompson-Course Technology.

Rahm, E. (2003). *Metadata management for heterogeneous information systems.* Invited talk at the 13th GI Workshop on Foundations of Database Systems (2001, June). Retrieved April 20, 2003: *http://dbs.uni-leipzig.de/en/Research/meta.html.*

Redman, T. (1992). *Data quality: Management and technology.* New York: Bantam.

Redman, T. (1996). *Data quality for the information age.* Boston, MA: Artech House.

Redman, T. (1998). The impact of poor data quality on the typical enterprise. *Communications of the ACM, 41*(2), 82.

Rifkin, G. (2002, October). GM's Internet overhaul. *MIT Technology Review, 105*(8), 66. Cambridge.

Rockart, J., & Short, J. (1989). IT in the 1990s: Managing organizational interdependence. *Sloan Management Review,* Winter, 7-17.

Ross, R. (2003, May). The business rule approach. *Computer, 36*(5), 85-87.

Scime, A. (2000). Learning from the World Wide Web: Using organizational profiles in information searches. *Informing Science, 3*(3), 136-173.

Segev, A., & Wang, R. (2001, November). *Data quality challenges in enabling eBusiness transformation.* Presentation at the Sixth International Conference on Information Quality (IQ-2001). Retrieved April 15, 2003: *http://web.mit.edu/tdqm/www/iqc/past/.*

Sergent, J. (2003, March 10). In Net vs. not: Which offers better shopping. *USA Today.* Retrieved March 10, 2003: *http://www.usatoday.com/usatonline/20030310/4930922s.htm.*

Shelby, R. (1992). *Information resource management's role in the 1990s.* Unpublished Auerbach book.

Shields, A., & Stein, P. (1989, September). *Requirements for a system to register and report on knowledge about the information_used and needed by a business* (Document #87-02-22). Unpublished IBM Business Systems-Internal Publication. Norwalk, CT.

Sterman, J. (2000). *Business dynamics: Systems thinking and modeling for a complex world.* New York: McGraw-Hill Irwin.

Tannenbaum, A. (2002). *Metadata solutions: Using metamodels, repositories, XML, and enterprise portals to generate information on demand.* Boston, MA: Addison-Wesley.

TechReference. Retrieved May 20, 2003: *http://searchcrm.techtarget.com/.*

Tiwana, A. (2001). *The essential guide to knowledge management: e-Business and CRM applications.* Upper Saddle River, NJ: Prentice Hall PTR.

U.S. Law. (1996, July). *Clinger-Cohen Act of 1996 introduced the concept and need for information resource management policies and practices.* Retrieved May 12, 2003: *http://www.dau.mil/jdam/contents/clinger_cohen.htm.*

Vaughn-Nichols, S. (2003, May). XML raises concerns as it gains prominence. *Computer, 36*(5), 14-16.

Wang, R., Allen, T., Harris, W., & Madnick, S. (2003, March). An information product approach for total information awareness. IEEE Aerospace Conference. Retrieved May 15, 2003: *http://web.mit.edu/tdqm/www/publications.shtml.*

Zachman, J. (1987). A framework for information systems architecture. *IBM Systems Journal, 26*(3), 276-92. Available: *http://www.zifa.com/.*

Chapter II

Mining for Web Personalization

Penelope Markellou
University of Patras, Greece and
Research Academic Computer Technology Institute, Greece

Maria Rigou
University of Patras, Greece and
Research Academic Computer Technology Institute, Greece

Spiros Sirmakessis
University of Patras, Greece and
Research Academic Computer Technology Institute, Greece

ABSTRACT

The Web has become a huge repository of information and keeps growing exponentially under no editorial control, while the human capability to find, read and understand content remains constant. Providing people with access to information is not the problem; the problem is that people with varying needs and preferences navigate through large Web structures, missing the goal of their inquiry. Web personalization is one of the most promising approaches for alleviating this information overload, providing tailored Web experiences. This chapter explores the different faces of personalization, traces back its roots and follows its progress. It describes the modules typically comprising a personalization process, demonstrates its close relation to Web mining, depicts the technical issues that arise, recommends solutions when possible, and discusses the effectiveness of personalization and the related concerns. Moreover, the chapter illustrates current trends in the field suggesting directions that may lead to new scientific results.

INTRODUCTION

Technological innovation has led to an explosive growth of recorded information, with the Web being a huge repository under no editorial control. More and more people everyday browse through it in an effort to satisfy their "primitive" need for information, as humans might properly be characterized as a species of *Informavores* who "have gained an adaptive advantage because they are hungry for further information about the world they inhabit (and about themselves)" (Dennett, 1991, p. 181). Based on the observation that humans actively seek, gather, share and consume information to a degree unapproached by other organisms, Pirolli and Card (1999, p. 3) took the informavores approach one step further and introduced the *Information Foraging Theory*[1] according to which, "when feasible, natural information systems evolve towards stable states that maximize gains of valuable information per unit cost" (see also Resnikoff, 1989). Under the information foraging assumption, people need information and the Web today provides open access to a large volume. Thus providing people with access to more information is not the problem; the problem is that more and more people with varying needs and preferences navigate through large and complicated Web structures, missing -in many cases- the goal of their inquiry. The challenge today is how to concentrate human attention on information that is useful (maximizing gains of valuable information per unit cost), a point eloquently made by H.A. Simon (as quoted by Hal Varian in 1995, p. 200), "...what information consumes is rather obvious: it consumes the attention of its recipients. Hence a wealth of information creates a poverty of attention and a need to allocate that attention efficiently among the overabundance of information sources that might consume it."

Personalization can be the solution to this information overload problem, as its objective is to provide users with what they want or need, without having to ask (or search) for it explicitly (Mulvenna et al., 2000). It is a multidiscipline area deploying techniques from various scientific fields for putting together data and producing personalized output for individual users or groups of users. These fields comprise information retrieval, user modeling, artificial intelligence, databases, and more. Personalization on the Web covers a broad area, ranging from check-box customization to recommender systems and adaptive Websites. The spectrum from customizable Websites (in which users are allowed, usually manually, to configure the site in order to better suit their preferences) to adaptive ones (the site undertakes to automatically produce all adaptations according to the user profile, recorded history, etc.) is wide and personalization nowadays has moved towards the latter end. We meet cases of personalization in use in e-commerce applications (product recommendations for cross-selling and up-selling, one-to-one marketing, personalized pricing, storefront page customization, etc.), in information portals (home page customization such as *my.yahoo.com*, etc.), in search engines (in which returned results are filtered and/or sorted according to the profile of the specific user or group of users), and e-learning applications (topic recommendations, student/teacher/administrator views, content adaptations based on student level and skills, etc.). And while recently there has been a lot of talking about personalization, one has to wonder whether it is hype or an actual opportunity. Doug Riecken, in his editorial article in the *Communications of the ACM Special Issue on Personalization* (2000), claims that it should be considered as an opportunity, but it must be defined clearly and it must be designed to be useful and usable, conditions that in the traditional HCI field

(Nielsen, 1994) are interpreted as allowing users to achieve their goals (or perform their tasks) in little time, with a low error rate, and while experiencing high subjective satisfaction.

The personalization technology is fast evolving and its use spreads quickly. In the years to come all Web applications will embed personalization components, and this philosophy will be part and parcel of many everyday life tasks (e.g., ambient computing, house of tomorrow). We are now at the phase of exploring the possibilities and potential pitfalls of personalization as implemented and designed so far. In our opinion this is a good point to review the progress, learn from our mistakes, and think about the "gray" areas and the controversies before planning for the future. This chapter aims to define personalization, describe its modules, demonstrate the close relation between personalization and Web mining, depict the technical issues that arise, recommend solutions when possible, and discuss its effectiveness, as well as the related concerns. Moreover, our goal is to illustrate the future trends in the field and suggest in this way directions that may lead us to new scientific results.

MOTIVATION FOR PERSONALIZATION

Taking things from the beginning, the roots of personalization — as we interpret it today — are traced back to the introduction of *adaptive hypermedia applications* in Brusilovsky's work of 1996 and its updated version of 2001. Adaptive hypermedia were introduced as an alternative to the traditional "one-size-fits-all" approach, building a model of the goals, preferences and knowledge of each individual user, and using this model throughout the interaction, in order to adapt to the user's specific needs.

Adaptations are differentiated depending on the amount of control a user has over them. Four distinct roles are defined in the process: adaptation *initiator, proposer, selector* and *producer* (Dieterich et al., 1993). Systems in which the user is in control of initiation, proposal, selection and production of the adaptation are called *adaptable* (Oppermann, 1994) ("in control" thereby meaning that the user can perform these functions, but can also opt to let the system perform some of them). In contrast, systems that perform all steps autonomously are called *adaptive*. Adaptability and adaptivity can coexist in the same application and the final tuning between the two should be decided taking into account convenience for the user, demands on the user, irritation of the user and the consequences of false adaptation. User control may be provided on a general level (users can allow or disallow adaptation at large), on a type level (users can approve or disapprove that certain types of adaptation take place) or on a case-by-case basis (Kobsa & Pohl, 2001).

As already mentioned, initial attempts of implementing personalization were limited to *check-box personalization,* in which portals allowed users to select the links they would like on their "personal" pages, but this has proved of limited use since it depends on users knowing in advance the content of their interest. Moving towards more intelligent (or AI) approaches, *collaborative filtering* was deployed for implementing personalization based on knowledge about likes and dislikes of past users that are considered similar to the current one (using a certain similarity measure). These techniques required users to input personal information about their interests, needs and/or preferences, but this posed in many cases a big obstacle, since Web users are not usually cooperative in revealing these types of data. Due to such problems, researchers resorted to *observational personalization,* which is based on the assumption that we can find clues about how to personalize information, services or products in records of users' previous navigational behavior (Mulvenna et al., 2000). This is the point at which *Web mining* comes into play; Web mining is defined as the use of data mining techniques for discovering and extracting information from Web documents and services and is distinguished as *Web content, structure* or *usage mining* depending on which part of the Web is mined (Kosala & Blockeel, 2000). In the majority of cases, Web applications base personalization on Web usage mining, which undertakes the task of gathering and extracting all data required for constructing and maintaining user profiles based on the behavior of each user as recorded in server logs.

Now that all necessary introductions are in place, we may proceed with formally introducing the central concept of this chapter. Defining a scientific discipline is always a controversial task, and personalization is no exception to this rule as, in the related bibliography, one may come across many definitions; we already referred to the definition found in Mulvenna et al. (2000) and we indicatively also quote the following one, which takes a more user-centric approach: "Personalization is a process that changes the functionality, interface, information content, or distinctiveness of a system to increase its personal relevance to an individual" (Blom, 2000). Eirinaki and Vazirgiannis (2003, p. 1) define it in a way that addresses adequately all primary aspects of person-alization as perceived in the specific context of this book: "Personalization is defined as any action that adapts the information or services provided by a web site to the knowledge gained from the users' navigational behavior and individual interests, in combination with the content and the structure of the web site". For the remainder of the chapter, we will use this as our working personalization definition.

PERSONALIZATION PROCESS DECOMPOSED

In this section we discuss the overall personalization process in terms of the discrete modules comprising it: *data acquisition, data analysis* and *personalized output.* We describe in detail the objectives of each module and review the approaches taken so far by scientists working in the field, the obstacles met, and when possible, the solutions recommended.

Data Acquisition

In the large majority of cases, Web personalization is a data-intensive task that is based on three general types of data: data about the user, data about the Website usage and data about the software and hardware available on the user's side.

*   **User data.** This category denotes information about personal characteristics of the user. Several such types of data have been used in personalization applications, such as:
    *   *Demographics* (name, phone number, geographic information, age, sex, educa-tion, income, etc.);

- *User's knowledge* of concepts and relationships between concepts in an application domain (input that has been of extensive use in natural language processing systems) or domain specific expertise;
- *Skills and capabilities* (in the sense that apart from "what" the user knows, in many cases it is of equal importance to know what the user knows "how" to do, or even further, to distinguish between what the user is familiar with and what she can actually accomplish);
- *Interests and preferences*
- *Goals and plans* (plan recognition techniques and identified goals allow the Website to predict user interests and needs and adjust its contents for easier and faster goal achievement).

There are two general approaches for acquiring user data of the types described above: either the user is asked *explicitly* to provide the data (using questionnaires, fill-in preference dialogs, or even via machine readable data-carriers, such as smart cards), or the system *implicitly* derives such information without initiating any interaction with the user (using acquisition rules, plan recognition, and stereotype reasoning).

- **Usage data.** Usage data may be directly observed and recorded, or acquired by analyzing observable data (whose amount and detail vary depending on the technologies used during Website implementation, i.e., java applets, etc.), a process already referenced in this chapter as Web usage mining. Usage data may either be:
  - Observable data comprising selective actions like clicking on an link, data regarding the temporal viewing behavior, ratings (using a binary or a limited, discrete scale) and other confirmatory or disconfirmatory actions (making purchases, e-mailing/saving/printing a document, bookmarking a Web page and more), or
  - Data that derive from further processing the observed and regard usage regularities (measurements of frequency of selecting an option/link/service, production of suggestions/recommendations based on situation-action correlations, or variations of this approach, for instance recording action sequences).

- **Environment data.** On the client side, the range of different hardware and software used is large and keeps growing with the widespread use of mobile phones and personal digital assistants (PDAs) for accessing the Web. Thus in many cases the adaptations to be produced should also take into account such information. Environment data address information about the available *software* and *hardware* at the client computer (browser version and platform, availability of plug-ins, firewalls preventing applets from executing, available bandwidth, processing speed, display and input devices, etc.), as well as *locale* (geographical information used for adjusting the language, or other locale specific content).
  After data have been acquired (a process that is in continuous execution for most of the cases), they need to be transformed into some form of internal representation

(modeling) that will allow for further processing and easy update. Such internal representation models are used for constructing individual or aggregate (when working with groups of users) profiles, a process termed *user profiling* in the relative literature. Profiles may be *static* or *dynamic* based on whether — and how often — they are updated. Static profiles are usually acquired explicitly while dynamic ones are acquired implicitly by recording and analyzing user navigational behavior. In both approaches, we have to deal with different but equally serious problems. In the case of explicit profiling, users are often negative about filling in questionnaires and revealing personal information online; they comply only when required and even then the data submitted may be false. On the other hand, in implicit profiling, even though our source of information is not biased by the users' negative attitude, the problems encountered derive once again from the invaded privacy concern and the loss of anonymity, as personalization is striving to identify the user, record the user's online behavior in as much detail as possible and extract needs and preferences in a way the user cannot notice, understand or control. The problem of loss of control is observed in situations in which the user is not in control of when and what change occurs and it is referenced in numerous HCI resources, such as Kramer et al. (2000), Mesquita et al. (2002), and Nielsen (1998) as a usability degrading factor. A more detailed discussion on the issues of privacy and locus of control can be found later in this chapter, under "Trends and Challenges in Personalization Research."

Data Analysis

User profiling dramatically affects the kinds of analysis that can be applied after the phase of data acquisition in order to accomplish more sophisticated personalization. The techniques that may be applied for further analyzing and expanding user profiles so as to derive inferences vary and come from numerous scientific areas that comprise artificial intelligence, machine learning, statistics, and information retrieval. In this chapter, we follow the approach of information retrieval and set our focus on deploying Web mining for analyzing user behavior and inferring "interesting" patterns, similarities, clusters and correlations among users and/or page requests. In the past years, several researchers have applied *Web usage mining* for constructing user profiles and making personalization decisions. Web usage mining uses server logs as its source of information and the process of deriving valuable information from them progresses according to the following phases (Srivastava et al., 2000): data preparation and preprocessing, pattern discovery and pattern analysis.

Data Preparation and Preprocessing

The objective of this phase is to derive a set of server sessions from raw usage data, as recorded in the form of Web server logs. Before proceeding with a more detailed description of data preparation, it is necessary to provide a set of data abstractions as introduced by the W3C1 (World Wide Web Consortium) for describing Web usage. A *server session* is defined as a set of page views served due to a series of HTTP requests from a single user to a single Web server. A *page view* is a set of page files that contribute to a single display in a Web browser window (the definition of the page view is necessary because for analyzing user behavior what is of value is the aggregate page view and not each one of the consecutive separate requests that are generated automatically for acquiring parts of the page view such as scripts, graphics, etc.). Determining which log entries refer to a single page view (a problem known as *page view identification*) requires information about the site structuring and contents. A sequential series of page view requests is termed *click-stream* and it is its full contents that we ideally need to know for reliable conclusions. A *user session* is the click-stream of page views for a single user across the entire Web, while a *server session* is the set of page views in a user session for a particular Website.

During data preparation the task is to identify the log data entries that refer to graphics or traffic automatically generated by spiders and agents. These entries in most of the cases are removed from the log data, as they do not reveal actual usage information. Nevertheless, the final decision on the best way to handle them depends on the specific application. After cleaning, log entries are usually parsed into data fields for easier manipulation.

Apart from removing entries from the log data, in many cases data preparation also includes enhancing the usage information by adding the missing clicks to the user click-stream. The reason dictating this task is client and proxy caching, which cause many requests not to be recorded in the server logs and to be served by the cached page views. The process of restoring the complete click-stream is called *path completion* and it is the last step for preprocessing usage data. Missing page view requests can be detected when the referrer page file for a page view is not part of the previous page view. The only sound way to have the complete user path is by using either a software agent or a modified browser on the client-side. In all other cases the available solutions (using for instance, apart from the referrer field, data about the link structure of the site) are heuristic in nature and cannot guarantee accuracy.

Except for the path completion issue, there remains a set of other technical obstacles that must be overcome during data preparation and preprocessing. More specifically, a major such issue is *user identification*. A number of methods are deployed for user identification and the overall assessment is that the more accurate a method is, the higher the privacy invasion problem it faces. Assuming that each IP address/agent pair identifies a unique user is not always the case, as many users may use the same computer to access the Web and the same user may access the Web from various computers. An embedded session ID requires dynamic sites and while it distinguishes the various users from the same IP/Agent, it fails to identify the same user from different IPs. Cookies and software agents accomplish both objectives, but are usually not well accepted (or even rejected and disabled) by most users. Registration also provides reliable identification but not all users are willing to go through such a procedure or recall logins and passwords. Alternatively, modified browsers may provide accurate records of user behavior even across Websites, but they are not a realistic solution in the majority of cases as they require installation and only a limited number of users will install and use them.

Last but not least, there arises the issue of *session identification*. Trivial solutions tackle this by setting a minimum time threshold and assuming that subsequent requests from the same user exceeding it belong to different sessions (or use a maximum threshold for concluding respectively).

Pattern Discovery

Pattern discovery aims to detect interesting patterns in the preprocessed Web usage data by deploying statistical and data mining methods. These methods usually comprise (Eirinaki & Vazirgiannis, 2003):

- *Association rule mining:* A technique used for finding frequent patterns, associations and correlations among sets of items. In the Web personalization domain, this method may indicate correlations between pages not directly connected and reveal previously unknown associations between groups of users with specific interests. Such information may prove valuable for e-commerce stores in order to improve Customer Relationship Management (CRM).

- *Clustering:* a method used for grouping together items that have similar characteristics. In our case items may either be users (that demonstrate similar online behavior) or pages (that are similarity utilized by users).

- *Classification:* A process that learns to assign data items to one of several predefined classes. Classes usually represent different user profiles, and classification is performed using selected features with high discriminative ability as refers to the set of classes describing each profile.

- *Sequential pattern discovery:* An extension to the association rule mining technique, used for revealing patterns of co-occurrence, thus incorporating the notion of time sequence. A pattern in this case may be a Web page or a set of pages accessed immediately after another set of pages.

Pattern Analysis

In this final phase the objective is to convert discovered rules, patterns and statistics into *knowledge* or insight involving the Website being analyzed. Knowledge here is an abstract notion that in essence describes the transformation from information to understanding; it is thus highly dependent on the human performing the analysis and reaching conclusions. In most of the cases, visualization techniques are used for "communicating" better the knowledge to the analyst.

Figure 1 provides a summarized representation of all described subtasks comprising the process of Web personalization based on usage mining.

The techniques mentioned so far for performing the various phases of data analysis apply Web usage mining in order to deliver Web personalization. This approach is indeed superior to other more traditional methods (such as collaborative or content based filtering) in terms of both scalability and reliance on objective input data (and not, for instance, on subjective user ratings). Nevertheless, usage-based personalization can also be problematic when little usage data are available pertaining to some objects, or when the site content changes regularly. Mobasher et al. (2000a) claims that for more effective personalization, both usage and content attributes of a site must be integrated into the data analysis phase and be used uniformly as the basis of all personalization decisions. This way semantic knowledge is incorporated into the process by representing domain ontologies in the preprocessing and pattern discovery phases, and using effective techniques to obtain uniform profiles representation and show how to use such profiles for performing real-time personalization (Mobasher & Dai, 2001).

Figure 1. Personalization Based on Web Mining

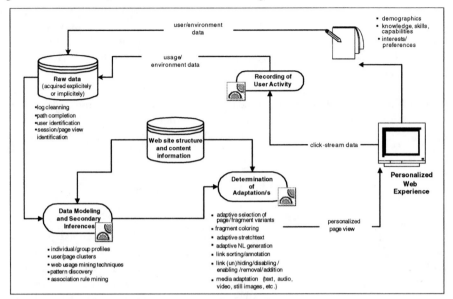

Personalized Output

After gathering the appropriate input data (about the user, the usage and/or the usage environment), storing them using an adequate representation and analyzing them for reaching secondary inferences, what remains is to explore and decide upon the kind of adaptations the Website will deploy in order to personalize itself. These adaptations can take place at different levels:

- *Content:* Typical applications of such adaptations are optional explanations and additional information, personalized recommendations, theory driven presentation, and more. Techniques used for producing such adaptations include adaptive selection of Web page (or page fragment) variants, fragment coloring, adaptive stretch-text, and adaptive natural language generation.

- *Structure:* It refers to changes in the link structure of hypermedia documents or their presentation. Techniques deployed for producing this kind of adaptation comprise adaptive link sorting, annotation, hiding and unhiding, disabling and enabling, and removal/addition. Adaptations of structure are widely used for producing adaptive recommendations (for products, information or navigation), as well as constructing personal views and spaces.

- *Presentation and media format:* in this type of personalized output the informational content ideally stays the same, but its format and layout changes (for example from images to text, from text to audio, from video to still images). This type of adaptations is widely used for Web access through PDAs or mobile phones, or in Websites that cater to handicapped persons.

In the majority of cases, personalized Websites deploy hybrid adaptation techniques.

Personalization requires the manipulation of large amounts of data and processing them at a speed that allows for low response times, so that adaptations take effect as soon as possible and the process remains transparent to the user. At the same time, in most personalization scenarios, and with the purpose of keeping the processing time very low, parts of the process are executed offline. An effect of this case is that the system delays in updating changing user profiles, since it is only natural that user preferences and even more often user needs change over time, requiring corresponding updates to the profiles. The trade-off between low response times and keeping profiles updated is usually determined on an application basis, according to the specific precision and speed requirements, or in other words, the fault and delay tolerance.

THEORY IN ACTION:
TOOLS AND STANDARDS

From the previous, it is obvious that personalizing the Web experience for users by addressing individual needs and preferences is a challenging task for the Web industry. Web-based applications (e.g., portals, e-commerce sites, e-learning environments, etc.) can improve their performance by using attractive new tools such as dynamic recommendations based on individual characteristics and recorded navigational history. However, the question that arises is how this can be actually accomplished. Both the Web industry and researchers from diverse scientific areas have focused on various aspects of the topic. The research approaches, and the commercial tools that deliver personalized Web experiences based on business rules, Website content and structure, as well as the user behavior recorded in Web log files are numerous. This section provides a tour around the most well known applications of Web personalization both at a research and a commercial level.

Letizia (Lieberman, 1995), one of the first intelligent agents, assists Web search and offers personalized lists of URLs close to the page being read using personal state, history and preferences (contents of current and visited pages). More specifically, the agent automates a browsing strategy consisting of a best-first search augmented by heuristics inferring user interest from her behavior.

WebWatcher (Armstrong et al., 1995; Joachims et al., 1997) comprises a "tour guide" Web agent that highlights hyperlinks in pages based on the declared interests and path traversal pattern of the current user, as well as previous similar users. WebWatcher incorporates three learning approaches: (a) learning from previous tours, (b) learning from the hypertext structure and (c) combination of the first two approaches.

A recommendation system that assists Web search and personalizes the results of a query based on personal history and preferences (contents and ratings of visited pages) is *Fab* (Balabanovic & Shoham, 1997). By combining both collaborative and content-based techniques, it succeeds to eliminate many of the weaknesses found in each approach.

Humos/Wifs (Ambrosini et al., 1997) has two components, the Hybrid User Modeling Subsystem and the Web-oriented Information Filtering Subsystem, assisting Web search and personalizing the results of a query based on an internal representation of user interests (inferred by the system through a dialogue). It uses a hybrid approach to user modeling (integration of case-based components and artificial neural network) and takes advantage of semantic networks, as well as a well-structured database, in order to perform accurate filtering.

Another agent that learns users' preferences by looking at their visit records and then provides them with updated information about the Website is *SiteHelper* (Ngu & Wu, 1997). The agent carries out two types of incremental learning: interactive learning, by asking user for feedback, and silent learning, by using the log files.

Personal WebWatcher (Mladenic, 1999) is a "personal" agent, inspired basically by WebWatcher, that assists Web browsing and highlights useful links from the current page using personal history (content of visited pages), while *Let's Browse* (Lieberman et al., 1999) implemented as an extension to Letizia, supports automatic detection of the presence of users, automated "channel surfing" browsing, dynamic display of the user profiles and explanation of recommendations.

The use of *association rules* was first proposed in Agrawal et al. (1993) and Agrawal and Srikant (1994). Chen et al. (1998) use association rules algorithms to discover "interesting" correlations among user sessions, while the definition of a session as a set of *maximal forward references* (meaning a sequence of Web pages accessed by a user) was introduced in Chen et al. (1996). This work is also the basis of *SpeedTracer* (Wu et al., 1998), which uses referrer and agent information in the pre-processing routines to identify users and server sessions in the absence of additional client side information, and then identifies the most frequently visited groups of Web pages. Krishnan et al. (1998) describe *path-profiling* techniques in order to predict future request behaviors. Thus content can be dynamically generated before the user requests it.

Manber et al. (2000) presents *Yahoo! personalization experience*. Yahoo! was one of the first Websites to use personalization on a large scale. This work studies three examples of personalization: Yahoo! Companion, Inside Yahoo! Search and My Yahoo! application, which were introduced in July 1996.

Cingil et al. (2000) describe the need for *interoperability* when mining the Web and how the various *standards* can be used for achieving personalization. Furthermore, they establish an architecture for providing Web servers with automatically generated, machine processable, dynamic user profiles, while conforming to users' privacy preferences.

Mobasher et al. (2000b) describe a general architecture for automatic Web personalization using Web usage mining techniques. *WebPersonalizer* (Figure 2) is an advanced system aiming at mining Web log files to discover knowledge for the production of personalized recommendations for the current user based on her similarities with previous users. These user preferences are automatically learned from Web usage data, eliminating in this way the subjectivity from profile data, as well as keeping them updated. The pre-processing steps outlined in Cooley et al. (1999a) are used to convert the server logs into server sessions. The system recommends pages from clusters that closely match the current session.

For personalizing a site according to the requirements of each user, Spiliopoulou (2000) describes a process based on discovering and analyzing *user navigational patterns*. Mining these patterns, we can gain insight into a Website's usage and optimality with respect to its current user population.

Usage patterns extracted from Web data have been applied to a wide range of applications. *WebSIFT* (Cooley et al., 1997, 1999b, 2000) is a Website information filter system that combines usage, content, and structure information about a Website. The information filter automatically identifies the discovered patterns that have a high degree of subjective interestingness.

Web Utilization Miner (WUM) (Spiliopoulou et al., 1999a, 1999b; Spiliopoulou & Faulstich, 1998; Spiliopoulou & Pohle, 2000) specifies, discovers, and visualizes interesting navigation patterns. In WUM the concept of navigation patterns includes both the sequence of events that satisfies the expert's constraints and the routes connecting those events.

Another Web usage miner designed for e-commerce applications is *MIDAS* (Buchner et al., 1999), in which a navigation pattern is a sequence of events satisfying the constraints posed by an expert who can specify, in a powerful mining language, which patterns have potential interest.

IndexFinder (Perkowitz & Etzioni, 2000b) is a Web management assistant, a system that can process massive amounts of data about site usage and suggest useful adaptations to the Web master. This assistant develops adaptive Websites that semi-automatically improve their organization and presentation by learning from visitor access patterns. Adaptive Websites are defined in Perkowitz and Etzioni (1997, 1998, 1999, 2000a).

Finally, Rossi et al. (2001) introduce an interesting approach based on the *Object-Oriented Hypermedia Design Method (OOHDM)*. They build Web application models

Figure 2.   A General Architecture for Usage-Based Web Personalization (Mobasher et al., 2000b)

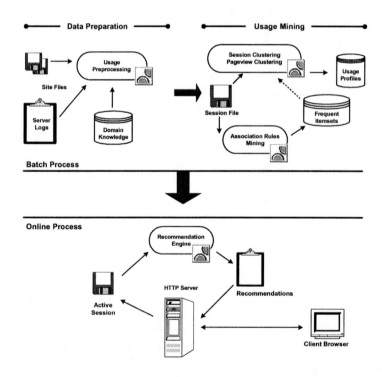

as object-oriented views of conceptual models and then refine the views according to users' profiles or preferences to specify personalization. In this context, the linking topology or the contents of individual nodes can be basically personalized.

Moreover, many vendors such as Blue Martini Software Inc., E.piphany, Lumio Software, Net Perceptions, Sane Solutions, WebSideStory Inc., and so forth provide a variety of commercial tools that support mining for Web personalization. Table 1 summarizes a list of the most representative current commercial applications. All these can be integrated directly into a Website server in order to provide users with personalized experiences.

As mentioned before, the techniques applied for Web personalization should be based on standards and languages ensuring interoperability, better utilization of the stored information, as well as personal integrity and privacy (Cingil et al., 2000).

Extensible Markup Language (XML)[2] is a simple, very flexible text format originally designed to meet the challenges of large-scale electronic publishing. XML plays an increasingly important role in the exchange of a wide variety of data on the Web and the *XML Query Language*[3] can be used for extracting data from XML documents.

Resource Description Framework (RDF)[4] is a foundation for processing metadata and constitutes a recommendation of W3C. It provides interoperability between applications that exchange machine-understandable information on the Web and its syntax can use XML. RDF applications include resource discovery, content description/ relationships, knowledge sharing and exchange, Web pages' intellectual property rights, users' privacy preferences, Websites' privacy policies, and so forth.

Platform for Privacy Preferences (P3P)[5] was developed by the W3C in 1999 and comprises a standard that provides a simple and automated way for users to gain more control over their personal information when visiting Websites. Personal profiling is a form of Website visitor surveillance and leads to a number of ethical considerations. Website visitors must be convinced that any collected information will remain confidential and secure. P3P enables Websites to express their privacy practices in a standard format that can be retrieved automatically and interpreted easily by user agents. P3P user agents allow users to be informed of site practices (in both machine and human readable formats) and to automate decision-making based on these practices when appropriate. Thus users need not read the privacy policies at every site they visit. However, while P3P provides a standard mechanism for describing privacy practices, it does not ensure that Websites actually follow them.

Open Profiling Standard (OPS)[6] is a proposed standard by Netscape that enables Web personalization. It allows users to keep profile records on their hard drives, which can be accessed by authorized Web servers. The users have access to these records and can control the presented information. These records can replace cookies and manual online registration. The OPS has been examined by the W3C, and its key ideas have been incorporated into P3P.

Customer Profile Exchange (CPEX)[7] is an open standard for facilitating the privacy-enabled interchange of customer information across disparate enterprise applications and systems. It integrates online/offline customer data in an XML-based data model for use within various enterprise applications both on and off the Web, resulting in a networked, customer-focused environment. The CPEX working group intends to develop open-source reference implementation and developer guidelines to speed adoption of the standard among vendors.

Table 1. Commercial Applications

Vendor	Application	Description
Accrue Software Inc. *http://www.accrue.com*	Accrue G2, Accrue Insight, Pilot Suite, Pilot Hit List	Analytic tools that allow companies to transform volumes of complex Web data into actionable information for building long-term, multi-channel customer relationships (by capturing users' decision-making process and behavior patterns).
Blue Martini Software Inc. *http://www.bluemartini.com*	Blue Martini Marketing	A comprehensive solution for customer analysis and marketing automation. Companies use the software to create a unified picture of customers, analyze their behavior for patterns and insights, and implement those insights through personalization and outbound marketing.
Coremetrics Inc. *http://www.coremetrics.com*	Coremetrics Marketforce	An online marketing analytics platform that captures and stores all visitor and customer activity to build LIVE (Lifetime Individual Visitor Experience) Profiles that serve as the foundation for all successful marketing initiatives (featuring essential tools to increase online sales, maximize marketing return on investment (ROI), and optimize site design).
E.piphany *http://www.epiphany.com*	E.piphany E.6	Integrated tool that merges analytical/operational CRM capabilities to drive intelligent, effective, and personalized interactions with customers on any touch point (including applications for marketing, sales, service, etc.).
Elytics Inc. *http://www.elytics.com*	Elytics Analysis Suite	Powerful customer-centric analytics tools and innovative visualization applications that allow companies to measure and optimize e-channel performance by improving customer segment response to online initiatives, marketing campaign and tactic effectiveness, content effectiveness, registration browse-to-buy conversions, and so forth.
IBM Corporation *http://www.ibm.com*	WebSphere Personalization, SurfAid (Express, Analysis, Business Integration)	Tools that allow Website content personalization matching the unique needs and interests of each visitor. By analyzing Web traffic and visitor behavior companies may gain rapid feedback in regard to site traffic, marketing campaigns, visitor geographies, site navigation and design effectiveness, visitor loyalty, site stickiness, and so forth.
Lumio Software *http://www.lumio.com*	Re:cognition Product Suite, Re:action, Re:search, Re:collect	Suite for optimizing customer experience by personalization/customization. It enhances the effectiveness of e-businesses by supporting behavioral data collection-analysis-storage, real-time knowledge deployment and key performance indicators measurement to continuously monitor the quality of the interactions with customers.
NCR Corporation *http://www.ncr.com*	Teradata Warehouse	Analytical CRM solution suite that enables personalized customer dialogues by event-driven optimization and achieving higher revenue and profitability while improving customer satisfaction.

Table 1. *(continued)*

	Commercial applications	
Vendor	Application	Description
Net Perceptions http://www.netperceptions.com	NetP 7	NetP 7 powers one-to-one interactions driving product penetration and increased revenue via call center, Website, outbound e-mail campaigns, and direct mail by delivering personalized offers to customers. It contains advanced analytics to build statistical models based on historical transaction data that form the basis for effective cross-sell, up-sell, targeted customer lists and alternative product recommendations for out-of-stock items.
NetIQ Corporation http://www.netiq.com	WebTrends Intelligence Suite, WebTrends Log Analyzer Series	Web analytics solutions deliver key insight into every element of Web visitor activity, allowing organizations to make smarter decisions in order to acquire, convert and retain more customers, resulting in higher returns on infrastructure and marketing investments and improved visitor-to-customer conversion rates.
Quest Software http://www.quest.com	Funnel Web Analyzer, Funnel Web Profiler	User profiling and Website traffic analysis tools that optimize Websites by analyzing how users interact with them and make informed decisions about what changes will improve users' experience (Client Click Stream analysis feature).
Sane Solutions http://www.sane.com	NetTracker 6.0 (Business Objects, Cognos, MicroStrategy)	NetTracker empowers business companies with easy-to-use, instant ad hoc analysis capabilities for answering very specific questions about individual visitors.
SAS http://www.sas.com	SAS Value Chain Analytics, SAS IntelliVisor, Enterprise Miner	Services for providing customized information, improving effectiveness of marketing campaigns by data mining and analytical techniques. They also help companies to reveal trends, explain known outcomes, predict future outcomes and identify factors that can secure a desired effect, all from collected demographic data and customer buying patterns.
SPSS Inc. http://www.spss.com	NetGenesis	A Web analytic software that interprets and explains customer behavior. It gathers and manages vast amounts of data, identifies which content brings the most value, builds loyal customers and determines the effectiveness of commerce and marketing campaigns. It addresses the distinct and complex needs of large businesses with dynamic, transaction driven and highly personalized Websites.
WebSideStory Inc. http://www.websidestory.com	HitBox Services Suite (Enterprise, Commerce, Wireless Website Analysis)	A broad range of market-proven services developed to help companies to optimize their online marketing performance (e.g., comprehensive online marketing analytics and optimization, essential Web traffic analysis, wireless Website analysis).

Personalized Information Description Language (PIDL)[8] aims at facilitating personalization of online information by providing enhanced interoperability between applications. PIDL provides a common framework for applications to progressively process original contents and append personalized versions in a compact format. It supports the personalization of different media (e.g., plain text, structured text, graphics, etc.), multiple personalization methods (such as filtering, sorting, replacing, etc.) and different delivery methods (for example SMTP, HTTP, IP-multicasting, etc.). It creates a unified framework for services to both personalize and disseminate information. Using PIDL, services can describe the content and personalization methods used for customizing the information and use a single format for all available access methods.

TRENDS AND CHALLENGES IN PERSONALIZATION RESEARCH

While personalization looks important and appealing for the Web experience, several issues still remain unclear. One such issue is *privacy preserving* and stems from the fact that personalization requires collecting and storing far more personal data than ordinary non-personalized Websites. According to Earp and Baumer (2003), there is little legal protection of consumer information acquired online — either voluntarily or involuntarily — while systems try to collect as much data as possible from users, usually without users' initiative and sometimes without their awareness, so as to avoid user distraction. Numerous surveys already available illustrate user preferences concerning online privacy (Kobsa & Schreck, 2003), with the requirement for preservation of anonymity when interacting with an online system prevailing.

A solution to this problem may come from providing *user anonymity,* even thought this may sound controversial, since many believe that anonymity and personalization cannot co-exist. Schafer et al. (2001) claim that "anonymizing techniques are disasters for recommenders, because they make it impossible for the recommender to easily recognize the customer, limiting the ability even to collect data, much less to make accurate recommendations". Kobsa and Schreck, (2003) on the other hand, present a reference model for pseudonymous and secure user modeling that fully preserves personalized interaction. Users' trust in anonymity can be expected to lead to more extensive and frank interaction, and hence to more and better data about the user, and thus better personalization. While this is a comprehensive technical solution for anonymous and personalized user interaction with Web services, a number of obstacles must still be addressed; hardly any readily available distributed anonymization infrastructures, such as mixes, have been put in place and anonymous interaction is currently difficult to maintain when money, physical goods and non-electronic services are being exchanged.

The deployment of personalized anonymous interaction will thus strongly hinge on social factors (i.e., regulatory provisions that mandate anonymous and pseudonymous access to electronic services). This will give the opportunity to holders of e-shops to apply *intelligent e-marketing* techniques with Web mining and personalization features, as in Perner and Fiss (2002). Intelligent e-marketing is part of the Web intelligence (Yao et al., 2001), where *intelligent Web agents (WA),* acting as computational entities, are making decisions on behalf of their users and self-improving their performance in dynamically changing and unpredictable task environments. WAs provide users with a user-friendly style of presentation (Cheung et al., 2001) that personalizes both interaction and content presentation (referenced in the bibliography as Personalized Multimodal Interface).

A relatively recent development that is foreseen to greatly affect Web personalization (and more specifically the Web mining subtasks) is the creation of the *semantic Web*. Semantic Web mining combines the two fast-developing research areas of semantic Web and Web mining with the purpose of improving Web mining by exploiting the new semantic structures in the Web. Berendt et al. (2002) give an overview of where the two areas meet today, and sketch ways of how a closer integration could be profitable. The Web will reach its full potential when it becomes an environment in which data can be shared and processed by automated tools, as well as by people. The notion of being able to semantically link various resources (documents, images, people, concepts, etc.) is essential for the personalization domain. With this we can begin to move from the current Web of simple hyperlinks to a more expressive, semantically rich web, in which we can incrementally add meaning and express a whole new set of relationships (hasLocation, worksFor, isAuthorOf, hasSubjectOf, dependsOn, etc.) among resources, making explicit the particular contextual relationships that are implicit in the current Web. The semantic Web will allow the application of sophisticated mining techniques (which require more structured input). This will open new doors for effective information integration, management and automated services (Markellos et al., 2003).

Moving away from the promising future potential of the personalization technology, perhaps it is interesting to return to its original motivation. Personalization has one explicit target: people. Users are being offered services or applications that need to be or should be personalized for ease of use, efficiency and satisfaction. Although in the past years different attempts have been proposed for evaluating personalization (Ramakrishnan, 2000; Vassiliou et al., 2002) a more systematic and integrated approach should be defined for its efficient assessment, justifying on a per application basis the use of such a resource demanding technology. In other words, despite the great potential and how smart a Website can be in changing itself in order to better suit the individual user, or how well it can anticipate and foresee user needs, the fact remains: systems are aware of only a fraction of the total problem-solving process their human partners undergo (Hollan, 1990), and they cannot share an understanding of the situation or state of problem-solving of a human (Suchman, 1987). Personalization, with all the automated adaptations it "triggers" transparently, is a blessing only if the human partner is allowed to control what is adapted automatically and how. This way, locus of control remains at the user side, where it should be. Other than that, numerous issues remain to be addressed: When is personalization required? What data should be used and is there a minimal efficient set? How should data be handled? Is personalization efficient for the user? What about the system's efficiency? Are there any criteria for the efficiency of the methods, in terms of accuracy, speed, privacy and satisfaction?

Technologically, the scene is set for personalization; it is fast developing and constantly improving. What is missing is its wider acceptance that will allow it to prove its full potential. The prerequisite for this final and crucial step is the investigation and resolution of issues connected with the human factor: ethics, trust, privacy, control, satisfaction, respect, and reassurance.

CONCLUSIONS

As the Web is growing exponentially, the user's capability to find, read, and understand content remains constant. Currently, Web personalization is the most promising approach to alleviate this problem and to provide users with tailored experiences. Web-based applications (e.g., information portals, e-commerce sites, e-learning systems, etc.) improve their performance by addressing the individual needs and preferences of each user, increasing satisfaction, promoting loyalty, and establishing one-to-one relationships. There are many research approaches, initiatives and techniques, as well as commercial tools that provide Web personalization based on business rules, Website contents and structuring, user behavior and navigational history as recorded in Web server logs.

Without disputing the enormous potential of the personalization technology, neither questioning the "noble" motivations behind it, the issue is still unclear: Does personalization really work? The answer is neither trivial nor straightforward. On the one hand the benefits could be significant not only for the Website visitor (being offered more interesting, useful and relevant Web experience) but also for the provider (allowing one-to-one relationships and mass customization, and improving Website performance). On the other hand, personalization requires rich data that are not always easily obtainable and in many cases the output proves unsuccessful in actually understanding and satisfying user needs and goals. Today, the situation is such that providers invest money on personalization technologies without any reassurances concerning actual added value, since users are negative towards the idea of being stereotyped. Finally, the ethical dimension of personalization should also be taken into account: online user activities are recorded for constructing and updating user profiles and this puts privacy in jeopardy.

Summarizing, in this chapter we explored the different faces of personalization. We traced back its roots and ancestors, and followed its progress. We provided detailed descriptions of the modules that typically comprise a personalization process and presented an overview of the interesting research initiatives and representative commercial tools that deploy Web usage mining for producing personalized Web experiences. Finally, we introduced and discussed several open research issues and in some cases, we provided recommendations for solutions.

REFERENCES

Agrawal, R., Imielinski, T., & Swami, A. (1993). Mining association rules between sets of items in large databases. *Proceedings of the ACM SIGMOD International Conference on Management of Data,* (pp. 207-216).

Agrawal, R., & Srikant, R. (1994). Fast algorithms for mining association rules. *Proceedings of the 20th VLDB Conference,* Santiago, Chile (pp. 487-499).

Ambrosini, L., Cirillo, V., & Micarelli, A. (1997). A hybrid architecture for user-adapted information filtering on the World Wide Web. *Proceedings of the 6th International Conference on User Modelling (UM'97),* (pp. 59-61). Springer-Verlag.

Armstrong, R., Joachims, D., Freitag, D., & Mitchell, T. (1995). WebWatcher: A learning apprentice for the World Wide Web. *Proceedings of the AI Spring Symposium on Information Gathering from Heterogeneous, Distributed Environments,* Stanford, California, USA (pp. 6-13).

Balabanovic, M., & Shoham, Y. (1997). Content-based collaborative recommendation. *Communications of the ACM, 40*(3), 66-72.

Berendt, B., Hotho, A., & Stumme, G. (2002). Towards semantic Web mining. In I. Horrocks & J. Hendler (Eds.), *Proceedings of the ISWC 2002, LNCS 2342* (pp. 264-278). Springer-Verlag Berlin.

Blom, J. (2000). Personalization - A taxonomy. *Proceedings of the CHI 2000 Workshop on Designing Interactive Systems for 1-to-1 Ecommerce.* New York: ACM. Available: *http://www.zurich.ibm.com/~mrs/chi2000/.*

Brusilovsky, P. (1996). Methods and techniques of adaptive hypermedia. *Journal of User Modeling and User-Adaptive Interaction, 6*(2-3), 87-129.

Brusilovsky, P. (2001). Adaptive hypermedia. In A. Kobsa (Ed.), *User modeling and user-adapted interaction, ten year anniversary, 11,* 87-110.

Buchner, M., Baumgarten, M., Anand, S., Mulvenna, M., & Hughes, J. (1999). Navigation pattern discovery from Internet data. *WEBKDD'99.* San Diego, California.

Chen, M., Park, J., & Yu, P. (1996). Data mining for path traversal patterns in a Web environment. *Proceedings of the 16th International Conference on Distributed Computing Systems,* (pp. 385-392).

Chen, M., Park, J., & Yu, P. (1998). Efficient data mining for path traversal patterns. *IEEE Transactions Knowledge and Data Engineering, 10*(2), 209-221.

Cheung, K., Li, C., Lam, E., & Liu, J. (2001). Customized electronic commerce with intelligent software agents. In S.M. Rahman & R.J. Bignall (Eds.), Internet commerce and software agents - Cases, technologies and opportunities (pp. 150-176). Hershey, PA: Idea Group Publishing.

Cingil, I., Dogac, A., & Azgin, A. (2000). A broader approach to personalization. *Communications of the ACM, 43*(8), 136-141.

Cooley, R., Mobasher, B., & Srivastava, J. (1997). Grouping Web page references into transactions for mining World Wide Web browsing patterns. *Knowledge and Data Engineering Workshop,* Newport Beach, CA (pp. 2-9).

Cooley, R., Mobasher, B., & Srivastava, J. (1999a). Data preparation for mining World Wide Web browsing patterns. *Knowledge and Information Systems, 1*(1), 5-32.

Cooley, R., Tan, P., & Srivastava, J. (1999b). *WebSIFT: The Web Site information filter system.* WEBKDD, San Diego, California. Available: *http://www.acm.org/sigkdd/proceedings/webkdd99/papers/paper11-cooley.ps.*

Cooley, R., Tan, P., & Srivastava, J. (2000). Discovering of interesting usage patterns from Web data. In M. Spiliopoulou (Ed.), *LNCS/LNAI Series.* Springer-Verlag.

Dennett, D.C. (1991). *Consciousness explained.* Boston, MA: Little, Brown and Co.

Earp, J., & Baumer, D. (2003). Innovative Web use to learn about consumer behavior and online privacy. *Communications of the ACM, 46*(4), 81-83.

Eirinaki, M., & Vazirgiannis, M. (2003, February). Web mining for Web personalization. *ACM Transactions on Internet Technology (TOIT), 3*(1), 1-27. New York: ACM Press.

Hollan, J.D. (1990). User models and user interfaces: A case for domain models, task models, and tailorability. *Proceedings of AAAI-90, Eighth National Conference on Artificial Intelligence,* (p. 1137). Cambridge, MA: AAAI Press/The MIT Press.

Joachims, T., Freitag, D., & Mitchell, T. (1997). WebWatcher: A tour guide for the World Wide Web. *Proceedings of the 15th International Joint Conference on Artificial Intelligence (JCAI97),* (pp. 770-775). Morgan Kaufmann Publishers.

Kobsa, A.J., & Pohl, W. (2001). Personalized hypermedia presentation techniques for improving online customer relationships. *The Knowledge Engineering Review, 16*(2), 111-155.

Kobsa, A., & Schreck, J. (2003). Privacy through pseudonymity in user-adaptive systems. *Transactions on Internet Technology, 3*(2), 149-183.

Kosala, R., & Blockeel, H. (2000). Web mining research: A survey. *SIGKDD Explorations, 2*(1), 1-15.

Kramer, J., Noronha, S., & Vergo, J. (2000). A user-centered design approach to personalization. *Communications of the ACM, 8*, 45-48.

Krishnan, M., Schechter, S., & Smith, M. (1998). Using path profiles to predict http request. *Proceedings of the 7th International World Wide Web Conference,* Brisbane, Qld., Australia, (pp. 457-467).

Lieberman, H. (1995). Letizia: An agent that assists Web browsing. *Proceedings of the 14th International Joint Conference Artificial Intelligence,* Montreal, CA, (pp. 924-929).

Lieberman, H., Van Dyke, N., & Vivacqua, A. (1999). Let's browse: A collaborative Web browsing agent. *Proceedings of the International Conference on Intelligent User Interfaces (IUI'99),* Redondo Beach, USA, (pp. 65-68). ACM Press.

Manber, U., Patel, A., & Robison, J. (2000). Experience with personalization on Yahoo! *Communications of the ACM, 43*(8), 35-39.

Markellos, K., Markellou, P., Rigou, M., & Sirmakessis, S. (2003). Web mining: Past, present and future. In S. Sirmakessis (Ed.), *Proceedings of the 1st International Workshop on Text Mining and its Applications, Studies in Fuzziness.* In press. Springer Verlag Berlin Heidelberg.

Mesquita, C., Barbosa, S.D., & Lucena, C.J. (2002). Towards the identification of concerns in personalization mechanisms via scenarios. *Proceedings of 1st International Conference on Aspect-Oriented Software Development,* Enschede, The Netherlands. Available: *http://trese.cs.utwente.nl/AOSD-EarlyAspectsWS/Papers/Mesquita.pdf.*

Mladenic, D. (1999). Text learning and related intelligent agents. *IEEE Intelligent Systems and their Applications, 14*(4), 44-54.

Mobasher, B., & Dai, H. (2003). A road map to more effective Web personalization: Integrating domain knowledge with Web usage mining. *Proceedings of the International Conference on Internet Computing 2003 (IC'03),* Las Vegas, Nevada.

Mobasher, B., Cooley, R., & Srivastava, J. (2000b). Automatic personalization based on Web usage mining. *Communications of the ACM, 43*(8), 142-151.

Mobasher, B., Dai, H., Luo, T., Sun, Y., & Zhu, J. (2000a). Integrating Web usage and content mining for more effective personalization. *Proceedings of the 1st International Conference on E-Commerce and Web Technologies (ECWeb2000),* Greenwich, UK, (pp. 165-176).

Mulvenna, M., Anand, S., & Bchner, A. (2000). Personalization on the Net using Web mining. *Communications of the ACM, 43*(8), 122-125.

Ngu, D., & Wu, X. (1997). SiteHelper: A localized agent that helps incremental exploration of the World Wide Web. *Proceedings of the 6th World Wide Web Conference,* Santa Clara, CA.

Nielsen, J. (1994). *Usability engineering.* Morgan Kaufmann.

Nielsen, J. (1998). Personalization is over-rated. Alertbox for October 4, 1998. Available: *http://www.useit.com.*

Perkowitz, M., & Etzioni, O. (1997). Adaptive Web sites: An AI challenge. *Proceedings of the 15th International Joint Conference on Artificial Intelligence.*

Perkowitz, M., & Etzioni, O. (1998). Adaptive Web sites: Automatically synthesizing Web pages. *Proceedings of the 15th National Conference on Artificial Intelligence.*

Perkowitz, M., & Etzioni, O. (1999). Adaptive Web sites: Conceptual cluster mining. *Proceedings of the 16th International Joint Conference on Artificial Intelligence.*

Perkowitz, M., & Etzioni, O. (2000a). Adaptive Web sites. *Communications of the ACM, 43*(8), 152-158.

Perkowitz, M., & Etzioni, O. (2000b). Towards adaptive Web sites: Conceptual framework and case study. *Artificial Intelligence, 118*(1-2), 245-275.

Perner, P., & Fiss, G. (2002). Intelligent E-marketing with Web mining, personalization, and user-adapted interfaces. In P. Perner (Ed.), *Advances in data mining 2002, LNAI 2394* (pp. 37-52). Berlin: Springer-Verlag Berlin Heidelberg.

Pirolli, P., & Card, S. (1999). Information foraging. *Psychological Review, 106*(4), 643-675.

Ramakrishnan, N. (2000). PIPE: Web personalization by partial evaluation. *IEEE Internet Computing, 4*(6), 21-31.

Resnikoff, H. (1989). *The illusion of reality* (p. 97). New York: Springer-Verlag.

Riecken, D. (2000, August). Personalized views of personalization. *Communications of the ACM, 43*(8), 27-28.

Rossi, G., Schwabe, D., & Guimaraes, R. (2001). Designing personalized Web applications. *Proceedings of the WWW10,* Hong Kong, 275-284.

Schafer, J., Konstan, J., & Riedl, J. (2001). E-commerce recommendation applications. *Data Mining and Knowledge Discovery, 5*(1), 115-153.

Smith, E., & Winterhalder, B. (eds.). (1992). Evolutionary ecology and human behavior. New York: de Gruyter.

Spiliopoulou, M. (2000). Web usage mining for Web site evaluation. *Communications of the ACM, 43*(8), 128-134.

Spiliopoulou, M., & Faulstich, L. (1998). *WUM: A Web utilization miner.* EDBT Workshop WebDB98, Valencia, Spain.

Spiliopoulou, M., & Pohle, C. (2000). Data mining for measuring and improving the success of Web sites. *Data Mining and Knowledge Discovery, Special Issue on Electronic Commerce.*

Spiliopoulou, M., Faulstich, L., & Wilkler, K. (1999a). A data miner analyzing the navigational behavior of Web users. *Proceedings of the Workshop on Machine Learning in User Modelling of the ACAI99,* Chania, Greece.

Spiliopoulou, M., Pohle, C., & Faulstich, L. (1999b). Improving the effectiveness of a Web site with Web usage mining. *Proceedings of the WEBKDD99,* San Diego, California (pp. 142-162).

Srivastava, J., Cooley, R., Deshpande, M., & Tan, P. (2000, January). Web usage mining: Discovery and applications of usage patterns from Web data. *ACM SIGKDD, 1*(2), 12-23.

Stephens, D., & Krebs, J. (1986). *Foraging theory*. Princeton, NJ: Princeton University Press.

Suchman, L.A. (1987). Plans and situated actions. Cambridge, UK: Cambridge University Press.

Varian, H. (1995, September). The information economy. *Scientific American,* 200-201.

Vassiliou, C., Stamoulis, D., & Martakos, D. (2002, January). The process of personalizing Web content: Techniques, workflow and evaluation. *Proceedings of the International Conference on Advances in Infrastructure for Electronic Business, Science, and Education on the Internet,* L'Aquila, Italy. Available: *http://www.ssgrr.it/en/ssgrr2002s/papers.htm.*

Wu, K., Yu, P., & Ballman, A. (1998). SpeedTracer: A Web usage mining and analysis tool. *IBM Systems Journal, 37*(1), 89-105.

Yao, Y., Zhong, N., Liu, J., & Ohsuga, S. (2001). Web intelligence (WI) research challenges and trends in the new information age. In N. Zhong et al. (Eds.), *WI 2001, LNAI 2198,* 1-17. Springer Verlag Berlin Heidelberg.

ENDNOTES

[1]   W3C. World Wide Web Consortium. Available: *http://www.w3.org.*

[2]   XML. Extensible Markup Language. Available: *http://www.w3.org/XML.*

[3]   XML Query Language. Available: *http://www.w3.org/TR/xquery/.*

[4]   RDF. Resource Description Framework. Model and Syntax Specification. Available: *http://www.w3.org/TR/REC-rdf-syntax/.*

[5]   P3P. Platform for Privacy Preferences Project. Available: *http://www.w3.org/P3P.*

[6]   OPS. Open Profiling Standard. Available: *http://developer.netscape.com/ops/ops.html.*

[7]   CPEX. Customer Profile Exchange. Available: *http://www.cpexchange.org/.*

[8]   PIDL. Personalized Information Description Language. Available: *http://www.w3.org/TR/NOTE-PIDL.*

SECTION II

CONTENT MINING

Chapter III

Using Context Information to Build a Topic-Specific Crawling System

Fan Wu
National Chung-Cheng University, Taiwan

Ching-Chi Hsu
Institute for Information Industry, Taiwan

ABSTRACT

One of the major problems for automatically constructed portals and information discovery systems is how to assign proper order to unvisited Web pages. Topic-specific crawlers and information seeking agents should try not to traverse the off-topic areas and concentrate on links that lead to documents of interest. In this chapter, we propose an effective approach based on the relevancy context graph to solve this problem. The graph can estimate the distance and the relevancy degree between the retrieved document and the given topic. By calculating the word distributions of the general and topic-specific feature words, our method will preserve the property of the relevancy context graph and reflect it on the word distributions. With the help of topic-specific and general word distribution, our crawler can measure a page's expected relevancy to a given topic and determine the order in which pages should be visited. Simulations are also performed, and the results show that our method outperforms the breath-first and the method using only the context graph.

INTRODUCTION

The Internet has now become the largest knowledge base in the human history. The Web encourages decentralized authoring in which users can create or modify documents locally, which makes information publishing more convenient and faster than ever. Because of these characteristics, the Internet has grown rapidly, which creates a new and huge media for information sharing and exchange. There are more than two billion unique and publicly accessible pages on the Internet, and the Internet is estimated to continue to grow at an accelerating rate, 7.3 million pages per day (Cyveillance, 2003). As a result of the tremendous size of information on the Web and its substantial growth rate, it is increasingly difficult to search for useful information on the Web.

Traditional information retrieval methods can be utilized to help users search for their needed information in a database. But they appear to be ineffective when facing this mammoth Web. Researchers have proposed many techniques to facilitate the information seeking process on the Web. Search engines are the most important and commonly used tools (Brown et al., 1998), which usually have large indexes of the Web and attempt to use a centralized architecture to solve the problem of information seeking in a decentralized environment. Web search engines are usually equipped with multiple powerful spiders that traverse the Web information space. But the engines have difficulties in dealing with such huge amounts of data. For example, Google *(http://www.google.com/)* claimed to be the largest search engine in the world, can only index about 60% of the Web. The other problem is that search engines usually return hundreds or thousands of results for a given query, which makes users bewildered in finding relevant answers for their information need (Lawrence 1999, 2000).

The general-purpose search engines, such as Altavista *(http://www.altavista.com/)*, offer high coverage of the possible information on the Web, but they often provide results with low precision. That is, the information does not match what the user wants. Directory search engines, such as Yahoo! *(http://yahoo.com.tw/)*, can limit the scope of its search upon such manually compiled collections of the Web contents that are related to some specified categories. The directory search engines return the results with higher precision, exhibiting the beauty of labor-intensive efforts. However, compiling a well-organized directory search engine for each directory would be tedious and impossible, and automatic construction of such an engine seems to have a long way to go.

The topic-specific search engine is another type of search engines that is constructed and optimized in accordance with domain knowledge. When users are aware of the topic or category of their need, a topic-specific search engine can provide the information with higher precision than a general, or directory search engine does. For example, ResearchIndex *(http://citeseer.nj.nec.com/cs/)* is a full-text index of scientific literature that aims at improving the dissemination and feedback of scientific literature. Travel-Finder *(http://www.travel-finder.com/)* is a topic-specific Web service designed to help individuals find travel professionals and travel information. LinuxStart *(http://www.linuxstart.com/)* is another topic-specific Web service that provides a deliberate hierarchy of Linux topics and a search engine for queries focused on Linux-related topics. Topic-specific search engines usually incorporate in their system domain knowledge and use focused crawlers to construct their data collection. The crawlers try not to traverse the off-topic areas, concentrating themselves on the links that lead to documents of interest. One of the major problems of the topic-specific crawler is how to assign a proper order to the unvisited pages that the crawler may visit later. The method to measure the importance of a document on the Web through linkage information has been adopted by the general and topic-specific search engines. But the topic-specific crawlers can further incorporate domain-specific knowledge to facilitate subjective search.

Text categorization provides a suitable way for Web page ordering. With text categorization, crawlers can classify each page into different categories and pick up those pages belonging to the interesting categories. For example, Chakrabarti et al. (1998, 1999a, 1999b) incorporated the manually compiled taxonomy from Yahoo! to build a topic-specific Web resource discovery system. This system provides users a Web-based administration interface to choose their favorite topics and choose examples to train the classifier. The system then utilizes the trained classifier as well as the canonical hierarchy to filter and rank the pages in the process of information discovery. However, it is difficult and time-consuming to manually build text classifiers for each topic. Many attempts have been made to automatically categorize documents. The machine learning paradigm has attracted much attention with its simplicity and effectiveness. With machine learning, a classifier that learns how to categorize the documents from training examples can be built.

Another problem for typical focused crawlers is that some sets of off-topic documents often lead to highly relevant documents. For example, lists of computer science papers are usually found on the pages of researchers' publication lists. These publication pages are usually referenced by the pages of the department member, which is an off-topic page in relation to the literature of computer science. Such a condition commonly occurs and causes problems in traversing the pages on the Web. An optimally focused crawler should sacrifice visiting several off-topic pages and then reach the highly relevant pages along the links. Typical focused crawlers have difficulties learning this phenomenon. Diligenti et al. (Diligenti, 2000) proposed a novel approach to build a model, called a *context graph*, for storing the information about link hierarchies and the distance from the off-topic pages to the target pages. We will study how context information affects the information discovery process in this chapter.

We organize the rest of this chapter as follow: Firstly, we briefly introduce the idea of the topic-specific crawler and its related issues. We discuss some important metrics for measuring the quality of Web pages. Many of them have been combined to determine the order of pages to traverse. Text categorization plays an important role in the most topic-distillation systems, so we will review this research topic. We also introduce some previous work for topic-specific crawling and discuss their problems. Then we propose a modified approach for the problems and discuss its important characteristics. We explain the design philosophy of our system and discuss some crucial design issues of the system. The future developments and application of the topic-specific crawlers are discussed. Finally, the conclusion of the chapter is given.

BACKGROUND

Huge amounts of data have been published on the Web. The accelerated growth of the Web has turned the Internet into an immense information space with diverse contents. Search engines are the most important and commonly used tools to facilitate the information seeking process on the Web. In order to achieve higher coverage of the Web, large-scale search engines use a software agent, called a *Web robot (http://www.robotstxt. org/wc/threat-or-treat.html, http://www.robotstxt.org/wc/guidelines.html),* to automatically collect data from the Web. The Web robot is a program that traverses the Web and recursively retrieves all documents to create a searchable index of the Web. Web robots usually start with a set of well-known URLs that may contain high-quality contents or a number of links to other parts of the Web. Different traversal strategies provide different views of the Web. A breadth-first strategy often leads to a broader view than a depth-first strategy. Some heuristics or ordering schemes can be incorporated if there are some other constraints (such as considerations of cost and storage, or quality and precision of documents).

Focused Crawler

A focused crawler (or topic-specific spider) is a goal-oriented Web robot, aiming at retrieving only the subset of the Web that is related to the given topics. The focused crawler analyzes the links it visits and determines the proper route to find the links that are more likely to lead to pages relevant to the topic. Figure 1 is a graph composed of the documents and their associated links, in which each node represents a Web page, and the edge between the nodes represents the link between the corresponding pages. In the figure, the node in black denotes an off-topic page, and the node in white denotes the on-topic one. The edges drawn in thick lines mean the links traversed by a traversal strategy, while the edges drawn in light lines mean the links not traversed by the traversal strategy. From Figure 1, we can see the differences in the traveled paths among the depth-first, breadth-first and focused crawlers. A focused crawler tries to identify the most promising links and avoids retrieving the off-topic documents. Its paradigm limits its search on the focused domain by adopting a strategy of filtering. The focused crawler does not treat all pages equally. Pages referring to the interested topic are more important than those referring to irrelevant topics.

Measuring (or predicting) whether a page can lead to the on-topic pages is an important task of focused crawlers. Given a Web page P, a focused crawler can exploit the information related to P for measuring the importance of the page (denoted as $I(P)$) (Cho et al., 1998). A page with higher $I(P)$ should be visited earlier, since the page has the higher probability of leading to a large number of important pages. There is a lot of literature that utilizes a variety of resources to better measure $I(P)$. We list some basic and commonly used measures below that are heuristics for evaluating the page importance. Some measures are topic-independent metrics, but some have the ability to distinguish the relevancy between the Web pages and the topic.

Backward and Forward Link Count

Intuitively, a page linked by many pages is more important than the one that is seldom referenced. This heuristic (called *backward-link count*), based on the concept of "citation count," is extensively used to evaluate the impact of published papers. The $I(P)$ of a page P measured from the metric of backward-link count is the number of other pages on the Web that point to page P. This heuristic attracts a lot of attention in measuring and analyzing Web linkage structure. However, evaluating this measurement is difficult since we do not have the entire topology of the Web.

Another related metric based on the link count is *forward-link count*. This idea is that a page with many outgoing links is valuable since it may be a Web directory or a Web resource depository. Clearly, the page with a larger forward-link count would provide crawlers with more opportunity to find other important pages. Thus the $I(P)$ of a page P measured from the metric of forward-link count is the number of pages on the Web that

Figure 1. Difference in Traveling Paths among the Different Traversal Strategies ((a), (b) and (c) are the paths of the depth-first, breadth-first and focused crawlers, respectively)

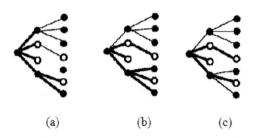

(a)   (b)   (c)

page *P* points to. This metric is usually used in conjunction with other factors to identify the index pages.

PageRank

The metric of PageRank, proposed by Page et al. (1998), is to evaluate the importance of a page from the link structure. This measure is successfully applied to the ranking mechanism in the Google search engine. The basic idea of PageRank is that the importance of a page *P* depends not only on how many links point to *P* but also on how important those links are. Precisely, the measure first obtains the weight of each link that points to page *P* by proportionally dividing the importance of such a page that has a link pointing to *P*, and then accumulates all the weights of those links that point to page *P*. Thus the value of the PageRank of page *P* is as follows:

$$I(P) = \sum_{Q \in B(P)} \frac{I(Q)}{c(Q)},$$

(1)

where *I(P)* and *I(Q)* are the importance (or PageRank value) of page *P* and *Q*, respectively; *B(P)* is the set of pages that have a link pointing to *P;* and *c(Q)* is the number of all links in page *Q*.

Figure 2 is an example illustrating Equation (1). Assume the importance of pages A and B is known beforehand, and *I(A)* and *I(B)* are 100 and 60, respectively. Then *I(D)*, for instance, is equal to the summation of the weights of the two links from pages A and B pointing to page D. The respective weights of the two links are 50 (= 100/2) and 20 (= 60/3). Thus, *I(D)* is 70. Note that the links of page D may reach page A through a finite number of pages and finally contribute to the importance of page A. Thus Equation (1) is recursive. It proves that the value of the PageRank of the links can be computed by starting with any subset of pages and iterating the computation until their values converge (Brin, 1998).

PageRank tries to model the human interests and attentions devoted to a specific Web page with a random walk model. Sometimes a surfer may arrive at page *P* by randomly

Figure 2. Values of the PageRank of the Pages are Propagated through Links (a page has a higher rank if the sum of the ranks of its back links is high)

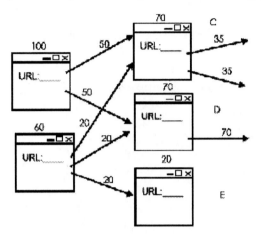

clicking links with some probability. Then the value of the PageRank of page *P*, incorporating the consideration of random surfing is:

$$I(P) = \beta + (1 - \beta) \times \sum_{Q \in B(P)} \frac{I(Q)}{c(Q)}, \qquad (2)$$

where β denotes the probability that the user randomly jumps to page *P* (Brin, 1998).

Authority and Hub

The metric of HITS (Hypertext Induced Topic Search), proposed by Kleinberg (1999), is often used to answer broad-topic queries and to find communities on the Web (Gibson et al., 1998). Its idea is based on the assumption that hyperlinks encode a considerable amount of latent human judgment. This type of judgment is the notion of authority. To be precise, the creator of page *P* having a link pointing to page *Q* has conferred authority on page *Q* to some extent. In addition, the creator of page *P* provides other pages that have links pointing to *P* the opportunities to find potential authorities.

The HITS algorithm tries to identify the set of the most related pages (called *root set* and denoted as S_σ hereafter) for a given query ε from a general search engine σ, and then evaluates the importance of the pages in S_σ. HITS first views the topology of the pages on the Web as a directed graph *G*. Graph *G* is represented as *G = (V, E)*, where *V* denotes a set of nodes in which each node in the set corresponds to a page on the Web, and *E* denotes a set of directed edges in which a directed edge *(P, Q)* exists in the set if there is a link from node *P* to node *Q*. Figure 3 expresses the steps: the first step is to submit query ε to search engine σ. The second step is to collect the first τ high-ranked pages derived from σ as the basic elements of S_σ. Then for each page *P* in S_σ, the next step is to construct two sets *A(P)* and *B(P)*, which respectively are the set of all pages that

Figure 3. Steps to find the Root Set from a User-Supplied Query

```
FindingRootSet ( σ , ε , τ , κ ) {
    Let  R_σ  denotes the top τ pages obtained by submitting  ε  to  σ ;
    Set  S_σ = R_σ ;
    For each page P∈ S_σ
        Let A(P) denotes the set of all pages that P points to;
        Let B(P) denotes the set of all pages pointing to P;
        Add all pages in A(P) to S_σ ;
        If |B(P) | ≤ κ  then
            Add all pages in B(P) to S_σ ;
        Else
            Add an arbitrary set of d pages from B(P) to  S_σ ;
        EndIf;
    EndFor;}
```

page P points to and the set of all pages that have a link pointing to page P. All the elements in $A(P)$ are inserted into S_σ directly. All the elements in set $B(P)$ are also inserted into S_σ if the number of set $B(P)$ is smaller than κ (a predefined number); otherwise (if the number of set $B(P)$ is larger than κ), an arbitrary set of κ pages in set $B(P)$ is inserted into S_σ.

After finding the root set, the HITS algorithm computes the authority and hub values for each page in the set. The idea is that a good authority should be pointed by a number of good hubs, and a good hub should point to a number of good authorities. The algorithm initially assigns a non-negative authority weight $x^{<o>}$ and a non-negative hub weight $y^{<o>}$ to each page, and then recursively updates the authority and hub weights of each referenced pages by the following equations, where $x_T^{<i>}$ and $y_T^{<i>}$ denote the authority and hub values of page T at the ith iteration ($T = P$ or Q).

$$x_P^{<i+1>} \leftarrow \sum_{(Q,P)\in E} y_Q^{<i>} \quad \text{and} \quad y_P^{<i+1>} \leftarrow \sum_{(P,Q)\in E} x_Q^{<i>} .$$

Finally, the high-quality pages are the ones with higher authority weight.

The HITS algorithm is a technique for locating high-quality documents related to a broad search topic and addresses another semantic ranking mechanism to evaluate the importance of a Web page. There are a lot of improvements for the HITS algorithms (Bharat et al., 1998; Chakrabarti et al., 1999a; Lawrence et al., 1999).

Textual Similarity

Textual similarity is used in the information retrieval community to measure the relevant degree between the document and the information the users need. Each document and the query are treated as an n-dimensional vector $<w_1, w_2, ..., w_n>$, where n is the number of unique terms in the vocabulary set, and w_i is the term-weight in the document (or the query) concerning the *i*th word in the vocabulary set. The degree of relevancy can be easily obtained by computing the similarity between query and document vectors. A vector matching operation, based on the cosine correlation (see Equation (3)), is used to measure the degree of textual similarity between the query and a document in the document collection. The resulting degree of the similarity can be used to rank the documents.

$$sim(d_i, q) = \frac{\vec{d_i} \cdot \vec{q}}{\left|\vec{d_i}\right| \times \left|\vec{q}\right|} = \frac{\sum_{j=1}^{n} w_{j,i} \times w_{j,q}}{\sqrt{\sum_{j=1}^{n} w_{j,i}^2} \times \sqrt{\sum_{j=1}^{n} w_{j,q}^2}},$$ (3)

where *q* is a query, is the *i*th document in the documents collection, and stands for the weight of the term in document *j*.

The term-weighting problem can be formulated as a clustering problem. Term Frequency/Inverse Documents Frequency (TFxIDF) is the common method to deal with term weighting by production of the TF (Term Frequency) and the IDF (Inverse Documents Frequency). TF, measuring the raw frequency of a term inside a document, provides for quantification of intra-cluster similarity; while IDF, measuring the inverse of the frequency of a term among the documents in the document collection, provides for quantification of inter-cluster dissimilarity. Further details about the term weighting can be found in Frakes et al. (1992).

Textural similarity has been applied to the World Wide Web (WWW) environment (Yang et al., 1999). A query Q drives the crawling process, and the importance of page P can be defined as the textual similarity between P and Q. However, there may be a difference in the computation of IDF in the WWW, since the crawling process cannot see the entire collection. Thus the IDF factor is estimated from the pages that have been crawled, or from some reference IDF terms that were computed at some other time.

Canonical Hierarchy

Text categorization (Yang et al., 1999) provides a suitable way for Web page ordering. Every Web page can be classified into different categories. The pages belonging to the interested category will be selected to users. This idea is based on the assumption that the probability of identifying the on-topic pages is higher if we always follow the links from Web pages belonging to the topic of interest. Thus the importance of a page can be determined by the category to which a page belongs.

From previous literature, the accuracy of classification by using a hierarchical taxonomy is better than that using a flat taxonomy. Therefore, many focused crawling systems utilized a hierarchy, such as Yahoo! and the Open Directory Project, to classify Web pages. In addition, they trained a text classifier and equipped it into the focused crawlers for classifying the Web pages. For example, Soumen Chakrabarti et al. (1999b) incorporated the manually compiled taxonomy from Yahoo! to build their topic-specific Web resource discovery system. Users can choose their favorite topic and select training examples to train the classifier through a Web-based administration interface of the system. The trained classifier, as well as the canonical hierarchy, is fed into a crawler to filter and rank the pages in the process of information discovery.

Reinforcement Learning

McCallum et al. (1999) created a topic-specific spider to find scientific papers on the Web. The Web spider incorporates the strategy of reinforcement learning, which is a branch of machine learning and concerns itself with optimal sequential decision-making. The strategy provides a formalism for measuring the adoption of actions that give no benefit immediately but gain benefit in the future. Reinforcement learning refers to the question of how an autonomous agent senses and acts in its environment. Whenever the agent performs an action in an environment, the trainer will provide a reward or penalty to indicate the appropriateness of the action. Based on the reward or penalty, the agent can learn to choose sequences of actions that will produce the greatest cumulative reward (Rennie et al., 1999).

The learning process of the agent can be formalized as a Markov decision process. The agent perceives a set S of distinct states and has a set A of actions that the agent can perform. The agent has a state-transition function T, $T: S{\times}A \rightarrow S$, and a reward function R, $R: S{\times}A \rightarrow V$. At discrete time step t, the agent senses the current state s_t of the environment, $s_t \in S$. Assume the agent chooses and performs an action a_t, $a_t \in A$. The environment then responds to the agent by a reward v, where $v \in V$ and $v = R(s_t, a_t)$, and leads the agent to the next state s_{t+1}, where $s_{t+1} = T(s_t, a_t)$. The goal of the learning process is to train the agent to have a control policy π, $\pi : S \rightarrow A$, which can maximize the total rewards over time.

RELEVANCY-CONTEXT-GRAPH APPROACH

Context Graph Approach

As Diligenti et al. (2000) mentioned, the major problem in focused crawling is how to assign proper credits to the unvisited pages that the crawler will visit. In the absence of a reliable credit assignment strategy, focused crawlers suffer from a limited knowledge of the topology of the Web. Thus focused crawlers usually incorporate domain-specific knowledge to facilitate subjective search.

When designing a page, Website designers usually assume that users will follow some paths, omit the off-topic information mentioned in those paths and finally reach their required pages. Dilegenti et al. (2000) proposed a novel approach to combine the context information within topic-specific crawling systems. They built a context model that can capture the link hierarchies rooted at a target page and, at the same time, encode the minimum distance from the off-topic page to the target page within that model. Those pages around the target pages are divided into several layers according to the distance away from target Web pages. The outer pages in the context graph will need more traversing steps to reach the target page. Figure 4 is a context graph that captures the link hierarchies in which each page in layer 1 has a link that directly points to the target page (in layer 0), each page in layer 2 has a link that points to some page in layer 1 (and then indirectly points to target page), and so on.

A context-focused crawler utilizes the capability of some general search engines to allow users to query for pages linking to a specified document. The resulting data are used to construct the representation of pages that occur within a certain link distance away

Figure 4. A Context Graph Keeps the Hierarchical Relationship between Contents and Layer Information within a Specific Topic

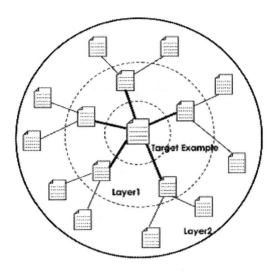

from the target documents. Then the representation is used to train a set of classifiers, which will assign documents to different categories based on the expected link distance away from the target document. That is, the classifiers are used to tell how many steps the current page is away from the target document. Based on the above discussion, two main stages are used in a focused crawler: (1) an initialization phase, during which a set of context graphs and the associated classifiers are constructed for each of the seed documents provided by the user; (2) a crawling phase that uses the classifiers to guide the search. The first stage of a crawling session is to extract the context from some general search engine within which seed pages can be found and then to encode this information in a context graph. Every derived seed document forms the first node of its associated context graph. Since the general search engine is capable of answering the parents for the specified page, each parent page is then inserted into the context graph as a node, and an edge is established between the target document node and the parent node. The similar work will be performed until a limited distance away from the target document is reached.

At the second stage, a set of classifiers is trained according to the different layers in which pages are located. A Naïve Bayes classifier is constructed for each layer. During crawling, the focused crawler will classify the downloaded pages into different classes, measuring in which layer the pages should be and putting them into the corresponding waiting queue. The crawler always retrieves the unvisited pages from the high-priority queues for crawling. Figure 5 is the framework of the focused crawler with several context graphs. In the initialization stage, a set of context graphs is constructed for the seed documents in the back crawl stage, and classifiers for different layers are trained in the learning stage. During the crawling stage, the crawler retrieves the pages from the Web, and the classifiers manage a set of queues containing the next page to be crawled.

Figure 5. System Architecture for Diligenti's Work

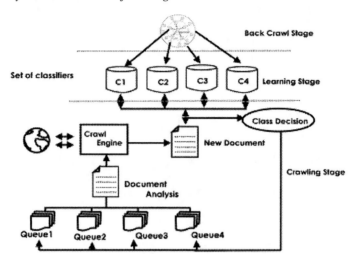

Relevancy-Context-Graph Model

The context-graph approach for topic-specific crawling is effective and efficient. The approach is based on the assumption that a common hierarchy exists on documents with the same topic. For example, the pages of computer science paper lists are usually found on the pages of researchers' publications, and these researchers' Web pages are usually referenced by the page with a list of laboratory members or department members. A nearly uniform hierarchy is expected to exist for such a topic. However, this assumption is not always true. The WWW is not a homogeneous and strictly organized structure. The topology of the related pages for some topics cannot form a uniform context graph.

Another problem with the context-graph approach is the amount of training data being different from layer to layer. It is natural and intuitive that more sample pages are found in the outer layers of the graph, and less sample pages found in the inner layers. This phenomenon is inclined to introduce a bias when we use these data to train the classifier for each layer. The classified result will tend to be dominated by the outer layer since the outer layer has more training data. As a result, this phenomenon leads the context-graph crawler to work like a breadth-first crawler.

We observed that hyperlinks of a page always provide semantic linkages between pages. In addition, we also observed that most pages are linked by other pages with related contents and that similar pages have links pointing to related pages. This assumption has been justified by Davison (2000). In his work, he shows the empirical evidence of topical locality on the Web, which implies topical locality mirrors spatial locality of pages on the Web. Based on this assumption, we propose an approach called the *Relevancy-Context-Graph* approach, which is similar to the context-graph approach. We also need to construct a context graph for each on-topic document. However, we treat it in a different way. Based on the topic locality assumption, the relevant pages should have semantic relationships to some degree through their links. To model this phenomenon, we use a number α, $\alpha \leq 1$ to present this relationship between pages. As Figure 6 suggests, the pages far away from the on-topic documents receive less relevancy value

Figure 6.   Context Graph with Relevancy Judgment: Pages Located in the nth Layer have the Relevant Degree α^n

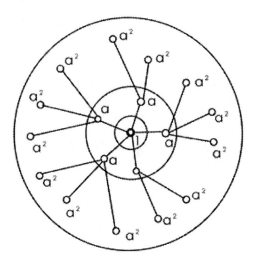

than the pages near the on-topic documents. For a given context graph, we can estimate the degree of relevancy for each page with respect to the on-topic document in such a way that the on-topic document itself (located in layer 0) will have the relevant degree 1; those pages located in layer 1 will have the relevant degree α, pages located in layer 2 have the relevant degree α^2, and so on.

We calculate the distributions of general feature words and the distributions of topic-specific feature words beforehand. In constructing the general word distribution, we use a task-oriented spider to crawl the Yahoo! taxonomy and retrieve all the referenced documents. Yahoo! is one of the largest manually-compiled Web directory search engines and contains more than 140,000 categories. We use these data to sample the Web and create the general-purpose language model. In constructing the topic-specific word distribution, we use the limited capability of search engines like AltaVista or Google to allow users to query the search engines for pages linking to a specified document. These data are used to construct the context graph for a given topic. After constructing the context graph, we can use Equation (4) to calculate the topic-specific word distribution:

$$P(w_i \mid t) = \frac{\displaystyle\sum_{\forall S \in G(t)} R_S \cdot C_{iS}}{\displaystyle\sum_{w_j} R_S \cdot C_{jS}} , \tag{4}$$

where $P(w_i \mid t)$ is the conditional probability of word w_i under the condition that is contained in topic t, $G(t)$ is the context graph for the topic t, R_s is the relevant degree of page S contained in $G(t)$, and C_{is} and C_{js} are the number of occurrence of word w_i and w_j in page S, respectively.

In the above equation, we consider the relevancy of a page as the weight to contribute to the distribution of the topic-specific feature words. It is reasonable that the feature of the words from the pages near the on-topic documents should be considered to be more important than the feature of the words from those pages far away from the on-topic documents. Thus the topic-specific relevancy of the occurrence of a word is proportional to the weight of its page.

When the crawler retrieves a document D, the relative degree of D with respect to the topic t should be assigned. Clearly, the higher the relative degree of D is, the higher the priority of D should be assigned for future crawling. We assign the priority to D according to the probability $P(t|D)$, which is the conditional probability relevant to the specified topic t when given the document D. According to the Bayes formula, we can convert the posteriori probability $P(t|D)$ from the prior probability $P(D|t)$. Then the priority of the newly retrieved document D is defined as follows:

$$P(t|D) = \frac{P(D|t)P(t)}{P(D)} \propto \frac{P(D|t)}{P(D)} = \frac{\sum_{w_i \in D} P(w_i|t)}{\sum_{w_i \in D} P(w_i)} \tag{5}$$

Note that the distributions of topic-specific feature words $P(w_i|t)$ are calculated from Equation (4). Thus in our approach, the rank of document D is calculated from the location of D in the context graph and the distribution of the feature words in D.

In Diligenti et al.'s work (2000), their focused crawler measures the priority of the pages according to which layer of the context graph the pages are located, and then retrieves the unvisited pages with the higher priority for crawling later. However, there does not often exist a uniform context graph for each topic, and a bias may occur since most pages are classified into the outer layers of the graph. In our approach, we calculate the distributions of feature words in a page for ranking the priority of the page instead. The priority calculation preserves the property of the context graph on the probabilities of feature words.

System Implementation

We divide the system into three subsystems according to their distinct functions. In Figure 7, we depict the three major building blocks of our topic-specific crawling system. The work of the data preparation subsystem collects necessary data from the Web, such as context graphs and general Web pages. The context graph is used to sample the word (or feature) distribution around the neighborhood of on-topic documents. When constructing context graphs, we retrieve the top N documents as on-topic documents, that is, the seed set of documents. After the seed documents have been retrieved, we recursively query the search engines, such as Google and AltaVista, to get the parent nodes of specified documents and finally construct each layer in the context graphs. The general Web pages are another kind of collected data. These data will be used to train a general language model, providing a way to estimate general word (or feature) distribution for Web documents. We can easily obtain the general Web pages from the Yahoo! directory search engine. Figure 8 shows the detail of the subsystem. In the subsystem, there are two major components: one is for constructing context graphs by

Figure 7. Three Major Subsystems of our Topic-Specific Crawling System

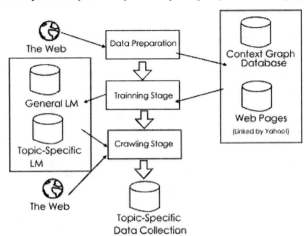

iteratively querying the search engines for parent nodes of a specified document; the other is for constructing the general language model referenced by the Yahoo! directory search engine.

All the data collected in the first subsystem are fed into the second subsystem (i.e., training subsystem), shown in Figure 7. The work of the subsystem is to train a topic classifier to have the capability to rank documents according to their relevancy to the specified topic. The subsystem tries to build two language models, general and topic-specific ones, respectively. Each language model provides the probability for the occurrence of a word. The major difference between these two language models is that the occurrence of a word in the topic-specific language model is weighted by the relevant degree. We treat both the language models as dictionaries with a word distribution probability. We use a huge hash table to implement the dictionary structure: each bucket of the hash table is composed of the exact word and its distribution probability. The distribution probability can be calculated to be the ratio of the occurrence of every individual word to the total words counted in the corpus. Note that all the words in the language models are exclusive of HTML tags and their attributes. The common words (also called stop words) are eliminated as well.

The third subsystem of the system shown in Figure 7 is used to cope with the crawling stage and the use of the learned knowledge for classification. The subsystem utilizes the trained data to determine the order for which pages should be visited first. There is a priority queue keeping all the unvisited URLs. When the crawler needs the next document to traverse, it pops the document with the highest priority from the queue. The document in the front of the queue is expected to rapidly lead to targets. The crawler then retrieves all the pages referenced by that document from the Web, calculates the scores of the new documents and puts the new documents back into the queue. In designing this subsystem, we need a robust HTML parser to look into the content of the page and parse all the referenced links. A robust HTTP protocol handler is also needed because some pages contain dead links, and some loops may be encountered when crawling. Figure 9 shows the details of the subsystem. The focused crawler uses the ordering function to reflect the possibility of finding the on-topic documents. The job controller

Figure 8. Details of the Subsystem for Data Preparation

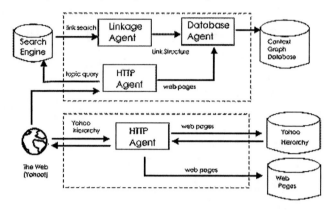

Figure 9. Details of the Subsystem of Crawling

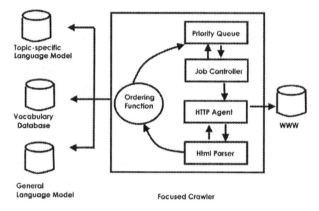

keeps popping up the unvisited URL with the highest priority to be retrieved first by the HTTP agent. The vocabulary database stores the thesaurus of feature words, domain knowledge of the topic, and so on.

EVALUATION

We compare the effectiveness of our crawling system to two crawlers: one is the breadth-first crawler and the other is the traditional focused crawler (Diligenti et al., 2000). The topic, "call for paper," is chosen for the evaluation. In the preparation of context graph training data, we limit the size of seed set (i.e., documents in layer 0) to be 30. All the words are extracted from HTML documents, exclusive of HTML tags and their attributes. All the on-topic documents are generated from the top 30 documents returned by the general text-based search engine. We use these 30 documents as seeds, and recursively find their up-links to construct their correspondent context graphs. The

Table 1. Statistics Summarizing the Context Graph for the Topic "Call for Paper"

Topic: Call for paper		
Vocabulary size: 211,060		
Layer	Number of nodes	Document size (byte)
0	30	305,131
1	179	7,053,497
2	1,359	35,267,685
3	13,926	347,270,949
4	25,191	791,967,774
Total	**40,685**	**1,181,865,036**

context graph data sets for the topic are summarized in Table 1. Note that the naïve α factor is set to 0.8 in the experiment to reflect the relevance relationship between two pages located in the two adjacent layers of the context graph.

To estimate the general word distribution, our spider traverses the Yahoo! taxonomy and retrieves all the referenced documents. There are fourteen top-level subjects in this experiment, in which each subject has a different number of child nodes and the depth can reach to 16. The characteristics of the Yahoo! hierarchy are shown in Figure 10. Then we start the three crawlers from the starting URL *http://www.cs.stanford.edu/* for the topics. Figure 11 shows the number of the relevant documents against the number of downloaded documents. From the figures, we can see our focused crawler keeps more focused on topic documents than the two others.

Figure 10. Distribution of the Number of Documents Pertaining to each one of the 14 Top-Level Subjects in Yahoo! Taxonomy (There are 571,356 documents referred by this taxonomy.)

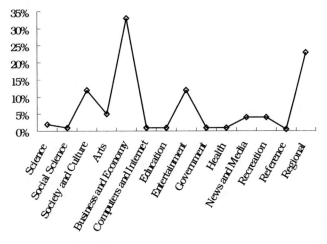

Figure 11.   Number of Relevant Documents against the Number of Downloaded Documents

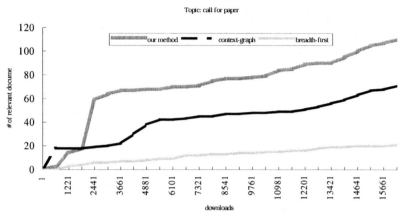

FUTURE TRENDS

General search engines are usually equipped with powerful crawlers that explore the Web exhaustively. It is reasonable for them to traverse the Web indiscriminately because general search engines aim at having a high coverage of the Web. Since the Web is growing at such a phenomenal pace, exhaustive crawling would take huge amounts of resources. In addition, a general search engine with a huge collection of documents is not always the best one. Without an appropriate quality control mechanism, users could get confused when they get thousands of results after a query submission to the general search engine.

Topic-specific crawling tries to solve this problem by means of controlling the quality of the retrieved data collection. The topic-specific search engines are becoming increasingly popular because they offer increased accuracy. They have other advantages such as less bandwidth and storage costs and capabilities of customizability as well. The personal search engine is the application of the focused crawling paradigm. Through recording the user's actions and analyzing his or her behavior from the data cached on the local disk, the personal search engine can be customized to provide personal service and meet individual needs.

The personal search engine still needs a lot of resources and energy to build and maintain, though its resource need is not as large as that of the general search engine. In addition, most people are familiar with the general search engines such as Yahoo! Thus, a simpler method that is based on the general search engines and can support customized service should be proposed. A personal document-filtering mechanism can equip browsers individually. The filtering mechanism learns the user interests from the cached data and the usage of the computer. Filtering can be seen as a special case of discriminating the documents into the relevant and non-relevant categories. The results of the queries from a general search engine could be filtered by this mechanism before the results are sent to the user. The mechanism re-ranks the search results to fit personal requirements, or the mechanism can further identify the results that the user is really interested in and discard the results that do not match that user's interest. Obviously, the personal document-filtering mechanism is also the application of the focused crawling paradigm, but it needs much fewer resources to build, as it is just post-processing of the stream of incoming documents from the general searching engines.

CONCLUSIONS

As the Web grows exponentially, it has become a crucial problem to provide effective search tools for searching with speed and precision. However, general search engines sometimes do not meet the user's demand, which may be solved by incorporating the systems with domain-specific knowledge. In this chapter, we propose a method to assign traversal order of unvisited pages for a topic-specific spider. Our method effectively estimates the proper order of unvisited pages and performs better than the pure context-graph and breadth-first spiders for a topic. We estimate the relevancy of a document according to the average expected distance away from the on-topic documents. The credit assignment for focused crawlers can be significantly improved by equipping the crawler with the capability of estimating the distance between current documents and the relevancy degree of the retrieved pages.

However, there are still some limitations in our method. First of all, we need a large amount of training data. These data could cost a lot of network bandwidth and storage. Secondly, we cannot handle complicated HTML layouts. Due to the popularity of the Web, more and more enhancements have been proposed and implemented in systems. Recently, most Web pages are not simply written in pure HTML; they often are created in HTML with the combination of script languages, such as JavaScript or VBScript, dynamically generated contents, and interactive embedded objects, such as a Java applet and Macromedia Flash. A focused crawler that can manage the rich hypertexts should be proposed for future use. Thirdly, we use a naïve a factor to reflect the relevance relationship between two pages that are located in two adjacent layers of the context graph. Traditional information retrieval uses cosine similarity to measure the content relevancy between two pages. Simply measuring the relevant relationship by contents will sometimes be ineffective. In fact, how to measure the relevancy in a hyperlinked environment is still a mystery. Perhaps algorithms similar to the HITS or PageRank algorithms should be incorporated to measure the relevancy degree between two pages.

REFERENCES

AltaVista. *http://www.altavista.com/*.

Bharat, K., & Henzinger, M. (1998). Improved algorithms for topic distillation in a hyperlinked environment. *Proceedings of the 21st Annual International ACM SIGIR Conference on Research and Development in Information Retrieval,* Melbourne, Australia, (pp. 104-111).

Brin, S., & Page, L. (1998). The anatomy of a large-scale hypertextual Web search engine. *Computer Networks and ISDN Systems, 30*(1-7), 107-117.

Brown, E.W., & Smeaton, A.F. (1998). Hypertext information retrieval for the Web. *ACM SIGIR Forum, 32*(2), 8-13.

Chakrabarti, S., Berg, M., & Dom, B. (1999a). Focused crawling: A new approach to topic-specific Web resource discovery. *Computer Networks, 31*(11-16), 1623-1640.

Chakrabarti, S., Berg, M., & Dom, B. (1999b). Distributed hypertext resource discovery through examples. *Proceedings of the 25th International Conference on Very Large Database (VLDB)*, (pp. 375-386).

Chakrabarti, S., Dom, B., Raghavan, P., & Kleinberg, J. (1998). Automatic resource compilation by analyzing hyperlink structure and associated text. *Computer Networks and ISDN Systems, 30*, 65-74.

Cho, J., Garcia-Molina, H., & Page, L. (1998). Efficient crawling through URL ordering. *Computer Networks, 30*(1-7), 161-172.

Cyveillance. (2003). *http://www.cyveillance.com/*.

Davison, B. (2000). Topical locality in the Web. *Proceedings of the 23rd International ACM SIGIR Conference on Research and Development in Information Retrieval*, (pp. 272-279).

Diligenti, M., Coetzee, F., Lawrence, S., Giles, C.L., & Gori, M. (2000). Focused crawling using context graphs. *Proceedings of the 26th International Conference on Very Large Database (VLDB 2000)*, (pp. 527-534).

Frakes, W.B., & Baeza-Yates, R. (1992). *Information retrieval: Data structures & algorithm*. NJ: Prentice Hall.

Gibson, D., Kleinberg, J., & Raghavan, P. (1998). Inferring Web communities from link topology. *Proceedings of the 9th ACM Conference on Hypertext and Hypermedia (HYPER-98)*, (pp. 225-234).

Google. *http://www.google.com/*.

Kleinberg, J. (1999). Authoritative sources in a hyperlinked environment. *Journal of the ACM, 46*(5), 604-632.

Lawrence, S. (2000). Context in Web search. *IEEE Data Engineering Bulletin, 23*(3), 25-32.

Lawrence, S., & Giles, C.L. (1999). Accessibility of information on the Web. *Nature, 400*, 107-109.

LinuxStart. *http://www.linuxstart.com/*.

McCallum, A., Nigam, K., Rennie, J., & Seymore, K. (1999). Building domain-specific search engines with machine learning techniques. *Proceedings of AAAI Spring Symposium on Intelligent Agents in Cyberspace*.

McCallum, A., Nigam, K., Rennie, J., & Seymore, K. (2000). Automating the construction of Internet portals with machine learning. *Information Retrieval Journal, 3*, 127-163.

Page, L., Brin, S., Motwani, R., & Winograd, T. (1998). *The PageRank citation ranking: Bring order to the Web*. Technical Report, Stanford University, CA.

Rennie, J., & McCallum, A. (1999). Using reinforcement learning to spider the Web efficiently. *Proceedings of the 16th International Conference on Machine Learning*, (pp. 335-343).

ResearchIndex. *http://citeseer.nj.nec.com/cs/*.

Travel-Finder. *http://www.travel-finder.com/*.

Yahoo! *http://www.yahoo.com/*.

Yang, Y., & Liu, X. (1999). A re-examination of text categorization methods. *Proceedings of the 22nd Annual International ACM SIGIR Conference on Research and Development in Information Retrieval (SIGIR'99)*, (pp. 42-49).

Chapter IV

Ontology Learning from a Domain Web Corpus*

Roberto Navigli
University of Rome "La Sapienza", Italy

ABSTRACT

Domain ontologies are widely recognized as a key element for the so-called semantic Web, *an improved, "semantic aware" version of the World Wide Web. Ontologies define concepts and interrelationships in order to provide a shared vision of a given application domain. Despite the significant amount of work in the field, ontologies are still scarcely used in Web-based applications. One of the main problems is the difficulty in identifying and defining relevant concepts within the domain. In this chapter, we provide an approach to the problem, defining a method and a tool, OntoLearn, aimed at the extraction of knowledge from Websites, and more generally from documents shared among the members of virtual organizations, to support the construction of a domain ontology. Exploiting the idea that a corpus of documents produced by a community is the most representative (although implicit) repository of concepts, the method extracts a terminology, provides a semantic interpretation of relevant terms and populates the domain ontology in an automatic manner. Finally, further manual corrections are required from domain experts in order to achieve a rich and usable knowledge resource.*

INTRODUCTION

The next generation of the World Wide Web, the so-called *semantic Web*, aims at improving the "semantic awareness" of computers connected via the Internet. The semantic Web requires that information be given a well-defined meaning through a machine-processable representation of the world, often referred to as an ontology.

The goal of a domain ontology is to reduce (or eliminate) the conceptual and terminological confusion among the members of a virtual community of users (for example, tourist operators, commercial enterprises, computer scientists) that need to share electronic documents and information of various kinds. This is achieved by identifying and properly defining a set of relevant concepts that characterize a given application domain. An ontology is therefore a *shared understanding* of some domain of interest (Uschold, 1996). In other words, an ontology is an explicit, agreed specification about a shared conceptualization. The construction of such a shared understanding, that is, a unifying conceptual framework, fosters *communication* and *cooperation* among people, *interoperability* among systems, *system engineering benefits* (reusability, reliability, and specification), and so forth.

Ontologies may have different degrees of formality but they necessarily include a vocabulary of terms with their meaning (definitions) and their relationships. Thus the construction of an ontology requires a thorough domain analysis that is accomplished by[1]:

- Carefully identifying *the vocabulary* that is used to describe the relevant concepts within the domain;
- Coding *complete and rigorous definitions* about the terms (concepts) in the vocabulary;
- Characterizing the *conceptual relations* among those terms.

The definition of the basic kinds and structures of concepts that are applicable in every possible domain usually requires the joint work of specialists from several fields, like philosophical ontologists and Artificial Intelligence researchers. The issue of identifying these very few "basic" principles, referred to as the *top ontology* (TO), is not a purely philosophical one, since there is a clear practical need of a model that has as much generality as possible, to ensure reusability across different domains (Smith et al., 2001).

Domain modelers and knowledge engineers are involved in the task of identifying the key domain conceptualizations, and describing them according to the organizational *backbones* established by the top ontology. The result of this effort is referred to as the *upper domain ontology* (UDO), which usually includes a few hundred application-domain concepts.

While many ontology projects eventually succeed in the definition of an upper domain ontology, very few projects can overcome the actual barrier of populating the third level that we call the *specific domain ontology* (hereafter, SDO), at the price of inconsistencies and limitations. On the other hand, general-purpose resources like Wordnet (Fellbaum, 1995), Cyc (Lenat, 1993) and EDR (Yokoi, 1993) — while dealing with thousands of concepts — do not encode much of the domain knowledge needed by specialized applications like information retrieval, document management, (semantic) Web services and so on.

Figure 1 reports the three levels of generality of a domain ontology.

It turns out that, although domain ontologies are recognized as crucial resources for the semantic Web (Berners-Lee, 1999), in practice, full-fledged resources are not available, and when available they are not used outside specific research or community environments.

We identify three features needed to build *usable* ontologies: *coverage*, *consensus* and *accessibility*.

Figure 1. Three Levels of Generality of a Domain Ontology

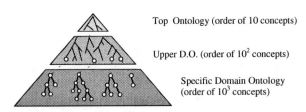

Top Ontology (order of 10 concepts)

Upper D.O. (order of 10^2 concepts)

Specific Domain Ontology
(order of 10^3 concepts)

- *Coverage:* the SDO must be sufficiently (for the application purposes) populated. Tools are needed to extensively support the task of identifying the relevant concepts and the relations among them.
- *Consensus:* reaching the consensus on a given issue is a difficult activity for one person and it gets even harder when the task involves a group of people and, in addition, the group is geographically dispersed. When a community decides to cooperate in a given domain, firstly, they have to agree on many basic issues; that is, they must reach a *consensus* of the business domain. Such a common view must be reflected by the domain ontology.
- *Accessibility:* tools are needed to easily integrate the ontology within an application that may clearly show its decisive contribution; for example, improving the ability to share and exchange information through the Web. This makes the ontology *accessible.*

The importance of ontologies in the field of information systems is always growing. Despite the significant amount of work carried out in recent years, ontologies are still scarcely applied and used. Research has mainly addressed the basic principles, such as knowledge representation formalisms, but limited attention has been devoted to more practical issues, such as techniques and tools aimed at the actual construction of an ontology (i.e., its actual *content*). Though recently a number of contributors proposed methods to extract terminology and word relations from domain data and Websites (Maedche et al., 2000, 2001; Morin, 1999; Vossen, 2001), there are two major drawbacks in the reported approaches:

- First, what is learned from available documents is mainly a list of *terms* and term relations. The definition (i.e., the *semantic interpretation*) of these terms is still left to the ontology engineer.
- Second, ontology learning has been investigated in isolation from ontology *engineering* (as also remarked in Maedche et al. (2000)) and ontology *validation* issues. This is a serious drawback, since an ontology in which the relevant concepts are not conformant with a domain view of a given community, will be scarcely used, or even disregarded.

Comprehensive ontology construction and learning has been an active research field in the past few years. Several workshops[2] have been dedicated to ontology learning and related issues. The majority of papers in this area propose methods to extend an existing ontology with unknown words (for example, Aguirre et al., 2000, and Alfonseca & Manandhar, 2002).

Alfonseca and Manandhar present an algorithm to enrich Wordnet with unknown concepts on the basis of hyponymy patterns. For example, the pattern *hypernism(N2,N1):appositive(N2,N1)* captures an hyponymy relation between Shakespeare and poet in the appositive NP: "Shakespeare, the poet...". This approach heavily depends upon the ability of discovering such patterns; however, it appears to be a useful complementary strategy with respect to OntoLearn. OntoLearn, in fact, is unable to analyze totally unknown terms. Berland and Charniak (1999) propose a method to extract whole-part relations from corpora and enrich an ontology with this information.

Few papers propose methods to extensively enrich an ontology with domain terms. For example, Vossen (2001) uses statistical methods and string inclusion to create syntactic trees, as we do (see Figure 4). However, no semantic disambiguation of terms is performed. Very often, in fact, ontology learning papers regard domain terms as concepts.

A statistical classifier for automatic identification of semantic roles between terms is presented in Gildea and Jurafsky (2001). In order to tag texts with the appropriate semantic role they use a training set of 50,000 sentences manually annotated within the FrameNet semantic labeling project, a resource that, unfortunately, is only partially available.

Finally, in Maedche and Staab (2000, 2001) an architecture is presented to help ontology engineers in the difficult task of creating an ontology. The main contribution of this work is in the area of ontology engineering, although machine learning methods are also proposed to automatically enrich the ontology with semantic relations.

In this chapter we describe a methodology and a tool aimed at building and assessing a domain ontology for intelligent information integration within a virtual community of users. The system has been developed and tested in the context of two European projects, *Fetish* (*http://fetish.singladura.com/index.php*) and *Harmonise* (*http://dbs.cordis.lu*), where it is used as the basis of a semantic interoperability platform for small and medium-sized enterprises operating in the tourism domain.

The main focus of the chapter is the description of *OntoLearn*, a tool for knowledge extraction from electronic documents, supporting the rapid construction of a domain ontology.

Figure 2 illustrates the proposed ontology engineering method, that is, the sequence of steps and the intermediate output produced in building a domain ontology.

As shown in Figure 2, *ontology engineering* is a complex process involving machine concept *learning* (*OntoLearn*), machine-supported concept *validation* (*Consys*) and *management* (*SymOntoX*).

OntoLearn explores available documents and related Websites to learn domain concepts, and to detect taxonomic relations among them. Concept learning is mainly based on the use of external, generic knowledge sources (specifically WordNet and SemCor, illustrated later). The subsequent processing step in Figure 2 is *ontology validation*. This is a continuous process supported by Web-based *groupware* aimed at consensus building, called *Consys* (Missikoff et al., 2001), to achieve a thorough validation with representatives of the communities that are active in the application domain.

Figure 2. Ontology Engineering Chain

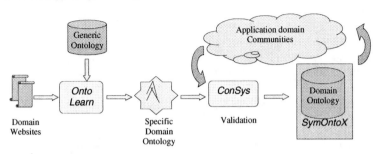

OntoLearn operates in connection with SymOntoX (Missikoff, 2002), an *ontology management* system used by the ontology engineers to define the concepts and their mutual connections, thus allowing a semantic net to be constructed. SymOntoX uses a knowledge representation method, referred to as *OPAL* (Object, Process, Actor modeling Language) (Missikoff, 2000), which is an extension of XML-based formalisms, such as RDF and OIL (*http://www.daml.org/2001/03/daml+oil-index*). The ontology engineers use the environment provided by SymOntoX to attach automatically learned concept sub-trees under the appropriate nodes of the upper domain ontology, to enrich concepts with additional information, and to perform consistency checks.

In the next section we describe in more detail the OntoLearn system, namely: terminology extraction from Websites, the knowledge-based semantic interpretation method, along with a summary of the knowledge representation scheme, the construction of a specific domain ontology and the possible integration of the domain ontology with WordNet. Finally, we present the results of the first year of experiments. Conclusions, further research and expected outcomes are discussed in the last section.

OntoLearn SYSTEM

The OntoLearn system consists of three main phases (shown in Figure 3). First, a domain terminology is *extracted* from a corpus of texts in the application domain (specialized Websites or documents exchanged among members of a virtual community), and *filtered* using statistical techniques and documents from different domains for contrastive analysis. The resulting terminology is the surface appearance of relevant domain concepts.

Second, terms are *semantically interpreted;* that is, unambiguous *concept* names are associated to the extracted terms.

Third, taxonomic (i.e., generalization/specialization) and similarity relations among concepts are detected, and a *specific domain ontology* (SDO) is generated. Ontology matching (i.e., the integration of SDO with the existing upper ontology) is performed with the aid of SymOntoX.

We assume that only a small *upper domain ontology* is available initially (a realistic assumption indeed); therefore, semantic interpretation is based on external (non domain-specific) knowledge sources, such as *WordNet* (Fellbaum, 1995) and the semantically tagged corpus *SemCor* (*http://mind.princeton.edu/wordnet/doc/man/semcor.htm*).

Figure 3. Architecture of OntoLearn

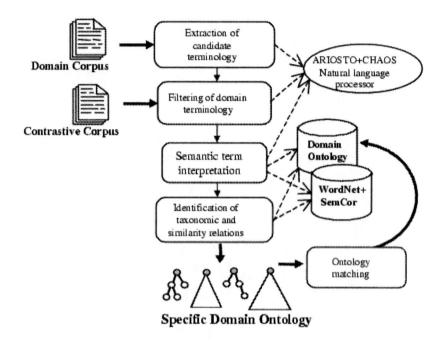

Specific Domain Ontology

WordNet is a large lexical knowledge base, whose popularity has recently been growing even outside the computational linguistic community. SemCor is a corpus of semantically annotated sentences; that is, every word is annotated with a sense tag selected from the WordNet sense inventory for that word.

Identification of Relevant Domain Terminology

The objective of this phase is to extract a domain terminology from the available documents. The documents are retrieved by browsing Websites with an initial set of domain terms (in our application domain, an initial upper ontology of about 300 terms was available), and then progressively specializing the search when new terms are learned.

A linguistic processor, ARIOSTO+CHAOS (Basili, 1996), is used to extract from the domain documents a list of syntactically plausible terminological patterns; for example, compounds (*credit card*), prepositional phrases (*board of directors*), adjective-noun relations (*manorial house*). Then, non-terminological (e.g., *last week*) and non-domain specific terms (e.g., *net income* in a tourism domain) are filtered out by using two measures based on information theory.

The first measure, called *Domain Relevance*, computes the conditional probability of occurrence of a candidate term in the application domain (e.g., tourism) with respect to other corpora that we use for a contrastive analysis (e.g., medicine, economy, novels, etc.).

More precisely, given a set of n domains $\{D_1, ..., D_n\}$ the domain relevance of a term t in the domain D_k is computed as:

$$DR_{t,k} = \frac{P(t \mid D_k)}{\max\limits_{1 \le j \le n} P(t \mid D_j)}$$

where $P(t \mid D_k)$ is estimated by:

$$E(P(t \mid D_k)) = \frac{f_{t,k}}{\sum\limits_{t' \in D_k} f_{t',k}}$$

where $f_{t,k}$ is the frequency of term t in the domain D_k.

The second measure, called *Domain Consensus* (*DC*), computes the *entropy* of the probability distribution of a term across the documents of the application domain. The underlying idea is that only terms that are *frequently* and *consistently* referred to in the available domain documents reflect some *consensus* on the use of that term. *DC* is an entropy, defined as:

$$DC_{t,k} = \sum\limits_{d \in D_k} \left(P_t(d) \log \frac{1}{P_t(d)} \right)$$

where $P_t(d)$ is the probability that a document d includes t. These two measures have been extensively evaluated in Velardi (2001) and Fabriani (2001).

Terminology filtering is obtained through a linear combination of the two filters:

$$DW_{t,k} = \alpha DR_{t,k} + (1-\alpha) DC_{t,k}^{norm}$$

where $DC_{t,k}^{norm}$ is a normalized entropy and $\alpha \in (0,1)$.

Let T be the terminology extracted after the filtering phase. Using simple string inclusion, a *forest* of *lexicalized trees* can be generated. Figure 4 is an example of lexicalized tree   extracted from our tourism corpus.

Clearly, lexicalized trees do not capture many taxonomic relations between terms, for example between *public transport service* and *bus service* in Figure 4.

Figure 4. A Lexicalized Tree

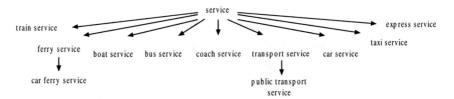

Semantic Interpretation of Terms

Semantic interpretation is a mapping between terms and concepts. To each term $t = w_n \cdot \ldots \cdot w_2 \cdot w_1$ (where w_i is an atomic word) the process of semantic interpretation associates the appropriate concept label. The idea is that although the string t is usually not included in the start-up ontology, there should be a conceptual entry for each possible sense of w_i ($i=1, \ldots, n$): for example, though there are no concepts associated with "*swimming pool*," we may find concept descriptions for "*swimming*" and "*pool*" individually. Therefore, it should be possible to compositionally create a definition for t, selecting the *appropriate* concept definition for w_i ($i=1, \ldots, n$), given the string context t in which it appears.

As we said, we use WordNet as a start-up ontology, since the upper domain ontology is initially quite poor. In WordNet, a word sense is uniquely identified by a set of terms called *synset*, (e.g., the sense #1 of *pool* is defined by { pool#1 }), and a textual definition called *gloss*, (e.g., "a hole that is (usually) filled with water"). Synsets are taxonomically structured in a lattice, with a number of "root" concepts called *unique beginners* (e.g., { entity#1, something#1 }). WordNet includes over 120,000 words (and over 170,000 synsets), but very few domain terms: for example, "*food*" and "*company*" are individually included, but not "*food company*" as a unique term.

Formally, a semantic interpretation is defined as follows: let $t = w_n \cdot \ldots \cdot w_2 \cdot w_1$ be a valid term belonging to a lexicalized tree   . The process of *semantic interpretation* is one that associates to each word w_k in t the appropriate WordNet synset $S^k_{i_k}$, where i_k is a sense number. The *sense*[3] of t is hence defined as:

$$S(t) = \{ S^k_{i_k} : S^k_{i_k} \in Synsets(w_k), w_k \in t \}$$

where $Synsets(w_k)$ is the set of synsets, each representing a distinct sense of the word w_k and $i_k \in \{ 1, \ldots, | Synsets(w_k) | \}$.

For instance:

$S(\text{"food company"}) = \{ \{ \text{food\#1, nutrient\#1} \}, \{ \text{company\#1} \} \}$

corresponding to sense #1 of *company* ("*an institution created to conduct business*") and sense #1 of *food* ("*any substance that can be metabolized by an organism to give energy and build tissue*").

Semantic interpretation is achieved by intersecting semantic information associated with each alternative sense of the words in t, and then selecting the "best" intersection. Semantic information is extracted from WordNet and represented in a diagrammatic form, according to a representation scheme described in the next subsection.

Semantic Representation of Concepts

Several types of lexical and semantic relations are supplied in WordNet, though these relations are neither systematically nor formally defined. As a first effort, we tried to establish a connection between the relations in WordNet and the concept representation scheme adopted in OntoLearn.

We define an ontology as a *semantic net,* constructed by supplying a set of concepts and their semantic relationships briefly reported in what follows. For each semantic relation a graphic symbol is provided: it will be used in constructing the diagrams (semantic nets) presented in the next sub-sections. We define $S \xrightarrow{R}{}^n T$ as

$S \xrightarrow{R} S_1 \xrightarrow{R} \ldots \xrightarrow{R} S_n \equiv T$, which is a chain of n instances of the relation R. We also define

$\xrightarrow{R_1,R_2}$ as $\xrightarrow{R_1} \cup \xrightarrow{R_2}$.

- *Generalization:* This is an asymmetric relation, often indicated as *is-a* relation, which links a concept to its more general concepts (e.g., *hotel is-a building*). Its inverse is called *specialization.* In the linguistic realm, this relation, defined between *synsets,* is called *hyperonymy* ($\xrightarrow{@}$) and its inverse *hyponymy* ($\xrightarrow{\sim}$). An example is shown in Figure 5.

- *Aggregation:* This is an asymmetric relation that connects a concept representing a whole to another representing a component. It is often indicated as *has-a* relation (e.g., *hotel has-a reception*). Its inverse is called *decomposition.* In the linguistic realm, this relation, defined between *synsets,* is called *meronymy* ($\xrightarrow{\#}$), and *holonymy* ($\xrightarrow{\%}$) its inverse. An example is shown in Figure 6.

Figure 5. An Example of Hyperonymy and Hyponymy — Book#2 is a Hyperonym of Hardcover#1, while Hardcover#1 is a Hyponym of Book#2

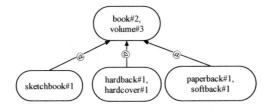

Figure 6. An Example of Meronymy and Holonymy — Car door#1 is a Meronym of Car#1, while Car#1 is a Holonym of Car door#1

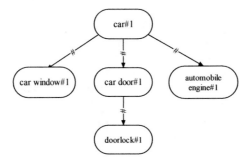

Figure 7. An Example of Similarity and Correlation

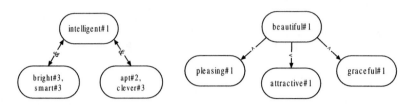

- *Similarity:* This is a symmetric relation that links two concepts that are considered similar in the given domain. A similarity degree is often indicated (e.g., *hotel similar-to [0.8] motel*).

  In the linguistic realm, this relation, defined between *synsets*, is called *synonymy* when the similarity degree is 1^4, while *similarity* ($\overset{\&}{\rightarrow}$) and *correlation* ($\overset{\wedge}{\rightarrow}$) are used to indicate progressively weaker levels of similarity (see Figure 7 for an example).

  In WordNet there is also a *dissimilarity* relation, called *antonymy* ($\overset{!}{\rightarrow}$), for example *liberal* and *conservative*, indicating a degree of similarity =0. Furthermore, the relation *pertainymy* ($\overset{\backslash}{\rightarrow}$) relates the nominal and adjectival realization of a concept (e.g., *mother* and *maternal*).

- *Relatedness:* This is a semantic relation that connects two concepts symmetrically related in the given domain. This relation assumes specific, domain dependent interpretations. For example, in *hotel related-to airport*, the relation subsumes *physical proximity*. This weakly defined relation does not have a counterpart in WordNet, but it can be induced from concept definitions and from the semantically annotated sentences in the SemCor corpus. Parsing the definition (i.e., the gloss in WordNet) of a given concept, and the semantically annotated sentences including that concept, we generate a linguistic counterpart of "relatedness," represented by the *gloss* relation ($\overset{gloss}{\rightarrow}$) and the *topic* relation ($\overset{topic}{\rightarrow}$). The idea is that if a concept c_2 appears in the definition of another concept c_1, or if c_2 appears in the near proximity of c_1 in an annotated sentence including c_1, then c_1 and c_2 are "related," that is, $c_1 \overset{gloss}{\rightarrow} c_2$ or $c_1 \overset{topic}{\rightarrow} c_2$, respectively. For example: "*The room(#1)s were very small but they had a nice view(#2)*" produces $room\#1 \overset{topic}{\rightarrow} view\#2$.

Term Disambiguation

Disambiguation of terms provides a semantic interpretation for the terms resulting from the terminology extraction step previously described. In order to disambiguate the words in a term $t = w_n \cdot \ldots \cdot w_2 \cdot w_1$ we proceed as follows:

(a)   If t is the first analyzed element of $\mathfrak{I}$, disambiguate the root node (w_1 if t is a compound) of $\mathfrak{I}$ either in a manual or an automatic way[5].

(b)   For any $w_k \in t$ and any synset S^k_i of w_k (i ranging from 1 to the number of senses of w_k), create a *semantic net*. Semantic nets are automatically created using the semantic relations described in the previous subsection, extracted from WordNet and SemCor (and, possibly, from the upper domain ontology).

To reduce the size of a semantic net, concepts at a distance greater than three edges from the net centre, S^k_i, are excluded. Figure 8 is an example of semantic net generated for sense #1 of *pool*.

Let then $SN(S^k_i)$ be the semantic network for sense i of word w_k.

(c)   Starting from the "head" w_1 of t, and for any pair of words w_{k+1} and w_k ($k=1,...,n$) belonging to t, intersect alternative pairs of semantic nets. Let $I = SN(S^{k+1}_i) \cap SN(S^k_j)$ be such an intersection for sense i of word $k+1$ and sense j of word k. Note that in each step k, the word w_k is already disambiguated, either as an effect of root disambiguation (for $k=1$) or as a result of step $k-1$.

(d)   For each intersection I, identify common *semantic patterns* in I in order to select the sense pairs (i, j) producing the "strongest" intersection (occasionally, more than one pair). To this end, given two arbitrary synsets S_1 and S_2, we use the following heuristics[6]:

1.   *color*, if S_1 is in the same adjectival cluster as *chromatic#3* and S_2 is a hyponym of a concept that can assume a colour like *physical object#1, food#1*, and so forth (e.g., $S_1 \equiv yellow\#1$ and $S_2 \equiv wall\#1$);

2.   *domain*, if the gloss of S_1 contains one or more domain labels and S_2 is a hyponym of those labels (for example, *white#3* is defined as "(of wine) almost colorless"; therefore it is the best candidate for *wine#1* in order to disambiguate the term *white wine*);

3.   *synonymy*, if

   (a) $S_1 \equiv S_2$ or (b) $\exists N \in Synset_{WN} : S_1 \xrightarrow{\ \ } N \equiv S_2$

Figure 8.   Part of the Semantic Net for the Concept Pool#1

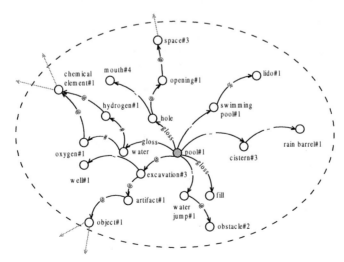

(for example, in the term *open air* both the words belong to synset { *open#8, air#2, ..., outdoors#1* });

4. *hyperonymy/meronymy path*, if:

$$\exists M \in Synset_{WN} : S_1 \overset{@,\#^{\leq 3}}{\to} M \overset{\leq 3_{\sim,\%}}{\leftarrow} S_2$$

(for instance, *mountain#1* $\overset{\#}{\to}$ *mountain peak#1* $\overset{@}{\to}$ *top#3* provides the right sense for each word of *mountain top*);

5. *hyponymy/holonymy path*, if:

$$\exists M \in Synset_{WN} : S_1 \overset{\sim,\%^{\leq 3}}{\to} M \overset{\leq 3_{@,\#}}{\leftarrow} S_2$$

(for example, in *sand beach*, *sand#1* $\overset{\%}{\to}$ *beach#1*);

6. *parallelism*, if:

$$\exists M \in Synset_{WN} : S_1 \overset{@^{\leq 3}}{\to} M \overset{\leq 3_{@}}{\leftarrow} S_2$$

(for instance, in *enterprise company*, *organization#1* is a common ancestor of both *enterprise#2* and *company#1*);

7. *gloss*, if:

(a) $S_1 \overset{gloss}{\to} S_2$ or (b) $S_1 \overset{gloss}{\leftarrow} S_2$

(for instance, in *picturesque village*, WordNet provides the example *"a picturesque village"* for sense 1 of *picturesque*; in *Website*, the gloss of *Web#5* contains the word *site*; in *waiter service*, the gloss of *restaurant attendant#1*, hyperonym of *waiter#1*, contains the word *service*);

8. *topic*, if $S_1 \overset{topic}{\to} S_2$ (like for the term *archeological site*, where both words are tagged with sense 1 in a SemCor file; notice that WordNet provides no mutual information about them);

9. *gloss+hyperonymy/meronymy path*, if:

$$\exists G, M \in Synset_{WN} : S_1 \overset{gloss}{\to} G \overset{@,\#^{\leq 3}}{\to} M \overset{\leq 3_{\sim,\%}}{\leftarrow} S_2$$
$$\vee \, S_1 \overset{gloss}{\to} G \overset{\sim,\%^{\leq 3}}{\to} M \overset{\leq 3_{@,\#}}{\leftarrow} S_2$$

(for instance, in *railways company,* the gloss of *railway#1* contains the word *organization* and *company#1* $\overset{@}{\rightarrow}$ *institution#1* $\overset{@}{\rightarrow}$ *organization#1*)

10. *gloss+parallelism,* if:

$$\exists G, M \in Synset_{WN} : S_1 \overset{gloss}{\rightarrow} G \overset{@\ \leq 3}{\rightarrow} M \overset{\leq 3\ @}{\leftarrow} S_2$$

(for instance, in *transport company,* the gloss of *transport#3* contains the word *enterprise* and *organization#1* is a common ancestor of both *enterprise#2* and *company#1*);

11. *gloss+gloss,* if:

$$\exists G \in Synset_{WN} : S_1 \overset{gloss}{\rightarrow} G \overset{gloss}{\leftarrow} S_2$$

(for example, in *mountain range, mountain#1* and *range#5* both contain the word *hill* so that the right senses can be chosen)

12. *hyperonymy/meronymy+gloss path,* if:

$$\exists G, M \in Synset_{WN} : S_1 \overset{@,\#\leq 3}{\rightarrow} M \overset{\leq 3\ \sim,\%}{\leftarrow} G \overset{gloss}{\leftarrow} S_2$$
$$\lor S_1 \overset{\sim,\%\leq 3}{\rightarrow} M \overset{\leq 3\ @,\#}{\leftarrow} G \overset{gloss}{\leftarrow} S_2;$$

13. *parallelism+gloss,* if:

$$\exists G, M \in Synset_{WN} : S_1 \overset{@\ \leq 3}{\rightarrow} M \overset{\leq 3\ @}{\leftarrow} G \overset{gloss}{\leftarrow} S_2.$$

Figure 9 shows a strong intersection between *mountain#1* and *top#3*. The bold arrows identify a pattern matching the "gloss+parallelism" heuristic (rule 10):

$$mountain\#1 \overset{gloss}{\rightarrow} land\#3 \overset{@}{\rightarrow}^2 location\#1 \overset{@}{\leftarrow} top\#3$$

(e)   Finally, for each intersection *I,* a vector is created measuring the number and weight of matching semantic patterns, as sketched in Figure 10. That is, while disambiguating the subterm $w_{k+1} \cdot w_k$ given the sense S_i^{k+1} for word w_{k+1} and all possible *n* senses of w_k, each intersection $SN(S_i^{k+1}) \cap SN(S_1^k), ..., SN(S_j^{k+1}) \cap SN(S_n^k)$ is evaluated as a vector, and the sum represents the "score" vector for S_j^{k+1}. If no mutual information is retrieved (that is, the sum is $\underline{0}$), the process is repeated between w_{k+1} and w_i (*i=k*-1, ..., 1) until a positive score is calculated.

Figure 9. Example of Intersecting Semantic Patterns for Mountain#1 and Top#3

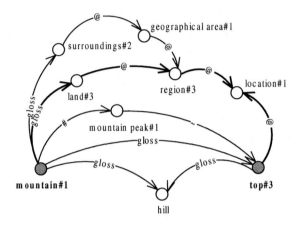

Figure 10. Evaluation of a Sense S of Term t with all Possible Senses of Term v (V_1, ..., V_n)

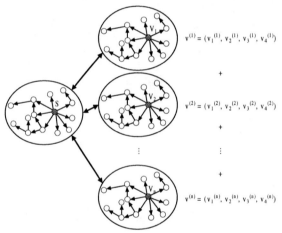

The best "score" vector (according to a lexicographic ordering) determines the sense for w_{k+1}. The process does not take into account the sense chosen for w_k in the previous iteration, because of a well-acknowledged polysemy of words coded in WordNet (Krovetz, 1997) (in fact, other senses may bring important information to the semantic interpretation process).

Refining the Gloss Relation

Starting from the work in Milhalcea (2001), we developed an algorithm for gloss disambiguation that relies on a set of heuristic rules and is based on multiple, incremental iterations. Here we describe the algorithm, report a running example and provide evaluation measures on a first set of domain glosses.

The Gloss Disambiguation Algorithm

A simplified formal description of the algorithm is reported in Figure 11. The algorithm takes as input the synset S whose gloss G we want to disambiguate. Two sets are used, P and D. D is a set of disambiguated synsets, initially including only the synset S. P is a set of terms to be disambiguated, initially containing all the terms from gloss G and from the glosses $\{G'\}$ of the direct hyperonyms of S. As clarified later, adding $\{G'\}$ provides a richer context for semantic disambiguation. The term list is obtained using our natural language processor to lemmatize words, and then removing irrelevant words. We use standard information retrieval techniques (e.g., stop words) to identify irrelevant terms.

When, at each iteration of the algorithm, we disambiguate one of the terms in P, we remove it from the set and add its interpretation (i.e., synset) to the set D. Thus, at each step, we can distinguish between *pending* and *disambiguated* terms (respectively the sets P and D). Notice again that P is a set of terms, while D contains synsets.

(a)   *Find monosemous terms:* The first step of the algorithm is to remove monosemous terms from P (those with a unique synset) and include their unique interpretation in the set D.

(b)   *Disambiguate polysemous terms:* Then, the core iterative section of the algorithm starts. The objective is to detect *semantic relations* between some of the synsets in D and some of the synsets associated to the terms in P. Let S' be a synset in D (an already chosen interpretation of term t') and S'' one of the synsets of a polysemous term $t'' \in P$ (i.e., t'' is still ambiguous). If a semantic relation is found between S' and S'', then S'' is added to D and t'' is removed from P.

To detect semantic relations between S' and S'', we apply a set of heuristics grouped in two classes, *Path* and *Context*, described in what follows.

Path Heuristics

The heuristics in class Path seek for *semantic patterns* from the node S' and the node S'' in the WordNet semantic network. A *pattern* is a chain of nodes (synsets) and arcs (directed semantic relations), where S' and S'' are at the extremes. We use the following heuristics to identify semantic paths ($S' \in D$, $S'' \in Synsets(t'')$, $t'' \in P$):

1.   *Hyperonymy path:* if $S' \stackrel{@}{\rightarrow}^n S''$ choose S'' as the right sense of t'' (e.g., thus we have $canoe\#1 \stackrel{@}{\rightarrow}^2 boat\#1$; i.e., a *canoe* is a kind of *boat*);

2.   *Hyperonymy/Meronymy path:* if $S' \stackrel{@,\#}{\rightarrow}^n S''$ choose S'' as the right sense of t'' (e.g., $archipelago\#1 \stackrel{\#}{\rightarrow} island\#1$);

3.   *Hyponymy/Holonymy path:* if $S' \stackrel{\sim,\%}{\rightarrow}^n S''$ choose S'' as the right sense of t'' (e.g., $window\#7 \stackrel{\%}{\rightarrow} computer\ screen\#1$);

4.   *Adjectival Similarity:* if S'' is in the same adjectival cluster than S', choose S'' as the right sense of t''. For example, *irritable#2* is defined as "*abnormally sensitive to a stimulus*" and *sensitive#1* is in the same cluster than *irritable#2*, so the first

sense of *sensitive* can be chosen;

5. *Parallelism:* if exists a synset T such that $S'' \overset{@}{\to} T \overset{@}{\leftarrow} S'$, choose S'' as the right sense of t'' (for example, *background#1* $\overset{@}{\to}$ *scene#3* $\overset{@}{\leftarrow}$ *foreground#2*);

Context Heuristics

The context heuristics use several available resources to detect co-occurrence patterns in sentences and contextual clues to determine a semantic proximity between S' and S''. The following heuristics are defined:

1. *Semantic co-occurrences:* word pairs may help in the disambiguation task if they always co-occur with the same senses within a tagged corpus. We use three resources in order to look for co-occurrences, namely:

   - the *SemCor corpus,* a corpus in which each word in a sentence is assigned a sense selected from the WordNet sense inventory for that word; an excerpt of a SemCor document follows:
     - **Color#1** was **delayed#1** until 1935, the **widescreen#1** until the **early#1 fifties#1**.
     - **Movement#7** itself **was#7** the **chief#1** and **often#1** the **only#1 attraction#4** of the primitive#1 movies#1 of the nineties#1.

   - the *LDC corpus,* a corpus in which each document is a collection of sentences having a certain word in common. The corpus provides a sense tag for each occurrence of the word within the document. Unfortunately, the number of documents (and therefore the number of different tagged words) is limited to about 200. An example taken from the document focused on the noun *house* follows:
     - Ten years ago, he had come to the **house#2** to be interviewed.
     - Halfway across the **house#1**, he could have smelled her morning perfume.

   - *gloss examples:* in WordNet, besides glosses, examples are sometimes provided containing synsets rather than words. From these examples, as for the LDC Corpus, a co-occurrence information can be extracted. With respect to LDC, WordNet provides examples for thousands of synsets, but just a few for the same word. Some examples follow:
     "Overnight **accommodations#4** are available."
     "Is there **intelligent#1** life in the universe?"
     "An **intelligent#1** question."

As we said above, only the SemCor corpus provides a sense for each word in a pair of adjacent words occurring in the corpus, while LDC and gloss examples provide the right sense only for one of the terms.

In either case, we can use this information *to choose the synset S'' as the right interpretation of t'' if the pair t' t'' occurs in the gloss and there is an agreement among (at least two of) the three resources about the disambiguation of the pair t' t''.* For example:

[…] Multnomah County may be short of general assistance money in its budget to handle an unusually high **summer#1 month#1**'s need […].

Later#1, Eckenfelder increased#2 the efficiency#1 of treatment#1 to between 75 and 85 percent#1 in the **summer#1 months#1**.

are sentences from the LDC Corpus and SemCor, respectively. Since there is a full agreement between the resources, one can easily disambiguate the gloss of *summer_camp#1: "a site where care and activities are provided for children during the summer months"*.

2.   *Common domain labels:* Domain labels are the result of a semiautomatic methodology described in Magnini (2000) for assigning domain labels (e.g., *tourism, zoology, sport*) to WordNet synsets[7]. This information can be exploited to disambiguate those terms with the same domain labels of the start synset S. Notice that a synset can be marked with many domain labels; therefore the algorithm selects the interpretation S'' of t if the following conditions hold together (the *factotum* label is excluded because it is a sort of topmost domain):

- *DomainLabels(S")* \ { factotum }$\subseteq$ *DomainLabels (S)* \ { factotum };
- There is no other interpretation S''' of t'' such that *DomainLabels (S''')* \ { factotum } $\subseteq$ *DomainLabels (S)* \ { factotum }.

For example, *boat#1* is defined as *"a small vessel for travel on water"*; both *boat#1* and *travel#1* belong to the *tourism* domain and no other sense of *travel* satisfies the conditions, so the first sense of *travel* can be chosen. Similarly, *cable car#1* is defined as *"a conveyance for passengers or freight on a cable railway;"* both *cable car#1* and *conveyance#1* belong to the *transport* domain and no other sense of *conveyance* satisfies the conditions, so the first sense of *conveyance* is selected.

(c)   *Update D and P.* During each iteration, the algorithm applies all the available heuristics in the attempt of disambiguating some of the terms in P, using all the available synsets in D. While this is not explicit in the simplified algorithm of Figure 11, the heuristics are applied in a fixed order that has been experimentally determined. For example, context heuristics are applied after Path heuristics 1-4, while Path heuristic 5 is applied only if no other heuristic applies. At the end of each iterative step, new synsets are added to D, and the correspondent terms are deleted from P. The next iteration makes use of these new synsets in order to possibly disambiguate other terms in P. Eventually, P becomes either empty or no new semantic relations can be found.

When the algorithm terminates, D \ { S } can be considered a first approximation of a *semantic definition of S*. For mere gloss disambiguation purposes, the tagged terms in the hyperonyms' gloss are discarded, so that the resulting set (*GlossSynsets*) now contains only interpretations of terms extracted from the gloss of S. At this stage, we can only distinguish the concepts extracted from the gloss of S from those in the gloss of its direct hyperonyms (respectively, in the dark and light gray ellipse in Figure 12), but the only available interpretations for semantic relations are those adopted in WordNet. WordNet relations, as already remarked, are not axiomatised, and often confuse the lexical and the semantic level.

Figure 11. Disambiguation Algorithm

```
DisambiguateGloss(S)

{G already disambiguated? }
if (GlossSynset(S) ≠ ∅) return

{ S is the starting point }
D := { S }
{ disambiguation  is  applied  the  terms  within  the  gloss of S
  and the glosses of its direct  hyperonyms }
P := Gloss(S) ∪ Gloss(Hyper(S))

{look for synsets associated to monosemous terms in P }
M := SynsetsFromMonosemousTerms(P)
D := D ∪ M
{ 'Terms' returns the terms contained in the gloss of M }
P := P \ Terms(M)

LastIteration:=D

{ until there is some heuristic to apply }
while(LastIteration ≠ ∅)
    NS := ∅ { new chosen synsets for disambiguating terms in the gloss of S }

        { for each just disambiguated synset S'}
        foreach (S' ∈ LastIteration)
            { look for connections between S' and the synsets to disambiguate }
            NS := NS ∪ Path-heuristics(S', P)

            NS := NS ∪ Context-heuristics(S', P)

        { D now contains all the new chosen synsets from the last iteration }
        D := D ∪ NS
        { remove the terms contained in the gloss of NS }
        P := P \ Terms(NS)
        { these results will be used in the next iteration }
        LastIteration := NS

{ stores the synsets chosen for some terms
  in the gloss of S }
foreach S' ∈ D
    if (Terms(S') ∩ Gloss(S) ≠ ∅)
        GlossSynsets(S) := GlossSynsets(S) ∪ { S' }

Return GlossSynsets(S)
```

A second, more precise approximation of a sound ontological definition for S is obtained by determining the nature of the semantic relations connecting S with each concept in $D \setminus \{ S \}$. This is an ongoing task and is discussed later in the chapter.

A Running Example

In the following, we present a sample execution of the algorithm on sense 1 of *retrospective*. Its gloss defines the concept as *"an exhibition of a representative selection of an artist's life work,"* while its hyperonym, *art exhibition#1,* is defined as *"an exhibition of art objects (paintings or statues)"*. Initially we have:

- $D = \{ retrospective\#1 \}$
- $P = \{$ *work, object, exhibition, life, statue, artist, selection, representative, painting, art* $\}$

The application of the monosemy step gives the following result:

- $D = \{$ *retrospective#1, statue#1, artist#1* $\}$
- $P = \{$ *work, object, exhibition, life, selection, representative, painting, art* $\}$

because *statue* and *artist* are monosemous terms in WordNet.

During the first iteration, the algorithm finds the matches:

retrospective#1 $\overset{@}{\rightarrow}^2$ *exhibition#2, statue#1* $\overset{@}{\rightarrow}^3$ *art#1* and *statue#1* $\overset{@}{\rightarrow}^6$ *object#1*

This leads to:

- $D = \{$ *retrospective#1, statue#1, artist#1, exhibition#2, object#1, art#1* $\}$
- $P = \{$ *work, life, selection, representative, painting* $\}$

During the second iteration, the hyponymy/holonymy heuristic finds that:

art#1 $\overset{\sim}{\rightarrow}^2$ *painting#1* (painting is a kind of art)

leading to:

- $D = \{$ *retrospective#1, statue#1, artist#1, exhibition#2, object#1, art#1, painting#1* $\}$
- $P = \{$ *work, life, selection, representative* $\}$

Since no new paths are found, the third iteration makes use of the LDC Corpus to find the co-occurrence *"artist life,"* with sense 12 of *life* (*biography, life history*):

- $D = \{$ *retrospective#1, statue#1, artist#1, exhibition#2, object#1, art#1, painting#1, life#12* $\}$
- $P = \{$ *work, selection, representative* $\}$

Notice that during an iteration, the co-occurrence heuristic is used only if all the other heuristics fail.

Figure 12. First Approximation of a Semantic Definition of Retrospective#1

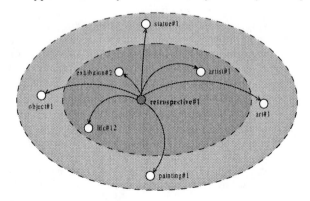

The algorithm stops because there are no additional matches. The chosen senses concerning terms contained in the hyperonym's gloss were of help during disambiguation, but are now discarded. Thus we have:

GlossSynsets(retrospective#1) = { *artist#1, exhibition#2, life#12* }

Evaluation of the Gloss Disambiguation Algorithm

A preliminary evaluation of the gloss disambiguation algorithm has been performed on a first set of 297 domain glosses. A more comprehensive assessment on general-purpose glosses is ongoing.

Two annotators manually assigned the appropriate WordNet sense to each term in a gloss, with a good inter-annotator agreement.

To assess the performance of the algorithm we used two usual evaluation measures: *recall* and *precision*. Recall provides the percentage of right senses with respect to the overall number of terms contained in the examined glosses. Precision measures the percentage of right senses with respect to all the retrieved gloss senses.

Table 1 gives an overview of the preliminary results. The algorithm runs with a 46.20% recall and a precision of 93.52%. A baseline precision is also provided, with a result of 82.89%, obtained with the first sense choice heuristic (notice that in WordNet the first sense of a term is also the most frequent).

Thanks to its good results, gloss disambiguation is a promising technique for improving the precision of term disambiguation, but we are also planning further applications to approach difficult tasks like Query Expansion, Information Retrieval, and so forth.

Creating Domain Trees

After semantic interpretation, all the terms in a tree $\Im$ are independently disambiguated. In this phase, in order to give concepts a semantic structure, we apply the following techniques:

(a) *concept clustering:* certain concepts are *fused* in a unique concept name on the basis of pertainymy, similarity and synonymy relations (e.g., respectively: *manor house* and *manorial house, expert guide* and *skilled guide, bus service* and *coach service*). Notice that we detect semantic relations between *concepts,* not words. For example, *bus#1* and *coach#5* are synonyms, but this relation does not hold for other senses of these two words;

(b) *taxonomic structuring:* hierarchical information in WordNet is used to detect is-

a relations between *concepts* (e.g., *ferry service* $\xrightarrow{@}$ *boat service*).

Since all the elements in $\Im$ are jointly considered, some interpretation error produced in the previous disambiguation step is corrected (this is due to the fact that hyperonymy relations involving the right sense may be found).

On the basis of these changes, each lexicalized tree $\Im$ is finally transformed into a *domain concept tree* Υ. Figure 13 shows the concept tree obtained from the lexicalized tree of Figure 4. For clarity, in the figure concepts are labelled with the associated terms (rather than with synsets), and numbers are shown only when more than one semantic

Table 1. Preliminary Results of the Gloss Disambiguation Algorithm

	# Terms	Retrieved senses	Right senses	Recall	Precision	Baseline
Domain glosses	1303	602	563	46.20%	93.52%	82.89%

Figure 13. A Domain Concept Tree

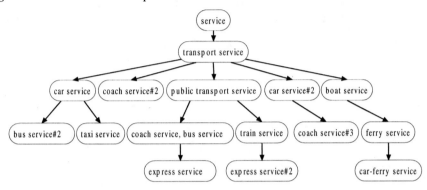

interpretation holds for a term, as for *coach service* and *bus service* (e.g., sense #3 of "bus" refers to "old cars").

Ontology Integration

It is not always the case that a basic core of domain concepts is already defined (Figure 14). This can happen because of a lack of agreement among experts or even because of the difficulty in the integration of different available domain resources.

In case it is not available, an upper domain ontology can be extracted from WordNet, through proper pruning and trimming, accomplished as follows:

- After the domain concept trees are attached under the appropriate nodes in WordNet in either a manual or an automatic manner, all branches not containing a domain node can be removed from the WordNet hierarchy;
- An intermediate node in the remaining WordNet hierarchy is pruned whenever the following conditions hold together[8]:
  i.   it has no "brother" nodes;
  ii. it has only one direct hyponym;
  iii. it is not the root of a domain concept tree;
  iv. it is not at a distance ≤ 2 from a WordNet *unique beginner* (this is to preserve a "minimal" top ontology).

Condition (i) prevents from hierarchy from being flat (the nodes in light grey in Figure 15 would be deleted, thus losing important semantic information). Condition (ii) must hold because a node with more than one hyponym is surely valuable, as it collocates at least two nodes under the same concept; conversely, a node with only one hyponym gives no additional information and provides no further classification. Condition (iii) is

Figure 14. How to Proceed when the Upper Domain Ontology is Not Defined?

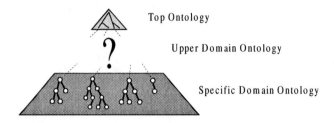

Figure 15. Pruning Steps over the Domain Concept Tree for "wine#1" (in dark grey)

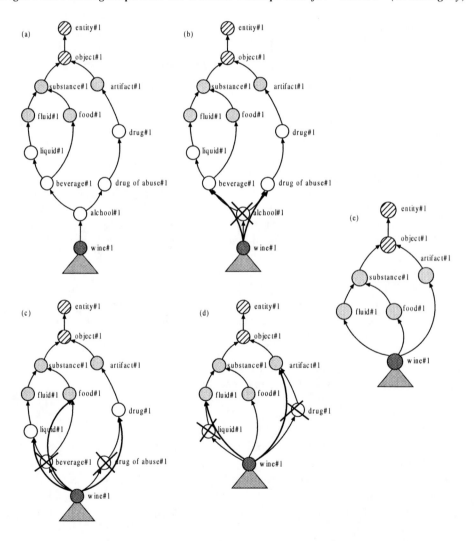

trivial: no domain node can be deleted. Also, condition (iv) is quite intuitive: nodes very high in the hierarchy represent the essential core of abstract concepts that cannot be deleted.

Figure 15 shows an example of pruning the nodes located over the domain concept tree with root *wine#1*. For the nodes in light grey the first condition does not hold, so they cannot be pruned, while shaded nodes belong to the upper part of the WordNet taxonomy, thus violating the fourth condition. The third condition prevents the concept *wine#1* from being deleted.

EVALUATION OF THE ONTOLEARN SYSTEM

The evaluation of ontologies is recognized to be an open problem[9]. Though the number of contributions in the area of ontology learning and construction has considerably increased in the past years, especially in relation to the forthcoming semantic Web, experimental data on the utility of ontologies are not available, besides (Farquhar et al., 1995) where an analysis of user distribution and requests is presented for the Ontology Server system. A better performance indicator would have been the number of users that access Ontology Server on a regular basis, but the authors mention that regular users are only a small percentage. Recent efforts are being made on the side of ontology evaluation tools and methods, but available results are on the methodological rather than on the experimental side. The ontology community is still in the process of assessing an evaluation framework.

We believe that, in absence of a commonly agreed-upon schema for analysing the properties of an ontology, the best way to proceed is evaluating an ontology within some existing application. Our current work is precisely in this direction: the results of a terminology translation experiment appear in Navigli et al. (2003), while an ontology-based text filtering experiment is still in progress.

In this chapter we presented an ontology learning method that is composed of various modules and algorithms. Therefore some kind of stand-alone evaluation of the output produced by OntoLearn is necessary. First, we provide an account of the feedback obtained from tourism experts participating in the Harmonise project (the Fetish project ended up with the need of tools for the construction of domain ontologies). Then, we evaluate the semantic disambiguation procedure, the key step of the OntoLearn methodology.

OntoLearn is a knowledge extraction system aimed at improving human productivity in the time-consuming task of building a domain ontology. Our experience in building a tourism ontology for the European project Harmonise reveals that, after one year of ontology engineering activities, the tourism experts were able to release the most general layer of the tourism ontology, manually identifying about 300 concepts. Then, we decided to speed up the process, developing the OntoLearn system. This produced a significant acceleration in ontology building, since in the next 6 months[10] the tourism ontology reached 3,000 concepts. Clearly, the definition of an initial set of basic domain concepts is crucial, so as to justify long lasting discussions. But once an agreement is reached, filling the lower levels of the ontology can still take a long time simply because it is a tedious and time-consuming task. Therefore we think that OntoLearn proved to be a useful tool within the Harmonise project.

The OntoLearn system has also been evaluated independently from the ontology engineering process. We extracted from a 1 million-word corpus of travel descriptions (downloaded from tourism Websites) a terminology of 3,840 terms, manually evaluated[11] by domain experts participating in the Harmonise project.

Two usual evaluation measures have been employed: *recall* and *precision*. Recall is defined as follows:

$$recall = \frac{\#\,correct\ terms}{\#\,domain\ relevant\ terms} \cdot 100$$

thus providing a percentage of the domain extracted terms with respect to the overall number of terms in the considered domain (which can only be estimated, of course).

Precision gives the percentage of domain terms with respect to all the retrieved terms. It is defined as:

$$precision = \frac{\#\,correct\ terms}{\#\,retrieved\ terms} \cdot 100$$

We obtained a precision ranging from 72.9% to about 80% and a recall of 52.74%. The precision shift is motivated by the well-known fact that the intuition of experts may significantly differ[12]. The recall has been estimated by submitting a list of about 6,000 syntactic candidates to the experts, asking them to mark truly terminological entries, and then comparing this list with that obtained by the filtering method for the identification of relevant domain terminology.

One of the novel aspects of OntoLearn with respect to current ontology learning literature is semantic interpretation of terms. Several experiments were performed to evaluate the semantic disambiguation algorithm. The evaluation was used to tune certain features of the algorithm (for example, the size of semantic nets, the weight of patterns, etc.).

First, we selected 650 complex terms from the set of 3,840, and we manually assigned the appropriate WordNet synset to each word composing the term. We used two annotators to ensure some degree of objectivity in the test set. These terms altogether contributed to the creation of 90 syntactic trees.

We found that the patterns involving the gloss relation contribute more than others to the precision of the algorithm. Certain patterns were found to produce a negative effect, and were removed. Among these is the *inverse gloss pattern* (heuristic 7[b]).

After the tuning phase, the process of semantic disambiguation led to an overall 84.5% precision, growing to about 89% for highly structured sub-trees such as those in Figure 13. In fact, the creation of domain trees significantly contributes to eliminating disambiguation errors (on the average, 5% improvement). The main results are reported in Figure 16. The dark columns show the results obtained when removing from the set of complex terms those including unambiguous words.

Figure 16. Precision Obtained Excluding Some of the Heuristics from the Term Disambiguation Section

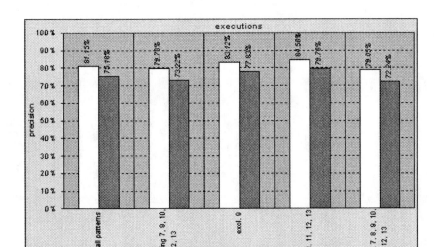

A consistent improvement is expected by the refinement of the gloss relations obtained through the gloss disambiguation algorithm. Currently, a full evaluation is ongoing.

Variations on the structure of semantic nets have also been considered, both including the information conveyed by certain kinds of relations (pertainymy, attribute, similarity) and applying some cuts on the quantity of hyponyms and on the higher part of WordNet's name hierarchy. The best result was reached when including all kinds of semantic relations and applying reasonable cuts.

Finally, we computed a sort of baseline, comparing the performance of the algorithm with that obtained by a method that always chooses the first synset for each word in a complex term. Recall that in WordNet the first sense is the most probable.

The results are shown in Figure 17. The increment in performance with respect to the baseline is higher (over 5%) when considering only polysemous terms. A 5% difference is not striking; however, the tourism domain is not very technical, and often the first sense is the correct one. We plan in the future to run experiments with more technical domains, for example economy, or software products.

Figure 17. Comparison with a Baseline

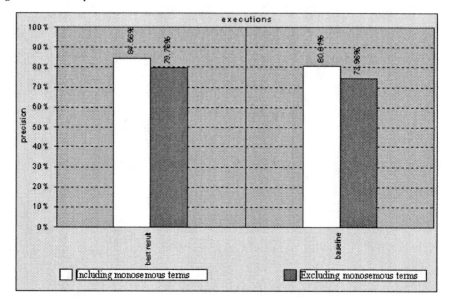

CONCLUSIONS AND FUTURE DEVELOPMENTS

In this chapter a method and the main ideas of the OntoLearn tool, aimed at supporting the ontology engineering process, have been presented. The method extracts domain concepts and detects semantic relationships among them. As mentioned in the previous section, the use of OntoLearn within the Harmonise project produced a remarkable increase of productivity in ontology building.

Setting aside the outcomes of a specific application (though real-world test beds do matter), we envisage several general advantages of OntoLearn with respect to ontology learning methods described in the literature:

- Many methods have been proposed to extract domain terminology or word associations from texts and use this information to build or enrich an ontology. *Terms* are, however, invariably identified with domain *concepts,* while we propose an actual *semantic interpretation* of terms.

- Thanks to semantic interpretation, we are able to detect not only taxonomic, but also other types of relations (e.g., similarity, pertainymy, relatedness). The amount of extracted semantic relations is being extended in our on-going work, exploiting the information obtained from the intersections of semantic nets and gloss disambiguation.

- Though WordNet is not an ontological standard for the semantic Web, it is *de facto* one of the most widely used general-purpose lexical databases, as also witnessed by the considerable funding devoted by the European Community to its extension (the EuroWordNet project[13]). An explicit relation between a domain ontology and WordNet may favour interoperability and harmonization between different ontologies.

- Ontology learning issues have been considered in strict connection with ontology engineering and validation issues. We conceived a general architecture, which we described only in a short form for the sake of brevity. The interested reader may refer to the referred papers for details.

However, ontology learning is a complex task and much is left to be done. Here we list some drawbacks or gaps of our method, which we are coping with in our ongoing developments:

- The semantic interpretation method requires that each term component have at least one synset in WordNet. If this is not the case (as it might happen in more technical domains), some context-based guess should be performed, as in Alfonseca and Manandhar (2002). A module that deals with such a problem is planned for the next version of OntoLearn.
- OntoLearn detects taxonomic relations starting from an initial lexicalized tree (Figure 4), structured on the basis of string inclusion. An ongoing extension of the algorithm attempts, in a subsequent step, to enrich a domain concept tree with "singleton" concepts whose originating terms have no words in common (e.g.,

  swimming pool $\xrightarrow{@}$ hotel facility), but this is outside the current scope of OntoLearn.
- OntoLearn detects taxonomic relations between complex concepts, and other types of semantic relations among the components of a complex concept. However, an ontology is usually more than this. The result of concept disambiguation in OntoLearn is more than a list of synsets, since we obtain semantic nets and intersections among them. This information, however, is not currently exploited to generate richer concept definitions. If available, a large resource like FrameNet could be used to add new relations, as in Gildea and Jurafsky (2001).
- Evaluation of gloss disambiguation is still in progress, but positive feedback shows that it will be useful for improving the precision of the semantic interpretation step and for defining concepts in terms of interconnected semantic nets. We also plan to employ these resources for query expansion and information retrieval tasks.
- A large-scale evaluation is still to be done. As we already pointed out, evaluation of ontologies is recognized as an open problem, and few results are available, mostly on the procedural ("how to") side. We partly evaluated OntoLearn in an automatic translation task (Navigli et al., 2003), and we are currently experimenting with an ontology-based text filtering system. In addition, it would be interesting to run OntoLearn on different domains, so as to study the effect of higher or lower levels of ambiguity and technicality on the output domain ontology.

REFERENCES

Agirre, E., Ansa, O., Hovy, E., & Martinez, D. (2000). Enriching very large ontologies using the WWW. *ECAI 2000 Ontology Learning Workshop.*

Alfonseca, E., & Manandhar, S. (2002, May). Improving an ontology refinement method with hyponymy patterns. *Language Resources and Evaluation* (LREC-2002), Las Palmas, Spain.

Basili, R., Pazienza, M.T., & Velardi, P. (1996). An empirical symbolic approach to natural language processing. *Artificial Intelligence, 85,* 59-99.

Berland, M., & Charniak, E. (1999). *Finding parts in very large corpora. Proceedings of the 37th Annual Meeting of the Association for Computational Linguistics (ACL-99).*

Berners-Lee, T. (1999). *Weaving the Web.* San Francisco, CA: Harper.

Fabriani, P., Velardi, P., & Missikoff, M. (2001, October). Using text processing techniques to automatically enrich a domain ontology. *Proceedings of ACM Conference on Formal Ontologies and Information Systems, ACM FOIS,* Ogunquit, Maine.

Farquhar, A., Fikes, R., Pratt, W., & Rice, J. (1995). *Collaborative ontology construction for information integration.* Technical report, Knowledge Systems Laboratory, Department of Computer Science.

Fellbaum, C. (1995). *WordNet: An electronic lexical database.* Cambridge: MIT Press.

Gildea, D., & Jurafsky, D. (2001). Automatic labelling of semantic roles. *Computational Linguistics, 99*(9).

Harabagiu, S., & Moldovan, D. (1999). *Enriching the WordNet taxonomy with contextual knowledge acquired from text.* AAAI/MIT Press.

Krovetz, R. (1997). Homonymy and polysemy in information retrieval. *Proceedings of ACL/EACL.*

Lenat, D.B. (1993). *CYC:* A large scale investment in knowledge infrastructure. *Communication of the ACM, 3*(11), 1993.

Maedche, A., & Staab, S. (2000). Semi-automatic engineering of ontologies from text. *Proceedings of the 12th International Conference on Software Engineering and Knowledge Engineering (SEKE'2000).*

Maedche, A., & Staab, S. (2001, May). Learning ontologies for the semantic Web. *Proceedings of the 2nd International Workshop on the Semantic Web,* Hong Kong, China.

Magnini, B., & Strapparava, C. (2000, June). Integrating subject field codes into WordNet. *Proceedings of LREC-2000, Second International Conference on Language Resources and Evaluation,* Athens, Greece.

Milhalcea, R., & Moldovan, D. (2001, June). eXtended WordNet: Progress report. *NAACL 2001 Workshop on WordNet and Other Lexical Resources,* Pittsburgh.

Missikoff, M. (2000). OPAL - A knowledge-based approach for the analysis of complex business systems. *LEKS, IASI-CNR,* Rome.

Missikoff, M., & Taglino, F. (2002, June). Business and enterprise ontology management with SymOntoX. *Proceedings of International Semantic Web Conference.*

Missikoff M., & Wang, X.F. (2001). Consys - A group decision-making support system for collaborative ontology building. *Proceedings of Group Decision & Negotiation 2001 Conference,* La Rochelle, France.

Morin, E. (1999). Automatic acquisition of semantic relations between terms from technical corpora. *Proceedings of 5th International Congress on Terminology and Knowledge Extraction, TKE-99.*

Navigli, R., Velardi, P., & Gangemi, A. (2003, January-February). Corpus driven ontology learning: A method and its application to automated terminology translation. *IEEE Intelligent Systems,* Special Issue on NLP, 22-31.

Smith, B., & Welty, C. (2001). Ontology: Towards a new synthesis. *Formal Ontology in Information Systems.* ACM Press.

Staab, S., & Maedche, A. (2001). Ontology learning for the semantic Web. *IEEE Intelligent Systems, 16*(2).

Uschold, M., & Gruninger, M. (1996). Ontologies: Principles, methods and applications. *The Knowledge Engineering Review, 11*(2).

Velardi, P., Missikoff, M., & Basili, R. (2001, July). Identification of relevant terms to support the construction of domain ontologies. *ACL-EACL Workshop on Human Language Technologies,* Toulouse, France.

Vossen, P. (2001, July). Extending, trimming and fusing WordNet for technical documents. *NAACL 2001 Workshop on WordNet and Other Lexical Resources,* Pittsburgh.

Yokoi, T. (1995). The EDR electronic dictionary. *Communications of the ACM, 38*(11), 15.

ENDNOTES

[*] This work has been partially supported by the European Project ITS – 13015 (FETISH) and ITS- 29329 (HARMONISE).

[1] "IDEF5 Ontology Description Capture Method Overview, " *http://www.idef.com/overviews/idef5.htm.*

[2] ECAI-2000 1st Workshop on *Ontology Learning (http://ol2000.aifb.uni-karlsruhe.de)* and IJCAI-2001 2nd Workshop on *Ontology Learning (http://ol2001.aifb.uni-karlsruhe.de).*

[3] The semantic interpretation of a term should be defined as a list, but here we use sets for convenience.

[4] Strict synonyms are those belonging to the same synset.

[5] Automatic root disambiguation can be performed in quite the same way as the procedure presented here by intersecting each root with its descendants and with all the other roots. However, a fully automatic procedure is a very delicate matter because choosing the wrong sense, that is, the wrong collocation for the root term in the hierarchy, would affect all its descendants in $\mathfrak{I}$.

[6] Some of these heuristics have been inspired by the work presented in Harabagiu (1999) and Milhalcea (2001).

[7] Domain labels have been kindly made available by the IRST to our institution for research purposes.

[8] The pruning step is performed from the bottom (the root domain node's hyperonyms) to the top of the hierarchy (the *unique beginners*).

[9] Consult the OntoWeb D.1.3 Tools Whitepaper *(http://www.aifb.unikarlsruhe.de/WBS/ysu/publications/eon2002_whitepaper.pdf).*

[10]   The time span also includes the effort needed to test and tune OntoLearn. Manual verification of automatically acquired domain concepts actually required few days.

[11]   Here manual evaluation is simply deciding whether an extracted term is relevant, or not, for the tourism domain.

[12]   This fact stresses the need of a consensus building groupware, such as Consys.

[13]   *http://www.hum.uva.nl/~ewn/.*

Chapter V

MARS:
Multiplicative Adaptive
Refinement Web Search

Xiannong Meng
Bucknell University, USA

Zhixiang Chen
The University of Texas - Pan American, USA

ABSTRACT

This chapter reports the project MARS (Multiplicative Adaptive Refinement Search), which applies a new multiplicative adaptive algorithm for user preference retrieval to Web searches. The new algorithm uses a multiplicative query expansion strategy to adaptively improve and reformulate the query vector to learn users' information preference. The algorithm has provable better performance than the popular Rocchio's similarity-based relevance feedback algorithm in learning a user preference that is determined by a linear classifier with a small number of non-zero coefficients over the real-valued vector space. A meta-search engine based on the aforementioned algorithm is built, and analysis of its search performance is presented.

INTRODUCTION

Vector space models and relevance feedback have long been used in information retrieval (Baeza-Yates & Ribeiro-Neto, 1999; Salton, 1989). In the n-dimensional vector space model, a collection of n index terms or keywords is chosen, and any document $\mathbf{d}$ is represented by an n-dimensional vector $\mathbf{d} = (d_1, ..., d_n)$, where d_i represents the relevance value of the i-th index term in the document. Let D be a collection of documents, R be the set of all real values, and R^+ be the set of all positive real values. It has been shown in Bollmann and Wong (1987) that if a user preference relation $\prec$ is a *weak order* satisfying some additional conditions then it can be represented by a linear classifier. That is, there is a query vector $\mathbf{q} = (q_1, ..., q_n) \in R^n$ such that:

$$\forall \mathbf{d}, \mathbf{d}' \in D, \mathbf{d} \prec \mathbf{d}' \Leftrightarrow \mathbf{q} \bullet \mathbf{d} < \mathbf{q} \bullet \mathbf{d}'. \tag{1}$$

Here, "$\bullet$" denotes the inner product of vectors. In general, a linear classifier over the vector space $[0,1]^n$ is a pair of $(\mathbf{q}, \theta)$ which classifies any document $\mathbf{d}$ as relevant if $\mathbf{q} \bullet \mathbf{d} > \theta$, or irrelevant otherwise, where the query vector $\mathbf{q} \in R^n$, the classification threshold $\theta \in R^+$, and $[0,1]$ denote the set of all real values between 0 and 1. Recall that $\mathbf{q} \bullet \mathbf{d}$ is usually used as the relevance rank (or score) of the document $\mathbf{d}$ with respect to user preference.

Let D_r be the set of all relevant documents in D with respect to a user's information needs (or search query). Assume that a user preference relation has a simple structure with only two levels, one level consisting of all relevant documents and the other consisting of all irrelevant documents, and within the same level no preference is given between any two documents. Then, finding a user preference relation satisfying the expression (1) is equivalent to the problem of finding a linear classifier $(\mathbf{q}, \theta)$ over $[0,1]^n$ with the property:

$$\forall \mathbf{d} \in D, \mathbf{d} \in D_r \Leftrightarrow \mathbf{q} \bullet \mathbf{d} > \theta, \tag{2}$$

where $\mathbf{q} \in R^n$ is the query (or weight) vector.

The goal of relevance feedback in information retrieval is to identify a user preference relation $\prec$ with respect to his/her information needs from documents judged by that user. Since user preference relations vary between users and may have various unknown representations, it is not easy for an information system to learn such relations. The existing popular relevance feedback algorithms basically use linear additive query expansion methods to learn a user preference relation as follows:

- Start with an initial query vector $\mathbf{q}_0$.

- At any step $k \geq 0$, improve the k-th query vector $\mathbf{q}_k$ to:

$$\mathbf{q}_{k+1} = \mathbf{q}_k + \alpha_1 \mathbf{d}_1 + ... + \alpha_s \mathbf{d}_s, \tag{3}$$

where $\mathbf{d}_1, ..., \mathbf{d}_s$ are the documents judged by the user at this step, and the updating factors $\alpha_i \in R$ for $i = 1, ..., s$.

One particular and well-known example of relevance feedback is Rocchio's similarity-based relevance feedback (Rocchio, 1971). Depending on how updating factors are used in improving the k-th query vector as in expression (3), a variety of relevance feedback algorithms have been designed (Salton, 1989). A similarity-based relevance feedback algorithm is essentially an adaptive supervised learning algorithm from examples (Chen & Zhu, 2000, 2002; Salton & Buckley, 1990). The goal of the algorithm is to learn some unknown classifier (such as the linear classifier in expression (1)) that is determined by a user's information needs to classify documents as relevant or irrelevant. The learning is performed by means of modifying or updating the query vector that serves as the hypothetical representation of the collection of all relevant documents. The technique for updating the query vector is linear addition of the vectors of documents judged by the user. This type of linear additive query updating technique is similar to what is used by the Perceptron algorithm (Rosenblatt, 1958). The linear additive query updating technique has a disadvantage: its *converging rate* to the unknown target classifier is slow (Chen & Zhu, 2000, 2002; Kivinen et al., 1997). In the real world of Web search, a huge number of terms (usually, keywords) are used to index Web documents. To make the things even worse, no users will have the patience to try, say, more than 10 iterations of relevance feedback in order to gain some significant search precision increase. This implies that the traditional linear additive query updating method may be too slow to be applicable to Web search, and this motivates the authors to design new and faster query updating methods for user preference retrieval.

MULTIPLICATIVE ADAPTIVE QUERY EXPANSION ALGORITHM

In this section, a multiplicative query updating technique is designed to identify a user preference relation satisfying expression (1) (Chen, 2001). The authors believe that linear additive query updating yields some mild improvement on the hypothetical query vector towards the target user preference. One wants a query updating technique that can yield *dramatic* improvements so that the hypothetical query vector can be moved towards the target in a much faster pace. The idea is that when an index term is judged by the user, its corresponding value in the hypothetical query vector should be boosted by a multiplicative factor that is dependent on the value of the term itself. If a document is judged as relevant, its terms are promoted by a factor. If a document is judged as irrelevant, its terms are demoted by a factor. The algorithm is described in Figure 1.

In this chapter, only non-decreasing updating functions $f(x)$: $[0,1] \rightarrow R^+$ are considered, because one wants the multiplicative updating for an index term to be proportional to the value of the term. The following two examples of algorithm MA are of particular interest.

Algorithm LMA: *In this algorithm, the updating function in algorithm MA is set to be* $f(x) = \alpha x$, *a linear function with a positive coefficient* $\alpha > 1$.

Algorithm ENL: *In this algorithm the updating function in algorithm MA is set to be* $f(x) = \alpha^x$, *an exponential function with* $\alpha > 1$.

The design of algorithm MA is enlightened by algorithm Winnow (Littlestone, 1988), a well-known algorithm equipped with a multiplicative weight updating technique. However, algorithm MA generalizes algorithm Winnow in the following aspects: (1) various updating functions may be used in MA, while only constant updating functions are used in Winnow; (2) multiplicative updating for a weight is dependent on the value

Figure 1. Algorithm MA (Multiplicative Adaptive Query Expansion Algorithm)

Algorithm $MA(q_0, f, \theta)$:
(i) Inputs:
      q_0: the non-negative initial query vector
      $f(x)$: $[0,1] \rightarrow R^+$, the updating function
      $\theta \geq 0$, the classification threshold
(ii) Set $k = 0$.
(iii) Classify and rank documents with the linear classifier (q_k, θ).
(iv) While (the user judged the relevance of a document **d**)
    {
       for (i = 1, ..., n)
       {
          /* $q_k = (q_{1,k}, ..., q_{n,k})$, $d = (d_1, ..., d_n)$ */
          if ($d_i \neq 0$)
          {
             /* adjustment */
             if ($q_{i,k} \neq 0$) set $q_{i,k+1} = q_{i,k}$ else set $q_{i,k+1} = 1$

             if (**d** is relevant) /* promotion */
                set $q_{i,k+1} = (1 + f(d_i)) q_{i,k+1}$
             else /* demotion */
                set $q_{i,k+1} = q_{i,k+1} / (1 + f(d_i))$
          } else /* $d_i == 0$ */
             set $q_{i,k+1} = q_{i,k}$
      } /* end of for */
    } /* end of while */
(v) If the user has not judged any document in the k-th step, then stop. Otherwise, let $k = k + 1$ and go to step (iv).

of the corresponding indexing terms, which is more realistic and applicable to real-valued vector space, while Winnow considers all the terms equally; and (3) finally, a number of documents which may or may not be counterexamples to the algorithm's current classification are allowed, while Winnow is an adaptive learning algorithm from equivalence queries, requiring the user to provide a counterexample to its current hypothesis. The equivalence query model is hardly realistic, because a user in reality has no knowledge about the information system or about the representation of his/her preference. What the user may do, and is able to do, is judge some documents as to what the user needs or does not need among those provided by the system.

Algorithm Winnow (Littlestone, 1987) and algorithm TW2 (Chen et al., 2002) can be derived from algorithm MA as follows:

Algorithm Winnow: *Algorithm MA becomes algorithm Winnow when the following restrictions are applied:*
- *The vector space is set to the binary vector space $\{0,1\}^n$.*
- *The initial query vector is set to $q_0 = (1,...,1)$.*
- *The updating function is chosen as $f(x) = \alpha$, a positive constant function.*
- *At step (iv), equivalence query is adopted. That is, the user is asked to judge at most one document that is a counterexample to the current classification of the algorithm.*

Algorithm TW2: *Algorithm MA becomes algorithm TW2 when the following restrictions are applied:*
- The vector space is set to the binary vector space $\{0,1\}^n$.
- The initial query vector is set to $q_0 = (0,\ldots,0)$.
- *The updating function is chosen as $f(x) = \alpha$, a positive constant function.*

The performance of algorithm MA is now analyzed when it is used to identify a user preference satisfying expression (2), a linear classifier $(\mathbf{q}, 0)$. Here is the case in which the threshold $\theta = 0$ is considered. The algorithm is said to make a classification error at step k when the user judged a document as a counterexample to the algorithm's current hypothesis. The total number of classification errors that algorithm MA will make can be estimated based on the worst-case analysis. Also, at most one counterexample is provided to the algorithm at each step. From now on to the end of the section, it is assumed that $\mathbf{q}$ is a non-negative query vector with m non-zero components and $\theta > 0$. Define:

$$\beta = \min\{q_i \mid q_i > 0, \quad 1 \leq i \leq n\}.$$

Definition: *Documents in the collection D are indexed with respect to a threshold δ, $0 < \delta \leq 1$, if for any document $\mathbf{d} = (d_1, \ldots, d_n) \in D$, either $d_i = 0$ or $\delta \leq d_i$, $1 \leq i \leq n$.*

In other words, when a document is indexed with respect to a threshold δ, any index term with a value below the threshold δ is considered not significant, and hence is set to zero. Recall that in the vector space model a document and its vector have equivalent meanings, so one may not distinguish between the two concepts.

Lemma: *Assume that documents are indexed with respect to a threshold δ. Let u denote the total number of promotions algorithm MA needs to find the linear classifier $(\mathbf{q}, 0)$. Let m denote the number of non-zero components in $\mathbf{q}$. Then:*

$$u \leq \frac{m \log \dfrac{\theta}{\beta \delta}}{\log(1 + f(\delta))}$$

Proof: Without loss of generality, it is further assumed that the m non-zero components of $\mathbf{q}$ are $q_1, \ldots, q_m$. When a promotion occurs at step k, a relevant document $\mathbf{d}$ is given to the algorithm as a counterexample to its classification. Because the document is indexed with respect to threshold δ, there is some i with $1 \leq i \leq m$ such that $\delta \leq d_i$. This means that the i-th component $q_{i,k}$ of the query vector $\mathbf{q}_k$ will be promoted to:

$$q_{i,k+1} = (1 + f(d_i))\, q_{i,k} > (1 + f(\delta))\, q_{i,k} \tag{4}$$

because f is non-decreasing. Since $q_{i,k}$ will never be demoted, it follows from expression (4) that $q_{i,k}$ can be promoted at most:

$$\frac{\log\frac{\theta}{\beta\delta}}{\log(1+f(\delta))} \tag{5}$$

times. Since each promotion yields a promotion for at least one $q_{i,k}$ for $1 \leq i \leq m$, the total number of promotions u is at most m times the value given in expression (5).

Theorem: *Assume that documents are indexed with respect to a threshold δ. Let T denote the total number of classification errors that algorithm MA makes in order to find the linear classifier (q, 0) over the real-valued vector space $[0,1]^n$. Let m denote the number of non-zero components in q. Then:*

$$T \leq \frac{[(1+f(1))(n-m)+\sigma](1+f(\delta))(1+\delta)}{f(\delta)\theta} + (\frac{(1+f(1))(1+f(\delta))(1+\delta)}{f(\delta)}+1)\frac{m\log\frac{\theta}{\beta\delta}}{\log(1+f(\delta))}$$

Where σ is the sum of the initial weights. (Hence, if $\theta = \frac{n}{k}$ is chosen, T = O(k log n).)

Proof: Without loss of generality, assume that the m non-zero components of q are

$q_1, ..., q_m$. The sum of the weights is estimated as $\sum_{i=1}^{n} q_{i,k}$. Let u and v be the number of promotion steps and the number of demotion steps occurring during the learning process, respectively. Let t_k denote the number of zero components in q_k at step k. Note that once a component of q_k is promoted to a non-zero value, it will never become zero again. For a promotion at step k with respect to a relevant document d judged by the user, for $i = 1, ..., n$, the following relation can be established:

$$q_i.k+1 = \begin{cases} q_{i,k}, & \text{if } d_i = 0, \\ (1+f(d_i)), & \text{if } d_i \neq 0 \text{ and } q_{i,k} = 0, \\ (1+f(d_i))q_{i,k}, & \text{if } d_i \neq 0 \text{ and } q_{i,k} \neq 0. \end{cases}$$

Since a promotion only occurs when:

$$q_k \cdot d = \sum_{i=1}^{n} d_i q_{i,k} = \sum_{d_i \neq 0 \text{ and } q_{i,k} \neq 0} q_{i,k} < \theta,$$

the following derivation can be carried out.

$$\sum_{i=1}^{n} q_{i,k+1} = \sum_{d_i \neq 0 \text{ and } q_{i,k}=0} q_{i,k+1} + \sum_{d_i \neq 0 \text{ and } q_{i,k} \neq 0} q_{i,k+1} + \sum_{d_i=0} q_{i,k+1}$$

$$= \sum_{d_i \neq 0 \text{ and } q_{i,k}=0} (1 + f(d_i)) + \sum_{d_i \neq 0 \text{ and } q_{i,k} \neq 0} (1 + f(d_i)) q_{i,k} + \sum_{d_i=0} q_{i,k}$$

$$\leq (1 + f(1)) t_k + \frac{1 + f(1)}{\delta} \sum_{d_i \neq 0 \text{ and } q_{i,k} \neq 0} \delta \, q_{i,k} + \sum_{i=1}^{n} q_{i,k}$$

$$\leq (1 + f(1)) t_k + \frac{1 + f(1)}{\delta} \sum_{d_i \neq 0 \text{ and } q_{i,k} \neq 0} d_i \, q_{i,k} + \sum_{i=1}^{n} q_{i,k} \qquad (6)$$

$$\leq (1 + f(1)) t_k + \frac{1 + f(1)}{\delta} \theta + \sum_{i=1}^{n} q_{i,k}.$$

For a demotion at step k with respect to an irrelevant document $\mathbf{d}$ judged by the user, for $i = 1, \dots, n$, it is true that:

$$q_{i,k+1} = q_{i,k} - (1 - \frac{1}{1 + f(d_i)}) q_{i,k} \leq q_{i,k} - (1 - \frac{1}{1 + f(\delta)}) q_{i,k}$$

Since a demotion occurs only when $\sum_{i=1}^{n} d_i q_{i,k} > \theta$, it can be seen that:

$$\sum_{i=1}^{n} q_{i,k+1} \leq \sum_{i=1}^{n} q_{i,k} - (1 - \frac{1}{1 + f(\delta)}) \sum_{i=1}^{n} q_{i,k}$$

$$\leq \sum_{i=1}^{n} q_{i,k} - \frac{f(\delta)}{1 + f(\delta)} \sum_{i=1}^{n} \frac{d_i}{1 + \delta} q_{i,k}$$

$$\leq \sum_{i=1}^{n} q_{i,k} - \frac{f(\delta)}{(1 + f(\delta))(1 + \delta)} \sum_{i=1}^{n} d_i \, q_{i,k} \qquad (7)$$

$$\leq \sum_{i=1}^{n} q_{i,k} - \frac{f(\delta)}{(1 + f(\delta))(1 + \delta)} \theta.$$

Let the sum of the initial weights be σ. Hence, after u promotions and v demotions:

$$\sum_{i=1}^{n} q_{i,k+1} \leq (1 + f(1)) \sum_{i=1}^{u} t_i + \sum_{i=1}^{n} q_{i,0} + \frac{(1 + f(1)) \theta \, u}{\delta} - \frac{f(\delta) \theta \, v}{(1 + f(\delta))(1 + \delta)}$$

$$\leq (1 + f(1))(n - m) + \sigma + \frac{(1 + f(1)) \theta \, u}{\delta} - \frac{f(\delta) \theta \, v}{(1 + f(\delta))(1 + \delta)}$$

Note that at any step the weights are never negative. It follows from the above relation that:

$$v \leq \frac{[(1+f(1))(n-m)+\sigma](1+f(\delta))\delta}{f(\delta)\theta} + \frac{(1+f(1))(1+f(\delta))u}{f(\delta)\delta} + u. \tag{8}$$

It follows from the Lemma expressions (6), (7) and (8) that the total number of promotions and demotions, that is, the total number of classification errors T, is bounded by:

$$T \leq u+v \leq \frac{[(1+f(1))(n-m)+\sigma](1+f(\delta))(1+\delta)}{f(\delta)\theta} + \frac{(1+f(1))(1+f(\delta))(1+\delta)u}{f(\delta)\delta} + u$$

$$\leq \frac{[(1+f(1))(n-m)+\sigma](1+f(\delta))(1+\delta)}{f(\delta)\theta} + (\frac{(1+f(1))(1+f(\delta))(1+\delta)}{f(\delta)\delta}+1)\frac{m\log\frac{\theta}{\beta\delta}}{\log(1+f(\delta))}$$

This completes our proof.

META-SEARCH ENGINE MARS

This section reports on the experimental meta-search engine MARS (Multiplicative Adaptive Refinement Search) that has been built using the algorithm MA to actually test the effectiveness and efficiency of the algorithm. MARS can be accessed from the URL specified at the end of the chapter. Figure 2 shows a general architecture of the meta-search engine MARS.

User queries to MARS are accepted from a Web browser. Besides entering the query, a user can also specify a particular general-purpose search engine he/she would like MARS to use and the maximum number of returned results (the larger the number is, the more time it takes to process). The QueryConstructor organizes the query into a format conforming to the specified search engine. One of the MetaSearchers sends the query to the general-purpose search engine. When the results are sent back from the general-purpose search engine, DocumentParser, DocumentIndexer and Ranker process the returned URLs and list them to the user as the initial search results. At this point, the rank is based on the original rank from the search engine. Constrained by the amount of space available on a typical screen, only the top 10 URLs (highest ranked) and the bottom 10 URLs (lowest ranked) are listed. Once the results are displayed, the user can interactively work with MARS to refine the search results. Each time the user can mark a number of particular URLs as relevant or not relevant. Upon receiving feedback from the user, MARS updates the weight assigned to each index term within the set of documents already returned from the specified search engine, according to the algorithm MA. If a document is marked as relevant, the weights of its index terms are promoted. If marked irrelevant, they are demoted. The refined results are sorted based on the ranking scores and then displayed back to the user for further relevance feedback. This process continues until the satisfactory results are found or the user quits the search.

Figure 2. Architecture of MARS

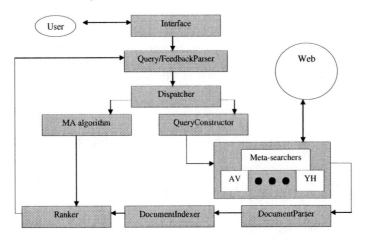

Figure 3. Interface of MARS

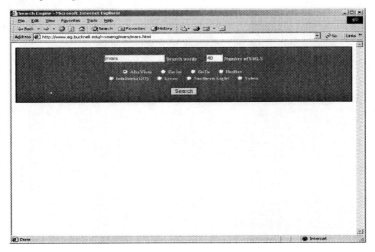

Figure 3 shows the user interface of MARS. Figure 4 shows the initial results returned by a general-purpose search engine with the search keyword being *"mars"*. Figure 5 shows the results after the user feedback has been processed by MARS.

Figure 4. Initial Results Returned by General-Purpose Search Engine

Figure 5. Results After User Feedback

EMPIRICAL PERFORMANCE ANALYSIS

Experiment Setting

The experiments were conducted in the summer of 2002. A collection of 72 random queries was sent to a general-purpose search engine (AltaVista was used in this study). Each of these queries resulted in a list of documents returned by the search engine. The number of returned documents was set to be 200, 150, 100, and 50, respectively. For each of the returned set of documents, the authors used the MARS meta-search engine that utilizes algorithm MA to interactively refine the search results. The returned documents from AltaVista would be marked as relevant or not relevant. The marked results were sent to MARS, which would promote or demote index terms of each document based on the feedback. The refined results were displayed to the user for possibly more feedback. For each query the process typically involved two to three rounds of feedback, until a satisfactory set of results was found.

At the time, the MARS meta-search engine was running on a Sun Ultra-10 workstation with 256 mega-bytes of memory. The code was written in a combination of C and C++, and the executables were generated by the GNU g++ compiler. The data collection process lasted about one month.

Statistics Collected

Three types of performance measures were collected and studied. The first is the precision-recall statistics. The information retrieval standard measurements of performance are *precision* and *recall*. The *precision* is defined as the ratio between the number of relevant documents returned and the total number of documents returned. The *recall* is defined as the ratio between the number of relevant documents returned and the total number of relevant documents. In many applied information retrieval systems such as the Web, such statistics as the total number of documents and the total number of relevant documents are not available. Two alternate measures are defined in this study to approximate the standard measurements. The set of documents returned by a search engine is defined as A. Then $|A|$ denotes the number of total returned documents. Assume a set of R documents in A is relevant to the search query judged by the user(s). For a given constant m (the number of top returned documents), define R_m to be the set of relevant documents among the top-m returned documents. Then the relative recall R_r and relative precision P_r are defined as follows:

$$R_r = \frac{|R_m|}{|R|}, \qquad P_r = \frac{|R_m|}{m}.$$

These two measures are used to assess the performance of MARS and compare it to that of AltaVista. The second performance measure is the relative placements of the relevant results. In standard precision-recall measurements, the precision *collectively* measures how many relevant results have been returned. It does not reflect the placement of individual results clearly. For example, if 5 out of the top 10 documents are relevant, at the tenth document, the precision is 50%. It does not show where these five relevant documents are, which could be placed as 1 through 5, or be placed as 6 through 10. Unless one goes back to each individual result, one would not know whether they are 1 through 5 or 6 through 10. These different placements, though the precision statistics are the same, make a difference in a practical information retrieval system such as a search engine. To alleviate this deficiency, the average rank L_m of the relevant documents in a returned set of m documents is defined as follows:

$$L_m = \frac{\sum_{i=1}^{C_m} L_i}{C_m}$$

where L_i is the rank of a relevant document i among the top-m returned documents, and C_m is the count of relevant documents among the m returned documents. The idea here is that the average rank should be as low as possible, which means all relevant documents are among the first returned documents; and the count C_m should be as large as possible, which means more relevant documents are among the top m documents. Note that $C_m \leq m$. The third statistic collected is the actual response time for the MARS meta-search engine to process and refine the queries. The response times are divided into two categories: the initial response time between the time issuing the query and the time receiving the response from an external search engine; and the time needed for the algorithm MA to refine the results. These two time measurements are called initial time and refine time.

Results and Analysis

The first set of statistics is reported in Table 1. The measurements were taken with $|A| = 200, 150, 100, 50$, respectively, and $m = 10$.

As can be seen from the table, MARS in general performs better than AltaVista. When the size of return documents is 200, MARS has an average precision of 65% and an average recall rate of 20%. While a 20% recall rate does not seem to be very high, notice that this is the result of 72 randomly selected queries. MARS was able, on the average, to list 20% of the total relevant documents in the top 10 positions. Note also that AltaVista holds the precision rate of 44% across different values of $|A|$ because no matter what the size of A is, the relevant documents among the top-m ($m=10$ in this case), R_m, remain the same for a general purpose search engine such as AltaVista. For MARS, because of the interactive user feedback, the value of R_m varies. The larger the value $|A|$ is, the more likely that the MA algorithm is able to move a relevant document to the top.

The second set of statistics, the average rank and count of relevant documents among the top-m returned documents, is reported in Table 2. The measurement is taken with $m = 20$; that is, the values in the table indicate the average rank and the average count of relevant documents among the top 20 documents. The *RankPower* P_m is defined as

Table 1. Relative Precision and Recall with 72 Queries and m = 10

	(50,10)		(100,10)		(150,10)		(200,10)	
	Precision	Recall	Precision	Recall	Precision	Recall	Precision	Recall
Mars	0.44	0.53	0.46	0.28	0.48	0.19	0.65	0.20
AltaVista	0.44	0.28	0.44	0.17	0.44	0.14	0.44	0.12

Table 2. Average Rank and Count of Relevant Documents among Top 20 Results

	Average Rank L_m	Average Count C_m	RankPower P_m
MARS	6.59	9.33	0.71
AltaVista	10.24	8.50	1.21

Table 3. Response Time in Seconds

	Mean	S.D.	95% C.I.	Max
Original	3.86	1.15	0.635	5.29
Refine	0.986	0.427	0.236	1.44

the ratio between the average rank and the count. The smaller the value of *RankPower*, the better it is. The results were obtained using the same set of 72 queries.

The data indicate that the average rank of relevant documents among the top 20 documents in MARS is 6.59 and the average count is 9.33. Note that in the best case where all top 20 documents are relevant, the average rank should be $(\sum_{i=1}^{20} i)/20 = 10.5$, the average count should be 20, and the *RankPower* is 10.5/20 = 0.525. The results show that although the average number of relevant documents does not increase dramatically (9.33 vs. 8.50), their ranks do (6.59 vs. 10.24). The *RankPower* of MARS (0.71) is much closer to the optimal value.

The statistics in the Table 3 indicate two measures, the original time and the refinement time. The values listed are mean, standard deviation, 95% confidence interval, and the maximum. One should note that the initial time is needed to get any search results from the external search engine whether or not the algorithm MA is involved. As can be seen, the time spent in refining the search results is very small relative to the time to get the initial result.

While the general statistics collected in the above tables show that algorithm MA performs very well under various conditions, some individual examples are of special interest. A couple of highly vague terms were chosen among the 72 queries — *memory* and *language* — to see how MARS handles them. These two words may mean completely differently in different areas. The term *memory* can mean human memory, or the memory chips used in computers; the term *language* can refer to spoken language or computer programming language. The examples show that the search precision improves dramatically with very limited relevance feedback in MARS compared to a general-purpose search engine such as AltaVista.

- *Memory:* The top 10 initial results sent back from AltaVista include two types of URLs, as expected. One is related to computer memory; the other is related to memory in human beings. Figure 6 shows the list (for space reason, only the top 10 results are listed). Relevant ones are preceded by an R, irrelevant ones by an X. There are five relevant documents in this list.

With one round of refinement in which a total of four URLs were marked (two marked in the top 10 list and two marked in the bottom 10 list), four of the original irrelevant URLs

Figure 6. Top 10 Initial Search Results for Keyword Memory

R   http://www.memorytogo.com/
 X http://memory.loc.gov/
 X http://lcweb2.loc.gov/ammem/ammemhome.html
R   http://www.datamem.com/
R   http://www.samintl.com/mem/index.htm
 X http://www.asacredmemory.com/
 X http://www.exploratorium.edu/memory/lectures.html
 X http://www.exploratorium.edu/memory/index.html
R   http://www.satech.com/glosofmemter.html
R   http://www.lostcircuits.com/memory/

Figure 7. Refined Search Results for Keyword Memory

R   http://www.streetprices.com/Electronics/...ware_PC
R   http://www.memorytogo.com/
 X http://www.crpuzzles.com/mem/index.html
R   http://www.linux-mtd.infradead.org/
R   http://fiberoptics.dimm-memory-infineon....owsides
R   http://www.ramplus.com/cpumemory.html
 X http://www.asacredmemory.com/
R   http://www.computersupersale.com/shopdis..._A_cat_
R   http://www.datamem.com/
R   http://www.lostcircuits.com/memory/

Figure 8. Top 10 Initial Search Results for Keyword Language

 X http://chinese.about.com/
R   http://www.python.org/
 X http://esl.about.com/
 X http://esl.about.com/homework/esl/mbody.htm
 X http://www.aliensonearth.com/catalog/pub/language/
 X http://kidslangarts.about.com/
 X http://kidslangarts.about.com/kids/kidslangarts/mb
 X http://pw1.netcom.com/~rlederer/rllink.htm
 X http://www.wordcentral.com/
 X http://www.win-shareware.com/html/language.html

were eliminated. The revised top 10 URLs are listed in Figure 7. The number of relevant documents now increases from five to eight, with relevant documents that the user has not seen before.

* *Language:* Similar to the term *memory*, the search results for *language* can be roughly divided into two classes, the ones related to human languages and the ones related to computer programming language. Figure 8 lists the original list of top 10 URLs returned from AltaVista. Assume the information about programming languages is of interest here.

Figure 9. Refined Search Results for Keyword Language

```
R    http://www.suse.de/lang.html
R    http://www.python.org/
   X http://www.eason.ie/flat_index_with_area...L400_en
R    http://www.w3.org/Style/XSL/
   X http://www.hlc.unimelb.edu.au/
   X http://www.transparent.com/languagepages/languages
R    http://caml.inria.fr/
R    http://home.nvg.org/~sk/lang/lang.html
R    http://www.ihtml.com/
   X http://www.aliensonearth.com/catalog/pub/language/
```

As can be seen in Figure 8, only one URL, *www.python.org,* is really relevant to the intention of the query. With a refinement of three URLs marked, one marked irrelevant from the top 10 list, one marked relevant from the top 10 list, and one marked relevant from the bottom 10 list (*www.suse.de/lang.html*), the refined list now contains six relevant URLs, shown in Figure 9, compared to only one before refinement. Of these six URLs, one was originally in the top 10 and was marked; one was originally in the bottom 10 and was marked; the other four were neither examined nor marked before at all. But they now showed up in the top 10 list!

APPLYING THE MA ALGORITHM TO PERSONALIZATION AND CLUSTERING

The multiplicative adaptive approach in the algorithm MA can be used in cooperation with other mechanisms to improve search accuracy. Here we discuss two such applications, personalization and clustering.

General-purpose search engines return a large number of URLs in response to a query. These returned URLs typically contain the keywords used in the query. But they are often not what the user is looking for because words alone without context usually cannot express the search intent accurately. For example, the search keywords *memory* or *language* will mean completely different things in different communities and in different contexts. Personalization and clustering are two techniques that can help alleviate this problem. In the PAWS-Cluster project (Meng & Chen, 2003), the algorithm MA is used in conjunction with a personalization component and a clustering component to improve search accuracies. When a list of search results is returned from a general-purpose search engine, the PAWS-Cluster sends the list through a personalizer or a cluster based on the user's selection. These results are then fed through the MA algorithm after the user has marked relevant or irrelevant on a part of the list, similar to the case in the MARS project. The MA algorithm re-calculates the score after promoting or demoting the original search results. The revised list is then presented to the user for further refinement. The architecture of PAWS-Cluster is presented in Figure 10. Note that the only difference between PAWS-Cluster and MARS architecture (Figure 2) is that the PAWS-Cluster contains two extra components, a personalizer and a cluster.

Figure 10. Architecture of PAWS-Cluster

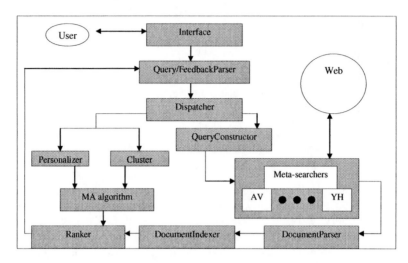

The Personalizer is a key part of PAWS-Cluster. People leave *digital traces* on the computers they use, especially on the computers dedicated to a single person. These traces include, among other things, email messages, digital news, work-related documents, personal documents and others. All these traces are distinct from one person to another because of the nature of their work, their personalities and other characteristics. When a person performs a search on the Web, the information interesting to that person is ultimately related to the digital trace left on her computer. If these digital traces are used to filter the search results returned from search engines before presenting to the user, one would expect the results be much more accurate. The user can collect her own profile on the client side. This collecting process is done periodically, not every time the user wants to search for something. The collection of this profile can be a part of the client software (browser) functionality. Also possible is to have a separate program perform this task. The key issues here are that the collecting process is initiated by individual users; the user knows exactly what is collected; and the results are not available to anyone else, including the search engines.

In the PAWS-Cluster project, the words that appeared in a user's documents on his/her desktop computer were used as the base of the profile. The profile consists of a number of the most frequently used words in the user's document collection. The collecting process simply traverses the directory tree of the user's computer, examining every document on its way. After some basic text processing, the results are sorted according to the appearance frequencies of these words. The top m words are kept as the profile.

When a URL is retrieved from a search engine along with its brief summary, a similarity measure is computed between the profile and the URL. The similarity is measured by the popular *cosine similarity* (Salton, 1989). A returned URL U along with its short summary contains a set of words; so does the user's profile P. U and P can be represented as an m-dimensional vector $<w_1, w_2, \ldots w_m>$ where the i-th component w_i

represents the significance of the i-th word in the vocabulary. Thus similarity S between a URL U and the profile P becomes as follows:

$$S = \sum_{i=1}^{m} \frac{w_{iu} w_{ip}}{|U \parallel P|}$$

Since a typical general-purpose search engine returns a long list of URLs when a search query is issued, it is easier to mark the URLs as clusters. The user would not have to examine every URL in a cluster. Rather the user only needs to examine a representative from a cluster. Once the cluster is marked relevant or not, the same MA algorithm is applied to each URL in the cluster. That is, the relevant documents are promoted and the irrelevant documents are demoted. The clusters are derived by the correlation similarities among the URLs.

If the correlation similarity between two URLs is greater than a given threshold, these two URLs are put into the same cluster.

The clustering algorithm takes two steps. First it computes pair-wise cosine similarities of all documents. This computation generates a similarity matrix $s[1:d][1:d]$ where $s[i][j]$ is the correlation similarity between document i and document j. The documents are then divided into clusters based on their correlation similarities. The algorithm goes through the correlation similarity matrix row by row and if the similarity between the two documents is greater than a given threshold, the two documents are put into the same cluster.

The following two examples illustrate how the system works. One is a personalization example, and the other is a clustering example. These experiments were performed during the winter of 2003.

- *Personalization Example:* Search keyword *memory*. Assume the initial search is meant for *computer memory chips*. Without personalization, the places for the relevant URLs are 2, 3, 7, 8, 10, or an average of 6 for the five relevant URLs returned by the general-purpose search engine. With personalization, the places become 1, 3, 5, 6, 8, 9, or an average of 5.3 for the six relevant URLs. For this example, at least, personalization helped bring more relevant URLs and placed the relevant URLs higher in the list.

- *Cluster Example:* Search keyword *xiannong,* first name of one of the authors. Before clustering, all relevant URLs are scattered among the returned URLs. After applying the cluster algorithms, many related URLs are clustered together. Some URLs that were seemingly un-related are now put into the same cluster because their contents (a brief description that was sent from the general-purpose search engine) are indeed related. Two examples are quoted here.

Cluster 13
http://www.cs.montana.edu/~bhz/pubs.html
http://www.cs.montana.edu/~bhz/recent.html
http://www.math.utah.edu/ftp/pub/tex/bib/toc/computsystscieng.html

In this example, the last URL contains one of the authors (Xiannong Meng) that appeared in the first two URLs as one of the co-authors in a list of publications of Binhai Zhu. In the original returned list, the places of these three URLs were 43, 44, and 64, respectively.

Cluster 14
http://www.asis.org/Publications/JASIS/vol52n8.html
http://www.commerce.uq.edu.au/isworld/publication/msg.08-07-1999.html

The first URL in Cluster 14 points to *JASIS* (*Journal of the American Society for Information Science and Technology*) in which the two authors published a paper. The second URL is the table of contents of another journal (*KAIS, Knowledge and Information Systems*) where the two authors published a separate paper. Originally, these two URLs were 42 places apart (48 and 90).

TRENDS AND CHALLENGES

Search engines have become dominant tools to find information over the Web in the few past years. How to accurately and efficiently locate a piece of information among hundreds or thousands of Web pages is an increasingly important and challenging issue. With an ever-growing number of Web pages available and the ambiguous nature of human languages, it is just not possible for a general-purpose search engine to return exactly what the user wants when a query is given in most cases. Refining what a general-purpose search engine will return in response to a search query becomes inevitable. Researchers are taking many different approaches to tackle the problem. The authors believe that adaptive refinement using relevance feedback is an important way of solving the problem. Some basic questions would have to be answered before real progresses can be made.

- *How to represent and capture user preferences:* This is a question that both ends of the search would have to answer. A user may use a particular set of vocabulary to represent his/her search intention. A search engine has to be able to capture and understand the true search intention when a query is received. Personalized profiles may help narrow this gap. But profiling raises the issues of privacy and scalability.

- *How to make adaptive refinement efficient:* Search engines can refine the search when receiving users' feedback. To effectively use the feedback to narrow the search results, the search engines would have to understand the feedback and be able to refine the search. AI techniques, machine learning in particular, may help improve this process.

- *Collaboration between search engines and browsers:* Currently the search engines and the browsers work as two independent camps. For adaptive refinement to succeed, browsers should understand how search engines work and carry out certain processing that is traditionally done by the search engines.

CONCLUDING REMARKS

The motivations of the work in this chapter come from the reality of Web search: Web search users usually have no patience to try, say, more than five iterations of relevance feedback for some intelligent search system in order to gain certain significant search precision increase. In contrast to the adoption of linear additive query updating techniques in existing algorithms, a new algorithm, multiplicative adaptive query expansion algorithm MA, is designed. The algorithm uses multiplicative query updating techniques to adaptively improve the query vector. Algorithm MA has been implemented in project MARS to show its effectiveness and efficiency. The algorithm has provable better performance than the popular Rocchio's similarity-based relevance feedback algorithm in learning a user preference determined by a linear classifier with a small number of non-zero coefficients over the real-valued vector space. Experiments indicate that algorithm MA substantially improves the search performance.

URL REFERENCES

[AV] *http://www.altavista.com/*.
[MA] *http://www.eg.bucknell.edu/~xmeng/mars/mars.html.*

REFERENCES

Baeza-Yates, R., & Ribeiro-Neto, B. (1999). *Modern information retrieval.* Reading, MA: Addison Wesley.

Bollmann, P., & Wong, S.K.M. (1987). Adaptive linear information retrieval models. *Proceedings of the 10th Annual International ACM SIGIR Conference on Research and Development in Information Retrieval.* New York: ACM Press.

Chen, Z. (2001). Multiplicative adaptive algorithms for user preference retrieval. *Proceedings of the 2001 Annual International Conference on Combinatorics and Computing, Lecture Notes in Computer Science 2108* (pp. 540-549). Heidelberg, Germany: Springer-Verlag.

Chen, Z., & Meng, X. (2000). Yarrow: A real-time client site meta search learner. *Proceedings of the AAAI 2000 Workshop on Artificial Intelligence for Web Search,* (pp. 12-17). Menlo Park, CA: AAAI Press.

Chen, Z., & Zhu, B. (2000). Some formal analysis of the Rocchio's similarity-based relevance feedback algorithm. In D.T. Lee & S.-H. Teng (Eds.), *Proceedings of the Eleventh International Symposium on Algorithms and Computation, Lecture Notes in Computer Science 1969* (pp. 108-119). Heidelberg, Germany: Springer-Verlag.

Chen, Z., & Zhu, B. (2002). Some formal analysis of the Rocchio's similarity-based relevance feedback algorithm. *Information Retrieval, 5*(1), 61-86. New York: Kluwer Academic Publishers.

Chen, Z., Meng, X., Fowler, R.H., & Zhu, B. (2001). Features: Real-time adaptive feature learning and document learning. *Journal of the American Society for Information Science, 52*(8), 655-665. New York: John Wiley & Sons.

Chen, Z., Meng, X., Zhu, B., & Fowler, R.H. (2002). WebSail: From on-line learning to Web search. *Journal of Knowledge and Information Science, 4*(2), 219-227. Heidelberg, Germany: Springer-Verlag.

Duda, R.O., & Hart, P.E. (1973). *Pattern classification and scene analysis.* New York: John Wiley.

Kivinen, J., Warmuth, M.K., & Auer, P. (1997). The perceptron algorithm vs. Winnow: Linear vs. logarithmic mistake bounds when few input variables are relevant. *Artificial Intelligence, 97*(1-2), 325-343. New York: Elsevier Publisher.

Littlestone, N. (1987). Learning quickly when irrelevant attributes abound: A new linear-threshold algorithm. *Machine Learning, 2*(4), 285-318. New York: Kluwer Academic Publishers.

Meng, X., & Chen, Z. (2003). Personalized Web search with clusters. *Proceedings of the 2003 International Conference on Internet Computing.* Athens, GA: CSREA Press.

Rocchio, J.J., Jr. (1971). Relevance feedback in information retrieval. In G. Salton (Ed.), *The smart retrieval system - Experiments in automatic document processing* (pp. 313-323). Englewood Cliffs, NJ: Prentice-Hall.

Rosenblatt, F. (1958). The perceptron: A probabilistic model for information storage and organization in the brain. *Psychological Review, 65*(6), 386-407. Washington, D.C.: American Psychology Association Publishing.

Salton, G. (1989). *Automatic text processing: The transformation, analysis, and retrieval of information by computer.* Reading, MA: Addison-Wesley.

Salton, G., & Buckley, C. (1990). Improving retrieval performance by relevance feedback. *Journal of the American Society for Information Science, 41*(4), 288-297. New York: John Wiley & Sons.

Wong, S.K.M., Yao, Y.Y., & Bollmann, P. (1988). Linear structures in information retrieval. *Proceedings of the 12th Annual International ACM-SIGIR Conference on Information Retrieval*, (pp. 219-232). New York: ACM Press.

Chapter VI

Exploiting Captions for Web Data Mining

Neil C. Rowe
U.S. Naval Postgraduate School, USA

ABSTRACT

We survey research on using captions in data mining from the Web. Captions are text that describes some other information (typically, multimedia). Since text is considerably easier to analyze than non-text, a good way to support access to non-text is to index the words of its captions. However, captions vary considerably in form and content on the Web. We discuss the range of syntactic clues (such as HTML tags) and semantic clues (such as particular words). We discuss how to quantify clue strength and combine clues for a consensus. We then discuss the problem of mapping information in captions to information in media objects. While it is hard, classes of mapping schemes are distinguishable, and a segmentation of the media can be matched to a parse of the caption.

INTRODUCTION

Non-text media are an important asset of the World Wide Web. Most of the world prefers to communicate with audio, images, and video rather than written text because these are more natural for the human brain. In addition, much of the world is illiterate and the increasing ubiquity of television and video games is hurting literacy. The Web is the first information technology that permits retrieval of media objects with much the same ease as text. If we could find them, we could get appropriate pictures of orchids or helicopters or quarterbacks in a few seconds without needing to search books or newspapers. Teachers could enliven their lectures with well-chosen images, audio, and video. And a news office could find the perfect picture instead of an adequate one.

Captions are valuable in data mining from the Web. They are text strings that explain or describe other objects, usually non-text or multimedia objects, and they are a form of metadata. Captions help understand and remember media (McAninch, Austin & Derks, 1992, 1993). Captions are especially valuable on the Web because only a small amount of text on Web pages with multimedia (1.2% in a survey of random pages [Rowe, 2002b]) describes the media objects. Thus, standard text browsers, when used to find media matching a particular description often do poorly; if they searched only the captions, they could do much better. Jansen, Goodrum, and Spink (2000) report that 2.65% of all queries in a sample of over 1,000,000 to the Excite search engine were attempting to find images, 0.74% were attempting to find video, and 0.37% were attempting to find audio, so multimedia retrieval was already important in 2000. It will undoubtedly increase in importance as the Internet becomes faster and more people provide Web multimedia resources.

Captions are also valuable because content analysis of media often does not provide the information that users seek. Nontext media do not usually tell when they were created or by whom, what happened before or after, what was happening outside the field of view when they were created, or in what context they were created; and nontext media usually cannot convey linguistic features like quantification, negation, tense, and indirect reference (Cohen, 1992). Furthermore, experiments collecting image-retrieval needs descriptions from users (Armitage & Enser, 1997; Jorgensen, 1998) showed users were rarely concerned with image appearance (e.g., finding a picture with an orange-red circle in the center), but rather, usually with meaning that only captions could provide (e.g., "dawn in the Everglades" or "labor organizing activities"). People seem to have a wide range of tasks for which multimedia retrieval is required, many not needing much understanding of the content of the media (Sutcliffe et al., 1997). This is fortunate because content analysis is often considerably slower and more unreliable than caption analysis because of the often much larger number of bits involved; most useful content analysis requires segmentation, an unreliable and costly process, as well as preprocessing and filtering that is hard to get correct (Flickner et al., 1995; Forsyth, 1999). So finding a caption to a media object simplifies analysis considerably.

But using captions from the Web entails two problems: finding them and understanding them. Finding them is hard because many are not clearly identified: Web page and caption formats and styles vary widely, and the mapping from the world of language to the world of visual or aural concepts is often not straightforward. Nonetheless, tools to address and often solve these problems are available. The somewhat restricted semantics of Web pages and captions can be exploited.

Commercial multimedia search engines that exploit text near media are available on the Web, most of them free. The major ones currently are *images.google.com, multimedia.lycos.com, www.altavista.com/image, multimedia.alltheweb.com, www.picsearch.com, www.gograph.com, gallery.yahoo.com, www.ditto.com, attrasoft.com/imagehunt, www.fatesoft.com/picture, www.ncrtec.org/picture.htm, www.webplaces.com/search, sunsite.berkeley.edu/ImageFinder.htm, www.icon bazaar.com/search, www.compucan.com/imagewolf-E.htm, www.goimagesearch.com,* and *www.animationlibrary.com.* But by no means has this software "solved" the problem of finding media. The copyright status of Web media objects is unclear in many countries, and pornographic images are also present on the Web, so search engines are

Table 1. Retrieval Performance (fraction of answers that are correct) in April 2003 with Five Image Search Engines on the World Wide Web

Keywords	images .google .com	multimedia .lycos .com	www .altavista .com/image	multimedia .alltheweb .com	www .picsearch .com
"moon"	0.75 (15/20)	0.94 (17/18)	0.87 (13/15)	0.20 (4/20)	0.81 (13/16)
"captain"	0.45 (9/20)	0.89 (16/18)	0.40 (6/15)	0.25 (5/20)	0.31 (5/16)
"closing"	0.40 (8/20)	0.50 (9/18)	0.93 (14/15)	0.00 (0/20)	0.06 (1/16)
"red orchid"	0.50 (10/20)	0.17 (3/18)	0.87 (13/15)	0.10 (2/20)	0.56 (9/16)
"quarterback throwing"	0.35 (7/20)	0.17 (3/18)	0.47 (7/15)	0.15 (3/20)	-- (0/0)
"angry crowd"	0.30 (6/20)	0.11 (2/18)	0.40 (6/15)	0.00 (0/20)	0.29 (2/7)
"American truck rear"	0.17 (3/18)	0.16 (3/18)	0.53 (8/15)	0.15 (3/20)	-- (0/0)
"missile on aircraft"	0.15 (3/20)	0.06 (1/18)	0.00 (0/15)	0.20 (4/20)	0.06 (1/16)
"diet soda bottle"	0.50 (1/2)	0.06 (1/18)	0.07 (1/15)	0.05 (1/20)	-- (0/0)
"Rockies skyline sunset"	-- (0/0)	0.17 (1/6)	0.27 (4/15)	0.17 (1/6)	-- (0/0)
"president greeting dignitaries"	0.00 (0/3)	-- (0/0)	0.00 (0/15)	-- (0/0)	-- (0/0)

cautious in what they index. (For these reasons, many Web browsers used by educational and government institutions do not permit access to most media-search engines (Finkelstein, 2003).) Also, the accuracy of keyword search for media is often significantly lower than that of keyword search for text. Table 1 shows accuracy, as judged by the author, for the best matches found for sample keywords entered in five image search engines. AltaVista appears to be the winner. But performance deteriorates considerably on larger queries, as much of the success on short queries was by exact matches to image-file names; this suggests "cheating" by some owners of images to get better exposure since, for instance, "red-orchid" is a vague and poor image name.

In general, commercial software needs to look good, and to do so it emphasizes precision (the fraction of answers found in all answers retrieved) as opposed to recall (the fraction of answers found of all possible answers on the Web). This is fine for users who are not particular about what media they retrieve on a subject; but users demand better quality from the Web today, and high-recall searches are necessary for important applications like systematic search for copyright infringement and checking policy compliance about content of Web pages. To increase recall, software needs to examine Web pages more carefully using the methods we shall discuss.

FINDING CAPTIONS ON WEB PAGES

We define a "caption" as any text that helps explain or describe a media object; their justification is that certain kinds of knowledge are best conveyed in words. The terms "media" and "multimedia" here include images, video, audio, and computer software. Images include photographs, drawings, diagrams, designs, backgrounds, and icons. Multimedia also includes text, and formatted text like tables and charts can have captions too. For the Web, multimedia are stored digitally, as bits and bytes, in files of a small number of formats. Table 2 lists extensions of common media types used with Web pages.

Table 2. Common File Extensions (ends of the file name) for Media Types on Websites

Media Type	Common Formats
Text	TXT, TBL, XLS, DOC, PPT
Image	JPG, JPEG, GIF, GIFF, PNG, TIF, TIFF, SVG
Video	MPG, MPEG, MOV, SWF, FLI, AVI
Audio	WAV, RAM, MID, ASX
Software	EXE, VBS

Syntactic Clues for Captions

Much text on a Web page near a media object is unrelated to that object. Thus we need clues to distinguish captions, allowing that there may be more than one caption for an object or more than one object for a caption (the latter is rarer). A variety of clues and ways to process them have been proposed in the literature (Favela & Meza, 1999; Hauptman & Witbrock, 1997; Mukherjea & Cho, 1999; Rowe, 1999, 2000b; Sclaroff et al., 1999; Srihari & Zhang, 1999; Swain, 1999; Watanabe et al., 1999) and we will summarize these ideas here.

About HTML

The language that built the Web was HTML (the Hypertext Markup Language) and it is still very popular today on the Internet. Web pages are text files whose names usually end in ".html" or ".htm" and are displayed by software called Web browsers. HTML defines key aspects of the appearance of Web pages through formatting tags inserted into text, delimited with angular brackets ("<" and ">"). Many tags have opposites indicated by a leading slash character, so for instance italics font is begun by "<i>" and turned off by "</i>". Larger-scale units like titles, headings, quotations, tables, and computer output also have explicit tags in HTML. Even prose paragraphs can be delimited by tags to ensure that a Web browser displays them properly. All these tags are useful in finding text units which could be captions.

Media is indicated in HTML by special tags, often by the "img" tag with argument "src" being the name of an image file to be displayed at that point on the page. Media files can also be the destinations of links in the "src" argument to the "href" hyperlink. Media can be specified with the HTML-4 "object" tag, which embeds complex objects in pages. Also used are "embed" for audio and video and "bgsound" for background sound. Media objects typically require considerably more storage space than that of the text of a Web page, so they are stored separately. Browsers can tell what kind of object a link points to by both the extension of its file name and the header information associated with the object when it is retrieved. The most popular image formats we found from our exhaustive survey of nearly all U.S. military ("*.mil") Websites in early 2002 (Rowe, 2002c), after the pruning of obviously uncaptioned images, were JPEG (683,404 images), GIF (509,464), PNG (2,940), and TIFF (1,639). The most popular audio formats were WAV (1,191), RAM (664), MID (428), and ASX (238). The most popular video formats were MPEG (8,033), SWF (2,038), MOV (746), FLI (621), AVI (490), and MP3 (397).

Sources of Captions in HTML Code

Several methods attach explicit captions to media on Web pages. "Alt" strings are text associated with media objects that is displayed, depending on the browser, when the user moves the mouse over the object or in lieu of the object on nonvisual browsers. Clickable text links to media files are also good since the text must explain the link; audio and video take time to load so are usually accessed that way. The "caption" tag indicates captions but is rarely used. Finally, a short caption can be the name of the media file itself suitably reformatted; for instance "northern_woodchuck31.gif" suggests a caption of "Northern woodchuck #31". All these provide likely but not guaranteed captions.

But many useful captions on Web pages are not marked so explicitly, particularly those reflecting traditional print layout. One convention is to center caption text above or below a displayed image in a different font size or style (e.g., italics) than the usual text. So the HTML text-appearance tags are moderate clues for captions. Titles and headings can also indicate captions as they generalize over a block of information, and they are helpful when better captions are unavailable. But they tend to be imprecise and to omit words, so they can be hard to decipher (Perfetti et al., 1987). Paragraphs above, below, or next to some media can also be captions (especially short paragraphs).

To illustrate, Figure 1 shows a sample Web page and Figure 2 shows its HTML source code. Four photographs, two graphics images, one hyperlink to an audio file, and one hyperlink to another page are specified in the source; both hyperlinks are followed by clicking on images. File names here provide useful clues for the five photographs but not so much for the two graphics images; one "alt" string is helpful; and the scope of two "center" commands helps connect text to image.

Another class of captions are embedded directly into the media, like characters drawn on an image (Wu, Manmatha & Riseman, 1997) or explanatory words spoken at the beginning of audio (Lienhart, 2000). These require specialized processing to extract, but this is usually not too hard because they should be made to contrast well with background information. Characters in images and video can be identified by methods of optical character recognition (Casey & Lecolinet, 1996); superimposed audio can be extracted using speech processing.

Captions can be attached through a separate channel of video or audio. For video an important instance is the "closed caption" associated with television broadcasts. Typically this transcribes the words spoken, though it occasionally describes visual information. Such captions are helpful for hearing-impaired people and for students learning the captioned language (Cronin, 1995; NCIP, 2003), but are only available for widely disseminated video. Similar captions are helpful for audio and for special applications of images like museums (The Dayton Art Institute, 2003), consistent with the endorsement by the World Wide Web Consortium (W3C, 1999) of captions to enhance Web access for the disabled.

Finally, "annotations" can function like captions, although they tend to emphasize analysis, opinion, background knowledge, or even advertisements more than description of their referent. Annotation systems have been developed to provide collaborative

Figure 1. Sample Web Page

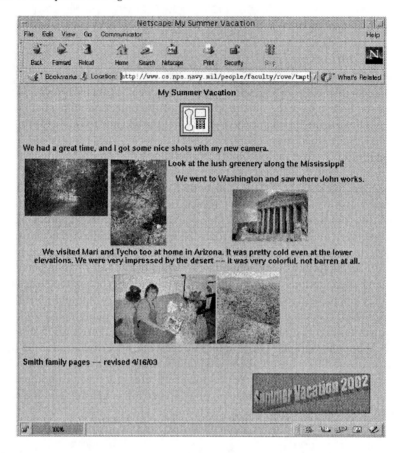

consensus (Sannomiya, 2001), which is especially helpful on the Web. Annotation can include physical parameters associated with the media such as the time, location, and orientation of the recording apparatus, to get clues as to speaker changes or extent of meetings (Kern et al., 2002). Unlike captions, Web annotations usually are stored on separate pages from their referents with links to them. Many annotation systems impose vocabulary limitations on the annotator so they can exploit fixed "ontologies" or concept hierarchies to classify objects. An exception is (Srihari & Zhang, 2000) where an expert user annotates in free text by guiding attention successively to parts of an image. Comments on the source code of a computer program are a form of annotation, and treating them like captions is facilitated by tools such as Javadoc in the Java programming language (Leslie, 2002).

Additional Clues for Captions

Besides HTML tags, several other clues suggest captions on Web pages. Length in characters is helpful: Captions usually average 200 characters, with few under 20 characters or over 1,000 characters. A likelihood distribution can be fitted. A strong clue

Figure 2. HTML Source Code for Figure 1

```
<title>My Summer Vacation</title>
<h1><center>My Summer Vacation</h1>
<a href="reveille.wav">
<img src="telephoneicon.gif"></a></center>
<p><i><h2>We had a great time, and I got some nice shots with my
 new camera.</h2></i></p>
<img align=left src="aspenRidgeRoadWheatland.jpg"
alt="Wisconsin where we stayed">
<img align=left src="Mississippi_side_channel.jpg">
<h2>Look at the lush greenery along the Mississippi!</h2>
<p><center><h2>We went to Washington and saw where John
works.</h2></p>
<img align=center src="supremecourt.jpg"></center>
<br><center><b><h2>We visited Mari and Tycho too at home in
Arizona.  It was pretty cold even at the lower elevations.  We
were very impressed by the desert -- it was very colorful, not
barren at all.</h2>
<img src="tycho_toy_00.jpg">
<img src="desert_saguaro.jpg"></b></center>
<hr><h2><i>Smith family pages -- revised 4/16/03</i></h2></a>
<a href="summer_vacation2.htm">
<img align=right src="summervacation.gif"</a>
```

is words in common of the proposed caption and the name of the media file (excluding punctuation), especially uncommon words. For instance, "Front view of woodchuck burrowing" matches "northern_woodchuck.gif". Nearness of the caption to the referent can be a clue; careful document image analysis (Satoh, Tachikawa & Yamaai, 1994) can do a better job of determining display adjacency than just counting characters between them in the HTML source code.

Image-related clues are the size of the image (uncaptioned images are more often small), the ratio of length to width (uncaptioned images have larger ratios), the image format (GIF is less likely to be captioned), and the use of certain words in the image file name (like "photo", "view", and "closeup" as positive clues and "icon", "button", and "bar" as negative clues). If image processing can be done, other evidence is the number of colors in the image and the frequency of the most common color. For Figure 1, the small size of telephoneicon.gif and summervacation.gif, "icon" in the first image's name, the length to width ratio of the second, and the limited number of colors in both all argue against their being captioned.

The number of occurrences of a media object on a page or site is also a useful clue. As a rule of thumb, objects occurring more than once on a page or three times on a site are unlikely (probability < 0.01) to have captions (Rowe, 2002b). Similarly, text that occurs multiple times on a page is not likely to be a caption. But headings and titles can be correctly ascribed to multiple media objects.

Another clue to a caption is consistency with known captions on the same page or at the same site. This is because organizations may specify a consistent page style ("look and feel") where, for instance, image captions are always a centered boldface single line

Table 3. Caption Candidates Derivable from the Figure 1 Web Page

Type	Caption	Media Object	Comments
title, h1, center	My Summer Vacation	reveille.wav (audio)	Weak candidate since object name different
filename	reveille	reveille.wav (audio)	Possible but not strong
title, h1, center	My Summer Vacation	telephoneicon.gif	Weak candidate since object name different
filename	telephoneicon	telephoneicon.gif	Possible but not strong
title, h1, center	My Summer Vacation	aspenRdigeRoadWheatland.jpg	Weak
p, i, h2	We had a great time, and I got some nice shots with my new camera.	aspenRidgeRoadWheatland.jpg	Possible but not strong since scope does not include media
filename	aspen ridge road wheatland	aspenRidgeRoadWheatland.jpg	Possible but not strong
alt	Wisconsin where we stayed	aspenRidgeRoadWheatland.jpg	Strong
title, h1, center	My Summer Vacation	Mississippi_side_channel.jpg	Weak candidate since object name different
filename	Mississippi side channel	Mississippi_side_channel.jpg	Possible but not strong
h2	Look at the lush greenery along the Mississippi!	Mississippi_side_channel.jpg	Possible but not strong by lack of scoping
title, h1, center	My Summer Vacation	supremecourt.jpg	Weak candidate since object name different
p, center, h2	We went to Washington and saw where John works.	supremecourt.jpg	Medium strength: object name different, but only good candidate for this image
filename	supremecourt	supremecourt.jpg	Possible but not strong
center, b, h2	We visited Mari....	supremecourt.jpg	Weak because of intervening line break
title, h1, center	My Summer Vacation	tycho_toy_00.jpg	Weak candidate since object name different
center, b, h2	We visited Mari....	tycho_toy_00.jpg	Good because overlap on unusual word "Tycho"
filename	Tycho toy 00	tycho_toy_00.jpg	Possible but not strong
title, h1, center	My Summer Vacation	desert_saguaro.jpg	Weak candidate since object name different
center, b, h2	We visited Mari....	desert_saguaro.jpg	Medium: Image reference crosses another image, but no text between images
filename	Desert saguaro	desert_saguaro.jpg	Possible but not strong
h2, i	Smith family pages – revised 4/16/03	summervacation.gif	Weak since better reference present
href (link)	summer vacation2	summervacation.gif	Strong since clickable link
filename	summervacation	summervacation.gif	Possible but not strong

under the image. This is helpful in recognizing, for instance, unusually short or long captions. This effect can be implemented by estimating default properties of the pages of a site and comparing caption candidates against these. For instance, *National Geographic* magazine tends to use multi-sentence captions in which the first sentence describes the image and subsequent sentences give background.

Table 3 shows the caption candidates obtained for Figure 1 using these principles.

Page Specification Languages beyond HTML

A variety of extensions to HTML can provide Web page designers with features in the direction of full programming languages. But generally these provide little additional caption information. JavaScript provides user-interface capabilities, but its media references are similar to HTML; it does allow file names to be assigned to variables that must then be decoded to determine the referent. Java Server Pages (JSP), Active Server Pages (ASP), and Java Servlets are popular extensions to HTML that support dynamically created Web pages. But they do not provide anything new for media or captions.

XML is increasingly popular as a language for data exchange that uses the same HTTP protocol as HTML. Mostly it is for transfer of text and numeric data, though the proposed SVG format will extend it to graphics. Media objects can be identified under XML, however, and several kinds of captions can be attached to them.

Page Crawlers for Multimedia

The Web is large and it is necessary to index caption-media pairs well in advance of queries, as with the text search engines. This requires a specialized Web "crawler" or "spider" (Heaton, 2002) to search for captioned media. It needs the usual tools of crawlers, including an HTML parser and a queue of page links found, but can ignore many hyperlinks like those to text pages and proprietary document formats, since its job is to catalog media links. It may or may not examine files of page markup languages like PDF (Adobe Acrobat) and PS (Postscript) depending on resources. These languages are harder to interpret than HTML but do contain captioned images, and major search engines like Google are now indexing them. A media crawler should also confirm the existence and type of the media it is indexing since there are plenty of mistakes about these things on Web pages; such checking does not require loading the page.

Semantic Clues for Captions

The above methods will generate many candidate captions for media objects. However, many of these will just be text that accidentally appears next to the media. So at some point one must investigate the candidates more closely and ascertain their meaning or semantics.

Word Semantics for Captions

Some words in captions suggest depiction, and thus serve both to confirm a caption and help explain its referent. Table 4 shows some examples. Many nouns and verbs of this kind can be found from a thesaurus system like Wordnet (Miller et al., 1990) as the subtypes ("hyponyms") in version 1.7 of "communication" in sense 2 ("something that is communicated by or to or between people or groups"), "representation" in sense 2 ("a creation that is a visible or tangible rendering of someone or something"), "communicate" in sense 1 ("transmit information"), "communicate" in sense 2 ("transmit thoughts or feelings"), "represent" in sense 9 ("create image or likeness of"), and "show" in sense 4 ("make visible or noticeable"), all of which represent important aspects of what captions provide. In addition, words relating to space (places and locations) and time (events and dates) are weak clues. Training data can suggest additional domain-dependent clue words, like animal names for a library of animal images.

The tense of verbs in captions is important, as generally present tenses refer to both the media itself (e.g., "The picture shows") and depicted events within it (e.g., "President congratulating award winners" using the present participle). This includes present progressive tenses, as in "The President is congratulating them". Past tenses often refer to undepicted events before the state the media depicts, but are also conventionally used

Table 4. Example Word Clues for Captions

	Nouns	**Verbs**	**Prepositions**
Images	picture, photograph, front, top	shows	above, beside
Audio	sound, music, excerpt	recorded	after, during
Video	clip, movie, video	taped	after, during
Software	program, demo, simulation	runs	into, for

for depicted objects in historical media, for example, "The President addressed Congress on January 18, 2003." Future tenses usually give goals unachieved and undepicted in the media.

Words can be more powerful clues with a limited or "controlled" vocabulary for describing media, like what librarians use in cataloging books, and this can be mandated in building specialized media libraries. Such a vocabulary can be significantly less ambiguous than unrestricted natural language, and its precise hierarchy permits unambiguous generalizations of terms for better keyword matching. Controlled-vocabulary media retrieval systems have been implemented at the U.S. Library of Congress in digitizing their media holdings (Arms, 1999) and at Getty Images Ltd. (Bjarnestam, 1998). But it is not feasible on most World Wide Web pages where no central control affects what is posted.

Structure of Referring Phrases

Individual words can be caption clues, but phrases can be even better. Table 5 gives some examples. A specialized grammar can recognize these and similar patterns. This is "partial parsing," parsing that need not analyze the whole sentence, used frequently in data mining applications. It must guess where a phrase starts, helped by indexing clue words.

If full parsing of caption candidates is possible (Guglielmo & Rowe, 1996; Srihari, 1995), another clue is that captions are mostly grammatical noun phrases, for example, "View of East Wing". Verbs predominantly occur in the form of participles attached to the head noun, for example, "East Wing viewed from south," unlike most English prose. But a few captions use imperatives (like "See at the left how we did it") to direct the reader's attention. Captions of other syntactic categories are usually cases of ellipsis on the head noun of a previous caption. For instance, "Mounted in a setting" after the previous caption "1 carat diamond on cutting tool" means "1 carat diamond mounted in a setting".

Not all words in a caption are equally likely to be represented in the media, and media search can be more successful if this is exploited. The implicit speech act often associated with descriptive captions is that the grammatical subjects of the caption correspond to the principal objects within the media (Rowe, 1994). For instance, "Stuffed panther in a

Table 5. Example Linguistic Referring Phrases found in Captions

Phrase	Restrictions	Media type
"the X above"	X is viewable	image
"the Figure shows X"	X is viewable	image
"Figure N: X"	N is a number, X is viewable	image
"side view of X"	X is viewable	image
"X beside Y"	X and Y are viewable	image
"look at the X"	X is viewable	image
"you can hear X"	X is audio	audio
"listen to X"	X is audio	audio
"X then Y"	X and Y are audio	audio/video
"shows X doing Y"	X is viewable and Y is a viewable act	video
"X during Y"	X and Y are viewable acts	image/video

museum case" has grammatical subject "panther," and we would expect to see all of it in the picture and probably centered in the picture; "museum" and "case" have no such guarantee. By contrast, "Museum case containing stuffed panther" implies that all of the case can be seen clearly but not necessarily the panther. "Museum case and stuffed panther" has a composite subject and thus both should be visible. Exceptions to this are undepictable abstract subjects, as in "Budget trimming in Washington". Wordnet permits quick checking if a subject is physical.

Other grammatical constructs can suggest features of the media:

- Present-tense principal verbs of caption sentences, subject gerunds, and participles attached to the principal noun can depict dynamic physical processes in video, audio, and software; for example, "greeting" in "President greeting dignitaries" for video and "cutting" in "Lawnmower cutting grass" for audio.
- Direct objects of such verbs, gerunds, and participles are usually fully depicted in the media when they are physical objects, like "computers" in "Students are using computers" and "bins" in "Workers loading bins".
- Objects of physical-location prepositions attached to the principal subject are also depicted in part (but not necessarily as a whole), like "case" in "Stuffed panther in museum case". Example prepositions are "within," "beside," "outside of," and "with" when used to mean accompaniment.
- If the subject of a caption sentence is an abstract term for a media object like "view" or "audio," objects of prepositions or participles attached to it are usually the true subjects, as in "View of North Rim" and "Scene showing damage to aircraft".

Figure 3. Classic Spatial Deixis Terms

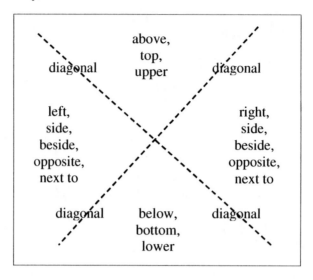

Fuzzy Deixis

Special linguistic expressions ("spatial deixis") refer to spatial relationships between captions and images, video, or parts of them. An example is "the right picture below". Such expressions are often "fuzzy" in that they do not define a precise area but associate a "suitability" at each point in a region of space (Matsakis et al., 2001). For instance, "below" defines a region downwards of some reference location, including things up to 45 degrees to either side, but preferring things more straight below. The most common spatial deixis terms are shown in Figure 3. It is important to distinguish the "deictic center" or the reference location of a referring expression, which on the Web page is usually the characters of the text itself. But it can also be a previously referenced object or set of objects, as in interpreting the word "right" in "the right picture below".

Language of Dynamic Media

Video and audio involve changes over time. So verbs and nouns referring to change are especially important in understanding them. Verbs involving physical motion like "go" and information transfer like "report" are common in describing video, as are their participles and gerunds and other related nouns like "song" and "segment". State-change nouns like "construction" are also common in video to summarize actions or their results. Software media is usually described by a narrower range of dynamic terms. Speech audio is similar to text and can be captioned similarly, and music audio is usually described only as a whole.

Mathematical Analysis of Clues

Which of these many clues about a caption candidate should we trust and how much? We must quantify them to answer that.

Filtering of Caption Candidates

To reduce processing effort it is helpful to first look for especially strong negative clues to rule out or "filter" caption candidates. Several mentioned above qualify: large size of the candidate, small size of the media object, duplicate occurrence of the media object, large distance of the candidate from the media object, and use of words very specific to noncaption text like "download," "click," "http," "index," and "page".

Filtering can recognize scope markers on caption-media connections. Lines (like from the "hr" tag in Figure 2), graphics, and captions themselves partition a Web page, and caption-media references rarely cross them. So for instance in Figure 1, the text "We visited Mari..." and the image "supremecourt.jpg" prevent assigning the caption "We had time..." to the images below "desert_saguaro.jpg" and "tycho00.jpg". Exceptions must be made for heading and title captions, which explicitly have broad scope, and adjacent media objects without intervening text, which can share the same captions.

The order of clue filtering is important for efficiency with large amounts of data. Generally speaking, filters should be applied in order of increasing values of the ratio of filter cost to filter-test failure probability, but full analysis can be complicated (Rowe, 1996).

Clue Strengths

To assess clue strengths, one model is that of "knowledge system" or "expert system" development (Stefik, 1995): We examine many Web pages and hypothesize clues for them using our intuition. This works when clues are not subtle, and many useful caption clues are obvious. Expert-system methodology is a well-developed branch of artificial intelligence, and a number of techniques from it can facilitate our task here, such as functional analysis of Web pages, use-case analysis, and validation and verification. But expert quantification of clues is often the most difficult part of expert-systems development, prone to numerous errors.

Another approach is to get statistics on a large and representative sample of pages on which captions are marked, and infer conditional probabilities of captions given the clues. Specifically, for each of a set of Web pages, people must identify the caption-media pairs present; then for each clue k, calculate $c_k/(c_k + n_k)$ where c_k is the number of occurrences of the clue in a caption and n_k is the number of occurrences of the clue in a noncaption. Clue appearances tend to be somewhat independent on Web pages because the pages often contain a good deal of variety. Thus clue appearance can be modeled as a binomial process with expected standard deviation $\sqrt{c_k n_k /(c_k + n_k)}$. The standard deviation can be used to judge whether a clue is statistically significant. A conditional probability that is two standard deviations away from the observed fraction of captions in the database is 95% certain to be significant, and one that is three standard deviations away is 99.6% certain to be significant. This standard deviation criterion rules out many potential clues, especially many word clues. Table 6 gives some example clues and their conditional probabilities in a sample of Web pages (Rowe, 2002b) with 2,024 possible text-media pairs in which the text was adjacent to the media. 21.1% pairs were confirmed to be caption-media pairs during exhaustive manual inspection, and statistical significance was generously defined to be more than one standard deviation away from 0.211.

Table 6. Sample Clues and Their Strengths in a Test Set (Rowe, 2002b)

Clue	Probability	Significant?
italics (<i>)	0.40	no
table datum (<td>)	0.47	yes
largest heading font (<h1>)	0.33	no
second largest heading font(<h2>)	0.49	yes
positive image words	0.31	yes
negative image words	0.19	no
positive caption words	0.31	yes
negative caption words	0.25	no
caption > 112 chars.	0.36	yes
caption < 31 chars.	0.15	yes
image diagonal > 330	0.28	yes
image diagonal < 141	0.09	yes
JPEG-format image	0.39	yes
GIF-format image	0.09	yes
digit in image filename	0.25	no
4 digits in image filename	0.40	yes
image in same directory as Web page	0.23	no
Web page name ends in "/"	0.14	yes
.com site	0.19	no
.edu site	0.21	no
.org site	0.16	no
.mil site	0.33	yes
centered text (<center>)	0.06	yes
title (<title>)	0.34	yes
alternative text (<alt>)	0.35	no
text-anchor link (<a>)	0.65	yes
image filename	0.04	yes
caption-suggestive wording	0.47	yes

Rowe (2002b) did recall-precision analysis of the importance of nine major categories of clues for image captions using a random sample of Web pages. Results showed that text-word clues were the most valuable in identifying captions, followed in order by caption type, image format, words in common between the text and the image filename, image size, use of digits in the image file name, and image-filename word clues; distance of the caption from the image was unhelpful in identifying a caption, at least for candidates within 800 characters of the media reference. Similar analysis of easily-calculated features of images, including number of colors, saturation of colors, frequency of the most common color, and average local variation in color, showed that only image size was significantly helpful.

Some other factors can weight clues. For instance, the probability of caption given a particular word in it depends on the word's relative location: Depictive words are four times as likely to occur early in the caption. Salton and Buckley (1988) provide a useful survey of some other general factors such as term frequency, inverse document frequency, term discrimination, and formulas including them.

Combining Evidence for a Caption-Media Pair

Best performance in identifying captions can be obtained by combining evidence from all available clues. This is a basic principle of data mining (Witten & Frank, 2000), and several approaches are possible. One popular way is a "linear model" in which we take a weighted sum of the clue probabilities, and label the text as a caption if the sum exceeds fixed threshold; linear regression can be used to find the best weights from a training set. But this tends to overrate candidates that are strong on one clue and weak on others.

A popular alternative is the multiplicative approach called Naive Bayes, which in this case would estimate the probability of a caption as:

$$p(caption \mid clues) = p(clue1 \mid caption)\, p(clue2 \mid caption)\, p(clue3 \mid caption)...p(caption) / p(clues)$$

where p means probability, p(X|Y) means the probability of X given Y, and "clues" means all clues together. We test whether this number exceeds a fixed threshold to decide if some given text is a caption. The probabilities on the right side can be obtained from statistics on a training set and are reliable given sufficient examples. This approach has the disadvantage of penalizing captions for one weak clue, which can be unfair for the less-certain clues. So the linear model idea can be embedded in the calculation by taking a weighted sum of several related weak clues, then using that sum in the product. This seems to work better for many applications than a pure linear model or Naive Bayes model.

Setting the threshold for both approaches is a classic problem of trading off precision and recall. Here precision means the fraction of the captions identified by the method that were actually captions, and recall means the fraction of the captions identified by the method of all the actual captions in the test set. If we value precision, we should set the threshold high; if we value recall, we should set the threshold low. In general, we must choose a threshold somewhere in between.

Adjusting Caption-Media Probabilities from their Context

Context should also affect the probability of a caption-media pair. For instance, in Figure 1 the paragraph "We visited Mari..." could go with either the images above or below. But the presence of stronger caption candidates for the images above — the text beside the vegetation pictures and above the Supreme Court picture — argues against further captions for those images. In general, strong candidate captions for some media object decrease the likelihoods of other candidates. This can be modeled mathematically by normalizing likelihoods (dividing the likelihoods by their sum) over all candidate captions on an image and/or normalizing likelihoods over all images that could be associated with a caption.

Another context issue is that media objects on the same page or at the same site tend to be captioned similarly in location and style, as mentioned earlier. We can model this by increasing the likelihoods of caption-media pairs that are consistent with those of their neighbors on the same page or same site. Likelihood changes can be done gradually in several cycles in a "relaxation" process from which a consensus gradually emerges.

Obtaining Training and Test Data from the Web

A problem for a statistics-based approach is that it needs a random sample of the Web. This is difficult because the Web is deliberately decentralized and has no comprehensive index. Browsers index the contents of pages, but do not provide listings of page links. One approach is to pick some known pages and do a random search from there, preferably a depth-first search on randomly chosen links to traverse a greater variety of pages (Rowe, 2002b). But pages with many links to them are more likely to be visited this way, especially index pages unrepresentative of a site. It would be better to observe the pages visited by a random set of users over a period of time, but that is difficult.

An alternative requiring less initial data could be to use "bootstrapping," a technique helpful in large data mining projects. Using an initial set of clues and their rough probability estimates obtained from an expert, one can rank caption-media pairs found by a semi-random search. The highest-rated caption-media pairs (say those ranking in the upper 10%) can be assumed to be captions, and conditional probabilities calculated on them. Resume searching randomly, now ranking new pages with revised clue probabilities for those clues shown to be statistically significant. Repeat the process of revising the probabilities several times, adding and dropping both clues and caption-media pairs as we proceed in a kind of feedback process. Eventually one has examined a large number of pages and obtained reliable clue probabilities.

MAPPING CAPTIONS TO MULTIMEDIA

Once we have identified a caption and an associated media object, we can match them or find the mapping between them. The justification for captioned media is that two modalities often provide information more efficiently than one modality could (Heidorn, 1997), but the information needs to be integrated. Evidence suggests that images are valuable in understanding natural-language utterances, independent of captions, by creating mental pictures and suggesting inferences about them (DiManzo, Adorni & Giunchiglia, 1986). Studies have shown eye movements in people comprehending descriptions of imaginary things (Spivey, 2000).

Studies of users have shown that they usually consider media data as "depicting" a set of objects (Armitage & Enser, 1997; Jorgensen, 1998) rather than a set of textures arranged in space or time. There are thus three concepts in any caption situation: real-world objects, the media objects representing the real-world objects, and the caption that references the media objects and relates them to the real-world objects. It should be noted that media access is usually just one part of the information that users seek: A user must be assigned to appropriate media with an appropriately chosen mix of methods (Srihari, Zhang & Rao, 2000).

"Deictic" is a linguistic term for expressions whose meaning requires assimilation of information from a referent outside the expression itself. Thus captions are deictic. Several theories have been proposed as to how various kinds of linguistic structures map to characteristics of their referent. Good work in particular has been done on the physical constraints entailed by spatial linguistic expressions (Di Tomaso et al., 1998; Giuchiglia et al., 1996; Mukerjee, 1998; Pineda & Garza, 2000). Unfortunately, few captions on the Web use spatial expressions. In the 1716 training examples of Web captions found by random search in Rowe (2002b), there were only 123 occurrences of any of the terms "right," "left," "above," "below," "beneath," "beside," "opposite," "next to," "side of," and "diagonal;" of these, only 33 referred to pictures as a whole and 36 referred to components of pictures. So Web caption interpretation should focus on other linguistic phenomena.

Correspondence in General between Captions and Media

Several kinds of relationships are possible between media and their captions. These can apply separately to each sentence of a multi-sentence caption.

- *Component-depictive:* The caption describes objects and/or processes that map to particular parts of the media. This is the traditional narrow meaning of "caption". For instance, a caption "President greeting dignitaries" with a picture that shows a President, several other people, and handshaking postures. Such captions are common, and are especially helpful when analogy and contrast of parts distinguishes media objects, as with botanical images (Heidorn, 1999).

- *Whole-depictive:* The caption describes the media as a whole. This is often signalled by media-type words like "view," "clip," and "recording". For instance, a caption "Recording of blue whale calls 8/12/92" with some audio.

- *Illustrative-example:* The media presents only an example of the phenomenon described by the caption. This occurs for captions too abstract to be depicted directly; for instance, "Labor unrest in the early 20th century" with a picture of a labor demonstration from 1910.

- *Metaphorical:* The media represents something analogous to the caption but does not depict it or describe it. For instance, the caption "Modern American poetry" with a picture of some trees. Variations on this kind of relationship occur with media that evoke emotional responses, like the caption "Stop police brutality" with a picture of police standing in a line.

- *Background:* The media represents some real phenomenon, but the caption only gives background information about it. For instance, the caption "The Civil War caused inflation" with a portrait of Abraham Lincoln. The house style of *National Geographic* magazine is generally to have all sentences of a caption except the first to be of this kind.

These distinctions are important because only with the first two does the text directly describe the media, and only with the first can prediction of the components of the media be done from the caption. Most research has focused on component-depictive captions. Within these there is considerable variation in content. Some captions focus more on the objects within the media, and some focus more on relationships or processes involving the objects. Some captions focus on small details that are of special importance. The total amount of detail can vary too; the World Wide Web Consortium recommends using both short captions and long captions together (WTC, 2003). So we cannot in general assume much about what a caption covers.

Media Properties and Structure

Whole-depictive caption sentences refer to the aggregate characteristics of the associated media object. Table 7 gives some examples. These can help distinguish between media objects matching a caption and avoid obviously incorrect matches by calculating properties of the media objects.

Many of the caption words that refer to such features are fuzzy, associated with a degree of suitability that is a function of position in a range of values. For instance, a picture is "big" with a probability that is monotonically increasing with the length of its

Table 7. Sample Aggregate Properties of Media Objects

Property	Media Type	Example Caption Phrase
size	image, video	big picture
scale	image, video, audio, software	closeup video
duration	video, audio, software	longer clip
color	image, video, software	infrared image
brightness	image, video	dark view
loudness	video, audio	busy excerpt
texture	image, video, audio	high-contrast image
shape	image, video, software	narrow photo
sound quality	video, audio	tinny recording
valuation	image, video, audio, software	difficult game

diagonal in pixels, say by a formula like $d^2/(10000 + d^2)$. Fuzzy terms are often context-dependent, so for instance a big icon is smaller than a big photograph. But this is less a problem in the restricted world of Web pages, with its narrow range of dimensions, durations, display parameters, and so forth, than it is for the real world. Formulas for fuzzy quantities can be obtained by tests with users.

Media objects also have a structure that can be referenced by component-depictive caption sentences. Although we have argued here that captions are the easiest way to understand media on the Web, there will always be valuable information in the sub-objects of a media object that captions do not think to convey. Images, audio, and video represent multidimensional spaces, and one can measure intensity of the signal at locations in those spaces. The gradient magnitude, or local change in the intensity, is an excellent clue to the boundaries between sub-objects in media objects. Color changes in an image suggest separate objects; changes in the frequency-intensity plot of audio suggest beginnings and ends of sounds (Blum et al., 1997); and many simultaneous changes between corresponding locations in two video frames suggest a new shot (Hauptmann & Witbrock, 1997). Partition of a media object into meaningful sub-objects is "segmentation" (Russ, 1995), and is central to many kinds of content analysis. But despite years of research, segmentation is not especially reliable because of the variety of the phenomena it must address. And when we have objects of multiple colors or textures, like a panther with spots or a beach with varying textures of gravel, domain-dependent knowledge must be used to group segmented regions into larger objects. Human faces are a classic example: Eyes, mouths, and hair contrast strongly with flesh.

Figure 4 shows an example of image segmentation, for the bottom left image in Figure 1. The Canny algorithm (Russ, 1995) was applied separately to the red, green, and blue image components of the original color image, and a union taken of the resulting region-partition edge cells. Dilation and erosion operations were used to simplify the segmentation and reduce noise. White represents areas in which significant changes in color are present for adjacent pixels; both white and black regions of the image can correspond

Figure 4. A Segmentation of the Lower Left Picture in Figure 1

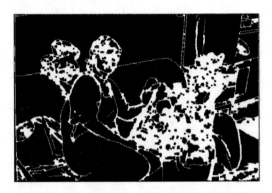

Figure 5. Example of Sonar Recording; Time is Horizontal Axis and Frequency is Vertical Axis

to objects. It can be observed that faces were extracted but not all their features. The widely varying colors of the child's clothes and toy caused difficulties for the segmentation as it merged them with furniture.

Figure 5 shows an example of natural audio spectrum, a sonar recording from deepsea sensors. The horizontal axis is time (the whole picture covers several minutes) and the vertical axis the frequency in the range one cycle-per-second to 128 cycles-persecond. Segmentation could extract the whale calls (the angled shapes in the upper frequencies), earthquakes (in the lower frequencies) and calibration signals (the episode toward the right end).

Table 8 shows the structure of some video, the CNN Headline News broadcast from 5:30 PM to 5:45 PM EST on May 4, 2003. Television video is hierarchically structured with strict timing constraints, and this structure can be inferred and exploited to understand what is going on (Gao, Xin & Xi, 2002).

Additional constraints can be exploited to understand media because media space obeys additional laws. For instance, objects closer to a camera appear larger, and gravity is downward, so inferences can often be made about distance to objects and support relationships between them in images. For video, objects in motion can be assumed to continue that motion unless explicitly prevented. For audio, many natural sounds decay exponentially in intensity when their cause is removed.

The subject of a media object can often be inferred even without a caption (Rowe, 2002a). Media on the Web are rarely selected at random, but rather are intended to illustrate something. The subject or subjects must be clear to accomplish this purpose. That means they are typically near the center of the media space, not "cut off" or touching

Table 8. Video Structure of 15 Minutes of a Television Newscast

High-level structure	Medium-level structure	Low-level structure (partial)
Introduction	30.0: Headlines	
	30.5: Short summaries	
Stories	31.5: First story: Iraqi weapons	Shot 1: 7 sec.
		Shot 2: 7 sec.
		Shot 3: 11 sec.
		Shot 4: 30 sec.
		Shot 5: 12 sec.
		Shot 6: 8 sec.
		Shot 7: 7 sec.
	33.0: Second story: Secretary of Defense discussing detainees	Shot 1: 21 sec.
		Shot 2: 57 sec.
		Shot 3: 9 sec.
	34.5: Third story: Democratic Presidential debate	Shot 1: 8 sec.
		Shot 2: 3 sec.
		Shot 3: 5 sec.
		Shot 4: 3 sec.
	35.0: Fourth story: Shuttle astronauts	Shot 1: 6 sec.
		Shot 2: 9 sec.
		Shot 3: 8 sec.
		Shot 4: 2 sec.
Advertisements	35.5: Teasers	Shot 1: 5 sec.
		Shot 2: 6 sec.
		Shot 3: 13 sec.
		Shot 4: 8 sec.
	36.0: Commercial advertisements	
Stories	38.0: Weather	
	39.5: Fifth story	
	40.0: Sixth story	
	40.5: Seventh story	
	41.0: Sports story 1	
	41.5 Sports story 2	
	42.0 Sports story 3	
	42.5 Sports stories 4 and 5	
	43.0 Sports story 6	
Advertisements	43.5 Teasers	
	44.0 Commercial advertisements	

edges of the media space, and well distinguished from nearby regions in intensity or texture. These criteria allow us to focus content analysis on the most important parts of the media object and thereby better match captions. They also provide another useful criterion for rating caption-media pairs, the size of the subject within the media object, since people generally prefer a higher-resolution representation of a subject.

Special Cases of Caption-Media Correspondence

While finding the caption-media correspondence for component-depictive captions can be difficult in general, there are several easier subcases. One is the recognition and naming of faces in an image using its caption (Houghton, 1999; Satoh, Nakamura & Kanda, 1999; Srihari, 1995). Names are distinctive capitalized structures in text, often associated with special words like "Mr.," "Prof.," and "President". Faces are distinctive visual features in images, with a distinctive range of flesh tones, and distinctive eye, mouth, and hair features in a rather narrow range of geometric configurations. So good candidate names and faces can be extracted from captions and images with less trouble than many other features. Name-face mappings can be disambiguated using visual-property and spatial-reference terms in the caption and looking to corresponding clues in the media and other captions. For instance, video of a television newscast showing a face often contains the spoken name, the name in the closed-caption, and the name written in graphics on the screen.

Similarly, dates and locations for associated media can often be extracted from captions with simple rules (Smith, 2002). Another important special case is captioned graphics, since the structure of graphics is easier to infer than the structure of camera images (Anderson & McCartney, 2003; Rajagopalan, 1996). Graphic objects like lines, polygons, and textures can map to particular caption words, and common sense or experience can often give match criteria. For instance, thin solid lines on a map often map to roads, circles to towns, numbers to numbers of roads, and text strings to names of towns. The proposed SVG image format has received considerable interest recently as a Web vector-graphics format that should be faster to download than current Web image formats, but is also easier to map to captions than the standard image formats (Arah, 2003).

Learning Connections between Captions and Media

The general case of matching component-depictive captions to media must match words of a caption to regions of the media. This must take into account the properties of the words, the properties of the regions, and the constraints relating them, and try to find the best matches. Statistical methods similar to those for identifying clues for captions can be used, except that we must now consider many different conceptual categories for which to assign words and regions, entailing problems of obtaining enough data. Graph matching methods (Gold & Rangarajan, 1996) can be used to efficiently match a subgraph of the semantic network corresponding to the caption to a subgraph corresponding to the media. Relaxation techniques, useful for many problems in vision, are helpful for this. Also helpful are advance knowledge about the settings and backgrounds of things described in captions (Sproat, 2001). For instance, when a caption says "President speaking" we expect to see a man in a suit with a microphone and a podium with insignia, and people seated or standing nearby.

To reduce the problem of manually specifying detailed knowledge about object appearance under many different conditions, machine-learning methods may help. Barnard et al. (2002) propose learning associations between words and image regions by using statistics over a training set of image-caption pairs, analogous to the learning of word associations in language understanding. Roy (2000, 2001) learns word-image associations, syntactic constraints, and semantic constraints from spoken descriptions in imitation of child language learning. Case-based or "best-match" reasoning can help with these learning tasks because instances of an object often cluster in multidimensional feature space (Barnard, Duygulu & Forsyth, 2001). Both approaches are exciting because they would permit much of the necessary data for caption understanding and mapping to be learned automatically from large data sets. But much more work needs to be done because both methods depend on high-quality caption and image processing. For instance, they will not work for Figure 4 because neither "tycho" (the child) nor "toy" in the name of the image file corresponds to a clear region of the image.

Dynamic Phenomena in Media and Media Sequences

Additional phenomena occur with media that extend over time (video, audio, and software). Physical-motion verbs and nouns can be depicted directly rather than just their subjects and objects, as with "Running leopard". As a start, dynamic phenomena can be categorized as translational (e.g., "go"), configurational ("develop"), property-change ("lighten"), relationship-change ("fall"), social ("report"), or existential ("appear"). Each needs domain-dependent knowledge to recognize in the media object.

Media objects also can occur in sets that are displayed on a page as sequences or structures in which position is important. Some examples are:

- The media are in increasing order of time. For instance, pictures may show key steps of a ceremony.
- The media represent different locations in some physical space. For instance, pictures may show New Year's celebrations.
- The media illustrate a hierarchy of concepts. For instance, pictures may show a vehicle and its components.
- The media represent functional or causal sequences. For instance, a visual repair manual for a vehicle may show the parts before and after disassembly.
- Media sets and sequences can also be embedded in other sets and sequences.

Such structures provide additional implicit semantics that can be exploited for retrieval. For instance, recognition that a set of pictures is in time sequence is helpful for retrieval when time is specified in a query even when the captions say nothing.

CONCLUSIONS

Multimedia is an increasing presence on the World Wide Web as a more natural match to the multimodality of humans than text. Captions usually provide an easier way to automatically understand media than media content analysis, which is often problematic and inconsistent. On the Web, something like a caption is usually nearby if we can recognize it. But there are ambiguities in what constitutes a caption, problems in interpreting the caption, problems in understanding multiple captions on the same object and multiple objects for the same caption, problems in understanding the media, at least superficially, and problems in matching the caption to the media. A key issue is how deep an understanding is necessary of captions and media to provide reliable indexing. This chapter suggests that much can be done without detailed understanding, but high-accuracy systems require more.

We envision future multimedia-retrieval technology as not much different from that of the present, just better. Keyword search will continue to provide the easiest access, and text will remain important to explain media objects on Web pages. As this chapter has shown, progress has been made in recent years on many technical issues needed to improve performance. Now a variety of results and tools are available for those building useful systems that permit us to illustrate articles, books, and presentations with perfectly matched pictures, sounds, video clips, and demonstration programs enhancing their information content.

REFERENCES

Anderson, M., & McCartney, R. (2003). Diagram processing: Computing with diagrams. *Artificial Intelligence, 145,* 181-226.

Arah, T. (2003). SVG: The future Web format. Available: *www.designer-info.com/ Writing/svg_format.htm.*

Armitage, L.H., & Enser, P. (1997). Analysis of user need in image archives. *Journal of Information Science, 23*(4), 287-299.

Arms, L. (1999, Fall). Getting the picture: Observations from the Library of Congress on providing access to pictorial images. *Library Trends, 48*(2), 379-409.

Barnard, K., Duygulu, P., & Forsyth, D. (2001). Clustering art. *Proceedings of IEEE Computer Society Conference on Computer Vision and Pattern Recognition,* (Vol. II, pp. 434-441).

Barnard, K., Duygulu, P., Forsyth, D., de Freitas, N., Blei, D., & Jordan, M. (2002). Matching words and pictures. Available: *http://www.cs.berkeley.edu/~kobus/ research/publications/JMLR/JMLR.pdf.*

Bjarnestam, A. (1998, February). Text-based hierarchical image classification and retrieval of stock photography. In J. Eakins, D. Harper & J. Jose (Eds.), *The challenge of image retrieval: Papers presented at the Research Workshop held at the University of Northumbria, Newcastle-on-Tyne, BCS Electronics Workshops in Computing.* Available: *http://www1.bcs.org.uk/homepages/686.*

Blum, T., Deislar, D., Wheaton, J., & Wold, E. (1997). Audio databases with content-based retrieval. In M. Maybury (Ed.), *Intelligent multimedia information retrieval* (pp. 113-135). Menlo Park, CA: AAAI Press/MIT Press.

Casey, E., & Lecolinet, R. (1996, July). A survey of methods and strategies in character segmentation. *IEEE Transactions on Pattern Analysis and Machine Intelligence, 18*(7), 690-706.

Cohen, P. (1992, November). The role of natural language in a multimodal interface. *Proceedings of Fifth Annual Symposium on User Interface Software and Technology,* Monterey, CA (pp. 143-149).

Cronin, B. (1995, Fall). The development of descriptive video services. *Interface, 17*(3), 1-4.

The Dayton Art Institute. (2003). Access art. Available: *http://tours.daytonart institute.org/accessart/index.cfm.*

DiManzo, M., Adorni, G., & Giunchiglia, F. (1986, July). Reasoning about scene descriptions. *Proceedings of the IEEE, 74*(7), 1013-1025.

Di Tomaso, V., Lombardo, V., & Lesmo, L. (1998). A computational model for the interpretation of static locative expressions. In P. Oliver & K.-P. Gapp (Eds.), *Representation and processing of spatial expressions* (pp. 73-90). Mahwah, NJ: Lawrence Erlbaum.

Favela, J., & Meza, V. (1999, September/October). Image-retrieval agent: Integrating image content and text. *IEEE Intelligent Systems, 14*(5), 36-39.

Finkelstein, S. (2003). BESS vs. image search engines. Available: *www.sethf.com/anticensorware/bess/image.php*.

Flickner, M., Sawhney, H., Niblack, W., Ashley, J., Huang, Q., Dom, B., Gorkani, M., Hafner, J., Lee, D., Petkovic, D., Steele, D., & Yanker, P. (1995, September). Query by image and video content: The QBIC System. Computer, 28(9), 23-32.

Forsyth, D.A. (1999, Fall). Computer vision tools for finding images and video sequences. *Library Trends, 48*(2), 326-355.

Gao, X., Xin, H., & Ji, H. (2002). A study of intelligent video indexing system. *Proceedings of Fourth World Congress on Intelligent Control and Automation, 3,* 2122-2126.

Giunchiglia, E., Armando, A., Traverso, P., & Cimatti, A. (1996, August). Visual representation of natural language scene descriptions. *IEEE Transactions on Systems, Man and Cybernetics, Part B, 26*(4), 575-589.

Gold, S., & Rangarajan, A. (1996, April). A graduated assignment algorithm for graph matching. *IEEE Transactions on Pattern Analysis and Machine Intelligence, 18*(4), 377-388.

Guglielmo, E.J., & Rowe, N. (1996, July). Natural-language retrieval of images based on descriptive captions. *ACM Transactions on Information Systems, 14*(3), 237-267.

Hauptman, G., & Witbrock, M. (1997). Informedia: News-on-demand multimedia information acquisition and retrieval. In M. Maybury (Ed.), *Intelligent multimedia information retrieval* (pp. 215-239). Menlo Park, CA: AAAI Press/MIT Press.

Heaton, J. (2002). *Programming spiders, bots, and aggregators in Java*. San Francisco, CA: Cybex.

Heidorn, P.B. (1997). *Natural language processing of visual language for image storage and retrieval*. Ph.D. dissertation, School of Information Sciences, University of Pittsburgh. Available: *http://www.isrl.uiuc.edu/~pheidorn/pub/VerbalImage/*.

Heidorn, P.B. (1999, November). The identification of index terms in natural language objects. *Proceedings of Annual Conference of the American Society for Information Science,* Washington, DC (pp. 472-481).

Houghton, R. (1999, September/October). Named faces: Putting names to faces. *IEEE Intelligent Systems, 14*(5), 45-50.

Jansen, B.J., Goodrum, A., & Spink, A. (2000). Search for multimedia: Video, audio, and image Web queries. *World Wide Web Journal, 3*(4), 249-254.

Jorgensen, C. (1998). Attributes of images in describing tasks. *Information Processing and Management, 34*(2/3), 161-174.

Kern, N., Schiele, B., Junker, H., Lukowicz, P., & Troster, G. (2002). Wearable sensing to annotate meeting recordings. *Proceedings of Sixth International Symposium on Wearable Computers,* (pp. 186-193).

Leslie, D. (2002, October). Using Javadoc and XML to produce API reference documentation. *Proceedings of ACM-SIGDOC Conference,* Toronto, Canada (pp. 109-109).

Lienhart, R. (2000, June). A system for effortless content annotation to unfold semantics in videos. *Proceedings of IEEE Workshop on Content-Based Access of Image and Video Libraries,* Hilton Head, SC (pp. 45-59).

Matsakis, P., Keller, J., Wendling, L., Marjarnaa, & Sjahputera, O. (2001, August). Linguistic description of relative positions in images. *IEEE Transactions on Systems, Man, and Cybernetics—Part B: Cybernetics, 31*(4), 573-588.

McAninch, C., Austin, J., & Derks, P. (1992-1993, Winter). Effect of caption meaning on memory for nonsense figures. *Current Psychology Research & Reviews, 11*(4), 315-323.

Miller, G., Beckwith, R., Fellbaum, C., Gross, D., & Miller, K. (1990, Winter). Five papers on Wordnet. *International Journal of Lexicography, 3*(4).

Mukherjea, S., & Cho, J. (1999). Automatically determining semantics for World Wide Web multimedia information retrieval. *Journal of Visual Languages and Computing, 10,* 585-606.

Mukherjee, A. (1998). Neat versus scruffy: A review of computational models for spatial expressions. In P. Oliver & K.-P. Gapp (Eds.), *Representation and processing of spatial expressions* (pp. 1-36). Mahwah, NJ: Lawrence Erlbaum.

NCIP (National Center to Improve Practice in Special Education). (2003). Video and captioning. Available: *http://www2.edc.org/NCIP/library/v&c/Toc.htm.*

Perfetti, C.A., Beverly, S., Bell, L., Rodgers, K., & Faux, R. (1987). Comprehending newspaper headlines. *Journal of Memory and Language, 26,* 692-713.

Pineda, L., & Garza, G. (2000, June). A model for multimodal reference resolution. *Computational Linguistics, 26*(2), 139-193.

Rajagopalan, R. (1996). Picture semantics for integrating text and diagram input. *Artificial Intelligence Review, 10*(3-4), 321-344.

Rowe, N. (1994). Inferring depictions in natural-language captions for efficient access to picture data. *Information Processing and Management, 30*(3), 379-388.

Rowe, N. (1996). Using local optimality criteria for efficient information retrieval with redundant information filters. *ACM Transactions on Information Systems, 14*(2), April, 138-174.

Rowe, N. (1999, Fall). Precise and efficient retrieval of captioned images: The MARIE project. *Library Trends, 48*(2), 475-495.

Rowe, N. (2002a, January/February). Finding and labeling the subject of a captioned depictive natural photograph. *IEEE Transactions on Data and Knowledge Engineering, 14*(1), 202-207.

Rowe, N. (2002b). MARIE-4: A high-recall, self-improving Web crawler that finds images using captions. *IEEE Intelligent Systems, 17*(4), July/August, 8-14.

Rowe, N. (2002c, July). Virtual multimedia libraries built from the Web. *Proceedings of Second ACM-IEEE Joint Conference on Digital Libraries,* Portland, OR (pp. 158-159).

Roy, D.K. (2000/2001). Learning visually grounded words and syntax of natural spoken language. *Evolution of Communication, 4*(1), 33-56.

Russ, J.C. (1995). *The image processing handbook* (2nd ed.). Boca Raton, FL: CRC Press.

Salton, G., & Buckley, C. (1988). Term-weighting approaches in automatic text retrieval. *Information Processing and Management, 24,* 513-523.

Sannomiya, T., Amagasa, T., Yoshikawa, M., & Uemura, S. (2001, January). A framework for sharing personal annotations on Web resources using XML. *Proceedings of Workshop on Information Technology for Virtual Enterprises,* Gold Coast, Australia, (pp. 40-48).

Satoh, S., Nakamura, Y., & Kanda, T. (1999, January-March). Name-It: Naming and detecting faces in news videos. *IEEE Multimedia, 6*(1), 22-35.

Satoh, T., Tachikawa, M., & Yamaai, T. (1994). Document image segmentation and text area ordering. *IEICE Transactions on Information and Systems, E77-01*(7), 778-784.

Sclaroff, S., La Cascia, M., Sethi, S., & Taycher, L. (1999, July/August). Unifying textual and visual cues for content-based image retrieval on the World Wide Web. *Computer Vision and Image Understanding, 75*(1/2), 86-98.

Smith, D. (2002, July). Detecting events with date and place information in unstructured texts. *Proceedings of Second ACM/IEEE-CS Joint Conference on Digital Libraries,* Portland, OR, (pp. 191-196).

Spivey, M.J., Richardson, D.C., Tyler, M.J., & Young, E.E. (2000, August). Eye movements during comprehension of spoken scene descriptions. *Proceedings of the 22nd Annual Meeting of the Cognitive Science Society,* Philadelphia, PA, (pp. 487-492).

Sproat, R. (2001). Inferring the environment in a text-to-scene conversion system. *Proceedings of International Conference on Knowledge Capture,* Victoria, British Columbia, Canada, (pp. 147-154).

Srihari, R. (1995). Use of captions and other collateral text in understanding photographs. *Artificial Intelligence Review, 8*(5-6), 409-430.

Srihari, R., & Zhang, Z. (1999). Exploiting multimodal context in image retrieval. *Library Trends, 48*(2), Fall, 496-520.

Srihari, R., & Zhang, Z. (2000, July-September). Show&Tell: A semi-automated image annotation system. *IEEE Multimedia, 7*(3), 61-71.

Srihari, R., Zhang, Z., & Rao, A. (2000). Intelligent indexing and semantic retrieval of multimodal documents. *Information Retrieval, 2*(2), 245-275.

Stefik, M. (1995). *Knowledge systems.* San Francisco: Morgan Kaufmann.

Sutcliffe, A., Hare, M., Doubleday, A., & Ryan, M. (1997). Empirical studies in multimedia information retrieval. In M. Maybury (Ed.), *Intelligent multimedia information retrieval* (pp. 449-472). Menlo Park, CA: AAAI Press/MIT Press.

Swain, M.J. (1999, February). Image and video searching on the World Wide Web. In D. Harper & J. Eakins (Eds.), *CIR-99: The challenge of image retrieval: Papers presented at the 2nd UK Conference on Image Retrieval, Newcastle-on-Tyne, BCS Electronics Workshops in Computing.* Available: *http://www1.bcs.org.uk/homepages/686.*

W3C. (1999). Web content accessibility guide. Available: http://www.w3.org/TR/WAI-WEBCONTENT/.

Watanabe, Y., Okada, Y., Kaneji, K., & Sakamoto, Y. (1999). Retrieving related TV news reports and newspaper articles. *IEEE Intelligent Systems, 14*(5), September/October, 40-44.

Witten, I., & Frank, E. (2000). *Data mining: Practical machine learning with Java implementations.* San Francisco: Morgan Kaufmann.

Wu, V., Manmatha, R., & Riseman, E. (1997, July). Finding text in images. *Proceedings of Second ACM Conference on Digital Libraries,* Philadelphia, PA, (pp. 3-12).

Chapter VII

Towards a Danger Theory Inspired Artificial Immune System for Web Mining

Andrew Secker
University of Kent, UK

Alex A. Freitas
University of Kent, UK

Jon Timmis
University of Kent, UK

ABSTRACT

The natural immune system exhibits many properties that are of interest to the area of Web mining. Of particular interest is the dynamic nature of the immune system when compared with the dynamic nature of mining information from the Web. As part of a larger project to construct a large-scale dynamic Web-mining system, this chapter reports initial work on constructing an e-mail classifier system. The Artificial Immune System for e-mail Classification (AISEC) is described in detail and compared with a traditional approach of naive Bayesian classification. Results reported compare favorably with the Bayesian approach and this chapter highlights how the Danger Theory from immunology can be used to further improve the performance of such an artificial immune system.

INTRODUCTION

Web-mining is an umbrella term used to describe three quite different types of data mining, namely content mining, usage mining and structure mining (Chakrabarti, 2003). Of these, we are concerned with Web content mining, which Linoff and Perry (2001) define as *"the process of extracting useful information from the text, images and other forms of content that make up the pages"* (p. 22).

The work in this chapter is concerned with performing text mining on the Web for the purposes of classification, but this is a hard task to achieve well. Firstly, the data contained on Web pages may be low quality, noisy and inconsistent in format, and secondly, the problem space may be vast. As of August 2003 the Internet's largest search engine, Google, indexes 3.3×10^9 Web pages (Google, 2003). Finally, the ease with which pages are published, moved or removed gives rise to an extremely dynamic medium.

It is our ultimate goal to construct a system to mine from the Web pages that the user will find interesting. That is, the user may consider them novel, surprising or unexpected. This is a slightly different problem from the classic classification task, as the class assigned to the page will depend not only on its content, but some current context. Work in Liu, Ma and Yu (2001) describes a system to mine surprising pages from competitors' Websites. At a high level it is possible that we may take inspiration from this, such as using a piece of user-specified information to infer the subject on which the user requires information and the interestingness of the retrieved result and thus lead to future work. Statistical techniques such as a naïve Bayesian algorithm (Mitchell, 1997) have proved successful when used for the classic classification task, but we propose the use of a system we believe may be more adaptable than a Bayesian algorithm: an Artificial Immune System.

Over the last few years, Artificial Immune Systems (AIS) have become an increasingly popular machine-learning paradigm. Inspired by the mammalian immune system, AIS seek to use observed immune components and processes as metaphors to produce algorithms. These algorithms encapsulate a number of desirable properties of the natural immune system and are turned towards solving problems in a vast collection of domains (deCastro & Timmis, 2002). There are a number of motivations for using the immune system as inspiration for both data mining and Web mining algorithms, which include recognition, diversity, memory, self-regulation, and learning (Dasgupta, 1999). Being based on an AIS algorithm, by its very nature the system will preserve generalization and forget little used information; thus giving a system such as this the ability to dynamically calculate interestingness based on context and adapt to changing user preferences. Being an adaptive learning system, it will not require expert set-up; instead it will learn, for example, a particular intranet structure and tailor itself to users' tastes.

In itself, an AIS based Web mining system would be a significant advance in the field of immune inspired algorithms. However it is our ultimate goal to go further than the areas of both Web mining and artificial immune systems have to date, by taking inspiration from an immunological theory called "Danger theory" (Matzinger, 2002a). We believe that algorithms inspired by this theory are suited to continuous learning tasks on large and dynamically changing data sets. In this theory, an immune response is launched based on a notion of perceived danger based on a current context, thus inspiring the context-dependent measure of interestingness required in the final system.

The scalability of immune based systems has been called into question (Kim & Bentley, 2001), and we believe the notion of a localized immune response in the Danger theory may offer some solutions by only activating the immune algorithm within context-dependent areas, as explained later.

Now that our final goal, a Web mining tool to retrieve interesting information from the Web, is defined, there are a number of steps we must take to reach it. The first is to show that an immune based algorithm can successfully perform a text mining task for the purposes of classification with an accuracy comparable to that of a standard technique such as a naïve Bayesian classifier. In this chapter we use a well known probabilistic technique, a naïve Bayesian classifier, for the purposes of comparison. This is a necessary step, as there are few references in the literature to turning immune inspired techniques to such a task. One exception is Twycross (2002) but the significant difference to this is we propose a system for continuous learning, thus making just this first stage a significant advance for the field which we can use as a step towards a Danger theory inspired system.

The algorithm named "AISEC" (Artificial Immune System for E-mail Classification) described in this chapter is a novel immune algorithm specifically designed for text mining and, as such, a first step towards our goal. In the following pages we begin by describing in a little more detail the background to the project, including an explanation of the artificial immune system paradigm and the Danger theory. We then describe the implementation and testing of the AISEC system, our first step towards the realization of an immune inspired Web content mining system. Finally, we conclude by discussing how the work in this chapter contributes to our goal, the strengths of an AISEC-like system, possible improvements and our ideas for the future of Web mining using immune inspired metaphors.

BACKGROUND

Although research into AIS began in the realm of computer security for virus detection and suchlike, some AIS based algorithms lend themselves particularly well to data mining, such as those described in Hunt and Cooke (1996). Watkins and Timmis (2002) describe the artificial immune system AIRS, which was shown to classify test data with an accuracy comparable to many standard algorithms. For a summary of a number of immune inspired algorithms for data mining, the reader is directed to Timmis and Knight (2002). One single reference can currently be found in the literature to an immune inspired system for text mining. Twycross (2002) details an AIS for classification of HTML documents into two classes: those which were on a given topic or not. The algorithm was tested on pages taken from the Syskill and Webert Web Page Ratings from the UCI data repository (Blake & Merz, 1998). This dataset consists of HTML pages, each on one of four different topics. The task was for this immune inspired system to predict if an unseen page was on a given topic or not when the system was trained using a number of example pages. The system was compared with a naïve Bayesian classifier and achieved a higher predictive accuracy in three out of four domains. The results showed that the system was relatively insensitive to the size of the training set, which was in contrast to the Bayesian system with which it was compared.

Artificial Immune Systems

Before we continue, we would like to briefly describe the important parts of an artificial immune system in the context of the natural immune system. Throughout we will only concentrate on the elements of the immune system relevant to the AISEC classification system described here. For a more general review of the immunology behind artificial immune systems the reader is directed towards the literature such as Sompayrac (1999).

The mammalian immune system works at three distinct levels, physical barriers (e.g., skin), the innate immune system and the adaptive immune system. AIS here are concerned with the latter, as only this exhibits the desirable properties for a computational intelligence system such as learning and memory. The natural immune system is based around a set of immune cells called *lymphocytes* and it is the manipulation of populations of these by various processes that gives the system its dynamic nature.

From a data mining perspective, an important component of a natural immune system is a *receptor*. These receptors are found on the surface of immune cells of the adaptive immune system called *B-cells* and *T-cells,* collectively known as lymphocytes. Each receptor is unique in shape and capable of binding to a slightly different range of molecular patterns from others. Typically, a receptor (Figure 1) will bind to proteins expressed on the surface of an invading cell, and any object capable of binding to one of these receptors by chemical interactions is called an *antigen*. A subset of the antigens are those that can harm the host, such as viruses and bacteria, and are referred to as pathogens. Similarly, at the core of an AIS is a set of immune cells, each described by a feature vector (Figure 1). The cell will represent a point in the solution space; a notion biologists refer to as a location in *shape space* (Figure 2C). In the system described in this chapter, the antigens are the objects to be classified and typically use the same representation as the immune cells, that is, a feature vector.

An *affinity function* may be defined to determine a measure of similarity between an immune cell and an antigen or between two immune cells. If the value calculated is greater than a threshold the antigen is said to be within the *recognition region* of the immune cell or that the lymphocyte will *recognize* the antigen. This reflects the natural system in which *regions of complementarity* are needed to provide enough electromagnetic force between an antibody's receptor and an antigen to pull these two cells together. In Figure 1, for example, the region of complementarity extends over the entire length of the receptor. The match between the receptor and antigen need not be exact and so when a binding takes place it does so with a certain strength, called an *affinity*. These terms are described diagrammatically in Figure 2.

Having discussed the representation of a lymphocyte and a notion of similarity between lymphocytes and antigens, we can now describe the processes that manipulate populations of these lymphocytes. We begin with the process by which lymphocytes are created. This creation occurs in the *bone marrow,* and the newly created lymphocytes are known as *naïve* lymphocytes, as they have not yet become stimulated. During generation, the shape of the cell's receptor is dictated by a random concatenation of different gene components. The receptor does require a basic shape to function and so elements taken from libraries of genes are used to encode the relevant parts of the receptor. It is the job of gene library algorithms to generate repertoires of immune cells. These gene libraries are used where the feature vector requires a certain structure,

Figure 1. Analogy between B-Cell Receptor and Artificial Immune Cell Feature Vector (The feature vector for the artificial cells could, for example, be a Boolean representation representing the presence or absence of words in a document.)

Figure 2. (A) Depicts a Lymphocyte (L) Binding with High Affinity to an Antigen (Ag_1); (B) Depicts a Binding between an Antigen (Ag_2) with Fewer Regions of Complementarity Compared with the Same Lymphocyte (This results in a bind with lower affinity, and so L may not become activated by Ag_2). (C) Shows the Relative Positions of L and the Complement of Ag_1 and Ag_2 in Shape Space. (Ag_1 is recognized by L, as the affinity between the two is higher than the affinity threshold.)

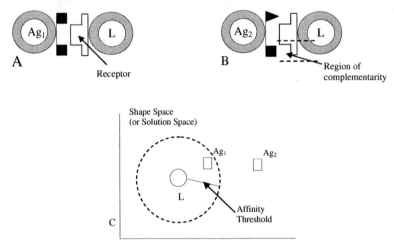

discrete or symbolic values are required or random generation of the feature vector is otherwise inappropriate.

Upon activation, the two types of lymphocytes will behave differently. Considering first a B-cell, whose job it is to tag an antigen for destruction, this B-cell must bind tightly to the antigen and stay bound until the antigen can be destroyed. It is quite possible for no B-cells in the body to have high enough affinity to bind. For this reason, an activated B-cell will begin a process of cloning and receptor mutation called *clonal selection*. Strong selective pressures during this proliferation process have the effect of maximizing affinity with the antigen and so increasing the effectiveness of the immune response. In the AIS world, an activated immune cell may adapt to new data in a similar way. Upon activation, the artificial cell may undergo a process of cloning with a rate proportional to the antigenic affinity. Each new clone is mutated with a rate inversely proportional to

Figure 3. (A) Cell Receptor Matches Pattern Belonging to the Host, Cell is Removed by Negative Selection; (B) Cell Receptor does not Match Antigenic Shape and so Cell is Left Unstimulated; (C) Cell Receptor Matches Foreign Antigenic Shape (unlike cell in B) and so is Selected for Cloning (Cell becomes activated and produces clones, some of which become memory cells. A modified version of a diagram from deCastro and Timmis (2002).)

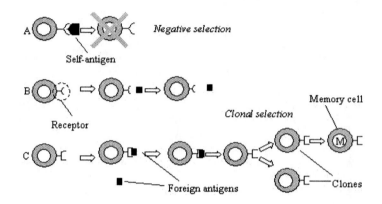

the affinity with the antigen. Both of these processes have the goal of moving the cell closer to the antigen within the solution space. An adaptation process such as this is a common paradigm found in many evolutionary algorithms, but asexual reproduction and mutation with rate dependent on some fitness measure are an important difference between AIS and these others. After the activation, a few clones with high affinities will live on to provide some memory of the event in the form of *memory cells,* although this is sill a point for debate. The process described above is summarized by Figure 3.

The fact that a lymphocyte may bind to any cell comes with a problem: If when T-cells (the body's powerful adaptive killers) are produced their receptor is in a random configuration, why do these not bind to cells of the host? In the natural system the body is purged of these cells before they are able to circulate and initiate an *auto-immune response* by a process called *negative selection* (Forrest, Perelson, Allen & Cherukuri, 1994), as depicted in Figure 3. Immature T-cells mature in a part of the body called the thymus where the chance of encountering a foreign antigen is negligible. While in the thymus these young T-cells will die upon binding with anything, and so it can be assumed that the only cells able to leave as mature cells are those that are not capable of binding to cells of the host. We say they are only capable of binding with *non-self.* Negative selection is a major component in a number of AIS algorithms. In these, a set of cells is compared against a set of patterns corresponding to self and the resulting affinities evaluated. Any antibody with a high affinity to an element of this self set will be eliminated, thus leaving antibodies capable of recognizing only non-self examples.

The thymus is one small part of the host and it would be impossible to remove all potentially self-reactive cells based on negative selection alone because not all "self" patterns may be present. The *two-signal* model as described in Matzinger (2002b) is used for purging self-reactive cells once they have left the thymus. A T-cell needs two signals to become activated. The recognition of an antigen by a T-cell is said to be signal one; the second signal or *co-stimulation* signal is a confirmation and is given to the T-cell by an *antigen presenting cell* upon proper presentation of the antigen. If the T-cell has received signal one in the absence of signal two, it has bound to a cell not properly presented, assumed to be part of the host and the T-cell is removed. This extra layer of protection allows potentially self-reactive cells to roam the body without beginning an *autoimmune* reaction.

Danger Theory

As described in the introduction it is our goal to take inspiration from a theory called the Danger theory to realize a unique Web mining system for discovery of interesting information. There are currently few AIS publications that even mention the existence of Danger theory. Notable exceptions are Williamson (2002) in which the author mentions Danger theory in a small section, and Aickelin and Cayzer (2002), which is currently the only paper dedicated to discussing the potential application of Danger theory to AIS. Now that we have explained the traditional view of the immune system, we can briefly describe the Danger theory, why it is significant and how we may put it to use.

Widely attributed to Polly Matzinger, the Danger theory (Matzinger, 2002a, 2002b) attempts to explain the nature and workings of an observed immune response in a way different from the more traditional view. This view is that immune cells cannot attack their host because any cells capable of doing so are deleted as part of their maturation by negative selection. However, this view has come under some criticism, as observations demonstrate that it may sometimes be necessary for the body to attack itself, and conversely the immune system may not attack cells it knows to be foreign. Matzinger argues that a more plausible way to describe the triggering of an immune response is a reaction to a stimulus the body considers *harmful*. This is conceptually a very small change but a complete paradigm shift in the field of immunology (Anderson & Matzinger, 2000). This model allows foreign and immune cells to exist together, a situation impossible in the traditional standpoint. However, when under attack, cells dying unnaturally may release a *danger signal* (Gallucci & Matzinger, 2001) that disperses to cover a small area around that cell: a *danger area*. It is within this and only within this area that the immune system becomes active and will concentrate its attack against any antigen within it.

As the immune response is initiated by the tissues themselves in the form of the release of danger signal, it is thought that the nature of this response may also be dictated by the tissues, another immunological paradigm shift. It has long been known that in a given part of the body an immune response of one class may be efficient, but in another may harm the host. Different types of danger signals may influence the type of immune response. This gives rise to a notion that tissues protect themselves and use the immune system to do so and is in stark contrast to the traditional viewpoint in which the roles are reversed and it is the immune system's role to protect tissues. There is still much debate in the immunological world as to whether the Danger theory is the correct explanation for observed immune function, but if the Danger theory is a good metaphor on which to base an artificial immune system then it can be exploited.

Danger Theory and Artificial Immune Systems

The concepts we identify in the Danger theory that we believe are of use are a context-dependent and localized response, the class of which may be determined also based on context. Firstly, the natural immune system reacts to a danger signal, but in an AIS this signal may signify almost anything. For example, in network security, a host may raise a danger signal if it is attacked, but in a text mining context, as suggested by Aickelin and Cayzer (2002), we may raise an "interesting document" signal, or in the context of e-mail classification a "mailbox is full" signal may be appropriate. This signal, whatever its nature, will be raised based on a current context, where this context may be some measure of interestingness or mailbox capacity for the above examples, which may change on a day-to-day basis. Furthermore, in the natural immune system when a cell begins to release a danger signal, the danger area is spatial. An example of a use of this spatial area in a Web mining system may be the generation of an "interesting" area around a document found on a Website. All pages within, say, one hyperlink of this page are also in the "interesting" area. Unlike the natural immune system, however, we are not constrained to a spatial area, and in Aickelin and Cayzer (2002) the possibility of a temporal danger area is also discussed. Finally the type of response may also be determined based on a current context. The Danger theory suggests that natural tissues release different types of danger signals based on the different type of pathogenic attacks. In a Web mining system, different types of signals may be released based on the type of media causing the stimulus. An interesting e-mail may release an "interesting" signal of one class while an interesting Web page may release a signal of one other class.

We have given some thought to the implementation of such an algorithm, details of which may be found in Secker, Freitas and Timmis (2003), although a number of interesting research questions still remain unanswered. For example, unlike most AIS algorithms, the tissue cells play a large part in a danger inspired system, but how should the behavior of these cells be implemented? For example, it may be helpful to implement a set of tissue cells in addition to the set of lymphocytes. Each individual cell may then react to a slightly different stimulus. Furthermore, we may also ask how the signal released by these cells should be interpreted. Should a signal from one cell be enough to stimulate an immune response or should activation occur only after a number of cells have been stimulated? If this latter approach is chosen we may then consider an activation function for the immune system such that a certain concentration of signals over a given space or time will initiate a response.

In this section we have posed a number of questions regarding the implementation of a danger inspired system. The final design of such a system and therefore the answers to these questions would be very much dependent upon the problem domain. It is these sorts of questions we would like our final Web mining system to answer, but before we can begin realization of such a system, we must first determine if an immune inspired algorithm is a suitable choice for the task of text mining.

Bayesian Classification

At the end of this chapter we compare the system proposed in the following section against a standard technique, in this case a naïve Bayesian classifier. Naïve Bayesian classifiers (Friedman & Kohavi, 2002; Mitchell, 1997; Weiss & Kulikowski, 1991) are a popular technique used for classification and especially popular for the classification of e-mail (see e-mail classification section), and we consider a brief explanation of the Bayesian learning paradigm a constructive addition at this stage.

In the classification task of machine learning it is our goal to assign a class to an instance based on the values of a number of attributes. A Bayesian classifier will not attempt to define a particular relationship between these attributes and the class of the instance; instead the probabilities of an instance belonging to each possible class is estimated, based on the training data, and the instance is assigned the class that is most probable. As Bayesian classifiers have roots in statistical mathematics, they possess properties that are mathematically provable, and therefore desirable for many applications. One of these is that it can be shown that in theory a Bayesian classifier will reach the smallest possible classification error given a sufficiently large training set. Although, in practice this may not be the case due to the need for simplifying assumptions, described later. In addition to this, probabilistic methods may be employed to deal with missing values and asymmetric loss functions; that is, situations in which the cost of misclassifying examples of one class may far outweigh the cost of misclassifying examples of another. For example, classifying an interesting e-mail as uninteresting and removing it is a lot less desirable than allowing uninteresting e-mail into the user's inbox (Diao, Lu & Wu, 2000).

The Bayes theorem is the cornerstone of Bayesian learning. Figure 4 describes how we can derive the equation used for the naïve Bayesian classifier from the Bayes theorem and an equation to return the most probable class given a set of features. As described by Mitchell (1997), the probability of observing hypothesis h given the training data D may be given by formula (1). In Bayesian learning we assign the most probable class v_{mp} from a finite set, V, based on a set of attribute values $<a_1,a_2...a_n>$ as described by formula (2). The Bayes theorem (1) and the equation to determine the most probable class (2) can be combined to produce (3) as shown in Figure 4.

In Figure 4 equation (3), $P(v_j)$ can be estimated simply by counting the frequency with which each class appears in the training data; however, the first term is a lot harder to determine. In practice we would need to see every possible instance in the problem space a number of times in order to provide reliable estimates. The naïve Bayes classifier introduces the assumption that attribute values are conditionally independent and therefore the probability of observing $a_1,a_2...a_n$ is the product of the probabilities of

Figure 4. Derivation of Naïve Bayesian Equation

$$P(h\,|\,D)=\frac{P(D\,|\,h)P(h)}{P(D)}\quad(1)$$

$$v_{mp}=\arg\max_{v_j\in V} P\left(v_j\,|\,a_1,a_2...a_n\right)\quad(2)$$

$$v_{mp}=\arg\max_{v_j\in V}\frac{P\left(a_1,a_2...a_n\,|\,v_j\right)P\left(v_j\right)}{P\left(a_1,a_2...a_n\right)}$$

$$v_{mp}=\arg\max_{v_j\in V} P\left(a_1,a_2...a_n\,|\,v_j\right)P\left(v_j\right)\quad(3)$$

Equation 1. Naïve Bayesian Classifier

$$v_{NB} = \operatorname*{argmax}_{v_j \in V} P\!\left(v_j\right) \prod_i P\!\left(a_i \mid v_j\right)$$

observing each attribute independently. This results in the approach used by the naïve Bayesian classifier as defined in Equation 1.

The terms in Equation 1 are usually calculated using frequency counts over the training data. However, it is quite likely that we will encounter a term unknown to the system. Assuming the frequency count to simply be 0 (i.e., P(new word|junk) = 0/100 = 0) would rule out this class entirely as this zero term results in the calculated probability for this class always evaluating to 0. A number of methods have been suggested for substituting a suitable probability for this value, although each comes with its own form of associated bias. Some implementations simply ignore this term, but a common strategy is to replace the probability with a small, non-zero number. Examples of this would be replacement with $1/n$, where n is the number of training examples, which has the advantage that this represents the increasing certainty that this element must have an almost-zero value with the increasing size of the training set. The probability may also be replaced by $1/m$ where m is the number of attributes and this is the strategy we adopt later in this chapter. For a worked example of naïve Bayesian classification used for classifying documents, the reader is referred to Mitchell (1997, p. 180).

E-Mail Classification

As explained later in this chapter it is our task to turn an AIS towards the classification of electronic mail (e-mail). There have been a number of strategies for this task discussed in the literature and the systems proposed broadly fall into two groups: spam filters and e-mail organizers. Spam (Graham, 2003) is a term used to describe e-mail that is unsolicited, sent in bulk and usually with a commercial objective. These systems typically classify incoming messages into only two classes, legitimate e-mail and spam e-mail, before these e-mails reach the user client. Two techniques that have been common are collaborative methods in which many users share their knowledge of junk e-mail to construct a central "blacklist" and rule-based in which rules are used for classification of incoming e-mail. Although as spam is constantly changing in content and style, the accuracy of both these techniques may suffer. For this reason, machine learning techniques are increasingly employed to tackle the problem of spam e-mail. Typically all these filters hide spam messages from the user, but for this to be acceptable safeguards may be usually put in place to ensure false classification of legitimate e-mail (which may be important to the user) is not removed accidentally. Androutsopoulos et al. (2000) is one such example in which this asymmetric loss function is accounted for. The authors compare a naïve Bayesian approach of spam removal to a memory based approach and assume that discarding a legitimate e-mail is as bad as classifying 999 spam e-mails as legitimate. The classifiers are biased accordingly. Recently, Cunningham et al. (2003) investigated a case-based approach to spam filtering with the added feature that, like the system we detail in this chapter, it may track concept drift. This is a phenomenon in which the concept of what the user finds interesting may change over time and so too may the content of uninteresting e-mails. An example of this may be the use of the word "ca$h" where the word "cash" was once used in spam e-mail such as advertisements.

E-mail organizers differ from spam filters in that they may work with more than two classes of email, and the job of this type of classifier tends to be to assign a folder to a message based on its content from within the user client; for example, assigning the labels "work" or "friends" to a message and assigning it the appropriate folder. Two e-mail organization systems from the literature are MailCat (Segal & Kephart, 1999), which integrated into the Lotus Notes client, and ifile (Rennie, 2000), which may integrate into the EXMH mail client. MailCat uses a Term Frequency-Inverse Document Frequency (TFIDF) approach to class assignment, a popular technique in the world of text mining. By contrast, ifile uses a naïve Bayesian technique (similar to that described in the previous section) to sort messages into folders. Four users tested the ifile system and the results show that users could expect a typical classification accuracy of between 85% and 90%. This Bayesian classification technique proves common in the literature. For example, Diao, Lu and Wu (2000) compare a naïve Bayesian system against the C4.5 decision tree algorithm, and find that although C4.5 can classify email with greater accuracy, the Bayesian system is more robust overall. Similarly, Yang and Park (2002) compare the TFIDF approach (described above) with a naïve Bayesian classifier and conclude that the Bayesian system provides a better classification accuracy in almost all cases. This TFIDF approach is also investigated in Brutlag and Meek (2000), who also compare this to discriminant classifiers and a classifier based on a language model approach. The results show that none of these three techniques is constantly superior and that the accuracy varies more between mail stores than the tested classifiers. A review of a number of research based and practical systems for spam email removal and more general e-mail organization can be found in Crawford, Kay and McCreath (2001).

AIS FOR E-MAIL CLASSIFICATION

As a step towards our goal we felt it was important to produce a text mining system based on an immune inspired algorithm. This must then be tested in a dynamic domain. For this reason we took the decision to gauge the performance of our text mining system on the task of e-mail. Our chosen task is to distinguish between e-mail the user would not be interested in, and legitimate e-mail which to the user is important or interesting, with the choice being made dependent upon previous experience. We consider e-mail classification to be essentially a Web content mining task as defined in the introduction, as the text contained in the e-mail is used for the purposes of classification and email is a part of the Internet environment. As explained in the introduction, this system has been written as a step towards an algorithm for mining interesting information from the Web, and so even though it is performing a task similar to a spam filter, as described in the previous section, we acknowledge it has no special measures to cope with this asymmetric loss function. The penalty for misclassifying an interesting document when the final system is run is not nearly as severe as misclassifying an e-mail. The novel system we propose posses a number of features, the combination of which dissociates it with those systems previously described. The main difference is that we address a continuous learning scenario. This contrasts with the vast majority of those systems above, which are trained once and then left to run. In addition to this we address concept drift, a feature implicit in the continuous learning scenario and a feature few other e-mail systems possess. One further advantage of an AIS is that our e-mail classifier requires no specific feature selection mechanisms. In contrast to some systems described, we do not pre-select a set of words from the training data; instead a selection is performed in a data-driven manner implicitly by the evolutionary operators.

"AISEC" Algorithm

AISEC seeks to classify unknown e-mail into one of two classes based on previous experience. It does this by manipulating the populations of two sets of immune cells. Each immune cell combines some features and behaviors from both natural B-cells and T-cells. For simplicity we refer to these as B-cells throughout. These two sets consist of a set of naïve (sometimes called free) B-cells and a set of memory B-cells, a biologically plausible notion as described in the background section. Once the system has been trained, each B-cell encodes an example of an uninteresting e-mail. New e-mails to be classified by the system are considered to be antigens. To classify an e-mail (antigen), it is first processed into the same kind of feature vector as a B-cell and presented to all B-cells in the system. If the affinity between the antigen and any B-cell is higher than a given threshold, it is classified as uninteresting; otherwise it is allowed to pass to the user's normal inbox. If the antigen (e-mail) is classified as uninteresting it will be removed to a temporary store. If the user deletes an e-mail from the temporary store it is confirmed to represent an uninteresting email. The B-cell that classified it as uninteresting is useful and is rewarded by promotion to a long-lived memory B-cell (assuming it was not already) and is selected for reproduction. This constant reproduction combined with appropriate cell death mechanisms gives the AISEC algorithm its dynamic nature. A high level outline of this process is shown in Figure 5.

Figure 5. High Level View of the AISEC Algorithm's Process after Initial Training

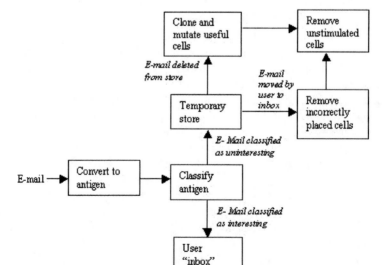

Once an e-mail has been placed in the user's inbox either by classification or by the user him or herself it is no longer accessible to the algorithm. When the user removes mail to save space, it is assumed he/she will do so by removing mail from the mail client's inbox, thus having no effect on the algorithm. As the folder where uninteresting e-mail is placed is nothing more than a temporary store, it should be emptied regularly.

During design a number of special considerations were given to the specialist nature of the text mining domain. The incorporation of these considerations in the final algorithm served to further distance our system from other AIS. These design decisions are discussed below:

- **Representation of one data class:** In a Web-mining context, learning types of documents a user finds interesting may be tiny compared with those a user finds uninteresting. B-cells therefore represent only the uninteresting e-mail class. This is a helpful simplification for the purposes of efficiency and more akin to the way the natural system works. Natural lymphocytes only encode possible pathogenic patterns and everything else is assumed harmless.

- **Gene libraries:** Two libraries of words, one for subject words and one for sender words are used. These contain words known to have been previously used in uninteresting e-mail. When a mutation is performed, a word from this library replaces a word from a cell's feature vector. Mutating a word in any other way, by replacing characters for example, would result in a meaningless string in almost all cases. All new cells entering the naïve cell set are mutants of existing cells.

- **Co-stimulation:** Uninteresting e-mail is not deleted but stored away. A B-cell must have become stimulated to classify this e-mail, so it can be assumed the first signal has already occurred. User feedback is then used to provide or not provide a second signal. At a time of the user's convenience this store may be emptied. It will be these user actions that will drive a number of dynamic processes. If an e-mail is deleted from this store by the user, the system has performed a correct classification; the user really was not interested in that e-mail and so a co-stimulation signal has occurred. The cell is rewarded by being allowed to reproduce. If, on the other hand, the user does not delete the e-mail, it is assumed the system has performed a misclassification, signal two does not occur and artificial cells may be deleted as appropriate.

- **Two recognition regions:** Around each B-cell is a recognition region: the region within which the affinity between this cell and an antigen is above a threshold. It is within this region a cell may stimulate another. A single region was found to be insufficient for both the triggering of evolutionary processes and classification. A smaller region, a classification region, was introduced for use in classification only. Empirical studies suggested the introduction of this second region was shown to increase the classification accuracy from around 80% to around 90% on the test set.

- **Cell death processes:** To both counteract the increase in population size brought about by reproduction and keep the system dynamic, cell death processes must be implemented. A naïve B-cell has not proved its worth and is simply given a finite lifespan when created, although it may lengthen its life by continually recognizing new pieces of data confirmed as uninteresting. Memory B-cells may also die, but these cells have proved their worth and it can be hard for the system to generate clones capable of performing well. For this reason, unlike naïve B-cells, memory cells are purged in a data driven manner. When a new memory cell, *mc,* is added to the memory cell set all memory cells recognizing *mc* have a stimulation counter reduced. When this count reaches zero they are purged from the system. This dissuades the system from producing an overabundance of memory cells providing coverage over roughly the same area, when one is quite sufficient.

The Algorithm in Detail

Before we begin, let us establish the following notational conventions:
- Let BC refer to an initially empty set of naïve B-cells
- Let MC refer to an initially empty set of memory B-cells
- Let Kt refer to the initial number of memory cells generated during training
- Let Kl refer to the clone constant that controls the rate of cloning
- Let Km refer to the mutation constant that controls the rate of mutation
- Let Kc refer to the classification threshold
- Let Ka refer to the affinity threshold
- Let Ksb refer to the initial stimulation count for naïve B-cells
- Let Ksm refer to the initial stimulation count for memory B-cells

Representation

A B-cell receptor holds information that may be extracted from a single e-mail, this is represented as a vector of two parts (Figure 6). One part holds words present in the subject field of a single e-mail and the second holds words present in the sender (and return address) fields of that particular e-mail. The actual words are stored in the feature vector because once set, the vector will not require updating throughout the life of the cell. This can be contrasted to the common practice of using a vector containing binary values as the receptor, each position in which represents the presence or absence of a word known to the system. As words are continually being added and removed from the system, each cell's vector would have to be updated as appropriate when this action occurs. The two sub-vectors are unordered and of variable length. Each B-cell will contain a counter used for aging the cell that is initialized to a constant value on generation and decremented as appropriate. This counter may be re-initialized if the B-cell is added to BC.

Affinity Measure

The *affinity* between two cells measures the proportion of one cell's feature vector also present in the other cell. It is used throughout the algorithm and is guaranteed to return a value between 0 and 1. The matching between words in a feature vector is case insensitive but otherwise requires an exact character-wise match. bc1 and bc2 are the cells we wish to determine the affinity between, as shown in Pseudocode 1.

Figure 6. B-Cell Structure

```
B-cell vector = <subject,sender>

subject = <word 1,word 2,word 3,...,word n>

sender = <word 1,word 2,word 3,...,word m>
```

Pseudocode 1. Affinity

```
PROCEDURE affinity (bc1, bc2)

    IF(bc1 has a shorter feature vector than bc2)

        bshort ← bc1, blong ← bc2

    ELSE

        bshort ← bc2, blong ← bc1

    count ← the number of words in bshort present in blong

    bs_len ← the length of bshort's feature vector

    RETURN count/bs_len
```

Algorithms and Processes

The AISEC algorithm works over two distinct stages: a training phase followed by a running phase. The running phase is further divided into two tasks, those of classifying new data and intercepting user feedback to allow the system to evolve. An overview of this algorithm is described in Pseudocode 2.

We now detail each of these three stages in turn: training, classification and the updating of the population based on user feedback. During the training stage the goal is to populate the gene libraries, produce an initial set of memory cells from training examples, and produce some naïve B-cells based on mutated training examples. As the

Pseudocode 2. AISEC Overview

```
PROGRAM AISEC

    train(training set)

    WAIT until (an e-mail arrives or a user action is intercepted)

        ag ← convert e-mail into antigen

        IF(ag requires classification)

            classify(ag)

            IF(ag is classified as uninteresting)

                move ag into user accessible storage

            ELSE

                allow e-mail to pass through

        IF(user is giving feedback on ag)

            update_population(ag)
```

Pseudocode 3. Training

```
PROCEDURE train(TE)

    FOREACH(te ∈ TE)

        process e-mail into a B-cell

        add subject words and sender words to appropriate library

    remove Kt random elements from TE and insert into MC

    FOREACH (mc ∈ MC)

        set mc's stimulation count to Ksm

    FOREACH (te ∈ TE)

        set mc's stimulation count to Ksb

        FOREACH (mc ∈ MC)

            IF(affinity(mc,te) > Ka)

                clones ← clone_mutate(mc,te)

                FOREACH (clo ∈ clones)

                    IF(affinity(clo,bc) >= affinity(mc,te))

                        BC ← BC ∪ {clo}
```

B-cells in the AISEC system represent one class, only the entire training set, here called TE, contains only e-mails the user has positively selected to be uninteresting. This is described in Pseudocode 3.

Now that the system has been trained it is available to begin two distinct functions. These are the classification of unknown e-mail and population update processes based on user feedback on the correctness of classification attempts. During the running phase the system will wait for either a new mail to be classified or an action from the user indicating feedback. Upon receipt of either of these, the system will invoke the necessary procedure as outlined in either Pseudocode 4 or Pseudocode 5. To classify an e-mail, an antigen, ag, is created in the same form as a B-cell, taking its feature vector elements from the information in the e-mail, then assigned a class based on the procedure described by Pseudocode 4.

To purge the system of cells that may match interesting e-mails, the AISEC algorithm uses the two-signal approach as outlined in the background section of this chapter. Signal one has occurred; that is, the instance has already stimulated a B-cell and been classified. Signal two comes from the user, in the form of interpreting the user's reaction to classified e-mail. It is during this stage that useful cells are stimulated and unstimulated cells are removed from the system. Antigen ag is the e-mail on which feedback has been given.

Pseudocode 4. Classification

```
PROCEDURE classify(ag) returns a classification for ag

    FOREACH (bc ∈ (BC ∪ MC))

        IF(affinity(ag,bc)) > Kc)

            classify ag as uninteresting

            RETURN

    classify ag as interesting

    RETURN
```

Pseudocode 5. Update B-Cell Population

```
PROCEDURE update population(ag)

    IF(classification was correct)

        FOREACH(bc ∈ BC)

            IF(affinity(ag,bc) > Ka)

                increment bc's stimulation count

        bc_best ← element of BC with highest affinity to ag

        BC ← BC ∪ clone_mutate(bc_best,ag)

        bc_best ← element of BC with highest affinity to ag

        mc_best ← element of MC with highest affinity to ag

        IF(affinity(bc_Best,ag)> affinity(mc_best,ag))

            BC ← BC \{bc_best}

            bc_best's stimulation count ← Ksm

            MC ← MC ∪ {bc_best}

            FOREACH(mc ∈ MC)

                IF(affinity(bc_best,mc) > Ka)

                    decrement mc stimulation count

                    add words from ag's feature vector to gene libraries

    ELSE
```

continued on the following page

Pseudocode 5.   (continued)

```
        FOREACH(bc ∈ (MC ∪ BC))

            IF(affinity(bc,ag) > Ka)

                remove all words in bc's feature vector from gene libraries

                delete bc from system

    FOREACH(bc ∈ BC)

        decrement bc's stimulation count

    FOREACH(bc ∈ (MC ∪ BC))

        IF(bc's stimulation count = 0)

            delete bc from system
```

The process of *cloning and mutation* that has been used throughout this section is detailed in Pseudocode 6. B-cell bc1 is to be cloned based on its affinity with B-cell bc2. Constants Kl and Km are used to control the rate of cloning and mutation. The symbol ⌊x⌋ denotes the "floor" of x; that is, the greatest integer smaller than or equal to the real-valued number x and that is necessary because num_clones and num_mutates must be integers.

Pseudocode 6.   Cloning and Mutation

```
PROCEDURE clone_mutate(bc1,bc2) returns set of B-cells

    aff ← affinity(bc1,bc2)

    clones ← ∅

    num_clones ← ⌊ aff * Kl ⌋

    num_mutate ← ⌊ (1-aff) * bc's feature vector length * Km ⌋

    DO(num_clones) TIMES

        bcx ← a copy of bc1

        DO(num_mutate) TIMES

            p ← a random point in bcx's feature vector

            w ← a random word from the appropriate gene library

            replace word in bcx's feature vector at point p with w

        bcx's stimulation level ← Ksb

        clones ← clones ∪ {bcx}

    RETURN clones
```

RESULTS

To determine the relative performance of AISEC, it was necessary to test it against another continuous learning system. The naïve Bayesian classifier explained previously was chosen as a suitable comparison algorithm. Even though the fundamental assumption of naïve Bayes, that all attributes are independent, is violated in this situation. Mitchell (1997) states, "*probabilistic approaches such as the one described here [naïve Bayesian] are among the most effective currently known to classify text documents*" (p. 180). An implementation of the naïve Bayesian classifier was implemented by the first author that was adapted to intercept input relating to classification accuracy in the same way as the AISEC system. This was done according to Equation 1, in which the set $V = \{$uninteresting, interesting$\}$, and $P(v_j)$ is the probability of mail belonging to class V_j and calculated based on the frequency of occurrence of class V_j. The term $P(a_i|v_j)$ is the probability of the e-mail containing word a_i given the e-mail belongs to class V_j. These probabilities are calculated using observed word frequencies over the data the system has been exposed to and so frequencies may be updated based on user input, much as in AISEC. The default probability assigned to an unknown word was $1/k$, where k is the total number of words known to the system.

Experimental Setup

Experiments were performed with 2268 genuine e-mails, of which 742 (32.7%) the first author manually classified as uninteresting and the remaining 1,526 (67.3%) were considered as of some interest. Due to the unsuitability of the few publicly accessible e-mail datasets that are traditionally used for single shot learning, unlike the continuous learning scenario discussed in this chapter, we were unable to test the system on a set of benchmark e-mails. All e-mails used were received by the first author between October 2002 and March 2003, and their date ordering was preserved. This temporal ordering is reflected in the order in which the e-mails are presented and should allow both systems to adapt to any drifting concepts and changing e-mail text. When processed, the sender information also included the return address, as this may be different from the information in the sender field. These fields were tokenized using spaces and the characters ".", ",", "(", ")", "!", "@", "<", ">" as delimiters. During the runs of the AISEC algorithm, the same values for all parameters were used. These values were arrived at by trial and error during testing and tend to work well over this dataset (see Table 1). The naïve Bayesian system was trained on the oldest 25 e-mails as both classes are required for training, and the AISEC system was trained on the oldest 25 uninteresting examples, only with the remainder of both used as a test set.

Unlike traditional single shot learning, where there is a fixed test set, we address continuous learning in which the system is continually receiving e-mails to be classified. Each time a new e-mail is classified the system can use the result of this classification (the information about whether or not the class assigned was correct) to update its internal representation. This continuous learning scenario calls for a slightly different measure of accuracy to that which is normally applied. Conceptually, as there is no fixed "test set" the system keeps track of its performance over the past 100 classification attempts. As each e-mail is classified, an average accuracy over these previous attempts is reported. The final classification accuracy is determined by taking the mean of all these values. As AISEC is non-deterministic, the result presented in Table 1 is the average of

Table 1. Parameter Values

Kc (classification threshold)	0.2
Ka (affinity threshold)	0.5
Kl (clone constant)	7.0
Km (mutation constant)	0.7
Ksb (Naïve B-cell stimulation level)	125
Ksm (Memory cell stimulation level)	25
Kt (initial number of memory cells)	20

Table 2. Results for Continuous Learning Task

Algorithm	Mean Classification Accuracy
Bayesian	88.05%
AISEC	89.09% ± 0.965

ten runs using a different random seed each time. The value after the "±" symbol represents the standard deviation. The result for the naïve Bayesian algorithm has no standard deviation associated with it, as, since it is a deterministic algorithm, just a single run was performed.

From Table 2 we can see that the AISEC algorithm can classify the e-mails in the given continuous test set with a slightly higher accuracy compared with the Bayesian approach, although we do not claim it classifies with higher accuracy in general. Instead, based on these results, we think it is reasonable to conclude that our algorithm performs with accuracy comparable to that of the Bayesian algorithm but with dynamics very different to that algorithm. We also undertook an experiment that assessed the performance of the algorithm when run in a traditional one-shot learning scenario. In this case the evolution of the system was stopped after the initial training e-mails and no feedback mechanisms were able to evolve the sets of B-cells from that point onwards. These results suggested the performance was surprisingly good, with mean predictive accuracies just 5% lower than with the user feedback mechanism. From this we suggest that the user feedback mechanisms are useful for the continued accuracy of the system, but not essential for this AIS to function well. This has been previously demonstrated by the AIS-based classifier, AIRS (Watkins & Timmis, 2002).

The line chart Figure 7 details the classification accuracy after the classification of each mail. This uses the accuracy measure described above and details the results for the entire test set apart from the first 100 e-mails. It can be seen that both algorithms are closely matched in general but there are certain areas where the changing data cause them to behave differently. Of interest are the areas between 1,000 and 1,250 and again between 1,900 and 2,100 e-mails classified. In both situations AISEC exhibits an increase in accuracy while there is a decrease in accuracy from the Bayesian algorithm. Even after manual inspection of the data the reasons for this were undetermined. We are currently considering a more rigorous and lengthy analysis of the test data to try to explain this interesting phenomenon. One suggestion would be that AISEC is faster to react to sudden changes. Consider, for example, a word that is very common among uninteresting

Figure 7. Change in Classification Accuracy Over Time

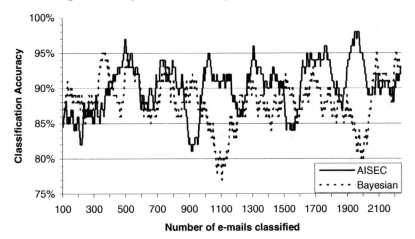

e-mail. The AISEC system will represent this as the presence of this word in a number of B-cells. The Bayesian system will represent this as a high frequency of occurrence in this class compared to the frequency of it appearing in the other class. Consider now that this word begins to be used in interesting e-mail. The AISEC system will react quickly by deleting any cells containing this word that would result in a misclassification. By contrast, the Bayesian system will react by only incrementing the frequency count of this word in the interesting class. Given the word has been common in uninteresting e-mail for some time, the frequency of occurrence in this class will still be large compared with frequency of occurrence in the interesting class and so will have a negligible effect on the final calculated class probability. Only after this word has been used many times in confirmed interesting e-mail the differences in the frequencies of usage may even out, and the difference in the probabilities of this word being used in each class significantly decreases.

CONCLUSIONS AND FUTURE WORK

As a first step towards a danger model-based artificial immune system for Web mining, we have described a novel immune inspired system for classification of e-mail. We have shown that an immune inspired algorithm written especially with text mining in mind may yield classification accuracy comparable to a Bayesian approach in this continuous learning scenario. We have gone some way to showing that an immune inspired system is capable of the specialized task of document classification using a text-mining approach. The results presented were generally encouraging, but it is clear there is still work to be done to optimize such a system. An increase in accuracy may be achieved by a change in the kind of features stored in the B-cell's feature vector, such as a measure of the relative importance of words and coupled with the necessary change in affinity function. An improvement in accuracy may also be made by the use of body text from the e-mail, stopword removal, stemming of words or perhaps the use of training data to optimize the algorithm's parameters.

We feel that the AISEC algorithm has shown that an AIS based algorithm can perform text-based classification with accuracy comparable with a naïve Bayesian classifier. We now wish to push forward with a more complex system. We would like to continue this project by investigating the use of Danger theory. This next step will be to extend AISEC to work in a danger-based scenario. In this scenario the concept of interestingness of an e-mail is more dynamic because it depends not only on the contents of the e-mail (as in this chapter) but also on the current status of the mailbox. In particular, when the mailbox is nearing capacity this may be interpreted as a danger signal and appropriate action taken. The ultimate goal of this work is to develop a Web mining system based on the danger model. The AISEC algorithm is one step in that direction and it is hoped that continued investigation will lead us further towards our goal.

REFERENCES

Aickelin, U., & Cayzer, S. (2002). *The danger theory and its application to artificial immune systems.* Paper presented at the First International Conference on Artificial Immune Systems (ICARIS 2002), Canterbury, UK, 141-148.

Anderson, C.C., & Matzinger, P. (2000). Danger: The view from the bottom of the cliff. *Seminars in Immunology, 12*(3), 231-238.

Androutsopoulos, I., Paliouras, G., Karkaletsis, V., Sakkis, G., Spyropoulos, C., & Stamatopoulos, P. (2000). *Learning to filter spam e-mail: A comparison of a naïve Bayesian and a memory-based approach.* Paper presented at the 4th European Conference on Principles and Practice of Knowledge Discovery in Databases, Lyon.

Blake, C.L., & Merz, C.J. (1998). *UCI Repository of machine learning databases.* Retrieved May 20, 2003: *http://www.ics.uci.edu/~mlearn/MLRepository.html.*

Brutlag, J.D., & Meek, C. (2000). *Challenges of the email domain for text classification.* Paper presented at the Seventeenth International Conference on Machine Learning (ICML 2000), USA, 103-110.

Chakrabarti, S. (2003). *Mining the Web (Discovering knowledge from hypertext data).* Morgan Kaufmann.

Crawford, E., Kay, J., & McCreath, E. (2001). *Automatic induction of rules for e-mail classification.* Paper presented at the Australian Document Computing Symposium (ADCS 2001), Australia, 13-20.

Cunningham, P., Nowlan, N., Delany, S.J., & Haahr, M. (2003). *A case-based approach to spam filtering that can track concept drift* (Technical report TCD-CS-2003-16). Dublin: Trinity College.

Dasgupta, D. (1999). An overview of AIS. In D. Dasgupta (Ed.), *Artificial immune systems and their applications* (pp. 3-21). Springer.

deCastro, L.N., & Timmis, J. (2002). *Artificial immune systems: A new computational intelligence approach.* Springer.

Diao, Y., Lu, H., & Wu, D. (2000). *A comparative study of classification based personal e-mail filtering.* Paper presented at the Fourth Pacific Asia Conference on Knowledge Discovery and Data Mining (PAKDD 2000).

Forrest, S., Perelson, A.S., Allen, L., & Cherukuri, R. (1994). *Self-nonself discrimination in a computer.* Paper presented at the IEEE Symposium on Research in Security and Privacy, Los Alamitos, USA, 202-212.

Friedman, N., & Kohavi, R. (2002). Bayesian classification. In W. Klosgen & J.M. Zytkow (Eds.), *Handbook of data mining and knowledge discovery* (pp. 282-288). Oxford University Press.

Gallucci, S., & Matzinger, P. (2001). Danger signals: SOS to the immune system. *Current Opinion in Immunology, 13*(1), 114-119.

Google. (2003). *Google homepage*. Retrieved May 23, 2003: *www.google.com.*

Graham, P. (2003). *A plan for spam*. Retrieved April 23, 2003: *http://www.paulgraham.com/ spam.html.*

Hunt, J.E., & Cooke, D.E. (1996). Learning using an artificial immune system. *Journal of Network and Computer Applications, 19*(2), 189-212.

Kim, J., & Bentley, P.J. (2001). *An evaluation of negative selection in an artificial immune system for network intrusion detection.* Paper presented at the Genetic and Evolutionary Computation Conference 2001 (GECCO 2001), San Francisco, USA, 1330-1337.

Linoff, G.S., & Berry, M.J.A. (2001). *Mining the Web (Transforming customer data into customer value).* Wiley.

Liu, B., Ma, Y., & Yu, P.S. (2001). *Discovering unexpected information from your competitors' web sites.* Paper presented at the Seventh International Conference on Knowledge Discovery and Data Mining (KDD 2001), San Francisco, USA, 144-153.

Matzinger, P. (2002a). The danger model: A renewed sense of self. *Science, 296,* 301-305.

Matzinger, P. (2002b). *The real function of the immune system or tolerance and the four D's.* Retrieved October 30, 2002: *http://cmmg.biosci.wayne.edu/asg/polly.html.*

Mitchell, T.M. (1997). Bayesian learning. In C.L. Liu & A.B. Tucker (Eds.), *Machine learning* (pp. 154-200). McGraw-Hill.

Rennie, J.D.M. (2000). ifile: An application of machine learning to mail filtering. *Proceedings of the KDD-2000 Workshop on Text Mining,* Boston, Massachusetts, USA.

Secker, A., Freitas, A.A., & Timmis, J. (2003). A danger theory inspired approach to Web mining. In J. Timmis, P. Bentley & E. Hart (Eds.), *Lecture notes in computer science, vol. 2787 (The Proceedings of the Second International Conference on Artificial Immune Systems)* (pp. 156-167). Springer.

Segal, R.B., & Kephart, J.O. (1999, May). *MailCat: An intelligent assistant for organizing e-mail.* Paper presented at the Third International Conference on Autonomous Agents (pp. 276-282).

Sompayrac, L. (1999). *How the immune system works.* Blackwell Science.

Timmis, J., & Knight, T. (2002). Artificial immune systems: Using the immune system as inspiration for data mining. In H.A. Abbass, R.A. Sarker & C.S. Newton (Eds.), *Data mining: A heuristic approach* (pp. 209-230). Hershey, PA: Idea Group Publishing.

Timmis, J., & Neal, M. (2001). A resource limited artificial immune system for data analysis. *Knowledge Based Systems, 14*(3-4), 121-130.

Twycross, J. (2002). *An immune system approach to document classification* (Technical Report HPL-2002-288). HP Labs, Bristol, UK.

Watkins, A., & Timmis, J. (2002). *Artificial Immune Recognition System (AIRS): Revisions and refinements.* Proceedings of The First International Conference on Artificial Immune Systems (ICARIS 2002), Canterbury, UK, 173-181.

Weiss, S.M., & Kulikowski, C.A. (1991). *Computer systems that learn.* Morgan Kaufmann.

Williamson, M.M. (2002). *Biologically inspired approaches to computer security* (Technical Report HPL-2002-131). HP Labs, Bristol, UK.

Yang, J., & Park, S.-Y. (2002). Email categorization using fast machine learning algorithms. *Discovery Science 2002,* 316-323.

Chapter VIII

XML Semantics

Yasser Kotb
Ain Shams University, Egypt

Katsuhiko Gondow
Tokyo Institute of Technology, Japan

Takuya Katayama
Japan Advanced Institute of Science and Technology, Japan

ABSTRACT

In this chapter, we consider the problem of checking the consistency of the semantics associated with extensible markup language (XML) documents. We propose a novel technique to add semantics to XML documents by attaching semantic information to the XML element tag attributes. We call this technique XML semantics. It is based on the same concept as attribute grammars (AGs), attaching and checking static semantics of programming languages through their attributes. Furthermore, we show how the attribute dependencies in this approach can be expressed in the SLXS language. The SLXS language is a new description language based on XML; we have designed it to describe the semantic dependencies of XML documents. By this approach we remain compliant with the XML core technology. Finally, we give a practical example to illustrate the power of our approach: we have successfully applied this approach to check the semantic consistency of the several holy books that are mentioned on the Religion 2 Website.

INTRODUCTION

The *Extensible Markup Language*, abbreviated *XML* (Bray, Paoli & Sperberg-McQueen, 2000), describes a class of data objects called XML documents and partially describes the behaviors of computer programs that process them. It is a useful way of describing declarative, structured documents. XML is a meta-language for describing markup languages. In other words, XML provides a facility to define tags and the structural relationships between them. However, XML lacks semantics in its construction (Psaila & Crespi-Reghizzi, 1999). XML specifies neither semantics nor a tag set. Since there is no predefined tag set, there cannot be any preconceived semantics. Meanwhile, *document type definitions (DTDs)* and other XML schemas (Thompson et al., 2001), which try to make XML documents more reliable and consistent, still lack the essential ability to describe semantics in XML documents.

Declarative structures, like XML, separate their semantic and syntax definitions, and have their own local descriptions that result in high readability and high maintainability. Therefore, the aim of this chapter is to propose a novel technique to add semantics to XML documents and to show how we can check the consistency of these semantics. This way is intended to use *attribute grammars (AGs)* (Knuth, 1968) in the area of Web content mining. By adding semantic information to XML attributes it is possible to describe the page's semantic dependencies, evaluate and check page consistency, and improve the automatic understanding of the page content. We focus primarily, but not only, on the design of a proper method to add semantics to XML documents by associating semantics with the element tag attributes. By extracting such a semantic description, we are able to notify document writers of semantic errors in XML documents. This method takes the advantage of attribute grammars. We use the positive characteristics of AGs in the sense that they provide a clear description by the functional computation of attributes. Of course we can add some semantics to XML documents by writing Java or Perl programs, but these programs are likely to be very ad-hoc, in the sense that:

- They tend to be large, including non-essential details, which results in low readability and low maintainability.
- They are located outside the data schema (DTD); syntax and semantics are loosely coupled, which implies that semantic checking cannot be forced upon XML users.

We propose a novel technique to add semantics to XML documents by attaching the semantic information to the XML element tag attributes (Kotb, Gondow & Katayama, 2002a). We called this *XML semantics*. This approach is based on the AGs concept of attaching and checking the static semantics of programming languages through their attributes.

Furthermore, in order to specify the attribute element tag dependencies in the XML documents, and to show how to compute automatically their values as functions of other attributes, we propose an XML-based specification language called **SLXS** *(Specification Language for XML Semantics)* (Kotb, Gondow & Katayama, 2002b). Any SLXS specification document must follow the predefined syntactic structure of an SLXS DTD. The complete list of SLXS DTD rules will be given and discussed later. SLXS allows us to describe the semantic consistency in a *functional, declarative,* and *local manner.* It uses the element tags only, without using any attributes attached to the element tags, which guarantees more readable and maintainable XML specification documents. Mainly, SLXS is used to automatically generate the necessary code for the attribute evaluation procedures and/or the functions that check the consistency of the semantics associated with an XML document. This code is called the *generated code*.

As a practical example to illustrate the real power of our approach, we have successfully applied it to check the semantic consistency of the several holy books that are mentioned in Religion 2.00 (Bosak, 1998). Religion 2.00 is a group of four religious works marked up for electronic publication from publicly available sources. It contains the four famous holy books in XML format: *The New Testament, The Old Testament, The Quran* and *The Book of Mormon.*

The remainder of this chapter is organized as follows: we start with an overview of the basic background of this research field and its significance, and then, we give a simple XML example that clarifies our ideas in the remainder of this chapter, and reviews briefly the basic concepts of attribute grammars and the relation to XML. Then we propose our novel technique for adding semantics to XML and the motivation for our work. These are followed by a discussion of specification language for XML semantics (SLXS) that is used to describe the different semantic dependencies in our XML documents. Next, we show a practical example of our approach that demonstrates the benefits of our technique. Finally, we mention some other related works and offer some conclusions.

BACKGROUND

In the production and dissemination of documents and hypertext on the Web, the trend towards mark-up languages is undeniable (Psaila & Crespi-Reghizzi, 1999). The hypertext mark-up language HTML is of course the best-known example, but HTML is just an instance of a document type designed at CERN for disseminating Web pages. Many different document types have been and are being defined for other purposes. The meta-notation for specifying document types and their grammars is provided by the *Standard Generalized Mark-up Languages (SGML)* (Goldfarb, 1991), and more recently, by its simplified and upgraded version of XML. Although the syntactic meta-notation of XML (and the mark-up languages in general) is easily checked, the semantic part of the mark-up specification is very poor. As a consequence, XML document type specifications can only be used to check the syntactic validity of a document, but are of no help for specifying transformations.

This serious weakness of XML has the undesirable consequence that application writers have to implement document transforming software using ad hoc techniques, which hinder portability, reuse, and extensibility. This is the main point of this research: we propose to introduce a new technique to add semantics to XML. This method uses attribute grammars in the area of Web content mining.

Web content mining uses the ideas and principles of data mining and knowledge discovery to screen more specific data. Another important aspect of Web content mining is the usage of the Web as a data source for knowledge discovery. This offers interesting new opportunities since more and more information regarding various topics is available on the Web. But the use of the Web as a provider of information is unfortunately more complex than working with static databases. Because of its very dynamic nature and its vast number of documents, there is a need for new solutions that do not depend on accessing complete data on the outset. In our approach, we concentrate on checking the semantic contents that are associated with XML documents. The reason for choosing XML rather than another mark-up language is that XML is rapidly emerging as the most widely adopted technology for information representation and exchange on the WWW.

In the remainder of this section, we introduce an XML example that plays a role in illustrating our ideas in the rest of the chapter. We will briefly introduce (informally) the basic concepts of attribute grammars and mention an AG example that corresponds to our running XML example. Finally, the possible connections between XML and AG will be discussed. Our aim in this section is to pay attention to the examples; both of them are artificial examples. The correspondence between these examples will clarify our discussions.

Running Example

Figure 1 shows an XML sample that represents the information of some book order and its corresponding total price. The total price of the order is copied from the total price of book list, while the total price of the book list itself is computed by summing the price associated with each book in the list. For simplicity, we consider here that the order consists of a single book list. In this example, we attach some semantic issues, which will be clarified shortly. We chose this example for its simplicity, as it is sufficient to explain the proposed techniques.

Attribute Grammars

Attribute Grammars (AGs) were introduced by Knuth (1968) to describe and implement the semantics of programming languages and, more generally, any syntax-directed computation. Moreover, it is used for implementing editors, compiler construction and compiler generator systems.

Our definition of attribute grammars is based on the works of Knuth (1968), Alblas (1991), and Katayama (1984). A survey with an extensive bibliography can be found in Deransart, Jourdan and Lorho (1988), and Alblas and Melichar (1991). AGs form an extension of the *context-free grammars (CFGs)* framework in the sense that the semantic information that is associated with programming language is constructed by attaching attributes to the grammar symbols representing these constructions. Each attribute has a set of possible values. Attribute values are defined by attribute evaluation rules associated with the production of the context-free grammar. These rules specify how to compute the values of certain attribute occurrences as a function of other attribute occurrences.

The attributes associated with a grammar symbol are divided into two disjoint classes, *synthesized attributes* and *inherited attributes*. The attribute evaluation rules associated with any grammar production define the synthesized attributes of the grammar symbol on its left side and the inherited attributes attached to the grammar symbols on its right side.

Example 1

To get the total price of a collection of books inside a bibliography of books, we can consider the classical attribute grammar that is depicted in Figure 2. The non-terminals of this grammar are: *bibliography, books, book, price, authors,* and *title.* The grammar is purely synthesized and the following attributes are used: *Price* represents the book price. *Total_price* represents the total price of the book order and book list, which is associated with both *"bibliography"* and *"books"* non-terminals. The grammar uses the auxiliary function *Value_Of* to get the equivalent value that represents the string of

Figure 1. Running XML Example

```
<?xml version="1.0"?>
<bibliography Total_price="520">
    <books Total_price="520">
        <book Isbn="3-540-54572-7" Price="120">
            <title> The art of compiler design </title>
            <authors Number="2">
                <author> Thomas Pittman </author>
                <author> James Peters </author>
            </authors>
        </book>
        <book Isbn="3-345-23454-7" Price="110">
            <title> C++ Programming Language </title>
            <authors Number="1">
                <author> Bjarne Stroustrup </author>
            </authors>
        </book>
        <book Isbn="0-201-48541-9" Price="150">
            <title> The Art of Computer Programming,
                    Volumes 1-3 Boxed Set</title>
            <authors Number="2">
                <author> Donald E. Knuth </author>
                <author> Donald Ervin Knuth </author>
            </authors>
        </book>
        <book Isbn="0-130-65198-2" Price="50">
            <title> The XML handbook </title>
            <authors Number="2">
                <author> Charles F. Goldfarb </author>
                <author> Paul Prescod </author>
            </authors>
        </book>
        <book Isbn="0-201-31006-6" Price="90">
            <title> The Java programming language </title>
            <authors Number="2">
                <author> Ken Arnold </author>
                <author> James Gosling </author>
            </authors>
        </book>
    </books>
</bibliography>
```

the *"NUMBER"*. The production rules of the grammar are given in Figure 2 together with its semantics rules.

Correspondence between XML and Standard Attribute Grammars

Apart from the semantics part in attribute grammars, both the syntactic part of AGs and XML can be considered as formalism tools defined over a syntactic structure: attribute grammar over CFG, and XML over *document-type definition (DTD)*. The major difference between the syntactic part of AG and DTD concerns the fact that DTD implements *extended context-free grammar (ECFG)* (Neven, 2000), whereas AG implements CFG. However, it is known from formal theory that every ECFG can be transformed

Figure 2. Production and Semantics Rules Associated with Example 1

Production Rules	Semantics Rules
bibliography → books	Total_price(bibliography) ← Total_price(books)
books → books book	Total_price (books) ← Total_price (books) + Price(book)
books → book	Total_price (books) ← Price(book)
book → title authors price	Price(book) ← Price(price)
price → NUMBER	Price(price) ← Value_Of(NUMBER)
authors → authors author	
authors → author	
author → STRING	
title → STRING	

in linear time into an equivalent CFG, by resolving each rule that contains a regular expression in its right hand to its equivalent plain context-free rule (Neven, 2000). XML lacks a distinction between inherited versus synthesized attributes, and more importantly does not support a semantic rules feature.

Both AG and XML are represented by a tree structure. For AGs, the *derivation tree* is used to check the syntactic validity of the given sentence in our grammar, as shown in Figure 3. At the same time, the attribute evaluation algorithms use the derivation tree to check the dependencies of the attributes. For XML, this tree is called a *DOM tree* (Wood et al., 1998), and it is used only to check the syntactic validity, as shown in Figure 4. In fact, AGs are well known for specifying semantics checkers for programming languages, while XML, like all markup languages, does not have semantics checkers at all.

In XML, the attributes that can be associated with tag elements are a kind of initialized lexical attributes that belong to a few predefined domains: *string, finite enumeration,* and *identification.* We can consider their attribute values as being static constants. In AGs, in addition to the available lexical attributes, semantic attributes denote another attribute kind that is evaluated during the attribute evaluation process or at the semantics phase. Moreover, attribute grammar attributes can hold any complex data structure for their values, like lists or sets, with auxiliary semantic functions implemented on these complex structures. In fact, the notion of semantic function is completely absent from markup specifications. Moreover, there is no distinction between inherited and synthesized attributes in the markup languages.

AGs define syntax-directed translators, from which the checker software can be built directly. XML has a serious weakness in this respect. The application writers have to implement document-transformation software using ad hoc techniques, which breaks the most important aspects of XML, namely, portability, reusability, and extensibility.

XML SEMANTICS APPROACH

Our approach to adding semantics to XML documents is achieved by attaching the semantic information to the XML documents through their element tag attributes. This approach is based on the same concept of attribute grammars as attaching and checking the static semantics for programming languages through their attributes. Attribute

Figure 3. Derivation Tree for AG Example 2

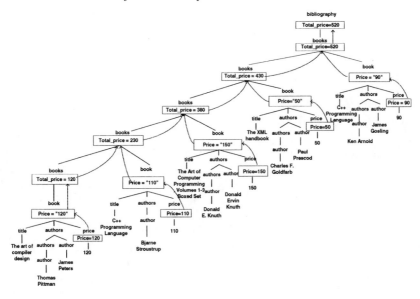

Figure 4. DOM Tree Structure for XML Example

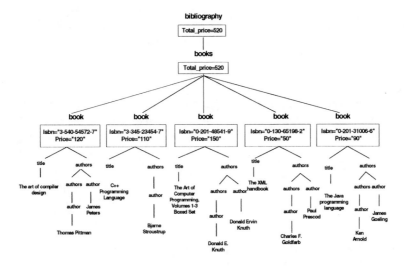

grammars have been shown to be a very useful and powerful concept for manipulating the static semantics of programming languages.

Starting from the syntactic analogy between AG and XML, as shown in previous sections, we argue that XML should benefit from integrating the semantic information through element tag attributes. We can illustrate this idea informally using our running example as follows: the total price of the collection of the book prices inside some books can be computed by associating the semantic information of the price for each book through its start element tag *"book"* using the attribute tag *"Price"* as follows:

<book Price = "100"> ...   </book>

and then associate the attribute element tag *"Total_price"* to the start element tag *"books"* as follows:

<books Total_price ="520"> ...   </books>

The value of the *"Price"* element tag attribute associated with each book is considered as a *static attribute* that acts as a lexical attribute in AGs, while the attribute *"Total_price"* is considered as an *evaluated attribute* that collects the semantic information from the inherited book prices, inside the books element tag, using the semantic operator *"SUM"*.

In the same manner, if we want to compute the average price for this book list, we can associate a new attribute *"Aver_price"* to the element tag *"books"* as follows:

<books Aver_price ="104"> ...   </books>

where the attribute *"Aver_price"* is considered as an evaluated attribute that depends on the book prices inside the element tag *"books"*.

Since every element tag can contain as many attributes as we like, we can compute the total and average price simultaneously by associating both attributes *"Total_price"* and *"Aver_price"* to *"books"* element tag as follows:

<books Total_price ="520" Aver_price ="104"> ...   </books>

Another new semantics concept that has been introduced to add semantics to XML is the *context attributes*. The value of a context attribute depends on the local context structure of the XML document. This new approach has been introduced to achieve consistent XML documents with respect to their own syntactic structure. For example, we associate the attribute *"Number"* to element tag *"authors"* to specify that the number of element tags *"author"* inside the element tag *"authors"* must be equal to the value of *"Number"*. Otherwise, it is considered an inconsistent value. As follows:

<authors Number="2">
    <author> Donald E. Knuth </author>
    <author> Donald Ervin Knuth </author>
</authors>

As another example, we can check the number of books in our list by associating the context attribute *"Books_number"* to the element tag *"books"* as follows:

<books Books_number ="5"> ...   </books>

In this case, the value of *"Books_number"* attribute must be equal to the number of element tag *"book"* in the given list.

The problem now is how to automatically evaluate and check the values of the evaluated and context attributes. We should specify these semantics in some formal method, like the role the semantics rule plays in AGs. Therefore, we propose a new meta-language, called *SLXS,* which is based on the XML structure (i.e., itself an XML document), as we will show later in this section.

Formally, we classify the XML element tag attributes into two types: *static attributes* and *dynamic attributes.* The former are considered as lexical attributes. The latter are used as intentional attributes, which carry the semantics and in turn can be separated into three subtypes, *evaluated attributes, context attributes,* and *copy attributes.* These attributes are evaluated by the evaluation algorithm and then compared with the corresponding extensional ones to check their semantic meaning. We assume that the evaluation of the dynamic attributes starts by giving them presumed values. Our semantics checker model, which checks the consistency of XML documents (Kotb, Gondow & Katayama, 2002c), is designed to report the inconsistent positions in the input XML document, and the expected correct values. As soon as we fix these inconsistent positions by giving them the correct values, we can repeat the checking of the desired input document until all XML element tag attributions become consistent. This repetition is necessary because some dynamic attributes may be interdependent. This way, we guarantee a consistent XML document.

Among the *evaluated attributes* there can be linear dependencies associated with the five different semantic operations: *sum, product, average, minimum,* and *maximum.* We have constrained the operations to these operations to simplify the discussion here. However, we argue that more semantic operations can be added to our approach. To achieve this, we suggest adding the implementation code for any new operators directly to the specification document SLXS, by writing program code inside the XML element CDATA. The reader can refer to Kotb (2003) for more details.

The *context attributes* are a new semantic approach that can be added to XML documents. These attributes contain some values depending on the local context structure of the XML documents, and provide additional information needed to achieve consistent document structure.

Another semantic concept called *copy attributes* has been introduced to copy semantic information value from some node in the derivation tree that is associated to the XML document to another node without any modification.

These dynamic (evaluated, context, and copy) attributes can be evaluated by generating separate evaluators for them. This method is based on the attribute grammar techniques that translate the AG description language into a set of recursive procedures (Jourdan, 1984; Katayama, 1984). It is an efficient method for evaluating attribute grammars and has practical importance. The basic idea behind this method is to consider non-terminal symbols of the grammar as functions that map their attribute dependencies to each other. The essential point is that AGs are completely compiled into a set of mutually-recursive procedures when the given AG is strictly non-circular. In our approach, we have borrowed this idea of generating mutually recursive procedures. We have proposed an *attribute evaluation generator algorithm* (Kotb, Gondow & Katayama, 2002a) to evaluate the attribute values and to check them with the static attributes that are explicitly provided in the source document. For each dynamic attribute that belongs to some element tag we associate a different procedure. The body of this procedure represents the dependency between this dynamic attribute and other attributes.

Although these semantic issues are quite simple, they can be extended to cover more semantic topics. The reason for simplicity is to achieve less complicated generated code. The code is generated from our XML semantics evaluator generator algorithm. This algorithm is used to generate the XML semantics evaluator procedures and checker functions from a given specification document. This specification document acts as a specification language or a meta-language that specifies our semantics for any desired XML document. Desired document means the XML document that is needed to check whether or not it is semantically consistent. For this purpose, we use SLXS language. These semantic rules depend on the attribute type. Therefore, we will return to our example to clarify the proposed language for different attribute types as follows:

1.   *Evaluated Attributes:* These are the attributes in an XML document for which we get values by evaluating them during our attribute evaluation process. Initially, these attributes have specified values that may be wrong. The values can be checked during our semantics checking process. We can get the correct values for these attributes by comparing the attribute values that exist in our document with those evaluated. For example, the attribute *"Total_price"* of the element tag *"books"* is an evaluated attribute depending on the attribute *"Price"* of element tag *"book"* through the **"SUM"** operation. This evaluated attribute semantic function can be specified with our specification language SLXS, as follows:

```
<Attr_Dependency>
        <Base_Attr>
            <Attr>
                    <Name>Total_price</Name>
                    <Elem>books</Elem>
            </Attr>
        </Base_Attr>
        <DependOn_Attr>
            <Attr>
                    <Name>Price</Name>
                    <Elem>book</Elem>
            </Attr>
        </DependOn_Attr>
        <Function>SUM</Function>
    </Attr_Dependency>
```

2.   *Context Attributes:* These are the attributes in XML documents whose values depend on the context structure of the document. We can check them directly within the specified context during semantics checking. For example, the attribute *"Number"* of the element tag *"authors"* is a context attribute depending on the number of author element tags *"author"* inside the element tag *"authors"*. This context attribute semantic function can be specified with our specification language SLXS as follows:

```
<Attr_Check>
        <Attr>
              <Name>Number</Name>
              <Elem>authors</Elem>
        </Attr>
        <Local_Context_Elem>author</Local_Context_Elem>
   </Attr_Check>
```

These kinds of attributes depend on the local context region structure. Although it seems like a syntactic problem within an XML document, it cannot check them against the DTD. Context attributes are a new semantics approach that can be added to XML documents. We suggest this to achieve consistent XML documents with respect to their own structure.

3.   *Copy Attributes:* These are the attribute instances that pass the attribute values without any modification through copy rules. Copy rules are the semantics equations that transfer the value of the right hand side to its left hand side without any modification. Formally, the attribute associated with the left hand side is called the *base attribute* and the attribute associated to right hand side is called the *depend_on attribute.* For example, the attribute *"Total_price"* of the element tag *"bibliography"* is a based attribute to the depend_on attribute *"Total_price"* of the element tag *"books".* We design SLXS to represent the copy rule as follows:

```
<Copy_Rule>
        <Base_Attr>
              <Attr>
                    <Name>Total_price</Name>
                    <Elem>bibliography</Elem>
              </Attr>
        </Base_Attr>
        <DependOn_Attr>
              <Attr>
                    <Name>Total_price</Name>
                    <Elem>books</Elem>
              </Attr>
        </DependOn_Attr>
   </Copy_Rule>
```

The complete SLXS specification document, which is associated with our running example, is shown in the next section.

SPECIFICATION LANGUAGE
FOR XML SEMANTICS

In order to define the attributes and the semantic dependencies among XML element attributions, we have proposed a new specification language called *SLXS (specification language for XML semantics)* (Kotb, Gondow & Katayama, 2002b). SLXS describes the semantic consistencies of XML documents in a *functional, declarative,* and *local* manner. It is based on XML technology; namely, it is an XML document that uses element tags only, without using any attributes attached to the element tags. This way, we guarantee more readable and maintainable XML specification documents. In addition, SLXS obeys the recommendations of experienced XML workers to avoid using attributes rather than element tags, as the attributes are more difficult to manipulate by program code and attribute values are not easy to test against the DTD. Mainly, SLXS is used to automatically generate the necessary code for the attribute evaluation procedures and/or the functions that check the consistency of the semantics associated with an XML document. This code is called the *generated code.*

The SLXS specification document must be validated with respect to a specified document type definition: we call it *SLXS DTD.* This SLXS DTD is fixed to our specification language. We argue that SLXS DTD would be extended to cover more semantic dependencies in a systematic way as our system itself is modified. In the following subsection we will discuss in detail the SLXS DTD.

SLXS DTD

SLXS DTD states what tags are used to describe contents of specification documents, which is used to specify the XML semantics, where each tag is allowed, and which tags can appear within other tags. This ensures that all the specification documentation is formatted in the same way. In addition, the XML semantics checker model (Kotb, Gondow & Katayama, 2002c) implements the XML semantics approach, and uses the SLXS DTD to properly verify and check the specification document's contents. The SLXS DTD is defined as follows:

```
<!— The DTD for SLXS Specification Language "SLXS.dtd" —>
<!ELEMENT XML_Semantics
          (Attrs_List, Eval_Attrs?, Copy_Attrs?, Context_Attrs?)>
<!ELEMENT Attrs_List (Attr)*>
<!ELEMENT Eval_Attrs (Attr_Dependency)*>
<!ELEMENT Attr_Dependency (Base_Attr, DependOn_Attr, Function)>
<!ELEMENT Copy_Attrs (Copy_Rule)*>
<!ELEMENT Copy_Rule (Base_Attr, DependOn_Attr)>
<!ELEMENT Context_Attrs (Attr_Check)*>
<!ELEMENT Attr_Check (Attr, Local_Context_Elem)>
<!ELEMENT Base_Attr (Attr)>
<!ELEMENT DependOn_Attr (Attr)>
<!ELEMENT Function (#PCDATA)>
<!ELEMENT Local_Context_Elem (#PCDATA)>
<!ELEMENT Attr (Name, Elem)>
<!ELEMENT Name (#PCDATA)>
<!ELEMENT Elem (#PCDATA)>
```

Where:
*   The element *XML_Semantics* defines the overall specification document structure for any XML document. It contains an element *Attrs_List,* optionally followed by the *Eval_Attrs, Copy_Attrs* and *Context_Attrs* elements, respectively.

- The element *Attr_List* defines the list of attributes in the desired XML document. It contains a list from *Attr* elements, which can be empty.
- The element *Eval_Attrs* defines the list of evaluated attributes in the desired document. It contains a list from *Attr_Dependency* elements, which can be empty.
- The element *Context_Attrs* defines the list of context attributes in the desired document. It contains a list from *Attr_Check* elements, which can be empty.
- The element *Copy_Attrs* defines the list of copy attribute dependency rules in the desired document. It contains a list from *Copy_Rule* elements, which can be empty.
- The element *Attr_Dependency* defines the evaluated attribute dependency. It contains, in order, the base attribute *(Base_Attr)*, the attribute that the base attribute depends on *(DependOn_Attr)*, and the applied function in this dependency *(Function)*.
- The element *Attr_Check* defines the context attribute. It contains the context attribute *(Attr)* and its associated local element tag name *(Local_Context_Elem)*.
- The element *Copy_Rule* defines the copy rule dependency. It contains, in order, the base attribute *(Base_Attr)* and the attribute that the base attribute depends on *(DependOn_Attr)*.
- The elements *Base_Attr* and *DependOn_Attr* define the base attribute and depend on attribute, respectively.
- The element *Attr* defines the attribute. It contains the attribute name *(Name)* and the element tag name *(Elem)* to which the attribute belongs.
- The elements *Name, Elem, Local_Context_Elem*, and *Function* allow only text as content. This is specified by the keyword *#PCDATA*. They define the attribute name, attribute belong element name, the local context element name and the function name, respectively.

SLXS Specification Document of the Running Example

In order to visualize the overall structure of SLXS specification language, we show the complete SLXS specification document that is associated with our running example. It is started by an XML document line declaration and followed by the validation line with the predefined SLXS DTD. Then, we specify the different semantic issues that may be in our XML document that must obey the constraints of the SLXS DTD.

```
<?xml version="1.0"?>
<!DOCTYPE XML_Semantics SYSTEM "SLXS.dtd">
<XML_Semantics>
    <Attrs_List>
        <Attr>
            <Name>Total_price</Name>
            <Elem>bibliography</Elem>
        </Attr>
        <Attr>
            <Name>Total_price</Name>
            <Elem>books</Elem>
        </Attr>
        <Attr>
```

```
                    <Name>Price</Name>
                    <Elem>book</Elem>
            </Attr>
            <Attr>
                    <Name>Number</Name>
                    <Elem>authors</Elem>
            </Attr>
        </Attrs_List>

        <Eval_Attrs>
            <Attr_Dependency>
                <Base_Attr>
                    <Attr>
                        <Name>Total_price</Name>
                        <Elem>books</Elem>
                    </Attr>
                </Base_Attr>
                <DependOn_Attr>
                    <Attr>
                        <Name>Price</Name>
                        <Elem>book</Elem>
                    </Attr>
                </DependOn_Attr>
                <Function>SUM</Function>
            </Attr_Dependency>
        </Eval_Attrs>

        <Context_Attrs>
            <Attr_Check>
                <Attr>
                    <Name>Number</Name>
                    <Elem>authors</Elem>
                </Attr>
                            <Local_Context_Elem>author</
Local_Context_Elem>
            </Attr_Check>
        </Context_Attrs>

        <Copy_Attrs>
            <Copy_Rule>
                <Base_Attr>
                    <Attr>
                        <Name>Total_price</Name>
                        <Elem>bibliography</Elem>
                    </Attr>
                </Base_Attr>
```

```
<DependOn_Attr>
    <Attr>
        <Name>Total_price</Name>
        <Elem>books</Elem>
    </Attr>
</DependOn_Attr>
    </Copy_Rule>
</Copy_Attrs>
</XML_Semantics>
```

A PRACTICAL EXAMPLE

This section is a case study applying the XML semantics approach to specify the consistency of the holy books published in XML format found at the Religion 2.00 Website (Bosak, 1998). Religion 2.00 is a site with the books of four major religions marked up for electronic publication. It contains four holy books in XML format: *The New Testament, The Old Testament, The Quran,* and *The Book of Mormon.* The goal of the study was to clarify the application of XML semantics in a problem domain, which is appreciated for the proposed approach, and to determine some of the strengths of XML semantics in this real domain.

We applied our approach to check the variant semantic consistency problems that exist inside these holy books. This included checking that the number of verses (or chapters) in each chapter (or book) was correctly written in the XML format document. We also checked that the XML document contained exactly the same number of chapters (and books) as in the real holy books. In addition, we computed the total number of verses in each book. In each case we found the Religion 2.00 Website to be semantically correct. In this chapter, we will apply our approach to add semantics to *The New Testament* holy book. However, we have succeeded in applying the same manner to other holy books.

The *New Testament* Semantics

In this section, we explain formally the several semantic issues associated with *The New Testament* XML format book. We have applied our approach to check the following semantic consistency problems:
1. The number of verses in each chapter was correctly written in the XML format document.
2. We checked that the XML format document contained exactly the same number of chapters as in the real *New Testament.*
3. We also checked that the XML format document contained exactly the same number of books as in the real *New Testament.*
4. We computed the total number of verses.
5. We computed the total number of verses in the whole real *New Testament.*

The *New Testament* SLXS Specification

In this section, we introduce the different attributes and their types that have been employed in the holy XML format document. These attributes will be used in checking

Table 1. Attributes Types

Attribute Name	Associated Element Tag	Attribute Type
Books_num	bookcoll	Context attribute
Total_verses_num	bookcoll	Evaluated attribute
Chapters_num	book	Context attribute
Sum_verses_num	book	Evaluated attribute
Verses_num	chapter	Context attribute

the *New Testament* semantic consistencies mentioned previously. In addition, we describe how to specify these semantic consistencies by the specification language SLXS.

Attributes

Table 1 shows the different attributes that are associated with the *New Testament* holy XML document to carry the semantic values. Moreover, we use these attributes to check whether the different positions in the holy XML document are consistent or not.

The SLXS Semantic Rules

In order to specify the former semantic consistencies, we have designed the following SLXS specification. The evaluated attributes *"Total_verses_num"* and *"Sum_verses_num"* are used to solve the 4th and 5th semantic problem, respectively. Both of them have been defined by "Attr_Dependency" part in the SLXS document. The *"Total_verses_num"* attribute depends on the *"Sum_verses_num"* through the *"SUM"* operator. Similarly, the evaluated attribute *"Sum_verses_num"* depends on the *"Verses_num"* attribute through *"SUM"* operator. In the other hand, the context attributes *"Verses_num," "Chapters_num"* and *"Books_num"* are used to check the first, second and third semantic problems and they are declared by "Attr_Check" portions in SLXS document. They depend on the local element tags *"v," "chapter"* and *"book,"* respectively.

```
<?xml version="1.0"?>
<!DOCTYPE XML_Semantics SYSTEM "SLXS.dtd">
<XML_Semantics>
    <Attrs_List>
        <Attr>
            <Name>Books_num</Name><Elem>bookcoll</Elem>
        </Attr>
        <Attr>
            <Name>Total_verses_num</Name><Elem>bookcoll</Elem>
        </Attr>
        <Attr>
            <Name>Chapters_num</Name><Elem>book</Elem>
        </Attr>
        <Attr>
            <Name>Sum_verses_num</Name><Elem>book</Elem>
```

```
            </Attr>
            <Attr>
                <Name>Verses_num</Name><Elem>chapter</Elem>
            </Attr>
        </Attrs_List>

        <Eval_Attrs>
            <Attr_Dependency>
                <Base_Attr>
                    <Attr>
                        <Name>Total_verses_num</Name>
                        <Elem>bookcoll</Elem>
                    </Attr>
                </Base_Attr>
                <DependOn_Attr>
                    <Attr>
                        <Name>Sum_verses_num</Name>
                        <Elem>book</Elem>
                    </Attr>
                </DependOn_Attr>
                <Function>SUM</Function>
            </Attr_Dependency>
            <Attr_Dependency>
                <Base_Attr>
                    <Attr>
                        <Name>Sum_verses_num</Name>
                        <Elem>book</Elem>
                    </Attr>
                </Base_Attr>
                <DependOn_Attr>
                    <Attr>
                        <Name>Verses_num</Name>
                        <Elem>chapter</Elem>
                    </Attr>
                </DependOn_Attr>
                <Function>SUM</Function>
            </Attr_Dependency>
        </Eval_Attrs>

        <Context_Attrs>
            <Attr_Check>
                <Attr>
                    <Name>Books_num</Name><Elem>bookcoll</Elem>
                </Attr>
                <Local_Context_Elem>book</Local_Context_Elem>
            </Attr_Check>
```

```
<Attr_Check>
    <Attr>
       <Name>Chapters_num</Name><Elem>book</Elem>
    </Attr>
    <Local_Context_Elem>
            chapter
    </Local_Context_Elem>
</Attr_Check>
<Attr_Check>
    <Attr>
       <Name>Verses_num</Name><Elem>chapter</Elem>
    </Attr>
    <Local_Context_Elem>v</Local_Context_Elem>
</Attr_Check>
    </Context_Attrs>
</XML_Semantics>
```

RELATED WORK

There are few attempts in this regard. The first approach to add semantics to XML was published by Psaila and Crespi-Reghizzi (1999). They provide a method for transforming the element description of DTD into an EBNF formal rule description and present the *semantic rule definition (SRD)*, which acts as meta-language that describes the semantics in the XML document and describes how to evaluate the semantics associated with XML. It is XML-based and employs DTD. In our approach, rather than semantic rule definitions, our specification language SLXS is a new method that is defined by using element tags, without using any attribute attached to the element tags. This guarantees more readable and maintainable XML documents. Furthermore, it obeys the recommendations of experienced XML workers to avoid using attributes in place of element tags; this is because attributes are more difficult to manipulate by program code and attribute values are not easy to test against a DTD. Meanwhile, it is easier to analyze this kind of XML document to extract the attribute dependencies during the implementation phase.

Although the new XML schema (Thompson et al., 2001) offers facilities for describing the structure and constraining the contents of XML documents, it still cannot solve the syntactic issues of the context attributes. For example, the XML schemas can specify the minimum and maximum occurrence of each element tag inside a given element tag, without depending on the tag value. Our approach directly specifies the exact occurrence number of the element tags, and those that depend on some attribute value associated with this tag.

Apart from the XML area, Neven (2000) has introduced a new form of attribute grammars (extended AGs) that work directly over extended context-free grammars rather than over standard context-free grammars. Viewed as a query language, extended AGs are particularly relevant, as they can take into account the inherent order of the children of a node in a document. Moreover, he has shown that two key properties of standard attribute grammars carry over to extended AGs: efficiency of evaluation and decidability of well-definedness.

CONCLUSIONS

We proposed a novel technique to add semantics to XML documents by attaching the semantic information to the XML element tag attributes. We called this XML semantics. This approach is based on the same concept of AGs as attaching and checking the static semantics of programming languages through their attributes. As a necessary step to specify the semantic that is associated with any XML document. We introduced a way to use XML as a specification language for XML semantics. We called this language SLXS. SLXS used to define the attributes and the semantics dependencies among XML element attributions. It is an XML document that obeys the specified syntactic structure for SLXS DTD.

Furthermore, we have successfully applied our approach in the real application domains. We have checked the different semantic consistencies of the several holy books that are mentioned in Religion 2.00 Website. In each case we found the Religion 2.00 Website to be semantically correct.

REFERENCES

Alblas, H. (1991). Attribute evaluation methods. In H. Alblas & B. Melichar (Eds.), *Attribute grammars, applications and systems, LNCS 545* (pp. 48-113). Prague: Springer-Verlag.

Alblas, H., & Melichar, B. (eds.). (1991). Attribute grammars, applications and systems, Prague, *LNCS 545*. New York: Springer-Verlag.

Bosak, J. (1998). *Religion 2.00.* Available: *http://www.ibiblio.org/xml/examples/religion/.*

Bray, T., Paoli, J., & Sperberg-McQueen, C.M. (2000). Extensible Markup Language (XML) 1.0 (2nd ed.). *W3C Recommendation 6 October 2000.* Available: *http://www.w3.org/TR/2000/REC-xml-20001006.*

Deransart, P., Jourdan, M., & Lorho, B. (1988). Attribute grammars, definitions, systems and bibliography. *LNCS 323.* Springer-Verlag.

Goldfarb, C.F. (1991). *The SGML handbook.* Oxford University Press.

Jourdan, M. (1984). Recursive evaluators for attribute grammars: An implementation. In B. Lorho (Ed.), *Methods and tools for compiler construction* (pp. 139-164). Cambridge University Press.

Katayama, T. (1984). Translation of attribute grammars into procedures. *ACM Transactions on Programming Languages and Systems, 6*(3), 344-369.

Knuth, D.E. (1968). Semantics of context-free languages. *Math. System Theory J.2,* 127-145.

Kotb, Y. (2003, September). *Checking consistency of XML documents by attribute grammar techniques.* Ph.D. dissertation, School of Information Science, Japan Advanced Institute of Science and Technology.

Kotb, Y., Gondow, K., & Katayama, T. (2002a). Checking consistency of XML semantics using attribute grammars. *Inter. Conf. on East-Asian Language Processing and Internet Information Technology, EALPIIT 2002,* 29-38.

Kotb, Y., Gondow, K., & Katayama, T. (2002b). The SLXS specification language for describing consistency of XML documents. *Fourth Workshop on Information and Computer Science (WICS2002),* IEEE Computer Society, 289-304.

Kotb, Y., Gondow, K., & Katayama, T. (2002c). The XML semantics checker model. *Third International Conference on Parallel and Distributed Computing, Applications and Technologies (PDCAT'02),* Japan, 430-438.

Neven, F. (2000). Extensions of attribute grammars for structured document queries. *7th International Workshop on Database Programming Languages* (Kinloch Rannoch, Scotland, 1999), *LNCS 1949,* Springer, 99-116.

Psaila, G., & Crespi-Reghizzi, S. (1999). Adding semantics to XML. In D. Parigot & V. Mernik (Eds.), *Proceedings of the Second Workshop on Attribute Grammars and their Applications (WAGA '99),* Amsterdam, The Netherlands, INRIA, (pp. 113-132).

Thompson, H. et al. (2001). XML schema part 1: Structures. *W3C Recommendation 2 May 2001.* Available: *http://www.w3.org/TR/xmlschema-1/.*

Wood, L. et al. (1998). Document Object Model (DOM). *Maintained by the W3C DOM WG.* Available: *http://www.w3.org/TR/REC-DOM-Level-1/.*

Chapter IX

Classification on Top of Data Cube

Lixin Fu
University of North Carolina, Greensboro, USA

ABSTRACT

Currently, data classification is either performed on data stored in relational databases or performed on data stored in flat files. The problem with these approaches is that for large data sets, they often need multiple scans of the original data and thus are often infeasible in many applications. In this chapter we propose to deploy classification on top of OLAP (online analytical processing) and data cube systems. First, we compute the statistics in various combinations of the attributes known as data cubes. The statistics are then used to derive classification models. In this way, we only scan the original data once, which improves the performance of classification significantly. Furthermore, our new classifier will provide "free" classification by eliminating the dominating I/O overhead of scanning the massive original data. An architecture that integrates database, data cube, and data mining is given and three new cube-based classifiers are presented and evaluated.

INTRODUCTION

Data classification is the process of building a model from available data called the *training data set* and classifying objects according to their attributes. Classification is a well-studied important problem (Han & Kamber, 2001). It has many applications. For example, it has been used in online classification of articles from registered newsgroups on the Internet into predefined subject categories, in the insurance industry, for tax and credit card fraud detection, for medical diagnosis, and so forth. Such data classification is one of the important topics in Web mining and Web services.

Currently, data classification is either performed on data stored in relational database management systems or performed on data stored in small flat files. The problem of existing classifiers built on these approaches is that for large data sets, they often need multiple scans of the original data and thus are infeasible in many real applications.

In this chapter we propose to deploy classification on top of OLAP (online analytical processing) and data cube systems. First, a multidimensional analysis is conducted on these large data sets. The output of this analysis is summarized data; for example, aggregates in various combinations of the attributes also known as data cubes (Gray et al., 1997). The aggregates are then used to derive classification models. In this way, we only scan the original data once, which improves the performance of classification significantly. Furthermore, since in the decision support systems data cubes are usually already precomputed (in terms of materialized views for example) for answering OLAP queries, our new classifier will provide "free" classification functions by eliminating the dominating I/O overhead of scanning the original data.

Our objectives in this chapter are:
- designing new classifiers built on data cubes and,
- proposing an architecture that takes the advantages of above new algorithms and integrates DBMS, OLAP systems, and data mining systems seamlessly.

The remainder of the chapter is organized as follows. First we give a brief summary of the related work. In the next two sections, statistics tree structures and related data cube computation algorithms are described as the foundation of later sections, and an architecture that integrates DBMS, OLAP, and data mining functions is proposed. After that, we present three new classifiers based on the data cube: pattern detection, cube-based naïve Bayesian classification, and cube-based decision tree classification. Lastly, we give the evaluation of these three algorithms, summarize the chapter, and discuss our future work directions related to classification.

BACKGROUND

Many popular classification algorithms are based on decision tree induction. Algorithm ID-3 generates a simple tree in a top-down fashion (Quilan, 1986). It chooses the attribute with the highest information gain as the split attribute. Data are partitioned into subsets recursively until the partitions contain samples of the same classes. Algorithm C4.5 extends the domain of classification in ID-3 from categorical domain to numerical domain (Quilan, 1993). It gives approaches to transform decision trees into rules. For continuous attribute A, the values are sorted and the midpoint v between two values is considered as a possible split. The split form is $A \leq v$. There are V-1 such splits if A has V values in its domain. For a categorical attribute, if its cardinality is small, all subsets of its domain can be a candidate split; otherwise, we can use a greedy strategy to create candidate splits.

Recent decision-tree classifiers focus on scalability issues for large data sets. SLIQ (Supervised Learning In Quest) uses Gini index as the classification function (Mehta, Agrawal & Rissanen, 1996). Presorting (for numerical attributes) and breadth-first searching avoid resorting at each node. SLIQ requires the use of an in-memory structure called "class list" and thus has poor performance for data sets whose "class list" structure is out of memory. SPRINT (Scalable PaRallelizable INduction of decision Trees) remedies this drawback of SLIQ and is easily parallelizable (Shafer, Agrawal & Mehta, 1996). It uses a different data structure called *attribute lists,* which are extracted column-wise from original relation and are composed of three columns: <attribute value, class value, transaction-id>. The transaction-id column is used to track where the records are to be partitioned. An attribute list is created for each attribute except the classifying attribute. Though the in-memory structure "class list" is taken out, it needs a hash tree for partitioning non-splitting attribute lists. Both SLIQ and SPRINT are still multi-pass algorithms for large data sets due to the necessity of external sorting and out-of-memory structures such as attribute lists.

Surajit et al. (Surajit Chaudhuri, Fayyad & Bernhardt, 1999) give a scalable classifier over a SQL database backend. They develop middleware that batches query executions and stages data into its memory or local files to improve performance. At its core is a data structure called count table or CC table, a four-column table (attribute-name, attribute-value, class-value, count). The CC table is sufficient for the computation of splits. The classifier has the complete freedom of evaluating the CC tables of the nodes in the decision tree in any order, not necessarily confined to breadth-first search or depth-first search. The middleware also contains a file-splitting technique to access less data for the lower-level nodes. The data mining client does not compute the CC tables. Instead, it requests the middleware for this service, which further initiates SQL queries against database backend without directly touching the physical data. In spite of these advantages, this classifier may still need multiple passes for the original data. On one hand, the DBMS cannot guarantee to scan only once to evaluate the SQL queries with UNIONs of GROUP_BYs. On the other hand, the CC tables computed for a node are not useful anymore in the computation of the CC tables for its descendants. In the computation of CC tables, the original data records have to be accessed again and again no matter whether they are in the server, in the memory, or in the local files of middleware.

Gehrke et al. give a uniform framework based on AVC-group (a data structure similar to CC tables but an independent work) for providing scalable versions of most decision tree classifiers without changing the quality of the tree (Gehrke, Ramakrishnan & Ganti, 1998). With usually much smaller sizes of CC tables or AVC-group than the original data or attribute lists in SPRINT, these two algorithms generally improve the mining performance. However, they, together with all other classification algorithms (as far as we know) including SLIQ and SPRINT, still need to physically access (sometimes in multiple scans) the original data set to compute the best splits through CC table or AVC-group, and partition the data sets into nodes according to the splitting criteria. Drastically different from these algorithms, our cube-based decision tree construction does not compute and store the F-sets (all the records belong to an internal node) to find best splits, nor does it partition the data set physically. Instead, we compute the splits through the data cubes, as shown in more detail below.

The BOAT algorithm (Gehrke, Ganti, Ramakrishnan & Loh, 1999) uses an optimistic approach to construct several levels of trees in two scans over the training data set. It constructs a decision tree and coarse split criteria from a large sample of original data using a statistical technology called *bootstrapping.* In a cleanup scan of data, discrepancies of the sample decision tree from the "real tree" are detected and corrected. For continuous attributes, the confidence interval of the best split provides guidance in obtaining an improved best split in the cleanup phase. BOAT is able to incrementally update the tree when the original data set has insertions and deletions.

An overview of data mining from a statistics perspective is shown in Elder IV and Pregibon (1996). A naïve Bayesian classifier (Duda & Hart, 1973) assumes class conditional independence and has classifying accuracy comparable to decision tree classifiers (Han & Kamber, 2001). AutoClass is another Bayesian classifier (Cheeseman & Stutz, 1996). If the attribute values are interdependent to one another for a given class value, which is often the case in many applications, Bayesian belief networks can be trained to reflect the conditional probability distribution of the attributes (Heckerman, 1996). Chan and Wong describe a method based on some concepts in statistics and information theory and prove that it is better than traditional classification algorithms based on decision trees (Chan & Wong, 1991). Other classification methods include back propagation (Lu, Setiono & Liu, 1995), association rule mining (Lent, Swami & Widom, 1997), k-nearest neighbor classifier (Duda & Hart, 1973), and so forth.

Since our new classifiers are built on top of the technologies of OLAP and data cube, the performance of cube computation has a direct influence on these classifiers. Next, we briefly introduce some of the cube systems and cube computation algorithms. To compute data cubes, various ROLAP (relational OLAP) systems, MOLAP (multidimensional OLAP) systems, and HOLAP (hybrid OLAP) systems are proposed (Chaudhuri & Dayal, 1997). Materialized views and indexing are often used to speed up the evaluation of data cubes and OLAP queries.

Materializing all the aggregate GROUP_BY views may incur excessive storage requirements and maintenance overhead for these views. A view selection algorithm proposed by Harinarayan et al. (Harinarayan, Rajaraman & Ullman, 1996) uses a greedy strategy to choose a set of views over the lattice structure under the constraint of a certain space or a certain number of views to materialize. Agarwal et al. (1996) overlap or pipeline the computation of the views so that the cost of the processing tree is minimized. Aside from scheduling the order of computing views are the choices of using sorting or hashing methods for the nodes in the processing tree. For sparse data, Zhao et al. proposed the chunking method and sparse data structure for sparse chunks (Zhao, Deshpande & Naughton, 1997).

For dimensions with small cardinalities, bitmap indexing is very effective (O'Neil, 1987). It is suitable for ad-hoc OLAP queries and has good performance due to quick bitwise logical operations. However, it is inefficient for large domains. In this case, encoded bitmap (Chan & Ioannidis, 1998) or B-trees (Comer, 1979) can be used. Other work related to indexing includes variant indexes (O'Neil & Quass, 1997), join indexes, and so forth.

Rather than computing all the data cubes, Beyer and Ramakrishnan (1999) develop the BUC (bottom-up cubing) algorithm for cubing only on group-bys that use clause HAVING COUNT(*) > X, where X is greater than some threshold. BUC builds cubes in a bottom-up fashion and employs the a priori property similar to association rule mining (Srikant & Agrawal, 1996) to eliminate non-frequent cube cells. However, this algorithm may still need multiple passes and it is not incrementally updateable. Johnson and Shasha

(1997) propose cube trees and cube forests for cubing. We have developed a dynamic multidimensional data structure called *Statistics Tree* (ST) to compute data cubes involving aggregation (Fu & Hammer, 2000; Hammer & Fu, 2001). In the next section, we will present these structures and related algorithms briefly.

STATISTICS TREES

Though much progress has been made, efficient computation of data cubes remains a very challenging problem because of the immense sizes of data warehouses, the curse of dimensionality (many dimensions with large domain sizes), and the complexity of queries. In addition, the administration (including computation, indexing and maintenance) of a large number of separate materialized views or multidimensional arrays is indeed a complex task that we desire to simplify. Another main drawback of ROLAP algorithms is that they are often multi-pass for large data sets. All of these challenges and dilemmas motivate us to develop a different evaluation strategy. We developed a dynamic multidimensional data structure called *Statistics Tree* (ST) (Fu & Hammer, 2000). Due to the large sizes of data warehouses, analytical processing usually focuses on summary information. Therefore, we only retain the aggregations of the cubes instead of the detailed records, which greatly reduced space and time costs. We call the OLAP queries that only involve aggregations *cube queries*. An ST is a multi-way, balanced tree whose leaf nodes contain the aggregates for a set of records consisting of one or more attributes. Leaf nodes are linked to facilitate storage and retrieval. Each level in the tree (except the leaf level) corresponds to an attribute. An internal node has one pointer for each domain value, and an additional "star" pointer represents the entire attribute domain. Internal nodes contain only pointers. Initially, the values in the leaf nodes are set to zero or undefined.

Populating the tree is done during a one-time scan of the data set: for each record, the tree is partially traversed based on the attribute values in the record; the leaf nodes at the end of the path are updated using the aggregation function (e.g., incremented by one in the case of the *count* function).

Figure 1 depicts a simple statistics tree corresponding to a data cube with three dimensions x_1, x_2, x_3 having cardinalities $d_1=2, d_2=3,$ and $d_3=4$ respectively. The contents of the tree are shown after inserting the record $(1,2,4)$ into an empty tree. The leaf nodes store the results of applying the aggregation function *count* to the data set. The update paths relating to the sample record are shown as solid thick lines in Figure 1. Notice that other aggregate functions such as *sum* can also be similarly implemented.

After the ST tree is initialized, and all the data cubes have been computed and stored in its leaves, the system is ready to evaluate cube queries issued by the users. CQL *(cube query language)* concisely specifies any subset of the full data cube that is composed of all the *core cube cells*. A core cube cell is a multidimensional rectangle with each attribute having a non-star value. A CQL expression returns an aggregated value for the covering cube cells. It is of form: *aggr* ^{measure} *(constraint; ...; constraint)*, where *aggr* is the aggregate operator: for example, *count, sum, min, max, avg,* and so forth, and *measure* is the measure of the data cube to track, for example, sales. There are three types of constraints for a dimension: (1) a single value including the special star value meaning

Figure 1. Statistics Tree after Processing Input Record (1,2,4)

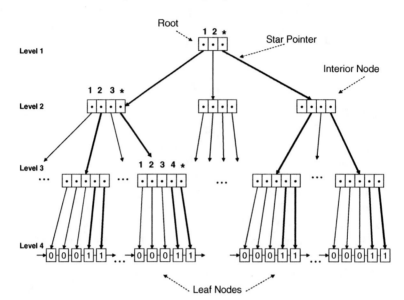

ALL; for example family car as the car type, (2) a range; for example [20, 30] as age of a customer, and (3) a partial set; for example {family car, truck}.

Cube queries are evaluated by traversing part of the ST. Starting from the root, one can follow all the pointers corresponding to the constrained attribute values specified in the query for the dimension of that node, to the next level nodes. Recursively descending level by level, eventually we reach the leaves. All the values in the fall-off leaves are summed up as the final answer to the input query.

In processing ad-hoc combinations of dimensional constraints, we differ from most existing algorithms, which only optimize certain group-by queries. Traditionally, the views represented as nodes in a view lattice structure are computed in a top-down fashion from one another. We compute collectively *all* the data cubes *at the same time.* Moreover, all the data cubes are packaged together into *one* compact data structure — ST. This significantly simplifies the management of all the otherwise separate cubes or views. ST can be regarded as a *super view.* It is not only space efficient, fast, compact, and interactive but also incrementally maintainable, self-indexing, and scalable.

If some dimensions have hierarchies in them, for example, day-month-year for the *time* dimension, we have optimized the computation of data cubes that have an arbitrary combination of different hierarchy levels. Though the constraints at high hierarchical levels in the query can be rewritten into those at the finest levels and the query can be evaluated by the ST at the finest levels (we call it the *base tree*), it is more efficient to compute and materialize more additional STs (we call them *derived trees;* together with the base tree, we call them a *family of ST trees*) for these queries. The derived trees contain the same dimensions of the base tree, but are at high hierarchy levels and much smaller than the base tree due to smaller cardinalities for high-level attributes. The I/O operations of retrieving the cubes from disks are greatly reduced. We have designed algorithms to choose candidate trees to materialize, derive them from the base tree, and select the proper trees in the family to evaluate the input query. In addition, CQL should also make some minor adjustments to accommodate hierarchy level information. Specifically, the constraints should also specify which dimension and which level of the dimension for the selected values. Interested readers may refer to Hammer and Fu (2001) for more details.

For dimensions with large cardinalities, we have designed new algorithms suitable for sparse data (Fu, 2004). STs are static structures, meaning that the shape of the tree is set and will not change by inserting more records once the number of dimensions and their cardinalities are given. The ST has exactly $(v+1)$ pointers for an internal node, where v is the cardinality of the attribute corresponding to the level of the node. The values are contiguous from 0 to $v-1$. There is a serious problem with this static ST structure: when many dimensions have large cardinalities the ST may not fit into memory! This often happens in applications. To fix this, we develop a new data structure called SST (sparse statistics trees) and the related algorithm to evaluate data cubes. SST is very similar to ST but the pointers are labeled with attribute values instead of implied contiguous values. When a new record is inserted into the SST, attribute values are checked along the paths with the existing entries in the nodes. If not matched, new entries will be added into the node and new subtrees are formed. Figure 2 shows an SST after inserting first two records (5, 7, 30) and (2, 15, 6). The paths accessed or newly created while inserting the second record are shown in dashed lines.

If the number of records is large in the training data set, at some point during the insertion process, SST may not fit into memory anymore. A cutting phase is started, which deletes the sparse leaves and saves them on disk for later retrieval to improve query accuracy. While evaluating a cube query after SST initialization, we first check the in-

Figure 2. SST Tree Example

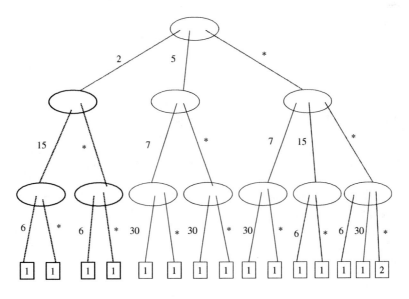

Figure 3. An Architecture of Data Warehouse with DBMS API

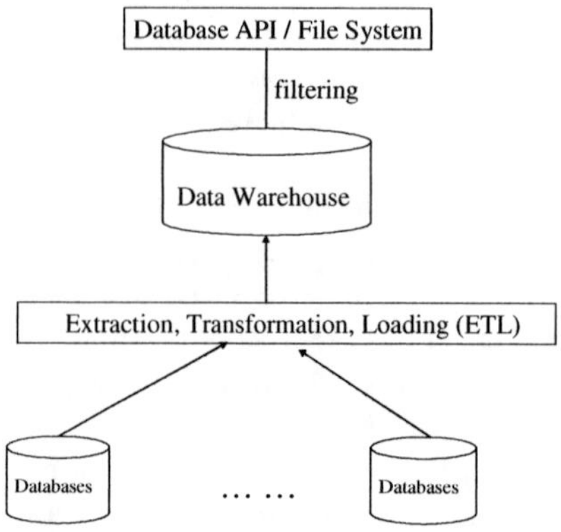

memory tree to quickly return a good approximation. If more accurate answers are required, we then retrieve the related leaves stored on disk.

ARCHITECTURE

Different from transactional processing systems, for example, commercial DBMS, OLAP and data mining are mainly used for analytical purposes at the organizational level. A data warehouse contains data extracted, cleaned, integrated, and loaded from multiple sources. "A data warehouse is a subject-oriented, integrated, time-variant, and nonvolatile collection of data in support of management's decision making process" (Inmon, 1996). The following is a general architecture for a data warehouse with a DBMS API interface.

There are some advantages of deploying data analysis on data warehouses instead of directly on operational databases. First, data are clean and consistent across the whole organization. Secondly, we can also use the existing infrastructure to manipulate and manage large amounts of data. Thirdly, the data warehouse DBMS can choose any interested subset of data to mine on, implementing an ad-hoc mining flexibility. Furthermore, our cube queries cannot return the specific detailing records themselves that satisfy certain constraints. In this case, DBMS is still necessary though OLAP and data mining algorithms can give "big picture" information and interesting patterns. OLAM (online analytical mining) system integrates OLAP with data mining and mining knowledge in multidimensional databases. A transaction-oriented commercial DBMS alone is not up to data mining and evaluating complex ad-hoc OLAP queries efficiently and effectively because DBMS have different workloads and requirements; for example, concurrency control and recovery. We need special OLAP servers (or data cube servers) and special data mining modules to answer some OLAP queries and data mining queries more efficiently. A natural solution is then to integrate these three systems tightly. Figure 4 is our proposed architecture for such an integrated system.

Figure 4. System Architecture that Integrates DBMS, OLAP, and OLAM

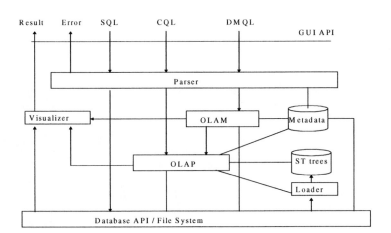

The undirected lines represent bi-directional information flows, except the top line representing GUI API. Users can submit SQL, CQL, and DMQL (data mining query language) queries through a common GUI API interface. The parser parses the user inputs and dispatches to the corresponding DBMS, OLAP, and OLAM engines if no syntactic errors are detected. Otherwise, the error messages are returned. Related metadata information is stored and will be used later by the data processing engines. The running results from the engines can be represented in various formats such as diagrams, tables, and so forth through a visualizer.

In addition to mining directly on databases or files, the OLAM engine can also be built on top of OLAP engines, which is the main topic of this chapter. The OLAP, or data cube server, instructs a loader to construct STs from databases or files so that later on the cube queries are evaluated using the initialized STs (or SSTs), which is significantly faster than using DBMS servers (Hammer & Fu, 2001).

After the ST is initialized, the data cubes can be extracted from the leaves to derive classification models. Next, we introduce a statistical model for pattern detection, which helps classification.

CUBE-BASED PATTERN DETECTION CLASSIFICATION

Pattern Detection Using Chi-Square Test

Given a training dataset with N records, each of which has d predictor attributes A_1, ..., A_j, ..., A_d, and the classifying attribute B, suppose that they are classified into C known classes L_p, $p = 1, 2, ..., C$ and that A_j has V values $\{a_{jk}| k = 1, 2, ..., V, j = 1, 2, ..., d\}$. Let us define:

O_{pk} = total number of records that belong to L_p
and have value a_{jk} for A_j

$$O_{p+} = \sum_{k=1}^{V} O_{pk}$$

$$O_{+k} = \sum_{p=1}^{C} O_{pk}$$

$$N' = \sum_{p,k} O_{pk} \leq N$$

$$E_{pk} = O_{p+} O_{+k} / N'$$

$$X_{pk} = \frac{(O_{pk} - E_{pk})}{\sqrt{E_{pk}}}$$

$$Y_{pk} = (1 - O_{p+} / N')(1 - O_{+k} / N')$$

$$Z_{pk} = \frac{X_{pk}}{\sqrt{Y_{pk}}}$$

This is under the assumption that being a member of L_p is independent from whether $A_j = a_{jk}$, E_{pk} is the expected total. A chi-square test can tell if A_j is dependent on the class labels. If statistic:

$$\chi^2 = \sum_{p,k} \frac{(O_{pk} - E_{pk})^2}{E_{pk}} > \chi_{d,\alpha}^2 ,$$

where $d = (C-1)(V-1)$, and α is a significance level, then with $(1-\alpha)$ confidence A_j is dependent on the class labels. Though the chi-square test can tell if the whole attribute is dependent on the class labels, it does not tell whether a record with a certain value, say $A_j = a_{jk}$, is classified to L_p. To this latter end, we need statistics such as Z_{pk}.

Using the statistic X_{pk}, the maximum likelihood estimate of its variance is Y_{pk} (Haberman, 1973) and Z_{pk} has a normal standard distribution. If $Z_{pk} > 1.96$, we can conclude with 95% confidence that the record with $A_j = a_{jk}$ will be classified to class L_p; if $Z_{pk} < -1.96$, and that record should be classified to a class other than L_p; otherwise, knowing that $A_j = a_{jk}$ does not provide us enough information about whether it should be classified to L_p.

To determine the class label of a future record, one can first retain the Z_{pk}s whose absolute values are above 1.96. The classification rules are of the form:

If a record with $A_j = a_{jk}$, then it is in L_p with a certainty $W(class = L_p/class \neq L_p \mid A_j = a_{jk})$. The weight evidence measure W can be defined by the difference of mutual information $I(class = L_p : a_{jk})$ and $I(class \neq L_p \mid A_j = a_{jk})$:

$$I(L_p : a_{jk}) = \log \frac{\Pr(L_p \mid a_{jk})}{\Pr(L_p)}$$

$$= \log \frac{O_{pk} / O_{+k}}{O_{p+} / N'}$$

$$W(Class = L_p / Class \neq L_p \mid a_{jk})$$

$$= I(Class = L_p : a_{jk}) - I(Class \neq L_p : a_{jk})$$

Mutual information $I(class = L_p : a_{jk})$ between L_p and a_{jk} measures the decrease of the uncertainty about classifying the record to L_p given $A_j = a_{jk}$.

Without the a priori knowledge of the correlation of the attributes, the weight of class membership prediction by all the attribute values is the sum of the weight of each attribute:

$$W_p = \sum_{j=1}^{V} W(Class = L_p / Class \neq L_p \mid a_{jk}) .$$

The predicted class label of an incoming record is the one with the maximum total weight $\max_p \{W_p\}$. This method can deal with noisy data. In addition, a record can be classified into multiple classes with a different strength of evidence. More details are given in Chan and Wong (1991).

Extraction of Statistics and Classification

Given the two-order statistics, for example, O_{pk}, we can classify objects using the above method. Fortunately, all the O_{pk}'s needed are already stored as some of the leaves of the related ST. To find the values of O_{pk}, first we construct a CQL expression with all constraints being star "*" values. The components corresponding to A_j and the classifying attribute B are replaced with a_{jk} and p respectively. The modified CQL expression is then used to traverse the ST. Starting from the root, follow the pointer corresponding to the first value to the node on the next lower level. Repeating the process will reach the leaf that holds the O_{pk} value. If the ST is stored on a disk, we will use the CQL expression to locate the position of O_{pk} and retrieve it. Once O_{pk}'s are extracted, other variables can be computed and the record is classified as above.

NAÏVE BAYESIAN CLASSIFICATION USING STATISTICS TREES

We also build a classifier that combines the techniques of the Naïve Bayesian classification algorithm and data cubing using STs. Naïve Bayesian classification is based on Bayes theorem:

$$P(L_p \mid A) = \frac{P(A \mid L_p)P(L_p)}{P(A)}$$

where $A = (a_{1k}, a_{2k}..., a_{dk})$ is the observed data sample, and $P(L_p \mid A)$ is the probability (also known as posterior probability) that A belongs to class L_p. The target class should be the one with the largest $P(L_p \mid A)$. Since the denominator $P(A)$ is the same, we only need to maximize the numerator. Under the assumption of class conditional independence:

$$P(A \mid L_p) = \prod_{j=1}^{d} P(A_j = a_{jk} \mid L_p)$$

$$P(A_j = a_{jk} \mid L_p) = \frac{O_{pk}}{O_{p+}}$$

$$P(L_p) = \frac{O_{p+}}{N'}$$

Sample A belongs to L_p if

$$P(A \mid L_p)P(L_p) \geq P(A \mid L_q)P(L_q),$$
$$for \; \forall \; 1 \leq q \leq C, q \neq p$$

As shown, O_{pk}s can be extracted directly from the ST and other variables can be computed according to the previous formulas. Both the cube-based pattern detection classifier and the cube-based Naïve Bayesian classifier are based on statistics theory. Their statistics can be simply extracted from STs. Computing all the cubes in the form of ST trees may be an over-kill, but they are free handy information as part of the analytical system to construct efficient classifiers.

CONSTRUCTION OF
DECISION TREES USING DATA CUBE
A General Decision Tree Construction Template

In decision tree classification, we recursively partition the training data set until the records in the sub-partitions are entirely or mostly from the same classes. The decision tree model is simple, easy to understand, and relatively fast to build compared to other methods (Quilan, 1993). When the data cubes have been computed, in this section we will design a new decision tree algorithm that builds a tree from data cubes *without accessing original training records*.

The internal nodes in a decision tree are called *splits*, predicates to specify how to partition the records. The leaves contain class labels into which the records satisfying the predicates in the root-to-leaf paths are classified. We consider binary decision trees, though multi-way trees are also possible. The following is a general template for almost all decision tree classification algorithms:

1. Partition (Dataset S)
2.   If (all records in S are of the same class) then return;
3.   Compute the splits for each attribute;
4.   Choose the best split to partition S into S_1 and S_2;
5.   Partition (S_1);
6.   Partition (S_2);

An initial call of Partition (training dataset) will setup a binary decision tree for the training data set. Our algorithm called *cubeDT (cube-based decision tree)* differs in the way of evaluating splits and partitioning from all existing decision tree algorithms of which we are aware. Before the evaluation of the splits, the domain values of the training records are all converted into integers starting from 0. For continuous attributes for example, the attribute values are replaced by the indexes of the intervals to which they belong. The ordinal and categorical attribute values are just simply converted into integers. The conversions can be done during the scanning of original training data and the computation of the data cubes using the methods from above.

Computing the Best Split for the Root

We use a gini-index to compute the splits at the root of the decision tree as follows:

$$gini(S) = 1 - \sum_{j=0}^{C-1} p_j^2, \text{ where } p_j \text{ is the frequency of class } j \text{ in } S$$

$$p_j = count(B = j) / n, n = |S|$$

$$gini(S) = \frac{n_1}{n} gini(S_1) + \frac{n_2}{n} gini(S_2), \text{ if } S \text{ is partitioned into } S_1 \text{ and } S_2, n_1 = |S_1|, n_2 = |S_2|$$

A split for continuous attribute A is of form *value(A)$\leq v$*, where v is the upper bound of some interval of index k $(k = 0, 1, ..., V-1$, where V is the total number of interval for A). To simplify, let us just denote this as $A \leq k$.

The following algorithm evaluates the best split for attribute A:

1.   x[j]=0, for j =0, 1, ..., C-1; CountSum = 0;
2.   minGini = 1; minSplit = 0;
3.   *for* i = 0 *to* V-1 *do*
4.   countSum ← countSum + count(A=i);
5. n_1= countSum; n_2 =n-countSum;
6.   squaredSumL, squaredSumH = 0;
7.   *for* j = 0 *to* C-1 *do*
8.   x[j] = x[j] + count(A=I; B = j); y = count(B=j) − x[j];
9.   squaredSumL ← squaredSumL+(x[j] /n_1)²;
10.   squaredSumH ← squaredSumH+(y /n_2)²;
11.   gini(S_1) = 1- squaredSumL;
12.   gini(S_2) = 1- squaredSumH;

13. $gini(S) = n_1 gini(S_1)/n + n_2 gini(S_2)/n;$
14.   *if* $gini(S) < minGini$ *then*
15. $MiniGini = gini(S); minSplit = i;$

Lines 1 and 2 initialize temporary variables countSum and array x, and current minimal gini index minGini and its split position miniSplit. Lines 3 through 15 evaluate all possible splits $A \leq i$ $(i=0, 1, ..., V-1)$ and choose the best one. Each split partition data set S into two subset $S_1 = \{r$ in $S \mid r[A] \leq i\}$ and $S_2 = S-S_1$. Line 4 tries to simplify the computation of the size of S_1 that is, $count(A \leq i)$ by prefix-sum computation. Similarly, array $x[j]$ is used to compute $count(A \leq i; B = j)$ for each class j $(j = 0, 1, ..., C-1)$ in lines 1 and 8.

For categorical attributes, the splits are of form $A \in T$, where T is a subset of A. Any subset of A is a candidate split. The size of T:

$n_1 = count(A \in T)$, and $n_2 = n-n_1$
$p_j = count(A \in T; B = j) / n_1$

Knowing how to compute these variables, we can similarly compute the gini(S) for each split and choose the best one, as we did for continuous attributes. The final split for the root is then the split with the smallest gini index among all the best splits of the attributes.

Partitioning and Computing Splits for Other Internal Nodes

The best split computed above is stored in the root. All other algorithms at this point partition the data set into subsets according to the predicates of the split. In contrast, cubeDT does not move data around. Instead, it just virtually partitions data by simply passing down the split predicates to its children without touching or querying the original data records anymore at this phase. The removal of the expensive process of data partitioning greatly improves the classification performance.

The computation of splits for an internal node other than the root is similar to the method in the previous section except that the split predicates along the path from the node to the root are concatenated as part of constraints in CQL. For example, suppose a table containing customer information has three predictor attributes: age, income, and credit-report (values are poor, good, and excellent). The records are classified into two classes: to buy or not to buy a computer. To compute the splits for income attribute, at the root node A, the split is of form: income $\leq v$, and $n_1 = count(income \leq v)$. Suppose the best split of A turns out to be "age ≤ 30," and now we are computing splits for income attribute at node B. Notice that value $n_1 = count(income \leq v; age \leq 30)$, and $n_2 = count(age \leq 30) - n_1$.

At node C, $n_1 = count(income \leq v; age > 30)$, and $n_2 = count(age > 30) - n_1$. All other variables are adjusted accordingly to compute the splits. Suppose that after computation and comparison the best split at B is "income $\leq \$40,000$". The diagram shown in Figure 5 gives the initial steps of evaluating splits of nodes A, B, and C.

Figure 5. Example of Computing Splits of Non-Root Internal Nodes

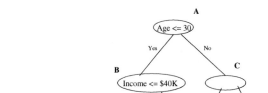

EVALUATION OF THE NEW CLASSIFIERS

In comparison with classifiers based on decision trees such as ID3, the classifier in has better classification accuracy. Our classifier will have the same accuracy but directly extract statistics from computed data cubes instead of computing from original data, thus providing classification for free. Studies show that the performance of a naïve Bayesian classifier is comparable with decision tree and neural network classifiers (Han & Kamber, 2001). In comparison with other data cube computation algorithms such as Bitmap and BUC, our cubing algorithms have better performance (Fu & Hammer, 2000).

Based on these studies, we naturally conclude that our statistical classifiers have the same or better accuracy but are much faster than decision tree classifiers such as ID-3, Bayesian classifiers, and neural network classifiers. Our cube-based decision tree construction algorithm has the same quality of SLIQ, SPRINT, and BOAT but is significantly faster due to direct computation of splits on data cube without actually partitioning and storing the F-sets.

CONCLUSIONS AND FUTURE WORK

In summary, in this chapter we propose new classifiers that extract some of the computed data cubes to set up statistical and decision tree models for classification. Once the data cubes are computed by scanning the original data once and stored in statistics trees, they are ready to answer OLAP queries. The new classifiers provide additional "free" classification that may interest users. Through the combination of technologies from data cubing and classification based on statistics and decision trees, we pave the way for integrating data mining systems and data cube systems seamlessly. An architecture to achieve this important integration has been proposed.

There is a clear trend of integrating DBMS, OLAP, and data mining into one comprehensive system that can deal with all kinds of queries. In industry, the data cube and data mining functionalities are usually provided by the third parties who build their products on top of DBMS systems. Our research goes one step further to integrated them together more tightly.

Our proposed classifiers based on statistics assume class conditional independence or do not use the prior knowledge concerning the interrelation of the attributes.

We will continue this research on the design of new classifiers that take advantage of correlation information of the attributes. We also plan to design other efficient data mining algorithms for data cubes.

REFERENCES

Agarwal, S., Agrawal, R., Deshpande, P., Naughton, J., Sarawagi, S., & Ramakrishnan, R. (1996). On the computation of multidimensional aggregates. *Proceedings of the International Conference on Very Large Databases,* Mumbai (Bomabi), India, (pp. 506-521).

Beyer, K., & Ramakrishnan, R. (1999). Bottom-up computation of sparse and iceberg CUBEs. In S.B. Davidson & C. Faloutsos (Eds.), *Proceedings of the 1999 ACM SIGMOD International Conference on Management of Data (SIGMOD '99)* (pp. 359-370). Philadelphia, PA.

Chan, C.Y., & Ioannidis, Y.E. (1998). Bitmap index design and evaluation. *Proceedings of the 1998 ACM SIGMOD International Conference on Management of Data (SIGMOD '98),* Seattle, WA (pp. 355-366).

Chan, K.C.C., & Wong, A.K.C. (1991). Statistical technique for extracting classificatory knowledge from databases. *Knowledge discovery in databases,* 107-124.

Chaudhuri, S., & Dayal, U. (1997). An overview of data warehousing and OLAP technology. *SIGMOD Record, 26*(1), 65-74.

Chaudhuri, S., Fayyad, U., & Bernhardt, J. (1999, March). Scalable classification over SQL databases. *15th International Conference on Data Engineering,* Sydney, Australia, 470.

Cheeseman, P., & Stutz, J. (1996). Bayesian classification (AutoClass): Theory and results. In U.M. Fayyad, G. Piatetsky-Shapiro, P. Smyth & R. Uthurusamy (Eds.), *Advances in knowledge discovery and data mining* (pp. 153-180). AAAI/MIT Press.

Comer, D. (1979). The ubiquitous Btree. *ACM Computing Surveys, 11*(2), 121-137.

Duda, R., & Hart, P. (1973). *Pattern classification and scene analysis.* New York: John Wiley & Sons.

Elder, J., IV, & Pregibon, D. (1996). A statistical perspective on knowledge discovery in databases. In U.M. Fayyad, G. Piatetsky-Shapiro, P. Smyth & R. Uthurusamy (Eds.), *Advances in knowledge discovery and data mining* (pp. 83-115). AAAI/MIT Press.

Fu, L. (2004). Processing ad-hoc cube queries over sparse data efficiently and interactively. *ICDE '04,* Boston, Massachusetts, USA (submitted).

Fu, L., & Hammer, J. (2000, November). CUBIST: A new algorithm for improving the performance of ad-hoc OLAP queries *ACM Third International Workshop on Data Warehousing and OLAP,* Washington, D.C., USA, 72-79.

Gehrke, J., Ganti, V., Ramakrishnan, R., & Loh, W.-Y. (1999, June). BOAT - Optimistic decision tree construction *Proceedings of 1999 International Conference Management of Data (SIGMOD '99),* Philadelphia, PA, (pp. 169-180).

Gehrke, J., Ramakrishnan, R., & Ganti, V. (1998). RainForest - A framework for fast decision tree construction of large datasets. *Proceedings of the 24th VLDB Conference (VLDB '98),* New York, USA, (pp. 416-427).

Gray, J., Chaudhuri, S., Bosworth, A., Layman, A., Reichart, D., Venkatrao, M. et al. (1997). Data cube: A relational aggregation operator generalizing group-by, cross-tab, and sub-totals. *Data Mining and Knowledge Discovery, 1*(1), 29-53.

Haberman, S.J. (1973). The analysis of residuals in cross-classified tables. *Biometrics, 29,* 205-220.

Hammer, J., & Fu, L. (2001, September). Improving the performance of OLAP queries using families of statistics trees. *3rd International Conference on Data Warehousing and Knowledge Discovery DaWaK 01,* Munich, Germany, 274-283.

Han, J., & Kamber, M. (2001). *Data mining: Concepts and techniques.* Morgan Kaufman Publishers.

Harinarayan, V., Rajaraman, A., & Ullman, J.D. (1996). Implementing data cubes efficiently. *SIGMOD Record, 25*(2), 205-216.

Heckerman, D. (1996). Bayesian networks for knowledge discovery. In U.M. Fayyad, G. Piatetsky-Shapiro, P. Smyth & R. Uthurusamy (Eds.), *Advances in knowledge discovery and data mining* (pp. 273-305). Cambridge, MA: MIT Press.

Inmon, W.H. (1996). *Building the data warehouse.* New York: John Wiley & Sons.

Johnson, T., & Shasha, D. (1997). Some approaches to index design for cube forests. *Bulletin of the Technical Committee on Data Engineering, IEEE Computer Society, 20*(1), 27-35.

Lent, B., Swami, A., & Widom, J. (1997). Clustering association rules. *Proceedings of the 13th International Conference on Database Engineering (ICDE '97),* Birmingham, UK, 220-231.

Lu, H., Setiono, R., & Liu, H. (1995, September). NeuroRule: A connectionist approach to data mining. In U. Dayal, P.M.D. Gray & S. Nishio (Eds.), *VLDB'95, Proceedings of 21st International Conference on Very Large Data Bases,* Zurich, Switzerland, (pp. 478-489). Morgan Kaufmann.

Mehta, M., Agrawal, R., & Rissanen, J. (1996, March). SLIQ: A fast scalable classifier for data mining. In P.M.G. Apers, M. Bouzeghoub & G. Gardarin (Eds.), *Advances in database technology - EDBT'96, 5th International Conference on Extending Database Technology,* Avignon, France, *Proceedings, 1057,* (pp. 18-32). Springer.

O'Neil, P. (1987). Model 204 architecture and performance. *Proceedings of the Second International Workshop on High Performance Transaction Systems,* Asilomar, CA (pp. 40-59).

O'Neil, P., & Quass, D. (1997). Improved query performance with variant indexes. *SIGMOD Record (ACM Special Interest Group on Management of Data), 26*(2), 38-49.

Quilan, J.R. (1986). Introduction of decision trees. *Machine Learning, 1,* 81-106.

Quilan, J.R. (1993). *C4.5: Programs for machine learning.* Morgan Kaufmann.

Shafer, J., Agrawal, R., & Mehta, M. (1996, September). SPRINT: A scalable parallel classifier for data mining. In T.M. Vijayaraman, A.P. Buchmann, C. Mohan & N.L. Sarda (Eds.), *VLDB'96, Proceedings of 22nd International Conference on Very Large Data Bases,* Mumbai (Bombay), India, (pp. 544-555). Morgan Kaufmann.

Srikant, R., & Agrawal, R. (1996, June). Mining quantitative association rules in large relational tables. In H.V. Jagadish & I.S. Mumick (Eds.), *Proceedings of the 1996 ACM SIGMOD International Conference on Management of Data,* Montreal, Quebec, Canada, *SIGMOD Record, 25(2),* 1-12. ACM Press.

Zhao, Y., Deshpande, P.M., & Naughton, J.F. (1997). An array-based algorithm for simultaneous multidimensional aggregates. *SIGMOD Record, 26*(2), 159-170.

SECTION III

STRUCTURE MINING

Chapter X

Data Cleansing and Validation for Multiple Site Link Structure Analysis

Mike Thelwall
University of Wolverhampton, UK

ABSTRACT

A range of techniques is described for cleansing and validating link data for use in different types of Web structure mining, and some applications are given. The main application area is Multiple Site Link Structure Analysis, which typically involves mining patterns from themed collections of Websites. The importance of data cleansing and validation stems from the fact that Web data are typically very messy. It involves extensive duplication of pages and page components, which when analyzing raw Web data may give meaningless results.

INTRODUCTION

Hyperlinks are important for their use in navigation within a site, and Web usage mining algorithms have been built to cluster site users based upon navigation patterns (Hafri et al., 2003) and to create site link structures from Web server logs (Wu & Ng, 2003). Links are also used for directing visitors to other sites, however, and links on other sites similarly provide a potential source of new visitors. Inter-site links, the focus of this chapter, are now routinely exploited by Web applications for a variety of purposes, including building search engine indexes, ranking search results, identifying clusters of topic-related pages, and extracting information about the behavior of Web authors. Such is the importance of links that there is a significant body of work that chooses them as the objects of study, for modeling their creation or for analyzing the structures produced by them (Barabási, 2002).

This chapter covers two different Web structure mining approaches, *link topology mining* and *link URL mining,* which use different raw data and methods. Link topology mining treats the Web as a graph with the pages as nodes and the links as either edges (directionless) or arcs (preserving the link direction), discarding all information about the content of the pages themselves. For link URL mining, the topology is used in conjunction with the URLs of the source and target of each page, allowing the mining of more concrete linking patterns. Typical outputs include information about the interconnectivity of sets of Websites or their linking practices. Both types of link mining can be used either on their own or in conjunction with other approaches to solve specific problems such as Web topic identification.

The techniques described in this chapter are primarily useful for a new type of Web structure mining, *Multiple Site Link Structure Analysis,* although they also have potential uses for Web Information Retrieval (IR). Web IR applications of link URL mining and link topology mining include heuristics to rank pages or cluster them by connectivity patterns, as well as to identify site types from their link structures alone. Multiple Site Link Structure Analysis (MSLSA) is the analysis of the link structure of a *collection* of Websites. The emphasis is on a finite collection of sites: more than one site but not the whole Web. The collection would typically have a unifying theme such as UK universities or U.S. libraries. The following are illustrative of the types of problems that might trigger an MSLSA investigation.

*   What are the patterns of interlinking and clustering of the Websites of different nations/industry sectors/groups of countries?
*   Which countries/types of site/sites do the Websites within a given nation/ industry/ sector/group of companies tend to link to?
*   Which Websites out of a given set appear to be having the most (link based) impact on the Web?

These questions can be useful for a variety of different interest groups, including Website managers. On a larger scale this includes managers with the responsibility to ensure that collections of sites are effective, from the level of the sites of a large company or university to the national level. The techniques are also being investigated on an international scale for the European Union *(www.webindicators.org)*.

The objective of this chapter is to present a state-of-the-art summary of data cleansing and validation techniques for link topology mining and link URL mining, mainly for MSLSA but also for Web IR. A range of types of application techniques will also be given. The choice of cleansing and validation as the focus of the chapter is due to the problematic nature of data collection and interpretation on the Web. Data cleansing is important because of the many types of problems in raw Web data, including the existence of duplicate sites. Data validation is critical for MSLSA (but not Web IR) in order to be able to interpret findings. Current research suggests that the statistical techniques that can successfully analyze link structure data will vary by the scope of the study and so it will not be fruitful to go into the details of individual case studies here.

An important theme that runs throughout the chapter is the application of *Alternative Document Models,* which systematically aggregate collections of Web pages for data cleansing and to allow different simultaneous scales of analysis.

BACKGROUND

A number of research areas have produced information about hyperlinks that is relevant to Web structure mining and this section offers a brief review of three of them. More information can also be found in the Web structure mining section of Kosala and Blockeel (2000), and the link structure analysis overviews of Henzinger (2001) and Chakrabarti et al. (2002).

Models of Web Growth

The most fundamental link structure research has evolved from theoretical physicists' abstract mathematical models for network growth. Whilst early work tackled a variety of kinds of networks simultaneously (Watts & Strogatz, 1998), later studies specialized to the Web. The main finding was that the Web does not grow at random but that new links tend to get connected to pages that are already major sources or targets of links. This 'rich gets richer' effect creates a scale-free network (Barabási & Albert, 1999; Barabasi et al., 2000). One consequence for the whole Web is that the distribution of links is not uniform or normal, but exhibits a power law, so that a small number of pages have a huge number of links. When this phenomenon was further investigated, it was found to vary by page type (Pennock et al., 2002), with some groups, such as university home pages, deviating significantly from a power law with a less uneven spread of links. Until recently, mathematical models have not incorporated factors that are known to effect the propensity to link between Websites such as geographical distance (Thelwall, 2002c), but still usefully illustrate general patterns.

An important implication of this research is that Web mining algorithms must not be based upon assumptions that 'average' linking behavior can be expected; instead, anomalies such as individual pages with huge numbers of links are endemic.

Link Structures in the Web

A strand of computer science research has studied the internal link structure of the Web graph from a topological perspective. In some analyses the direction of the links are preserved, in others not. Broder et al. (2000) dissected two large AltaVista crawls of the Web from 1999, each of about 200 million pages and 1.5 billion links. They found that if the direction of the links was ignored then 90% of the pages were connected together in one huge component. At the center were a quarter of the pages, named the Strongly Connected Component (SCC), which was a set such that starting at any page and following links in their original direction would yield the whole of the rest of the SCC. Half of the rest of the pages could either trace a link path into the SCC, or could be linked to by a path from the SCC, only following links in the correct direction. The results do not cover the 'whole' Web, only AltaVista crawls, and presumably most pages in the crawl have been found by following links, with a minority found by user submission of URLs.

Nevertheless, the highly interconnected nature of the core of the Web can be seen. This phenomenon is a natural result of the power law of Web linking and in particular the existence of a few extremely highly interconnected sites such as Yahoo! that can connect otherwise disparate pages. Research into the Web graph has spawned specialist workshops on the topic and a similar exercise on academic Websites (Thelwall & Wilkinson, 2003b). Although the original purpose of the research was to optimize Web crawler design the results are useful background for Web link algorithms in general, and cluster mining in particular.

Link Analysis for Information Retrieval

Although the link structure of the Web has been important since the creation of the first crawlers such as the World Wide Web Worm, link structure analysis came into existence as a result of two algorithms designed to rank pages in response to user queries: Google's PageRank (Brin & Page, 1998) and Kleinberg's (1999) HITS. The success of Google in particular seems to have given rise to expectations that links could profitably be used in Web Information Retrieval algorithms.

PageRank is an algorithm that assigns a global importance rating to Web pages based upon link structures alone. The underlying principle is that more important Web pages will be more frequently linked to. Early search engines relied upon the contents of pages to judge their relevance to a user's query. This is error-prone, however, particularly for popular queries. For example, it would be difficult to find authoritative pages for 'Netscape' based upon contents alone since so many contain the word 'Netscape,' but the Netscape home page would have a very high PageRank since so many pages link to it. Link based ranking is problematic, nevertheless, because site home pages are more frequently linked to than the pages containing useful information and some links are more influential than others — for example, Yahoo! links would be a more reliable quality indicator than those from obscure personal home pages. PageRank avoids these problems to some extent by recursively incorporating the importance of links in its calculation. Nevertheless, it cannot get around the problem that almost all links between different sites seem to be created unsystematically and so small differences in link counts, for example between 0 and 1, are unreliable quality indicators. As a consequence, subsequent research has found at most minor improvements in Web IR algorithms from the incorporation of links (Hawking et al., 2000; Savoy & Picard, 2001).

DATA COLLECTION METHODS
Web Crawlers

Web mining applications need a carefully conducted data collection stage. The use of a crawler to gather data is an obvious choice, whether a personally designed version or a publicly available one such as Harvest-NG (*http://Webharvest.sourceforge.net/ng/*). The practicalities of crawling the Web will depend upon the scale of the investigation, because of the resources that will be consumed (storage space, CPU time and network bandwidth). For an investigation of moderate size small test crawls can be used to judge whether a full-scale crawl would be practical. For basic crawler coverage issues see

Thelwall (2001a, 2002a), and for design issues there are standard textbooks (Heaton, 2002; Pallman, 1999).

Web crawling for data mining has its own unique set of problems related to accuracy and coverage. The problem of accuracy has two components: finding all relevant pages and not recording multiple copies of the same page. Crawlers work by following links and so will miss pages on a site that are not linked. Lawrence and Giles (1999) term the pages that can be found by following links from the home page the "publicly indexable set," making it clear that complete site coverage is not claimed. Note that crawlers are likely to miss some links that human users can see, such as those embedded in JavaScript, Java or Shockwave.

The problem of duplicate pages is in a sense more troublesome because it is partially avoidable and so crawlers should be designed to compare all fetched pages and discard duplicates. This can be made feasible for large crawls by calculating numerical key codes from the text of each page and comparing the numbers, at least initially, instead of the whole pages (Heydon & Najork, 1999). This strategy should catch most cases in which pages are duplicated, with the exception being pages containing dynamic elements such as text hit counters. A common source of duplicate URLs is the situation in which the home page of a directory can be retrieved either by name or by specifying the directory root.

Mirror sites can present a problem of coverage rather than accuracy because in a typical Web structure mining investigation the whole Web will not be crawled and so the original sites of some mirror sites may not be included. As a result, heuristics or human judgments may be needed to decide whether a given set of pages should be ignored as a mirror site or not. In university Webs, for example, it is common to find several copies of Sun's Java documentation. It is undesirable to crawl such duplicated sets of pages since an analysis of their links would give information about the original creators rather than the new hosts. Fortunately, Sun's Java documentation has a standard set of URL structures and so regular expressions can be built to avoid crawling them. Other mirror sites can also be found either after the crawl at the anomaly identification stage or by human monitoring of the crawl, or checking of its results. A regular expression list for URLs that should not be crawled is a good idea, not just for software documentation but also for other undesired types of pages, such as automatically generated online Web server logs. It may also be desirable to ban e-mail archives, Web discussion lists and bulletin boards simply because they represent a different kind of communication medium than Web pages.

If human monitoring of crawls is employed then the operator can compile a banned list for each site to supplement the generic regular expressions applied to all sites. Examples of these can be found at the Cybermetrics database site *(cybermetrics.wlv.ac.uk/ database)*.

Commercial Search Engines

It is possible to obtain summary data about the whole Web (or at least the portion crawled) by sending queries to commercial search engines. The advanced interfaces of many allow queries specific to links, such as one for all pages that link to a given URL. At the time of writing, AllTheWeb and AltaVista allowed the most flexible queries, including the use of Boolean operators. For example, to find all pages in the .edu domain that link to Cambridge University the request would be:

domain:edu AND link:cam.ac.uk

This can be used either to obtain an approximate count of the number of pages involved, or to get the URLs of the first 1,000 by successive queries. As a simple example of how this could be used for data mining purposes, for a given Website a search engine could be used to count the number of pages that link to it from the .com, .edu and .mil domains, and for a set of universities these three inlinks counts could be compared across the set, patterns identified and outliers noted. Note that the results will not be perfect for two reasons. First, AltaVista uses heuristics to guess at the results to avoid a huge amount of processing. Second, the link command would match cam.ac.uk anywhere in a link URL, and not necessarily just the domain name. As a result of these and other problems (e.g., Bar-Ilan, 2001), care should be taken in interpreting the results. Search engines are not an ideal source for academic research in particular because their coverage and reporting algorithms are outside of the public domain. There is little choice, however, for any applications that require information that can only be obtained from very large Web crawls.

Search engines tend to have allowable usage policies that do not allow enquiries from automated processes. In the case of Google an alternative is available through the Google API *(http://www.google.com/apis/)*, although this has a maximum requests limit per day. Nevertheless, the restrictions mean that it may not be possible to use search engines as part of a fully automated data mining exercise.

Existing Data Sources

There are a number of places on the Web that supply data sets from Web crawls. These sources may be useful for testing algorithms, or in some circumstances for the actual data to be used, avoiding the need for direct crawling. Perhaps the best known are TREC Web collections (trec.org) which include the HTML of large coherent sets of Web pages, although they are designed for Web Information Retrieval algorithm evaluation purposes (Hawking et al., 2001). The 18Gb collection for 2003 was a crawl of 125 million pages from the .gov domain *(es.cmis.csiro.au/TRECWeb/)*. The TREC data are sold on storage media such as DVDs.

The Internet Archive *(www.archive.org)* hosts a huge database of large-scale crawls of the Web and allows researchers access to its raw data and borrowed time on computers for processing. This is a logical alternative to commercial search engine databases because although its coverage may not be the largest or freshest, researchers can gain direct access to the data through writing their own software. Compared to the TREC data the coverage is also much larger.

One Website contains a set of files containing the link structure (only) of national systems of university Websites *(cybermetrics.wlv.ac.uk/database/)*. The files are of up to 2Gb in size and can be used for the testing of algorithms without the need for either a crawler or text parsing software to extract raw link structure data. See also the WebIR site resource list *(www.webir.org/resources.html)*.

DATA CLEANSING

Web links are problematic as a data source when attempting to obtain a meaningful interpretation. For instance if twice as many Web pages in France link to the UK than Germany then this could be taken as evidence of a closer online connection with the UK than Germany. But this could be a faulty diagnosis if technical factors have inflated one count, and also 'online connection' is quite vague: what precisely should be inferred from the value of link counts? These key problems will be addressed in this section and the next two.

There are many potential causes of inflated link counts. Since the Web is unregulated, there is nothing to stop an individual author from creating millions of pages that link to wherever they choose. Some may do this as a part of an attempt to fool the ranking systems of search engines. In other cases links may be replicated throughout a site for perfectly innocent reasons, perhaps in a navigation bar to acknowledge the Website's design company. Nevertheless, both cases are undesirable when counting links because to compare two link counts, each link in both should ideally have been created with a similar level of care, and for similar reasons. But if one count contains mostly those created by individuals and another mostly replicated links then it would be meaningless to compare them. For a small-scale link counting exercise it may be possible to visit all links and employ a method to manually weed out the undesired ones, but on a larger scale this will be too time consuming. As a result much link mining research has been devoted to designing data cleansing measures to minimize the impact of spurious links.

For link URL mining it is important to distinguish between different types of links. Any link between a pair of pages is an *inlink* for the target page and an *outlink* for the source. The same terminology can be extended to sites and other identifiable entities so that site inlinks, for instance, are links targeted at any page in a site from any page outside of the site.

Alternative Document Models

Data cleansing for link URL mining is mainly concerned with eliminating duplicate or similar links. One technique for this is to change the method of counting so that replicated links in a site are ignored. The new counting methods, known as Alternative Document Models (ADMs), employ content units of different sizes (Thelwall, 2002e; see also Bharat, Chang, Henzinger & Ruhl, 2001). Although the individual Web page is the natural unit of information on the Web, it is artificial and arbitrary. For example, one author may place an entire book online in a single huge page, whereas another could split a similar one into thousands of individual section-based pages. Moreover, it is easy to use authoring tools to replicate features of a Web page throughout a site, so that the different pages would only be partially unique entities. An alternative to the page is to aggregate all pages into coherent multiple page 'documents' and to use these as the basic units. The implication of this for link counting would be that duplicate links to or from the same document could be ignored, even if source and/or target URLs were not identical.

Let a URL in standard form be http://sd/pf where f is the file name (if any), p is the path (if any), d is the site specification part of the domain name and s the rest (if any). The site specification part is the canonical domain name at the level sold by domain name registrars. For .com sites this will be the second level domain, for example, sun.com, whereas for UK sites this would be the third level domain, for example, sun.co.uk. The s part is typically only www., or otherwise specifies the subsite. Here are two examples.

$$http://www.scit.wlv.ac.uk/ukinfo/map.htm$$
$$s = www.scit. \quad d = wlv.ac.uk \quad p = ukinfo/ \qquad f = map.htm$$

$$http://www.netscape.com/$$
$$s = www. \qquad d = netscape.com \qquad\qquad p \;\&\; f \; are \; empty.$$

The importance of the ADMs is in identifying when two links should be treated as identical. If there is a link from http://s_0d_0/p_0f_0 to http://s_1d_1/p_1f_1 and a second link from http://s_2d_2/p_2f_2 to http://s_3d_3/p_3f_3 then the conditions below diagnose when these should be regarded as duplicates.

- *File ADM* $s_i = s_{i+2}$, $d_i = d_{i+2}$, $p_i = p_{i+2}$ and $f_i = f_{i+2}$ for i = 0,1.
- *Directory ADM* $s_i = s_{i+2}$, $d_i = d_{i+2}$ and $p_i = p_{i+2}$ for i = 0,1.
- *Domain ADM* $s_i = s_{i+2}$ and $d_i = d_{i+2}$ for i = 0,1.
- *Site ADM* $s_i = s_{i+2}$ for i = 0,1.

Example

Suppose that pages a.com/1.htm and a.com/2.htm contain two links each, one to b.com/3.htm and one to c.b.com/4.htm. Then the file ADM would record four links from site a.com to site b.com, the directory and domain ADMs would record two, and the site ADM just one.

Hybrid ADMs have also been employed, using a different one for link sources and targets (Thelwall & Wilkinson, 2003a), which can give better results for collections of large sites. The effect of applying the site ADM is to count no more than one link between any pair of sites, which should eliminate most cases of replicated links, but this may be too extreme, eliminating too many links that are not duplicates or similar. For any given data set the ADM to be used can be chosen in several different ways. TLD Spectral Analysis, described later, is the generic method, but the results of the three sections below can also help. For example, the ADM chosen could be the one that gives results without anomalies, with the highest correlation with an external source, or which best fits a theoretical model.

There are several problems and oversimplifications with the ADM definitions.
- IP addresses will need to be converted to domain names when possible.
- A policy should be adopted for port numbers and username-password pairs in URLs, for example, ignoring them or treating them as one of the four URL components used above.
- A policy should be adopted for malformed URLs — either to ignore them or to employ an automatic correction heuristic.
- Non-standard URLs must be ignored or converted to standard form.

A final point on the use of ADMs is that they are only a heuristic and that along with the elimination of replicated URLs they will remove non-replicated ones too, in an indiscriminate fashion. Results support their use, however (Thelwall, 2002; Thelwall & Harries, 2003; Thelwall & Wilkinson, 2003a).

Summary Statistics for Outlier Identification

Manual intervention and checking of data is less appealing than a fully automated technique, such as the ADMs, but can be necessary. Since huge data sets may be involved it is likely to be impractical to manually check the whole data set for anomalies such as replicated links and so software support will be needed. For example, summary statistics can be calculated from the data set and used to help identify the largest anomalies (Aguillo & Thelwall, 2003). These could be simple frequency counts for each link target URL or ADM document. A set number of the most highly targeted URLs can then be manually investigated to see whether they are anomalies. The kinds of anomalies that can be expected are replicated links in navigation bars and credit links placed in pages by Web authoring software or Web design companies. A policy will be needed for dealing with the various types found that will depend upon the particular problem that is being investigated by the research. If ADMs are being used then they should automatically eliminate most anomalies.

Example

An investigation into links from Spanish university Websites (Thelwall & Aguillo, 2003) found that the third highest target of links *(http://www.zope.org/credits)* origi-nated from a single site with a huge number of automatically generated links to this page, actually created by the Zope software used to construct the site. The 3,335 links clearly do not reflect a widespread interest in Zope by Spanish academics, just a single application. The domain ADM successfully reduces these multiple links to a single domain link, a better reflection of the impact of Zope. Alternatively, the URL target could have been removed as a manually identified anomaly.

Correlation with External Data

If there are expected values or trends for link counts from the data then comparing the actual data to the expected trend can be used to identify anomalies (Thelwall, 2001b, 2002e). For example, it may be expected that the number of links to each site is approximately proportional to site size. A graph of inlinks against size could then be used to identify unusual cases for further investigation or standard statistical measurements for outliers used such as Mahalanobis distance, which have the advantage of being potentially fully automated. This procedure is similar to that used in traditional statistics when investigating a data set before applying a statistical test to it.

Example

A significant correlation between counts of links to UK universities per staff member and the research ratings of the universities has been used as evidence that research and link creation are related in some way (Thelwall, 2002e). One small institution was identified as being an outlier because it conducted mainly types of research that did not tend to use the Web.

Mathematical Modeling

One way to identify outliers is to develop a specific theoretical model of linking for the space and assess the extent to which the model fits the data. Although this could be achieved using the Web growth models described above, it can also be applied to summary statistics.

The specifics of any mathematical model would depend on the collection of Websites studied, but the general approach will be illustrated with the example of a set of UK university Websites. A model that has been applied is to assume that the number of links both to and from a university site should be proportional to its research productivity (Thelwall, 2002b). As a result, plotting link counts against the product of the research productivities of the two universities should give a straight line. The outliers will be points that do not obey the predictions of the model. A version of this was used to demonstrate the existence of a geographic trend in the data (Thelwall, 2002c), which could be used to build an improved model:

$$\lambda_{A,B} = \partial_{A,B} \rho_A \rho_B$$

where $\lambda_{A,B}$ is the expected number of links from university A to university B, $\partial_{A,B}$ is a function of the distance between A and B, and ρ_A, ρ_B is the research productivity of A and B respectively.

If a model does fit the data then this is also a step towards data validation, but if a reasonable model does not fit well at all then this may indicate either a problem with the data or an unreasonable theory.

Topological Cleansing

If link data from a crawl are to be used in topological algorithms then data cleansing specific to preserving *topological* structure is needed. In the crawling process the duplication of pages should have been largely eliminated, but the links in other pages can still point to the duplicates rather than the originals (if such a distinction makes sense). Ideally, a table of duplicate URLs can be built during the crawl and then applied to the links in the link database so that no links are left pointing to a page that is not in the data set because of being judged a duplicate.

A particular duplication problem is caused when a site has duplicate domain names, giving at least two URLs for every page. In UK universities it is common to have duplicate short and long domain names, for example wlv.ac.uk and wolverhampton.ac.uk, and in UK businesses it is common to have a co.uk and a com domain name. Cases such as these can be batch processed with regular expressions. Further issues relating to the concept of the publicly indexable Web are discussed by Cothey (2003).

Other Approaches

There are some examples of studies with different types of data cleansing. Broder et al. (2000) explain that AltaVista's standard crawl employs a range of (unpublished) filters and heuristics in its operation, "to avoid overloading web servers, avoid robot traps (artificial infinite paths), avoid and/or detect spam (page flooding), deal with connection time outs". This yields a partial crawl of the known URLs. It is not known whether the crawling incorporates any kind of duplicate identification. The Broder et al.

(2000) link typology analysis used AltaVista's database for a 'whole Web' study after employing the heuristic that any page with at least five inlinks and not crawled by AltaVista would be artificially added: those with less inlinks were experimentally assessed as being likely to be an incorrect URL or missing page. This type of heuristic is necessary when the crawler itself is outside of the control of the researcher. See Cothey (2003) for a further discussion of issues around crawling.

Others using search engines for raw data but without insider access to the original database need to know that AltaVista employs a second set of filters to its database before deploying it. These are designed to remove duplicate and similar pages, eliminate spam, and for other unspecified reasons (Broder et al., 2000). Arasu, Cho, Garcia-Molina, Paepcke and Raghavan (2001) give a good survey of heuristics for page crawling, but these are for effective and efficient operation from a Web IR perspective rather than for accuracy.

Duplicate identification is a particular problem for link topology mining because of the problem of deciding what to do with links to pages that have been removed as duplicate. These appear to have been ignored in all reported cases so far, but a logical alternative would be to redirect them to original URLs. This does not seem to have been done in any published research, however. The TREC (2002) .gov test collection includes a table of duplicate URLs to allow users to test different approaches for dealing with duplication.

ADVANCED DATA CLEANSING: TLD SPECTRAL ANALYSIS

This section describes a technique to select the best ADM to apply to a set of Websites when correlation and modeling techniques are not available (Thelwall, 2004). The approach is to make a series of theoretical assumptions about the links in the Websites studied in order to devise goodness of fit tests to identify the best fitting ADM. The testing is centered around the problem of reporting summary statistics for the TLDs of link targets from links originating from the Websites but can be used as a data cleansing step prior to the application of other analyses, such as interlinking pattern description. The basic approach can be generalized to *any* link properties for which frequency distributions can be calculated.

The ITTD Model of Linking Behavior

The Independent TLD Target Distribution (ITTD) model is a set of assumptions about linking behavior that can be tested in order to select the best fitting ADM for a set of Websites. It is likely that no ADM provides a perfect fit but it is still useful to choose the one that provides the best match across the whole set. The approach will work best if the sites form a coherent group, such as university Websites in a country or commercial Websites from one industry sector, because it would be more reasonable to expect a common pattern of linking behavior amongst similar sites. The following are the three assumptions of the ITTD model.
1.   Each Website is constructed from a finite collection of "documents," however defined.

2.   The TLDs of site outlinks obey a common probability distribution across the documents of all the Websites.

3.   The TLDs of the site outlinks are statistically independent of each other.

Based upon the above assumptions, if the documents in the sites are correctly identified, then the proportion of links from each Website in the set that target each TLD should be approximately the same. To test how well an ADM fits a set of Websites it is therefore sufficient to compute these proportions across the set of Websites and then use a measure of the extent to which they vary to assess goodness of fit.

Suppose that two Websites A and B link only to .com and .org sites. Let n_A, n_B be the total number of outlinks from A and B, and c_A, c_B be the number of links to .com sites from A and B respectively. The links to .org sites would therefore be the differences n_A-c_A and n_B-c_B. Applying the ITTD model, all of these links are assumed to come from a common distribution and we can estimate the probability that any link targets a .com site by $(c_A + c_B) / (n_A + n_B)$. The actual proportions in each site, c_A/n_A and c_B/n_B, are likely to be slightly different from this, but if the model is correct and the total number of links in each site is not small, then the difference should not be large. The key question is how to measure the difference. One way is to calculate the probability of each site's link distribution being a random sample from the distribution, with parameters estimated by the aggregated data from all sites. This is theoretically appealing, if computationally problematical for large sites, but is not practical because the results will be heavily dependant upon the total number of documents involved. This means that if two ADMs were compared on this basis then the one at the lower level of aggregation would almost certainly appear to be less likely.

Goodness of Fit Tests

The difficulty in using a theoretical probability model to pick the best fitting ADM means that a new procedure is needed. The purpose must be to pick an ADM that best fits the ITTD assumptions in a way that does not intrinsically favor ADMs with a smaller total number of documents, resulting from a higher level of aggregation. This leads logically to tests of variability in the proportion of links that target different TLDs across the sites in the set.

A simple test is to calculate the proportion outlinks in each site that target .com domains. The standard deviation of this set of proportions is then a simple variability statistic and a low value would mean that the sites targeted similar proportions of .com sites, consistent with the ITTD assumptions. The ADM producing the lowest standard deviation should be selected.

Example

To illustrate the calculations, Table 1 shows the calculations used to choose between the file and domain ADM. The Domain ADM is selected because of its lower standard deviation — there appears to be an anomalously high level of linking to the .com domain at the file level from site B, which is the cause of the poor showing of the file ADM.

An alternative test along the same lines is to select two groups of TLDs and calculate for each site the proportion of links targeting the first group out of just the links

Table 1.

Site	File ADM			Domain ADM		
	Total site outlinks	.com outlinks	Proportion of .com links	Total site outlinks	.com outlinks	Proportion of .com links
A	400	200	0.500	250	120	0.480
B	800	700	0.875	75	40	0.533
C	300	175	0.583	120	70	0.583
Standard deviation			0.197			0.052

targeting the two groups. This could be repeated for multiple disjoint groups of TLDs, calculating standard deviations for the proportions each time to give independent tests of goodness of fit. To illustrate the grouping approach, one link to {.net} could be compared to those to {.gov, .mil, .org} so that for each site the proportion calculated would be the number of links targeting .net divided by the number of links targeting .net, .gov, .mil or .org. This approach depends upon sites in the test set being broadly similar in size. In particular, sites with very low numbers of links should be removed because the proportion of links to any TLD will have a much higher variability when based upon a small number.

Ideally, results from any approach would point to the same TLD as being the best. In practice, however, it is unlikely to be clear-cut. Application designers will need to choose a test that works on their kind of data. Currently, no testing has been conducted to compare approaches and select the best one. Note that all goodness of fit tests are necessarily heuristic because, in addition to ADMs themselves being simplifications of Web publishing patterns, link creation is not an isolated activity: authors tend to preferentially link to pages that are already linked to (Pennock et al., 2002). Hence assumption 3 in particular is unlikely to be valid in practice.

VALIDATION

Since Web data are typically very messy, it is desirable to validate it in order to be able to interpret results with some confidence. Some of the data cleansing techniques described above are useful for this: particularly mathematical modeling and correlation with external data sources. Both of these can, if successful, support the validity of interpretations of the data. For example, studies of inter-university linking have hypothesized that counts of links to a university should correlate with its research productivity and have successfully checked this (Thelwall, 2001b). Note that the reliability of such as test may be undermined if the same correlation techniques are also used for data cleansing.

Even if the above techniques support the validity of the data, *random URL sampling* should also be undertaken as part of the validation process. By visiting a selection of the links a pattern may be identified to help interpret link data. Previous attempts at this have found the classification of link types very difficult (Wilkinson, Harries, Thelwall & Price, 2003), and so this is likely to be time-consuming. This stage will probably need manual intervention to classify the pages. An alternative approach that can be fully automated is to apply a set of simplifying assumptions to turn the classification exercise into an automated content analysis (Neuendorf, 2002). The exact assumptions will depend on the type of sites being investigated and the reason why they are being investigated.

APPLICATION 1: MULTIPLE SITE LINK STRUCTURE ANALYSIS-DESCRIPTIVE STATISTICS FOR SETS OF WEBSITES

This section covers techniques for describing sets of Websites and mining patterns from them once the data have been cleansed and validated. The techniques described are indicative of the range available, but individual studies are likely to require a selection that depends upon their overall goals.

Summary Statistics

Some applications of Web link mining simply require the reporting and interpretation of summary statistics (Polanco et al., 2001; Thelwall, 2001bc, 2002cd; Thelwall & Smith, 2002; Thelwall, Tang & Price, 2003). This may be particularly applicable to very large Web spaces and an example of this is a 'health check' for Spanish university Websites (Thelwall & Aguillo, 2003). The kind of summary statistics that could be reported include the following.

- Site inlink counts, site outlink counts, either in normalized or raw form.
- A breakdown of site outlinks by top-level domain or by others of the ADM levels.
- A compilation of the most frequently targeted documents in the sites, or by the sites.

The reporting of summary statistics will be most useful if they can be compared to similar numbers from another Web space. It may be possible to design an investigation with the aim of comparing two or more spaces.

Note that it should not be assumed that TLDs are accurate descriptions of sites; for example, many .com sites are not commercial. Other TLDs are more reliable, such as .gov and .edu. If this is a problem then random sampling should be used to estimate the percentage of documents in the category that match the apparent TLD content.

Interlinking Pattern Description

When dealing with a relatively small number of Websites, graphical or statistical techniques can be employed to suggest link structure relationships between sites. For a small set of Websites, simple network diagrams can be used (Thelwall, 2001c). For example, this technique was used for the universities of 13 countries in the Asia-Pacific region (Thelwall & Smith, 2002). The countries were arranged in a circle and arrows drawn between each pair with thickness proportional to the (normalized or un-normalized) count of links from the arrow source country to its target country. For clarity, a minimum width threshold was chosen below which an arrow was not drawn. This procedure is best carried out by a macro drawing language for speed and precision. In the above example Visual Basic for Applications in Corel Draw 7 was used. It is useful to produce more than one diagram if the areas are not of a similar size. A raw link count version is useful to give an overall perspective on link 'traffic'. Normalization can be achieved by dividing link counts by the size of the source space, the target space or both. Each gives a different perspective on the data. If search engines are used for raw data then the advanced search facilities allow mining of related information such as linguistic patterns (Thelwall, Tang & Price, 2003).

Pathfinder network scaling may be appropriate when there are too many sites to use network diagrams. In other cases standard statistical clustering techniques can be employed, such as multi-dimensional scaling, cluster analysis and factor analysis. The success of each one will be dependent upon the underlying structure of the actual data set. They have all been applied to a set of university Websites with partial success (Polanco et al., 2001; Thelwall, 2002d), but problems were caused by overlapping geographic and research productivity trends that made all three techniques not ideal. In cases such as these, alternative techniques such as mathematical modeling or simulations may be needed.

The raw data for a clustering exercise can be direct link counts, colink counts or coupling counts. Two documents are *coupled* if they both link to the same documents, and *colinked* if a document links to both of them. A coupling (or colink) count is the number of documents that couple (or colink) them. A high count is an indicator of similarity in either case. It is not clear yet whether counts of colinks, links, or couplings are consistently superior to the others as similarity measures (Thelwall & Wilkinson, 2004).

APPLICATION 2: WEB IR

Web structure mining algorithms have significant uses as part of larger Web IR applications, with the prime example being Google's PageRank. For Web IR applications the validation stage is not necessarily a precursor to the application: typically the validation stage will come afterwards in the form of evaluating the results of the algorithm on a test set. The data cleansing stage will also need to be fully automated to give an efficient algorithm.

In the next subsection a topological clustering procedure will be described in detail but first an overview will be given of a link URL mining method to categorize sites (Amitay et al., 2003). The algorithm is designed to identify the type of a site from eight categories using only link structures, including statistics such as page inlink and outlink counts. The rationale for the algorithm is that different site types will have different characteristic link signatures. Rule mining based upon a test set was used to create decision rules to choose categories for sites.

Topological Community Mining

Documents need to be clustered on the Web for applications including information retrieval and interface design. Clustering is normally achieved using the text of Web pages only, or with the aid of link structures. The vector space model can be used for text based clustering, for example (Baeza-Yates & Ribeiro-Neto, 1999). Kleinberg's (1999) HITS algorithm, and later improvements (e.g., Kitsuregawa et al., 2002) use text and links. A topological clustering algorithm that only uses link structure is likely to be less effective than a combined one, but can be useful for Information Retrieval as part of a multi-layered approach, and for other applications where it is the link structure itself that is of interest. The terminology *community identification* can be used for topological cluster mining to indicate that the clustering is based upon connections rather than any measures of document content similarity.

Topological clustering for huge Web spaces has become possible through the development of a new fast algorithm, the Community Identification Algorithm (CIA) (Flake et al., 2002). Fundamental to the CIA is the idea that Web pages may form natural communities based upon link structures alone, where a community is, loosely speaking, a collection of pages that connect better to each other than to the rest of the Web. Broder et al. (2000) showed that the Web is highly connected and so it would not be effective to equate the term community with the connected components of the Web. An algorithm must be used that is able to identify a group of documents as a community even though they also link to other pages outside of the group.

The CIA solves the problem of finding a community that contains a given seed set of documents by formulating it as a maximal flow problem, which is solved using an existing fast algorithm (Ford & Fulkerson, 1956). Let G be a directed graph and E a seed set of nodes. The task is to find a subgraph E' with $E \subset E' \subset G$ such that E' is in some sense well connected to the seed set relative to the rest of the graph.

To implement the algorithm, the graph G is extended by adding links in the opposite direction to all existing links, when this does not cause duplication. This results in a graph that is symmetrical in the sense that between any pair of nodes there is either no link or two links, one in each direction. All links are then given a flow capacity k. Artificial source and sink nodes are then added to the graph with links added from the source to each community member in E and given an infinite capacity, and links added from each node in the original G to the sink and given a capacity of 1. Applying the maximal flow algorithm to the network produces a minimum cut, which splits the nodes of G into two, with one part containing all those from E. The size of E' is potentially dependent on the parameter k, with larger values giving bigger communities, but in the nature of the algorithm E' should always be well connected to E. If k is greater than the number of arrows in the network then all nodes connected to any node in the initial community will find themselves in the community calculated by the CIA, but if $k = 1$ then the algorithm will return only the original community.

In order to mine information from the link structure of a large area of the Web we need to repeatedly apply the CIA, since each application yields only one community. It is a local rather than global clustering approach. The problem is in choosing the seed sets, the parameter k and a method for combining the results. The easiest choice of seed set is a single Web document, repeating the algorithm for each document in the set, allowing systematic coverage of the whole space (Thelwall, 2003). It would be possible to extend this with other systematic choices of seed set, for example all linked pairs of nodes, if computing resources are available, but single seed nodes are the minimum for systematic coverage.

The parameter k can be varied in order to identify an appropriate value for the needs of the mining task. For example $k = 2, 4, 8, 16, 32$ would give a range of average community sizes. It might be found that 8 is the most effective, for example. Low values will tend to produce very small communities whereas large values will tend to produce at least one very big community, and so a middle value is likely to be needed.

The result of applying the algorithm for one value of k and all seed sets will be a list of communities. Some will be identified only once, whereas others may be identified multiple times from different seed sets. A graph of the sizes of the communities found will be useful to visualize the spread so that the results of different k values can be compared. The communities identified are likely to overlap and so it is most useful where this is not a problem. For example, if the question was to find all documents that could possibly be regarded as being in the same community as a given one then this could be the union of all communities containing it, with duplication not being an issue.

The CIA can be applied to any ADM level and so the same clustering can be conducted for files, directories, domains and sites. For a given document, the community structure of higher-level aggregation documents containing it can also be reported and compared. This has been termed a layered approach: simultaneously identifying structures in different aggregation levels of the Web.

FUTURE TRENDS

Much of the Web link analysis described here has been concerned with data cleansing and validation. Most research has focused on university Websites, although the European Union has financed a project that includes creating indicators for science policy makers based upon link statistics *(www.wiserweb.org)*. Another project funded by the Canadian Social Sciences and Humanities Research Council is attempting to derive business intelligence from link structures. This is now the major challenge: to develop viable applications. The purpose of the analyses could be to identify trends, report summary statistics, identify outliers, or to cluster the documents in the space. The use of the Web is so widespread, and with so much commercial content, that there is a lot of scope for different data mining applications. Full-scale applications will have to tackle the problem of data cleansing, and the amount of human involvement required to execute this stage effectively. The extent and role of interaction in data mining generally is a controversial issue (Ankerst, 2002) and although the data cleansing techniques can be fully automated in principle, for example using the spectral analysis technique to automatically identify the correct ADMs, it remains to be seen whether this will be effective in practice.

A second challenge is to incorporate link algorithms such as the CIA into IR systems. Pure link based algorithms need to be used in conjunction with text-based ones and it remains to be shown that the two can be effectively merged together. Additionally, the most effective way of incorporating CIA results needs to be identified. In particular, which k values and which ADMs produce the most useful communities?

CONCLUSIONS

This chapter has described techniques for mining the link structure of the Web based exclusively on the links themselves, either for incorporation in Web IR applications or to report on an aspect of the link structure of a group of sites: summarizing link counts or link target types, or describing interlinking patterns. The focus of the chapter, however, has been data cleansing and validation, as a result of raw Web link data typically being messy and problematic to interpret.

The key tool for many of the techniques is the Alternative Document Model concept, a set of heuristics for grouping pages into larger multiple-page documents. ADMs are needed in data cleansing to provide a mechanism to remove anomalies caused by multiple links created for a common reason. They also provide a different perspective on a Web space, even when they are not used for validation.

The future for link URL mining and link topology mining is in developing new applications and a coherent set of analysis techniques to exploit the advances already made. The research area is small at the moment but successful new applications, particularly those with a commercial context, will allow it to grow.

REFERENCES

Amitay, E., Carmel, D., Darlow, A., Lempel, R., & Soffer, A. (2003). The connectivity sonar: Detecting site functionality by structural patterns. *Proceedings of ACM HyperText 03*, pp. 38-47.

Ankerst, M. (2002). Report on the SIGKDD-2002 panel. The perfect data mining tool: Interactive or automated? *SIGKDD Explorations, 4*(2). Available: *http://www.acm.org/sigs/sigkdd/explorations/issue4-2/ankerst.pdf*.

Arasu, A., Cho, J., Garcia-Molina, H., Paepcke, A., & Raghavan, S. (2001). Searching the Web. *ACM Transactions on Internet Technology, 1*(1), 2-43.

Baeza-Yates, R., & Ribeiro-Neto, B. (1999). *Modern information retrieval.* New York: ACM.

Barabási, A.L. (2002). *Linked: The new science of networks.* Cambridge, MA: Perseus Publishing.

Barabási, A.L., & Albert, R. (1999). Emergence of scaling in random networks. *Science, 286,* 509-512.

Barabási, A.L., Albert, R., & Jeong, H. (2000). Scale-free characteristics of random networks: The topology of the World Wide Web. *Physica A, 281,* 69-77.

Bar-Ilan, J. (2001). Data collection methods on the Web for informetric purposes - A review and analysis. *Scientometrics, 50*(1), 7-32.

Bharat, K., Chang, B., Henzinger, M., & Ruhl, M. (2001). Who links to whom: Mining linkage between Web sites. *IEEE International Conference on Data Mining (ICDM '01),* San Jose, California.

Brin, S., & Page, L. (1998). The anatomy of a large scale hypertextual Web search engine. *Computer Networks and ISDN Systems, 30*(1-7), 107-117.

Broder, A., Kumar, R., Maghoul, F., Raghavan, P., Rajagopalan, S., Stata, R., Tomkins, A., & Wiener, J. (2000). Graph structure in the Web. *Journal of Computer Networks, 33*(1-6), 309-320.

Chakrabarti, S., Joshi, M.M., Punera, K., & Pennock, D.M. (2002). The structure of broad topics on the Web. *Proceedings of the WWW2002 Conference.* Available: *http://www2002.org/CDROM/refereed/338/]*.

Cothey, V. (2005, to appear). Web-crawler reliability. *Journal of the American Society for Information Science and Technology.*

Flake, G.W., Lawrence, S., Giles, C.L., & Coetzee, F.M. (2002). Self-organization and identification of Web communities. *IEEE Computer, 35,* 66-71.

Ford, L.R., & Fulkerson, D.R. (1956). Maximal flow through a network. *Canadian Journal of Mathematics, 8*(3), 399-404.

Hafri, Y., Djeraba, C., Stanchev, P., & Bachimont, B. (2003). A Markovian approach for Web user profiling and clustering. *Lecture Notes in Artificial Intelligence 2637*, 191-202.

Hawking, D., Bailey, P., & Craswell, N. (2000). ACSys TREC-8 experiments. *Information Technology: Eighth Text Retrieval Conference (TREC-8)*, NIST, Gaithersburg, MD, USA, 307-315.

Hawking, D., Craswell, N., Thistlewaite, P., & Harman, D. (2001). Results and challenges in Web search evaluation. *Computer Networks, 31*(11-16), 1321-1330.

Heaton, J. (2002). *Programming spiders, bots and aggregators in java.* Sybex.

Henzinger, M.R. (2001). Hyperlink analysis for the Web. *IEEE Internet Computing, 5*(1), 45-50.

Heydon, A., & Najork, M. (1999). Mercator: A scalable, extensible Web crawler. *World Wide Web, 2,* 219-229.

Kitsuregawa, M., Toyoda, M., & Pramudiono, I. (2002). WEB community mining and WEB log mining: Commodity cluster based execution. *Proceedings of the 13th Australasian Database Conference* (ADC2002), Melbourne, Australia.

Kleinberg, J. (1999). Authoritative sources in a hyperlinked environment. *Journal of the ACM, 46*(5), 604-632.

Kosala, R., & Blockeel, H. (2000). Web mining research: A survey. *ACM SIGKDD Explorations, 2*(1), 1-15.

Lawrence, S., & Giles, C.L. (1999). Accessibility of information on the Web. *Nature, 400,* 107-109.

Neuendorf, K. (2002). *The content analysis guidebook.* CA: Sage.

Pallman, D. (1999). *Programming bots, spiders and intelligent agents in Microsoft visual C++.* Microsoft Press.

Pennock, D.M., Flake, G.W., Lawrence, S., Glover, E., & Giles, C.L. (2002). Winners don't take all: Characterizing the competition for links on the Web. *Proceedings of the National Academy of Science, 99*(8), 5207-5211.

Polanco, X., Boudourides, M.A., Besagni, D., & Roche, I. (2001). *Clustering and mapping Web sites for displaying implicit associations and visualising networks.* University of Patras.

Savoy, J., & Picard, J. (2001). Retrieval effectiveness on the Web. *Information Processing & Management, 37*(4), 543-569.

Thelwall, M. (2001a). A Web crawler design for data mining. *Journal of Information Science, 27*(5), 319-325.

Thelwall, M. (2001b). Extracting macroscopic information from Web links. *Journal of the American Society for Information Science and Technology, 52*(13), 1157-1168.

Thelwall, M. (2001c). Exploring the link structure of the Web with network diagrams. *Journal of Information Science, 27*(6), 393-402.

Thelwall, M. (2002a). Methodologies for crawler based Web surveys. *Internet Research: Electronic Networking and Applications, 12*(2), 124-138.

Thelwall, M. (2002b). A research and institutional size based model for national university Web site interlinking. *Journal of Documentation, 58*(6), 683-694.

Thelwall, M. (2002c). Evidence for the existence of geographic trends in university Web site interlinking. *Journal of Documentation, 58*(5), 563-574.

Thelwall, M. (2002d). An initial exploration of the link relationship between UK university Web sites. *ASLIB Proceedings, 54*(2), 118-126.

Thelwall, M. (2002e). Conceptualizing documentation on the Web: An evaluation of different heuristic-based models for counting links between university Web sites. *Journal of the American Society for Information Science and Technology, 53*(12), 995-1005.

Thelwall, M. (2003). A layered approach for investigating the topological structure of communities in the Web, *Journal of Documentation, 59*(4), 410-429.

Thelwall, M. (2004). Methods for reporting on the targets of links from national systems of university Web sites. *Information Processing & Management, 40*(1), 125-144.

Thelwall, M., & Aguillo, I. (2003). La salud de las Web universitarias españolas. *Revista Española de Documentación Científica, 26*(3), 291-305.

Thelwall, M., & Harries, G. (2003). The connection between the research of a university and counts of links to its Web pages: An investigation based upon a classification of the relationships of pages to the research of the host university. *Journal of the American Society for Information Science and Technology, 54*(7), 594-602.

Thelwall, M., & Harries, G. (2004, in press). Can personal Web pages that link to universities yield information about the wider dissemination of research? *Journal of Information Science, 30*(3).

Thelwall, M., & Smith, A. (2002). A study of the interlinking between Asia-Pacific university Web sites. *Scientometrics, 55*(3), 363-376.

Thelwall, M., & Wilkinson, D. (2003a). Three target document range metrics for university Web sites. *Journal of the American Society for Information Science and Technology, 54*(6), 489-496.

Thelwall, M., & Wilkinson, D. (2003b). Graph structure in three national academic Webs: Power laws with anomalies. *Journal of the American Society for Information Science and Technology, 54*(8), TREC (2002). The .GOV test collection. Available: *http://es.cmis.csiro.au/TRECWeb/govinfo.html.*

Thelwall, M., & Wilkinson, D. (2004). Finding similar academic Web sites with links, bibliometric couplings and colinks. *Information Processing & Management, 40*(3), 383-385.

Thelwall, M., Tang, R., & Price, E. (2003). Linguistic patterns of academic Web use in Western Europe. *Scientometrics, 56*(3), 417-432.

Watts, D.J., & Strogatz, S.H. (1998). Collective dynamics of 'small-world' networks. *Nature, 393*, 440-442.

Wilkinson, D., Harries, G., Thelwall, M., & Price, E. (2003). Motivations for academic Web site interlinking: Evidence for the Web as a novel source of information on informal scholarly communication. *Journal of Information Science, 29*(1), 59-66.

Wu, E.H., & Ng, M.K. (2003). A graph-based optimization algorithm for Website topology using interesting association rules. *Lecture Notes in Artificial Intelligence 2637*, 178-190.

Chapter XI

Extracting and Customizing Information Using Multi-Agents

Mohamed Salah Hamdi
UAE University, United Arab Emirates

ABSTRACT

Rapidly evolving network and computer technology, coupled with the exponential growth of the services and information available on the Internet, has already brought us to the point where hundreds of millions of people should have fast, pervasive access to a phenomenal amount of information, through desktop machines at work, school and home, through televisions, phones, pagers, and car dashboards, from anywhere and everywhere. The challenge of complex environments is therefore obvious: software is expected to do more in more situations, there are a variety of users (Power/Naive, Techie/ Financial/Clerical, ...), there are a variety of systems (Windows/NT/Mac/Unix, Client/Server, Portable, Distributed Object Manager, Web, ...), there are a variety of interactions (Real-time, Data Bases, Other Players, ...), and there are a variety of resources and goals (time, space, bandwidth, cost, security, quality, ...). To cope with such environments, the promise of information customization systems is becoming highly attractive. In this chapter we discuss important problems in relationship to such systems and smooth the way for possible solutions. The main idea is to approach information customization using a multi-agent paradigm.

INTRODUCTION

The recent proliferation of personal computers and communication networks has a strong scientific, intellectual and social impact on the society.

Using a computer network, geographically distributed people can communicate, coordinate, and collaborate their work efforts across time and space barriers. The quality of the results of exploiting this technology depends on how well individual knowledge can be communicated among the members; that is, how well members can gather the appropriate set of knowledge. The challenge faced is therefore how to turn the scattered, diverse knowledge available into a well-structured knowledge repository. The general framework for this is that of knowledge management, which is suggested as a methodology for creating, maintaining and exploiting a knowledge repository (Drucker et al., 1998; Liebowitz and Wilcox, 1997; Schreiber et al., 2000).

The recent popularity of the World Wide Web (Web) has provided a tremendous opportunity to expedite the dispersement of various information creation/diffusion infrastructures. The mass of content available on the Web raises important questions over its effective use. With largely unstructured pages authored by a massive range of people on a diverse range of topics, simple browsing has given way to filtering as the practical way to manage Web-based information. Today's online resources are therefore mainly accessible via a panoply of primitive but popular information services such as search engines.

Search engines are very effective at filtering pages that match explicit queries. Unfortunately, most people find articulating what they want extremely difficult, especially if forced to use a limited vocabulary such as keywords. The result is large lists of search results that contain a handful of useful pages, defeating the purpose of filtering in the first place.

Search engines also require massive memory resources (to store an index of the Web) and tremendous network bandwidth (to create and continually refresh the index). These systems receive millions of queries per day, and as a result, the CPU cycles devoted to satisfying each individual query are sharply curtailed. There is no time for intelligence. Furthermore, each query is independent of the previous one and no attempt is made to customize the responses to a particular individual.

What is needed are systems that act on the user's behalf and that can rely on existing information services that do the resource-intensive part of the work. These systems will be sufficiently lightweight to run on an average PC and serve as personal assistants. Since such an assistant has relatively modest resource requirements it can reside on an individual user's machine, which facilitates customization to that individual. Furthermore, if the assistant resides on the user's machine, there is no need to turn down intelligence. The system can have substantial local intelligence and information customization becomes possible.

The work described here discusses some ideas aiming at improving the reduction of information overflow, which is so common today in Web search results. It should be understood in the broader framework of Web mining. Web mining includes the discovery of document content, hyperlink structure, access statistics and other interesting connections of information on the Web. It is interdisciplinary in nature, spanning across such fields as information retrieval, natural language processing, information extraction, machine learning, database, data mining, data warehousing, knowledge management, user interface design, and visualization. Web mining is moving the World Wide Web to a more useful environment in which users can quickly and easily find the information they need (Scime, 2004).

The main idea in this research project is to do information customization based on a multi-agent approach. In the following we will discuss some important points in relationship with information customization, modeling user's interest and task context, and multi-agent systems, and then describe an application example (see also Hamdi, 2003a, 2003b, 2003c).

BACKGROUND

Since the beginning of recorded history, people have been fascinated with the idea of non-human artificially intelligent embodied creatures acting as assistants. People have, for example, often embraced the romantic dream of robots as butlers who would someday putter about the living room performing mundane household tasks. Though automata of various sorts have existed for centuries, it is only with the development of computers, control theory, and artificial intelligence (AI) since the 1950s that anything resembling autonomous assistants/agents has begun to appear.

Alan Turing, famous for his work on computability (Turing, 1937), posed the question, "Can machines think?" (Turing, 1959, p. 433). His test, in which a person communicates via a teletype with either a person or a computer, became known as the Turing test. The Turing test requires a conversational computer to be capable of fooling a human at the other end. It is the Turing test that inspired the birth of the artificial intelligence community in the 1950s. At that time, and after some work with neural networks (deemed a failure at the time due to the difficulty of learning weights), AI researchers were focusing on symbolic search-based systems and on exploring heuristic search to prove logic theorems. Initial successes thus led to heuristic search of symbolic representations becoming the dominant approach to AI. The 1960s saw much progress. LISP (McCarthy, 1960) was just invented and the course was set for representing the world with symbols and using logic to solve problems (McCarthy & Hayes, 1969). At the same time, the General Problem Solver (Newell et al., 1959) which, given a suitable representation, could solve any problem, was created. Problems solved were in simple, noise and error-free symbolic worlds, with the assumption that such solutions would generalize to allow larger, real-world problems to be tackled. Researchers did not worry about keeping computation on a human time-scale, using the increases in hardware performance to constantly increase the possible search space size, thus solving increasingly impressive problems. During the 1970s, search became well understood (Nilsson, 1971). Symbolic systems still dominated, with continuing hardware improvements allowing steady, successful progress. Robots were created, for example Shakey (Nilsson, 1984), that lived in special block worlds, and could navigate around and stack blocks sensibly. Such simplified worlds avoided the complexity of real-world problems. The assumption underpinning all the symbolic research, that simple symbolic worlds would generalize to the real world, was about to be found wanting. In the 1980s, expert systems were created to try to solve real problems. It has been realized that "common sense" (McCarthy, 1983) was required in addition to specialized domain knowledge to solve anything but simple microworld problems. A sub-field of AI, knowledge representation, came into being to examine approaches to representing the everyday world. Unfortunately, the idea of "common sense" proved impossible to represent, and knowledge-based systems were widely viewed to have failed to solve real-world problems. At the same time, the back-propagation algorithm (Rumelhart et al., 1986) caused a resurgence of interest in connectionist approaches, previously deemed a failure. The late 1980s and early 1990s saw the decline of search-based symbolic approaches. Researchers focused on the creation of embodied, grounded systems using the "world as its own best model" (Brooks, 1991, p. 583). This had some initial successes; however, it too failed to scale up to real-world problems of significant complexity. Connectionist approaches were aided by new parallel hardware in the early 1990s, but the complexity of a parallel architecture led such systems to fail in the marketplace. Towards the end of the 1990s, knowledge engineering, widely seen as costly and hard to re-use, was superseded by machine learning techniques. Pattern-learning algorithms (Mitchell, 1997) could classify suitable domains of knowledge with as much accuracy as manual classification. Hybrids of traditional and embodied AI started to appear as new approaches. The dream of indirect human computer interaction (Kay, 1990; Negroponte, 1970) coupled with early ideas on intelligence (Minsky, 1986) led to the new field of agent-based computing. Experiments with interface agents that learned about their user (Maes, 1994), and multi-agent systems in which simple agents interact to achieve their goals (Wooldridge & Jennings, 1995) dominated the research. Such agent systems were all grounded in the real world, using proven AI techniques to achieve concrete results.

The gauntlet thrown down by early researchers has been variously taken up by new ones in distributed artificial intelligence, robotics, artificial life, distributed object computing, human-computer interaction, intelligent and adaptive interfaces, intelligent search and filtering, information retrieval, knowledge acquisition, end-user programming, programming-by-demonstration, and a growing list of other fields.

Information Customization

The impact of the digital computer and the changing role of information are becoming obvious. The rapid evolution of technology and the changes being wrought are exciting and announce the coming of the information revolution. New terminology and metaphors have appeared in rapid succession: Cyberspace, the information super-highway, and softbots are just some examples.

A major part of the information revolution is the Internet. There is suddenly so much information that is potentially visible through the computer screen. The range and diversity of these online resources are what make the research significant and interesting. Coping with the characteristics of openness (the sum of knowledge present cannot be characterized) and frequent change marks a change for artificial intelligence (AI) systems. AI researchers are now more than interested observers. These resources (online resources) represent a complex and dynamic environment and are a wonderful experimental test-bed for investigating artificial intelligence issues such as intelligent search, knowledge representation, and so forth. Conversely, effective utilization of the resources will require intelligence.

Building software that can interact with the range and diversity of the online resources is a challenge, and the promise of Information Customization (IC) systems is becoming highly attractive.

IC systems are different from conventional search engines or database systems. Not all information is easy to find. Most people using, for example, the Internet to search for specific information report some frustrating experiences. From the user's perspective, two problems frequently arise when using the search engine. First, the words might not match exactly and hence nothing is returned by the search engine. Second, and much more common, is that too many URLs are returned by the search engine. Furthermore, each query is independent of the previous one. No attempt is made to customize the responses of the search engine to a particular individual. The result is homogenized, least-common-denominator service and no personalization is possible.

Even when the relevant information is easy to find, it will be perhaps boring and time-consuming for the user to perform this task and it would be wonderful if an IC system could identify and present the information with little or no user intervention. The system should also be able to update the presentation as new information becomes available. This will release the user from continually observing the resources. This raises, of course, questions about robustness and persistence of the system.

Important Characteristics of IC Systems

IC systems tend, by their very nature, to be distributed — the idea of a centralized IC system is an oxymoron. Distributed systems have long been recognized as one of the most complex classes of computer systems to design and implement. A great deal of research effort has been devoted to understanding this complexity, and to developing formalisms and tools that enable a developer to manage it (Andrews, 2000). Despite this research effort, the problems inherent in developing distributed systems can in no way be regarded as solved. So, in building an IC system, it is vital not to ignore the lessons learned from the distributed systems community. The IC system developer must therefore recognize and plan for problems such as synchronization, mutual exclusion for shared resources, deadlock, and livelock.

IC systems are often expected to be adaptive. Adaptive software is software that adapts, with little or no intervention by a programmer, to changes in the environment in which it runs. Such an adaptive solution will be able to add feedback for performance characteristics and allow the program to make choices autonomously. As a result, the system is able to change its behavior based on its previous experience.

We also expect an IC system to act even if all the details are not specified, or the situation changes. This is the property of autonomy; that is, the system is able to exercise control over its own actions. Other considerations such as pro-activeness (the program does not simply react in response to the environment) and mobility (where the program runs) are also of importance.

Finally, an IC system, in order to be accepted, should be robust; that is, a working system, accessible seven days a week, twenty-four hours a day. Speed is also expected: virtually all widely used systems begin transmitting useful (or at least entertaining) information within seconds. Of course, there should be an added value when using IC systems: any increase in sophistication had better yield a tangible benefit to users.

Modeling Users and Tasks

An IC system is software that acts, in accordance with a user's preferences, in an environment. In reality, different users have different preferences, the environment is constantly changing, and the target is really a cloud of related products. One should therefore expect continual change and the solution is to design a flexible, evolvable system, and make it easy for end-users to make changes (note that it is hard to stop them from making bad changes).

User modeling (Kobsa, 1990) comes in two varieties, behavioral and knowledge-based. Knowledge-based user modeling is typically the result of questionnaires and studies of users, hand-crafted into a set of heuristics. Behavioral models are generally the result of monitoring the user during an activity. Stereotypes (Rich, 1979) can be applied to both cases, classifying the users into groups (or stereotypes), with the aim of applying generalizations to people in those groups.

To realize an IC system acting in accordance with a user's preferences, one may hope that the designers choose the best choices to meet the specification. However, in reality, much information is lost during design: Making goals Boolean is an arbitrary process, specification is warped to match the achievable, design rationale is left informal or is lost, and there is often a need to start all over in a new environment. The solution is therefore to capture how much criteria are worth and let the program make the best choices, given a particular environment and criteria.

The typical user profiling approach for IC systems is therefore behavior-based, using a binary or a multi-class behavioral model representing what users find interesting and uninteresting. Machine learning techniques are then used to access potential items of interest in respect to the behavioral model.

According to the machine learning paradigm (see Mitchell, 1997 for a comprehensive introduction to machine learning), a general inductive process automatically builds an automatic document (the term document refers here to any source of information available to the user) classifier by learning, from a set of pre-classified documents, the characteristics of the categories of interest. The general inductive process (also called the *learner*) automatically builds a classifier for a category c_i by observing the characteristics of a set of documents manually classified under c_i or "not classified" under c_i by a domain expert; from these characteristics, the inductive process gleans the characteristics that a new unseen document should have in order to be classified under c_i. In machine learning terminology, the classification problem is an activity of *supervised* learning, since the learning process is "supervised" by the knowledge of the categories and of the training instances that belong to them. The advantages of this approach are an accuracy comparable to that achieved by human experts, and a considerable savings in terms of expert labor power, since no intervention from either knowledge engineers or domain experts is needed for the construction of the classifier or for its porting to a different set of categories when the classifier is ported to a completely different domain.

There are a lot of effective machine learning algorithms based on two or more classes. The *train-and-test* approach, for example, relies on the availability of an *initial corpus* of documents pre-classified under a set of categories. A document is a *positive example* of a category if it is classified under this category. Otherwise it is a *negative example* of that category. Once a classifier has been built it is desirable to evaluate its effectiveness. In this case, prior to classifier construction the initial corpus is split into two sets, not necessarily of equal size: a *training (and validation) set* used for inductively building the classifier by observing the characteristics of these documents; and a *test set* used for testing the effectiveness of the classifier. Each document in the test set is fed to the classifier, and the classifier decisions are compared with the expert decisions. A measure of classification effectiveness is based on how often the classifier decisions match the expert decisions.

An alternative is the *k-fold cross-validation* approach (Mitchell, 1997), in which k different classifiers are built by partitioning the initial corpus into k disjoint sets and then iteratively applying the train-and-test approach on pairs consisting of one of those disjoint sets as test set and the remaining documents in the corpus as training set. The final effectiveness figure is obtained by individually computing the effectiveness of each classifier and then averaging the individual results in some way (see Sebastiani, 2002).

Systems based on behavioral models and employing a learning technology are classified according to the type of information required by the learning technique and the way the user model is represented. Algorithms requiring an explicit training set employ supervised learning, while those without a training set use unsupervised learning techniques (Mitchell, 1997). There are three general ways to learn about the user: monitor the user, ask for feedback or allow explicit programming by the user. Monitoring the user's behavior produces unlabelled data, suitable for unsupervised learning techniques. This is generally the hardest way to learn, but is also the least intrusive. If the monitored behavior is assumed to be an example of what the user wants, a positive example can be inferred. Asking the user for feedback, be it on a case-by-case basis or via an initial training set, produces labeled training data. Supervised learning techniques can thus be employed, which usually outperform unsupervised learning. The disadvantage is that feedback must be provided, requiring an investment of an often significant effort in the system by the user. User programming involves the user changing the system explicitly. Programming can be performed in a variety of ways, from complex programming languages to the specification of simple cause/effect graphs. Explicit programming requires significant effort by the user.

Modeling the user's changing interest and task contexts by creating adaptive user profiles will help in capturing worthy criteria and solving the problem of information customization by linking these semantic aspects (often formulated in human terms) into queries (syntactic structures).

User profiles are of great importance for information extraction and information customization since they are essential for deciding what kind of information is needed, where this information can be found, how this information can be retrieved, and how this information should be presented to the user. User profiles will therefore have a great influence on the solution to be adopted for implementing an IC system. In our case they will have a strong impact on the multi-agent system to be created.

Agent and Multi-Agent Approaches

A convenient metaphor for building software to interact with the range and diversity of online resources is that of an agent. An agent is a person or program that performs some task on your behalf. We would like to have a program that navigates the online resources to find the specific information that is strongly suspected to be there. You care about the result, and are happy to delegate the process to an assistant. You expect an agent to act even if all the details are not specified, or the situation changes. You expect an agent to communicate effectively with other agents.

Agents can be viewed as a new model for developing software to interact over a network. This view has emerged because of the predominance of networks in the world. Information, knowledge, and electronic resources in general, are distributed across a network and programs and methods are needed to access them and present them in a customized manner. Using agents adds a layer of abstraction that localizes decisions about dealing with local peculiarities of format, knowledge conventions, and so forth, and thus helps to understand and manage complexity. Agents should therefore be seen as an abstraction that appears to provide a powerful way of conceptualizing, designing, and implementing a particularly complex class of software systems.

Agents can be thought of as a natural extension to object-oriented programming. Objects not only provide data encapsulation, but they also provide a modular way of modeling a system in terms of its entities and the interactions among those entities. On the other hand, objects are passive entities; they change their state only in response to method invocations (i.e., member function calls), and they have no control over when those invocations will occur. In contrast, agents are active and self-motivated. Each agent has its own thread of control, and runs independently of the other agents. Agents interact among themselves by sending and receiving messages, but the messages are not in the form of function calls. It is possible to multicast a message to a group of agents, and each recipient agent is free to ignore a message or deal with it at a later time.

While the original work on agents was instigated by researchers intent on studying computational models of distributed intelligence, a new wave of interest has been fueled by two additional concerns of a practical nature: simplifying the complexities of distributed computing and overcoming the limitations of current user interface approaches. Both of these can essentially be seen as a continuation of the trend toward greater abstraction of interfaces to computing services. On the one hand, there is a desire to further abstract the details of hardware, software, and communication patterns by replacing today's program-to-program interfaces with more powerful, general and uniform agent-to-agent interfaces; on the other hand there is a desire to further abstract the details of the human-to-program interface by delegating to agents the details of specifying and carrying out complex tasks. Harrison et al. (1995) argue that while it is true that point solutions not requiring agents could be devised to address many if not all of the issues raised by such problems, the aggregate advantage of agent technology is that it can address all of them at once.

Multi-agent systems are systems composed of multiple interacting agents, in which each agent is a coarse-grained computational system in its own right. The hypothesis/ goal of multi-agent systems is creating a system that interconnects separately developed agents, thus enabling the ensemble to function beyond the capabilities of any singular agent in the set-up. To arrive at a multi-agent solution, concepts such as those found in object-oriented computing, distributed computing, expert systems, and so forth are necessary but do not suffice because distributed computing modules are usually passive and dumb. Also, their communications are usually low-level while multi-agent systems require high-level messages. Lastly, and importantly, multi-agent systems applications require a cooperation-knowledge level, while these systems (as object-oriented computing, expert systems, etc.) typically operate at the symbol and knowledge levels (Newell, 1982).

The approach of multi-agent systems seems to be a suitable framework for developing IC systems since many of the properties of IC systems or requirements on these systems such as being autonomous, in that they are able to exercise control over their actions and act without user intervention, being adaptive (learning), in that they are able to change their behavior based on their previous experience, and being proactive (goal-oriented), in that they are able to take actions that involve resource identification, query formulation and refinement, retrieval, and information organization for their users, coincide with those required on multi-agent systems and on agent-based systems in general.

When speaking about agents and the properties of agents, some further clarifications are necessary. One should normally avoid prescriptive arguments about how a word should be used. Russell and Norvig (1995) put it this way: "The notion of an agent is meant to be a tool for analyzing systems, not an absolute characterization that divides the world into agents and non-agents" (p. 33). The only concepts that yield sharp edge categories are mathematical concepts, and they succeed only because they are content-free. Agents "live" in the (real) world, and real-world concepts yield fuzzy categories.

Even though there is no generally agreed upon clear-cut definition for agents, most proposed definitions are based on either the assumption that "agents act or can act" or on the assumption that "agents act in place of another with permission" (the latter is based on the former). Most agent criteria are therefore often related to the following points :
- An agent is part of and situated in an environment.
- An agent senses and acts autonomously.
- No other is required for input/output.
- An agent has its own agenda (event driven or program).
- Acting may affect later sensing.
- An agent acts continually (over a period of time).

Because the class of systems satisfying such criteria seems to be too large, the following agent properties are often needed for classification purposes (Franklin & Graesser, 1997):
- *Reactive (sensing and acting):* responds in a timely fashion to changes in the environment.
- *Autonomous:* exercises control over its own actions.
- *Goal-oriented (pro-active, purposeful):* does not simply act in response to the environment.
- *Temporally continuous:* is a continuously running process.
- *Communicative (socially able):* communicates with other agents, perhaps including people.
- *Learning (adaptive):* changes its behavior based on its previous experience.
- *Mobile:* able to transport itself from one machine to another.
- *Flexible:* actions are not scripted.
- *Having character:* believable "personality" and emotional state.

For a more thorough discussion of agent-based systems and their properties see Bradshaw (1997b), Franklin and Graesser (1997) and Stuart (2000).

Furthermore, and as rationale and justification for deciding to adopt an agent-based solution, an IC system is an inherently distributed system. This means that a system of multiple, interacting, autonomous agents is a natural model of the way the resources invoked by the IC system are distributed. In addition to this, there are specific advantages with respect to the IC system as opposed to more traditional distributed information systems. With reference to the presentation of information to the user, agents are appropriate because: (1) the autonomy of the agent enables it to encapsulate the interests of a particular user and tailor its responses to reflect those interests; (2) the fact that an agent can anticipate the user's needs means that it can act to identify pertinent information of which the user may be unaware; and (3) an agent is able to exploit user profile information to perform its task more suitably.

Agents are also appropriate because they have the ability to manage scarce resources, and because they allow existing systems to be integrated in a comparatively clean and straightforward manner. For existing systems to be made available to the user, they must provide an interface that is consistent with other resources, and that supports the flexible interaction required. Such resources may be "wrapped up" as agents to provide this flexible and consistent interface (Genesereth & Ketchpel, 1994; Jennings et al., 1993).

A final advantage in the use of agents is their ability to record, maintain and communicate information *about* the system, as well as the information within the system. In particular, to satisfy a user's request, the agents within the system must maintain a record of the information repositories and software tools available, and how appropriate they are for various tasks. This mediation of system information is useful for any large, distributed information system, and it is especially useful if the availability of resources may change over time, which is the case in IC systems. Wiederhold (1992) proposed the concept of a mediator in information system architectures as a way of managing the volume of information within such systems. Put simply, a mediator is an agent that develops and maintains an abstraction of the information or resources within the system.

Web Mining

Given the vast and ever-growing amount of information available in the Web and the fact that search engines do not seem to help much, how does the average user quickly find what he or she is looking for?

As mentioned earlier, IC systems seem to be the appropriate solution. The approach is to personalize the Web space — create a system that responds to user queries by potentially aggregating information from several sources in a manner that is dependent on the user's identity.

Existing commercial systems seek to do some minimal personalization based on declarative information directly provided by the user, such as their zip code, or keywords describing their interests, or specific URLs, or even particular pieces of information they are interested in (e.g., price for a particular stock). More elaborate solutions are eagerly awaited from applying new information customization techniques; that is, developing specific IC systems specialized on the Web — Web mining systems.

Current Web mining research aims at creating systems that (semi-) automatically tailor the content delivered to the user from a Website. This is usually done by mining the Web — both the contents, as well as the user's interaction (Cooley et al., 1997). Web mining, when looked upon in data mining terms, can be said to have three operations of interests — clustering (finding natural groupings of users, pages, etc.), associations (which URLs tend to be requested together), and sequential analysis (the order in which URLs tend to be accessed). As in most real-world problems, the clusters and associations in Web mining do not have crisp boundaries and often overlap considerably. In addition, bad exemplars (outliers) and incomplete data can easily occur in the data set, due to a wide variety of reasons inherent to Web browsing and logging. Thus, Web mining and personalization require modeling of an unknown number of overlapping sets in the presence of significant noise and outliers, (i.e., bad exemplars). Moreover, the data sets in Web mining are extremely large. The Web contains a mix of many different data types, and so in a sense subsumes text data mining, database data mining, image mining, and so on. The Web contains additional data types not available on a large scale before, including hyperlinks and massive amounts of (indirect) user usage information. Spanning across all these data types there is the dimension of time, since data on the Web change over time. Finally, there are data that are generated dynamically, in response to user input and programmatic scripts.

To mine data from the Web is therefore different from mining data from other sources of information. Interesting results are expected from novel mixings of these different data types to achieve novel goals. Also, any discussion of data mining from the Web requires a discussion of issues of scale (Hearst, 1997). In addition, scalable robust techniques to model noisy data sets containing an unknown number of overlapping categories should be developed (Krishnapuram et al., 2001).

CASE STUDY: E-LEARNING

Having decided on a research direction, the following question emerges. What constitutes a good domain and problem? The key characteristic of an interesting domain is that there are a variety of resources in differing formats but there is some common overall structure. Too much structure reduces the problem to known methods. Too little structure makes the problem very difficult. Having structure is useful to guide the search and identification of relevant information.

We will illustrate our ideas using an example consisting of an e-learning application. In this application a student registered in many courses seeks course materials from the sites (of different natures) of different lecturers. These diverse resources can be physically distributed. They are also dynamic so that course materials can be added, updated or deleted. The student profile, which contains the courses being attended currently by the student, the courses already attended by the student, and possibly other additional information, changes also over time because the student can, for example, leave a course or register in a new one (and have in this way another different profile). This means that the customized presentation of information for the student should be updated continuously as new information becomes available. This happens with no user intervention using an autonomous multi-agent system.

The Bee-Gent System

As a solution to the problems of network communication, we use Bee-gent (Bonding and Encapsulation Enhancement Agent) (Kawamura et al., 2000), a communication framework based on the multi-agent model. The Bee-gent framework is comprised of two types of agent. "Agent Wrappers" are used to agentify (i.e., provide an agent interface) existing applications, while "Mediation Agents" support inter-application co-ordination by handling all communications. The mediation agents move from the site of an application to another, where they interact with the agent wrappers. The agent wrappers themselves manage the states of the applications they are wrapped around, invoking them when necessary.

The Bee-gent system has many desirable features. The mediation agent manages the coordinating interactions of the various applications in a unified manner. It is easy to maintain consistency because it is not necessary to divide and distribute the coordinating interactions on the basis of each individual application, and therefore development is simplified. It is also easy to modify the system configuration and the coordinating interactions because these interactions are encapsulated.

When the mediation agent migrates it carries its own program, data and current state. Frequency of communication is reduced compared to a purely message-based system and network loads are decreased largely because communication links can be disconnected after launch of the mediation agent. Processing efficiency is improved because the mediation agent communicates with the applications locally.

The agent wrappers provide the common interfaces. Application interoperability increases and therefore it is easier to build open systems. Large-scale system development becomes easier because procedures for handling application co-ordination do not have to be known explicitly. Applications are agentified by the agent wrappers. It is possible to protect information in a superior manner and to control process priorities by autonomously dealing with requests from the mediation agents. Flexible interactions that change according to the situation are possible because the agentified applications and the mediation agents communicate using the ACL (Agent Communication Language).

The methods of information exchange and communication are highly suited to Internet and Web computing. Migration and communication of the mediation agents adopt the HTTP protocol. Bee-gent adopts XML/ACL (eXtensible Markup Language) as the representation format of the agent communication language ACL. XML/ACL is likely to become highly popular as an information representation format.

Implemented Example

The implemented sample provides a service to a student that checks whether lecturers are offering information that matches the profile of the student and informs the student of the information found. The process flow of this sample is shown in Figure 1.

The components of the system are (the terms "Student" and "TeacherX" are used just as names for the different applications (active parts, i.e., agents) in the system in order to distinguish between them. It should therefore be understood that humans are not being conceived as part of the system):

- Student (USR).
- Teacher1 (T1).
- Teacher2 (T2).

Figure1. Process Flow through a Multi-Agent System for Extracting Information.

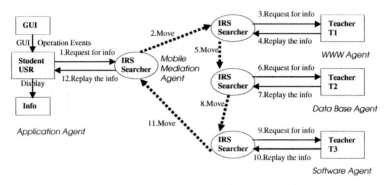

IRS: Information Retrieval Service   GUI: Graphical User Interface

- Teacher3 (T3).
- Mediation agent providing the information retrieving service (Searcher).

The student (USR) and the three teachers (T1, T2, T3) in this example are technically applications, each of them existing within an agent wrapper; that is, they represent different agents of the system (Figure 1). The student uses a Graphical User Interface (GUI) to update his or her profile and search for information matching that profile. The agent wrapper for the user application (USR) creates a mediation agent (Searcher), which travels to the three agent wrappers of the teacher applications to retrieve the needed information.

The behaviors of the agent wrappers that wrap the applications and the mediation agent are defined by interaction protocols. The interaction protocols consist of the states of the components, the transitions, the message exchanges and the migration of the mediation agent. An agent wrapper or a mediation agent in a given state performs the action whose precondition coincides with the current state. The state of the agent changes to the next state according to a transition rule. An interaction protocol is therefore defined by specifying the preconditions of the possible states, the actions and the transition rules.

Each of the agents (mediation agent or agent wrappers) is implemented in Java with a class that represents the agent body and a set of classes that represent the different states (each class defines a state). The behaviors of an agent are specified on the basis of the current state and the state transition rules. First, one should list all the names of the states the agent can enter. Next, define the class for each state. Then specify the actions to be executed in the state (consisting of the agent's own processes and the interactions with other agents). Also, one has to specify the next states the agent enters according to the result of the action executions. An agent usually starts its activity from an "INIT" state and terminates all its action executions in an "END" state.

The mediation agent realizes services by interacting with the agent wrappers on the basis of conversations (sending and receiving XML (eXtensible Markup Language) messages by invoking a method called sendXML()).

The application T1 in the example was in reality a Web page that contains information published by the first teacher (Teacher1). This page contains a link called *"Courses"* that points to another page that was structured as follows: the page contains a list of all the course names that are given by the corresponding teacher, together with four additional links under the name of each course: *Syllabus, Course Notes, Old Exams, Other Information.* The role of the agent wrapper for this application was to follow the link *"Courses,"* to look up the course names for which information is required, and finally, to return the information about each of these courses in form of four URLs: one for the *Syllabus,* one for the *Course Notes,* one for the *Old Exams,* and the last one for *Other Information.*

The second teacher (Teacher 2) is a somewhat conservative one and takes no stock in Web pages. He is maintaining a simple database about the courses he is offering. The information contained in the database is as follows: for each course, the name of the course, a short syllabus in textual form, and the FTP address of a zipped file (the zipped file contains course notes, slides, old exams and any other kind of additional information that concerns the course) are stored. The application T2 is therefore a database application for answering queries about the courses offered by Teacher 2.

The third teacher (Teacher 3), unlike Teacher 2, is very active in research in the domain of agents. He has just finished a recent agent project and he is proud of presenting his agent that supplies information about the courses he is offering in a customized and pretty manner. The application T3 is therefore an intelligent agent offering information about the courses given by Teacher 3.

The application USR in the implemented example gives the student the opportunity to update his profile, to initiate a query to look up information that is of interest to him, and finally, to see the result returned by the system or follow the returned URLs to obtain more details.

In this way the student is able to obtain up-to-date information at any time without needing to consult all the sites of the different instructors. The student needs only to initiate a query and the system will do the rest.

The agent wrapper of the application T1 was implemented as follows:

- Search the Web page of the teacher for the link *courses.*
- Open the Web page corresponding to that link.
- For each "course name" for which information is searched (needed) do the following:
  - Search this Web page for the "course name" (the "course name" is extracted automatically from the student profile by the agent wrapper for the user application (USR) and communicated to the agent wrapper of the teacher application (Web page of the teacher) by the mediation agent, as shown in Figure 1).
  - If the "course name" was found, then: search the Web page for four links: *Syllabus, Course Notes, Old Exams, Other Information,* occurring immediately after the "course name" and return the corresponding URLs, together with the "course name;" that is, store them temporarily before communicating them back to the mediation agent.
- Report all the information found to the mediation agent.

The agent wrapper for the application T2 is responsible for starting the application according to the conditions of the application, transforming requests for information about the courses (this information is communicated by the mediation agent) into queries to the database system, collecting the results of the queries, and finally replying these results to the mediation agent. The results consist of the syllabus for each course in textual form, followed by a FTP address where a zipped file containing course notes, slides, old exams and any other kind of additional information that concerns the course can be downloaded.

Even though there is no need for wrapping the application T3 since it is already an agent, the mediation agent should be able to invoke and to benefit from the services offered by the agent T3; that is, there should be some way of understanding between the mediation agent and the agent T3. In this case, this is the responsibility of the agent wrapper for T3.

In our example, the resources invoked by the system (Web page of Teacher 1, database system of Teacher 2, and intelligent agent of Teacher 3) were as shown in Figure 2. The profile of each student consisted of the student's name, id, and names of the courses in which the student is registered in the current semester, in addition to other information concerning his or her study. One of the students, for example, was registered in the current semester in the courses "Artificial Intelligence," "Compiler Design," and "Database Systems". By clicking on the icon "Search Info" on the user screen a search is initiated by the multi-agent system and finally the information found by the system is displayed on the user screen. The information consists in this case of the following:

- Four URLs for *Syllabus, Course Notes, Old Exams, Other Information* for the course "Artificial Intelligence" given by Teacher 1.
- A pretty collection of information (proposed by agent T3) about the course "Artificial Intelligence" given by Teacher 3.
- Four URLs for *Syllabus, Course Notes, Old Exams, Other Information* for the course "Compiler Design" given by Teacher 1.
- A short syllabus in textual form for the course "Database Systems" given by Teacher 2, followed by the FTP address of a zipped file containing additional information about the course.
- A pretty collection of information (proposed by agent T3) about the course "Database Systems" given by Teacher 3.

The student can see the corresponding information immediately or follow the different links, and as sketched in the example, the student needs only to state *what* he or she wants. In this case the student wants information about the courses he or she is registered in for the current semester; this is reflected by the student's profile. The system is responsible for deciding *which* resources to invoke. In this case the system will consult the Web page of Teacher 1, the database system of Teacher 2, and the intelligent agent of Teacher 3. In general, however, there should be some strategy for discovering the location of potentially useful information; for example, among the whole Web, among a reasonable part of the Web, among a set of databases, or among any other heterogeneous set of resources. The system is also responsible for the *how* to invoke the resources once found. In this case, each of the resources (the Web page of Teacher 1, the database system of Teacher 2, and the intelligent agent of Teacher 3) is invoked (searched, queried, or conversed) by the agent wrapper, which is created manually (by the programmer). The mediation agent, also created manually, travels between the agent wrappers transporting queries and collecting answers to the queries. In general, however, the creation of the mediation agent and the agent wrappers, that is, the creation of the whole multi-agent system, should be automated. The multi-agent system to be created depends on the resources to be invoked, their locations and the profile of the student. The automation task may therefore be very difficult: the resources can be numerous and may have very different formats (they may be unstructured Web pages, databases, agents) and this complicates the creation of the agent wrappers (how to wrap an unknown application), as well as the creation of the mediation agent (which route to take to navigate to the different agent wrappers, how to communicate with the different agent wrappers).

Of course, the system in its current state is still simple and there are many ways for improvement. These are discussed in the following section.

Discussion

In the following we focus on three interesting points. The first point concerns the identification of relevant information from dynamic resources with little or no user intervention; that is, identification of the application or the site that may help in finding the relevant information. In the current system this issue is hard-coded into the architecture of the system. In general, however, heuristics (semantic aspects) extracted from common sense knowledge, for example, by imitating humans (i.e., make an exploratory study to investigate the activities of humans as they try to identify sites (applications, Websites) that may be useful, (i.e., contain useful information)) can be incorporated into the system to help locate the sites. The idea of incorporating "common sense" is not new. It goes back to the 1980s, as artificial intelligence researchers were examining approaches to representing the everyday world (see for example McCarthy, 1983). Similar ideas were also investigated in Sterling (1997).

In addition, the user interaction can be exploited to label the information (as positive and negative examples) for learning purposes. The system asks its users to label its answers as correct or not (suitable or not). The feedback it receives from its users can be used to continually improve its performance. It might be used as training data for an algorithm that attempts to learn the conventions underlying the resource (application or site) placement. This can be done in a similar way as discussed in Shakes et al. (1997).

Incorporating such learning capabilities is of great importance, especially because people may find articulating what they want hard, but they are very good at recognizing it when they see it. This insight leads to the utilization of relevance feedback, where people rate applications or sites as interesting or not and the system tries to find those that match the interesting examples (positive examples) and do not match the not interesting examples (negative examples). With sufficient positive and negative examples, modern machine learning techniques can classify new sites with impressive accuracy.

A long-term aim, therefore, will consist of automating the creation of the multi-agent system that implements the IC system, that is, making it possible to wrap each application or site that was identified to be appropriate (by observing the user activities, learning, or using any other suitable method) and changing the mediation agent appropriately.

Figure 2. Resources Invoked in the Implemented Example

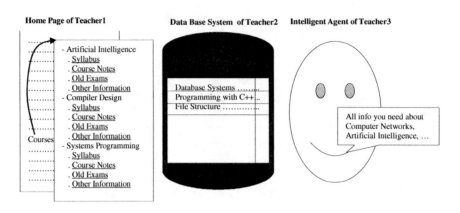

The second point concerns the customized presentation of current information, that is, presenting the information really needed by the user. In the current system this issue is hard-coded into the mediation agent. In general, however, task context and user preferences (interests), which are modeled in form of user profiles, can be used to automate query formulation. User profiles are semantic aspects expressed in human terms. Queries are syntactic structures. An appropriate method should be developed to link them together. A long-term aim, therefore, will consist of automating the creation of the mediation agent from the user profile.

The third point is tightly related to the two previous ones and concerns the creation of the profile of the user, which is of great importance for knowing which kind of information is needed by the user, where this information can be found, and how this information can be retrieved. In the current system this issue is mastered mainly by the user (student), who is responsible for changing his or her profile. In general, however, automation is also possible in this case (even partially), especially in the part concerning the user preferences in which machine learning techniques can be applied. The acquisition of user profiles by unobtrusive monitoring of browsing behavior and application of supervised machine learning techniques with an appropriate representation to extract user preferences can be explored. This can, for example, be done in a similar way as discussed in Stuart et al. (2001), where research papers published online are recommended to researchers who need to know about new papers in their general field of interest, and older papers relating to their current work. The success of the acquisition of user profiles using machine learning techniques depends of course on the domain of application.

Systems working on a person's behalf and incorporating these capabilities will enforce a powerful abstraction: a person is able to state *what* he/she wants (or at least is able to recognize *what* he/she wants when he/she sees it), and the IC system is responsible for deciding *which* resources to invoke in response and *how* to do so.

Such a system is able to use software tools and services on a person's behalf. Tool use is one of the hallmarks of intelligence (Etzioni, 1997). In many cases, IC systems rely on the same tools and utilities available to human computer users.

CONCLUSIONS

In this chapter we were able to demonstrate an example of how the multi-agent paradigm can be used to approach a solution for the problem of information customization. Many of my students have had the opportunity to run the system and test it. It was interesting to observe that the most fascinating point for them was to see the system presenting the information found in a somehow customized manner for each individual student. The example is simple but the results are encouraging and future work will be focused on improving the system and studying how such simple examples built with insight should lead to identification of key difficulties, useful abstractions and a general method for solving the problem and revelation of the issues.

In general, at an early stage of research as we are currently at with IC systems, an experimental approach that eschews formalism and models in favor of building systems is preferred. It is necessary to have real examples of systems to think about. Having gathered enough experience with useful IC systems, the challenge will be to make them more intelligent by inventing new AI techniques and extending familiar ones. This should be done while keeping the IC systems usable and useful.

RELATED WORK

Because of the information overload problem created by the unstructured nature of the Web, the trend to use intelligent agents as a promising solution for assisting and facilitating the processes of information extraction and information customization was increasing in recent years. Brown et al. (1995), Etzioni and Weld (1995), Hermans (1996) and Oliver (1996) are just some examples.

The intelligent agent's roles normally revolve around satisfying user demands for information. In general, the agents involved take on the task of gathering information to meet a variety of user needs. In Brown et al. (1995), for example, it is suggested that a more comprehensive framework would include both supply and demand agents. Supply agents provide information to demand agents. Specifically, supply agents effectively configure information for information consumers. Demand agents search for needed information.

These agents are typically designed to search the Web for information to meet user goals. There are several types of these agents being developed in recent times. One example is Internet SoftBot, which was developed at the University of Washington (Etzioni & Weld, 1995). Softbot is a prototype implementation of a high-level assistant. In contrast to systems for assisted browsing or information retrieval, the Softbot can accept high-level user goals and dynamically synthesize the appropriate sequence of Internet commands to satisfy those goals (Etzioni & Weld, 1995). A third type of agent may exist, called a broker agent, which matches supply agent capabilities with demand agent needs (Brown et al., 1995).

Agents could also play various roles in an agent-enabled system architecture. Some could act in the role of intelligent user interface managers, drawing on the resources of other agents working behind the scenes (Arens et al., 1991; Browne et al., 1990; Kay, 1990; Neal & Shapiro, 1994; Sullivan & Tyler, 1991). Such agents would work in concert to help coordinate the selection of the appropriate display modes and representations for the relevant data (Bradshaw & Boose, 1992), incorporating semantic representations of the knowledge in the documents to enhance navigation and information retrieval (Boy, 1992; Bradshaw & Boy, 1993; Gruber et al., 1992; Lethbridge & Skuce, 1992; Mathe & Chen, 1994). Because the layout and content of the views would be driven by context and configuration models rather than by hand-crafted user-interface code, significant economies could be realized as the data and software components are reused and semi-automatically reconfigured for different settings and purposes. Some agents might be represented explicitly to the user as various types of personal assistants (Maes, 1994). Ideally, each software component would be "agent-enabled;" however for practical reasons components may at times still rely on traditional inter-application communication mechanisms rather than agent-to-agent protocols.

Though research in the domain of intelligent agents had been ongoing for more than twenty years, agents really became a buzzword in the popular computing press (and also within the artificial intelligence and computing communities) around 1994. During that year several key agent-related publications appeared. A report entitled "Intelligent agents: The new revolution in software" (Guilfoyle & Warner, 1994) wildly speculated on market sector totals for agent software and products by the year 2000. The first of now several special issues of the *Communications of the ACM* on agents appeared in 1994 and it included articles like "Agents that reduce work and information overload" (Maes, 1994) and "How might people interact with software agents" (Norman, 1994). Then there was a *Byte* article on "The network with smarts" (Reinhardt, 1994). Indeed, during late 1994 and throughout 1995 and 1996, there was an explosion of agent-related articles in the popular computing press. It is no coincidence that this explosion coincided with that of the Web. The field has clearly matured since with the publication of certain key papers and books, including Wooldridge and Jennings (1995), Nwana (1996), Bradshaw (1997a), Jennings and Wooldridge (1998) and Nwana and Azarmi (1997), amongst others. Several annual and biennial conferences now grace the area, including the International Conference on Multi-Agent Systems (ICMAS), the International Conference on the Practical Application of Intelligent Agents and Multi-Agent Technology (PAAM), and the International Conference on Autonomous Agents (AA). ICMAS, PAAM and AA held their first conferences in 1995, 1996 and 1997 respectively. These conferences and numerous other agent-oriented national and international workshops, many agent special issues of journals, agent books, agent standardization initiatives such as FIPA, the *Journal of Autonomous Agents and Multi-Agent Systems* (JAMAS), the book "Readings in Agents" (Huhns & Singh, 1998), initiatives such as the AgentLink Network of Excellence, and so forth all bear testimony to a quickly maturing area.

Despite the narrow scope of early agent research, a fair number of useful agent systems have been developed. In contrast to former days, information has long lost its automatic association with text. In addition to text there are graphics, image, speech, video, and mixtures of all these information types. These "new" information types gain significance not only in everyday life but also within the professional realm of enterprises that are faced with today's information flood. As a consequence, the methods and algorithms devised in the early days of agents have to be reconsidered, adapted, or even re-developed. New agent methods and algorithms are now emerging because of the efforts of both IT professionals in companies and agent researches in academia. The agent systems emerging must have the ability to cope with hypermedia information, for example, hypertexts and a multitude of different media. The problem in enterprises is often that it is unknown at the time of purchasing or devising new systems what kind of information must be considered and — above all — in what form this information will be available when the agent system is in operation. An important problem is therefore: how agent systems can be used to find and deal with unknown information.

Some current agent research work is therefore focusing on issues such as:

- Adaptive choice of and balanced access to sources: the emphasis here is on collaborative learning of how to select information sources/search engines based on the principle of maximum expected utility and on improving resource utilization and global performance (load balancing) (Sen et al., 1999).
- Cooperative and adaptive distributed data mining: the emphasis here is on collaborative learning of how and when to apply methods for knowledge representation and discovery in distributed information sources (Romaniuk, 2000).

There are also many other problems that arise when using agents to implement IC systems. The major problem of Internet and Web, namely the huge amount of heterogeneous information sources consisting of large volumes of (non-, semi-) structured, volatile (dangling links, relocated), redundant (mirrored, copied) data, causes an "information overload" of the user. This complicates the process of searching for relevant information ("needle-in-the-hay-stack") and the process of coping with system, structural and semantic heterogeneity (Sheth et al., 1999).

The impact of heterogeneity and globalization on information overload is sketched by the following problems and steps towards solving them:

- How to reconcile differences in data structure: reconcile different data models, content representation (schematic).
- How to deal with semi-structured or unstructured data: define appropriate wrapper and translator.
- What about media data?: extract and correlate various heterogeneous audio, video and image data.
- How to cope with differences in underlying terminologies: choose and map different domain ontologies used to describe content of information sources (semantics).
- How to reconcile contextual heterogeneity: differentiate between implicitly assumed contextual interpretations.
- How to cope with differences in query languages: use specific languages and operations for retrieving information.
- How to properly model content of sources: different levels of abstraction of information modeling at sources.
- How to query and fuse content from sources: identify/focus and keep track on which source has what subset of relevant information and combine partially relevant information from sources.
- How to discover relevant information resources: determine and keep track of relevant information sources, formulate appropriate requests to *(potentially millions of)* sources.

For these reasons, a framework that offers not only basic agent functionality but also the thread of control and the structure of the yet unknown agent application to be devised should be developed. This framework should allow a great deal of flexibility to a system developer and provide, at the same time, maximum support.

User modeling is typically knowledge-based or behavior-based. Knowledge-based approaches engineer static models of users and dynamically match users to the closest model. Behavior-based approaches use the user's behavior itself as a model, often using machine learning techniques to discover useful patterns of behavior. User modeling changed in the 1990s, moving from the static hand-crafted representations of the 1980s to dynamic behavior-based models. There are also approaches that try to bring together ideas from knowledge-based and behavior-based modeling to address the problem domain by allowing domain knowledge to be used when constructing the user profile. Kobsa (1990) provides a good survey of user modeling techniques.

Another important point in relationship with IC systems concerns their evaluation. Evaluation of IC systems and real-world knowledge acquisition systems in general, as Shadlbolt (1999) discusses, is both tricky and complex. A lot of evaluations are performed with user log data simulating real user activity or with standard benchmark collections. Although these evaluations are useful, especially for technique comparison, they must be backed up by real- world studies so we can see how the benchmark tests generalize to the real-world setting. A comparison of IC systems is also difficult since there are no widely used standards for reporting results. Where machine learning techniques are employed, standard tests such as precision and recall provide useful metrics for comparing learning algorithms. However, the best test of an IC system's ability to help a user is a user trial. Unfortunately, user trials in the literature do not follow a consistent methodology. These problems are also seen in the more general agent domain, where it has yet to be conclusively demonstrated if people really benefit from such information systems (Nwana, 1996).

FUTURE DIRECTION OF WORK

The next step for this work is to focus on automating the creation of the student profile and then on automating the multi-agent system; that is, creating the mediation agent directly from the student profile and knowing which sites should be wrapped by agent wrappers, also based on the knowledge contained in the student profile, and creating the agent wrappers. In a first step, the automation of the student profile creation may be done partially by adopting a behavioral user model based on monitoring the student and asking the student for relevance feedback. The statistical information generated by these approaches is then fed to some form of machine learning algorithm. In this way it will be possible to capture the student preferences concerning the sites that should be visited for collecting information. This will help in generating the agent wrappers of the multi-agent system. It will also be possible to capture the student preferences concerning the type of information that should be extracted from those sites. This will help in generating the mediation agent.

The idea of building a profile that is understandable by the users could be extended to actually visualizing the knowledge contained within it. This will allow the system to engage the user in dialogue about what exactly the user is interested in. The knowledge elicited from this dialogue should allow further improvements to the system. Additionally, visualizing the profile knowledge will allow users to build a better conceptual model of the system, helping to engender a feeling of control and eventually trust in the system and improved user understanding.

REFERENCES

Andrews, G.R. (2000). *Foundations of multithreaded, parallel, and distributed programming*. Addison-Wesley.

Arens, Y., Feiner, S., Foley, J., Hovy, E., John, B., Neches, R., Pausch, R., Schorr, H., & Swartout, W. (1991). *Intelligent user interfaces*. Report ISI/RR-91-288, USC/ Information Sciences Institute, Marina del Rey, California, USA.

Boy, G.A. (1992). Computer-integrated documentation. In E. Barrett (Ed.), *Sociomedia: Mutimedia, hypermedia, and the social construction of knowledge* (pp. 507-531). Cambridge, MA: MIT Press.

Bradshaw, J.M. (Ed.) (1997a). *Software agents*. Boston, MA: MIT Press.

Bradshaw, J.M. (1997b). An introduction to software agents. In J.M. Bradshaw (Ed.), *Software agents* (pp. 3-46).Menlo Park, CA: AAAI Press.

Bradshaw, J.M., & Boose, J.H. (1992). *Mediating representations for knowledge acquisition*. Seattle, WA: Boeing Computer Services.

Bradshaw, J.M., & Boy, G.A. (1993). *Adaptive documents*. Internal Technical Report EURISCO.

Brooks, R.A. (1991). Intelligence without reason. *Proceedings of the 1991 International Joint Conference on Artificial Intelligence,* (pp. 569-595).

Brown, C., Gasser, L., O'Leary, D.E., & Sangster, A. (1995). AI on the WWW supply and demand agents. *IEEE Expert, 10*(4), 50-55.

Browne, D., Totterdell, P., & Norman, M. (eds.). (1990). *Adaptive user interfaces*. San Diego, CA: Academic.

Cooley, R., Mobasher, B, & Srivastava, J. (1997, November). Web mining: Information and pattern discovery on the World Wide Web. *Proceedings of the 9th IEEE International Conference on Tools with Artificial Intelligence* (ICTAI'97), Newport Beach, California, USA.

Drucker, P.F., Dorothy, L., Susan, S., Brown, J.S., Garvin, D.A., & Harvard Business Review (1998). *Harvard Business Review on knowledge management*. Harvard Business School Press.

Etzioni, O. (1997). Moving up the information food chain: Deploying softbots on the World Wide Web. *AI Magazine, 18*(2), 11-18.

Etzioni, O., & Weld, D.S. (1995). Intelligent agents on the Internet: Fact, fiction, and forecast. *IEEE Expert, 10*(4), 44-49.

Franklin, S., & Graesser, A. (1997). Is it an agent, or just a program?: A taxonomy for autonomous agents. *Proceedings of the Third International Workshop on Agent Theories, Architectures, and Languages,* published as *Intelligent agents III,* (pp. 21-35). Springer-Verlag.

Genesereth, M.R., & Ketchpel, S.P. (1994). Software agents. *Communications of the ACM, 37*(7), 48-53.

Gruber, T.R., Tenenbaum, J.M., & Weber, J.C. (1992). Toward a knowledge medium for collaborative product development. In J.S. Gero (Ed.), *Proceedings of the Second International Conference on Artificial Intelligence in Design.*

Guilfoyle, C., & Warner, E. (1994). Intelligent agents: The new revolution in software. *Ovum Report, BCS Expert Systems 94 Conference (Applications Track),* Cambridge, UK, (pp. 359-371).

Hamdi, M.S. (2003a, May). An agent-based Aapproach for intelligent user interfaces. *Proceedings of the Fourth International Conference on Intelligent Processing and Manufacturing of Materials* (IPMM-03), Sendai, Japan.

Hamdi, M.S. (2003b, June). Information extraction using multi-agents. *Proceedings of the 2003 International Conference on Internet Computing* (IC'03), Las Vegas, Nevada, USA.

Hamdi, M.S. (2003c, September). Automation of information extraction. *Proceedings of the Seventh International Conference on Automation Technology* (Automation 2003), National Chung Cheng University, Chia-yi, Taiwan, ROC.

Harrison, C.G., Chess, D.M., & Kershenbaum, A. (1995). *Mobile agents: Are they a good idea?* IBM Research Report RC 19887.

Hearst, M. (1997). Distinguishing between Web data mining and information access. *Proceedings, Knowledge Discovery KDD-97,* Newport Beach, CA.

Hermans, B. (1996). Intelligent software agents on the Internet: An inventory of currently offered functionality in the information society & a prediction of (near-) future developments. Ph.D. dissertation, Tilbury University, Tilbury, The Netherlands.

Huhns, M.H., & Singh, M.P. (1998). *Readings in agents.* San Francisco, CA: Morgan Kaufmann.

Jennings, N.R., & Wooldridge, M. (1998). *Agent technology: Foundations, applications, and markets.* London: Springer.

Jennings, N.R., Vagra, L.Z., Aarnts, R.P., Fuchs, J., & Sharek, P. (1993). Transforming stand-alone expert systems into a community of cooperating agents. *International Journal of Engineering Applications of AI, 6*(4), 317-331.

Kawamura, T., Hasegawa, T., Ohsuga, A., & Honiden, S. (2000). Bee-gent: Bonding and encapsulation enhancement agent framework for development of distributed systems. *Systems and Computers in Japan, 31*(13), 42-56.

Kay, A. (1990). User interface: A personal view. In B. Laurel (Ed.), *The art of human-computer interface design* (pp. 191-207). Reading, MA: Addison-Wesley.

Kobsa, A. (1990). User modeling in dialog systems: Potentials and hazards. *AI & Society: The Journal of Human and Machine Intelligence. 4*(3), 214-231.

Krishnapuram, R., Joshi, A., Nasraoui, O., & Yi, L. (2001). Low complexity fuzzy relational clustering algorithms for Web mining. *IEEE Transactions Fuzzy Systems, 9*(4), 596-607.

Lethbridge, T.C., & Skuce, D. (1992). Beyond hypertext: Knowledge management for technical documentation. *Proceedings of the 10ᵗʰ Annual International Conference on Systems Documentation,* Ottawa, Ontario, Canada, (pp. 313-322).

Liebowitz, J., & Wilcox, L. (1997). *Knowledge management and its integrative elements.* CRC Press.

Maes, P. (1994). Agents that reduce work and information overload. *Communications of the ACM, 37*(7), 31-40.

Mathe, N., & Chen, J. (1994). A user-centered approach to adaptive hypertext based on an information relevance model. *Proceedings of the Fourth International Conference on User Modeling,* Hyannis, MA, (pp. 107-114).

McCarthy, J. (1960). Recursive functions and symbolic expressions. *CACM, 3*(4), 184-195.

McCarthy, J. (1983). Some expert systems need common sense. In P. Heinz (Ed.), *Computer culture: The scientific, intellectual and social impact of the computer 426* (pp. 129-137). 1994 Annals of The New York Academy of Sciences.

McCarthy, J., & Hayes, P.J. (1969). Some philosophical problems from the standpoint of artificial intelligence. *Machine Intelligence, 4*(1), 463-502.

Minsky, M. (1986). *The society of mind.* New York: Simon and Schuster.

Mitchell, T.M. (1997). *Machine learning.* New York: McGraw-Hill.

Neal, J.G., & Shapiro, S.C. (1994). Knowledge-based multimedia systems. In J.F.K. Buford (Ed.), *Multimedia system* (pp. 403-438). Reading, MA: Addison-Wesley.

Negroponte, N. (1970). *The architecture machine: Towards a more human environment.* Cambridge: MIT Press.

Newell, A. (1982). The knowledge level. *Artificial Intelligence, 18*(1), 87-127.

Newell, A., Shaw, J.C., & Simon, H. (1959). A general problem-solving program for a computer. *Computer and Automation, 8*(7), 10-16.

Nilsson, N.J. (1971). *Problem-solving methods in artificial intelligence.* New York: McGraw-Hill.

Nilsson, N.J. (1984, April). *Shakey the robot.* SRI A.I. Center, Technical Note 323.

Norman, D. (1994). How might people interact with agents. *Communications of the ACM, 37*(7), 68-76.

Nwana, H.S. (1996). Software agents: An overview. *The Knowledge Engineering Review, 11*(3), 205-244.

Nwana, H.S., & Azarmi, N. (Eds.). (1997). Software agent and soft computing: Towards enhancing machine intelligence. *Lecture notes in artificial intelligence 1198.* New York: Springer-Verlag.

Oliver, J.R. (1996). *On artificial agents for negotiation in electronic commerce.* Ph.D. dissertation, University of Pennsylvania.

Reinhardt, A. (1994). The network with smarts. *Byte, 19*(10), 51-64.

Rich, E. (1979). User modeling via stereotypes. *Cognitive Sciences, 3*(1), 329-354.

Romaniuk, S.G. (2000). Using intelligent agents to identify missing and exploited children. *IEEE Intelligent Systems, 15*(2), 27-30.

Rumelhart, D.E., Hilton, G.E., & Williams, R.J. (1986). Learning internal representations by error propagation. In D.E. Rumelhart & J.L McClelland (Eds.), *Parallel distributed processing.* Cambridge, MA: MIT Press.

Schreiber, G., de Hoog, R., Akkermans, H., Anjewierden, A., Shadbolt, N., & van de Velde, W. (2000). *Knowledge engineering and management.* MIT Press.

Scime, A. (2004). Guest editor's introduction: Special issue on web content mining. *Journal of Intelligent Information Systems, 22*(3), 211-213.

Sebastiani F. (2002). Machine learning in automated text categorization. *ACM Computing Surveys (CSUR), 34*(1), 1-47.

Sen, S., Biswas, A., & Gosh, S. (1999). Adaptive choice of information sources. In M. Klusch (Ed.), *Intelligent information agents.* Springer.

Shadbot, N., O'Hara, K., & Crown, L. (1999). The experimental evaluation of knowledge acquisition techniques and methods: History, problems and new directions. *International Journal of Human-Computer Studies, 51*(4), 729-755.

Shakes, J., Langheinrich, M., & Etzioni, O. (1997). Dynamic reference sifting: A case study in the home page domain. *Proceedings of the 6th International World Wide Web Conference,* Santa Clara, California, USA, (pp. 189-200).

Sheth, A., Kashyap, V., & Lima, T. (1999). Semantic information brokering: How can a multi-agent approach help? *Proceedings of Cooperative Information Agents III,* LNAI 1652. Springer.

Sterling, L. (1997). On finding needles in WWW haystacks. *Proceedings of the 10th Australian Joint Conference on Artificial Intelligence,* AI'97, Perth, Australia. Published as *Advanced topics in artificial intelligence,* (pp. 25-36). Springer-Verlag.

Stuart, E.M. (2000, August). *Interface agents: A review of the field.* Technical Report Number: ECSTR-IAM01-001, ISBN: 0854327320, University of Southampton.

Stuart, E.M., David, C.D., & Nigel, R.S. (2001, October). Capturing knowledge of user preferences: Ontologies in recommender systems. *Proceedings of the First International Conference on Knowledge Capture* (K-CAP 2001), Victoria, B.C., Canada.

Sullivan, J.W., & Tyler, S.W. (eds.). (1991). *Intelligent user interfaces.* New York: Association of Computing Machinery.

Turing, A.M. (1937). On computable numbers with an application to the Entscheidungs problem. *Proceedings of London Math. Soc.,* 2(43), 544-546.

Turing, A.M. (1950). *Computing machinery and intelligence. Mind, 49,* 433-460.

Wiederhold, G. (1992). Mediators in the architecture of future information systems. *IEEE Computer, 25*(3), 38-49.

Wooldridge, M.J., & Jennings, N.R. (1995). Intelligent agents: Theory and practice. *The Knowledge Engineering Review, 10*(2), 115-152.

Chapter XII

Web Graph Clustering for Displays and Navigation of Cyberspace

Xiaodi Huang
The University of Southern Queensland, Australia

Wei Lai
Swinburne University of Technology, Australia

ABSTRACT

This chapter presents a new approach to clustering graphs, and applies it to Web graph display and navigation. The proposed approach takes advantage of the linkage patterns of graphs, and utilizes an affinity function in conjunction with the k-nearest neighbor. This chapter uses Web graph clustering as an illustrative example, and offers a potentially more applicable method to mine structural information from data sets, with the hope of informing readers of another aspect of data mining and its applications.

INTRODUCTION

A graph is suitable for World Wide Web (WWW) navigation. Nodes in a graph can be used to represent URLs and edges between nodes represent links between URLs. We can look at the entire cyberspace of the WWW as one graph — a huge and dynamic growing graph. It is, however, impossible to display this huge graph on the computer screen.

Most current research interests are moving towards using "site mapping" methods (Chen, 1997; Maarek & Shaul, 1997) in an attempt to find an effective way of constructing a structured geometrical map for a single Website (a local map). This can guide the user through only a very limited region of cyberspace, and does not help the user in his/her overall journey through cyberspace.

Huang et al. (1998) proposed an online exploratory visualisation approach, which provides a major departure from traditional site-mapping methods. This approach does not pre-define the geometrical structure of a specific Website (a part of cyberspace), but incrementally calculates and maintains the visualisation of a small subset of cyberspace online corresponding to the change in the user's focus. In other words, following the user's orientation, a sequence of Web sub-graphs is automatically displayed with the smooth animation. This feature enables the user to logically explore the entire cyberspace without requiring the whole structure of cyberspace to be known.

In real applications, graphs may be huge in terms of the number of nodes and edges. Many graph drawing algorithms have been developed (Battista, 1998), but most of them have difficulty dealing with large graphs with thousands of nodes. Clustering graphs is one efficient method to draw large graphs even though other techniques exist, such as fisheye view, hyperbolic geometry (Burchard, 1995) and distortion-oriented presentation (Leung & Apperly, 1994). A clustered graph can significantly reduce visual complexity by replacing a set of nodes in a cluster with one abstract node. Moreover, a hierarchically clustered graph can find superimposed structures over the original graph through a recursive clustering process.

The Web graph has recently been used to model the link structure of the Web. The studies of such graphs can yield valuable insights into Web algorithms for crawling, searching and discovery of Web communities. This chapter proposes a new approach to clustering the Web graph. The proposed algorithm identifies a small subset of the graph as "core" members of clusters, and then incrementally constructs the clusters using a selection criterion. Two qualitative criteria are proposed to measure the quality of graph clustering. We have implemented our algorithm and demonstrated a set of arbitrary graphs with good results.

This chapter is organized as follows. The next section introduces the background of our prototype system of Web navigation using graph layout. We then discuss some issues on graph clustering, followed by our approach described in detail. We present an empirical evaluation of a set of arbitrary graph clustering by using our approach. After the applications are briefly provided, this chapter ends with the summary of our work.

BACKGROUND

Examples of Web Graph Displays

We first have a quick look at our Web graph display system. Our system can ensure that any online Web sub-graph, as shown in Figure 1, has no overlapping node images and fits in the window. Three kinds of modes for the user's interaction are provided. In the mode *LayoutAdjust,* the user can adjust a Web sub-graph layout. If the user clicks a node in the Web sub-graph, the sub-graph of this node switches between invisibility and visibility. Figure 2 shows the result after the user clicks the nodes - Phone, Fax and Teaching in the graph shown in Figure 1. If the user clicks these nodes again, their sub-graphs would become invisible (i.e., they would disappear, as shown in Figure 1). In this way the user can make a node's sub-graph visible or invisible by direct manipulation.

Figure 1. A Web Sub-Graph Display

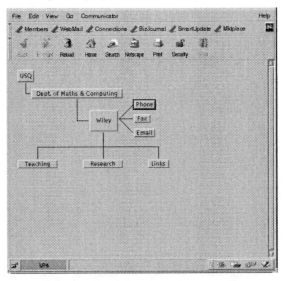

Figure 2. Some Sub-Graphs become Visible after the User's Interaction

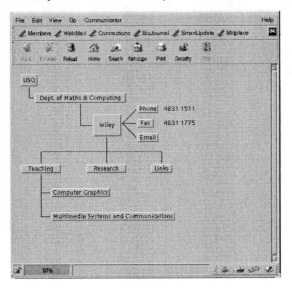

When a node's sub-graph becomes visible, our system checks whether this new sub-graph overlaps any part of the current display graph. If so, those overlapping parts of the sub-graph become invisible automatically. Given that the node with the label *Research* is clicked, the sub-graph associated with this node appears and the sub-graph associated with the node *Teaching* automatically disappears, as shown in Figure 3.

Each node in the Web graph is linked to a URL. For example, the node with the label Computer Graphics is linked to the Website of the unit 66333 - Computer Graphics. The

Figure 3. A Sub-Graph becoming Visible Makes Another One Invisible

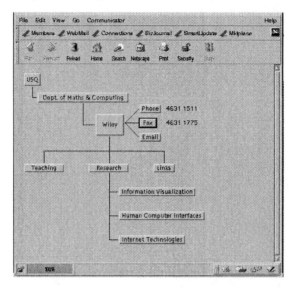

Figure 4. A Web Page Corresponding to a Node is Shown

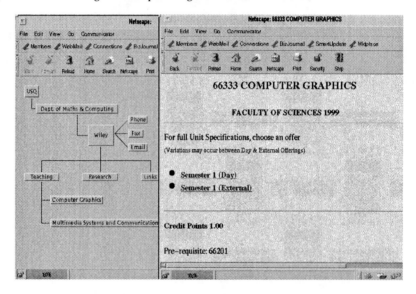

detailed Web page content associated with a node in a Web sub-graph will be displayed by easily clicking this node in the *ShowPage* mode. Figure 4 shows the result of the user's selection of the node with the label Computer Graphics in the ShowPage mode.

In the third interaction mode, called the *Navigation* mode, triggered by clicking the right mouse button, the user can change the focused node to traverse another Web sub-graph. With the current focused node Wiley in the *Navigation* mode, if the user clicks the nodes Links and then its child node CNN, a Web sub-graph corresponding to this

Figure 5. Another Website and Its Web Graph

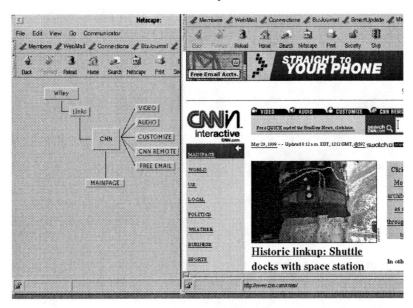

new current focused node CNN will be presented as indicated in the left window in Figure 5. A Web sub-graph can keep track of the user's navigation by recording the history nodes visited, two nodes — Wiley and Links in the above navigation, for example. Further, all other nodes linking to the CNN node in the Website are dynamically added in this way: our system analysed the source HTML file of the CNN Website and extracted all the hyperlinked URLs in this file to generate those new nodes in the Web sub-graph. The system can navigate from one Website to another in the same way.

The user can readily switch between the three interaction modes. If the user within the *ShowPage* mode clicks the node CNN, the CNN Web page appears (Figure 5). At the same time, the user can also change to the *LayoutAdjust* mode by clicking the left mouse button.

Our online Web sub-graph is formed dynamically on the basis of the user's focus. When the user changes the focus (i.e., click a node in the *Navigation* mode), the Web sub-graph is updated by dropping old nodes and adding new ones. This is similar to driving a car: new views arrive in the front and old views vanish in the back.

Automatic Graph Layout Techniques

The automatic graph layout techniques used in our system can ensure that a Web graph layout fits in the display window and has no overlaps.

The most difficult editing function for a Web graph is layout — assigning a position for each node and a curve for each edge. The assignment must be chosen to maximize the readability of the resulting picture. A good layout is like a picture — worth a thousand words, while a poor layout can confuse or mislead the user. This problem is called the graph drawing problem — how to create a nice layout automatically. Automatic layout can release the user from the time-consuming and detail-intensive chore of generating a readable diagram. However, most existing systems that incorporate diagrams such as CASE tools do not support automatic layout. The diagram layouts in these systems have to be adjusted manually by the user using the mouse.

Most classical graph drawing algorithms (Battista, 1998) produce aesthetically pleasing abstract graph layouts. These algorithms can be applied to draw practical graphs as long as the nodes take very little space. The reason is that such algorithms were often originally designed for abstract graphs in which the nodes occupy little or no space. The images of nodes in graph applications can, however, be represented as circles, boxes, diamonds or other shapes, and may contain a considerable amount of text and graphics. Moreover, the nodes are used to represent sub-graphs in some systems (Eades, 1990; Huang, 1998), and may be quite unpredictable in their sizes and shapes. Applying such algorithms to practical graphs may therefore result in overlapping nodes and/or edge-node intersections. Algorithms that exemplify this problem can be found in Eades (1991) and Lai (2002). Producing diagrams that are symmetric and well spread out, these classical algorithms have great potential for wide use of visualisation of network structures, if we can remove the probably produced overlapping nodes of nontrivial size in such diagrams.

We are interested in the problem of how to display diagrams, namely how to lay out practical graphs in applications. The term abstract graph layout refers to layout techniques for abstract graphs where nodes are negligible in size, while the term practical graph layout implies those for practical graphs where nodes vary in shape and size.

Our approach makes use of existing classical graph drawing algorithms by applying one of them to a practical graph first. Some post-processes of avoiding overlaps of node images and edge-node intersections by rearranging the graph layout are then employed (Eades, 1991; Lai, 2002). Additionally, this approach to adjusting a graph layout can preserve the mental map of the original graph (Eades, 1991; Misue, 1995).

The critical part of our approach is to remove overlapping nodes. We use the techniques for removing overlaps of node images and edge-node intersections (Eades, 1991; Lai, 2002). We have experimented with these techniques using many sets of overlapping nodes and found that it is quite effective.

When the number of nodes in a graph becomes large enough, the user cannot perceive all elements at the same time. This is another import issue in graph layout. This problem can be solved by clustering the graph, which forms sub-graphs and sub-graph nodes. One of these clustering techniques will be introduced in the following sections.

ISSUES ON GRAPH CLUSTERING

Generally speaking, the purpose of cluster analysis is to organize data into meaningful groups: data objects in the same group are highly similar while those in different groups are dissimilar. Clustering is a process of finding such groups based on chosen semantics. According to these semantics, two kinds of clustering approaches can be roughly classified: content-based clustering and structure-based clustering. Content-based clustering uses semantic aspects of data such as category labels. In contrast, structure-based clustering takes advantage of structural information about data. Moreover, structure-based clustering is domain-independent; thus it is suitable for graph visualization.

During the clustering of a graph, a metric of the nodes in the graph is required to measure its complexity. Based on this metric, existing approaches of partitioning graphs (Erez Hartuv, 2000; Matula, 1969, 1970) can loosely be divided into the following groups: *connectivity based partitions,* which use standard concepts from Graph Theory such as components, cliques, and *k*-cores; *distance partitions from selected subsets,* which utilize neighborhoods of "central" nodes; *neighborhood based partitions,* in which a cluster is a set of units with similar neighborhoods such as degree partition, regular partition, and colorings; and *other approaches,* such as eigen-vector methods. These approaches have proven useful in graph partitioning. Some of these approaches cannot, however, be directly applied into graph visualization because they depend on a good initial embedding of a graph, the creation of which is expensive, particularly for a large graph.

In graph visualization, a node structural metric is used in different forms. One simple example of such a metric is the degree of a node, for example, the number of edges connected to the node. A metric more specific to trees, called the Strahler metric, is applied to tree graphs, in which nodes with the highest Strahler metric values generate a skeleton or backbone, which is then emphasized (M.I. Herman, 1998; M.S. Herman, 1999). Using the distance metric, Botafogo et al. (1991) constructed a *distance matrix* that has as its entries the distances of every node to every other node, to identify hierarchies in an organization.

A clustered graph can be laid out more quickly than the original graph, as the clustered nodes and edges reduce the graph complexity. Relatively speaking, the storage space of a clustered graph is less than that of the original graph. Furthermore, clustering nodes provides a basis for navigation and context clustering, which is accomplished by three possible approaches (Kimelman, 1994):

- *Ghosting:* deemphasizing nodes, or relegating nodes to the background.
- *Hiding:* not displaying nodes with a metric under a cutoff value.
- *Grouping:* grouping nodes under a new supernode representation.

We propose a new approach to graph clustering and have developed an algorithm for graph clustering. This algorithm identifies a small subset of the graph as "core" members of clusters, and then incrementally constructs the clusters by a selection criterion.

APPROACH TO GRAPH CLUSTERING

To describe our algorithm for graph clustering, we provide the following definitions.

Definitions

Supposing a given Web graph $G = (V, E)$ and an integer k, we partition G into subgraphs $G_1, G_2, ..., G_k$, such that:

$$G = \cup_{i=1}^{k} G_i \text{ and } G_i \cap G_j = \phi, i \neq j$$

An optimization criterion of this partition is the well-known Minimum Cuts.

Given a subset T of V, the cut $\delta(T)$ induced by T is the subset of edges $(i, j) \in E$ such that $|\{i,j\} \cap T| = 1$. That is, $\delta(T)$ consists of all those edges with exactly one endpoint in T. Actually, for each edge $e \in E$, if there is a nonnegative cost (or capacity) c_e, the cost of a cut $\delta(T)$ is then the sum of the costs of the edges in that cut:

$$c(\delta(T)) = \sum_{e \in \delta(T)} c_e$$

The minimum cut is to find a cut with the minimum cost measured by the above equation. Since all the costs in our Web graph are 1s, the minimum cut thus becomes the problem of finding a cut with as few edges as possible in the graph.

A graph can be partitioned into different clusters in various ways. So we need a quantitative function to measure the quality of clustering. In general, a good clustering algorithm should produce clusters with high "homogeneity (or cohesion)" and low "separation (or coupling)". The nodes in a cluster are highly connected to other nodes in the same cluster. At the same time, the nodes in different clusters are separated with a minimum cut.

To measure the homogeneity of a cluster, we use the following function:

$$\eta(C_i) = \begin{cases} \dfrac{2}{|C_i|(|C_i|-1)} \displaystyle\sum_{v_i, v_k \in C_i} |\{e_{lk}\}| & |C_i| \neq 1 \\ 1 & |C_i| = 1 \end{cases} \tag{2.1}$$

According to the above function, if the nodes in C_i are completely connected, then the cluster C_i will have $|C_i|(|C_i|-1)/2$ edges in total and namely $\eta(C_i) = 1$. Additionally, for a singleton cluster $|C_i| = 1$, we also define the value of its homogeneity as 1.

Definition 1. *Homogeneity of Clusters:* Given a graph $G = (V, E)$ and its subgraphs G_1, $G_2, ..., G_m$, then the average homogeneity of all clusters in G is:

$$C_H(G) = \frac{1}{|S|} \sum_i^{|S|} \eta(C_i)$$

where $|S|$ is the number of clusters in G, $|C_i|$ the number of nodes in the cluster C_i, and $\eta(C_i)$ determined by equation (2.1).

Obviously, the value range of homogeneity is [0, 1]. Observe that the bigger the value of $C_H(G)$ is, the more cohesive the nodes in the clusters are.

To measure the degree of separation between two clusters, a function is required to accurately quantify the relative costs of the clustering. The sum of the edge costs in a minimum cut between two clusters is related to the sizes of the separated clusters. For this reason, a measurement of separation between two clusters can be given by:

$$\delta(C_i, C_j) = \frac{c(\delta(T))}{|C_i \| C_j |} = \frac{1}{|C_i \| C_j |} \sum_{v_l \in C_i, v_k \in C_j} c_{lk} \qquad (2.2)$$

where $i \neq j$ and c_{lk} is the cost of the edge between nodes v_1 and v_k with exactly one endpoint in the cut set. In our approach, we have $c_{lk} = 1$ if the nodes v_l and v_k are directly connected.

For a totally unconnected graph, namely without a cost for any cuts, we have $\delta(C_i, C_j) = 0$ based on the above function. On the other hand, if clusters C_i and C_j are a complete bipartite graph where every pair of nodes in C_i and C_j are adjacent, then we have $\delta(C_i, C_j) = 1$.

Definition 2. *Separation of Clusters:* Given a graph $G = (V, E)$ and its subgraphs G_1, G_2, ..., G_k, we use the arithmetic average as the measurement of the separations among the clusters:

$$C_S(G) = \frac{1}{n} \sum_{1 \leq i, j \leq k; i \neq j} \delta(C_i, C_j)$$

where n is the number of pairs of clusters whose member node(s) are directly connected, $0 < n \leq k(k - 1)/2$ and $\delta(C_i, C_j)$ is determined by equation (2.2).

Note that the smaller the value of $C_S(G)$ is, the less the cost of the cut. With the above definitions, the graph clustering problem can be defined as follows.

Definition 3. *Maximum Homogeneity of Graph Clustering:* Given a connected graph $G = (V, E)$ and an integer m, the G is partitioned into subgraphs G_1^l, G_2^l, $\cdots$, G_m^l, in the l different ways. If the following conditions hold true:

(1) $G = G^l = \cup_{i=1}^{m} G_i^l$

(2) $G_i^l \cap G_j^l = \phi, for \ \ i \neq j$

(3) $p = \arg \max_{l=1,\cdots,m} \{C_H(G^l)\}$

(4) $0 \leq C_H(G^l) \leq 1$

Then G_1^p, G_2^p, $\cdots$, G_m^p are called *Maximum Homogeneity clusters* of graph G.

Definition 4. *Minimum Coupling of Graph Clustering:* Given a connected graph $G = (V, E)$ and an integer m, the G is partitioned into subgraphs G_1^l, G_2^l, $\cdots$, G_m^l, in the l different ways. If the following conditions hold true:

(1) $G = G^l = \cup_{i=1}^m G^l_i$

(2) $G^l_i \cap G^l_j = \phi, for\, i \neq j$

(3) $p = \arg\min_{l=1,\cdots,m} \{C_s(G^l)\}$

(4) $0 \leq C_s(G^l) \leq 1$

Then $G^p_1, G^p_2, \cdots, G^p_m$ are called *Minimum Coupling of Graph Clusters* of graph G. In what follows, a few definitions used in the following algorithms are provided:

Definition 5. *Node degree:* The degree of a node v in a graph denoted by $\deg(v)$ is the number of edges incident with node v. The sum of the degrees of G is $2|E|$, that is:

$$\sum_{i=1}^{|V|} \deg(v_i) = 2\,|\,E\,|$$

Since every edge has exactly two endpoints, the average degree of G is $\mu = \overline{Deg}(G) = 2\,|\,E\,|\,/\,|V\,|$.

Definition 6. *Seed nodes:* A set of nodes whose degrees are greater than $\mu + \tau$, denoted by S, where τ is a threshold.

We usually define τ as a value related to σ because the *standard deviation* (a statistics term) σ is a measurement of how spread the distribution of the degrees is. In the special case of a fully connected graph, namely if the degree of every node is equal to μ, there will be no seed node. We can then start to construct the clusters from any node in G.

In order to introduce the k-nearest neighbor search, we define a distance function as follows:

Definition 7. *Distance Function $D(v,u)$:* A function used to compute the distance between nodes v and u where v and $u \in G$. It is actually the minimum length of all pairs of paths joining them, which is equal to the number of edges in the shortest path if such path exists, otherwise $D(v, u) = \infty$. The shortest path can be found by using Dijkstra's algorithm.

Definition 8. *K-nearest Neighbor Search:* For a query node $q \in G$ and a query parameter k, the k-nearest neighbor search returns a set k-$NN(q) \subset G$ that contains at least k nodes in G, and in which the following conditions hold:

$$D(u,q) \leq D(w,q), \forall u \in k\text{-}NN(q), \forall w \in G - k - NN(q), u \neq w$$

Consequently, the result set is $\{w \in G - k - NN(v) \,|\, D(w,v) \leq k\}$. For example, 1-NN (v) represents a set of nodes with which the node v incidents. Note that the node v is not included in the set of k-$NN(v)$.

Definition 9. *Affinity Function:* Given a connected graph $G = (V, E)$, the affinity of *node v to Cluster C can be measured by:*

$$f(v, C, k) = \frac{|C \cap k\_NN(v)|}{\deg(v)} \text{ where } v \notin C$$

Obviously, we have $0 \leq f(v, C, 1) \leq 1$.

We will use these definitions to describe our algorithm in the following section.

Algorithm

The algorithm presented here has two steps: find the seed nodes (Figure 7) and build a cluster around each such node recursively (Figure 8). It detects as previously defined seed nodes the nodes whose degrees have greater than the average degree of the nodes in the graph. These nodes are potentially used as initial members of different clusters later. In some cases, two or more seed nodes are, however, densely connected and they are not far away in the graph. This suggests they should be within one cluster. Two seed nodes will be combined into one seed node, provided that they share the nodes of their *k-NN*, and the number of the shared nodes is no less than half a degree of one of them. Each member of the reduced seed node set is a core candidate for each cluster. After this, the algorithm begins with successively adding *1-NN* nodes of seed nodes into corresponding clusters, and then each newly added node in the clusters again expands appropriate nodes in its *1-NN* respectively and so on, until the affinity criterion of a node

Figure 7. An Algorithm to Find Seed Nodes

```
Input: graph G=(V,E); seed set: S ← φ; threshold : k and τ
Output: S
Compute the degrees of nodes in G, deg(v).
Compute the average degree μ and standard derivation of the degrees δ
//Find the seed nodes S
for each v ∈ V
    if deg(v) ≥ μ + τ then
            S ← S ∪ {v}
    end if
end for
for S = φ then STOP
for each v ∈ S
    if max |(k - NN(v) + {v}) ∩ (k - NN(u) + {u})| ≥ deg(u)/2 then
       u∈S-{v}
            S ← S \{u}
    end if
end for
```

is not satisfied. Each cluster accepts a node as its new member based on a defined affinity function, which measures how the affinity of the node is relevant to existing member nodes in the cluster. Specially, the value of a node affinity to a cluster, formally defined in Definition 9, is calculated by the number of the shared nodes in both *1-NN* of the node and the existing member nodes of the cluster. The clusters competitively choose a node as their new member according to the rule: the node is with the highest affinity to a cluster. If the affinities of a node to all the clusters are equivalent, the node will become a singleton cluster. This procedure processes iteratively until no more nodes can be added to any cluster by following the above rule. Finally, the remaining nodes not belonging to any cluster must belong to chains. Such chains are then divided among their closest clusters, or remain as independent singleton clusters.

The neighboring nodes are found in an incremental manner in our algorithm. In other words, having found the k nearest neighbours, the algorithm does not make a computation from scratch to obtain the set of $k+1$ nearest neighbour; instead it just continually

Figure 8. Algorithms to Aggregate Nodes by Local Search

```
// Construct the clusters around core candidate nodes
Input: seed set S = {s₁, s₂, ..., sₘ}
Output: clusters Cᵢ(i=1,2,…,m)
for each sᵢ ∈ S
    If 1_NN(sᵢ) ≠ 1_NN(sⱼ)(i ≠ j = 1, …, m) then
    Cᵢ ← Cᵢ ∪ {sᵢ} ∪ 1 - NN(sᵢ)
    else
    k = arg max {f(1_NN(sᵢ),Cᵢ,1)}
         i=1,?,m
    Cₖ ← Cₖ ∪ {sᵢ} ∪ 1 - NN(sᵢ)
    end if
end for
for i =1 to m
for each v ∈ V - Cᵢ

    k = arg max {f(v,Cᵢ,1)}
         i=1,?,m
    if f(v, Cₖ, 1) > 0.5 then
    Cₖ ← Cₖ ∪ {v}
    end if
end for
end for
// This is an optional algorithm for handing the remaining node chain
for each v ∈ V - Cᵢ do

    i = arg min {D(v,u) | u ∈ Cᵢ}
         i=1,…,|S|
Cᵢ ← Cᵢ ∪ {v}
end for
```

explores the additional neighbours of current clustered nodes. The incremental nearest neighbor algorithm ranks the next available unclassified nodes in terms of their affinities to newly classified members of the clusters, and then a cluster chooses the node with highest affinity as its new member. The formal description of the algorithm is presented in Figure 7 and Figure 8.

The algorithm can be summarized as follows:
1. Identify a small subset S whose members have high degrees in G.
2. Remove the node(s) in S that is (are) highly connected to other node(s) and each remaining node in S is called a core candidate.
3. With a core candidate as its first member, each cluster incrementally classifies available nodes that have the highest affinities to the existing members of the cluster. That is, each member of each cluster continually absorbs the nodes in its *1-NN* until the expansion criterion is not satisfied.

The time complexity of the algorithm is $O(|S|^2)$.

EXPERIMENTS

We have implemented our algorithm in a prototype called PGD by using Java programming language. In this section, we present the clustering results of a set of arbitrary graphs by applying our approach, and discuss some features. Note that we will use one node to represent all the member nodes in a cluster in the following clustered figures.

The seed node set of Graph 1 in Figure 9 is $\{v_4, v_7, v_9, v_{10}, v_{14}\}$. The node v_9 has even affinities to other nodes v_4, v_7, v_{10} and v_{14}, and the node v_9 is thus a singleton cluster. It is actually also a bridge node between clusters $v_{1-4}, v_{5-8}, v_{14-17}$ and v_{10-13}. Note that all members in this seed node set are the core candidates for the corresponding clusters.

Graph 2 in Figure 10 was specially designed for testing our algorithm for dealing with a remaining node chain during clustering. First, the nodes v_1-v_5 and v_6-v_{11} are constructed into two clusters C_1 (v_1-v_5) and C_2 (v_6-v_{11}). The node v_9 then aggregates one member of its 1-NN, node v_{12}, into C_2. That is, the node v_{12} becomes a new member of C_2. However, the node v_{12} cannot continually accept node v_{13} into its cluster C_2, because only one node of 1-NN (v_{13}) (node v_{12}) is within C_2. This aggregation process thus stops at the node v_{12} (Figure 10(b)) Additionally, the remaining node chain v_{13}-v_{16} can be optionally combined into C_2 with the optional algorithm provided (Figure 10(c)). Or they just remain as different singleton clusters. This is reasonable in that the nodes in C_1 and C_2 are densely connected while the nodes v_{13}-v_{16} are relatively not.

Graph 3 in Figure 11 shows different clustered results of a remaining node chain with different criteria. The clusters C_1 (v_1-v_3) and C_2 (v_4-v_8) are firstly built. (Node v_4 has more affinity to C_2 (v_5 and v_6) than to C_1 (v_3), so v_4 will be put into C_2) Then the remaining node chain v_9-v_{11} is generated. With the loose criterion:

$$\max\{|1 - NN(v) \cap \{u \mid u \in C_2\}|\} \geq \deg(v)/2 \ ,$$

nodes v_9-v_{11} will be incrementally aggregated into C_2:

Figure 9. Initial and Clustered Graph 1

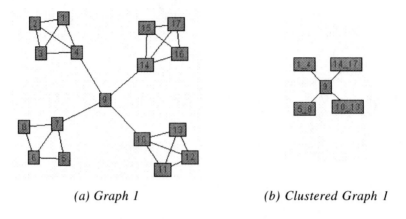

(a) Graph 1   (b) Clustered Graph 1

Figure 10. Initial and Clustered Graph 2

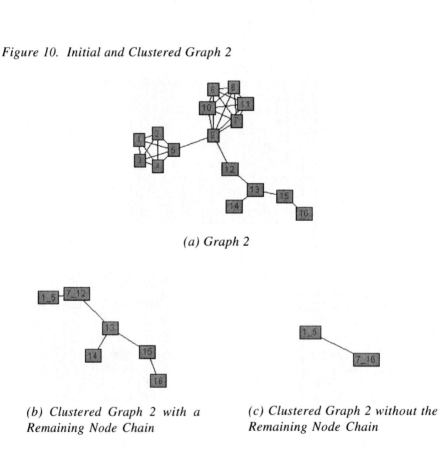

(a) Graph 2

(b) Clustered Graph 2 with a
Remaining Node Chain

(c) Clustered Graph 2 without the
Remaining Node Chain

Figure 11. Initial and Clustered Graph 3

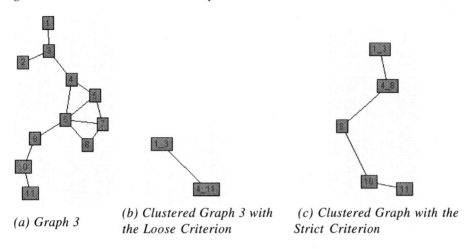

(a) Graph 3
(b) Clustered Graph 3 with the Loose Criterion
(c) Clustered Graph with the Strict Criterion

$$v_9 \in 1\text{-}NN(v_6) \to v_{10} \in 1\text{-}NN(v_9) \to v_{11} \in 1\text{-}NN(v_{10})\,(\text{Figure } 11(b)).$$

However, they will be singleton clusters with a strict criterion:

$$\max\{|1\text{-}NN(v)\cap\{u\,|\,u\in C_2\}\,|\} > \deg(v)/2$$

The result is shown in Figure 11(c).

Figures 12 and 13 show another two examples of well-clustered Graphs 4 and 5 by our approach.

In our experiments, the parameters are $k=1$, that is, *1-NN* and $\tau = 0$. If we want to reduce the number of clusters of a given graph, for example, we should specify $\tau = \sigma$, and then $\mu + \tau = 3.569$ for Graph 3 in Figure 11. Based on Definition 6, only the node v_6 (Figure 11(b)) can be a seed node, and the nodes v_1, v_2 and v_3 will be singleton clusters with the loose criterion.

Figure 12. Initial and Clustered Graph 4

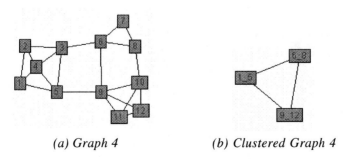

(a) Graph 4   (b) Clustered Graph 4

Figure 13. Initial and Clustered Graph 5

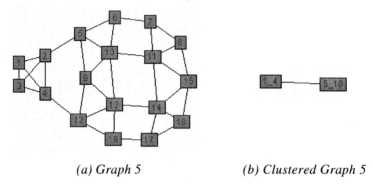

       (a) Graph 5   *(b) Clustered Graph 5*

Table 1. Parameters for Clustering Graphs 1-5

Graph	1	2		3		4	5
$|V|$	12	16		11		12	18
$\overline{Deg(G)}$	3.294	3.875		2.363		3.500	3.778
σ	0.470	1.668		1.206		0.978	0.808
$|C|$	5	6	2	2	5	3	2
$C_H(G)$	1	1	0.863	0.511	0.873	0.933	0.642
$C_S(G)$	0.25	0.634	0.018	0.042	0.567	0.095	0.036

The experimental results for clustering are reported in Table 1. Some parameters are also illustrated in Figure 14. Our approach has fast running time, and can find a good clustering solution.

Figure 14. Quality of the Clustered Graphs

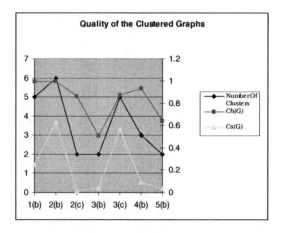

RELATED WORK

Although there are numerous algorithms for cluster analysis in the literature, we briefly review those that are closely related to the structure of a graph, and compare them with our approach.

Matuala (1969, 1970, 1972, 1987) used a high connectivity in similarity graphs to cluster analysis, which is based on a cohesiveness function. The function defines every node and edge of a graph to be the maximum edge-connectivity of any sub-graph containing that element. The k-connected sub-graphs of the graph are obtained by deleting all elements with cohesiveness less than k in the graph, where k is a constant value. It is, however, hard to determine the values of connectivity in real clustering applications with this approach.

There is some recent work related to the clustering of a graph. The HCS algorithms (Shamir, 2000) use a similarity graph as the input data, partitioning recursively a current set of elements into two subsets. Highly connected sub-graphs are then identified as kernels that are considered as clusters, if the number of their edges exceeds half that of their corresponding nodes. Unfortunately the result of the clustering is not uniquely determined. Using the same basic scheme as HCS to form kernels, the CLICK algorithm (Shamir, 2000) builds on a statistical model, including the following processing: singleton adoption, a recursive clustering process on the set of remaining singletons, and an iterative merging step. The CAST (Amir Ben-Dor, 1999) starts with a single element and uses a single parameter t. Elements are added or removed from the cluster if their affinity is larger or lower than t, until the process stabilizes.

The features of our approach differ from previous work in the following aspects:
1. Our approach does not require the initial layout of a graph, and is suitable for clustering any types of graphs, including tree graphs, since it is based purely on the structure of a graph. Actually, the approach presented here is a novel method of graph partitioning so that it can be applicable to graph partition as well.
2. Without the need to be specified in advance (does not like k-means), the number of clusters is automatically detected on the basis of the distribution of node degrees of a given graph.
3. The number of clusters can be easily adjusted by specifying different values of the thresholds.
4. A proposed simple affinity function, as an expansion condition, is based on the degree of a node. The clusters are gradually expanded by local search with k-nearest neighbour. Essentially, the algorithm identifies the number of clusters at a "global" level, and grows the nodes into the clusters by local search.
5. The definitions of homogeneity and separation are provided to formally measure the quality of graph clustering.

APPLICATIONS

The WWW can be considered as a graph where nodes are static html pages and edges are hyperlinks between these pages. This graph is called the Web graph. It has been the subject of a variety of recent work aimed at understanding the structure of the World Wide Web (Albert, 1999; Broder, 2000; Dill, 2001; Kleimberg, 1999; R. Kumar, 2000;

S.R. Kumar, 1999; Papadimitriou, 2001; Watts, 1998).

The main findings about the WWW structure are as follows:

1. A *power-law* distribution of degrees (Albert, 1999; S.R. Kumar, 1999): in-degree and out-degree distribution of the nodes of the Web graph follows the power law. The probability that a Web page has in-degree i is proportional to $1/i^x$, where the latest estimation for x is 2.1. The out-degree of a Web page is also distributed with a power law with exponent roughly equal to 2.7. The average number of links per page is about 7.

2. A *bow-tie* shape (Broder, 2000): the Web's macroscopic structure, which can be naturally broken into four pieces: SCC, a *Strongly Connected Component* (a central core), where all the pages can reach one another along directed links; *IN,* which consists of pages that can reach the *SCC,* but cannot be reached from it; *OUT,* which consists of pages that are accessible from the *SCC,* but do not link back to it. Finally, *TENDRILS,* which contains pages that cannot reach the *SCC,* and cannot be reached from the *SCC*.

3. The average path length between two Web pages: 16 (Broder, 2000) and 19 (Albert, 1999).

4. *Small world phenomenon* (Kleimberg, 1999; Watts, 1998): Six degrees of separation between any two Web pages. It is almost true in a strongly connected component part of the Web graph if allowing traversal of both out-links and in-links, but not true in general.

5. *Cyber-communities* (S.R. Kumar, 1999): groups of individuals who share a common interest, together with the most popular Web pages among them. A bipartite clique in the Web graph can be interpreted as a core of such a community, defined by a set of fans, all pointing to a set of authorities, and the set of authorities, all pointed to by the fans. The size of the bipartite cliques is relatively small, ranging from three to ten. Over 100,000 such communities have been recognized in a sample of 200M pages on a Web crawl.

6. Self-similarity structure (Dill, 2001): the Web shows a fractal structure in many different ways. A graph can be viewed as the outcome of a number of similar and independent stochastic processes. At various scales, there are "cohesive collections" of Web pages (for example, pages on a site, or pages about a topic) and these collections are structurally similar to the whole Web (i.e., they exhibit the *bow-tie* structure and follow power-law of the in-degree and out-degree). The central regions of such collections are called "Thematically Unified Clusters" (TUCs), and they provide the navigational backbone of the Web.

Link analysis plays an import role in understanding of the Web structure. There are two well known algorithms for ranking pages: Page Rank (Page, 1998) and HITS (Kleinberg, 1999).

The study of the Web graph is not only fascinating in its own right, but also yields valuable insight into Web algorithms for crawling, searching and prediction of the Web structure. The Web graph is actually a special case of a general graph, and we can employ some existing graph theoretic approaches to classify the Web graph.

Our approach is based on the theoretical properties of a graph so that it potentially has wide applications. Here we apply it to Web visualization. In our prototype called PGD, there is a Web crawler program that builds the graph of a Website, with a starting address:

http://www.it.swin.edu.au, and a depth: 5. The program applies a depth-first search algorithm to explore the Web and create a graph as shown in Figure 15(a). Figure 15(b) shows the layout of its clustered graph applied by the proposed algorithm, where white nodes are the member nodes of their black and nearby clustered nodes. Our approach actually identifies the dense sub-graphs in the Web graph and then classifies them. From the clustered Web graph, we reach the following conclusions:

Figure 15. Layout of the Clustered Web Graph

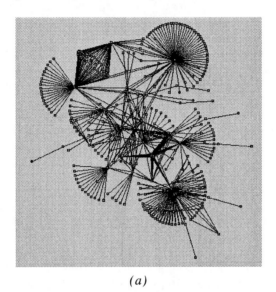

(a)

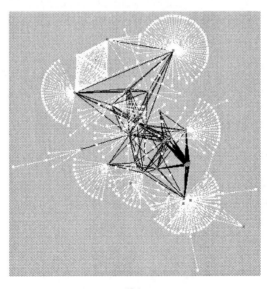

(b)

1.   The clustered graph can reduce visual complexity. In large graphs, we will only display the clustered nodes and relative edges. Although there are several existing approaches to lay out large graphs, such as Hyperbolic tree (Munzner & Burchard, 1995) and multilevel clustered graphs (Eades & Feng, 1997), our approach has a feature of automatically clustering nodes based on the connectivity of a graph.

2.   There is a possible Web community around the clustered node. We describe the properties of the Web communities derived as two distinct types of dense subgraphs in Web graphs, where the link density is greater among members than between members and the rest of the network (Flake, Lawrence, Giles & Coetzee, 2002). A Web community is a set of Web pages having a common topic and so far various graph theoretical approaches have been proposed to potentially extract Web communities from the Web graph, such as HITS (Flake, Lawrence, Giles & Coetzee, 2002), bipartite graph (Kitsuregawa, 2001) and Maximum Flow algorithm (Flake & Giles, 2002). All these approaches assume the dense part of a Web graph as a potential Web community. We can identify a Web community by analysing the member nodes in the clusters in our approach.

3.   Classification of Web pages. Hyperlinks contain high-quality semantic clues to the topic of a Web page. Pages on the same or related topics tend to be linked more frequently than those on unrelated topics (Chakrabarti, 1999).

SUMMARY

In this chapter, we have presented a new approach to clustering graphs. The approach produced good results in our experiments and applied into the visualization of a Website. Our approach is a graph theoretic approach and it thus has wide applications. For example, if the input graph is a similarity graph, where nodes correspond to elements and edges connect elements with similarity values above some thresholds, it can be used to classify the elements. The future improvements may use a weighted Web graph, and thus consider clustering the weighted Web graph.

REFERENCES

Albert, A.L.B., &. Albert, R. (1999). Emergence of scaling in random networks. *Science*, 286.

Amir Ben-Dor, R.S., & Yakhini, Z. (1999). Clustering gene expression patterns. *Journal of Computational Biology, 6*(3-4), 281-297.

Battista, G.D., Eades, P., Tamassia, R., & Tollis, T. (1998). *Graph drawing: Algorithms for the visualization of graphs*. Prentice Hall.

Botafogo, R.A., Rivlin, E., & Schneiderman, B. (1991). Structural analysis of hypertexts: Identifying hierarchies and useful metrics. *ACM Transactions on Information Systems, 10*(2), 142-180.

Brin, S., &. Page, L. (1998). *The anatomy of a large-scale hypertextual Web search engines*. Paper presented at the Proceedings of the Seventh WWW Conference.

Broder, A., Maghoul, R.K.F., Raghavan, P., Rajagopalan, S., Stata, R., Tomkins, A., & Wiener, J. (2000). Graph structure in the Web. Paper presented at the *Ninth International WWW Conference*, Amsterdam, The Netherlands.

Burchard, T.M., &. Burchard, P. (1995). Visualizing the structure of the World Wide Web in 3D hyperbolic space. Paper presented at the *Proceedings of VRML '95, special issue of Computer Graphics, ACM SIGGRAPH*, New York.

Chakrabarti, B.D., Kumar, S., Raghavan, P., Rajagopalan, S., Tomkins, A., Gibson, D., & Kleinberg, J. (1999). Mining the Web's link Structure. *IEEE computers,* 60-66.

Chen, Y. & Koutsofios, E. (1997). WebCiao: A Website visualisation and tracking system. Paper presented at the *Proceedings of WebNet '97 Conference*.

Dill, S., Kumar, R., McCurley, K., Rajagopalan, S., Sivakumar, D., & Tomkins, A. (2001). Self-similarity in the Web. Paper presented at the *Proceedings 27th VLDB*.

Eades, P., & Feng, Q.-W. (1997). Multilevel visualization of clustered graphs. Paper presented at the *Symposium on Graph Drawing GD '96*, Berlin.

Eades, P., &. Wei, L. (1990). Visual interface design for relational systems. Paper presented at the *Proceedings of the Fifth Australian Software Engineering Conference*.

Eades, P., &. Wei, L. (1991). Algorithms for disjoint node images. *Australian Computer Science Communications, 14*(1), 253-265.

Flake, G.W., Lawrence, S., & Giles, C.L. (2002). Efficient identification of Web communities. Paper presented at the *Proceedings of the Sixth International Conference on Knowledge Discovery and Data Mining*.

Flake, G.W., Lawrence, S., Giles, C.L., & Coetzee, F. (2002). Self-organization and identification of Web communities. *IEEE Computers,* 66-70.

Hartuv, E., & Shamir, R. (2000). A clustering algorithm based on graph connectivity. *Information Processing Letters, 76*(4-6), 175-181.

Herman, I., Delest, M., & Melancon, G. (1998). Tree visualization and navigation clues for information visualization. *Computer Graphics Form, 17*(2), 153-165.

Herman, I., Delest, M., Melançon, G., Duke, M., & Domenger, J.-P. (1999). Skeletal images as visual cues in graphs visualization. Paper presented at the *Data Visualization '99. Proceedings of the Joint Eurographics and IEEE TCVG Symposium on Visualization*.

Huang, M.L., Eades, P., & Cohen, R.F. (1998). WebOFDAV - Navigating and visualising the Web on-line with animated context swapping. Paper presented at the *Proceedings of the 7th International World Wide Web Conference*.

Kimelman, D., Leban, B., Roth, T., & Zernik, D. (1994). Reduction of visual complexity in dynamic graphs. Paper presented at the *Proceedings of the Symposium on Graph Drawing GD 1993*.

Kitsuregawa, P.K.R., &. Kitsuregawa, M. (2001). An approach to relate the Web communities through bipartite graphs. Paper presented at the *Proceedings of the Second International Conference on Web Information Systems Engineering*.

Kleimberg, J. (1999). *The small world phenomenon: An algorithmic perspective.* (Technical Report), Cornell University.

Kleinberg, J.M. (1999). Authoritative sources in a hyperlinked environment. *Journal of the ACM, 46*(5), 604-632.

Kumar, R., Raghavan, P., Rajagopalan, S., Sivakumar, D., Tomkins, A., & Upfal, E. (2000). Stochastic models for the web graph. Paper presented at the *Proceedings of the IEEE symposium on Foundations of Computer Science.*

Kumar, R., Raghavan, P., Rajagopalan, S., & Tomkins, A. (1999). Trawling the Web for emerging cyber communities. Paper presented at the *Proceedings of the 8th WWW Conference.*

Lai, W., &. Eades, P. (2002). Removing edge-node intersections in drawings of graphs. *Information Processing Letters, 81,* 105-110.

Leung, Y.K., & Apperly, M.D. (1994). A review and taxonomy of distortion-oriented presentation techniques. *ACM Transactions on Computer-Human Interaction, 1*(2), 126-160.

Maarek, Y.S. & Shaul, I.Z.B. (1997). WebCutter: A system for dynamic and tailorable site mapping. Paper presented at the *Proceedings of the Sixth International World Wide Web Conference.*

Matula, D.W. (1969). The cohesive strength of graphs. In G. C. a. S. F. Kapoor (Ed.), *The many facets of Graph Theory* (Vol. 110, pp. 215-221): Lecture Notes in Mathematics.

Matula, D.W. (1970). Cluster analysis via graph theoretic techniques. Paper presented at the *Proceedings of Louisiana Conference on Combinatorics, Graph Theory and Computing*, Winnipeg.

Matula, D.W. (1972). K-Components, clusters and slicings in graphs. *SIAM J. Appl. Math, 22*(3), 459-480.

Matula, D.W. (1987). Graph theoretic techniques for cluster analysis algorithms. In V. Ryzin (Ed.), *Classification and clustering* (pp. 95-129).

Misue, K., Eades, P., Lai, W., & Sugiyama, K. (1995). Layout adjustment and the mental map. *Journal of Visual Languages and Computing, 6*, 183-210.

Munzner, T., & Burchard, P. (1995, December). Visualizing the structure of the World Wide Web in 3D hyperbolic space. Paper presented at the *VRML'95 Symposium*, San Diego, CA.

Papadimitriou, C.H. (2001). Algorithms, games and the Internet. Paper presented at the *STOC.*

Shamir, R. (2000). CLICK: A clustering algorithm for gene expression analysis. In R. S. S. Miyano, & T. Takagi (Eds.), *Currents in Computational Molecular Biology* (pp. 6-7). Universal Academy Press.

Watts, D.J., & Strogatz, S.H. (1998). Collective dynamics of small-world networks. *Nature, 393,* 440-442.

SECTION IV

USAGE MINING

Chapter XIII

Integrating Semantic Knowledge with Web Usage Mining for Personalization

Honghua Dai
DePaul University, USA

Bamshad Mobasher
DePaul University, USA

ABSTRACT

Web usage mining has been used effectively as an approach to automatic personalization and as a way to overcome deficiencies of traditional approaches such as collaborative filtering. Despite their success, such systems, as in more traditional ones, do not take into account the semantic knowledge about the underlying domain. Without such semantic knowledge, personalization systems cannot recommend different types of complex objects based on their underlying properties and attributes. Nor can these systems possess the ability to automatically explain or reason about the user models or user recommendations. The integration of semantic knowledge is, in fact, the primary challenge for the next generation of personalization systems. In this chapter we provide an overview of approaches for incorporating semantic knowledge into Web usage mining and personalization processes. In particular, we discuss the issues and requirements for successful integration of semantic knowledge from different sources, such as the content and the structure of Web sites for personalization. Finally, we present a general framework for fully integrating domain ontologies with Web usage mining and personalization processes at different stages, including the preprocessing and pattern discovery phases, as well as in the final stage where the discovered patterns are used for personalization.

INTRODUCTION

With the continued growth and proliferation of e-commerce, Web services, and Web-based information systems, personalization has emerged as a critical application that is essential to the success of a Website. It is now common for Web users to encounter sites that provide dynamic recommendations for products and services, targeted banner advertising, and individualized link selections. Indeed, nowhere is this phenomenon more apparent as in the business-to-consumer e-commerce arena. The reason is that, in today's highly competitive e-commerce environment, the success of a site often depends on the site's ability to retain visitors and turn casual browsers into potential customers. Automatic personalization and recommender system technologies have become critical tools, precisely because they help engage visitors at a deeper and more intimate level by tailoring the site's interaction with a visitor to her needs and interests.

Web personalization can be defined as any action that tailors the Web experience to a particular user, or a set of users (Mobasher, Cooley & Srivastava, 2000a). The experience can be something as casual as browsing a Website or as (economically) significant as trading stocks or purchasing a car. Principal elements of Web personalization include modeling of Web objects (pages, etc.) and subjects (users), categorization of objects and subjects, matching between and across objects and/or subjects, and determination of the set of actions to be recommended for personalization. The actions can range from simply making the presentation more pleasing to anticipating the needs of a user and providing customized information.

Traditional approaches to personalization have included both content-based and user-based techniques. Content-based techniques use personal profiles of users and recommend other items or pages based on their content similarity to the items or pages that are in the user's profile. The underlying mechanism in these systems is usually the comparison of sets of keywords representing pages or item descriptions. Examples of such systems include Letizia (Lieberman, 1995) and WebWatcher (Joachims, Freitag & Mitchell, 1997). While these systems perform well from the perspective of the end user who is searching the Web for information, they are less useful in e-commerce applications, partly due to the lack of server-side control by site owners, and partly because techniques based on content similarity alone may miss other types of semantic relationships among objects (for example, the associations among products or services that are semantically different, but are often used together).

User-based techniques for personalization, on the other hand, primarily focus on the similarities among users rather than item-based similarities. The most widely used technology user-based personalization is collaborative filtering (CF) (Herlocker, Konstan, Borchers & Riedl, 1999). Given a target user's record of activity or preferences, CF-based techniques compare that record with the historical records of other users in order to find the users with similar interests. This is the so-called *neighborhood* of the current user. The mapping of a visitor record to its neighborhood could be based on similarity in ratings of items, access to similar content or pages, or purchase of similar items. The identified neighborhood is then used to recommend items not already accessed or purchased by the active user. The advantage of this approach over purely content-based approaches that rely on content similarity in item-to-item comparisons is that it can capture "pragmatic" relationships among items based on their intended use or based on similar tastes of the users.

The CF-based techniques, however, suffer from some well-known limitations (Sarwar, Karypis, Konstan & Riedl, 2000). For the most part these limitations are related to the scalability and efficiency of the underlying algorithms, which requires real-time computation in both the neighborhood formation and the recommendation phases. The effectiveness and scalability of collaborative filtering can be dramatically enhanced by the application of Web usage mining techniques.

In general, *Web mining* can be characterized as the application of data mining to the content, structure, and usage of Web resources (Cooley, Mobasher & Srivastava, 1997; Srivastava, Cooley, Deshpande & Tan, 2000). The goal of Web mining is to automatically discover local as well as global models and patterns within and between Web pages or other Web resources. The goal of *Web usage mining,* in particular, is to capture and model Web user behavioral patterns. The discovery of such patterns from the enormous amount of data generated by Web and application servers has found a number of important applications. Among these applications are systems to evaluate the effectiveness of a site in meeting user expectations (Spiliopoulou, 2000), techniques for dynamic load balancing and optimization of Web servers for better and more efficient user access (Palpanas & Mendelzon, 1999; Pitkow & Pirolli, 1999), and applications for dynamically restructuring or customizing a site based on users' predicted needs and interests (Perkowitz & Etzioni, 1998).

More recently, Web usage mining techniques have been proposed as another user-based approach to personalization that alleviates some of the problems associated with collaborative filtering (Mobasher et al., 2000a). In particular, Web usage mining has been used to improve the scalability of personalization systems based on traditional CF-based techniques (Mobasher, Dai, Luo & Nakagawa, 2001, 2002).

However, the pure usage-based approach to personalization has an important drawback: the recommendation process relies on the existing user transaction data, and thus items or pages added to a site recently cannot be recommended. This is generally referred to as the "new item problem". A common approach to resolving this problem in collaborative filtering has been to integrate content characteristics of pages with the user ratings or judgments (Claypool et al., 1999; Pazzani, 1999). Generally, in these approaches, keywords are extracted from the content on the Website and are used to either index pages by content or classify pages into various content categories. In the context of personalization, this approach would allow the system to recommend pages to a user, not only based on similar users, but also (or alternatively) based on the content similarity of these pages to the pages the user has already visited.

Keyword-based approaches, however, are incapable of capturing more complex relationships among objects at a deeper semantic level based on the inherent properties associated with these objects. For example, potentially valuable relational structures among objects such as relationships between movies, directors, and actors, or between students, courses, and instructors, may be missed if one can only rely on the description of these entities using sets of keywords. To be able to recommend different types of complex objects using their underlying properties and attributes, the system must be able to rely on the characterization of user segments and objects, not just based on keywords, but at a deeper semantic level using the domain ontologies for the objects. For instance, a traditional personalization system on a university Website might recommend courses in Java to a student, simply because that student has previously taken or shown interest in Java courses. On the other hand, a system that has knowledge of the underlying domain ontology might recognize that the student should first satisfy the prerequisite requirements for a recommended course, or be able to recommend the best instructor for a Java course, and so on.

An *ontology* provides a set of well-founded constructs that define significant concepts and their semantic relationships. An example of an ontology is a relational schema for a database involving multiple tables and foreign keys semantically connecting these relations. Such constructs can be leveraged to build meaningful higher-level knowledge in a particular domain. Domain ontologies for a Website usually include concepts, subsumption relations between concepts (concept hierarchies), and other relations among concepts that exist in the domain that the Web site represents. For example, the domain ontologies of a movie Website usually include concepts such as "movie," "actor," "director," "theater," and so forth. The genre hierarchy can be used to represent different categories of movie concepts. Typical relations in this domain may include "Starring" (between actors and movies), "Directing," "Playing" (between theaters and movies), and so forth.

The ontology of a Website can be constructed by extracting relevant concepts and relations from the content and structure of the site, through machine learning and Web mining techniques. But, in addition to concepts and relations that can be acquired from Web content and structure information, we are also interested in usage-related concepts and relations in a Website. For instance, in an e-commerce Website, we may be interested in the relations between users and objects that define different types of online activity, such as browsing, searching, registering, buying, and bidding. The integration of such usage-based relations with ontological information representing the underlying concepts and attributes embedded in a site allows for more effective knowledge discovery, as well as better characterization and interpretation of the discovered patterns.

In the context of Web personalization and recommender systems, the use of semantic knowledge can lead to deeper interaction of the visitors or customers with the site. Integration of domain knowledge allows such systems to infer additional useful recommendations for users based on more fine grained characteristics of the objects being recommended, and provides the capability to explain and reason about user actions.

In this chapter we present an overview of the issues related to and requirements for successfully integrating semantic knowledge in the Web usage mining and personalization processes. We begin by providing some general background on the use of semantic knowledge and ontologies in Web mining, as well as an overview of personalization based on Web usage mining. We then discuss how the content and the structure of the site can be leveraged to transform raw usage data into semantically-enhanced transactions that can be used for semantic Web usage mining and personalization. Finally, we present a framework for more systematically integrating full-fledged domain ontologies in the personalization process.

BACKGROUND
Semantic Web Mining

Web mining is the process of discovering and extracting useful knowledge from the content, usage, and structure of one or more Web sites. Semantic Web mining (Berendt, Hotho & Stumme, 2002) involves the integration of domain knowledge into the Web mining process.

For the most part the research in semantic Web mining has been focused in application areas such as Web content and structure mining. In this section, we provide a brief overview and some examples of related work in this area. Few studies have focused on the use of domain knowledge in Web usage mining. Our goal in this chapter is to provide a road map for the integration of semantic and ontological knowledge into the process of Web usage mining, and particularly, in its application to Web personalization and recommender systems.

Domain knowledge can be integrated into the Web mining process in many ways. This includes leveraging explicit domain ontologies or implicit domain semantics extracted from the content or the structure of documents or Website. In general, however, this process may involve one or more of three critical activities: domain ontology acquisition, knowledge base construction, and knowledge-enhanced pattern discovery.

Domain Ontology Acquisition

The process of acquiring, maintaining and enriching the domain ontologies is referred to as "ontology engineering". For small Web sites with only static Web pages, it is feasible to construct a domain knowledge base manually or semi-manually. In Loh, Wives and de Oliveira (2000), a semi-manual approach is adopted for defining each domain concept as a vector of terms with the help of existing vocabulary and natural language processing tools.

However, manual construction and maintenance of domain ontologies requires a great deal of effort on the part of knowledge engineers, particularly for large-scale Websites or Websites with dynamically generated content. In dynamically generated Websites, page templates are usually populated based on structured queries performed against back-end databases. In such cases, the database schema can be used directly to acquire ontological information. Some Web servers send structured data files (e.g., XML files) to users and let client-side formatting mechanisms (e.g., CSS files) work out the final Web representation on client agents. In this case, it is generally possible to infer the schema from the structured data files.

When there is no direct source for acquiring domain ontologies, machine learning and text mining techniques must be employed to extract domain knowledge from the content or hyperlink structure of the Web pages. In Clerkin, Cunningham and Hayes (2001), a hierarchical clustering algorithm is applied to terms in order to create concept hierarchies. In Stumme, Taouil, Bastide, Pasquier and Lakhal (2000) a Formal Concept Analysis framework is proposed to derive a concept lattice (a variation of association rule algorithm). The approach proposed in Maedche and Staab (2000) learns generalized conceptual relations by applying association rule mining. All these efforts aim to *automatically* generate machine understandable ontologies for Website domains.

The outcome of this phase is a set of formally defined domain ontologies that precisely represent the Website. A good representation should provide machine understandability, the power of reasoning, and computation efficiency. The choice of ontology representation language has a direct effect on the flexibility of the data mining phase. Common representation approaches are vector-space model (Loh et al., 2000), descriptive logics (such as DAML+OIL) (Giugno & Lukasiewicz, 2002; Horrocks & Sattler, 2001), first order logic (Craven et al., 2000), relational models (Dai & Mobasher, 2002), probabilistic relational models (Getoor, Friedman, Koller & Taskar, 2001), and probabilistic Markov models (Anderson, Domingos & Weld, 2002).

Knowledge Base Construction

The first phase generates the formal representation of concepts and relations among them. The second phase, knowledge base construction, can be viewed as building mappings between concepts or relations on the one hand, and objects on the Web. The goal of this phase is to find the instances of the concepts and relations from the Website's domain, so that they can be exploited to perform further data mining tasks. Learning algorithms plays an important role in this phase.

In Ghani and Fano (2002), a text classifier is learned for each "semantic feature" (somewhat equivalent to the notion of a concept) based on a small manually labeled data set. First, Web pages are extracted from different Websites that belong to a similar domain, and then the semantic features are manually labeled. This small labeled data set is fed into a learning algorithm as the training data to learn the mappings between Web objects and the concept labels. In fact, this approach treats the process of assigning concept labels as filling "missing" data. Craven et al. (2000) adopt a combined approach of statistical text classification and first order text classification in recognizing concept instances. In that study, learning process is based on both page content and linkage information.

Knowledge-Enhanced Web Data Mining

Domain knowledge enables analysts to perform more powerful Web data mining tasks. The applications include content mining, information retrieval and extraction, Web usage mining, and personalization. On the other hand, data mining tasks can also help to enhance the process of domain knowledge discovery.

Domain knowledge can improve the accuracy of document clustering and classification and induce more powerful content patterns. For example, in Horrocks (2002), domain ontologies are employed in selecting textual features. The selection is based on lexical analysis tools that map terms into concepts within the ontology. The approach also aggregates concepts by merging the concepts that have low support in the documents. After preprocessing, only necessary concepts are selected for the content clustering step. In McCallum, Rosenfeld, Mitchell and Ng (1998), a concept hierarchy is used to improve the accuracy and the scalability of text classification.

Traditional approaches to content mining and information retrieval treat every document as a set or a bag of terms. Without domain semantics, we would treat "human" and "mankind" as different terms, or, "brake" and "car" as unrelated terms. In Loh et al. (2000), a concept is defined as a group of terms that are semantically relevant, for example, as synonyms. With such concept definitions, concept distribution among documents is analyzed to find interesting concept patterns. For example, one can discover dominant themes in a document collection or in a single document; or find associations among concepts.

Ontologies and domain semantics have been applied extensively in the context of Web information retrieval and extraction. For example, the ARCH system (Parent, Mobasher & Lytinen, 2001) adopts concept hierarchies because they allow users to formulate more expressive and less ambiguous queries when compared to simple keyword-based queries. In ARCH, an initial user query is used to find matching concepts within a portion of concept hierarchy. The concept hierarchy is stored in an aggregated form with each node represented as a term vector. The user can select or unselect nodes in the presented portion of the hierarchy, and relevance feedback techniques are used to modify the initial query based on these nodes.

Similarly, domain-specific search and retrieval applications allow for a more focused and accurate search based on specific relations inherent in the underlying domain knowledge. The CiteSeer system (Bollacker, Lawrence & Giles, 1998) is a Web agent for finding interesting research publications, in which the relation "cited by" is the primary relation discovered among objects (i.e., among published papers). Thus, CiteSeer allows for comparison and retrieval of documents, not only based on similar content, but also based on inter-citation linkage structure among documents.

CiteSeer is an example of an approach for integrating semantic knowledge based on Web structure mining. In general, Web structure mining tasks take as input the hyperlink structure of Web pages (either belonging to a Website or relative to the whole Web), and output the underlying patterns (e.g., page authority values, linkage similarity, Web communities, etc.) that can be inferred from the hypertext co-citations. Another example of such an approach is the PageRank algorithm, which is the backbone of the Google search engine. PageRank uses the in-degree of indexed pages (i.e., number of pages referring to it) in order to rank pages based on quality or authoritativeness. Such algorithms that are based on the analysis of structural attributes can be further enhanced by integrating content semantics (Chakrabarti et al., 1998). Web semantics can also enhance crawling algorithms by combining content or ontology with linkage information (Chakrabarti, van den Berg & Dom, 1999; Maedche, Ehrig, Handschuh, Volz & Stojanovic, 2002).

The use of domain knowledge can also provide tremendous advantages in Web usage mining and personalization. For example, semantic knowledge may help in interpreting, analyzing, and reasoning about usage patterns discovered in the mining phase. Furthermore, it can enhance collaborative filtering and personalization systems by providing concept-level recommendations (in contrast to item-based or user-based recommendations). Another advantage is that user demographic data, represented as part of a domain ontology, can be more systematically integrated into collaborative or usage-based recommendation engines. Several studies have considered various approaches to integrate content-based semantic knowledge into traditional collaborative filtering and personalization frameworks (Anderson et al., 2002; Claypool et al., 1999; Melville, Mooney & Nagarajan, 2002; Mobasher, Dai, Luo, Sun & Zhu, 2000b; Pazzani, 1999). Recently, we proposed a formal framework for integrating full domain ontologies with the personalization process based on Web usage mining (Dai & Mobasher, 2002).

WEB USAGE MINING
AND PERSONALIZATION

The goal of personalization based on Web usage mining is to recommend a set of objects to the current (active) user, possibly consisting of links, ads, text, products, and so forth, tailored to the user's perceived preferences as determined by the matching usage patterns. This task is accomplished by matching the active user session (possibly in conjunction with previously stored profiles for that user) with the usage patterns discovered through Web usage mining. We call the usage patterns used in this context *aggregate usage profiles* since they provide an aggregate representation of the common activities or interests of groups of users. This process is performed by the recommendation engine which is the online component of the personalization system. If the data collection procedures in the system include the capability to track users across visits, then the recommendations can represent a longer term view of user's potential interests based on the user's activity history within the site. If, on the other hand, aggregate profiles are derived only from user sessions (single visits) contained in log files, then the recommendations provide a "short-term" view of user's navigational interests. These recommended objects are added to the last page in the active session accessed by the user before that page is sent to the browser.

The overall process of Web personalization based on Web usage mining consists of three phases: data preparation and transformation, pattern discovery, and recommendation. Of these, only the latter phase is performed in real-time. The data preparation phase transforms raw Web log files into transaction data that can be processed by data mining tasks. A variety of data mining techniques can be applied to this transaction data in the pattern discovery phase, such as clustering, association rule mining, and sequential pattern discovery. The results of the mining phase are transformed into aggregate usage profiles, suitable for use in the recommendation phase. The recommendation engine considers the active user session in conjunction with the discovered patterns to provide personalized content.

Figure 1. General Framework for Web Personalization Based on Web Usage Mining — The Offline Pattern Discovery Component

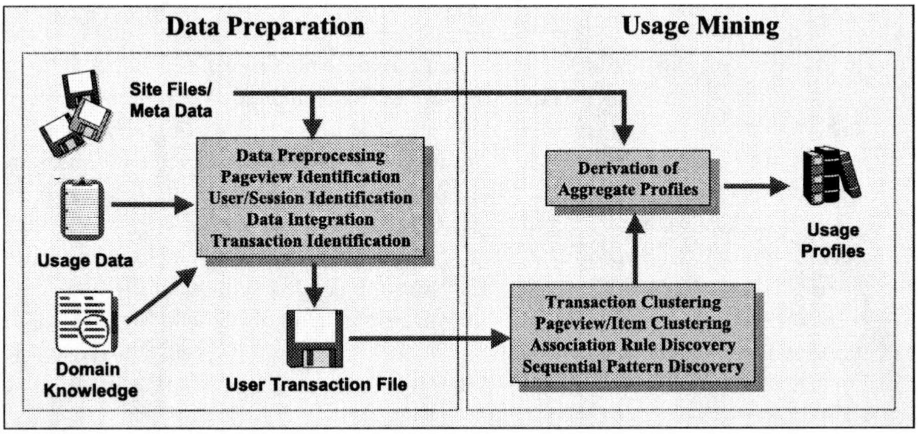

Figure 2. General Framework for Web Personalization Based on Web Usage Mining — The Online Personalization Component

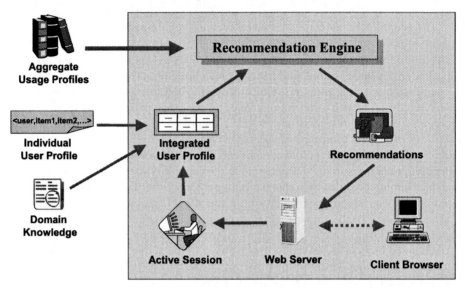

The primary data sources used in Web usage mining are the server log files, which include Web server access logs and application server logs. Additional data sources that are also essential for both data preparation and pattern discovery include the site files (HTML, XML, etc.) and meta-data, operational databases, and domain knowledge. Generally speaking, the data obtained through these sources can be categorized into four groups (see also Cooley, Mobasher, & Srivastava, 1999; Srivastava et al., 2000).

- **Usage data:** The log data collected automatically by the Web and application servers represents the fine-grained navigational behavior of visitors. Depending on the goals of the analysis, this data needs to be transformed and aggregated at different levels of abstraction. In Web usage mining, the most basic level of data abstraction is that of a *pageview*. Physically, a pageview is an aggregate representation of a collection of Web objects contributing to the display on a user's browser resulting from a single user action (such as a clickthrough). These Web objects may include multiple pages (such as in a frame-based site), images, embedded components, or script and database queries that populate portions of the displayed page (in dynamically generated sites). Conceptually, each pageview represents a specific "type" of user activity on the site, e.g., reading a news article, browsing the results of a search query, viewing a product page, adding a product to the shopping cart, and so on. On the other hand, at the user level, the most basic level of behavioral abstraction is that of a *server session* (or simply a *session*). A session (also commonly referred to as a "visit") is a sequence of pageviews by a single user during a single visit. The notion of a session can be further abstracted by selecting a subset of pageviews in the session that are significant or relevant for the analysis tasks at hand. We shall refer to such a semantically meaningful subset of pageviews as a *transaction*. It is important to note that a transaction does not refer simply to product purchases, but it can include a variety of types of user actions as captured by different pageviews in a session.

- **Content data:** The content data in a site is the collection of objects and relationships that are conveyed to the user. For the most part, this data is comprised of combinations of textual material and images. The data sources used to deliver or generate this data include static HTML/XML pages, image, video, and sound files, dynamically generated page segments from scripts or other applications, and collections of records from the operational database(s). The site content data also includes semantic or structural meta-data embedded within the site or individual pages, such as descriptive keywords, document attributes, semantic tags, or HTTP variables. Finally, the underlying domain ontology for the site is also considered part of content data. The domain ontology may be captured implicitly within the site, or it may exist in some explicit form. The explicit representation of domain ontologies may include conceptual hierarchies over page contents, such as product categories, structural hierarchies represented by the underlying file and directory structure in which the site content is stored, explicit representation of semantic content and relationships via an ontology language such as RDF, or a database schema over the data contained in the operational databases.

- **Structure data:** The structure data represents the designer's view of the content organization within the site. This organization is captured via the inter-page linkage structure among pages, as reflected through hyperlinks. The structure data also includes the intra-page structure of the content represented in the arrangement of HTML or XML tags within a page. For example, both HTML and XML documents can be represented as tree structures over the space of tags in the page. The structure data for a site is normally captured by an automatically generated "site map" which represents the hyperlink structure of the site. A site mapping tool must have the capability to capture and represent the inter- and intra-pageview relationships. This necessity becomes most evident in a frame-based site where portions of distinct pageviews may represent the same physical page. For dynamically generated pages, the site mapping tools must either incorporate intrinsic knowledge of the underlying applications and scripts, or must have the ability to generate content segments using a sampling of parameters passed to such applications or scripts.

- **User data:** The operational database(s) for the site may include additional user profile information. Such data may include demographic or other identifying information on registered users, user ratings on various objects such as pages, products, or movies, past purchase or visit histories of users, as well as other explicit or implicit representation of users' interests. Obviously, capturing such data would require explicit interactions with the users of the site. Some of this data can be captured anonymously, without any identifying user information, so long as there is the ability to distinguish among different users. For example, anonymous information contained in client-side cookies can be considered a part of the user's profile information, and can be used to identify repeat visitors to a site. Many personalization applications require the storage of prior user profile information. For example, collaborative filtering applications, generally, store prior ratings of objects by users, though, such information can be obtained anonymously, as well.

For a detailed discussion of preprocessing issues related to Web usage mining see Cooley et al. (1999). Usage preprocessing results in a set of n pageviews, $P = \{p_1, p_2, \cdots, p_n\}$, and a set of m user transactions, $T = \{t_1, t_2, \cdots, t_m\}$, where each t_i in T is a subset of P. *Pageviews* are semantically meaningful entities to which mining tasks are applied (such as pages or products). Conceptually, we view each transaction t as an l-length sequence of ordered pairs:

$$t = \left\langle (p_1^t, w(p_1^t)), (p_2^t, w(p_2^t)), \cdots, (p_l^t, w(p_l^t)) \right\rangle,$$

where each $p_i^t = p_j$ for some j in $\{1, \cdots, n\}$, and $w(p_i^t)$ is the weight associated with pageview p_i^t in transaction t, representing its significance (usually, but not exclusively, based on time duration).

For many data mining tasks, such as clustering and association rule discovery, as well as collaborative filtering based on the kNN technique, we can represent each user transaction as a vector over the n-dimensional space of pageviews. Given the transaction t above, the transaction vector $\vec{t}$ is given by: $t = \left\langle w_{p_1}^t, w_{p_2}^t, \cdots, w_{p_n}^t \right\rangle$, where each $w_{p_i}^t = w(p_j^t)$, for some j in $\{1, \cdots, n\}$, if p_j appears in the transaction t, and $w_{p_i}^t = 0$, otherwise. Thus, conceptually, the set of all user transactions can be viewed as an $m \times n$ transaction-pageview matrix, denoted by TP.

Given a set of transactions as described above, a variety of unsupervised knowledge discovery techniques can be applied to obtain patterns. These techniques such as clustering of transactions (or sessions) can lead to the discovery of important user or visitor segments. Other techniques such as item (e.g., pageview) clustering and association or sequential pattern discovery can be used to find important relationships among items based on the navigational patterns of users in the site. In each case, the discovered patterns can be used in conjunction with the active user session to provide personalized content. This task is performed by a recommendation engine.

REQUIREMENTS FOR
SEMANTIC WEB USAGE MINING

In this section, we present and discuss the essential requirements in the integration of domain knowledge with Web usage data for pattern discovery. Our focus is on the critical tasks that particularly play an important role when the discovered patterns are to be used for Web personalization. As a concrete example, in the last part of this section we discuss an approach for integrating semantic features extracted from the content of Web sites with Web usage data, and how this integrated data can be used in conjunction with clustering to perform personalization. In the next section, we go beyond keyword-based semantics and present a more formal framework for integrating full ontologies with the Web usage mining and personalization processes.

Representation of Domain Knowledge

Representing Domain Knowledge as Content Features

One direct source of semantic knowledge that can be integrated into mining and personalization processes is the textual content of Web site pages. The semantics of a Web site are, in part, represented by the content features associated with items or objects on the Web site. These features include keywords, phrases, category names, or other textual content embedded as meta-information. Content preprocessing involves the extraction of relevant features from text and meta-data.

During the preprocessing, usually different weights are associated with features. For features extracted from meta-data, feature weights are usually provided as part of the domain knowledge specified by the analyst. Such weights may reflect the relative importance of certain concepts. For features extracted from text, weights can normally be derived automatically, for example as a function of the term frequency and inverse document frequency (tf.idf) which is commonly used in information retrieval.

Further preprocessing on content features can be performed by applying text mining techniques. This would provide the ability to filter the input to, or the output from, other mining algorithms. For example, classification of content features based on a concept hierarchy can be used to limit the discovered patterns from Web usage mining to those containing pageviews about a certain subject or class of products. Similarly, performing learning algorithms such as, clustering, formal concept analysis, or association rule mining on the feature space can lead to composite features representing concept categories or hierarchies (Clerkin, Cunningham, & Hayes, 2001; Stumme et al., 2000).

The integration of content features with usage-based personalization is desirable when we are dealing with sites where text descriptions are dominant and other structural relationships in the data are not easy to obtain, e.g., news sites or online help systems, etc. This approach, however, is incapable of capturing more complex relations among objects at a deeper semantic level based on the inherent properties associated with these objects. To be able to recommend different types of complex objects using their underlying properties and attributes, the system must be able to rely on the characterization of user segments and objects, not just based on keywords, but at a deeper semantic level using the domain ontologies for the objects. We will discuss some examples of how integrated content features and usage data can be used for personalization later in this Section.

Representing Domain Knowledge as Structured Data

In Web usage mining, we are interested in the semantics underlying a Web transaction or a user profile which is usually composed of a group of pageview names and query strings (extracted from Web server logs). Such features, in isolation, do not convey the semantics associated with the underlying application. Thus, it is important to create a mapping between these features and the objects, concepts, or events they represent.

Many e-commerce sites generate Web pages by querying operational databases or semi-structured data (e.g., XML and DTDs), from which semantic information can be easily derived. For Web sites in which such structured data cannot be easily acquired, we can adopt machine learning techniques to extract semantic information. Furthermore, the domain knowledge acquired should be machine understandable in order to allow for further processing or reasoning. Therefore, the extracted knowledge should be represented in some standard knowledge representation language.

DAML+OIL (Horrocks & Sattler, 2001) is an example of an ontology language that combines the Web standards from XML and RDF, with the reasoning capabilities from a description logic *SHIP(DL)*. The combinations of relational models and probabilistic models is another common approach to enhance Web personalization with domain knowledge and reasoning mechanism. Several approaches to personalization have used Relational Models such as Relational Markov Model (Anderson et al., 2002). Both of these approaches provide the ability to represent knowledge at different levels of abstraction, and the ability to reason about concepts, including about such relations as subsumption and membership.

In Dai & Mobasher (2002), we adopted the syntax and semantics of another ontology representation framework, *SHOQ(D)*, to represent domain ontologies. In *SHOQ(D)*, the notion of *concrete datatype* is used to specify literal values and *individuals* which represent real objects in the domain ontology. Moreover, *concepts* can be viewed as sets of individuals, and *roles* are binary relations between a pair of concepts or between concepts and data types. The detailed formal definitions for concepts and roles are given in Horrocks & Sattler (2001) and Giugno & Lukasiewicz (2002). Because our current work does not focus on reasoning tasks such as deciding subsumption and membership, we do not focus our discussion on these operations. The reasoning apparatus in *SHOQ(D)* can be used to provide more intelligent data mining services.

Building "Mappings" Between Usage-Level and Domain-Level Instances

During usage data preprocessing or post processing, we may want to assign domain semantics to user navigational patterns by mapping the pageview names or URLs (or queries) to the instances in the knowledge base. To be more specific, instead of describing a user's navigational path as: "$a_1, a_2, ..., a_n$" (where a_i is a URL pointing to a Web resource), we need to represent it using the instances from the knowledge base, such as: "movie(name=Matrix), movie(name=Spiderman), ..., movie(name=Xman)." With the help of a pre-acquired concept hierarchy, we may, for example, be able to infer that the current user's interest is in the category of "Action&Sci-Fi." We refer to this "semantic" form of usage data as "Semantic User Profiles." These profiles, in turn, can be used for semantic pattern discovery and online recommendations. In the context of personalization applications, domain-level (semantic) instances may also need to be mapped back to Web resources or pages. For example, a recommendation engine using semantic user profiles may result in recommendations in the form of a movie genre. This concept must be mapped back into specific pages, URLs, or sections of the site relating to this genre before recommendations can be relayed to the user.

Using Content and Structural Characteristics

Classification algorithms utilizing content and structural features from pages are well-suited for creating mappings from usage data to domain-level instances. For example, in Craven et al. (2000) and Ghani & Fano (2002) classifiers are trained that exploit content or structural features (such as terms, linkage information, and term proximity) of the pageviews. From the pageview names or URLs we can obtain the corresponding Web content such as meta-data or keywords. With help from text classification algorithms, it is possible to efficiently map from keywords to attribute instances (Ghani & Fano, 2002).

Another good heuristics used in creating semantic mappings is based on the anchor text associated with hyperlinks. If we can build the complete user navigational path, we would be able to acquire the anchor text for each URL or pageview name. We can include the anchor text as part of the content features extracted from the body of documents or in isolation. However, whereas the text features in a document represent the semantics of the document, itself, the anchor text represents the semantics of the document to which the associated hyperlink points.

Using Query Strings

So far, we have overlooked the enormous amount of information stored in databases or semi-structured documents associated with a site. Large information servers often serve content integrated from **multiple** underlying servers and databases (Berendt, & Spiliopoulou, 2000). The dynamically generated pages on such servers are based on queries with multiple parameters attached to the URL corresponding to the underlying scripts or applications. Using the Web server query string recorded in the server log files it is possible to reconstruct the response pages. For example, the following are query strings from a hypothetical online bookseller Web site:

http://www.xyz.com/app.cgi?action=viewitem&item=1234567&category=1234

http://www.xyz.com/app.cgi?action=search&searchtype=title&searchstring= web+mining

http://www.xyz.com/app.cgi?action=order&item=1234567&category=1234& couponid=3456

If the background database or semi-structured documents are available, then we can access the content of the instances in the response pages via the name-value pairs from the query strings. This enriches our knowledge base of user interest. In the above bookseller Web site example, if we were able to access background database, we would be able to get the content of item "1234567" in category "1234". In this case, we could have the book name, price, author information of this item. We could recommend other books in the same content category or written by the same author. More generally, in well-designed sites, there is usually an explicitly available semantic mapping between query parameters and objects (such as products and categories), which would obviate the need to reconstruct the content of dynamic pages.

Levels of Abstraction

Capturing semantic knowledge at different levels of abstraction provides more flexibility both in the mining phase and in the recommendation phase. For example, focusing on higher-level concepts in a concept hierarchy would allow certain patterns to emerge which otherwise may be missed due to low support. On the other hand, the ability to drill-down into the discovered patterns based on finer-grained subconcepts would provide the ability to give more focused and useful recommendations.

Domain knowledge with attributes and relations requires the management of a great deal more data than is necessary in traditional approaches to Web usage mining. Thus, it becomes essential to prune unnecessary attributes or relations. For example, it may be possible to examine the number of distinct values of each attribute and generalize the attributes if there is a concept hierarchy over the attribute values. In Han & Fu (1995) a multiple-level association rule mining algorithm is proposed that utilizes concept hierarchies. For example, the usage data in our hypothetical movie site may not provide enough support for an association rule: "Spiderman, Xmen → Xmen2", but mining at a higher level may result in obtaining a rule: "Sci-Fi&Action, Xmen → Xmen2". In Anderson et al. (2002) relational Markov models are built by performing shrinkage (McCallum et al., 1998) between the estimates of parameters at all levels of abstractions relative to a concept hierarchy. If a pre-specified concept hierarchy does not exist, it is possible to automatically create such hierarchies through a variety of machine learning techniques, such as hierarchical agglomerative clustering (Stumme et al., 2000).

Integration of Semantics at Different Stages of Knowledge Discovery

The semantic information stored in the knowledge base can be leveraged at various steps in the knowledge discovery process, namely in the preprocessing phase, in the pattern discovery phase, or during the post-processing of the discovered patterns.

Preprocessing Phase

The main task of data preprocessing is to prune noisy and irrelevant data, and to reduce data volume for the pattern discovery phase. In Mobasher, Dai, Luo, & Nakagawa (2002), it was shown that applying appropriate data preprocessing techniques on usage data could improve the effectiveness of Web personalization. The concept level mappings from the pageview-level data to concepts can also be performed in this phase. This results in a transformed transaction data to which various data mining algorithms can be applied. Specifically, the transaction vector t given previously can be transformed into

a vector $t' = \left\langle w_{o_1}^t, w_{o_2}^t, \cdots, w_{o_k}^t \right\rangle$, where each o_j is a semantic object appearing in one of

the pageviews contained in the transaction, and $w_{o_j}^t$ is a weight associated with that object in the transaction. These semantic objects may be concepts appearing in the concept hierarchy or finer-grained objects representing instances of these concepts.

Pattern Discovery Phase

Successful utilization of domain knowledge in this phase requires extending basic data mining algorithms to deal with relational data to concept hierarchies. As an example, consider a distance-based data mining technique such as clustering. The clustering of flat single-relation data (such as Web user transactions) involves the computation of similarities or distance among transaction vectors. In such cases, normally simple vector-based operations are used. However, in the presence of integrated domain knowledge represented as concept hierarchies or ontologies, the clustering algorithms will have to perform much more complex similarity computations across dimensions and attributes. For example, even if the two user transactions have no pageviews in common, they may still be considered similar provided that the items occurring in both transactions are themselves "similar" based on some of their attributes or properties. The integration of domain knowledge will generate "semantic" usage patterns, introducing great flexibility as well as challenges. The flexibility lies in the pattern discovery being independent of item identities. The challenge is in the development of scalable and efficient algorithms to perform the underlying computational tasks such as similarity computations. We discuss this issue further below.

Post-Processing Phase

Exploiting domain knowledge in this phase can be used to further explain usage patterns or to filter out irrelevant patterns. One possibility is to first perform traditional usage mining tasks on the item-level usage data obtained in the preprocessing phase, and then use domain knowledge to interpret or transform the item level user profiles into "domain-level usage profiles" (Mobasher & Dai, 2002) involving concepts and relations in the ontology. The advantage of this approach is that we can avoid the scalability issues that can be endemic in the pattern discovery phase. The disadvantage is that some important structural relationships may not be used during the mining phase resulting in lower quality patterns.

Aggregation Methods for Complex Objects

To characterize patterns discovered through data mining techniques, it is usually necessary to derive aggregate representation of the patterns. An example of this situation is clustering applications. In the context of Web user transactions, clustering may result in a group of sessions or visitors that are considered similar because of their common navigational patterns. The vector representation of these transactions facilitates the aggregation tasks: the centroid (mean vector) of the transaction cluster acts as a representative of all of the transactions in that cluster. However, in the case of semantically enhanced transactions, the aggregation may have to be performed independently for each of the attributes associated with the objects contained in the cluster.

For example, clustering may result in a group of users who have all visited pages related to several movies. To be able to characterize this group of users at a deeper semantic level, it would be necessary to create an aggregate representation of the collection of movies in which they are interested. This task would require aggregation along each dimension corresponding to the attributes of "movie" instances, such as "genre", "actors", "directors", etc. Since each of these attributes require a different type of aggregation function depending on the data type and the domain, it may be necessary to associate various aggregation functions with the specification of the domain ontology, itself. In the next section we present one approach for solving this problem.

Measuring Semantic Similarities

Measuring similarities (alternatively, distances) among objects is a central task in many data mining algorithms. In the context of Web usage mining this may involve computing similarity measures among pageviews, among user transactions, or among users. This also becomes a critical task in personalization: a current user's profile must be matched with similar aggregate profiles representing the discovered user pat-terns or segments. As in the case of the aggregation problem discussed above, when dealing with semantically enhanced transactions, measuring similarities poses additional challenges. This is because the similarity of two transactions depends on the similarities of the semantic objects contained within the transactions.

Let us again consider the *static* vector model for representing a Web transaction t (or a user profile): $t = \langle w^t_{p_1}, w^t_{p_2}, ..., w^t_{p_n} \rangle$. Computing similarity between two such vectors is straightforward and can be performed using measures such as cosine similarity, Euclidean distance, Pearson correlation (e.g., in case the weights represent user ratings).

When such vectors are transformed according to the underlying semantics, however, the computation of similarities will involve the computation of semantic similarities among the concepts or objects, possibly using different domain-specific similarity measures. Let A and B be two transformed transactions, each represented as a set of semantic objects in a site:

$$A = \{a_1, a_2, \cdots, a_m\} \text{ and } B = \{b_1, b_2, \cdots, b_l\}.$$

The computation of vector similarity between A and B, $Sim(A,B)$, is dependent on the semantic similarities among the component objects, $SemSim(a_i, b_j)$. For instance, one approach might be to compute the weighted sum or average of the similarities among object pairs, such as in:

$$Sim(A, B) = \frac{\sum_{a \in A} \sum_{b \in B} SemSim(a,b)}{|A| \cdot |B|}$$

In general, computing the semantic similarity, $SemSim(a,b)$, is domain dependent and requires knowledge of the underlying structure of among objects. If both objects can be represented using the same vector model (e.g., pages or documents represented as bags of words), we can compute their similarity using standard vector operations. On the other hand, if their representation includes attributes and relations specified in the domain ontology, we need to first make sure that the objects can be classified under a common ontological schema and then measure similarities along the different dimensions corresponding to each attribute. The notion of semantic matching among objects and classes has been a subject of considerable study recently (Rodriguez & Egenhofer, 2003; Palopoli, Sacca, Terracina, & Ursino, 2003; Ganesan, Garcia-Molina, & Widom, 2003).

For example, such an approach was used in Jin & Mobasher (2003) in the context of collaborative filtering with movies. In this work, association analysis was first performed on the "genre" attribute to define a genre hierarchy. Furthermore, the "year" attribute was discretized into intervals, while other attributes, such as "cast", were treated as a bag of words. These preprocessing steps allowed for the definition of appropriate similarity measures for each attribute. Finally, the semantic similarity between two movies, i and j, was defined as a linear combination of attribute-level similarities:

$$SemSim(i, j) = \alpha_1 * CastSim(i, j) + \alpha_2 * DirectorSim(i, j) + \alpha_3 * GenreSim(i, j) + ...,$$

where, α_i are predefined weights for the corresponding attributes.

Example: Using Content Features for Semantic Web Usage Mining

As an example of integrating semantic knowledge with the Web usage mining process, let us consider the especial case of using textual features from the content of Web pages to represent the underlying semantics for the site. As noted earlier, each pageview p can be represented as a k-dimensional feature vector, where k is the total number of extracted features (words or concepts) from the site in a global dictionary. This vector can be given by:

$$p = \langle fw(p, f_1), fw(p, f_2), \cdots, fw(p, f_k) \rangle$$

where $fw(p, f_j)$ is the weight of the jth feature in pageview p, for $1 \le j \le k$. For the whole collection of pageviews in the site, we then have an $n \times k$ pageview-feature matrix $PF = \{p_1, p_2, \cdots, p_n\}$.

There are now at least two basic choices as to when content features can be integrated into the usage-based personalization process: pre-mining integration or post-mining integration.

The pre-mining integration involves the transformation of user transactions, as described earlier, into "content-enhanced" transactions containing the semantic features of the pageviews. While, in practice, there are several ways to accomplish this transformation, the most direct approach involves mapping each pageview in a transaction to one or more content features. The range of this mapping can be the full feature space, or feature sets (composite features) which in turn may represent concepts and concept categories. Conceptually, the transformation can be viewed as the multiplication of the transaction-pageview matrix TP, defined earlier, with the pageview-feature matrix PF. The result is a new matrix $TF = \{t_1, t_2, \cdots, t_n\}$, where each t_i is a k-dimensional vector over the feature space. Thus, a user transaction can be represented as a content feature vector, reflecting that user's interests in particular concepts or topics.

Various data mining tasks can now be performed on the content-enhanced transaction data. For instance, if we apply association rule mining to such data, then we can get a group of association rules on content features. As an example, consider a site containing information about movies. This site may contain pages related to the movies themselves, actors appearing in the movies, directors, and genres. Association rule mining process could generate a rule such as: {"British", "Romance", "Comedy" ⇒ "Hugh Grant"}, suggesting that users who are interested in British romantic comedies may also like the actor Hugh Grant (with a certain degree of confidence). During the online recommendation phase, the user's active session (which is also transformed into a feature vector) is compared with the discovered rules. Before recommendations are made, the matching patterns must be mapped back into Web pages or Web objects. In the above example, if the active session matches the left hand side of the association rule, the recommendation engine could recommend other Web pages that contain the feature "Hugh Grant".

The post-mining integration of semantic features involves combining the results of mining (performed independently on usage and content data) during the online recommendation phase. An example of this approach was presented in Mobasher et al. (2000b), where clustering algorithms were applied to both the transaction matrix TP and the transpose of the feature matrix PF. Since both matrices have pageviews as dimensions, the centroids of the resulting clusters in both cases can be represented as sets of pageview-weight pairs where the weights signify the frequency of the pageview occurrence in the corresponding cluster. We call the patterns generated from content data "content profiles", while the patterns derived from usage data are called "usage profiles". Though they share the same representation, they have different semantics: usage profiles represent a set of transactions with similar navigational behavior, while content profiles contain groups of Web pages with (partly) similar content.

Specifically, given a transaction cluster (respectively, a feature cluster) cl, we can construct the usage (respectively, content) profile pr_{cl} as a set of pageview-weight pairs by computing the centroid of cl:

$$pr_{cl} = \{\langle p, weight(p, pr_{cl})\rangle \mid weight(p, pr_{cl}) \geq \mu\},$$

where:

- the significance weight, $weight(p, pr_{cl})$, of the page p within the usage (respectively, content) profile pr_{cl} is given by:

$$weight(p, pr_{cl}) = \frac{1}{|cl|} \cdot \sum_{s \in cl} w(p, s)$$

- $w(p,s)$ is the weight of page p in transaction (respectively, feature) vector s in the cluster cl; and
- the threshold μ is used to focus only on those pages in the cluster that appear in a sufficient number of vectors in that cluster.

Each such profile, in turn, can be represented as a vector in the original n-dimensional space of pageviews. This aggregate representation can be used directly in the recommendation phase: given a new user, u who has accessed a set of pages, P_u, so far, we can measure the similarity of P_u to the discovered profiles, and recommend to the user those pages in matching profiles which have not yet been accessed by the user. Note that this approach does not distinguish between recommendations emanating from the matching content and usage profiles. Also note that there are many other ways of combining usage profiles and content profiles during the online recommendation phase. For example, we can use content profiles as the last resort in the situation where usage profiles can not provide sufficient number of recommendations.

A FRAMEWORK FOR ONTOLOGY-BASED PERSONALIZATION

At a conceptual level, there may be many different kinds of objects within a given site that are accessible to users. At the physical level, these objects may be represented by one or more Web pages. For example, our hypothetical movie site may contain pages related to the movies, actors, directors, and studios. Conceptually, each of these entities represents a different type of semantic object. During a visit to this site, a user may implicitly access several of these objects together during a session by navigating to various pages containing them. In contrast to content features, ontological representation of domain knowledge contained in the site makes it possible to have a uniform architecture to model such objects, their properties, and their relationships. Furthermore, such a representation would allow for a more natural mapping between the relational schema for the backend databases driving Web applications and the navigational behavior of users.

In this section we will present a general framework for utilizing domain ontologies in Web usage mining and personalization. Figure 3 lays out a general process for such an integrated approach. In keeping with our earlier discussion, it is composed of three main phases: preprocessing, pattern discovery and online recommendation. Each of these phases must take into account the object properties and their relationships as specified in a domain ontology.

We assume that the site ontology is already available (either specified manually, or extracted automatically using ontology learning techniques). The goal of the preprocessing phase is to transform users' navigational transactions into "semantic transaction" by mapping accessed pages and resource to concepts and objects of the specified ontology. The goal of the pattern discovery phase is to create aggregate representation of groups of semantic objects that are implicitly accessed by similar users, thus providing a semantic characterization of user segments with common behavior or interests. Finally,

Figure 3. A General Framework for Personalization Based on Domain Ontologies

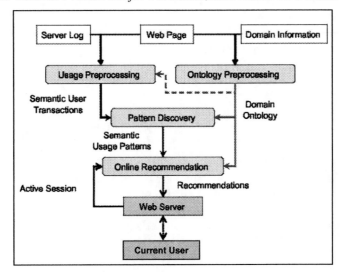

in the recommendation phase, the discovered semantic patterns are utilized in conjunction with an ongoing record of a current user's activity (including, possibly the user's stored profile) to recommend new resources, pages, or objects to that user.

Knowledge Representation

General ontology representation languages such as DAML+OIL (Horrocks, 2002) provide formal syntax and semantics for representing and reasoning with various elements of an ontology. These elements include "individuals" (or objects), "concepts" (which represent sets of individuals), and "roles" (which specify object properties). In DAML+OIL, the notion of a concept is quite general and may encompass a heterogeneous set of objects with different properties (roles) and structures. We, on the other hand, are mainly interested in the aggregate representations for groups of objects that have a homogenous concept structure (i.e., have similar properties and data types). For example, we may be interested in a group of movie objects, each of which has specific values for properties such as "year", "genre", and "actors." We call such a group of objects a *class*. Thus, in our framework, the notion of a class represents a restriction of the notion of a concept in DAML+OIL. It should be noted, however, that the users of a Web site, in general, access a variety of objects belonging to different classes. Thus, this homogeneity assumption would imply that semantic objects within user transactions must first be classified into homogenous classes as a preprocessing step.

More specifically, we define a *class* C as a set of objects together with a set of *attributes*. These attributes together define the internal properties of the objects in C or relationships with other concepts that involve the objects in C. Thus attributes of a class correspond to a subset of the set of roles in the domain ontology. We denote the domain of values of an attribute r as D_r. Furthermore, because we are specifically interested in aggregating objects at the attribute level, we extend the notion of a role to include a domain-specific combination function and an ordering relation.

More formally, a class C is characterized by a finite set of attributes AC, where each attribute a in AC is defined as follows.

Definition: Let C be a class in the domain ontology. An *attribute a AC* is a 4-tuple, where
$$a = \langle T_a, D_a, \prec_a, \psi_a \rangle$$
- T_a is the *type* for the values for the attribute a.
- D_a is the domain of the values for a;
- $\prec_a$ is an ordering relation among the values in D_a; and
- ψ_a is a *combination function* for the attribute a.

The "type" of an attribute in the above definition may be a concrete datatype (such as "string" or "integer") or it may be a set of objects (individuals) belonging to another class.

In the context of data mining, comparing and aggregating values are essential tasks. Therefore, ordering relations among values are necessary properties for attributes. We associate an ordering relation $\prec_a$ with elements in D_a for each attribute a. The ordering relation $\prec_a$ can be null (if no ordering is specified in the domain of values), or it can define a partial or a total order among the domain values. For standard types such as values from a continuous range, we assume the usual ordering. In cases when an attribute a

represents a concept hierarchy, the domain values of a are a set of labels, and $\prec_a$ is a partial order representing the "is-a" relation.

Furthermore, we associate a data mining operator, called the *combination function*, ψ_a, with each attribute a. This combination function defines an aggregation operation among the corresponding attribute values of a set of objects belonging to the same class. This function is essentially a generalization of the "mean" or "average" function applied to corresponding dimension values of a set of vectors when computing the centroid vector. In this context, we assume that the combination function is specified as part of the domain ontology for each attribute of a class. An interesting extension would be to automatically learn the combination function for each attribute based on a set of positive and negative examples.

Classes in the ontology define the structural and semantic properties of objects in the domain which are "instances" of that class. Specifically, each object o in the domain is also characterized by a set of attributes A_o corresponding to the attributes of a class in the ontology. In order to more precisely define the notion of an object as an instance of a class, we first define the notion of an instance of an attribute.

Definition: Given an attribute $a = \langle T_a, D_a, \prec_a, \psi_a \rangle$ and an attribute $b = \langle T_b, D_b, \prec_b, \psi_b \rangle$, b is an *instance* of a, if $D_b \subseteq D_a$, $T_b = T_a$, $\psi_b = \psi_a$, and $\prec_b$ is a restriction of $\prec_a$ to D_b. The attribute b is a *null instance* of a, if Db is empty.

Definition: Given a class C with attribute set $A_C = \{a_1^C, a_2^C, \cdots, a_n^C\}$, we say that an object o is *an instance of* C, if o has attributes $A_o = \{a_1^o, a_2^o, \cdots, a_n^o\}$ such that each is a, possibly null, instance of a_1^C.

Based on the definitions of attribute and object instances, we can now provide a more formal representation of the combination function ψ_a. Let C be a class and $\{o_1, o_2, \cdots, o_m\}$ a set of object instances of C. Let $a \in A_C$ be an attribute of class C. The combination function ψ_a can be represented by:

$$\psi_a\left(\left\{\langle a_{o_1}, w_1 \rangle, \langle a_{o_2}, w_2 \rangle, \cdots, \langle a_{o_m}, w_m \rangle\right\}\right) = \langle a_{agg}, w_{agg} \rangle,$$

where each belonging to object o_i is an instance of the attribute a, and each w_i is a weight associated with that attribute instance (representing the significance of that attribute relative to the other instances). Furthermore, a_{agg} is a *pseudo instance* of a meaning that it is an instance of a which does not belong to a real object in the underlying domain. The weight w_{agg} of a_{agg} is a function of $w_1, w_2, \dots, w_n$.

Given a set of object instances, of a class C, a *domain-level aggregate profile* for these instances is obtained by applying the combination function for each attribute in C to all of the corresponding attribute instances across all objects $o_1, o_2, \dots, o_n$.

Ontology Preprocessing

The ontology preprocessing phase takes as input domain information (such as database schema and meta-data, if any) as well as Web pages, and generates the site ontology. For simple Web sites, ontologies can be easily designed manually or derived semi-automatically from the site content. However, it is more desirable to have automatic ontology acquisition methods for a large Web site, especially in Web sites with dynamically generated Web pages. E-commerce Web sites, for instance, usually have well-structured Web content, including predefined metadata or database schema. Therefore it is easier to build automatic ontology extraction mechanisms that are site-specific.

There have been a number of efforts dealing with the ontology learning problem (Clerkin et al., 2001; Craven et al., 2000; Maedche & Staab, 2000). A wide range of information, such as thesauri, content features, and database schema can help to identify ontologies. Many of these approaches have focused on extracting ontological information from the Web, in general. In Berendt et al. (2002) the notion of "Semantic Web Mining" was introduced, including a framework for the extraction of a concept hierarchy and the application of data mining techniques to find frequently occurring combinations of concepts.

An Example

As an example, let us revisit our hypothetical movie Web site. The Web site includes collections of pages containing information about movies, actors, directors, etc. A collection of pages describing a specific movie might include information such as the movie title, genre, starring actors, director, etc. An actor or director's information may include name, filmography (a set of movies), gender, nationality, etc. The portion of domain ontology for this site, as described, contains the classes **Movie, Actor** and **Director** (Figure 4). The collection of Web pages in the site represents a group of embedded objects that are the instances of these classes.

In our example, the class **Movie** has attributes such as *Year, Actor* (representing the relation "acted by"), *Genre,* and *Director.* The *Actor* and *Director* attributes have values that are other objects in the ontology, specifically, object instances of classes **Actor** and **Director,** respectively. The attribute *Year* is an example of an attribute whose datatype is positive integers with the usual ordering. The attribute *Genre* has a concrete datatype whose domain values in D_{Genre} are a set of labels (e.g., "Romance" and "Comedy"). The ordering relation $\prec_{Genre}$ defines a partial order based on the "is-a" relation among subsets of these labels (resulting in a concept hierarchy of Genres, a portion of which is shown in Figure 4).

Figure 4. Ontology for a Movie Web Site

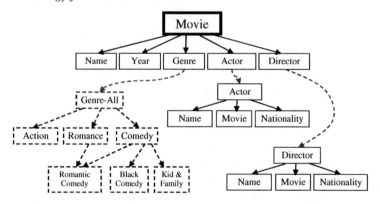

Figure 5 shows a **Movie** instance "About a Boy" and its related attributes and relations extracted from a Web page. The schema of the class **Movie** is shown at the bottom left portion of the figure. Here we treat the classes **Genre** and **Year** as attributes of the class **Movie**. The instances of the ontology are shown at the bottom right of the figure. The *Genre* attribute contains a partial order among labels representing a concept hierarchy of movie genres. We use a restriction of this partial order to represent the genre to which the **Movie** instance belongs. The diagram also shows a keyword bag containing the important keywords in that page.

An attribute *a* of an object *o* has a domain D_a. In cases when the attribute has unique a value for an object, D_a is a singleton. For example, consider an object instance of class **Movie,** "About a Boy" (see Figure 5). The attribute *Actor* contains two objects "H. Grant" and "T. Collette" that are instances of the class **Actor** (for the sake of presentation we use the actors' names to stand for the object instances of **Actor**). Therefore, D_{Actor} = { "H. Grant", "T. Collette"}. Also, a real object may have values for only some of the attributes. In this case the other attributes have empty domains. For instance, the attribute *Director* in the example has an empty domain and is thus not depicted in the figure. We may, optionally, associate a weight with each value in the attribute domain D_a (usually in the range [0,1]). This may be useful in capturing the relative importance of each attribute value.

For example, in a given movie the main actors should have higher weights than other actors in the cast. In our example, the object "H. Grant" has weight 0.6 and the object "Toni Collette" has weight 0.4. Unless otherwise specified, we assume that the weight associated with each attribute value is 1. In the object *o* shown in Figure 5, the domain for the attribute *Genre* is the set of labels {Genre-All, Action, Romance, Comedy, Romantic Comedy, Black Comedy, Kids & Family}. The ordering relation $\prec^o_{Genre}$ is a restriction of $\prec_{Genre}$ to the subset {Genre--All, Comedy, Romantic Comedy, Kids & Family}.

Figure 5. Example of Ontology Preprocessing

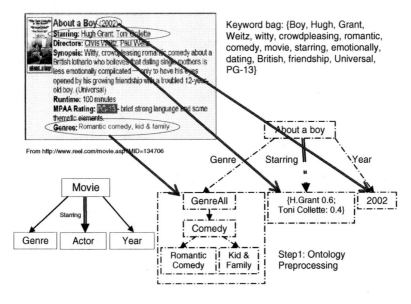

Pattern Discovery

As depicted in Figure 3 domain ontologies can be incorporated into usage preprocessing to generate semantic user transactions, or they can be integrated into pattern
discovery phase to generate semantic usage patterns. In the following example, we will
focus on the latter approach.

Given a discovered usage profile (for example, a set of pageview-weight pairs
obtained by clustering user transactions), we can transform it into a domain-level
aggregate representation of the underlying objects (Dai & Mobasher, 2002). To distinguish between the representations we call the original discovered pattern an "item-level"
usage profile, and we call the new profile based on the domain ontology a "domain-level"
aggregate profile. The item-level profile is first represented as a weighted set of objects:
$pr = \{\langle o_1, w_1 \rangle, \langle o_2, w_2 \rangle, \cdots, \langle o_n, w_n \rangle$ in which each o_i is an object in the underlying domain
ontology and w_i represents o_i's significance in the profile pr. Here we assume that, either
using manual rules, or through supervised learning methods, we can extract various
object instances represented by the pages in the original page- or item-level usage
profile. The transformed profile represents a set of objects accessed together frequently
by a group of users (as determined through Web usage mining). Objects, in the usage
profile, that belong to the same class are combined to form an aggregated pseudo object
belonging to that class. An important benefit of aggregation is that the pattern volume
is significantly reduced, thus relieving the computation burden for the recommendation
engine. Our goal is to create an aggregate representation of this weighted set of objects
to characterize the common interests of the user segment captured by the usage profile
at the domain level.

Given the representation of a profile pr as a weighted set of objects, the objects in
pr may be instances of different classes $C_1, C_2, ..., C_k$ in the ontology. The process of
creating a domain-level aggregate profile begins by partitioning pr into collections of
objects with each collection containing all objects that are instances of a specified class
(in other words, the process of classifying the object instances in pr). Let G_i denote the
elements of pr that are instances of the class C_i.

Having partitioned pr into k groups of homogeneous objects, $G_1, ..., G_k$, the problem
is reduced to creating aggregate representation of each partition G_i. This task is
accomplished with the help of the combination functions for each of the attributes of C_i
some of whose object instances are contained in G_i. Once the representatives for every
partition of objects are created, we assign a significance weight to each representative
to mark the importance of this group of objects in the profile. In our current approach the
significance weight for each representative is computed as the weighted sum of all the
object weights in the partition. However, significance weight can be computed using
other numeric aggregation functions.

Examples Continued: Generating Domain-Level Aggregate Profiles

To illustrate the semantic aggregation process, let us return to our movie site
example. The aggregation process requires that a "combination function" be defined for
each attribute of an object in the domain ontology. Figure 6 and 8 show an example of
such process. Each movie object has attribute "Name", "Actor", "Genre" and "Year". For
the attribute *Name*, we are interested in all the movie names appearing in the instances.
Thus we can define ψ_{Name} to be the union operation performed on all the singleton *Name*

attributes of all movie objects. On the other hand, the attribute *Actor* contains a weighted set of objects belonging to class **Actor**. In fact, it represents the relation "Starring" between the actor objects and the movie object. In such cases we can use a vector-based weighted mean operation as the combination function. For example, we will determine the aggregate weight of an actor object *o* by:

$$w_o' = \left(\sum_i w_i \cdot w_o\right) / \sum_i w_i.$$

Applying ψ_{Actor} in our example will result in the aggregate actor object $\{\langle S, 0.58\rangle, \langle T, 0.27\rangle, \langle U, 0.09\rangle\}$. As for the attribute *Year*, the combination function may create a range of all the *Year* values appearing in the objects. Another possible solution is to discretize the full *Year* range into decades and find the most common decades that are in the domains of the attribute. In our example, using the range option, this may result in an aggregate instance [1999, 2002] for the *Year* attribute.

The attribute *Genre* of **Movie** contains a partial order representing a concept hierarchy among different *Genre* values. The combination function, in this case, can perform tree (or graph) matching to extract the common parts of the conceptual hierarchies among all instances. Extracting the common nodes from this hierarchy may also depend on the weights associated with the original objects leading to different weights on the graph edges. For example, given that the higher weight Movies 1 and 2 have "Romance" in common, this node may be selected for the aggregate instance, even though it is not present in Movie 3. However, the weight of "Romance" may be less than that of "Comedy" which is present in all three movies.

Figure 6 shows the item-level usage profile and its representation as a weighted set of objects, as well as the resulting domain-level aggregate profile. Note that the original item-level profile gives us little information about the reasons why these objects were commonly accessed together. However, after we characterize this profile at the domain-

Figure 6.   Creating an Aggregate Representation of a Set of Movie Objects

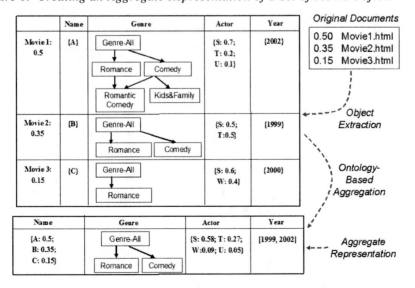

level, we find some interesting patterns: they all belong to *Genre* "Comedy" (and to a lesser degree "Romance), and the actor *S* has a high score compared with other actors.

Online Recommendation Phase

In contrast to transaction-based usage profiles, semantic usage profiles capture the underlying common properties and relations among those objects. This fine-grained domain knowledge, captured in aggregate form enables more powerful approaches to personalization. As before, we consider the browsing history of the current user, i.e., active session, to be a weighted set of Web pages that the user has visited. The same transformation described in the last subsection can be used to create a semantic representation of the user's active session. We call this representation the *current user profile*.

Figure 7 presents the basic procedure for generating recommendations based on semantic profiles. The recommendation engine matches the current user profile against the discovered domain-level aggregate profiles. The usage profiles with matching score greater than some pre-specified threshold are considered to represent this user's potential interests. A successful match implies that the current user shares common interests with the group of users represented by the profile. The matching process results in an *extended user profile* which is obtained by applying the aggregation process described above to the domain-level profiles and the original user profile.

The recommendation engine then instantiates the user's extended profile to real Web objects and will recommend them to the user. We can also exploit structural relationships among classes during the recommendation process. For example, if a concept hierarchy exists among objects, and the recommendation engine can not find a good match for a user profile at a certain concept level, then it can generalize to a more abstract level (e.g., from "romantic comedy" to "romance").

This approach has several advantages over traditional usage-based personalization. First, it retains the user-to-user relationships that can be captured by the discovered usage profiles. Secondly, in contrast to standard collaborative filtering, it provides more flexibility in matching aggregate usage profiles with the current user's activity because the matching process involves comparison of features and relationships, not exact item

Figure 7. Online Recommendation Enhanced by Domain Ontologies

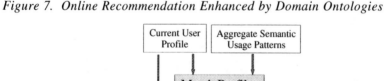

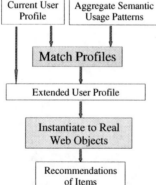

identities. Thirdly, the items do not have to appear in any usage profiles in order to be recommended, since fine-grained domain relationships are considered during the instantiation process. The previous example shows that this approach can also be used to solve the "new item" problem. Furthermore, it can alleviate the notorious "sparsity" problem in collaborative filtering systems by allowing for "fuzzy" comparisons between two user profiles (or ratings). The basis for matching profiles does not have to be similar ratings on the same items. The comparison can be based on showing interest in different objects with similar properties (for example, purchasing items that have same brand). Therefore, even if the raw transaction or rating data is sparse, the semantic attributes of items or users can be used to indirectly infer potential interest in other items.

CONCLUSIONS

We have explored various approaches, requirements, and issues for integrating semantic knowledge into the personalization process based on Web usage mining. We have considered approaches based on the extraction of semantic features from the textual content contained in a site and their integration with Web usage mining tasks and personalization both in the pre-mining and the post-mining phases of the process. We have also presented a framework for Web personalization based on full integration of domain ontologies and usage patterns. The examples provided throughout this chapter reveal how such a framework can provide insightful patterns and smarter personalization services.

We leave some interesting research problems for open discussion and future work. Most important among these are techniques for computing similarity between domain objects and aggregate domain-level patterns, as well as learning techniques to automatically determine appropriate combination functions used in the aggregation process.

More generally, the challenges lie in the successful integration of ontological knowledge at every stage of the knowledge discovery process. In the preprocessing phase, the challenges are in automatic methods for the extraction and learning of the ontologies and in the mapping of users' activities at the clickstream level to more abstracts concepts and classes. For the data mining phase, the primary goal is to develop new approaches that take into account complex semantic relationships such as those present in relational databases with multiple relations. Indeed, in recent years, there has been more focus on techniques such as those based relational data mining. Finally in the personalization stage, the challenge is in developing techniques that can successfully and efficiently measure semantic similarities among complex objects (possibly from different ontologies).

In this chapter we have only provided an overview of the relevant issues and suggested a road map for further research and development in this area. We believe that the successful integration of semantic knowledge with Web usage mining is likely to lead to the next generation of personalization tools which are more intelligent and more useful for Web users.

REFERENCES

Anderson, C., Domingos, P., & Weld, D. (2002). Relational markov models and their application to adaptive Web navigation. *Proceedings of the Eighth ACM SIGKDD International Conference on Knowledge Discovery and Data Mining* (KDD-2002), Edmonton, Alberta, Canada.

Berendt, B., & Spiliopoulou, M. (2000). Analysing navigation behaviour in Websites integrating multiple information systems. *VLDB Journal, Special Issue on Databases and the Web, 9*(1), 56-75.

Berendt, B., Hotho, A., & Stumme, G. (2002). Towards semantic Web mining. *Proceedings of the First International Semantic Web Conference* (ISWC02), Sardinia, Italy.

Bollacker, K., Lawrence, S., & Giles, C.L. (1998). Citeseer: An autonomous Web agent for automatic retrieval and identification of interesting publications. *Proceedings of the Second International Conference on Autonomous Agents*, Minneapolis, Minnesota.

Chakrabarti, S., Dom, B., Gibson, D., Kleinberg, J., Raghavan, P., & Rajagopalan, S. (1998). Automatic resource list compilation by analyzing hyperlink structure and associated text. *Proceedings of the 7th International World Wide Web Conference*, Brisbane, Australia.

Chakrabarti, S., van den Berg, M., & Dom, B. (1999). Focused crawling: A new approach to topic-specific Web resource discovery. *Proceedings of the 3rd World Wide Web Conference*, Toronto.

Claypool, M., Gokhale, A., Miranda, T., Murnikov, P., Netes, D., & Sartin, M. (1999). Combining content-based and collaborative filters in an online newspaper. *Proceedings of the ACM SIGIR '99 Workshop on Recommender Systems: Algorithms and Evaluation*, Berkeley, California.

Clerkin, P., Cunningham, P., & Hayes, C. (2001). Ontology discovery for the semantic Web using hierarchical clustering. *Semantic Web Mining Workshop at ECML/PKDD-2001*, Freiburg, Germany.

Cooley, R., Mobasher, B., & Srivastava, J. (1997). Web mining: Information and pattern discovery on the World Wide Web. *Proceedings of the International Conference on Tools with Artificial Intelligence*, 558-567, Newport Beach. IEEE Press.

Cooley, R., Mobasher, B., & Srivastava, J. (1999). Data preparation for mining World Wide Web browsing patterns. *Journal of Knowledge and Information Systems, 1*(1), 5-32.

Craven, M., DiPasquo, D., Freitag, D., McCallum, A., Mitchell, T., Nigam, K., & Slattery, S. (2000). Learning to construct knowledge bases from the World Wide Web. *Artificial Intelligence, 118*(1-2), 69-113.

Dai, H., & Mobasher, B. (2002). Using ontologies to discover domain-level Web usage profiles. *Proceedings of the 2nd Semantic Web Mining Workshop at ECML/PKDD 2002*, Helsinki, Finland.

Ganesan, P., Garcia-Molina, H., & Widom, J. (2003). Exploiting hierarchical domain structure to compute similarity. *ACM Transactions on Information Systems, 21*(1), 63-94.

Getoor, L., Friedman, N., Koller, D., & Taskar, B. (2001). Learning probabilistic models of relational structure. *Proceedings of the 18th International Conference on Machine Learning.*

Ghani, R., & Fano, A. (2002). Building recommender systems using a knowledge base of product semantics. *Proceedings of the Workshop on Recommendation and Personalization in E-Commerce*, 2nd International Conference on Adaptive Hypermedia and Adaptive Web Based Systems, Malaga, Spain.

Giugno, R., & Lukasiewicz, T. (2002). P-SHOQ(D): A probabilistic extension of SHOQ(D) for probabilistic ontologies in the semantic Web. *Proceedings of the 8th European Conference on Logics in Artificial Intelligence*, Cosenza, Italy.

Han, J., & Fu, Y. (1995). Discovery of multiple-level association rules from large databases. *Proceedings of the 1995 International Conference on Very Large Data Bases* (VLDB95), Zurich, Switzerland.

Herlocker, J., Konstan, J., Borchers, A., & Riedl, J. (1999). An algorithmic framework for performing collaborative filtering. *Proceedings of the 22nd ACM Conference on Research and Development in Information Retrieval* (SIGIR'99), Berkeley, CA.

Horrocks, I. (2002). DAML+OIL: A description logic for the semantic Web. *IEEE Data Engineering Bulletin, 25*(1), 4-9.

Horrocks, I., & Sattler, U. (2001). Ontology reasoning in the SHOQ(D) description logic. *Proceedings of the 17th International Joint Conference on Artificial Intelligence*, Seattle, WA.

Hotho, A., Maedche, A., & Staab, S. (2001). Ontology-based text clustering. *Proceedings of the IJCAI-2001 Workshop Text Learning: Beyond Supervision*, Seattle, WA.

Jin, X., & Mobasher, B. (2003). Using semantic similarity to enhance item-based collaborative filtering. *Proceedings of The 2nd IASTED International Conference on Information and Knowledge Sharing*, Scottsdale, Arizona.

Joachims, T., Freitag, D., & Mitchell, T. (1997). Webwatcher: A tour guide for the World Wide Web. *Proceedings of the 15th International Conference on Artificial Intelligence*, Nagoya, Japan.

Lieberman, H. (1995). Letizia: An agent that assists Web browsing. *Proceedings of the 1995 International Joint Conference on Artificial Intelligence*, Montreal, Canada.

Loh, S., Wives, L.K., & de Oliveira, J.P. (2000). Concept-based knowledge discovery in texts extracted from the Web. *SIGKDD Explorations, 2*(1), 29-39.

Maedche, A., & Staab, S. (2000). Discovering conceptual relations from text. *Proceedings of the European Conference on Artificial Intelligence* (ECAI00), Berlin.

Maedche, A., Ehrig, M., Handschuh, S., Volz, R., & Stojanovic, L. (2002). Ontology-focused crawling of documents and relational metadata. *Proceedings of the 11th International World Wide Web Conference* (WWW02), Honolulu, Hawaii.

McCallum, A., Rosenfeld, R., Mitchell, T., & Ng, A. (1998). Improving text classification by shrinkage in a hierarchy of classes. *Proceedings of the 15th International Conference on Machine Learning*, Madison, Wisconsin.

Melville, P., Mooney, R.J., & Nagarajan, R. (2002). Content-boosted collaborative filtering for improved recommendations. *Proceedings of the 18th National Conference on Artificial Intelligence* (AAAI02), Edmonton, Alberta, Canada.

Mobasher, B., Cooley, R., & Srivastava, J. (2000a). Automatic personalization based on Web usage mining. *Communications of the ACM, 43*(8), 142-151.

Mobasher, B., Dai, H., Luo, T., & Nakagawa, M. (2001). Effective personalization based on association rule discovery from Web usage data. *Proceedings of the 3rd ACM Workshop on Web Information and Data Management* (WIDM01), Atlanta, Georgia.

Mobasher, B., Dai, H., Luo, T., & Nakagawa, M. (2002). Discovery and evaluation of aggregate usage profiles for Web personalization. *Data Mining and Knowledge Discovery, 6*, 61-82.

Mobasher, B., Dai, H., Luo, T., Sun, Y., & Zhu, J. (2000b). Integrating Web usage and content mining for more effective personalization. *E-Commerce and Web Technologies: Proceedings of the EC-WEB 2000 Conference*, Lecture Notes in Computer Science (LNCS) 1875, 165-176. Springer.

Palopoli, L., Sacca, D., Terracina, G., & Ursino, D. (2003). Uniform techniques for deriving similarities of objects and subschemes in heterogeneous databases. *IEEE Transactions on Knowledge and Data Engineering, 15*(1), 271-294.

Palpanas, T., & Mendelzon, A. (1999). Web prefetching using partial match prediction. *Proceedings of the 4th International Web Caching Workshop* (WCW99), San Diego, CA.

Parent, S., Mobasher, B., & Lytinen, S. (2001). An adaptive agent for Web exploration based on concept hierarchies. *Proceedings of the International Conference on Human Computer Interaction*, New Orleans, LA.

Pazzani, M. (1999). A framework for collaborative, content-based and demographic filtering. *Artificial Intelligence Review, 13*(5-6), 393-408.

Perkowitz, M., & Etzioni, O. (1998). Adaptive Websites: Automatically synthesizing Web pages. *Proceedings of the 15th National Conference on Artificial Intelligence*, Madison, WI.

Pitkow, J., & Pirolli, P. (1999). Mining longest repeating subsequences to predict WWW surfing. *Proceedings of the 2nd USENIX Symposium on Internet Technologies and Systems*, Boulder, Colorado.

Rodriguez, M.A., & Egenhofer, M.J. (2003). Determining semantic similarity among entity classes from different ontologies. *IEEE Transactions on Knowledge and Data Engineering, 15*(2), 442-456.

Sarwar, B.M., Karypis, G., Konstan, J., & Riedl, J. (2000). Analysis of recommender algorithms for e-commerce. *Proceedings of the 2nd ACM E-Commerce Conference* (EC'00), Minneapolis, MN.

Srivastava, J., Cooley, R., Deshpande, M., & Tan, P. (2000). Web usage mining: Discovery and applications of usage patterns from Web data. *SIGKDD Explorations, 1*(2), 12-23.

Spiliopoulou, M. (2000). Web usage mining for Web site evaluation. *Communications of ACM, 43*(8), 127-134.

Stumme, G., Taouil, R., Bastide, Y., Pasquier, N., & Lakhal, L. (2000). Fast computation of concept lattices using data mining techniques. *Proceedings of the Knowledge Representation Meets Databases Conference* (KRDB00), Berlin.

Chapter XIV

Web Usage Mining in Search Engines

Ricardo Baeza-Yates
Universidad de Chile, Chile

ABSTRACT

Search engine logs not only keep navigation information, but also the queries made by their users. In particular, queries to a search engine follow a power-law distribution, which is far from uniform. Queries and related clicks can be used to improve the search engine itself in different aspects: user interface, index performance, and answer ranking. In this chapter we present some of the main ideas proposed in query mining and we show a few examples based on real data from a search engine focused on the Chilean Web.

INTRODUCTION

Given the rate of growth of the Web, scalability of search engines is a key issue, as the amount of hardware and network resources needed is large and expensive. In addition, search engines are popular tools, so they have heavy constraints on query answer time. So, the efficient use of resources can improve both scalability and answer time. One tool to achieve these goals is Web mining. In this chapter we focus on Web usage mining of logs of queries and user clicks to improve search engines and Websites. We do not consider other kinds of Web mining such as link analysis (Chakrabarti, 2002), content mining, or Web dynamics (Levene & Poulovassilis, 2003).

There are few papers that deal with the use of query logs to improve search engines, because this information is usually not disclosed. The exceptions deal with strategies for caching the index and/or the answers (Markatos, 2000; Saraiva et al., 2001; Xie &

O'Hallaron, 2002), and query clustering using click-through data associated with queries (obtaining a bipartite graph) for ranking or related goals (Beeferman & Berger, 2000; DirectHit, 1997; Wen, Nie & Zhang, 2001; Xue et al., 2002; Zhang & Dong, 2003). Other papers are focused on user behavior while searching, for example detecting the differences among new and expert users or correlating user clicks with Web structure (Baeza-Yates & Castillo, 2001; Holscher & Strube, 2000; Pradumonio et al., 2002). Recently, there has been some work on finding queries related to a Website (Davison et al., 2003) and weighting different words in the query to improve ranking (Schaale et al., 2003).

The main goal of this chapter is to show how valuable it is to perform log query mining, by presenting several different applications of this idea combined with standard usage mining. Although past research has focused on the technical aspects of search engines, analyzing queries has a broader impact in Web search and design in two different aspects: *Web findability* and *information scent*. Web findability[1] or ubiquity is a measure of how easy it is to find a Website when search engines are the main access tools. To improve findability, there are several techniques. One is to use query log analysis of Website search and include in the Website text the most used query words.

Information scent (Pirolli, 1996) is how good a word is with respect to words with the same semantics. For example, polysemic words (words with multiple meanings) may have less information scent. The most common queries are usually the ones with more information scent. When analyzing Web search queries we find words that are found (or not found) on a site but have more or a similar information scent to words in the home page, and words that are not found that imply new information that needs to be added.

This chapter is organized as follows. We start with some basic concepts followed by some primary statistics of search engine usage. Next we present two applications of the search engine log. First, using the query distribution, we present an inverted file organization with three levels: precomputed answers, and main and secondary memory indexes. We show that by using half the index in main memory we can answer 80% of all queries, and that using a small number of precomputed answers we can improve the query answer time on at least 7% (Baeza-Yates & Saint-Jean, 2003b). Second, we present an algorithm that uses queries and clicks to improve ranking (Zhang & Dong, 2003) by capturing semantic relations of queries and Web pages. We conclude with some open problems.

PRELIMINARIES

Zipf's Law

Zipf's law was introduced in the late 1940s to describe several empirical observations such as the distribution of the population of cities or the frequency of words in English written text (Zipf, 1932). If F_i is the frequency of the *i-th* most frequent event, we have that $F_i \sim 1/i^\alpha$ where α is a constant, and the parameter of the distribution. In a log-log graph, α is the slope (without the sign) of the line. In the case of words, it means that there are few very frequent words (usually called stop words) and many unusual words. In Figure 1, the first part of the curve is the frequent words, while the last part of the curve is the unusual words. Perhaps, due to this distribution, the number of distinct words in a text (vocabulary) does not grow linearly, but follows a sublinear curve of the form

$N=O(T^\beta)$ (Heaps' law), with T the total number of words, and β around 0.5 for English text (Baeza-Yates & Ribeiro-Neto, 1999) and a bit larger for the Web (around 0.6).

Inverted Files

The main components of an inverted file are the vocabulary or list of unique words and the posting file, which holds the occurrences in the text of each word in the vocabulary. For each word we basically have a list of pointers to Web pages plus some additional information that is used for ranking the results. The exact implementation depends on the retrieval model used and if we want to use full addressing (for example to answer sentence queries) or just point to Web pages to save space. As the words in the text are not uniform, the posting file has few long lists as well as many more short lists, following the Zipf distribution, which can be compressed efficiently (Baeza-Yates & Ribeiro-Neto, 1999).

Due to the Heaps' law, we can assume that the vocabulary always fits in main memory. In practice, the vocabulary of a large search engine has several million words that will point to hundreds of millions of Web pages. Due to the constraints imposed by concurrent access to search engines, the inverted file should be in main memory (RAM), but as it is too large, part of the index will be in secondary memory (disk), with the subsequent loss in query answer time.

Web Log Data

For our experiment we use about 800,000 pages from a vertical search engine targeted on the Chilean Web, TodoCL (TodoCL, 2000). We define the Chilean Web as all .cl domains plus all Websites with IP addresses provided by Chilean ISPs. In this set of pages we find $T=151,173,460$ words, from which $N=2,067,040$ were unique, thus establishing the vocabulary. The average length of a word in the vocabulary is $\bar{x}=8.46$. The number of documents where a word appears follows a Zipf's distribution with parameter α about 1.5 as seen in Figure 1 (the model is fitted in the main part of the graph).

Figure 1. Words in the Vocabulary vs. their Number of Occurrences in Web Pages

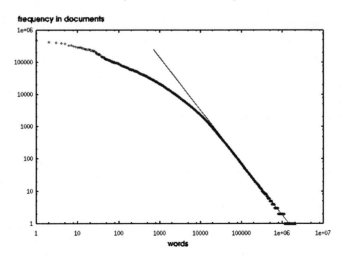

The query set, from the same search engine, is a two-month log from 2001 that consists of 738,390 queries containing 777,351 words (that is, an average of 1.05 words per query), where the unique words are $C=465,021$.

SEARCH ENGINE USAGE

In this section we present basic statistics about the queries. Figure 2 shows that the frequency of query words also follow Zipf's law, with the parameter $\alpha = 1.42$. This is larger than the parameter 0.59 obtained by Saraiva et al. (2001), perhaps due to language and cultural differences.

The standard correlation among the frequency of a word in the Web pages and in the queries is 0.15, which is very low. That is, words in the content of the Web pages follow a Zipf's law distribution that is very different from the distribution of the words in the query, as is depicted in Figure 3 (any correlation would show as a line in the figure.) There are many common words in both the queries and the content, most of them articles, pronouns, and so forth (that is, *stop words*), but also other words like *Chile*. Examples of popular queries that do not find many answers are *Hentai, Mexico, DivX, covers,* and *melodies.* This implies that what people search for is different from what people publish on the Web.

The search engine log also registers the number of answer pages seen and the pages selected after a search. Many people refine a query, adding and removing words, but most see very few answer pages. Table 1 shows the comparison of four different search engines (Baeza-Yates & Saint-Jean, 2003a; Silverstein et al., 1999; Spink, Jansen et al., 2002; Spink, Ozmutlu et al., 2002; Wolfram, 2001). Clearly, the default query operation is dominant (in the case of TodoCL, only 15% are phrase queries).

The navigation graph can be complicated even in a search engine. Figure 4 shows the transitions between different states, indicating the proportion of users that took that

Figure 2. Frequency of Query Words in a Log-Log Graph

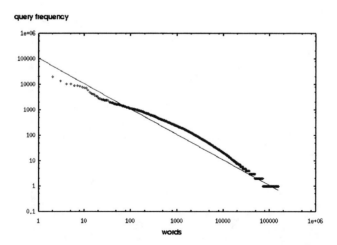

Figure 3. Word Query Frequency vs. Number of Documents that Contain Each Word

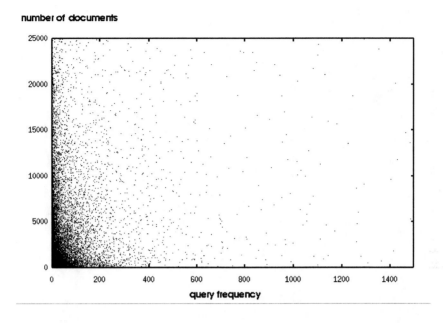

Table 1. Query Statistics for Four Search Engines

Measure	AltaVista	Excite	Fast	TodoCL
Words per query	2.4	2.6	2.3	1.1
Queries per user	2	2.3	2.9	—
Answer pages per query	1.3	1.7	2.2	1.2
Boolean queries	< 40%	10 %	—	16%

path. The number in each state represents the probability of a user being in that state. From the diagram we can see that:

- Advanced search is not used.
- Few people refine queries.
- Less than 10% of the users browse the directory[2].

This means that instead of posing a better query, a trial and error method is used. Table 2 gives the most popular queries for three search engines (in the case of TodoCL we have translated them to English), which shows that they are very similar and independent of the country and the language. Further studies of queries have been done for Excite (Spink, Jansen et al., 2002; Wolfram, 2001) and Fast (Spink et al., 2001), showing that the focus of the queries has shifted in recent years from leisure to e-commerce.

Figure 4. State Diagram of User Behavior in TodoCL

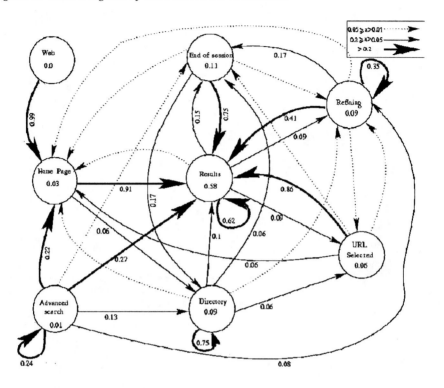

Table 2. Most Frequent Queries in Three Search Engines (2001)

Excite	Fast	TodoCL
free	free	Chile
sex	download	photos
Christmas	sex	free
nude	pictures	sex
pictures	nude	history
new	mp3	mp3
pics	hotel	videos
music	Windows	music
games	pics	Argentina
stories	crack	Ley
woman	software	university
university	education	sell

INDICES BASED IN QUERY DISTRIBUTION

In this section we show a simple storage model for a search engine, which uses main memory efficiently, while improving scalability (Baeza-Yates & Saint-Jean, 2003b). Since few words are queried frequently, what is important is the growth of the most frequently queried subset of words, rather than the growth of the overall vocabulary on the Web pages. In this section we only use single word queries, which are more than 95% of all queries.

Storing part of the index in main memory can be considered as static caching of inverted lists, but in practice is not the same because current search engines must have large portions of the index in main memory to achieve fast answer time. In the sequel, we consider that our scheme and caching are orthogonal. That is, we can devote part of the main memory to do dynamic caching of the answers and of the inverted lists that are in secondary memory. Alternatively, we could add compression.

Basic Scheme

Let M be the available main memory. We always assume that the vocabulary fits in main memory (as it grows sub-linearly, it is a small percentage of the inverted file). So we have the vocabulary and part of the lists in main memory. The rest of the word lists go to secondary memory.

Recall that N is the number of words of the vocabulary and let L_i be the number of documents where the *i-th* word appears, where the words $1..N$ are ordered by decreasing query frequency. For each word in the vocabulary we need to store the word itself (let x_k be the length of the *k-th* word) and a pointer to the corresponding occurrence list (say 4 bytes). In each list element, we need at least an integer as a Web page identifier plus information for ranking (for example, the frequency of the word in the Web page). Let b be the number of bytes per list element, which depends on the exact implementation of the inverted file. Hence, the average space needed by the inverted file, in bytes, is:

$$E = \sum_{k=1}^{N} (4 + x_k + bL_k) = \underbrace{(4 + \bar{x})\, N}_{V} + b \sum_{k=1}^{N} L_k$$

where $\bar{x}$ is the average length of the vocabulary words, and V the space needed by the vocabulary. Notice that by using $\bar{x}$ we are assuming independence between the word length and the query word frequency. In fact, for our data, the correlation is -0.02, almost nothing.

If $E \leq M$, everything fits in RAM. However, when $E > M$, part of the inverted file must be stored on disk. We could assume that memory paging and disk buffering will improve the access time, but over this we do not have control. Most inverted files use a hashing table for the vocabulary, which implies a random order for the words. If we put in this order the lists of the inverted file until we run out of main memory and the rest on the disk, many words that are frequently queried (because the correlation is small) will be on the disk. The optimal arrangement would be to store in main memory the subset of query words that maximizes the total frequency and still fits in memory. The rest of the word lists would go to secondary memory. Formally, we have to find the variables $i_1,...,i_p$ such that they maximize the sum of the query frequencies of the words $i_1, ..., i_p$ with the restriction that $V + b \sum_{j=1}^{p} L_{ij} \leq M$. The optimal solution will depend on each data set.

As the distribution is so biased, a nearly optimal solution is to put in main memory the lists of the most frequent query words that fit. Let p be the largest number of words in the vocabulary such that:

$$V + b \sum_{j=1}^{p} L_j \leq M .$$

Then, the lists of the p most queried words will be in main memory. This heuristic is not optimal because there will be a few cases in which it would be better to replace a word with a large posting list with two or more words with smaller overall lists of similar size or smaller, but at the same time larger total query frequency. Nevertheless, we show next that this solution is quite good.

Using our data, Figure 5 shows the difference between the heuristic (curve below) and a random order (curve above, basically a diagonal). In the x-axis we have the portion of query words that have their list in main memory. The y-axis shows the portion of the index that must be in main memory to reach that proportion of queries. The vertical line at the end is the words that are never queried. The gap in the diagonal line is two of the most frequently queried words, which in our heuristic are at the beginning (the dots of the graphs are plotted in multiples of 100 words).

Figure 5. Query Frequency vs. Memory — Random Order and our Heuristic

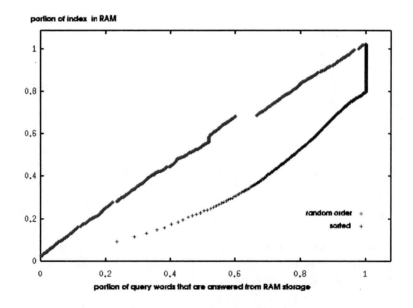

From this example we can see that:

- To reach 100% of the queries, we only need to have 80% of the index in main memory. This is because more than 75% of the words are never queried (but have short posting lists).
- To reach 50% of the queries we only need 20% of the index in memory.
- With 50% of the index in memory, we can answer 80% of the queries.

Hence, this simple heuristic reduces the usage of memory in at least 20% without increasing the query answer time.

Improving the Query Answer Time: Precomputed Answers

Precomputed answers can be considered as static caching of answers, but they are conceptually different because precomputed answers could have better quality, for example with manual intervention (e.g., main links related to a query as in Yahoo!). If we have precomputed answers for the most frequent queries, answer time is improved, as we do not have to access the index. However, more memory with respect to the index information of these words might be needed, decreasing the value of p and increasing the search time for other words. This implies that there is an optimal number of precomputed answers. We consider the precomputed answers as a cache memory, even though it is in main memory.

Notice that with our data, only 2,000 precomputed answers can resolve 20% of the queries. On the other hand, to answer 50% of the queries we need around 100,000 precomputed answers, which requires too much space.

Assume that each precomputed answer needs W bytes of memory (for example, 80 URLs with the text context and other attributes such as size and date). Then we must have:

$$kW + V + b \sum_{i=k+1}^{p+k} L_i \le M$$

where the words $k+1$ to $p+k$ have their lists stored in main memory. We want to find k and p that optimize the query answer time. Hence we have three sections of memory: precomputed answers, index in memory, and index in disk.

The query answer time is given by:

$$t = \frac{\beta_1 \sum_{i=1}^{k} F_i + \beta_2 \sum_{i=k+1}^{p+k} F_i + \beta_3 \sum_{i=p+k+1}^{C} F_i}{\sum_{i=1}^{C} F_i}$$

where we recall that C is the number of unique words in the queries and F_i is the query frequency of the i-th word. In addition, β_1, β_2, and β_3 are constants that represent the relative answer time of precomputed answers, index in memory, and index in disk, respectively. In the examples that follow we use the following set of values: $M=400MB$, $W=40KB$, $b=8$, $\beta_1=1$, $\beta_2=5$, and $\beta_3=50$. This implies $V=24.56MB$, which is only 6% of the memory. We have chosen W considering 512 bytes per URL, so we have 80 URLs in the

Figure 6. Query Answer Time as a Function of the Number of Precomputed Answers

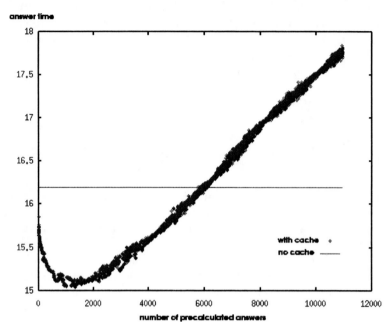

precomputed answer. If more answers are needed we have to go to the inverted file in disk and we assume that this event happens with negligible probability. As we have seen in the previous section, the average number of results seen by users is less than 20 (Silverstein et al., 1999; Spink et al., 2001) and only 12 using our data (but other values for W are possible).

Figure 6 shows the query answer time depending on k (this fixes p); here we can observe that the optimal point is 1338 precomputed answers, improving the answer time approximately 7% (the line is the answer time for $k=0$). Hence, the precomputed answers take 13% of the memory, which implies that in our example the 81% of the memory left is taken by the most frequently queried part of the inverted file.

RANKING BASED ON
USER QUERIES AND CHOICES

The relation of pages chosen after a query and the query itself provide valuable information. After a query, a user usually performs a click to view one answer page. Each click is considered a positive recommendation of that page (in most cases bad pages are not clicked). In Zhang and Dong (2002), an algorithm based on these relations is proposed to improve ranking: MASEL (Matrix Analysis on Search Engine Log).

The MASEL Algorithm

The basic idea is to use the query log to find relations among users, queries, and clicks on answers. It is assumed that in a short period of time, the IP address is used by a single user (not always true because of proxies and dynamic IPs).

The algorithm considers users, queries, and clicked pages, using a recursive definition among those three elements in the spirit of authorities and hubs (Kleinberg, 1998). The hypothesis is that good users make good queries, good queries return good answers, and good answers are clicked by good users.

Given a query q^*, and a time interval $[t_{now}-T, t_{now}]$, the algorithm has four steps:

- From the query log obtain all users that have asked q^*. We denote by U those users.
- Find from the logs the set Q of all the queries posed by users in U.
- Using the search engine (or another technique), find the set R of relevant clicked pages for all the queries in Q.
- Compute the ranking using the iterative process outlined below.

The period of the log analysis T is a parameter of the algorithm. Let $m=|U|$, $s=|R|$, and $n=|Q|$. We define u_i as a variable that represents the quality of the user i, q_j as the quality of query j, and r_k as the quality of the page k. We use normalized values, such that the sum of each the qualities adds up to 1, although we are just interested in the relative order. We compute these values iteratively (normalizing after each iteration). We define the users depending on their queries:

$$u_i = \sum_{j=1}^{n} a_{ij}q_j, \quad \text{where} \quad a_{ij} = \begin{cases} num(i,j) & \text{if } j = q^* \\ \alpha num(i,j) & \text{if } j \neq q^* \end{cases}$$

where $num(i,j)$ represents how many times the user i asked query j and $0<\alpha<1$ weights queries different from q^*. We define queries in function of the pages that they answer:

$$q_j = \sum_{k=1}^{s} b_{jk}r_k, \quad \text{where} \quad b_{jk} = \begin{cases} sim(j,k) & \text{if } j = q^* \\ \beta sim(j,k) & \text{if } j \neq q^* \end{cases}$$

where $sim(j,k)$ is the similarity of page k with query j and $0<\beta<1$ weights queries different from q^*. Finally, pages are defined by the clicks done by users:

$$r_k = \sum_{i=1}^{m} c_{ki}u_i, \quad \text{where} \quad c_{ki} = hit(k,i,\{q^*\}) + \gamma hit(k,i,Q-\{q^*\})$$

where $hit(k,i,S)$ is the number of times that user i clicked in page k while doing a query in S and $0<\gamma<1$ weights the queries different from q^*. In matrix form we have:

$$\vec{u} = A\vec{q}, \qquad \vec{q} = B\vec{r}, \qquad \vec{r} = C\vec{u}$$

which implies

$$\vec{u} = A\vec{q} = A(B\vec{r}) = A(B(C\vec{u})) = (ABC)\vec{u}$$

$$q = B\vec{r} = B\,(C\vec{u}) = B(C(A\vec{q}\,) = (BCA)\vec{q}$$

$$\vec{r} = C\vec{u} = C\,(A\vec{q}\,) = \;C(A(B\vec{r}\,)) = (CAB)\vec{r}$$

This defines an iterative method to compute u, q, and r. With this we obtain a ranking for the r_k values.

The parameter T is crucial for the effectiveness of the algorithm. If T is too large, the matrices are large and the algorithm is slower. In addition we add many queries that are not related to q^*. On the other hand, if T is small, the method does not work and we are wasting useful log information. In fact, T is inversely proportional to the query frequency.

Experimental Results

MASEL was proposed for an image search engine, where the precision of answers is low. To give some simple examples, we tried this idea for text, where the results were quite good (Baeza-Yates & Saint-Jean, 2003a). Typically, the first two or three answers were a good complement to the search engine ranking. For example, for the word *cars* (in Spanish) we used $T=24$ and $T=48$ hours. For 24 hours the results were:

www.chileautos.cl/link.asp
www.chileautos.cl/personal.htm
www.autoscampos.cl/frmencabau.htm
rehue.csociales.uchile.cl/publicaciones/moebio/07/bar02.htmm

The first three are relevant, while the last one is not. For 48 hours we had:

www.mapchile.cl/
fid.conicyt.cl/acreditacion/normas.htm
www.clancomunicaciones.cl/muni_vdm/consejo.htm

where the last two are not relevant, but the first is relevant without containing the word *cars;* it is a site of maps. This example shows the potential of MASEL to find semantic relations through two persons that asked different questions. It also shows the sensitivity of the value T.

Figure 7 shows the precision for three Spanish words of different frequency of occurrence: software, *banco* (bank), and *empresas* (enterprises). The most popular word, *software,* has good results with smaller T. Bank, for $T=72$, has excellent precision, which decreases with larger T. This is because *bank* has many meanings and the main meaning refers to a commercial bank. However, with larger T, other meanings start to appear in the query log. Clearly, the value of T depends on the frequency of the word and if the word is polysemic or not. In this case, as in link analysis, we can have *topic drifting* in the answers.

Figure 7. Precision of the Answer vs. T *in Hours for Three Spanish Words*

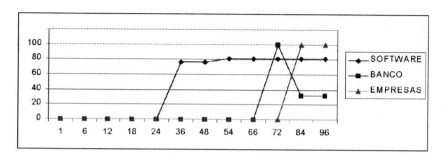

If the word does not have the dominant meaning or it is not frequent, this technique is not useful, as there are not enough data in a log of only several days. The issue of topic drifting could be reduced by changing the parameters ±, ², and ³.

CONCLUSIONS

In our examples there are several lines for further research. They include better understanding of queries and their evolution in time; analysis of how the changes in the query distribution affects the performance of a given index layout; study of the best combination of index layout based on query distribution, dynamic caching and compression; and inclusion of Boolean and phrase queries in the index layout problem.

We are currently doing additional research in Web query mining to improve Web findability and information scent, as well as using queries to focus Web crawlers. For example, if we represent a given interest by a query vector Q using the vector model (Baeza-Yates & Ribeiro-Neto, 1999), a crawler can try to maximize the similarity of a retrieved vector page p with Q. This technique is used by focused crawlers or search agents (Baeza-Yates & Piquer, 2002). We can extend the idea by representing all past queries in a search engine as a vector Q_t which is updated using a time based average, with the last queries q by using a moving average: $Q_{t+1} = \alpha Q_t + (1-\alpha) q$, where α weights past versus current queries.

REFERENCES

Baeza-Yates, R., & Castillo, C. (2001). *Relating Web structure and user search behavior* (extended poster). Tenth World Wide Web Conference, Hong Kong, China.

Baeza-Yates, R., & Piquer, J.M. (2002). Agents, crawlers and Web retrieval. *Cooperative Information Agents (CIA) 2002,* Springer LNCS, Madrid, Spain.

Baeza-Yates, R., & Ribeiro-Neto, B. (1999). *Modern information retrieval.* UK: ACM Press/Addison-Wesley. Available: *sunsite.dcc.uchile.cl/irbook/.*

Baeza-Yates, R., & Saint-Jean, F. (2003a). *Query analysis in a search engine and its application to rank Web pages* (in Spanish), BID 10, Barcelona, Spain.

Baeza-Yates, R., & Saint-Jean, F. (2003b). A three level search engine index based in query log distribution. *SPIRE 2003,* Manaus, Brazil.

Baeza-Yates, R., Poblete, B., & Saint-Jean, F. (2003). *The evolution of the Chilean Web: 2001-2002* (in Spanish). Center for Web Research *(www.cwr.cl),* University of Chile.

Beeferman, D., & Berger, A. (2000). Agglomerative clustering of a search engine query log. *Proceedings of the Conference on Knowledge Discovery and Data Mining,* Boston, MA, (pp. 407-416).

Chakrabarti, S. (2002). *Mining the Web: Discovering knowledge from hypertext data.* San Francisco, CA: Morgan Kaufmann.

Davison, D., Deschenes, D., & Lewanda, D. (2003). *Finding relevant Website queries* (poster), WWW12, Budapest, Hungary, 20 - 24.

Directhit: Home Page. (1997). *www.directhit.com.*

Hölscher, C., & Strube, G. (2000, May). Web search behavior of Internet experts and newbies. *WWW9,* Amsterdam, The Netherlands.

Kleinberg, J. (1998). Authoritative sources in a hyperlinked environment. *Proceedings of Ninth Symposium on Discrete Algorithms.*

Levene, M., & Poulovassilis, A. (Eds.). (2003). *Web dynamics.* Springer.

Markatos, E.P. (2002). On caching search engine query results. *Proceedings of the 5th International Web Caching and Content Delivery Workshop.*

Pirolli, P. (1997). Computational models of information scent-following in a very large browsable text collection. *Human Factors in Computing Systems: Proceedings of the CHI '97 Conference*, (pp. 3-10). New York: ACM Press.

Pramudiono, I., Takahiko, S., Takahashi, K., & Kitsuregawa, M. (2002). User behavior analysis of location Aaware search engine. *Mobile Data Management,* 139-145.

Saraiva, P.C., de Moura, E.S., Ziviani, N., Meira, W., Fonseca, R., & Ribeiro-Neto, B. (2001). Rank-preserving two-level caching for scalable search engines. *Proceedings of the 24th Annual International ACM Conference on Research and Development in Information Retrieval,* New Orleans, Louisiana, USA (pp. 51-58).

Schaale, A., Wulf-Mathies, C., & Lieberam-Schmidt, S. (2003). *A new approach to relevancy in Internet searching - the "Vox Populi Algorithm",* arXiv.org e-Print archive.

Silverstein, C., Henzinger, M., Marais, H., & Moricz, M. (1999). Analysis of a very large AltaVista query log. *SIGIR Forum, 33*(3), 6-12.

Spink, A., Jansen, B.J., Wolfram, D., & Saracevic, T. (2002). From e-sex to e-commerce: Web search changes. *IEEE Computer, 35*(3), 107-109.

Spink, A., Ozmutlu, S., Ozmutlu, H.C., & Jansen, B.J. (2002). U.S. versus European Web searching trends. *SIGIR Forum, 26*(2).

Spink, A., Wolfram, D., Jansen, B.J., & Saracevic, T. (2001). Searching the Web: The public and their queries. *Journal of the American Society for Information Science and Technology, 52*(3), 226-234.

TodoCL: Home Page. (2000). *www.todocl.cl.*

Wen, J-R., Nie, J-Y., & Zhang, H-J. (2001). Clustering user queries of a search engine. *WWW10,* Hong Kong.

Wolfram, D. (2000). A query-level examination of end user searching behaviour on the Excite search engine. *Proceedings of the 28th Annual Conference Canadian Association for Information Science.*

Xie, Y., & O'Hallaron, D. (2002). *Locality in search engine queries and its implications for caching*. Infocom.

Xue, G-R., Zeng, H-J., Chen, Z., Ma, W-Y., & Lu, C-J. (2002). Log mining to improve the performance of site search. *First International Workshop for Enhanced Web Search* (MEWS 2002), Singapore, 238-245. IEEE CS Press.

Zhang, D., & Dong, Y. (2002). A novel Web usage mining approach for search engine. *Computer Networks, 39*(3), 303-310.

Zipf, G. (1932). Selective studies and the principle of relative frequency in language. Cambridge, MA: Harvard University Press.

ENDNOTES

[1]   We have found Web pages using this term with our semantic as far back as 1995.

[2]   TodoCL uses ODP (dmoz.org) as Google does.

Chapter XV

Efficient Web Mining for Traversal Path Patterns

Zhixiang Chen
The University of Texas - Pan American, USA

Richard H. Fowler
The University of Texas - Pan American, USA

Ada Wai-Chee Fu
The Chinese University of Hong Kong, Hong Kong

Chunyue Wang
The University of Texas - Pan American, USA

ABSTRACT

A maximal forward reference of a Web user is a longest consecutive sequence of Web pages visited by the user in a session without revisiting some previously visited page in the sequence. Efficient mining of frequent traversal path patterns, that is, large reference sequences of maximal forward references, from very large Web logs is a fundamental problem in Web mining. This chapter aims at designing algorithms for this problem with the best possible efficiency. First, two optimal linear time algorithms are designed for finding maximal forward references from Web logs. Second, two algorithms for mining frequent traversal path patterns are devised with the help of a fast construction of shallow generalized suffix trees over a very large alphabet. These two algorithms have respectively provable linear and sublinear time complexity, and their performances are analyzed in comparison with the a priori-like algorithms and the Ukkonen algorithm. It is shown that these two new algorithms are substantially more efficient than the a priori-like algorithms and the Ukkonen algorithm.

INTRODUCTION

Because of its significant theoretical challenges and great application and commercial potentials, Web mining has recently attracted extensive attention (e.g., Buchner et al., 1998, 1999; Catledge & Pitkow, 1995; Chen et al., 1998; Cooley et al., 1997). Surveys of recent research in Web mining can be found in Kosala and Blockeel (2000) and Srivastava et al. (2000). One of the major concerns in Web mining is to discover user traversal (or navigation) path patterns that are hidden in vast Web logs. Such discovered knowledge can be used to predict where the Web users are going, that is, what they are seeking, so that it helps the construction and maintenance of real-time intelligent Web servers that are able to dynamically tailor their designs to satisfy users' needs (Perkowitz & Etzioni, 1998). It has significant potential to reduce, through prefetching and caching, Web latencies that have been perceived by users year after year (Padmanabhan & Mogul, 1996; Pitkow & Pirolli, 1999). It can also help the administrative personnel to predict the trends of users' needs so that they can adjust their products to attract more users (and customers) now and in the future (Buchner & Mulvenna, 1998).

Traversal path pattern mining is based upon the availability of traversal paths that must be obtained from raw Web logs. A maximal forward reference of a Web user, a longest consecutive sequence of Web pages visited by the user without revisiting some previously visited page in the sequence, is a typical traversal path pattern (Chen et al., 1998; Cooley et al., 1999). This chapter studies the problem of efficient mining of frequent traversal path patterns that are large sequences of maximal forward references. The previously known algorithms for the problem are the two a priori-like algorithms *FullScan* and *SelectiveScan* designed in Chen, Park and Yu (1998).

This chapter aims at designing algorithms for mining traversal path patterns with the best possible efficiency. The main contributions are summarized as follows. First, two algorithms, ISMFR (Interval Session Maximal Forward References) and GSMFR (Gap Session Maximal Forward References), are given for finding maximal forward references from raw Web logs. The first algorithm is designed for *interval sessions* of user accesses and the second for *gap sessions*. The two algorithms have linear, hence optimal, time complexity, and are substantially more efficient than the sorting based method devised in Chen, Park and Yu (1998) for finding maximal forward references. Second, the problem of mining frequent traversal path patterns from maximal forward references is investigated with the help of a fast construction of *shallow* generalized suffix trees over a very large alphabet (Chen et al., 2003a, 2003b). Precisely, a *shallow* generalized suffix tree is built for a set of maximal forward references obtained by the algorithm ISMFR (or GSMFR) such that each tree node contains the frequency of the substring represented by that node. Once such a tree is built, a simply traversal of the tree outputs frequent traversal path patterns, that is, frequent substrings, with respect to some given frequency threshold parameter. Two algorithms, SbSfxMiner (Sorting Based Suffix Tree Miner) and HbSfxMiner (Hashing Based Suffix Tree Miner), are designed to overcome some well-understood obstacles of suffix tree construction (Gusfield, 1997, pp. 116-119): the complexity of suffix tree construction is dependent on the size of the underlying alphabet and a suffix tree does not have nice locality properties to support memory paging. These two algorithms, SbSfxMiner and HbSfxMiner, have respectively provable sublinear and linear time complexity. Performances of these two algorithms are analyzed in comparison with the two a priori-like algorithms FullScan and SelectiveScan in Chen, Park and Yu

(1998) and the Ukkonen algorithm for linear time suffix construction (Ukkonen, 1995). It is shown that these two new algorithms are substantially more efficient than FullScan, SelectiveScan and the Ukkonen algorithm as well. In short, algorithm HbSfxMiner has optimal complexity in theory, while algorithm SbSfxMiner has the best empirical performance.

The rest of the chapter is organized as follows. The problem formulation is given and is followed with the review of related work. Algorithms ISMFR and GSMFR are then designed for finding maximal forward references from raw Web logs. Next, characteristics of maximal forward references are given. The chapter then discusses *shallow* generalized suffix trees. In the next section, algorithms SbSfxMiner and HbSfxMiner are designed for mining frequent traversal path patterns, and their performances are comparatively analyzed. Finally, conclusions are given.

PROBLEM FORMULATION

The Web has a natural graph structure: pages in general are linked via hyperlinks.

When a user surfs the Web, she may move forward along the graph via selecting a hyperlink in the current page. She may also move backward to any page visited earlier in the same session via selecting a *backward* icon. A forward reference may be understood as the user looking for her desired information. A backward reference may mean that the user has found her desired information and is going to look for something else. A sequence of consecutive forward references may indicate the information for which the user is looking. A maximal forward reference is defined as the longest consecutive sequence of forward references before the first backward reference is made to visit some previously visited page in the same session. Thus, the last reference in a maximal forward sequence indicates a content page (Chen et al., 1998; Cooley et al., 1999) that is desired by the user. Under such understanding, when a user searches for desired information, her information needs can be modeled by the set of maximal forward references that occurred during her search process.

Figure 1. Illustration of Traversal Path Patterns

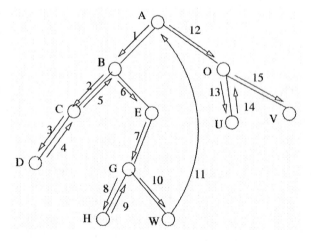

Suppose that the Web log contains the traversal path *{A, B, C, D, C, B, E, G, H, G, W, A, O, U, O, V}* for a user as shown in Figure 1. Starting at *A*, one has forward reference sequences *AB*, *ABC* and *ABCD*. Then, at *D* a backward reference to *C* is made, meaning that *ABCD* is a maximal forward reference. Now, some caution shall be paid to *C*. Here, even though a backward reference is made to *B*, one shall not consider *ABC* as a maximal forward reference, because the current backward reference is the second backward reference (the first is $D \rightarrow C$). At *B*, a forward reference is made to *E*, and thus begins new forward reference sequences *ABE*, *ABEG* and *ABEGH*. *ABEGH* is a maximal forward reference, because the first backward reference occurs at *H* after the forward reference *E*. Similarly, one can find the other maximal forward references *ABEGW*, *AOU* and *AOV*. When *D*, *H*, *W*, *U* and *V* are the pages desired by the user, the set of the maximal forward references *ABCD*, *ABEGH*, *ABEGW*, *AOU*, and *AOV* precisely describes the user's needs and her actual search behaviors as well.

A *large reference sequence* with respect to some given frequency threshold parameter α is defined as a consecutive subsequence that occurs at least α many times in a set of maximal forward references. A *maximal reference sequence* with respect to α is a large reference that is not contained in any other large reference sequence. In the above example, when the frequency threshold parameter α is 2, one has large reference sequences *A, B, E, G, O, AB, BE, EG, AO, ABE, BEG*, and *ABEG*, and the maximal reference sequences are *ABEG* and *AO*. A maximal reference sequence corresponds to a frequent traversal path pattern, that is, the *hot* access pattern of users. The goal in this chapter is to design algorithms for mining frequent traversal path patterns, that is, frequent or maximal reference sequences, with the best possible efficiency.

Once large reference sequences are determined, maximal references sequences can be obtained in a straightforward manner (Chen, Park & Yu, 1998).

The traversal path *A, B, C, D, C, B, E, G, H, G, W, A, O, U, O, V* of the user in the above example is recorded in the *referrer log*, and so are traversal paths of all the other users.

A *referrer log* is a typical configuration of Web logs, where each traversed link is represented as a pair *(source, destination)*. In this chapter, one assumes that Web logs are referrer logs. The high-level design of the approaches to mining frequent traversal path patterns is as follows: first, one finds maximal forward references from Web logs. Second, one builds a generalized suffix tree for the set of maximal forward references. Last, one traverses the tree to generate large or maximal reference sequences.

RELATED WORK

The problem of mining frequent traversal path patterns resulted in an algorithm for finding frequent traversal path patterns from a Web log (Chen, Park & Yu, 1998). That algorithm works in two phases. First, the log is sorted according to user IDs to group every user's references as a traversal path. Next, each traversal path is examined to find maximal forward references. The time complexity of the algorithm is $O(N \log N)$, where *N* denotes the number of records in the log. At the next step, two a priori-like algorithms, *FullScan* and *SelectiveScan*, were designed for mining large reference sequences from maximal forward references, and the performances of these two algorithms were analyzed.

Cooley et al. (1999) have detailed discussions of various data preparation tasks. The maximal forward references, called *transactions*, were also examined as a finer level characterization of user access sessions. But no explicit algorithms were given to find maximal forward references, and mining frequent traversal path patterns was not studied there. The work in Xiao and Dunham (2001) studied the application of generalized suffix trees to mining frequent user access patterns from Web logs. However, the patterns in Xiao and Dunham (2001) are not traversal path patterns as considered in the usual settings in much of the literature (such as Chen et al., 1998; Padmanabhan & Mogul, 1996; Pitkow & Pirolli, 1999; Su et al., 2000) and in the context of this chapter. The patterns in that paper are in essence frequent consecutive subsequences of user access sessions, while traversal paths corresponding to the underlying hyperlink structure were not of concern. Furthermore, that paper relies on the Ukkonen's *suffix link* algorithm to construct a suffix tree and hence cannot overcome the well-understood obstacles of suffix tree construction (Gusfield, 1997, pp. 116-119), that is, the complexity dependence on the size of the underlying alphabet and the lack of good locality properties to support memory paging.

Many researchers have been investigating traversal or surfing path patterns in order to model users' behaviors and interests. The uncovered model can be used in many applications such as prefetching and caching to reduce Web latencies (Padmanabhan & Mogul, 1996; Pitkow & Priolli, 1999; Su et al., 2000). The N-gram approaches are used to find most frequent subsequences of the paths, and sometimes the most frequent longest subsequences are the most interesting. Once those subsequences are obtained, methods such as first order or higher order Markov-chains can be applied to predict users' behaviors or interests. Other researchers have also considered user access sessions as ordered sequences (Masseglia et al., 1999). They have also studied how to identify the longest repeating subsequences of the ordered sessions to find associations of those sequences. In all those papers, a user's surfing path is considered as an ordered sequence of consecutive references. In other words, a user's surfing path is the user's access session in order. This is different from the maximal forward references studied in Chen et al. (1998), Cooley et al. (1999) and in the present chapter.

In Chen, Fu and Tung (2003), optimal algorithms are designed for finding user access sessions from very large Web logs. Since maximal forward references are finer level characterizations of sessions, as carefully examined in Cooley et al. (1999), the algorithms in Chen, Fu and Tung (2003) cannot be applied directly to the problem of finding maximal forward references. However, these algorithms were improved in Chen, Fowler and Fu (2003) to find maximal forward references with optimal time complexity.

FINDING MAXIMAL FORWARD REFERENCES

Sessions

The basic idea of finding maximal forward references is as follows. The algorithm reads the Web log once sequentially, and generates sessions on the fly. While a session is generating, maximal forward references within that session are also generated. Although it is easy to understand that a *session* or *visit* is the group of activities performed by a user from the moment she enters a server site to the moment she leaves the site, it is not an easy task to find user sessions from Web logs. Due to security or privacy, a user's identity is often not known, except for the client machine's IP address or host name. When the log is examined, it is not clear when a session starts or when it ends. Some users access the Web, page after page, at a very fast pace. Others access the Web at a very slow pace, visiting one for a while, doing something else, and then visiting another. Local caching and proxy servers cause other difficulties.

Researchers have proposed cut-off thresholds to approximate the start and the end of a session (Berendt et al., 2001; Chen et al., 2003; Cooley et al., 1999). One may also propose a maximum 30-minute gap between any two pages accessed by the user in a session. If the gap limit is exceeded, then a session boundary should be inserted between the two pages. As in Cooley et al. (1999), Chen et al. (2003) and Berendt et al. (2001), the following two types of sessions are considered in this chapter:

- α-interval sessions: the duration of a session may not exceed a threshold of α. That is, one assumes that a user should not spend too much time on each session. So a value α is given to limit the time a user can have for a session. Usually, α may be set to 30 minutes.

- β-gap sessions: the time between any two consecutively accessed pages may not exceed a threshold of β. That is, it is assumed that a user should not be *idle* for too much time between any two consecutive accesses in any session. So a value β is given to limit the time a user can be *idle* between two consecutive accesses in a session. Usually, β may also be set to 30 minutes.

Certainly, there are exceptions to α and β limits. For example, a person may need to spend a few hours to find a correct tour map of Hong Kong over the Web, so the session exceeds the α limit. However, these two kinds of limits are quite accurate in Web usage analysis (Berendt et al., 2001). A more sophisticated consideration would allow adaptive (or variable) limits for different users in particular applications. This is not trivial, due to precise modeling of user behaviors, and is beyond the scope of this chapter.

Data Structures

The proposed algorithms maintain the following data structures. A URL node structure is defined to store the URL and the access time of a user access record and a pointer to point to the next URL node. A user node is also defined to store the following information for the user: the user ID, usually the hostname or IP address in the access record; the start time, that is, the time of the first access record entered into the user node; the current time, that is, the time of last access record entered into the user node; the URL node pointer pointing to the linked list of URL nodes; a forward reference tag indicating whether the last reference of the user is a forward reference or not; the counter recording the total number of URL nodes added; and two user node pointers to respectively point to the previous user node and the next. Finally, a head node is defined with two members, one pointing to the beginning of the two-way linked list of user nodes and the other storing the total number of valid records that have been processed so far.

The user nodes and URL linked lists cannot be allowed to exceed the limit of RAM.

This difficulty is overcome with the sorted property of the Web log as follows: it is not a concern how many user nodes there may be. When an access record of a new user arrives, a user node is created for her. When a new access record of some existing user arrives, the time of this new record and start time (or the current time) of the user node is checked to determine whether the α threshold is exceeded for interval sessions (or the β threshold is exceeded for gap sessions). To do so requires knowing how to control the size of the URL linked list for the user. After a certain number of valid user access records have been processed, all those user nodes with start (or current) times beyond the α (or β) threshold in comparison with the time of the most recent record processed are purged, and thus the number of user nodes is under control.

Finding Maximal Forward References from Interval Sessions

At the high level design, the algorithm repeats the following tasks until the end of the Web log: read a user access record r from disk to RAM. Test whether r is valid or not; if r is valid then add r to its corresponding user node D in the user node linked list. Compare the start time of D with the time $t(r)$ to see whether a new session of the user begins or not. If yes, then output the URLs in D's URL linked list in order as a maximal forward reference sequence, and reset D with information in r; otherwise use r to search D's URL linked list to find maximal forward reference sequences. Finally, check if a γ number of valid records have been processed so far, where γ is tunable parameter that is dependent on the size of the underlying RAM. If yes, then purge all the old user nodes and output their sessions. The formal description of the algorithm, called ISMFR, is given in Algorithm 1.

Algorithm 1.

```
Algorithm ISMFR (Interval Session Maximal Forward References):
    input:
        infile: input web log file
        outfile: output user access session file
        α: threshold for defining interval sessions
        γ: threshold for removing old user nodes
    begin
1.      open infile and outfile
2.      createHeadNode(S); S.head = null; S.counter=0
3.      while (infile is not empty)
4.          readRecord(infile,r)
5.          if (isRecordValid(r))
6.              n = findRecord(S,r)
7.              if (n is null)
8.                  addRecord(S, r)
9.                  else if (t(r) − n.startTime ≤ α)
10.                     n.currentTime = t(r)
11.                     findMaxFRS(n.urlListPtr, n.forwardReferenceTag, r)
12.                 else
13.                     writeMaxFRSAndReset(outfile, n, r)
14.                 S.counter=S.counter+1
15.                 if (S.counter > γ )
16.                     purgeNodes(outfile, S, t(r)); S.counter=1
17.              cleanList(outfile,S);
18.      close infile and outfile
    end
```

Algorithm 2.

Algorithm GSMFR (Gap Session Maximal Forward References):
    input: the same as ISMFR except
        $\beta > 0$ is used to replace α

    The body is also the same as ISMFR except that
    Line 9 is replaced by
    9.   else if $(t(r) - n.cuurentTime \leq \beta)$

    and Line 16 is replaced by
    16.   purge2Nodes(outfile, S, t(r)); S.counter=1

Finding Maximal Forward Reference Sequences from Gap Sessions

The algorithm, called GSMFR, is similar to algorithm ISMFR. They differ at steps 9 and 16. At step 9 GSMFR checks to decide whether a new session begins or not, and whether the *time gap* between the current record and the last record of the same user is beyond the threshold β or not. At step 16, algorithm GSMFR will call function *purge2Nodes(outfile, S, t(r))* to check, for every user node in the user linked list *S.head*, whether the *time gap* between the current record and the last record of the user node is beyond the threshold β or not. If so, it purges the user node in a similar manner as algorithm ISMFR. The description of GSMFR is given in Algorithm 2.

Performance Analysis

When the parameters α, β and γ are given, it is quite easy to see that both algorithms ISMFR and GSMFR have $\theta(N)$ optimal time complexity, where N denotes the number of user access records in the Web log. It should be pointed out that different thresholds α, β and γ may be needed for different applications. The only explicitly reported algorithm for finding maximal forward references from Web logs is the sorting-based algorithm SMF (Chen, Park & Yu, 1998).

To compare the two algorithms ISMFR and GSMFR with the SMF algorithm uses five Web logs, *L100MB, L200MB, L300MB, L400MB* and *L500MB,* with 100 to 500 megabytes of user access records collected from the Web server of the Department of Computer Science, the University of Texas - Pan American. The computing environment is a Gateway Dell E-5400 PC with 512 megabytes of RAM and 20 GB of hard disk. The *sort* command in the DOS environment, which supports standard external file sorting, is utilized. All programs were implemented in Microsoft Visual C++ 6.0, setting $\alpha = \beta = 30$ minutes and $\gamma = 500$, and using the same *isRecordValid( )* function for the three algorithms. Performance comparisons are illustrated in Figure 2. The empirical analysis shows that both algorithms ISMFR and GSMFR have almost the same performance, and are substantially much faster than the sorting based algorithm SMF.

Figure 2. Performances of Algorithms ISMFR and GSMFR

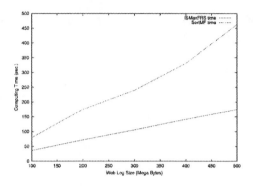

(a) ISMFR vs. SMF

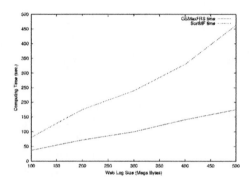

(b) GSMFR vs. SMF

PROPERTIES OF
MAXIMAL FORWARD REFERENCES

The properties of maximal forward references of the five logs *L100MB*, *L200MB*, *L300MB*, *L400MB* and *L500MB* have been examined. When the parameters α and β are set to 30 minutes to define interval sessions and gap sessions, it is obvious that the length of a maximal forward reference, or the number of URLs in it, is small. (Users on average will not make too many clicks along a path, though Web indexers may.) Distributions, accumulative distributions and average lengths of maximal forward references are shown in Figure 3. Part (a) of Figure 3 shows the number of maximal forward references for each given length on the x-axis. Part (b) shows the accumulative number of maximal forward references with lengths less than or equal to a given value on the x-axis. Part (c) shows average lengths of maximal forward references in Web logs of sizes on the x-axis. Part (d) shows sizes of sets of maximal forward references from Web logs of sizes on the x-axis.

In summary, when the parameters β and α are set to 30 minutes to define interval sessions and gap sessions, maximal forward references in the five Web logs have the following three properties:

Figure 3. Properties of Maximal Forward References (MFRs)

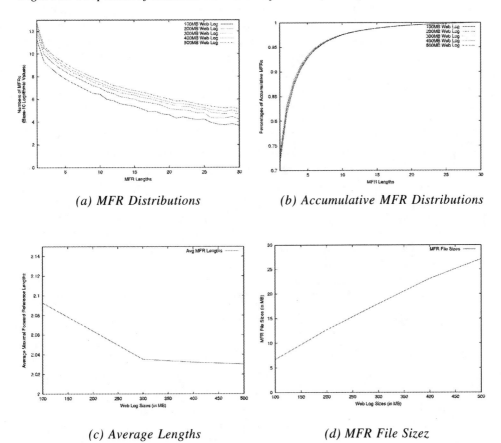

(a) *MFR Distributions*   (b) *Accumulative MFR Distributions*

(c) *Average Lengths*   (d) *MFR File Sizez*

1. Almost all maximal forward references have a length ≤ 30.
2. More than 90% maximal forward references have lengths less than or equal to four, and the average length is about two.
3. The number of unique URLs is 11,926.

In addition, the sizes of five maximal forward reference files corresponding to the five Web logs range from 6.7 megabytes to 27.1 megabytes. One must caution readers that the above three properties are not typical to the Web logs considered here.

"Shallow" Generalized Suffix Trees Over a Very Large Alphabet

Suffix trees are old data structures that become new again and have found many applications in data mining and knowledge discovery as well as bio-informatics. The first linear-time algorithm for constructing suffix trees was given by Weiner (1973). A different but more space efficient algorithm was given by McCreight (1976). Almost 20 years later, Ukkonen (1995) gave a conceptually different linear time algorithm that allows online construction of a suffix tree and is much easier to understand. These algorithms build, in their original design, a suffix tree for a single string S over a given alphabet Σ. However, for any set of strings $\{S_1, S_2, ..., S_n\}$ over Σ, those algorithms can be easily extended to build a tree to represent all suffixes in the set of strings in linear time. Such a tree that represents all suffixes in strings $S_1, S_2, ..., S_n$ is called a *generalized* suffix tree. Usually, a set of strings $S_1, S_2, ..., S_n$ is represented as $S_1\$S_2\$...\$S_n\$$.

One typical application of generalized suffix trees is the identification of frequent (or longest frequent) substrings in a set of strings. This means that generalized suffix trees can be used to find frequent traversal path patterns of maximal forward references, simply because such patterns are frequent (or longest frequent) substrings in the set of maximal forward references, when maximal forward references are understood as strings of URLs. Figure 4 illustrates a suffix tree for the string *mississippi,* and generalized suffixed trees for *mississippi$missing$* and *mississippi$missing$sipping$*. Notice that in the generalized suffix trees, a counter is used at each internal node to indicate the frequency of the substring labeling the edge pointing to the node.

For any given set of strings $S_1, S_2, ..., S_n$ over an alphabet Σ, let:

$$m = \sum_{i=1}^{n} |S_i|.$$

It is well understood (Gusfield, 1997, pp. 116-119) that the linear time (or space) complexity of Weiner, Ukkonen, and McCreight algorithms have all ignored the size of the alphabet Σ, and that memory paging was not considered for large trees and hence cannot be stored in main memory. Notice that suffix trees or generalized suffix trees do not have nice locality properties to support memory paging. When both m and $|\Sigma|$ are very large, the time complexity of those classical algorithms is $O(m|\Sigma|)$ and the space complexity is $\theta(m|\Sigma|)$. In particular, as pointed out in the fifth section, the alphabet Σ in the case of mining frequent traversal path patterns is 11,926 (the number of unique URLs), which is too big to be ignored, and m ranges from 6.7 megabytes to 27.1 megabytes and hence the $\theta(m|\Sigma|)$ space requirement is far beyond the main memory limit of a reasonable computer. Therefore, the challenges of applying generalized suffix trees to efficient mining of frequent traversal path patterns are how to overcome the efficiency dependence on the size of an alphabet in building a generalized suffix tree for a set of maximal forward references, and how to find innovative ways to scale down the space requirement. As one has learned from the fifth section, in the case of mining frequent traversal path patterns, on the one hand the size of the alphabet Σ (the set of all URLs) is very large, and files of maximal forward references are also very large. On the other hand, each maximal forward reference has a short length, less than or equal to some small constant (when a threshold is used to delimit sessions); the vast majority have just several URLs, and the average length is even smaller. Thus, the generalized suffix tree for the sequence of maximal forward references in a Web log is *shallow and very flat*. In the case of the logs in the fifth section, the width of the first level of the tree is $s=|\Sigma|=$

Figure 4. A Suffix Tree and Two Generalized Suffix Trees

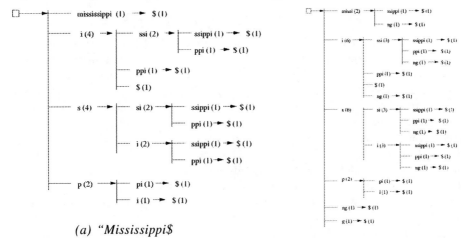

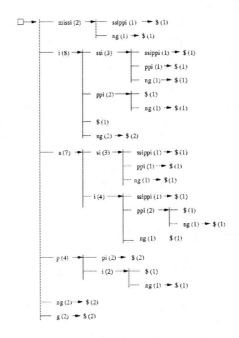

(a) "Mississippi$

(b) "Mississippi$missing$

(c) "Mississippi$missing$sipping$

11,926; the height of each of the *s* subtrees of the root is no more than 30; more than 90% of those subtrees have a height no greater than four; and the average height is just slightly more than two. In general, if a generalized suffix tree has a depth bounded by some small constant, then we call it a *shallow* generalized suffix tree.

MINING FREQUENT
TRAVERSAL PATH PATTERNS

It is assumed in this section that either algorithm ISMFR or GSMFR has obtained maximal forward references. Fast construction of shallow generalized suffix trees over a very large alphabet is studied (Chen et al., 2003a). The techniques developed there will be used here to design algorithms with the best possible efficiency for mining frequent traversal path patterns. Let Σ be the alphabet of all URLs in maximal forward references. For any maximal forward reference S over Σ with a length of n (i.e., S has n URLs in it), $S[1:n]$ denotes S, where $S[i]$ is the i-th URL in S. One uses RstUkkonen(SuffixTree sft, NewString str) to denote the restricted version of the Ukkonen algorithm for building a generalized suffix as follows: it takes an existing generalized suffix tree sft and a new string $str[1:n]$ as input and adds the suffix $str[1:n]$ to sft but ignores all the suffixes $str[2:n]$, $str[3:n]$, ..., $str[n:n]$. When no confusion arises, letters means URLs, and strings means maximal forward references.

Consider a generalized suffix tree sft of a set of strings. For each subtree t of sft such that the root of t is a child of the root of sft, let $t.first()$ denote the first letter that occurred at t. Here the subtree t contains exactly all suffixes starting with the letter $t.first()$, and any two distinct subtrees must have distinct first letters (Chen et al., 2003a). Furthermore, a simple traversal of the subtree t can generate all the frequent (or longest frequent) substrings starting with the letter $t.first()$. For example, the first letter that occurred at the top subtree in Figure 4(c) is m, and all suffixes starting with m in the strings *mississippi\$missing\$sipping\$* are contained in that subtree. This critical observation leads to the designs of the new algorithms: the strategy is to organize all suffixes starting with the same letter into a group and build a subtree for each of such groups. A more or less related strategy has been devised in Hunt et al. (2001), but the strings considered there are over a small alphabet and the method used to build subtrees is of quadratic time complexity.

In the following two subsections, N is used to denote the number of strings in a given set of strings, and a percentage parameter pct is used to determine the frequency threshold $pct * N$.

Algorithm SbSfxMiner

The key idea for designing algorithm SbSfxMiner is as follows. Read strings sequentially from an input file, and for every string $s[1:n]$ output its n suffixes to a temporary file. Then sort the temporary file to group all the suffixes starting with the same letter together. Next, build a generalized suffix tree for each group of such suffixes. (Precisely, the tree here is a subtree of the conventional generalized suffix tree.) Finally, traverse the tree to output all frequent (or longest frequent) substrings. It follows from the properties of maximal forward references in the fifth section that the size of the temporary file is about $O(N)$. Sorting this file takes $O(N \log N)$ time. By the property of the Ukkonen algorithm, building a generalized suffix tree for a group of strings takes $O(N)$ time. Hence, the whole process is of sublinear time. The description of SbSfxMiner is given in Algoritm 3.

Algorithm 3.

```
Algorithm SbSfxMiner:
    input:
            infile: maximal forward reference file
            tmpfile: temperary file
            pct: frequencey threshold = pct * N
            outfile: frequenct maximal forward reference pattern file
    Begin
1.          infile.open(); tmpfile.open()
2.          while (infile  is not empty)
3.                  readMFR(infile, s)
4.                  for (i = 1, i ≤ n; i + +)
5.                          tmpfile.append(s[i:n])
6.          infile.close();outfile.open()
7.          sort(tmpfile);  createSuffixTree(sft)
8.          while (tmpfile is not empty)
9.                  readMFR(tmpfile, s)
10.                 if (sft.empty() or sft.first() == s[1])
11.                         RstUkkonen(sft, s)
12.                 else if (sft.first() ≠ s[1])
13.                         traverseOutput(sft, outfile, pct)
14.         createSuffixTree(sft)
15.         traverseOutput(sft,outfile, pct)
16.         tmpfile.close(); outfile.close()
    end
```

Algorithm HbSfxMiner

The key idea of designing algorithm HbSfxMiner is to eliminate the sorting process to group all suffixes with the same starting letter together. The new approach is to design a fast function to map each letter to a unique integer, and to use this function to map suffixes with the same starting letter into a group. Because URLs have a nice directory path structure, such a function can be designed with constant time complexity. In the general case, one may use a hashing function to replace the function so that it will be more efficient in computing hashing values of letters. Because sorting is not required, the time complexity of the new algorithm is linear. The following is the detailed description of Algorithm 4.

Performance Analysis

Using the five Web logs *L100MB, L200MB, L300MB, L400MB* and *L500MB* as mentioned in the fifth section, the algorithms SbSfxMiner and HbSfxMiner are compared with the Ukkonen algorithm (Ukkonen, 1995) and the SelectiveScan algorithm (Chen, Park & Yu, 1998). Since it was known that SelectiveScan is more efficient than FullSacn (Chen, Park & Yu, 1998), it is not necessary to compare the new algorithms with FullScan. For SelectiveScan, only times for *pct=0.2* are shown. It has much worse performance for smaller values of *pct*. The computing environment is the same as that in Session 4, and all programs were also implemented using Microsoft Visual C++ 6.0. The empirical results are shown in Figure 5.

Algorithm 4.

Algorithm HbSfxMiner:
    input:
        infile: maximal forward reference file
        f: a function from letter to integer
        pct: frequencey threshold =*pct*N*
        outfile: frequenct maximal forward reference pattern file
    Begin
  1.   infile.open(); outfile.open()
  2.   createSuffixTrees(sft, size)
  3.   while (infile is not empty)
  4.   readMFR(infile, s)
  5.   for $(i = 1; i \le n; i++)$
  6.   RstUkkonen(sft[f(s[i])], s[i:n])
  7.   for $(i = 1; i < size; i++)$
  8.   traverseOutput(sft[i], outfile, *pct*)
  9.   tmpfile.close(); outfile.close()
    end

Figure 5. Performance of Four Algorithms

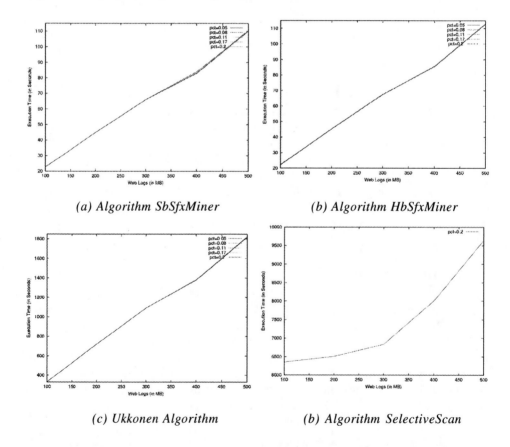

(a) Algorithm SbSfxMiner

(b) Algorithm HbSfxMiner

(c) Ukkonen Algorithm

(b) Algorithm SelectiveScan

It is clear that the new algorithms have the best performance. When carefully examined, algorithm SbSfxMiner performs even better than HbSfxMiner. The reason is that the computing of the underlying mapping function, though a constant time for each computation, exceeds the sorting time when accumulated for so many substrings in the file.

CONCLUSIONS

The problem of mining frequent traversal path patterns from very large Web logs is fundamental in Web mining. In this chapter, the two algorithms ISMFR and GSMFR are designed for finding maximal forward references from very large Web logs, and two other algorithms, SbSfxMiner and HbSfxMiner, are devised for mining frequent traversal path patterns from large sets of maximal forward references. When SbSfxMiner and HbSfxMiner are respectively combined with algorithms ISMFR or GSMFR, two algorithms are obtained for mining frequent traversal path patterns from Web logs directly. These two algorithms have respectively linear and sublinear complexity, and have substantially better performance than the two a priori-like algorithms in Chen, Park and Yu (1998) and the Ukkonen algorithm (Ukkonen, 1995) in the case of mining frequent traversal patterns.

ACKNOWLEDGMENTS

The authors thank the two anonymous referees and Professor Anthony Scime for their valuable comments on the draft of this chapter. The work of the first two and the last authors is supported in part by the Computing and Information Technology Center of the University of Texas-Pan American.

REFERENCES

Berendt, B., Mobasher, B., Spiliopoulou, M., & Wiltshire, J. (2001). Measuring the accuracy of sessionizers for Web usage analysis. *Proceedings of the Workshop on Web Mining at the First SIAM International Conference on Data Mining*, (pp. 7-14).

Borges, J., & Levene, M. (1999). Data mining of user navigation patterns. *Proceedings of the WEBKDD'99 Workshop on Web Usage Analysis and User Profiling*, (pp. 31-39).

Buchner, A.G., Baumgarten, M., & Anand, S.S. (1999). Navigation pattern discovery from Internet data. *Proceedings of the WEBKDD'99 Workshop on Web Usage Analysis and User Profiling*, (pp. 25-30).

Buchner, A.G., & Mulvenna, M.D. (1998). Discovering Internet marketing intelligence through online analytical Web usage mining. *ACM SIGMOD RECORD*, 54-61.

Catledge, L., & Pitkow, J. (1995). Characterizing browsing behaviors on the World Wide Web. *Computer Networks and ISDN Systems, 27*(6), 1065-1073.

Chen, M.S., Park, J.S., & Yu, P.S. (1998). Efficient data mining for path traversal patterns. *IEEE Transactions on Knowledge and Data Engineering, 10*(2), 209-221.

Chen, Z., Fowler, R.H., & Fu, A. (2003). Linear time algorithms for finding maximal forward references. *Proceedings of the IEEE International Conference on Information Technology: Coding & Computing,* (pp. 160-164).

Chen, Z., Fowler, R.H., Fu, A., & Wang, C. (2003a). Fast construction of generalized suffix trees over a very large alphabet. *Proceedings of the Ninth International Computing and Combinatorics Conference, Lecture Notes in Computer Science LNCS 2697,* (pp. 284-293).

Chen, Z., Fowler, R.H., Fu, A., & Wang, C. (2003b). Linear and sublinear time algorithms for mining frequent traversal path patterns from very large Web logs. *Proceedings of the Seventh International Database Engineering & Applications Symposium.*

Chen, Z., Fu, A., & Tung, F. (2003). Optimal algorithms for finding user access sessions from very large Web logs. *World Wide Web, 6*(3), 259-279.

Cooley, R., Mobasher, B., & Srivastava, J. (1997). Web mining: Information and pattern discovery on the World Wide Web. *Proceedings of the IEEE International Conference Tools with AI,* (pp. 558-567).

Cooley, R., Mobasher, B., & Srivastava, J. (1999). Data preparation for mining World Wide Web browsing patterns. *Journal of Knowledge and Information Systems, 1*(1), 5-32.

Gusfield, D. (1997). *Algorithms on strings, trees, and sequences.* Cambridge University Press.

Hunt, E., Atkinson, M.P., & Irving, R.W. (2001). A database index to large biological sequences, *Proceedings of the 27th International Conference on Very Large Data Bases,* (pp. 139-148).

Kosala, R., & Blockeel, H. (2000). Web mining research: A survey. *SIGKDD Explorations, 2*(1), 1-15.

Masseglia, F., Poncelet, P., & Cicchetti, R. (1999). An efficient algorithm for Web usage mining. *Networking and Information Systems Journal, 2*(5-6), 571-603.

McCreight, E.M. (1976). A space-economical suffix tree construction algorithm. *Journal of Algorithms, 23*(2), 262-272.

Padmanabhan, V.N., & Mogul, J.C. (1996). Using predictive prefetching to improve World Wide Web latency. *Computer Communication Review, 26,* 22-36.

Perkowitz, M., & Etzioni, O. (1998). Adaptive Web pages: Automatically synthesizing Web pages. *Proceedings of AAAI/IAAI'98,* (pp. 727-732).

Pitkow, J., & Pirolli, P. (1999). Mining longest repeating subsequences to predict World Wide Web Surfing. *Proceedings of the Second USENIX Symposium on Internet Technologies & Systems,* (pp. 11-14).

Srivastava, J., Cooley, R., Desphande, M., & Tan, P. (2000). Web usage mining: Discovery and applications of usage patterns from Web data. *SIGKDD Exploration, 1*(2), 12-23.

Su, Z., Yang, Q., Lu, Y., & Zhang, H. (2000). WhatNext: A prediction system for Web requests using N-gram sequence models. *Proceedings of the First International Conference on Web Information Systems Engineering,* (pp. 200-207).

Ukkonen, E. (1995). On-line construction of suffix trees. *Algorithmica, 14*(3), 249-260.

Weiner, P. (1973). Linear pattern matching algorithms. *Proceedings of the 14th IEEE Annual Symposium on Switching and Automata Theory,* (pp. 1-11).

Xiao, Y., & Dunham, M. (2001). Efficient mining of traversal patterns. *Data & Knowledge Engineering, 39,* 191-214.

Chapter XVI

Analysis of Document Viewing Patterns of Web Search Engine Users

Bernard J. Jansen
The Pennsylvania State University, USA

Amanda Spink
University of Pittsburgh, USA

ABSTRACT

This chapter reviews the concepts of Web results page and Web page viewing patterns by users of Web search engines. It presents the advantages of using traditional transaction log analysis in identifying these patterns, serving as a basis for Web usage mining. The authors also present the results of a temporal analysis of Web page viewing, illustrating that the user — information interaction is extremely short. By using real data collected from real users interacting with real Web information retrieval systems, the authors aim to highlight one aspect of the complex environment of Web information seeking.

INTRODUCTION

The Web has dramatically changed the way people locate information. One can define Web mining as:

> *the discovery of and analysis of useful information from the World Wide Web. This describes the automatic search of information resource available on-line, i.e., Web content mining, and the discovery of user access patterns from Web services, i.e., Web usage mining (Cooley, Mobasher & Srivastava, 1997).*

Information viewing characteristics of users are central aspects of this view of Web mining. As the Web has become a worldwide phenomenon (Cole, Suman, Schramm, Lunn & Aquino, 2003), we need an understanding what searching trends are emerging, including both how people utilize Web search engines in the search process to locate Web documents and how searchers are visiting and viewing the documents that the search engine locates.

There is a growing body of Web research concerning how users interact with Web search engines. There are also reports on the number of results pages viewed. When a Web search engine user submits a query, the search engine returns the results in "chunks" of usually about 10 results. We refer to these "chunks" as results pages, and the search engine presents results within these pages to the user sequentially from the topmost ranked results page to the maximum number of results pages retrieved by the search engine. However, there has been little large-scale research examining the pattern of interactions between Web search engine users and the actual Web documents presented by these results pages.

In this chapter, we summarize research on the results page viewing activities of users of Web search engines. We examine general searching characteristics including the number of results pages viewed. We then examine the number of Web documents that users view, analyzing the relationship between sessions, queries, and Web pages viewed. We also explore the temporal relationships of these interactions.

We begin with a review of the literature, followed by the methodology we utilized to analyze actual Web queries submitted by users to Web search engines. We use these queries to examine trends in searching. Specifically, we examine results pages accessed, and page viewing or click-through data (i.e., the Web page/s a user visits when following a hyperlink from a search engine results page), including the temporal aspects of this viewing. Click-through data shows great promise in the area of Web mining to isolate relevant content, identify searchers' usage patterns, and evaluate Web search engine system performance (Joachims, 2002). We then discuss the implications of these results for Web search engine users, search engine designers, and the designers of Websites. We conclude with directions of future research in this area.

BACKGROUND

There has been limited research examining the results pages and little analysis of the Web page viewing patterns of Web search engine users. There is a growing body of literature in information science that examines how people search on the Web (Hölscher & Strube, 2000; Jansen & Pooch, 2001; Jansen, Spink & Saracevic, 2000; Spink, Jansen, Wolfram & Saracevic, 2002). This research provides insight into how people search for information on the Web, and provides a framework for considering the Web document viewing and search process. Jansen and Pooch (2001) present an extensive review of the Web searching literature, reporting that Web searchers exhibit different search techniques than do searchers on other information systems.

Hölscher and Strube (2000) examined European searchers and report information on sessions, queries, and terms, noting that experts exhibit different searching patterns than novices. Jansen, Spink and Saracevic (2000) conducted an in-depth analysis of the user interactions with the Excite search engine. Spink, Jansen, Wolfram and Saracevic (2002) analyzed trends in Web searching, reporting that Web searching has remained relatively stable over time, although they noted a shift from entertainment to commercial searching. This stream of research provides useful information and a methodology for examining Web searchers and their patterns of results pages viewing.

Focusing specifically on results page access patterns, Jansen, Spink and Pedersen (under review) present temporal results of results page viewing activities on the Alta Vista Web search engine. The queries examined for this study were submitted to Alta Vista on September 8, 2002 and span a 24-hour period. The queries were recorded in four transaction logs (*general*, *audio*, *image*, and *video*) and represent a portion of the searches executed on the Web search engine on this particular date. The original general transaction log contains approximately 3,000,000 records. Each record contains three fields: (1) *Time of Day:* measured in hours, minutes, and seconds from midnight of each day as recorded by the Alta Vista server; (2) *User Identification:* an anonymous user code assigned by the Alta Vista server; and (3) *Query Terms:* terms exactly as entered by the given user.

For the temporal analysis, the researchers compared the results from this analysis to results from a 1998 study of Alta Vista searchers. Silverstein, Henzinger, Marais and Moricz (1998) used a transaction log with several fields, including: (1) *Time Stamp:* measured in milliseconds from 1 January 1970, (2) *Cookie:* the cookie filename used to identify a user computer, and (3) *Query:* terms exactly as entered by the given user. The queries in the 1998 study were submitted to Alta Vista during the period August 2 through September 13, 1998. The total transaction log contained 993,208,159 requests, just under a billion records.

Table 1 shows an increase in the percentage of users viewing more than the first results page, which when combined with other increased interactions may indicate an increased persistence in locating relevant results.

Table 2 presents a more detailed view of the results pages viewing of Alta Vista Web users.

Jansen, Spink and Pedersen (forthcoming) also present results page viewing of searchers using a multimedia ontology.

Table 3 presents these results.

Table 1. Overview Results for Data Analysis of 1998 and 2002

	Alta Vista 1998		Alta Vista 2002	
Sessions	285,474,117		369,350	
Queries	993,208,159		1,073,388	
Terms				
Unique			369,350	9.5%
Total			1,073,388	100%
Results Pages Viewed				
1 page	718,615,763	85.2%	781,483	72.8%
2 pages	63,258,430	7.5%	139,088	13.0%
3+ pages	13,674,409	7.3%	150,904	14.1%

Table 2. Results Pages Viewed for 2002

Number of Results Pages Viewed	Occurrences	%	Occurrences	%
1	846,213,351	85.2%	781,483	72.8%
2	74,490,612	7.5%	139,088	13.0%
3	29,796,245	3.0%	60,334	5.6%
4	42,707,951 *	4.3%	27,196	2.5%
5			16,898	1.6%
6			11,646	1.1%
7			6,678	0.6%
8			4,939	0.5%
9			3,683	0.3%
>=10			21,398	2.0%

Note: For the 1998 figure, calculated based on distinct queries only, 153,645,993.
* Number and percentages are for session of 4 and more.

Table 3. Result Page Viewing of General, Audio, Image, and Video Searching in 2002

	General	Audio	Image	Video
Sessions	369,350	3,181	26,720	5,789
Queries	1,073,388	7,513	127,614	24,265
Terms				
Unique	297,528 (9.5%)	6,199 (33.4%)	71,873 (14.1%)	8,914 (19.1%)
Total	3,132,106 (100%)	18,544 (100%)	510,807 (100%)	46,708 (100%)
Results Pages Viewed				
1 page	781,483 (72.8%)	5,551 (73.9%)	80,455 (63.0%)	13,357 (55.0%)
2 pages	139,088 (13.0%)	1,070 (14.2%)	14,498 (11.1%)	3,905 (16.1%)
3+ pages	150,904 (14.1%)	892 (11.9%)	32,661 (25.65)	1,949 (28.9%)

When comparing among the four types of searching (general, audio, image, and video) in Table 3, we see that video searchers viewed more results pages than other searchers, with only 55% of video searchers viewing only one results page.

There has been less research focusing on European users of Web search engines, relative to users of U.S. search engines. Three studies have examined this area of Web searching (Cacheda & Viña, 2001a; Hölscher & Strube, 2000; Spink, Ozmutlu, Ozmutlu & Jansen, 2002). Hölscher and Strube (2000) examined European searchers on the Fireball search engine, a predominantly German search engine, and reported on the use of Boolean and other query modifiers. The researchers note that experts exhibit different searching patterns than novice users. Cacheda and Viña (2001a, 2001b) reported statistics from a Spanish Web directory service, BIWE.

Table 4 provides the key results for the Fireball and BIWE studies.

Table 4 shows that users of European search engines view even fewer results pages than users of U.S. search engines.

Most of the existing Web searching literature focuses on human searching and page viewing. However, much searching is now done using automated processes such as agents and meta-searching tools. Jansen, Spink and Pedersen (2003a, 2003b) conducted two studies of agent searching on Web search engines. In the first study (Jansen, Spink & Pederson, 2003a), the queries examined were submitted to Alta Vista on September 8,

Table 4. Results Pages Comparison of Fireball and BIWE Study

	Fireball Study		BWIE Study	
Sessions	Not Reported		71,810 *	
Queries	451,551		105,786	
Terms				
Unique	Not Reported		18,966	16%
Total	Not Reported		116,953	
Results Pages Viewed				
1 page	9261367	60%	48,831	68%
2 pages	6545887	40%	9,335	13%
3+ pages			13,644	19%

* Data reported using 71,810 initial queries.

Table 5. Agents' Searching Characteristics for Top Agents

		Number	Percentage
Sessions		22	
Queries		219,718	
Terms	Unique	277,902	60%
	Total	459,537	
Results Pages Viewed Per Query			
1 page		18,8747	86%
2 pages		17,155	8%
3+ pages		13,816	6%

2002. The researcher culled the agent submissions from the original transaction logs. The researchers examined sessions with over 10,000 queries.

Table 5 displays the results of this analysis.

Agents exhibit the same characteristic as human Web searchers, a very low tolerance for wading through a lot of results. In fact, Web agents appear to have an even lower tolerance for viewing a large number of results. For 86% of the agents, only the first set of results was viewed, which is 30% higher than human Web searchers.

The researchers conducted a follow-up study (Jansen, Spink & Pederson, 2003b) with a larger set of agent submissions. The results are displayed in Table 6.

Table 6 shows for over 2,500 agents, most still viewed only one results page.

Spink, Jansen, Wolfram and Saracevic (2002), as part of a body of research studying Web searcher and Web search engine interaction, analyzed three data sets culled from more than one million queries submitted by more than 200,000 users of the Excite Web search engine, collected in September 1997, December 1999, and May 2001. This longitudinal benchmark study shows that public Web searching is evolving in certain directions, specifically in the area of result pages viewed.

Table 7 shows the results pages aspect of this study.

Table 6. Aggregate Results for General Search Trends

	Agent Searching Data During Interactions with Alta Vista	
Sessions	2,717	
Queries	896,387	
Terms		
Unique	570,214	17.7%
Total	3,224,840	
Results Pages Viewed		
1 page	760,071	85%
2 pages	67,755	8%
3+ pages	68,561	8%

Table 7. Comparative Statistics for Excite Web Query Data Sets

Variables	1997	1999	2001
Result pages viewed per query			
1 page	28.6%	42.7%	50.5%
2 pages	19.5%	21.2%	20.3%
3+ pages	51.9%	36.1%	29.2%

Generally, from Table 7, we see that users are viewing fewer results pages in 2001 relative to 1997. Over 50% of the users by 2001 viewed no more than only one results page.

VIEWING OF RESULTS PAGES AND WEB DOCUMENTS

In general, from a summation of this literature, Web searching sessions are very short as measured in number of queries. There has been less analysis of session temporal length, but it is assumed to be short. Users view a very limited number of results pages. The studies cited previously illustrate that the majority of Web searchers, approximately 80%, view no more than 10 to 20 results.

However, the page viewing characteristics of Web searchers have not been analyzed at any finer level of granularity. We do not know how many Web documents Web searchers actually view (i.e., pages viewed). In this chapter, we present research results to address these issues by examining the page viewing patterns of actual Web search engine users.

More specifically, the overall research questions driving this study (Jansen & Spink, 2003), are:
(1)   How many results pages do Web search engine users examine?
(2)   How many Web documents do Web search engine users view when searching the Web?
(3)   How relevant are the Web documents that they are viewing?

To address the first research question, we obtained, and quantitatively analyzed, actual queries submitted to AlltheWeb.com, a major Web search engine at the time owned by FAST. From this analysis, we could determine the number of result pages the searcher viewed. In addition to capturing the user's query, we also captured the Web document that the user viewed for each query, which addresses the second research question. For the third research question, we evaluate a subset of click-through data from this transaction log to determine whether or not the Web document contained relevant information.

Data Collection

The queries examined for this study were submitted to FAST, a major Web search engine on February 6, 2001 and span a 24-hour period. They were recorded in a transaction log and represent a portion of the searches executed on the Web search engine on this particular date. The transaction log held a large and varied set of queries (over one million records). In our analysis, we generally use the procedure and terminology outlined in Jansen and Pooch (2001).

Briefly, the metrics we used and addressed by Jansen and Pooch (2001) include:

(1)   *Session.* The *session* is the entire sequence of queries entered by a searcher. We identified a searcher as a unique *User Identification* and applied no temporal cut-off. We attempted to exclude sessions from softbots using numerical limitation. However, currently, there is no way to precisely identify all of these automated searches (Silverstein, Henzinger, Marais & Moricz, 1999).

(2)   *Query.* A set of queries compose a session. We define a *query* as a string of zero or more characters submitted to a search engine. This is a mechanical definition as opposed to an information seeking definition (Korfhage, 1997). We refer to the first query by a particular searcher as an *initial query.* A subsequent query by the same searcher that is identical to one or more of the searcher's previous queries is a *repeat query.*

(3)   *Term.* A *term* is a string of characters separated by some delimiter such as a space or some other separator. In our analysis, we used a blank space as the separator.

Each record within the transaction log contains three fields: (1) *Time of Day:* measured in hours, minutes, and seconds from midnight of each day as logged by the Web server; (2) *User Identification:* an anonymous user code assigned by the FAST server; (3) *Query Terms:* terms exactly as entered by the given user, and (4) *Page Viewed:* the uniform resource locator (URL) that the searcher viewed after entering the query. With these fields, we located a user's initial query and recreated the chronological series of actions by each user in a session.

Data Analysis

A term is any series of characters separated by white space. A query is the entire string of terms submitted by a searcher in a given instance. A session is the entire series of queries submitted by a user during one interaction with the Web search engine. A results page is the chunk of results presented by the search engine. The Web page is the Web document located at the URL locator presented by the Web search engine in the results page.

When a searcher submits a query, then views a document, and returns to the search engine, the FAST server logs this second visit with the identical user identification and query, but with a new time (i.e., the time of the second visit). This is beneficial information in determining how many of the retrieved results the searcher visited from the search engine, but unfortunately it also skews the results in analyzing how the user searched on the system.

To address the first research question, we collapsed the data set by combining all identical queries submitted by the same agent to give the unique queries in order to analyze sessions, queries and terms and pages of results viewed.

For the second research question, we utilized the complete un-collapsed sessions in order to obtain an accurate measure of the temporal length of sessions and the number of pages visited.

For the third research question, we randomly selected 530 records from the transaction log. Each record contained the query submitted by the Web search engine user and the Web page viewed after the user submitted that query. Three independent raters reviewed these 530 queries for relevance, assigning a binary relevance judgment of 1 (for relevant) or 0 (for not relevant) based on the rater's interpretation of the query.

Relevance is a standard measure utilized in information retrieval to evaluate the effectiveness of a query based on the documents retrieved (Saracevic, 1975). The reviewers received training regarding the judgment process and were given instructions for determining relevance. Inter-rater agreement across the three raters was found to be quite high (0.95). From these relevance rankings, we were able to calculate relative precision (i.e., the ratio of the number of relative documents retrieved to the number of documents retrieved at a certain point in the results listing).

RESULTS
General Searching Characteristics

Table 8 presents an overview of the analysis.

Overall, the relationship between the number of sessions and queries, the ratio of unique terms relative to the total number of terms, and the percentages of pages viewed correspond closely to that reported in other Web searching studies (Montgomery &

Table 8. Overview Data

Sessions	153,297	
Queries	451,551	
Terms		
Unique	180,998	13%
Total	1,350,619	
Session size		
1 query	81,036	53%
2 queries	28,117	18%
3+ queries	44,144	29%
Pages of Results		
1 page	244,441	54%
2 pages	86,976	19%
3+ pages	43,509	27%

Faloutsos, 2001; Silverstein, Henzinger, Marais & Moricz, 1999), leading us to believe that the data from this transaction log represents searches submitted by the typical population of Web users. Jansen and Pooch (2001) also noted similarities among users of a variety of Web search engines.

Number of Result Pages Viewed

From an analysis of Table 8, some patterns emerge. Some 53% of the users entered one query and about 54% of the users viewed only one page of results. The relationship between the number of queries submitted and the number of results pages viewed is parallel, with about equal percentages of queries submitted and results pages viewed. This may imply some relationship between the sufficiency (Jansen, Spink & Saracevic, 1998) of the retrieved results relative to the user's information need. For example, if the results from the first query were relevant and satisfied the information there would be no need for the user to submit additional queries.

Table 9 presents a more in-depth analysis of the number of pages viewed per query submitted.

There is a sharp decrease in the number of viewings between the first and second and the second and third results pages, with very few users viewing more than four or five results pages. As with previous Web studies, these Web users have a low tolerance for wading through large numbers of Web documents.

Figure 1 displays the trend in results page viewing using the data displayed in Table 9.

Table 9. Results Pages Viewed

Number of Results Pages Viewed	Occurrences	Percentage
1	24,4441	54.1%
2	86,976	19.3%
3	43,509	9.6%
4	24,880	5.5%
5	14,999	3.3%
6	9,706	2.1%
7	6,583	1.5%
8	4,570	1.0%
9	3,219	0.7%
>=10	4,391	2.8%

Figure 1. Viewing of Results Pages

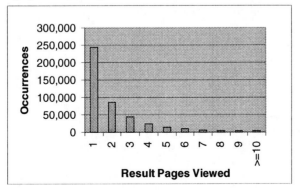

Table 10. Pages Viewed per Session

Number of Pages Viewed	Occurrences	Percentage
1	42,499	27.62%
2	22,997	14.95%
3	15,740	10.23%
4	11,763	7.65%
5	9,032	5.87%
6	7,157	4.65%
7	5,746	3.73%
8	4,563	2.97%
9	3,869	2.51%
>=10	29,370	19.09%

Figure 2. Viewing Web Pages

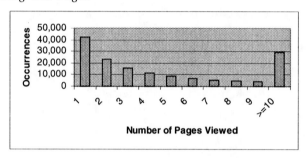

Web Documents Viewed by Users

Although most users viewed only the first one or two results pages, this does not tell us the actual number of Web pages they actually visited (i.e., pages viewed). They may have viewed all results presented, or they may have viewed none. To address this issue, Table 10 shows the number of pages viewed per session.

The mean number of Web results viewed was 8.2, with a standard deviation of 26.9. Previous studies report that most Web searchers rarely visit more than the first results page, which usually displays 10 results. While 10 results is in line with the average, our analysis shows that over 66% of searchers examine fewer than five pages in a typical session and almost 30% view only one document in a given session.

Figure 2 displays the trend in page viewing using the data from Table 10.

Web Documents Viewed by Query

This low number of viewed pages holds when we move from the session level of analysis to the query level.

Table 11 presents the number of pages viewed per query.

The mean number of pages viewed per query is 2.5, with a standard deviation of 3.9. FAST users viewed five or less documents per query over 90% of the time. The largest number of users by far viewed only one Web page per query, just fewer than 55%.

Figure 3 displays the trend in page viewing by query using the data from Table 11.

Table 11. Pages Viewed per Query

Number of Pages Viewed	Occurrences	Percentage
1	274,644	54.3%
2	95,532	18.9%
3	47,770	9.4%
4	27,625	5.5%
5	16,800	3.3%
6	11,024	2.2%
7	7,653	1.5%
8	5,231	1.0%
9	3,802	0.8%
>=10	15,473	3.1%

Figure 3. Viewing of Web Pages by Query

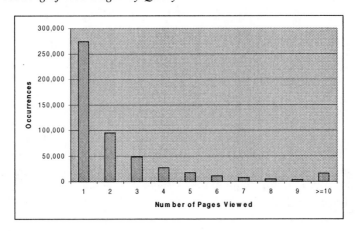

Session Duration

Table 12 presents the session duration, as measured from the time the first query is submitted until the user departs the search engine for the last time (i.e., does not return).

With this definition of search duration, we can measure the total user time on the search engine and the time spent viewing the first and all subsequent Web documents, except the final document. Unfortunately, this final viewing time is not available since the Web search engine server records the time stamp. Naturally, the time between visits from the Web document to the search may not have been entirely spent viewing the Web document.

However, this may not be a significant issue, as shown from the data in Table 12. The mean session duration was two hours, 21 minutes and 55 seconds, with a standard deviation of four hours, 45 minutes, and 36 seconds. However, we see that the longer session durations skewed our result for the mean. Fully 52% of the sessions were less than 15 minutes. This is in line with earlier reported research on Web session length (He, Göker & Harper, 2002). Over 25% of the sessions were less than five minutes.

Table 12. Session Duration

Session Duration	Occurrences	Percentage
< 5 minutes	55,966	26.2%
5 to 10 minutes	13,275	6.2%
10 to 15 minutes	41,987	19.7%
15 to 30 minutes	19,314	9.1%
30 to 60 minutes	30,955	14.5%
1 to 2 hours	8,691	4.1%
2 to 3 hours	21,901	10.3%
3 to 4 hours	2,635	1.2%
> 4 hours	18,605	8.7%

Document Viewing Duration

While session length has been addressed, what has not been previously reported in the literature is the duration of pages viewed by Web search engine users, which is presented in Table 13.

The mean time spent viewing a particular Web document was 16 minutes and two seconds, with a standard deviation of 43 minutes and one second. However, some lengthy page views skewed our mean. Over 75% of the users viewed the retrieved Web document for less than 15 minutes. Nearly 40% of the users viewed the retrieved Web document for less than 3 minutes. Perhaps more surprisingly, just fewer than 14% of the users viewed the Web document for less than 30 seconds. These results for Web document viewing are substantially less than has been previously reported using survey data (CyberAtlas, 2002).

Table 13. Duration of Page Views

Page View Duration	Occurrences	Percentage
< 30 seconds	46,303	13.9%
30 to 60 seconds	16,754	5.0%
1 to 2 minutes	48,059	14.5%
2 to 3 minutes	16,237	4.9%
3 to 4 minutes	47,254	14.2%
4 to 5 minutes	15,203	4.6%
5 to 10 minutes	47,254	14.2%
10 to 15 minutes	14,047	4.2%
15 to 30 minutes	41,215	12.4%
30 to 60 minutes	9,054	2.7%
> 60 minutes	30,592	9.2%

Table 14. Relevance Results for Pages Viewed

Relevance Score	Number of Documents	Percentage
3	199	37.5%
2	74	14.0%
1	103	19.4%
0	154	29.1%
	530	

RELEVANCE OF PAGES VIEWED

This portion of the study involved using a random subset of records from the FAST transaction log, which included the Website the searcher actually visited. Three independent raters visited the sites and evaluated the Web document to determine relevance. This analysis helps address the question of whether search sessions are short because the searchers are finding the information that they need or because they are not finding the information they need and just giving up or going elsewhere. The results are reported in Table 14.

Three independent raters viewed 530 URLs and evaluated these pages for relevance based on their interpretation of the query submitted. Each rater assigned a relevance Web document a rating of one. A non-relevant page received a rating of zero. So, the maximum score a Web page could receive was three, meaning that all three reviewers rated the page relevant.

Approximately 52% of the time, two or more raters evaluated a page to be relevant. Over 48% of the time, two or more raters evaluated a page to be not relevant. These percentages, taken in total, represent precision for this set of results retrieved by this search engine. This confirms earlier survey data that users were finding relevant findings on Web search engines (Spink, Bateman & Jansen, 1999). Assuming a relevance score of two or higher indicates a relevant document, Web users would generally need to view about two documents to find a relevant one.

SUMMARY

There are some clear patterns concerning the number of results pages viewed by FAST users. Approximately 54% of the users view only one results page. This finding is similar to the percentage of users that enter only one query (53%) and the percentage of relevant documents (52%). The similarity among these percentages would seem to indicate several things. One, the information needs of a majority of Web searchers are not extremely complex, given they require only one query. Two, Web search engines appear to do a good job of indexing and ranking Web documents in response to these queries, based on the majority of users viewing only one results page. Three, it appears that on average about 50% of the documents that a person views will be relevant, implying that the typical Web user will have to view about two Web documents to find a relevant document. This is supported by our analysis of Web documents viewed, with 43% of users in our sample viewing two or fewer Web documents.

From our results, Web search engine users on average view about eight Web documents. However, our analysis shows that over 66% of searchers examine fewer than five, with more than one in three Web searchers viewing only one document in a given session. Users on average view about two to three documents per query. Over 55% of Web users view only one result per query.

Not only are the session lengths of Web search engines users short in terms of number of queries submitted and documents viewed, but they are also short temporally. Over half the sessions were less than 15 minutes and about 25% of the sessions were less than five minutes.

The mean time spent viewing a particular Web document was just over 16 minutes. However, 75% of the users spent less than 15 minutes viewing the retrieved Web document. Twenty percent of the Web users view a Web document for less than a minute. These results would seem to indicate that the initial impression of a Web document is extremely important, as Web searchers are typically not going to spend a great deal of time combing the document to find the relevant information.

From our analysis, it appears that generally the precision Web users can expect is about 50%, meaning that one out of every two of the Web documents viewed will be relevant to their query. Given the large number of documents that most Web search engines retrieve, 50% is rather high. However, note that this analysis is for Web documents viewed, not documents retrieved. This has significant implications for Web search engines and Web page designers. It is clear the Web search engine users are making relevance determination based solely on the document summary that is displayed in the search engines results page.

This study contributes to the Web searching literature in several important ways. First, the data come from users submitting real queries and viewing actual Web pages. Accordingly, they provide a realistic glimpse into how users search, without the self-selection issues or altered behavior that can occur with lab studies or survey data. Second, our sample is quite large, with approximately 150,000 users. Third, we obtained data from a popular search engine and one of the largest search engines on the Web in terms of both document collections. Finally, it provides a detailed examination of the Web document viewing patterns and viewing duration of Web users.

As with any research, there are limitations that should be recognized. The sample data come from one major Web search engine, introducing the possibility that the queries do not represent the queries submitted by the broader Web searching population. However, Jansen and Pooch (Jansen & Pooch, 2001) have shown that characteristics of Web sessions, queries, and terms are very consistent across search engines. Another potential limitation is that we do not have information about the demographic characteristics of the users who submitted queries, so we must infer their characteristics from the demographics of Web searchers as a whole. Third, we do not have information about the browsing patterns of the users once they leave the search engine to visit a Web document. It is possible that they are browsing using the hypermedia structure of the Web. However, given the duration between departing and returning to the search engine, this is unlikely in most situations. Finally, it is possible that the click-through data we used in the relevance evaluation are not representative of the total transaction log.

FUTURE TRENDS

Our results provide important insights into the current state of Web searching and Web usage. The short session lengths, combined with short queries have been issues for designers of Web information systems. This does not seem to be a successful strategy to maximize recall or precision, the standard metric for information retrieval system performance. However, it appears that Web search engine users are finding relevant information with this searching strategy. This may indicate the need for new metrics for evaluation of Web information systems. More importantly, a precision of approximately 50% would indicate there is room for continued improvement in Web search engine design.

ACKNOWLEDGMENTS

We thank Excite, AlltheWeb.com and AltaVista for providing the Web query data sets without which we could not have conducted this research.

REFERENCES

Cacheda, F., & Viña, Á. (2001a, July). Experiences retrieving information in the World Wide Web. *Proceedings of the 6th IEEE Symposium on Computers and Communications,* Hammamet, Tunisia, (pp. 72-79).

Cacheda, F., & Viña, Á. (2001b, October). Understanding how people use search engines: A statistical analysis for e-business. *Proceedings of the e-Business and e-Work Conference and Exhibition 2001*, Venice, Italy, (pp. 319-325).

Cole, J.I., Suman, M., Schramm, P., Lunn, R., & Aquino, J.S. (2003, February). *The UCLA Internet report surveying the digital future year three* [website]. UCLA Center for Communication Policy. Available: *http://www.ccp.ucla.edu/pdf/UCLA-Internet-Report-Year-Three.pdf*.

Cooley, R., Mobasher, B., & Srivastava, J. (1997, November). Web mining: Information and pattern discovery on the World Wide Web. *Proceedings of the 9th IEEE International Conference on Tools with Artificial Intelligence* (ICTAI'97), Newport Beach, CA, (pp. 558-567).

CyberAtlas. (2002). *November 2002 Internet usage stats* [website]. Nielsen//NetRatings Inc. Retrieved 1 January, 2002 from: *http://cyberatlas.internet.com/big_picture/traffic_patterns/article/0,,5931_1560881,00.html*.

He, D., Göker, A., & Harper, D.J. (2002). Combining evidence for automatic Web session identification. *Information Processing & Management, 38*(5), 727 - 742.

Hölscher, C., & Strube, G. (2000). Web search behavior of Internet experts and newbies. *International Journal of Computer and Telecommunications Networking, 33*(1-6), 337-346.

Jansen, B.J., & Pooch, U. (2001). Web user studies: A review and framework for future work. *Journal of the American Society of Information Science and Technology, 52*(3), 235-246.

Jansen, B.J., & Spink, A. (2003, June). An analysis of Web information seeking and use: Documents retrieved versus documents viewed. *Proceedings of the 4th International Conference on Internet Computing*, Las Vegas, Nevada, (pp. 65–69).

Jansen, B.J., Spink, A., & Pederson, J. (2003a, June). Monsters at the gates: When softbots visit Web search engines. *Proceedings of the 4th International Conference on Internet Computing,* Las Vegas, Nevada, (pp. 620-626).

Jansen, B.J., Spink, A., & Pederson, J. (2003b, October). Web searching agents: What are they doing out there? *Proceedings of the 2003 IEEE International Conference on Systems, Man & Cybernetics*, Washington, DC, (pp. 10-16).

Jansen, B.J., Spink, A., & Pederson, J. (Forthcoming). A view from above: A temporal analysis of Web searching on alta vista. *Information Processing & Management.*

Jansen, B.J., Spink, A., & Pederson, J. (Under review). Trend analysis of alta vista Web searching. *Journal of the American Society for Information Science and Technology.*

Jansen, B.J., Spink, A., & Saracevic, T. (1998). Searchers, the subjects they search, and sufficiency: A study of a large sample of excite searches. *Proceedings of the 1998 World Conference on the WWW and Internet,* Orlando, Florida.

Jansen, B.J., Spink, A., & Saracevic, T. (2000). Real life, real users, and real needs: A study and analysis of user queries on the Web. *Information Processing and Management, 36*(2), 207-227.

Joachims, T. (2002). Optimizing search engines using clickthrough data. *Proceedings of 8th ACM SIGKDD International Conference on Knowledge Discovery and Data Mining,* Edmonton, Alberta, Canada, (pp. 133–142).

Korfhage, R. (1997). *Information storage and retrieval.* New York: Wiley.

Montgomery, A., & Faloutsos, C. (2001). Identifying Web browsing trends and patterns. *IEEE Computer, 34*(7), 94-95.

Saracevic, T. (1975). Relevance: A review of and a framework for the thinking on the notion in information science. *Journal of the American Society of Information Science, 26*(6), 321-343.

Silverstein, C., Henzinger, M., Marais, H., & Moricz, M. (1999). Analysis of a very large Web search engine query log. *SIGIR Forum, 33*(1), 6-12.

Spink, A., Bateman, J., & Jansen, B.J. (1999). Searching the Web: A survey of excite users. *Journal of Internet Research: Electronic Networking Applications and Policy, 9*(2), 117-128.

Spink, A., Jansen, B.J., Wolfram, D., & Saracevic, T. (2002). From e-sex to e-commerce: Web search changes. *IEEE Computer, 35*(3), 107-111.

Spink, A., Ozmutlu, S., Ozmutlu, H.C., & Jansen, B.J. (2002). U.S. versus European Web searching trends. *SIGIR Forum, 32*(1), 30-37.

Chapter XVII

A Java Technology Based Distributed Software Architecture for Web Usage Mining

Juan M. Hernansáez
University of Murcia, Spain

Juan A. Botía
University of Murcia, Spain

Antonio F.G. Skarmeta
University of Murcia, Spain

ABSTRACT

In this chapter we focus on the three approaches that seem to be the most successful ones in the Web usage mining area: clustering, association rules and sequential patterns. We will discuss some techniques from each one of these approaches, and then we will show the benefits of using METALA (a META-Learning Architecture) as an integrating tool not only for the discussed Web usage mining techniques, but also for inductive learning algorithms. As we will show, this architecture can also be used to generate new theories and models that can be useful to provide new generic applications for several supervised and non-supervised learning paradigms. As a particular example of a Web usage mining application, we will report our work for a medium-sized commercial company, and we will discuss some interesting properties and conclusions that we have obtained from our reporting.

INTRODUCTION

When we face the challenge of data recovering from the Internet, or Web mining (WM), we can consider it from two main perspectives: Web resources mining and Web usage mining (WUM). Still, we can split the first one into Web content mining and Web structure mining. While the differences between these resource mining areas sometimes are not clear, WUM is more clearly defined, but it is not isolated either. It aims to describe the behaviour of the users who are surfing the Web. Many techniques and tools have been proposed, giving partial solutions to some of the WUM problems. All the proposed techniques and ideas are showing their importance in many areas, including Web content and Web structure mining.

One of the most accepted definitions for *Web usage mining* is that it is "the application of data mining techniques to large Web data repositories in order to extract usage patterns" (Cooley, Tan & Srivastava, 1999). As we know, Web servers around the world record data about user interaction with the Web pages hosted in the Web servers. If we analyze the Web access logs of different Websites we can know more about the user behaviour and the Web structure, making easier the improvement of the design of the sites among many other applications.

Analyzing data from the access logs can help organizations and companies holding the Web servers to determine the ideal life cycle of their products, the customer needs, effectiveness of new launched products, and more. In short, WUM can support marketing strategies across products over some specific groups of users, and improve the presence of the organization by redesigning the Internet Websites. Even if the organization is based on intranet technologies, WUM can warn of a more effective infrastructure for the organization, and can also warn of improvements and faults of the workgroup communication channels.

This chapter is organized as follows: in the first section, we introduce the three approaches intended for solving the WUM problems and challenges: *clustering, association rules* and *sequential patterns.* We will focus on the techniques that we have integrated in our own architecture, having one technique of each approach. Then, in the second section, we present our software architecture for automated data analysis processes, called *METALA*. We will show how this architecture can be used to support the WUM techniques and models, as well as other data analysis methods like *machine learning,* and how we integrated some algorithms of each one of these three approaches. As an example of a WUM application provided by METALA, in the third section we summarize our work for a medium-sized industrial company, which wanted to know more about the usage of its Website, and about the strengths and flaws of the site and how to improve it. From this work we have proposed some ideas to face the problems we found when applying the WUM techniques. Finally, in the fourth section we give our conclusions and discuss our future work.

WEB USAGE MINING TECHNIQUES

As we have already mentioned, there are three main Web usage mining approaches. They are *clustering, association rules* and *sequential patterns.* Most of the WUM techniques can be included in one of these approaches, and some others may be hybrid.

Notice that these techniques are not exclusive to the WUM field: most of them are based on generic algorithms and ideas taken from other more general fields, such as data mining or databases. We first introduce clustering in the first subsection. Then, we overview association rules in the second subsection. We finally discuss sequential patterns in the third subsection.

Clustering

Hartigan (1975) states that Clustering is the "grouping of similar objects from a given set of inputs." That is, given some points in some space, a clustering process groups the points into a number of clusters, where each cluster contains the *nearest* (in some sense) points. This approach is widely used in WUM. The key concept of clustering is the distance measurement used to group the points into clusters. Nevertheless, there are many clustering algorithms and variants of these algorithms.

Nasraoui et al. (2002) introduced the clustering algorithms that we have implemented in our architecture, to be shown in the second section. We have chosen these algorithms for our architecture as they are specifically intended for the WM purpose, and because they have been proved to be efficient during the WM process. All these algorithms are based on the simple K-means algorithm, which must be outlined before we can go further.

The K-means algorithm is one of the best known clustering algorithms. It was first introduced by McQueen (1967). It is an iterative algorithm that divides a set of data samples in a number (K, given) of clusters. For this, we first randomly choose the prototypes of each cluster. Then each data sample is classified into the cluster whose prototype is closer to the sample. After that, the prototypes of each cluster are moved to the arithmetic mean of samples in corresponding cluster. As soon as the prototypes stop moving, the algorithm finalizes and the samples remain in the current clusters. The prototypes are also known as the *centroids* or centers of the clusters.

We now review the WM overall process in which we have applied the algorithms of Nasraoui et al. (2002). We start from the logs stored in the Web server, and we must first preprocess the logs in order to limit the noise of the data and to prevent the algorithms from wrong accesses. A good explanation of the preprocess phase can be found in the work of Cooley, Mobasher and Srivastava (1999). For the WM purpose, we must use a discrete version of the K-means basic algorithm, because the centroids (also named *medoids*) are going to be *sessions* of accesses to Web pages (URL accesses) and not just continuous data to be recomputed in each iteration by modifying its numerical values.

As we can see, for the clustering purpose, we consider a *session* as the minimum meaningful data unit. The meaning of the session is the same as the one from the Web servers field: a Web session is a group of URLs accessed by an user during a period of time. There is a session expiration time of the Web server such that if the user stops accessing the Website and exceeds that time, the session ends.

We next define a *distance measurement* between sessions. For this we first identify unique URLs in all the sessions (i.e., a URL that is not repeated in a single session but can appear in other sessions). Then, we can define a distance measurement between sessions by just computing the cosine of the angle between them. That is, if two sessions contain exactly the same URLs, they have a similarity of 1, or 0 otherwise. But this similarity measurement has a drawback: it ignores the URL structure. For example, consider two sessions with the only accesses {/courses/cmsc201} and {/courses/cmsc341}, and also consider the pair {/courses/cmsc341} and {/research/grants}. According to the cosine, the similarity of the sessions will be zero. However, it is clear that the two first sessions are more similar than the other two, because both users seem to be interested in courses. Thus we define a new *syntactic* similarity measurement, at the level of URLs. The new similarity measurement basically measures the overlapping existing between the paths of two URLs. Now, we can define a similarity measurement between user sessions, using this URL level based similarity. In some cases the cosine of the angle of two sessions will give a more intuitive similarity measurement and it will be also used.

Now we can study the algorithms. We first consider the *Fuzzy C-Medoids algorithm (FCMdd)*. Let $X = \{x_i | i=1, ..., n\}$ be a set of n objects. Let $r(x_i,x_j)$ be the distance from the object x_i to the object x_j. Let $V = \{v_1,v_2,...,v_c\}$, with $v_i \in X$, a subset of X with cardinality c. The elements of V are the *centroids*. Let X_c be the set of all subsets V of X with cardinality c. Each V represents a specific choice of the prototypes for the c clusters in which we wish to partition the data. In the WUM area, X is the total Web sessions set computable from the access log file.

The key concept of the FCMdd algorithm is the possibilistic or fuzzy membership of x_j into the cluster i. This membership set is denoted by u_{ij} and can be heuristically defined in many ways. There are four possible solutions for u_{ij} (two are fuzzy and two are possibilistic). Here we just present one of the fuzzy solutions:

$$u_{ij} = \frac{\left(\frac{1}{r(x_j,v_i)}\right)^{1/(m-1)}}{\sum_{k=1}^{c}\left(\frac{1}{r(x_j,v_k)}\right)^{1/(m-1)}}$$

(1)

where the constant $m \in (1,\infty)$ is the "fuzzifier". The larger m, the less the difference between the memberships of the different sessions to the different clusters (i.e., the borders among clusters are fuzzier).

With the fuzzy FCMdd algorithm, once we have computed the centroids of the different clusters, we must characterize them in order to interpret the results of the WUM process. This can be simply done by using the weights of the URLs stored in the sessions, which must be placed in the clusters whose centroid is closer. Then, the weights values are computed by dividing the number of times the URL access appears in the cluster by the cardinality of the cluster. Most relevant URLs are then used to tell what the cluster represents.

About the flaws and advantages of the algorithm, we can say that in the worst case, the complexity of FCMdd is $O(n^2)$, due to the step of computing the new centroids. However, it is possible to obtain good results by reducing the amount of candidate objects to be considered when computing the new centroids. If we consider k objects, where k is a small constant, the complexity reduces to $O(k \times n)$. The problem with the

FCMdd algorithm is that it is not *robust*. This means that it is very sensitive to *outliers* (noise in the data) so sometimes it cannot provide good clusters. The problem of handling outliers can be solved with another fuzzy algorithm: *Fuzzy C-Trimmed Medoids Algorithm (FCTMdd)* (also known as *Robust Fuzzy C-Medoids algorithm*). This algorithm can only use the fuzzy version of the membership u_{ij}, stated in equation 1. The "trimmed" values will be those whose distance to the harmonic mean of a subset of objects of X is over a specific threshold. We will just keep the first s objects obtained by sorting candidate values in ascending order of distance.

The complexity of the robust algorithm is still $O(n^2)$ in the worst case. But like with FCMdd, we can consider just k candidate objects to make it almost linear, although we have to add the time of computing the s objects. Note that both algorithms may converge to a local minimum. Thus, it is advisable to try many random initializations to increase the accuracy of the results.

There are other clustering techniques applicable in WM, such as the system from Yan et al. (1996) based on the Leader algorithm (Hartigan, 1975), the BIRCH algorithm (Zhang et al., 1997) or the ROCK algorithm (Guha et al., 2000).

Association Rules

The problem of mining association rules between sets of items in large databases was first stated by Agrawal et al. (1993), and it opened a brand new family of techniques in the WUM area. The original problem can be introduced with an example: imagine a market where customers buy different items. They have a "basket" with different acquired products, and we can establish relations between the bought products. Finding all such rules is valuable for cross-marketing, add-on sales, customer segmentation based on buying patterns, and so forth. But the databases involving these applications are very large, so we must use fast algorithms for this task.

If we move the original problem statement to the WM area, we can think of the "baskets" as the users that accessed a Website, the items in the "basket" as the pages of the Website visited and the products as all the pages of the Website. Thus, we can find rules relating the requested URLs of the Website. For example, a rule can say that in 100 cases, 90% of the visitors to the Website of a restaurant who visited the index page also visited both the restaurant menu page and the prices page. The rule should be written:

[index⇒menu,prices](support=100, confidence=90%)

This way the restaurant may know the hit rate of the menu and prices pages from the index page, among other interesting associations.

In this section we just consider the Apriori algorithm (Agrawal & Srikant, 1994), which has been integrated in our architecture. From this algorithm lots of techniques and new algorithms have been proposed, but most of them are just refinements of some of the phases of the basic Apriori algorithm.

The Apriori algorithm is a fast algorithm intended for solving the association rules problem stated above, and it is the algorithm we have included in our METALA architecture for the association rules approach. Before explaining the algorithm, we must state a formal definition of the problem. Let $I=\{i_1,i_2,...,i_m\}$ be a set of literals, called items.

In WM, these are the URLs requested by users. Let D be a set of *transactions* (called web sessions in WM), in which each transaction is a set of items so that the set of items T is contained in I $(T{\subseteq}I)$. There is a unique identifier associated with each transaction. We can say that a transaction T contains X, a set of some of the items of I, if $X{\subseteq}T$. One *association rule* is an implication of the form $X{\rightarrow}Y$, where $X \subseteq I$, $Y \subseteq I$, and the intersection $X{\cap}Y$ is empty. The rule $X{\Rightarrow}Y$ is true for the set of transactions D with *confidence c* if the $c\%$ of the transactions of D containing X also contain Y. The rule $X{\Rightarrow}Y$ has *support s* in the set of transactions D if the $s\%$ of the transactions of D contain $X{\cup}Y$.

The problem of discovering such association rules can be divided into two subproblems:

1. Finding all the sets of items with a support over a certain threshold. The support for a set of items is defined as the number of transactions containing the set (i.e., the number of transactions in which a group of URLs appears). These sets are called *large itemsets* or *litemsets*.

2. Using the litemsets to generate the desired rules. For example, assume that *ABCD* and *AB* are litemsets. We can know if $AB \Rightarrow CD$ by calculating the confidence of

    the rule, which is the ratio $\dfrac{\mathbf{support(ABCD)}}{\mathbf{support(AB)}}$. If this confidence is over a certain

    threshold, the rule holds, and besides the rule has the minimum support because *ABCD* is a *large itemset*.

To solve the first subproblem, we can use the algorithm AprioriTid. It passes several times over the data. In the first pass, from the individual items (individual URLs) we get the *large itemsets* (i.e., those with a minimum support previously set; in WM, this is equivalent to setting a threshold, for example 2, and checking which URLs appear in at least two transactions). In each next pass, we start from the set computed in the previous pass. We use this set of candidate itemsets to generate new possible *large itemsets*.

That is, starting from the sets of URL groups with enough support, we build a new set of items made from all the valid combinations of initial URLs (these new combinations are called candidate itemsets). A combination is valid in a transaction if all the subgroups of URLs of the new formed group contain only URLs belonging to such transaction. Once we have checked that some candidates have enough support, the process starts again. It will end when no new sets of large itemsets can be formed.

Once we have got all the large itemsets we can face subproblem 2: getting the association rules existing between the groups of URLs; that is, given a confidence threshold, for each subset $s \subset l$ where s is a subset of items contained in the set of items l, we generate a rule $s \Rightarrow (l - s)$ *if support(l) / support(s)* $\geq$ *confidence*. A fast algorithm to solve this problem is needed (Agrawal & Srikant, 1994).

We now consider the advantages and disadvantages of using Apriori. Its advantages are clear: it solves the problem statement of association rules, and to do it efficiently it takes advantage of the observation that a k-itemset can be frequent only if all its subsets of k-1 items are frequent. Nevertheless, if we consider the computational complexity of the algorithm, it is clear that the cost of the k-th iteration of Apriori strictly depends on both the cardinality of the candidate set C_k and the size of the database D. In fact, the number of possible candidates is, in principle, exponential in the number m of items appearing in the various transactions of D.

Thus, many techniques have been proposed to improve its efficiency, especially the process of counting the support of the candidate itemsets and the process of identifying the frequent itemsets. For the first problem many techniques have been proposed. We can mention hashing (Park et al., 1995), reduction of the number of transactions (Han & Fu, 1995), partitioning (Savasere et al., 1995) sampling (Toivonen, 1996) and dynamic count of itemsets (Brin et al., 1997). The second problem could be stated as follows: we are given m items, and thus there are 2^m potentially frequent itemsets, which form a lattice of subsets over I. However, only a small fraction of the whole lattice is frequent. Most of the algorithms that address this problem only differ in the way they prune the search space to make the candidate generation phase more efficient. And most of these algorithms need to pass more than once over the database, which is too expensive. Zaki et al. (1997) propose a hybrid approach, called *itemset clustering,* which includes several algorithms in which the preprocessed database is scanned just once.

Sequential Patterns

Srivastava et al. (2000) state that the techniques of sequential pattern discovery attempt to find inter-session patterns such that the presence of a set of items is followed by another item in a time-ordered set of sessions or episodes. By using this approach, Web marketers can predict future visit patterns that will be helpful in placing advertisements aimed at certain user groups. Other types of temporal analysis that can be performed on sequential patterns include trend analysis, change point detection, or similarity analysis.

We can find more applications in the Internet area: for example, consider Web hyperlink predicting. If we could know the pages to be requested by the user, we would be able to do precaching with these pages in each connection and therefore speed up the overall browsing process and save bandwidth.

Agrawal and Srikant (1995) considered again the pattern discovery problem (Agrawal et al., 1993) to find an application for sequential pattern discovery. Previously, we have seen that one pattern consisted of an unsorted set of items. Now, the set of items is sorted and the problem consists of, given a sorted sequence, being able to predict a possible continuation of the sequence.

The algorithms proposed by Agrawal and Srikant (1995) have been implemented in the METALA architecture (to be shown in the second section) to have a representation of the sequential patterns approach.

We will see now the new problem statement: given a database D of customer transactions, each transaction has an unique customer identifier, a transaction time and the items acquired in the transaction. An *itemset* is a non-empty set of items, and a *sequence* is an ordered list of *itemsets*. A customer supports a sequence s if s is contained in the sequence for the client. The *support* for a sequence is defined as the fraction of all customers supporting this sequence. Given D, the problem of mining sequential patterns is discovering among all the sequences the *maximal* ones, that is, those sequences that exceed the minimum support threshold and are not contained in any other sequence. Each of these maximal sequences is called *sequential pattern*. The sequence satisfying the minimum support is named *large sequence.*

Three new algorithms were proposed: *AprioriAll, AprioriSome* and *DynamicSome*. All the algorithms have the same phases, and they only differ in the way they perform the *sequence phase* shown below. The phases are the following:

1. *Sort phase:* the original database *D* is sorted using the customer identifier as the primary key and the transaction time as the secondary. This way we get a database of sequences of customers.
2. *Litemset phase:* in this phase we compute the set *L* of all *litemsets,* just like in the same phase of the association rules version of the Apriori algorithm, but only with one difference: we must change the *support* definition. Here is the fraction of customers choosing the itemset in some of their (possibly) several transactions.
3. *Transformation phase:* it is necessary to quickly determine whether a given set of large sequences is contained in a sequence of a customer. Thus, we transform *D* into D_T, for example removing those items that do not belong to any sequence and cannot support anything.
4. *Sequence phase:* using the set of itemsets we compute the desired sequences. Read below.
5. *Maximal phase:* find the maximal sequences from the total of large sequences. For this, starting from the set of large sequences *S,* we must use an algorithm for computing maximal sequences (Agrawal & Srikant, 1995).

The way the *sequence phase* is performed determines the form of the algorithms presented. This phase makes multiple passes over the data. In each pass, we start with an initial set of large sequences. We use this set to generate new potential large sequences, called *candidate* sequences. The AprioriAll algorithm generates the candidates in a similar way as the association rules version of the Apriori algorithm. However, AprioriSome and DynamicSome do it in a different way. They have two distinguished phases: one forward, in which all the large sequences of certain length are computed, and another backwards, where we find the remaining large sequences. Notice that DynamicSome has an additional advantage: it can generate the candidates on-the-fly.

As in the case of the association rules version of the Apriori algorithm, it is not an easy task determining the computational complexity of the presented algorithms. These algorithms have problems when the database of sequences is large or the sequential patterns to be mined are numerous and/or long. There are some other algorithms that try to minimize these problems by reducing the generation of candidate subsequences, for example, Freespan (Han et al., 2000). We can mention some other interesting sequential pattern discovery researches, such as the work of Schechter et al. (1998) or Pitkow and Pirolli (1999).

METALA ARCHITECTURE

METALA is a software architecture that aims to guide the engineering of information systems that support *multi-process inductive learning* (MIL). METALA is defined on the basis of four different layers of abstraction (Figure 1): (1) the object oriented (OO) layer, (2) the middleware layer and (3) the agents layer. The fourth layer is the METALA application.

Figure 1. Abstraction Layers of METALA

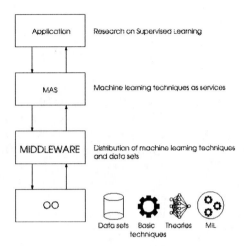

In the *OO layer,* basic software support tasks are addressed like, for example, training data access and management, machine learning algorithms dynamic behaviour and extensibility mechanisms, learning processes remote monitoring, models management, and so forth. This is the most extensive layer. It defines the ground level tools to work on inductive learning.

The basic unit of learning data in METALA is the *instance.* It is compound by a set of values referring to a particular example in the learning data source. A data source is a set of instances. Instances can be indexed via a cursor named *access.* Data sources can be organized inside a *repository.*

Learning algorithms are seen in the architecture as possible services to offer and use. Dynamic behaviour of any inductive technique is defined via a deterministic finite automata (DFA), as shown in Figure 2.

Figure 2. Behaviour that all Learning Services must Show

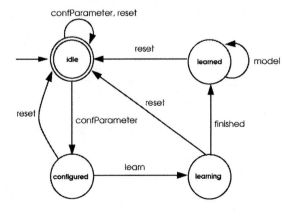

The most important transition in the DFA is from the *configured* state to the *learning* one by the *learn* token. This token corresponds to a method call in all algorithms. A learning process can be prolonged in time and METALA includes a special mechanism to inform the client when the process has finished, the *listener*. A listener is an object, owned by the client, which receives progress and termination calls from the learning process while the client is doing other tasks. The usual operation has the following sequence: configuring an experiment for a learning technique, launching it (i.e., testing a learning technique with the specified configured parameters), monitoring the progress of the experiment and finally, if the experiment ends successfully, getting the knowledge *model* associated to the experiment for later evaluation and/or utilization. The models are the pieces of knowledge that a concrete learning algorithm induces from data. Models can be stored, recreated and visualized.

METALA is *extendable*. It allows the integration of new techniques by using some basic interfaces that all new algorithms must support. Extendability is considered for both algorithms and models. Any new learning technique added to METALA must have a matching model representation.

We now move on the *middleware layer:* it uses the entire framework defined in the OO layer to produce a distributed learning tool. The distribution mechanisms are very technology dependent. The current system is developed with Java and RMI (Sun Microsystems, 1998). With RMI all must be coded in Java, an easy language to learn and use. In this layer we define the *information model* of METALA. It is based on the concept of directory (a hierarchical database that stores data about entities of interest). The directory allows the coordination between the *agents* of the system (read below). It also stores all the needed information about knowledge models, learning techniques and launched experiments.

The *agent layer* is built on the middleware layer. By looking into the directory provided by the information model of METALA, an agent can locate the rest of the agents (and its corresponding services) in the system. In Figure 3, we can see the agent layer of METALA.

There are four kinds of agents. The *user agent* is the front-end to the user. It shows the directory to the user and allows executing and monitoring learning techniques, as well as visualizing and evaluating the obtained models.

The *machine learning agent* (MLA) provides the learning techniques for a specific user and the behaviour of the monitoring task (i.e., which data should be displayed and updated when executing a particular experiment of a particular learning technique). The *directory service agent* (DSA) offers necessary services to access to the directory. Finally, the *data repository agent* (DRA) provides the leaning data needed for executing the learning techniques from the MLA.

In Figure 3 we can see that data may come from different sources: plain text files, relational databases and LDAP databases. Note that in this distributed framework any agent can work in a remote or local manner. Other important features of METALA are the following:

- It is *extendable:* it comes with a methodology to integrate new inductive learning algorithms and models, even new paradigms for learning. Note that METALA was originally intended only for supervised inductive learning. This led us to consider models in a different way, since no inferences are performed by WUM techniques such as clustering or association rules, which are non-supervised ones. Displayed

Figure 3. Organization of Agents in the METALA Architecture

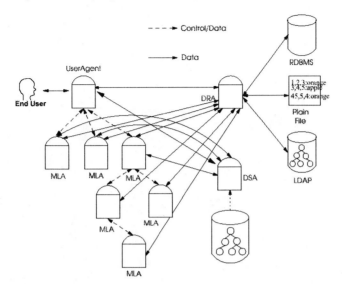

models have more informative power, in this case, than the error estimation measures needed by the supervised learning techniques. We even created a graphical URL recommender tool (Mobasher et al., 2002) integrated into the METALA architecture (Figure 4) based on the information provided by the new WUM models. So the system was positively influenced in the sense that higher software particularization can be done to transform a generic inductive learning tool into a WM tool.

- It is *distributed:* agents can be located at different hosts, to make efficient use of available servers.
- It is *flexible:* all agents can be totally independent and this feature allows an easy adaptation to almost any particular execution condition.
- It is *scalable:* it correctly supports the growth of both pending learning tasks to perform and available servers to manage.
- It is *autonomous:* it is capable of deciding the best way to distribute machine learning tasks among the available learning servers (Botia et al., 2001).
- It is *multi-user:* different users can make use of inductive learning algorithms and the other services that the system offers at the same time; METALA allows management of users and all of them have their own user space to read and write produced results.
- It *is educational:* it is clear that METALA is a good assistance tool for knowing the main paradigms of inductive learning. At the present time, with our architecture we can do research on basic techniques like induction of artificial neural networks (Bishop, 1995), decision trees and rules (Quinlan, 1993), genetic algorithms (Goldberg, 1989) and on induction of classification theories by naive bayes (Witten & Frank, 2000). We can also test other high-level techniques that perform what we named *multi-process inductive learning* (MIL), such as boosting (Freund & Schapire,

Figure 4. URL Recommender Tool (The model used in this case is shown on the left panel. The tool control panel is on the right side. On top of this panel we can see the values of the parameters used for the model of the left side. Below we can select the data source containing the URLs visited by a user. At the bottom we can choose the desired values of support and confidence for getting the recommendations, and the recommendations provided by the tool based on these values and on the observed visited URLs.)

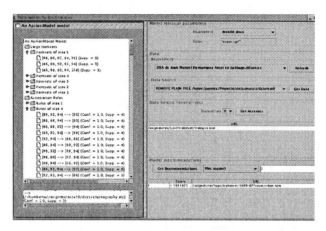

1996), bagging (Breiman, 1996) and landmarking (Bensusan & Giraud-Carrier, 2000; Fürnkranz & Petrak, 2001). Besides, we have added the capability of researching WM techniques of the most important approaches.

It is also clear that our system is not comparable to others such as SpeedTracer (Wu et al., 1997) in the sense that we are neither looking for a particular technique that we consider the most appropriate for WUM, nor for particular statistical reports. Nowadays, it is commonly accepted that no single supervised machine learning technique behaves better than the rest in any classification and/or regression task (Wolpert, 1996; Wolpert & Macready, 1995). This fact is called the *selective superiority problem* (Brodley, 1993). We believe that we can also apply this fact for non-supervised machine learning techniques, like the WM ones. We offer the possibility of choosing the technique that the user considers more suitable for a particular problem. METALA is extendable and the generated models are usable for creating new applications and tools (see Figure 4 for an example); we can add any learning algorithm that we consider interesting, testing it and generating any reports (see following section) and applications just coding with the provided METALA methodology.

AN APPLICATION EXAMPLE

We now show an example of an application in the real world of some of the WUM algorithms implemented in the METALA architecture. We report here the work we have performed for a medium-size industrial company. This company requested from us a report about its Website. The main targets were to get some valuable information about groups of users and their preferences and about the Website structure. We had at our disposal three years of Web access logs and the *topology* of the Website, which did not change too much during the three years. The Website was structured hierarchically, and under the root node (which was a page including links for selecting language) we found two nodes with exactly the same tree structure, with information pages for the two languages that we could select at the root node.

The WUM algorithms used for the reporting were the association rules Apriori algorithm and the clustering fuzzy C-medoids algorithm. We used the *robust* version of the fuzzy C-medoids algorithm, since it provides more accurate results. We considered unnecessary to use any algorithm of the third WUM approach (sequential patterns), as it was not applicable to this problem.

In order to write the report, we analyzed separately the results for the two algorithms and for the three years. We performed several experiments with all the cases to increase the reliability of the results. Then, we compared and combined the results, removing possibly wrong values (with the Apriori algorithm there are no wrong results, but with the clustering fuzzy robust algorithm, misclassifying objects in the clusters is possible since it contains some random components). Analyzing the results and getting the conclusions useful for the company was not an easy task (see the next subsection for ideas addressing this issue), and it required a lot of human interpretation. Nevertheless, we created a fully qualified report providing interesting results and ideas for improving the presence of the company Website and for easily improving its design and technical structure. The most interesting conclusions can be summed up as follows:

- Thanks to the Apriori algorithm, we knew the hit rate of some pages, on condition that its parent page was visited. We focused on the pages with several links where we realized that only one of them had a low hit rate. For such pages we gave the advice of improving the format of the link to make it more attractive to users. Sometimes pages providing general information presented links where only the first ones were clicked. Hence we proposed distributing the links in a non-sequential manner, to give more hit probability to the links presented at the bottoms of the pages. We also proposed linking these sequential pages to each other to improve the overall hit rate.

- We observed that some pages with a high hit rate in the previous years had a low hit rate with the new naming. Thus, we recommended again changing the name, or providing some new pages with the old name, with new content or directly linking to the pages with the old name, because it seemed that users were not able to reach the newly named pages as before.

- One of the most successful pages of the Website was the chat page. This page provided excellent opportunities to the company to meet the needs of the users, and to meet the requests for information from users about the company products. However, this application was placed in a place that was not easily reachable (by the obtained rules we realized that the paths traversed to reach the chat were very diverse). Thus we proposed making it accessible from the main browsing bar of the Website. This had a potential risk, however: users using the chat as incidental entertainment. But we considered that this industrial company was specialized enough to not attract such users.

- Analyzing the clusters created by the clustering algorithm, we also realized that most of the users of the chat application used only one of the languages that the Web was intended for, although users in both languages frequently accessed the Website. After checking the chat page, we realized it was written for only one of the languages, and thus we advised redesigning it in order to avoid losing potential customers of the other language.

- Another very important page of the Website was the contact request form. This page put the company directly in contact with its potential customers. We found some clusters profiling users surfing the main pages of the Website, looking for general information about the company and its products. The request form was included in such clusters. Looking in the Apriori results, we discovered that those URLs belonged to long time sessions. Thus, we recommended giving more content to the general browsing pages, providing frames, java applets, other information not directly related to the company, and so forth. The objective was to retain the users surfing the Website long enough to, if she is remotely interested in the company, use the contact request form.

- Evaluating others clusters, we found that some of the products were preferred by users using one language, whereas other products were preferred by the other language users. Thus we recommended that the company study this result, and we advised introducing minor changes to the content of the pages of products to make them more attractive to the users of the other language.

- We also found a case where a page was not being properly accessed, as we found a rule relating very specific URLs but for different languages. After checking the pages, we discovered that some documents were available for the two languages but they were presented in a confusing format, so that users chose the documents randomly. We thus recommended modifying the format.

- Concerning the technical part of the Website, we notice some interesting facts. Some association rules associated URLs being loaded at the same time (for example documents or plugins in a Web page) but the confidence of the rules was not the same when the pages were one in the consequent and the other in the antecedent. Although the difference was not too big, it was significant enough to deserve a study. We discovered that such pages frequently consisted of calling to *Macromedia Flash* documents or to Java applets. So we concluded that some users could not access to these pages and we recommended providing more information about how to get the appropriate plugins, and also designing an alternative version of the pages for the users just interested in the *hard* information content of the pages, or for users that cannot get the plugins. For the users who cannot use the chat, which was a JAVA applet, we advised providing a direct link to the contact request form, to make it easier for them to access the company.

- Some more technical results were provided by the clustering algorithm. We found some clusters relating pages in both languages, in a significant proportion. Since both language versions of the Website contained exactly the same information, these results made no sense for us. To find an explanation we incorporated a statistic analysis process to the algorithms. This way we could discover that many accesses came from automatic Internet information indexers, such as "robots" and "spiders". These tools index information by traversing the hierarchy of the Web in some order, and thus the results they produce may be difficult to interpret.

Conclusions from the Reporting

We got some interesting ideas from the reporting. The integrated WUM algorithms proved to be useful for the mining purpose, but the results we obtained required a lot of human interpretation. It is necessary to develop automatic mechanisms allowing a fast interpretation of the mining results. As we were writing the report, some repeating tasks were identified:

*   For the *Apriori* algorithm, identifying the *interesting* rules was made in the following manner: most of the rules associate index and general-browsing (browsing bars, frames, etc.) pages, so we opt to pay more attention to the more specific URLs, that is, those Web pages located deeper in the Website hierarchy. Thus, the *topology* of the Web site turned out to be very important to identify interesting rules.

    Another "rule of thumb" we used in order to identify interesting rules was focusing on the consequent of the rules. The most interesting rules had a more specific URL in the consequent. If a rule was $A{\rightarrow}B$ and A could only be reached from B, the rule says nothing because obviously we had to visit B to reach A. The rule $B{\rightarrow}A$ would be more interesting, since it gives us an idea of the possibility of visiting B when we are visiting its parent A, and thus we would get the hit rate of B. Nevertheless, if we study the association rules version of the Apriori algorithm we find that no time order is considered when obtaining the rules; that is, the accessed URLs are stored with no timestamp. So we cannot know if a rule $A{\rightarrow}B$ indicates A occurring before B or just the opposite. However, since we have the topology of the Web and the confidence and support of the rule, it is easy to infer time order. Chronological order of the accesses turned out to be a very important issue to be considered, and maybe integrated, in our future work. Taking into account the length of the considered sessions may be an important factor, too.

*   For the *robust fuzzy C-medoids* algorithm, the results are the clusters and the weights of the associated URLs. To analyze these results, we prune out those clusters with low cardinality. We set a threshold of how interesting the URLs should be *(score)*, and only show those URLs above this threshold. Since the Website was hierarchically structured, we could group the URLs in more general topics by just adding the score of the contained URLs. The most interesting clusters were those with higher cardinality and URL weights, but also those with more specific URLs, the same as before with the association rules.

    Analyzing the clusters was easier than analyzing the association rules, but some human interaction was still needed. The clusters with higher cardinality are not always the most interesting ones. Sometimes we look for the *unexpectedness* of the clusters (or, in the case of Apriori, of a rule) and it is not easy checking this. Some interesting work has been made in this sense (Cooley, 2003). Deciding whether a result is unexpected or wrong is difficult, and the topology of the Website, and even the access logs themselves, are needed sometimes.

    Finally, the idea of incorporating a kind of analytical tool was interesting. Thanks to the information provided by the statistics analysis we could discover that many accesses recorded in the Web access logs came from "robots" and "spiders" that automatically index information for Web searchers and other Internet applications. Such tools and agents use some kind of algorithms to scan the Website in a prefixed order. This behaviour is not of our interest, since we are looking for understanding and to model the human behaviour while interacting with the Web. We think that the unexpected results that came from these accesses should be pruned out. This gave us the idea of considering the *user agent* field (Luotonen, 1995) of the log in the mining process, because we must determine if the access corresponds to a human user. We also consider incorporating some other fields of the log, as they may provide interesting information. For example, in the event that we do not have at our disposal the topology of the Website, it would be important to use the "Referrer" field of the log, as we may reconstruct the topology of a Website, or at least of a part of it.

CONCLUSIONS AND FUTURE WORK

In this chapter we have studied one technique from the three most important groups of techniques to perform Web mining on Web usage log files. We have passed through clustering, association rules and sequential patterns. Then we have introduced the tool that we developed to work with some of these algorithms in real world applications. The METALA tool was originally developed to study the generic problem of meta-learning. However, its utility as a tool to manage WUM has been proved in this chapter. Moreover, we also have included in this chapter the results obtained from the application of the tool to a medium-sized company.

Our current and future work consists of migrating the current architecture and information model of METALA to a J2EE (JAVA 2 Enterprise Edition) Application Server and to use Enterprise JavaBeans (Sun Microsystems, 2001), which drastically simplifies the complexity of the current METALA system and offers new capabilities. We are also integrating new Web mining techniques and learning paradigms, researching new Web mining applications and tools using the obtained WUM models, and testing the performance of the new implementation with huge-sized data sources (a critical issue when analyzing Web server logs). Finally, we are researching a way for automatically suggesting to the user the algorithm(s) and configuration parameters that best fit the user needs for a particular problem.

ACKNOWLEDGMENTS

This work is supported by the Spanish CICYT through the project TIC2002-04021-C02-02.

REFERENCES

Agrawal, R., & Srikant, R. (1994). Fast algorithms for mining association rules. *Proceedings of the 20th International Conference on Very Large Data Bases* VLDB, (pp. 487-499).

Agrawal, R., & Srikant, R. (1995). Mining sequential patterns. *Eleventh International Conference on Data Engineering,* 3-14.

Agrawal, R., Imielinski, T., & Swami, A.N. (1993). Mining association rules between sets of items in large databases. *Proceedings of the 1993 ACM SIGMOD International Conference on Management of Data,* (pp. 207-216).

Bensusan, H., & Giraud-Carrier, C. (2000). *If you see la Sagrada Familia, you know where you are: Landmarking the learner space.* Technical report.

Bishop, C.M. (1995). *Neural networks for pattern recognition.* Clarendon Press.

Botía, J.A., Skarmeta, A.G., Garijo, M., & Velasco, J.R. (2001). Handling a large number of machine learning experiments in a MAS based system. *Workshop on Multi-Agent Systems Infrastructure and Scalability in Multi-Agent Systems.*

Breiman, L. (1996). Bagging predictors. *Machine Learning, 26*(2), 123-140.

Brin, S., Motwani, R., Ullman, J.D., & Tsur, S. (1997). Dynamic itemset counting and implication rules for market basket data. SIGMOD 1997, *Proceedings ACM SIGMOD International Conference on Management of Data, 5,* (pp. 255-264).

Brodley, C.E. (1993). Addressing the selective superiority problem: Automatic algorithm/model class selection. *Machine Learning: Proceedings of the Ninth International Conference,* (pp. 1-10).

Cooley, R. (2003). The use of Web structure and content to identify subjectively interesting Web usage patterns. *ACM Transactions on Internet Technology, 3*(2), 93-116.

Cooley, R., Mobasher, B., & Srivastava, J. (1999). Data preparation for mining World Wide Web browsing patterns. *Knowledge and Information Systems, 1*(1), 5-32.

Cooley, R., Tan, P-N., & Srivastava, J. (1999). Discovery of interesting usage patterns from Web data. *WEBKDD,* 163-182.

Freund, Y., & Schapire, R.E. (1996). Experiments with a new boosting algorithm. *International Conference on Machine Learning,* 148-156.

Fürnkranz, J., & Petrak, J. An evaluation of landmarking variants. *Proceedings of the ECML/PKDD-01 Workshop: Integrating Aspects of Data Mining, Decision Support and Metalearning,* (pp. 57-68).

Goldberg, D.A. (1989). *Genetic algorithms in search, optimization and machine learning.* Addison-Wesley.

Guha, S., Rastogi, R., & Shim, K. (2000). ROCK: A robust clustering algorithm for categorical attributes. *Information Systems, 25*(5), 345-366.

Han, J., & Fu, Y. (1995, September). Discovery of multiple-level association rules from large databases. *Proceedings of the 1995 International Conference on Very Large Data Bases VLDB'95,* Zurich, Switzerland, 420-431.

Han, J., Pei, J., Mortazavi-Asl, B., Chen, Q., Dayal, U., & Hsu, M-C. (2000). FreeSpan: Frequent pattern-projected sequential pattern mining. *2000 International Conference on Knowledge Discovery and Data Mining.*

Hartigan, J. (1975). *Clustering algorithms.* John Wiley.

Luotonen, A. (1995). The common Logfile format. Available: *http://www.w3.org/Daemon/User/Config/Logging.html.*

McQueen, J. (1967). Some methods for classification and analysis of multivariate observations. *Proceedings of the Fifth Berkeley Symposium on Mathematical Statistics and Probability,* (pp. 281-297).

Mobasher, B., Dai, H., Luo, T., & Nakagawa, M. (2002). Discovery and evaluation of aggregate usage profiles for Web personalization. *Data Mining and Knowledge Discovery, 6,* 61-82.

Nasraoui, O., Krishnapuram, R., Joshi, A., & Kamdar, T. (2002). Automatic Web user profiling and personalization using robust fuzzy relational clustering. E-commerce and intelligent methods. In the series *Studies in fuzziness and soft computing.*

Park, J.S., Chen, M.S., & Yu, P.S. (1995). An effective hash based algorithm for mining association rules. *Proceedings of the 1995 ACM SIGMOD International Conference on Management of Data,* (pp. 175-186).

Pitkow, J.E., & Pirolli, P. (1999). Mining longest repeating subsequences to predict World Wide Web surfing. *USENIX Symposium on Internet Technologies and Systems.*

Quinlan, J.R. (1993). C4.5: Programs for machine learning. *The Morgan Kaufmann series in machine learning.* Morgan Kaufmann.

Savasere, A., Omiecinski, E., & Navathe, S. (1995). An efficient algorithm for mining association rules in large databases. *Proceedings of the 21st VLDB Conference,* (pp. 432-443).

Schechter, S., Krishnan, M., & Smith, M.D. (1998). Using path profiles to predict HTTP requests. *7th International World Wide Web Conference, 30,* 457-467.

Srivastava, J., Cooley, R., Deshpande, M., & Tan, P-N. (2000). Web usage mining: Discovery and applications of usage patterns from Web data. *SIGKDD Explorations, 1*(2), 12-23.

Sun Microsystems. (1998). Java remote method invocation specification. Available: *http://java.sun.com/j2se/1.4.2/docs/guide/rmi/spec/rmiTOC.html.*

Sun Microsystems. (2001). *Enterprise JavaBeans specification, Version 2.0.* Available: *http://java.sun.com/products/ejb/docs.html.*

Toivonen, H. (1996). Sampling large databases for association rules. *Proceedings of the 1996 International Conference on Very Large Data Bases, 9,* (pp. 134-145).

Witten, I.A., & Frank, E. (2000). *Data mining. Practical machine learning tools and techniques with JAVA implementations.* Morgan Kaufmann.

Wolpert, D.H. (1996). The lack of a priori distinctions between learning algorithms. *Neural Computation,* 1341-1390.

Wolpert, D.H., & Macready, W.G. (1995). *No free lunch theorems for search.* Technical report, Santa Fe Institute.

Wu, K., Yu, P.S., & Ballman, A. (1997). SpeedTracer: A Web usage mining and analysis tool. *Internet Computing, 37*(1), 89.

Yan, T., Jacobsen, M., Garcia-Molina, H., & Dayal, U. (1996). From user access patterns to dynamic hypertext linking. *Fifth International World Wide Web Conference,* Paris, France, 1007-1118.

Zaki, M.J., Parthasarathy, S., Ogihara, M., & Li, W. (1997). New algorithms for fast discovery of association rules. *Third International Conference on Knowledge Discovery and Data Mining,* 283-296.

Zhang, T., Ramakrishnan, R., & Livny, M. (1997). BIRCH: A new data clustering algorithm and its applications. *Data Mining and Knowledge Discovery, 1*(2), 141-182.

Chapter XVIII

Web Usage Mining:
Algorithms and Results

Yew-Kwong Woon
Nanyang Technological University, Singapore

Wee-Keong Ng
Nanyang Technological University, Singapore

Ee-Peng Lim
Nanyang Technological University, Singapore

ABSTRACT

The rising popularity of electronic commerce makes data mining an indispensable technology for several applications, especially online business competitiveness. The World Wide Web provides abundant raw data in the form of Web access logs. However, without data mining techniques, it is difficult to make any sense out of such massive data. In this chapter, we focus on the mining of Web access logs, commonly known as Web usage mining. We analyze algorithms for preprocessing and extracting knowledge from such logs. We will also propose our own techniques to mine the logs in a more holistic manner. Experiments conducted on real Web server logs verify the practicality as well as the efficiency of the proposed techniques as compared to an existing technique. Finally, challenges in Web usage mining are discussed.

INTRODUCTION

The rate of growth of the World Wide Web (Web) may be slowing down, but *Online Computer Library Center* researchers concluded that the Web would continue to grow rapidly in their annual review of the Web (Dean, 2000). In addition, Forrester Research affirmed the continued popularity of electronic commerce through its prediction that global online trade would expand to \$12.8 trillion by 2006 (Sharrard, Kafka & Tavilla, 2001). Hence, to stay competitive and profitable in a fast paced environment like the Web, companies must be able to extract knowledge from their Web access logs, Web transaction logs and Web user profiles to ensure the success of *Customer Relationship Management* (CRM) (Berson, Smith & Thearling, 2000). However, the immense amount of Web data makes manual inspection virtually impossible and thus, data mining techniques become indispensable in the quest for cutting-edge knowledge. In fact, electronic commerce has even been touted as the killer domain for data mining (Kohavi, 2001).

Our focus here is on *Web Usage Mining* (WUM), which we define as the extraction of meaningful user patterns from Web server access logs using data mining techniques. For brevity, we shall use the term *logfile* to refer to a Web server access log. WUM is fast gaining importance because of the wide availability of logfiles as well as its applicability in CRM (Woon, Ng & Lim, 2002b). In addition, it has diversified applications such as Web personalization (Mobasher, Cooley, & Srivastava; Mobasher, Dai, Luo, Sun & Zhu, 2000), Website structuring (Masseglia, Poncelet & Teisseire, 1999; Perkowitz & Etzioni, 1999; Spiliopoulou, 2000), marketing (Buchner & Mulvenna, 1998), user profiling (Heer & Chi., 2002; Mobasher et al., 2000), caching and prefetching (Yang, Zhang & Li, 2001).

Unfortunately, as most logfiles are originally meant for debugging purposes, they are non-ideal candidates for WUM raw data (Kohavi, 2001). However, due to their adoption by a vast number of existing Web servers, we postulate that they will not be replaced as the *de facto* Web data sources in the near future. Sources of logfiles include Web servers, Web clients, proxy servers and application servers (Kohavi, 2001; Srivastava, Cooley, Deshpande & Tan, 2000). A standard logfile has the following format (Consortium, 1995): [*remotehost logname username date request status bytes*] where:

- *remotehost* is the remote hostname or its IP address,
- *logname* is the remote logname of the user,
- *username* is the username with which the user has authenticated himself,
- *date* is the date and time of the request,
- *request* is the exact request line as it came from the client,
- *status* is the HTTP status code returned to the client, and
- *bytes* is the content-length of the document transferred.

The following is a fragment of a common logfile:

ntu.edu.sg - - [30/May/2003:00:01:15 -0400] ⌐GET /html/faq.html HTTP/1.0⌐ 200 4855

155.69.181.254 - - [1/Jun/2003:00:03:22 -0400] ⌐GET /pub/home.html HTTP/1.0⌐ 200 165

As observed in the example, the fields *logname* and *username* are usually not recorded. Therefore, it is difficult to identify the activities of individual users. An extended format is also available to capture demographic data and session identifiers but we shall only focus on the standard common logfile format because of its wider adoption and fewer privacy/security concerns (Hallam-Baker & Behlendorf, 1996).

There are several existing works on logfile mining but they deal separately on specific issues of mining and make certain assumptions without taking a *holistic* view, and thus have limited practical applicability (Chen, Park & Yu, 1996, 1998; Cooley, Mobasher & Srivastava, 1997a; Gaul & Schmidt-Thieme, 2000; Joshi & Krishnapuram, 2000; Nanopoulos, Katsaros & Manolopoulos, 2001, 2002; Pei, Han, Mortazavi-Asl & Zhu, 2000). Some take the Website structure into consideration; some focus only on traversal patterns; some consider the amount of time spent on a page. In this chapter, we shall examine such work and then introduce a more holistic version (which takes into consideration all of the above issues) of WUM, termed TRALOM2 (*TRAnsactionized LOgfile Mining 2*) to effectively and correctly identify transactions as well as to mine useful knowledge from logfiles. TRALOM2 is actually an enhancement of TRALOM, our previous work (Woon et al., 2002b).

We also introduce a data structure called the *WebTrie* to efficiently hold useful preprocessed data so that TRALOM2 can be done in an *online* and *incremental* fashion; online means being able to mine the latest data with little overhead while incremental means being able to re-use past mining data. We will build upon our previous preliminary work on TRALOM and WebTrie and deal with more issues here. Together with the WebTrie, TRALOM2 has been shown to be useful and viable by experiments conducted on a variety of real logfiles. The rest of the chapter is organized with the following objectives in mind:

*   Provide extensive background knowledge to WUM.
*   Survey prominent existing work on WUM.
*   Show how WUM can be improved with a more holistic approach.
*   Discuss exciting challenges for future research.
*   Conclude the chapter with a concise summary.

BACKGROUND

In this section, the phases of WUM are first briefly discussed and then prominent existing work is elaborated.

Phases of Web Usage Mining

Phase 1: Preprocessing

Several problems exist during the preprocessing phase where logfiles are transformed into a form that is suitable for mining. The following are preprocessing tasks that have been identified (Cooley, Mobasher & Srivastava, 1999):

1. *Data Cleaning:* The logfile is first examined to remove irrelevant entries such as those that represent multimedia data and scripts or uninteresting entries such as those that belong to top/bottom frames.
2. *User Identification:* Since several users may share a single machine name, certain heuristics are used to identify users (Pitkow, 1997).
3. *Session Identification:* After a user is identified, his/her page accesses must be divided (sessionized) into individual sessions (Berendt, Mobasher, Spiliopoulou & Wiltshire, 2001).
4. *Path Completion:* Some accesses are not captured by the logfile and this may result in *incomplete paths* (requests made to a page not directly linked to the last requested page) in the log data. This is probably due to the use of local caches or

proxy servers. Some solutions include *cache busting* (using cache specific headers to stop page caching) or the use of navigation history (Pitkow, 1997).

5.   *Transaction Identification:* Once a session of completed paths is determined, page references must be grouped into logical units representing Web transactions before any mining can be carried out.

Phase 2: Mining

There are four main mining techniques that can be applied to Web access logs to extract knowledge, but we will focus on algorithms based on *association rule mining* (ARM) and sequential mining because of their complexity, applicability and popularity. Here are the four techniques:

1.   *Sequential-pattern-mining-based:* Allows the discovery of temporally ordered Web access patterns

2.   *Association-rule-mining-based:* Finds correlations among Web pages

3.   *Clustering-based:* Groups users with similar characteristics

4.   *Classification-based:* Groups users into predefined classes based on their characteristics

The above techniques help in the design of better Websites as well as in the development of effective marketing strategies. However, generally, users are not willing to disclose personal information and may tend to give false information (Cooley, Mobasher & Srivastava, 1997b). Hence, it is more practical to assume the anonymity of users for WUM in general, especially for non-commercial sites where user registration is not required, and to disregard clustering and classification.

Phase 3: Applying Mining Results

The last phase of WUM involves the analysis and translation of mining results into useful actionable tasks such as the following:

•   Re-design Websites so that correlated pages are found together.

•   Improve access time by prefetching pages frequently accessed sequentially.

•   Improve caching by storing pages frequently revisited.

•   Enhance surfing experience by relocating pages in such a way that users need not visit unnecessary pages to get to their desired pages.

Existing Work

In this section and throughout the rest of the chapter, the sample logfile in Table 1 will be used for illustration purposes. At this point in time, we assume that user sessions can be accurately determined. This logfile contains a total of five Web pages, *A*, *B*, *C*, *D* and *E*, and the bracketed numbers are their respective access times in seconds. Note that it is not possible to determine the access time of the last page of every session, as logfiles do not capture data that can determine when a user actually finishes reading a page. The last column contains the average access times of pages in a session.

Chen et al. pioneered work in path traversal pattern mining and popularized research in this area (Chen et al., 1996). The authors coined the term *mining traversal patterns*, which means the capturing of user access patterns in distributed information providing

Table 1. A Sample Logfile

Session ID	Web Access Sequence	Average Access Time (s)
100	A(4) B(3) C(21) B(5) D(4) E	7.4
200	B(4) D(2) B(5) C(17) E	7
300	C(4) D(5) E	4.5
400	A(6) B(24) D	15

environments such as the Web. The procedure for mining traversal patterns consists of three steps:

1. *Determine transactions:* The authors assumed that backward references (revisitations of pages) are used only for ease of traveling and are focused on the discovery of forward reference patterns. The moment a backward reference occurs, a forward reference path is considered terminated and is termed a *maximal forward reference* (MFR), which represents a transaction.

2. *Determine large reference sequences:* A *large reference sequence* is an MFR that appears frequently enough to satisfy a minimum support threshold. From the set of MFRs, large reference sequences are determined using algorithms based on the concepts of ARM with one slight modification for the self-join procedure during candidate generation. The following modification is necessary because unlike an itemset, an MFR has consecutive references: For any two distinct reference sequences, $\{a_1...a_{k-1}\}\{b_1...b_{k-1}\} \in L_{k-1}$, they are combined to form a k-reference sequence only if either $\{a_1...a_{k-1}\}$ contains $\{b_1...b_{k-2}\}$ or $\{b_1...b_{k-1}\}$ contains $\{a_1...a_{k-2}\}$.

3. *Determine maximal reference sequences*: A *maximal reference sequence* is a large reference sequence that is not contained in any other maximal reference sequence.

Chen et al. do not make any distinction between references used for various purposes and may discover too many sequences from the transactions identified using the MFR technique. The MFR technique *over-evaluates* subsequences found at the beginning of a sequence; such subsequences are given higher importance. For example, consider session 100 of Table 1. For brevity, we shall use the term S_x to denote session X of Table 1. The resultant set of MFRs is $\{ABC, ABDE\}$. Although the subsequence $\{AB\}$ appears only once in S_{100}, it appears twice in the set of MFRs. In addition, the assumption that backward references are used only for ease of traveling is only applicable in certain cases. For example, in S_{200}, page D is only accessed for 2 seconds, which suggests that the user may think that D is an irrelevant page and travel back quickly to B. However, the incorrect subsequence $\{BD\}$ would be discovered by the MFR technique. Finally, it uses the classic association rule mining algorithm, *Apriori* (Agrawal & Srikant, 1994) to discover frequent sequences; this limits its scalability because Apriori is known to scale poorly with respect to both the database and frequent itemset sizes because of its need for candidate itemset generation (Das, Ng & Woon, 2001; Han, Pei & Yin, 2000). Punin et al. also used the MFR method to discover frequent sequences of pages (Punin, Krishnamoorthy & Zaki, 2001). The authors also proposed the use of association mining on sessions with duplicated pages and path information removed.

To group Web pages into more meaningful transactions, Cooley et al. proposed a novel way of identifying transactions based on the assumption that a user uses a page either for navigation or for its content (Cooley et al., 1997a). A transaction can then be defined in the following two ways:

1. *Navigation-Content:* A navigation-content transaction contains all navigation pages leading to content pages and the content pages themselves for a given user. Mining such transactions yields frequent traversal paths to content pages.

2. *Content:* A content-only transaction contains only content pages for a given user. Mining such transactions yields correlations among content pages.

Assuming that the amount of time a user spends on a page is indicative of the type of the page, the authors introduced a *reference length* (RL) (duration of viewing reference) transaction identification method. In this method, the user must supply the percentage *n* of navigation references in a log so that a cut-off time *c* can be calculated using a chi-squared distribution to decide if a reference is for navigation or content purposes. Experiments are conducted to mine association rules from transactions identified by both the reference length and MFR techniques. The experiments revealed that the reference length method performed better for content-only transactions. The RL method is more practical than MFR, as it takes into consideration the dimension of access time. However, *n* can only be determined accurately by an expert and there is a need to scan the entire logfile once first before *c* can be computed. In addition, since users may be accessing a site using heterogeneous systems with varying bandwidth connections and varying network traffic, content pages may be mistaken for navigation pages for systems with broadband connections used during off-peak periods. Recently, Cooley suggested that WUM could enjoy greater success if it considers the content and structure of a Website (Cooley, 2003). Through experiments with an electronic commerce site, he showed how knowing the important frames of a Website and knowing the concept hierarchy of products could aid in discovering useful knowledge with WUM. Hence, knowledge of the content and structure of Websites yield good *filters* during the preprocessing and result-analysis phase.

The use of *wildcards* in navigation paths is first proposed by Spiliopoulou et al. (Spiliopoulou & Faulstich, 1998) and explored further by Gaul et al. (Gaul & Schmidt-Thieme, 2000). Such paths are known as *generalized subsequences* and contain an additional wildcard symbol * which denotes arbitrary subsequences. Generalized subsequences are effectively used only by experts in building specific queries. Spiliopoulou et al. also introduced *aggregate trees,* which are similar to *FP-trees* (Han et al., 2000). An aggregate tree is a trie that stores navigation paths and the number of times a particular path is visited. It is useful for obtaining support counts of paths but grows exponentially with respect to the number of pages on a site.

Nanopoulos et al. argued that the technique of Chen et al. is not resistant to *noise* (Nanopoulos & Manolopoulos, 2000). Noise in this context means random page accesses that are not intended by a user. The authors proposed a technique that takes into consideration the structure of a site as well as *subpath* containment in obtaining support counts (Nanopoulos & Manolopoulos, 2000). For example, the path {ACD} is a subpath of S_{100} and is thus supported by S_{100}. The authors assumed that the graph structure of a site is available to determine the validity of candidate paths and designed an Apriori-like algorithm similar to that of Chen et al. to mine frequent paths. Pei et al. followed up on this technique by proposing a faster scalable mining technique, which is based on the non-Apriori-like ARM algorithm, *FP-growth* (Han et al., 2000). FP-growth achieves impressive speed-ups against Apriori because it only scans the database twice and does not need to generate and test candidate itemsets. It uses a compact data structure to store pertinent database information efficiently based on a minimum support threshold. Similarly, Pei et al. introduced a new data structure called *Web access pattern tree* (WAP-tree) to store compressed access pattern information (Pei et al., 2000). It first assumes that transaction identification is already done correctly and builds the WAP-tree from the database given a minimum support threshold. It then proceeds to mine for frequent sequences recursively. However, we contend that this notion of noise is farfetched, as its occurrence is minimal. Even if noise consistently exists, it would be advantageous to detect it and capitalize on it. Moreover, by using subpath containment, too many frequent paths may be found.

All in all, much work has been done in WUM and most researchers make assumptions (which may not be applicable in all scenarios) to support their approach. Hence, the challenge remains for a more general and yet efficient technique for WUM. In the next section, we discuss our approach in meeting this challenge.

TRANSACTIONIZED LOGFILE MINING

In this section, we present TRALOM2 (Transactionized Logfile Mining 2), a holistic solution to the problem of WUM. TRALOM2 is more holistic than existing approaches, as it takes into consideration all the available information from logfiles and does not make too many specific assumptions. It is an enhanced version of TRALOM (Woon et al., 2002b). We will formally define TRALOM2 and explain how *sessionization* (session identification) and *transactionization* can be carried out appropriately. We then introduce a data structure, the WebTrie, that holds important information extracted in real time from logfiles and allows mining to be done in a timely and incremental manner. Finally, algorithms to efficiently mine transactionized logfiles are presented.

SESSIONIZATION

Firstly, all entries are removed from the logfile except successful HTTP requests for HTML files and image files. Unlike all the discussed existing work on Web usage mining, we do not disregard image files because they may contain important content (maps, product images etc.) and affect the calculation of access times of entries. Previously, in TRALOM, we have removed images without such consideration. On the one hand, a navigation page with many images to load would give the impression that the user is spending a lot of time viewing the content in it. On the other hand, the images themselves may be the actual desired content. Therefore, in TRALOM2, we use an image content proportion value γ to allow users to set the amount of content stored in images. The image entries will not be included in the final sessions but they are used to compute the access times of HTML pages that appear after the image entries in the following way: HTML page access time = $\gamma \times$ (sum of access times of all images after previous HTML page and before current HTML page). Setting $\gamma = 0$ means disregarding all images, while setting $\gamma = 1$ means all images contain important content. All entries are then mapped to unique integers. Next, as Berendt et al. (2001) discovered a 30-minute session duration heuristic delivers the best results, it will be used here to group entries into sessions.

TRANSACTIONIZATION

Once a session has been identified, it is important to determine whether a page is used for content or navigation purposes (Cooley et al., 1997a). A content page is a page perceived by a user to contain content information, while a navigation page is one perceived to contain link information to reach a content page. Before we describe the *Transactionization Algorithm* (TA), here are formulation preliminaries: Let the *universal pageset*, $U=\langle p_1, p_2, ..., p_n \rangle$, be a set of *pages* found in a Website and let n be the total number. A *k-conset* is an unordered set of k unique content pages. A *k-traset* is an ordered set of $(k-1)$ unique navigation pages and a content page as its last page. Let $D_c \subseteq P$ (U) be a set of consets. Let $D_t \subseteq P$ (U) be a set of trasets. Let $s_m = \langle p_1, p_2, ..., p_m \rangle$ be a session identified from the logfile using a 30-minute window with m pages. Let a_p be the access time of page p. Let A_{sm} be the average access time of a page given by $\frac{1}{m-1}\Sigma_{p=1}^{m-1}a_p$

in a session s_m. Let $\oplus$ be an append operator; for a k-traset $X = \{p_1, ..., p_k\}$, $X \oplus \{p_i\}$ results in $X = \{p_1, ..., p_k, p_i\}$.

A conset contains only pages that are accessed for their content rather than their links. A traset contains a sequence of navigation pages and a content page as its last page. A page is considered to be a content page if its access time is greater than the average access time of all the pages in a session. This is appropriate, as it is logical that users spend more time on a content page than a navigation page. A study on tasks undertaken by users revealed that users spend an average time of about 75 seconds and 10 seconds on content and navigation pages respectively (Byrne, John, Wehrle & Crow, 1999). Recently, Cockburn et al. conducted an empirical analysis of Web use and showed that the most frequently occurring time gap between subsequent page accesses was just about a second, which meant that navigation pages are accessed most frequently (Cockburn & McKenzie, 2001). Therefore, since users usually spend much more time on content pages and access navigation pages more frequently, it is reasonable to conclude that this approach is feasible. Our method differs from that of Cooley et al. as we do not require the user to make a good guess of the percentage of navigation pages and we save one logfile scan (Cooley et al., 1997a). In addition, TA can also be applied on a session the moment it arrives because there is no need to calculate a suitable cut-off time based on all the sessions. Finally, since we use the average access time of pages in each session, our technique is not affected by varying bandwidth and traffic conditions across sessions. TA consists of the following steps:

1: Initialize $D_c = D_t = \varnothing$
2: for each session $s_n \in D$ do
3:     Initialize conset $X = \varnothing$
4:     Initialize traset $Y = \varnothing$
5:     Compute average access time of session s_n, A_{s_n}
6:     for each page $p_i \in s_n$ where $i = 0 ... n$ do
7:         if $i = n$ then
8:             $X = X \cup \{p_i\}$
9:             $Y = Y \oplus \{p_i\}$
10:        else
11:            if access time of page p_i, $a_{p_i} \geq A_{s_n}$ then

```
12:                         Y = Y ⊕ {p_i}
13:                         D_t = D_t ∪ {Y}
14:                         Initialize traset Y = ∅
15:                         if p_i ∉ X then
16:                             X = X ∪ {p_i}
17:                         end if
18:                     else if p_i ∈ Y at position m then
19:                         Remove all pages in Y from position m+1 onwards
20:                     else
21:                         Y = Y ⊕ {p_i}
22:                     end if
23:             end if
24:     end for
25:     D_c = D_c ∪ {X}
26:     D_t = D_t ∪ {Y}
27: end for
```

The basic idea of TA is to determine the nature (content or navigation) of a page using its access time and then to assign it to meaningful sets. For each page in a session, we first check if it is the last page (step 7). If it is and since we cannot determine the access time of the last page, we assume it is a content page and add it to both conset X and traset Y. For every other page, we check if its access time is greater than or equal to the average access time of pages in that particular session (step 11). If it is, then we conclude that it is a content page and append it to Y and add Y to D_t. This is because every traset ends with one content page. We will only add this content page to X if it does not exist in X (step 15), as we are only interested in finding correlations between different pages with consets. If a page p is a navigation page and already exists in Y, it is assumed that since a user has returned to a previously traversed page without reaching a content page, the user has not found what he/she wants, and thus the intermediate navigation pages are actually mistakes and should not be included (step 18).

Example: Both TA and MFR are applied on the logfile in Table 1, and Table 2 shows the extracted content, traversal and MFR transactions. We shall illustrate TA step by step using the Web access sequence of S_{100}: When $C(21)$ is encountered, a traset $\langle ABC \rangle$ is added to D_t and C is added to a conset X because it has an access time that is greater than the average access time. Finally, when the last page E is encountered, another traset $\langle BDE \rangle$ is added to D_t and E is added to conset X, which is then added to D_c. An interesting observation is that a page can be both a content and a navigation page. This is due to different user perceptions. We weed out rare perceptions with the use of the support threshold. In the example, page B can be identified as both a content and navigation page. However, it is clear that it will not contribute to a frequent conset as it occurs only once in D_c but will more likely contribute to a frequent traset as it appears three times as a navigation page in D_t. Another observation is that transactions identified by MFR have longer lengths. This is undesirable as such longer transactions will result in several rules being mined and since such transactions contain both content and navigation pages, mined rules may be misleading. For example, if the minimal support count is two, $\langle ABD \rangle$ will be a frequent sequence; in S_{100}, it is a series of navigation pages while in S_{400}, it has

Table 2. Extracted Transactions from Table 1

D_c	D_t	MFR Transactions
{CE}	⟨ABC⟩	⟨ABC⟩
{CE}	⟨BDE⟩	⟨ABDE⟩
{DE}	⟨BC⟩	⟨BD⟩
{BD}	⟨E⟩	⟨BCE⟩
	⟨CD⟩	⟨CDE⟩
	⟨E⟩	⟨ABD⟩
	⟨AB⟩	
	⟨D⟩	

more content pages. Hence, there is no way of deciding whether this sequence should be used to aid in the design of navigation or content pages.

WebTrie

Before introducing the WebTrie, an additional set called a *paset* has to be defined: A *k-paset* is an ordered set of *k* unique pages and may contain a mixture of content and navigation pages. The WebTrie is specifically designed to mine pasets.

Definition 1 (WebTrie): *A WebTrie consists of a tree node w that has an integer label representing a navigation page and an integer representing its support. We use w_p to refer to a tree node that corresponds to a page $p \in U$ and β_{w_p} to represent its support count. Let $C(w_p)$ be the support-ordered set of child nodes of node w_p. If $C(w_p) \neq \varnothing$, then $C(w_p) \subseteq \{w_m, ..., w_n\}$ where $1 \leq m \leq n \wedge \beta_{w_m} \geq \beta_{w_{m+1}}$.*

Note that an implicit virtual root node *R* is needed to link all the WebTries together. The WebTries under *R* are sorted in support-descending order, in which the leftmost WebTrie has the highest support count. For brevity, we shall refer to the set of WebTries built for a logfile as the WebTrie henceforth. The WebTrie is constructed using all the 1-pasets and 2-pasets in D_t. For construction details, refer to our previous work (Woon et al., 2002b). Note that WebTrie is created/updated on the fly each time TA identifies a traset; it is considered to be constructed *online* because at any point in time, it reflects the actual current state of the logfile. Like the SOTrieIT (Das et al., 2001), the WebTrie is *support-independent* and thus does not require any user input to begin construction. In addition, it is also *incremental,* as it needs not be rebuilt from scratch whenever new log entries arrive or when different support thresholds are used. Figure 1 shows the WebTrie constructed from D_t found in Table 2. The bracketed numbers are the support counts.

Figure 1. A WebTrie

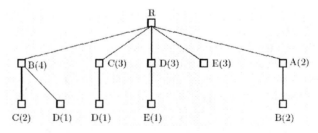

Mining Algorithms

In this section, the algorithms for discovering knowledge from consets and trasets efficiently are discussed. Here are formulation preliminaries: A conset $T \in D_c$ is said to support a conset X iff $X \subseteq T$. Let σ_x be the *support count* of a conset X, which is the number of consets in D_c that support X. A paset $X = \langle x_1, x_2, \ldots x_j \rangle$ is said to be a *consecutive subsequence* of a traset $Y = \langle y_1, y_2, \ldots y_k \rangle$, $X \blacktriangleright Y$, if $\exists i$ s.t. $y_{i+m} = x_m$ for $1 \le m \le j$. A traset $T \in D_t$ is said to support a paset X iff $X \blacktriangleright T$. Let α_x be the *support count* of an paset X, which is the number of trasets in D_t that support X. Let S be the *support threshold* where $0 \le S \le 1$ and $|D|$ be the number of transactions in a transaction database D. A conset X is *large* or *frequent* if $\sigma_x \ge |D_c| \times S$. A paset X is *large* or *frequent* if $\sigma_x \ge |D_t| \times S$. A *Web Usage Rule* (WUR) is an implication of the form $X \rightarrow Y$, where X and Y are sets of frequent consets and $X \cap Y = \varnothing$. The WUR $X \rightarrow Y$ holds in the database D_c with *confidence* $c\%$ if no less than $c\%$ of the content transactions in D_c that contain X also contain Y. A *Web Traversal Blueprint* (WTB) is a set of all frequent pasets.

A WUR is analogous to an association rule, and thus, all the advancements of ARM can be brought to bear on mining WURs. We will not elaborate on WUR mining because it is straightforward after we have modeled it as an ARM problem. Formerly, we have presented an algorithm, which we now term WTBD1 (WTB Discovery 1), to mine for the WTB. WTBD1 uses the WebTrie constructed from Dt given a support threshold S. From past experiments, it was observed that WTBD1 performed badly whenever there are many frequent pasets having a size greater than two. This is due to the huge number of candidate pasets being generated by the recursive function *FindTrail* and the need to scan the database to confirm their actual support counts. To eliminate this candidate generation problem, we introduce an improved version of WTBD1, called the WTBD2 algorithm:

1: Let l be the size of the largest traset in D_t
2: Initialize set $L_j = \varnothing$ for $1 \le j \le l$
3: for each WebTrie tree node $w_{pi} \in C(R)$ do
4:     if $\beta_{w_{pi}} \ge |D_t| \times S$ then
5:         $L_1 = L_1 \cup p_i$
6:         Invoke FindTrail $(\{w_{pi}\}, w_{pi}, 2)$
7:     else
8:         Exit for each loop
9:     end if
10: end for

Procedure FindTrail (paset X, WebTrie tree node *parent*, int k)
1: for each WebTrie tree node $w_{pi} \in C(parent)$ do
2:     if $w_{pi} \in X$ then
3:         Continue loop with other nodes
4:     end if
5:     if $\beta_{w_{pi}} \ge |D_t| \times S$ then
6:         paset $Y = X \oplus \{p_i\}$
7:         if $(k == 2) \vee (\alpha_Y \ge |D_t| \times S)$ then
8:             $L_K = L_K \cup Y$
9:             Invoke FindTrail $(Y, w_{pi}, k + 1)$

10:                    end if
11:        else
12:                    Exit for each loop
13:        end if
14: end for

The main idea is to reduce the number of database scans by earlier database scans to eliminate the need for candidate paset generation. Unlike WTBD1, WTBD2 only invokes the new procedure *FindTrail* recursively on frequent pasets (steps 7-10 of FindTrail). This is intuitive because if a paset has been found to be infrequent, it will still be infrequent even if pages are appended to it. Therefore, by scanning the database earlier (step 7 of FindTrail), unnecessary calls to *FindTrail* as well as candidate paset generation can be avoided.

Example: Given a support threshold of 25%, applying WTBD2 on the WebTrie in Figure 1 yields the following results: WTB = $\{\langle B\rangle, \langle C\rangle, \langle D\rangle, \langle E\rangle, \langle A\rangle, \langle BC\rangle, \langle AB\rangle\}$. We run a standard ARM algorithm on the consets found in Table 2 and the following are the frequent consets found: $\{B\}, \{C\}, \{D\}, \{E\}, \{BD\}, \{CE\}, \{DE\}$. Using the same support, applying the MFR algorithm on the same original logfile found in Table 1 yields the following large sequences: $\langle A\rangle, \langle B\rangle, \langle C\rangle, \langle D\rangle, \langle E\rangle, \langle AB\rangle, \langle BC\rangle, \langle BD\rangle, \langle DE\rangle, \langle ABD\rangle$. It is clear that the MFR method discovers more sequence patterns but since it does not differentiate between consets and pasets, the mined knowledge is difficult to apply. In addition, it has also missed one frequent conset $\{CE\}$. The reason is because pages C and E are not consecutive pages as seen in S_{100} and S_{300}. However, it is obvious that correlated content pages need not necessarily be consecutive pages, although navigation pages must be consecutive. If we check the results of our algorithms against the original logfile found in Table 1, we would discover useful insights. For example, the frequent paset $\langle BC\rangle$ tells us that BC is an important path to a content page. We can see from S_{100} and S_{200} that this insight is meaningful because to reach the content page C, we must go through navigation page B. The frequent conset $\{CE\}$ tells us that content pages C and E are often accessed in a session and are thus correlated. A check from S_{100} and S_{200} confirms this.

Summary

TRALOM2 is an attempt to provide a more holistic and yet efficient solution to the problem of WUM. Its strength and usefulness stem from the following features:

- **Content Proportion Value:** The downloading of unimportant images would affect the identification of content and navigation pages in techniques like TRALOM and RL. TRALOM2 addresses this issue by introducing a content proportion value to specify the amount of content in images.

- **Transactionization:** TRALOM2 applies a transactionization technique to split a logfile into two different databases for two different mining tasks so as to discover meaningful knowledge. Previous approaches do not split the logfile and would end up discovering knowledge that is distorted.

- **Average Page Access Time:** Unlike the RL method that requires a user parameter, TRALOM2 uses a simple yet reliable way to differentiate between a content and a navigation page. By using only the average page access time in a session, transactionization can be carried out incrementally because the average page access time can be determined using the page information in the session alone; the RL method requires information from all the sessions.

- **WebTrie:** TRALOM2 uses the WebTrie to store preprocessed information in an incremental fashion, and hence, there is no need to rebuild the WebTrie each time new sessions are logged. The WebTrie can be re-used repeatedly when mining at different support thresholds. None of the existing methods employ such a re-usable data structure.

- **Association Rule Mining Plug-in:** For discovery of Web usage rules, TRALOM2 allows the plugging in of any ARM algorithm. Current techniques require ARM algorithms to be modified before they can be used, and thus they could not easily plug in faster algorithms.

- **Lack of sensitive assumptions:** TRALOM2 only makes one assumption: duplicated navigation pages that do not lead to content pages are mistakes. This assumption is only invalid in cases in which users are not interested in content pages and would like to explore the structure of a Website.

Experiments

This section evaluates the performance and practicality of the TRALOM2 techniques by conducting experiments on a Pentium-4 machine with a CPU clock rate of 2.4 GHz, 1 GB of main memory and running on a Windows 2000 platform. The algorithms are implemented in Java and the real logfiles can be freely downloaded (Danzig, Mogul, Paxson & Schwartz, 2000). These logfiles were created in 1995 and were also used in a workload characterization study for Web servers (Arlitt & Williamson, 1996). They are useful as they are obtained from diversified environments, as seen in Table 3. Table 4 shows the details of the transactionized logfiles and the construction time of WebTries. We have set the content proportion value γ of images to 0.25, as we assume that images at the three sites do not contain much content; this is speculative but it suffices to show the effect of γ on TRALOM2. The bracketed numbers are the details of the transactionized logfiles in our previous work in which images are totally disregarded and thus removed even before sessionization, that is, $\gamma = 1$.

As seen from Table 4, the conset databases of $\mathcal{D}_1$ and $\mathcal{D}_2$ are reduced by half while that of $\mathcal{D}_3$ has almost doubled. The reduction of conset databases is due to an increase

Table 3. Real Logfiles

Symbol	Duration	Size (MB)	Number of Unique URLs	Source
$\mathcal{D}_1$	1 week	168	8436	Internet access provider for the Metro Baltimore
$\mathcal{D}_2$	1 month	200	941	NASA Kennedy Space Center
$\mathcal{D}_3$	7 months	228	2981	University of Saskatchewan

Table 4. Transactionization and WebTrie Details

	$|D_c|$	$|D_t|$	Average size of consets	Average size of trasets	Time to process one traset for WebTrie (ms)
$\mathcal{D}_1$	49K (97K)	171K (209K)	2.4 (2)	2.1 (1.3)	104 (0.28)
$\mathcal{D}_2$	38K (88K)	121K (299K)	3.2 (2.7)	2.7 (1.3)	746 (0.41)
$\mathcal{D}_3$	78K (46K)	132K (241K)	2.1 (3.4)	1.8 (1.3)	13 (0.23)

in the size of each conset (see column 4 of Table 4), which in turn is caused by more pages being identified as content pages in a session. By setting $\gamma = 0.25$, the average access time of a session would be decreased (if a few pages have many images that have long loading time in the session) and more pages would have an access time greater than the average. However, in the case of $\mathcal{D}_3$, the average size of consets has decreased. This is probably due to the fact that most pages in a session need to load several images and with $\gamma = 0.25$ now, such pages would have a shorter access time compared to the scenario in which $\gamma = 1$, and thus would not qualify as content pages. Another observation is that in all three databases, the average size of trasets has increased and this causes a huge increase in the time to process each traset for the construction of the WebTrie (see columns 5 and 6 of Table 4).

Due to the lack of a fair metric for comparing various logfile mining algorithms, only three algorithms are used in the experiments: Apriori (for conset mining), WTBD1 and WTDB2. Hence, our objective here is to prove the practicality of our approach, while comparison issues are discussed in the next section. Figures 2, 3 and 4 show the performance of the three algorithms on $\mathcal{D}_1$, $\mathcal{D}_2$ and $\mathcal{D}_3$ at varying minimum support thresholds. Note that execution times are plotted on a log scale. The construction time of the WebTrie is not reflected in the performance figures due to amortization (the WebTrie can be re-used for several different support thresholds). This premise is reasonable because the optimal support threshold cannot be known a priori and must be adjusted by the user through experiments with various support thresholds.

From the three figures, it can be seen that WTBD1 performs terribly at low support thresholds (in many cases, its computation time is not plotted, as it exceeds 1,000s). In all cases, WTBD2 outperforms WTBD1 by a wide margin, especially at the lower support thresholds, by eliminating the need for candidate paset generation. Conset mining generally takes a longer time even though its database D_c is much smaller than D_t. Probably, this is due to the use of the classic Apriori algorithm that also involves candidate generation. Fortunately, conset mining has the advantage of having the ability to plug in faster ARM algorithms whenever they are available, and thus, minimal work is needed to speed up conset mining.

Figure 2. Execution Times for $\mathcal{D}_1$ at Varying Minimum Support Thresholds

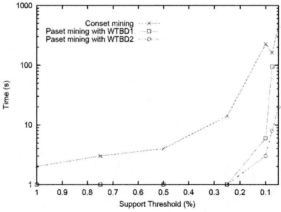

Figure 3. Execution Times for $\mathcal{D}_2$ at Varying Minimum Support Thresholds

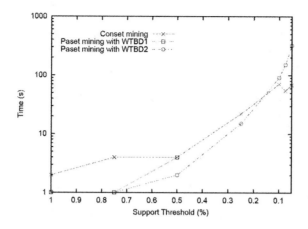

Figure 4. Execution Times for $\mathcal{D}_3$ at Varying Minimum Support Thresholds

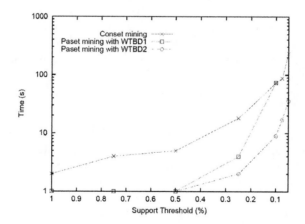

Another striking observation is that paset mining takes less than a second for high support thresholds. This is because the WebTries hold information that allows frequent pasets of lengths 1 and 2 to be discovered almost instantly without database scans. This characteristic is highly desirable, as analysts need to make adjustments to the support threshold quickly, especially at higher support thresholds. However, it can be seen that performance degrades exponentially for WTBD1 as the support threshold is lowered. This is due to the need to scan D_t several times to determine whether a candidate paset of size 3 and above is frequent. WTBD2 fairs much better and can perform within 200s in all three logfiles, even at a low threshold of 0.05%. The performance difference between WTBD1 and WTBD2 is most evident in $\mathcal{D}_2$ because it contains longer trasets; there are many more and longer frequent pasets, and thus, many more candidate pasets are generated by WTBD1.

Figure 5. Number of Frequent k-consets and k-pasets in $\mathcal{D}_1$, $\mathcal{D}_2$ and $\mathcal{D}_3$ at a Minimum Support Threshold of 0.05%

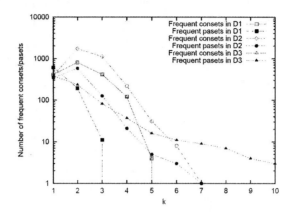

Finally, Figure 5 shows the number of mined frequent *k*-consets and *k*-pasets in the three logfiles at a minimum support threshold of 0.05%. The number of frequent consets discovered is generally larger than that of frequent pasets except in $\mathcal{D}_3$. Therefore, it is obvious that the support thresholds for conset and paset mining should be different and adjusted accordingly. Another observation is that there are many more consets and pasets of size 3 and below. If the objective is to uncover long frequent patterns, then such shorter patterns would be redundantly generated.

CHALLENGES

As Web technology matures and WUM becomes more popular and understood, we postulate that Web logging will become more pervasive at the application server side. This is because at the application layer, more comprehensive information about the users can be recorded, making sessionization and transactionization techniques redundant. Classification and clustering techniques can then be carried out more effectively. However, as the change to application server logging incurs additional costs, existing sites would probably stick to traditional server logging for a while. In any case, the following challenges for WUM remain:

- Several WUM techniques exist but they all work well for certain situations in which their assumptions are valid. Therefore, it is desirable to have a way to select the best algorithm for a particular scenario. Previously, we have proposed a novel comparison framework termed WALMAGE *(Web Access Log Mining AlGorithm Evaluator)* for this purpose (Woon, Ng & Lim, 2002a). WALMAGE allows us to evaluate the suitability of WUM algorithms by providing a set of cognitive measures to describe Web scenarios as well as logfile mining algorithms and a suitability measure to determine the best algorithm for the scenario. However, WALMAGE needs to be further improved by incorporating more cognitive theories before it can be of practical use.

- With wider availability and cheaper costs of Web connections, logfiles will certainly grow exponentially. Thus, the scalability of WUM algorithms including TRALOM2 needs to be improved in order to perform WUM in a timely manner.
- For big organizations, logfiles are usually distributed across several global systems. Hence, the parallelization of WUM algorithms would greatly enhance performance in such situations.
- Due to the proliferation of Web crawlers, robots and agents, there exists a critical need to accurately detect entries logged by such entities as such entries may create illusionary WUM results.
- Currently, most WUM research uses non-commercial logfiles for testing their methods. More experiments are needed on commercial logfiles before WUM methods can be proven to be really useful as competitive business tools.

CONCLUSIONS

The importance of Web usage mining is unquestionable with the rising importance of the Web not only as an information portal but also as a business edge. Web access logs contain abundant raw data that can be mined for Web access patterns, which in turn can be applied to improve the overall surfing experience of users. By taking into consideration the strengths and weaknesses of existing approaches, we have designed a more holistic and efficient Web usage mining algorithm called TRALOM2. Experiments conducted on real logs show the viability of our approach. However, much work is still needed to make Web usage mining more useful in the electronic commerce domain.

REFERENCES

Agrawal, R., & Srikant, R. (1994). Fast algorithms for mining association rules. *Proceedings of the International Conference on Very Large Databases*, Santiago, Chile, pp. 487-499.

Arlitt, M. F., & Williamson, C. L. (1996). Web server workload characterization: the search for invariants. *Proceedings of the ACM SIGMETRICS Conference on Measurement and Modeling of Computer Systems*, Philadelphia, Pennsylvania, 126-137.

Berendt, B., Mobasher, B., Spiliopoulou, M., & Wiltshire, J. (2001). Measuring the accuracy of sessionizers for Web usage analysis. *Proceedings of the International Workshop on Web Mining*, Chicago, 7-14.

Berson, A., Smith, S., & Thearling, K. (2000). *Building data mining applications for CRM*. New York: McGraw-Hill.

Buchner, A.G., & Mulvenna, M.D. (1998). Discovering Internet marketing intelligence through online snalytical Web usage mining. *ACM SIGMOD Record, 27*(4), 54-61.

Byrne, M.D., John, B.E., Wehrle, N.S., & Crow, D.C. (1999). The tangled Web we wove: A taskonomy of WWW use. *Proceedings of the International Conference on Human Factors in Computing Systems*, Pittsburgh, Pennsylvania, 544-551.

Chen, M.S., Park, J.S., & Yu, P.S. (1996). Data mining for path traversal patterns in a Web environment. *Proceedings of the 16th International Conference on Distributed Computing Systems*, Hong Kong, 385-392.

Chen, M.S., Park, J.S., & Yu, P.S. (1998). Efficient data mining for path traversal patterns. *IEEE Transactions on Knowledge and Data Engineering, 10*(2), 209–221.

Cockburn, A., & McKenzie, B. (2001). What do Web users do? An empirical analysis of Web use. *International Journal of Human-Computer Studies, 54*(6), 903–922.

Consortium, W.W.W. (1995). The common logfile format. Available: *http://www.w3.org/Daemon/User/Config/ Logging.html#common-logfile-format.*

Cooley, R. (2003). The use of Web structure and content to identify subjectively interesting Web usage patterns. *ACM Transactions on Internet Technology, 3*(2), 93-116.

Cooley, R., Mobasher, B., & Srivastava, J. (1997a). Grouping Web page references into transactions for mining World Wide Web browsing patterns. *Proceedings of the IEEE Knowledge and Data Engineering Workshop,* Newport Beach, CA, 2-9.

Cooley, R., Mobasher, B., & Srivastava, J. (1997b). Web mining: Information and pattern discovery on the World Wide Web. *Proceedings of the 9th International Conference on Tools with Artificial Intelligence,* Newport Beach, CA, 558-567.

Cooley, R., Mobasher, B., & Srivastava, J. (1999). Data preparation for mining World Wide Web browsing patterns. *Knowledge and Information Systems, 1*(1), 5-32.

Danzig, P., Mogul, J., Paxson, V., & Schwartz, M. (2000). The Internet traffic archive. Available: *http://ita.ee.lbl.gov/html/../index.html.*

Das, A., Ng, W.K., & Woon, Y.K. (2001). Rapid association rule mining. *Proceedings of the 10th International Conference on Information and Knowledge Management,* Atlanta, Georgia, 474-481.

Dean, N. (Ed.). (2000). *OCLC researchers measure the World Wide Web.* Online Computer Library Center (OCLC) Newsletter.

Gaul, W., & Schmidt-Thieme, L. (2000). Mining Web navigation path fragments. *Proceedings of the Workshop on Web Mining for E-commerce - Challenges and Opportunities,* Boston, MA.

Hallam-Baker, P.M., & Behlendorf, B. (1996). *Extended log file format.* Available: *http://www.w3.org/TR/WD-logfile.html.*

Han, J., Pei, J., & Yin, Y. (2000). Mining frequent patterns without candidate generation. *Proceedings of the ACM SIGMOD Conference,* Dallas, Texas, 1–12.

Heer, J., & Chi., E.H. (2002). Separating the swarm: Categorization methods for user access sessions on the Web. *Proceedings of the ACM CHI Conference on Human Factors in Computing Systems,* Minneapolis, Minnesota, 243–250.

Joshi, A., & Krishnapuram, R. (2000). On mining Web access logs. *ACM SIGMOD Workshop on Research Issues in Data Mining and Knowledge Discovery,* 63-69.

Kohavi, R. (2001). Mining e-commerce data: The good, the bad, and the ugly. *Proceedings of the 7th ACM SIGKDD International Conference on Knowledge Discovery and Data Mining,* San Francisco, California, 8-13.

Masseglia, F., Poncelet, P., & Teisseire, M. (1999). Using data mining techniques on Web access logs to dynamically improve hypertext structure. *ACM SigWeb Letters, 8*(3), 13-19.

Mobasher, B., Cooley, R., & Srivastava, J. (2000). Automatic personalization based on Web usage mining. *Communications of the ACM, 43*(8), 142–151.

Mobasher, B., Dai, H., Luo, T., Nakagawa, M., Sun, Y., & Wiltshire, J. (2000). Discovery of aggregate usage profiles for Web personalization. *Proceedings of the Workshop on Web Mining for E-commerce - Challenges and Opportunities,* Boston, MA.

Mobasher, B., Dai, H., Luo, T., Sun, Y., & Zhu, J. (2000). Combining Web usage and content mining for more effective personalization. *Proceedings of the International Conference on E-commerce and Web Technologies.*

Nanopoulos, A., & Manolopoulos, Y. (2000). Finding generalized path patterns for Web log data mining. *Proceedings of the East-European Conference on Advances in Databases and Information Systems, 215–228.*

Nanopoulos, A., Katsaros, D., & Manolopoulos, Y. (2001). Effective prediction of Web-user accesses: A data mining approach. *Proceedings of the WEBKDD Workshop,* San Francisco, CA, USA.

Nanopoulos, A., Katsaros, D., & Manolopoulos, Y. (2002). A data mining algorithm for generalized Web prefetching. *IEEE Transactions on Knowledge and Data Engineering* (To appear).

Pei, J., Han, J., Mortazavi-Asl, B., & Zhu, H. (2000). Mining access patterns efficiently from Web logs. *Proceedings of the Pacific-Asia Conference on Knowledge Discovery and Data Mining,* Kyoto, Japan.

Perkowitz, M., & Etzioni, O. (1999). Adaptive Web sites: Conceptual cluster mining. *Proceedings of the 16th International Joint Conference on Artificial Intelligence, 264–269.*

Pitkow, J. (1997). In search of reliable usage data on the WWW. *Proceedings of the 6th International World Wide Web Conference,* Santa Clara, California, 451-463.

Punin, J.R., Krishnamoorthy, M.S., & Zaki, M.J. (2001). Logml: Log markup language for Web usage mining. *Proceedings of the WEBKDD Workshop,* San Francisco, California, 88-112.

Sharrard, J., Kafka, S.J., & Tavilla, M.J. (2001). Global online trade will climb to 18% of sales. Available: *http://www.forrester.com/ER/Research/Brief/Excerpt/0,1317, 13720,00.html.*

Spiliopoulou, M. (2000). Web usage mining for Web site evaluation. *Communications of the ACM, 43*(8), 127-134.

Spiliopoulou, M., & Faulstich, L.C. (1998). WUM: A Web Utilization Miner. *Proceedings of the International Workshop on the Web and Data Bases,* Valencia, Spain, 109–115.

Srivastava, J., Cooley, R., Deshpande, M., & Tan, P.N. (2000). Web usage mining: Discovery and applications of usage patterns from Web data. *SIGKDD Explorations, 1*(2), 12-23.

Woon, Y.K., Ng, W.K., & Lim, E.P. (2002a). Evaluating Web access log mining algorithms: A cognitive approach. *Proceedings of the 1st International Workshop on Mining for Enhanced Web Search,* Singapore.

Woon, Y.K., Ng, W.K., & Lim, E.P. (2002b). Online and incremental mining of separately grouped Web access logs. *Proceedings of the 3rd International Conference on Web Information Systems Engineering,* Singapore.

Yang, Q., Zhang, H.H., & Li, T. (2001). Mining Web logs for prediction models in WWW caching and prefetching. *Proceedings of the 7th ACM SIGKDD International Conference on Knowledge Discovery and Data Mining,* San Francisco, California, 473-478.

SECTION V

CONCLUSION

Chapter XIX

The Scent of a Newsgroup:
Providing Personalized Access to Usenet Sites through Web Mining

Giuseppe Manco
Italian National Research Council, Italy

Riccardo Ortale
University of Calabria, Italy

Andrea Tagarelli
University of Calabria, Italy

ABSTRACT

Personalization is aimed at adapting content delivery to users' profiles: namely, their expectations, preferences and requirements. This chapter surveys some well-known Web mining techniques that can be profitably exploited in order to address the problem of providing personalized access to the contents of Usenet communities. We provide a rationale for the inadequacy of current Usenet services, given the actual scenario in which an increasing number of users with heterogeneous interests look for information scattered over different communities. We discuss how the knowledge extracted from Usenet sites (from the content, the structure and the usability viewpoints) can be suitably adapted to the specific needs and expectations of each user.

INTRODUCTION

The term *knowledge discovery in databases* is usually devoted to the (iterative and interactive) process of extracting valuable patterns from massive volumes of data by exploiting *data mining* algorithms. In general, data mining algorithms find hidden structures, tendencies, associations and correlations among data, and mark significant information. An example of data mining application is the detection of behavioural models on the Web. Typically, when users interact with a Web service (available from a Web server), they provide enough information on their requirements: what they ask for, which experience they gain in using the service, how they interact with the service itself. Thus, the possibility of tracking users' browsing behaviour offers new perspectives of interaction between service providers and end-users. Such a scenario is one of the several perspectives offered by Web mining techniques, which consist of applying data mining algorithms to discovery patterns from Web data. A classification of Web mining techniques can be devised into three main categories:

- *Structure mining.* It is intended here to infer information from the topology of the link structure among Web pages (Dhyani et al., 2002). This kind of information is useful for a number of purposes: categorization of Websites, gaining an insight into the similarity relations among Websites, and developing suitable metrics for the evaluation of the relevance of Web pages.

- *Content mining.* The main aim is to extract useful information from the content of Web resources (Kosala & Blockeel, 2000). Content mining techniques can be applied to heterogeneous data sources (such as HTML/XML documents, digital libraries, or responses to database queries), and are related to traditional Information Retrieval techniques (Baeza-Yates & Ribeiro-Neto, 1999). However, the application of such techniques to Web resources allows the definition of new challenging application domains (Chakrabarti, 2002): Web query systems, which exploit information about the structure of Web documents to handle complex search queries; intelligent search agents, which work on behalf of users based both on a description of their profile and a specific domain knowledge for suitably mining the results that search engines provide in response to user queries.

- *Usage mining.* The focus here is the application of data mining techniques to discover usage patterns from Web data (Srivastava et al., 2000) in order to understand and better serve the needs of Web-based applications and end-users. Web access logs are the main data source for any Web usage mining activity: data mining algorithms can be applied to such logs in order to infer information describing the usage of Web resources. Web usage mining is the basis of a variety of applications (Cooley, 2000; Eirinaki & Vazirgiannis, 2003), such as statistics for the activity of a Website, business decisions, reorganization of link and/or content structure of a Website, usability studies, traffic analysis and security.

Web-based information systems depict a typical application domain for the above Web mining techniques, since they allow the user to choose contents of interest and browse through such contents. As the number of potential users progressively increases, a large heterogeneity in interests and in the knowledge of the domain under investigation is exhibited. Therefore, a Web-based information system must tailor itself to different user requirements, as well as to different technological constraints, with the ultimate aim of personalizing and improving users' experience in accessing the system. Usenet turns out to be a challenging example of a Web-based information system, as it encompasses a very large community, including government agencies, large universities, high schools, and businesses of all sizes. Here, newsgroups on new topics are

continuously generated, new articles are continuously posted, and (new) users continuously access the newsgroups looking for articles of interest. In such a context, the idea
of providing personalized access to the contents of Usenet articles is quite attractive,
for a number of reasons.

1. First of all, the hierarchy provided by the newsgroups is often inadequate, since
    too many newsgroups deal with overlapping subjects, and even a single newsgroup
    dealing with a specific topic may contain rather heterogeneous threads of discus-
    sion. As an example, the newsgroup **comp.lang.java.programmer** (which
    should deal with programming issues in the Java programming language) contains
    threads that can be grouped in different subtopics, dealing respectively with
    "typing," "networking," "debugging," and so forth. As a consequence, when
    looking for answers to a specific query one can frequently encounter the *abun-
    dance problem*, which happens when too many answers are available and the
    degree of relevance of each answer has to be suitably weighted. By contrast, one
    can even encounter the *scarcity problem,* which usually happens when the query
    is too specific and many viable answers are missed. Hence, articles in the hierarchy
    provided by the newsgroups need better (automatic) organization according to
    their contents, in order to facilitate the search and detection of relevant information.
2. Answers to specific threads, as well as references to specific articles, can be
    analysed from a *structural* point of view. For example, the graph structure of the
    accesses to articles (available from users' access logs) can be investigated to allow
    the identification of *hub* and *authoritative* articles, as well as users with specific
    areas of expertise. Thus, the analysis of the graphs devised from both accesses and
    reactions to specific articles is clearly of greater impact to the purpose of providing
    personalized access to the Usenet service.
3. Since users can be tracked, their preferences, requirements and experiences in
    accessing newsgroups can be evaluated directly from the access logs. As a
    consequence, both available contents and their presentation can be adapted
    according to the user's profile, which can be incrementally built as soon as the user
    provides sufficient information about his/her interaction with the service. More-
    over, the experience provided by the interaction of a given user can be adapted to
    users exhibiting a similar profile, thus enabling a *collaborative system* in which
    experiences are shared among users.

As a matter of fact, Usenet and the Web share strong similarities. Hence, the
application of well-known Web mining techniques from literature to Usenet should, in
principle, allow similar benefits of mining traditional Web contents. Nevertheless, the
application of the above techniques must take into account the intrinsic differences
between the two contexts. To this purpose, the contribution of this chapter is the analysis
and, where necessary, the revising of suitable Web mining techniques with the aim of
tailoring them to the Usenet environment.

The goal of this chapter is to survey some well-known Web mining techniques that
can be profitably exploited to address the problem of providing personalized access to
the contents of Usenet communities available from the Web. In such a context, the
problem of providing personalized access to the Usenet communities can be ideally
divided into three main phases: *user profiling,* the process of gaining an insight about
the preferences and tastes of Usenet visitors through an in-depth analysis of their

browsing behaviour; *content profiling,* the process of gaining an insight about the main issues and topics appearing in the content and in the structure of the articles; and *personalization,* the adoption of ad-hoc strategies to tailor the delivery of Usenet contents to a specific profile.

For brevity's sake, only the most prominent adaptations required to apply these techniques to the Usenet environment are illustrated in detail. We mainly point out the possibility of accessing newsgroups from a Web interface (such as, e.g., in **groups.google.com**), and envisage a Web-based service capable of providing personalized access by exploiting Web mining techniques. A Web-enabled Usenet access through a Web server has some major advantages with respect to the traditional access provided by NNTP (Net News Transfer Protocol) servers. In particular, from a user point of view, a Web-based service exhibits the advantage of offering ubiquitous and anytime access through the Web, without the need of having a predefined client other than a Web browser. In addition, a user can fruitfully exploit further consolidated Web-based services (such as, e.g., search engine capabilities). From a service provider point of view, it offers the possibility of tracking a given user in his/her interaction with the service for free, by exploiting traditional Web-based techniques.

Throughout this chapter, a particular emphasis is given on clustering techniques tailored for personalization. Although a number of different approaches exist (Deshpande & Karypis, 2001; Mobasher et al., 2001), we believe that those based on clustering are particularly promising since they effectively allow the partition of users on the basis of their browsing behaviours, which reliably depict user profiles. Moreover, since clusters provide objective descriptions for the corresponding profiles, such an approach is also able to act on the process of content delivery in order to address the specificities of each profile: any change in the details of a particular profile is soon captured by clustering and, consequently, exploited in the delivery process.

INFORMATION CONTENT OF
A USENET SITE

Usenet operates in a peer-to-peer framework that allows the users to exchange public messages on a wide variety of topics including computers, scientific fields, politics, national cultures, and hobbies. Differing from e-mail messages, Usenet articles (formatted according to the RFC-1036 Usenet news standard) are concerned with public discussions rather than personal communications and are grouped, according to their main subject, into newsgroups. Practically speaking, newsgroups are collections of articles sharing the same topics. Newsgroups can be organized into hierarchies of topics. Information about the hierarchy can be found in the newsgroup names themselves, which contain two or more parts separated by periods. The first part of the name indicates the top-level hierarchy to which the newsgroup belongs (the standard "Big Seven" top-level hierarchies are: comp, misc, news, rec, sci, soc, talk). Reading from left to right, the various parts of the name progressively narrow the topic of discussion. For example, the newsgroup comp.lang.java.programmer contains articles discussing programming issues concerning the Java programming language. Notice that, although the newsgroup hierarchy is highly structured, articles can be posted to multiple newsgroups. This

Figure 1. Example of a Web Interface to Usenet News

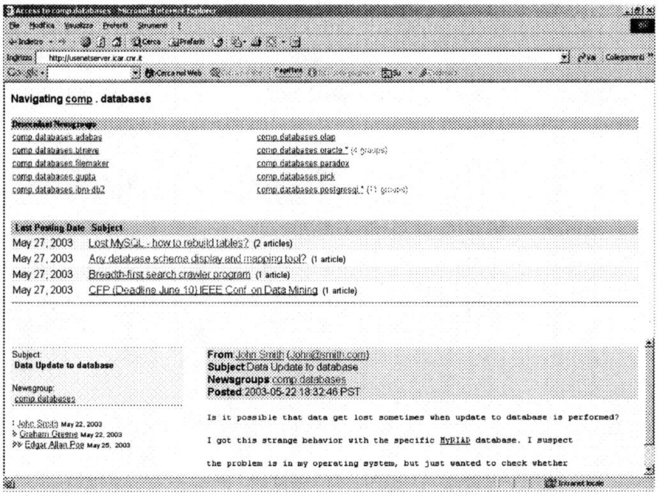

usually happens when articles contain more than one topic of discussion: for example, an article concerning the use of an Oracle JDBC Driver can be posted to both comp.lang.java.programmer and comp.databases.oracle.

In our scenario, Usenet articles can be accessed by means of a Web server, which allows both the visualization of articles, and the navigation of newsgroup hierarchies. An example of such an interface is provided in Figure 1. Users can navigate the hierarchy of newsgroups by accessing highly structured pages, in which hyperlinks point to specific portions of the hierarchy.

A crucial aspect in the information delivery process is the quality of information itself. Information quality is guaranteed neither in a typical Web setting nor in a Usenet scenario. However, while information related to a given topic of interest is scattered on the Web, Usenet simplifies the process of information locating. Indeed, articles are typically grouped in threads: a thread contains an initial article, representing an argument of discussion raised by some user, and a chain of answers to the initial article. Users only have to look within those threads semantically related to the topic under investigation. This allows us to narrow the search space and, as a consequence, to obtain a recall higher than the one typically achievable by traditional information retrieval approaches on the Web. Also, the process of thread selection corresponds to the sense disambiguation of the topic of interest. This, in turn, leads to an increase in the degree of accuracy of the inferred knowledge. Moreover, since Usenet allows the user to focus on a specific set of threads, the possibility of the individual news articles having been written by authoritative people is not less likely than it is on the Web (provided that an effective technique for narrowing the search space, depending on the specific topic of interest, can be devised for the Web itself). Yet, Usenet is a source of information whose inferable knowledge is often complementary with respect to the contents within Web pages. As an example, consider the scenario in which a user is interested in finding detailed information on a specific topic like "using Java Native Interface and Java Servlets running under Apache Tomcat". Querying and posting to Usenet newsgroups allows the satisfaction of the specific request. This ultimately corresponds to benefit from the depicted collaborative environment, by obtaining both references to dedicated Websites and reports from other users' experiences.

Two main information sources can be detected in a Usenet environment: *access logs,* describing users' browsing behaviour, and *Usenet repositories,* representing the articles a user may access. We now analyse such information sources in more detail.

Web Logs: Mechanisms for Collecting User Clickstream

Usage data are at the basis of any Web usage mining process. These data can be collected at different levels on an ideal communication channel between a generic user and the Website currently accessed: at client level, proxy-server level, and Website level. Sources at different levels take into account different segments of Web users and, as a consequence, highlight distinct browsing patterns (Cooley, 2000). Precisely, sources at the client level focus on *single user/single site* (or even *single user/multi site*) browsing behaviour. Information related to *multi user/multi site* navigational behaviour is collected at the proxy-server level. Finally, sources at the Website level reveal usage patterns of *multi user/single site* type. Since the user profiling phase aims to gain an insight into the browsing strategies of visitors, we focus on the sources of usage data at Website level. It is worth noticing that in such a context usage mining techniques are only exploited to silently infer user preferences from their browsing sessions. This finally does not raise *privacy violation* issues: since users are not tracked at the client side, their identity is unknown and any invasive technology, such as cookies, is not leveraged to try to recognize the user across their repeated transactions. Furthermore, information extracted from browsing data is mediated on a huge number of user sessions, which makes the proposed Web usage mining techniques non-invasive of user privacy.

Web logs represent a major approach to tracking user behaviour. By recording an incoming request to a Web server, Web logs explicitly capture visitors' browsing behaviour in a concurrent and interleaved manner. A variety of ad-hoc formats have been devised for organizing data within Web logs: two popular formats are CLF (Common Log Format) and ECLF (Extended Common Log Format). ECLF, recently introduced by the W3C, improves CLF by adding a number of new fields to each entry that have been revealed as being particularly useful for demographic analysis and log summaries (Eirinaki & Vazirgiannis, 2003). ECLF logs can also include cookies, that is, pieces of information uniquely generated by Web servers to address the challenging task of tracking users during their browsing activities.

The main limitation that affects Web logs is that they do not allow for the reliable capture of user behaviour. For instance, the viewing time perceived at the Website level may be much longer than it actually is at the client level. This is typically due to a number of unavoidable reasons, such as the client bandwidth, the transmission time necessary for the Web server to deliver the required resource and the congestion status of the network. Also, Web logs may not record some user requests. Such a loss of information usually happens when a user repeatedly accesses the same page and caching is present. Typically, only the first request is captured; subsequent requests may be served by a cache, which can be either local to the client or part of an intermediate proxy-server. These drawbacks must be taken into account while extracting usage patterns from Web logs: a variety of heuristics have been devised in order to pre-process Web logs in a such a way as to reduce the side effects of the above issues.

Data about user behaviour can also be collected through alternative approaches (Cooley, 2000), which allow the overcoming of the traditional limitation affecting the exploitation of Web logs: the impossibility of capturing information other than that in the HTTP header of a Web request. Among them, we mention ad-hoc tracking mechanisms for defining meaningful application-dependent logs describing user browsing activities at the required degree of detail. Indeed, the exploitation of new technologies for developing Web (application) servers (such as, e.g., JSP/PHP/.NET frameworks) leads to two main advantages in processing usage data collections. Firstly, it can capture information that is not typically addressed by Web logs, such as request parameters and state variables of an application. Secondly, it guarantees the reliability of the information offered. A format for the generic entry of an application log, suitably thought for the Usenet environment, can be devised. It may consist of (at least) three fields. *User* is a field that refers to the identity of the user who made the request: it can either be an IP address or a unique user-id. *Time* is a time stamp for the request. *Request* logs the details (such as the level in the newsgroup hierarchy, or the topics) of the request.

Content Data: Finding Structure within News Articles

News articles are the primary information source of Usenet. Different from generic text documents (to which at first sight they could be assimilated), some relevant features properly characterize them, as well as e-mail messages:

*   Articles are usually rather short in size. This may look like a sociological observation, since the size of an article depends on a set of factors such as the topic involved, user preferred behaviour, and degree of interaction required. Nevertheless, newsgroups are conceived as a means of generating discussions, which typically consist of focused questions and (rather) short replies.
*   Text documents usually exhibit only unstructured features (words occurring in the text). By contrast, news articles result in a combination of important structural properties (such as sender, recipients, date and time, and whether the article represents a new thread or a reaction in a given thread), and unstructured components (*Subject, Content, Keywords* headers).
*   Also, news articles may contain junk (unsolicited) information. This eventually results in a loss of recall in information delivery, and performance worsening due to the waste of bandwidth and server storage space. Although junk information is quite typical in a Web setting, the presence of spam articles is still more problematic in the Usenet environment, mainly due to duplicate copies or conversational threads including many useless articles (e.g., replies). Many techniques and tools for spam filtering have been developed in the last seven years, mainly aimed at classifying messages as either spam or non-spam. Among them we mention (Androutsopoulos et al., 2000; Drucker et al., 1999). Clearly, such techniques can be used to improve the quality of the information contained in a Usenet server, thus allowing the concentration only on significant data sources.

We now briefly review how to extract relevant information from a collection of news articles. This requires a study on the representation of both structured and unstructured features of a news article. Concerning text contents, the extraction of relevant features is usually performed by a sequence of well-known text operations (Baeza-Yates &

Ribeiro-Neto, 1999; Moens, 2000), such as *lexical* analysis, *removal of stopwords, lemmatisation* and *stemming*. The above text operations associate each article with a set of terms that are assumed to best reflect the textual content of the article. However, such terms have different discriminating power, that is, their relevance in the context where they are used. Many factors may contribute in weighting relevant terms: statistics on the text (e.g., size, number of different terms appearing in), relationships between a term and the document containing it (e.g., location, number of occurrences), and relationships between a term and the overall document collection (e.g., number of occurrences).

A commonly used weighting function is based on the finding that the most significant terms are those occurring frequently within a document, but rarely within the remaining documents of the collection. To this purpose, the weight of a term can be described as a combination of its frequency of occurrence within a document (*Term Frequency - TF*) and its rarity across the whole collection (*Inverse Document Frequency - IDF*). A widely used model complying with the above notion is the *vector-space model* (Baeza-Yates & Ribeiro-Neto, 1999), in which each article is represented as a n-dimensional vector **w**, where n is the number of available terms and each component w_j is the (normalized) *TF.IDF* weight associated with a term j:

$$w_{ji} = (tf_{ji} \cdot idf_j) \Big/ \sqrt{\sum_p (tf_{pi} \cdot idf_p)^2} \;.$$

It is well-known from literature that this model tends to work quite well in practice despite a number of simplifying assumptions (e.g., term independence, absence of word-sense ambiguity, as well as of phrase-structure and word-order).

From each article, further features can be extracted from both the required headers (such as *From, Date, Newsgroups* and *Path*) and the optional headers (such as *Followup-To, Summary, References*). In particular, discriminating information can be obtained by exploiting the hierarchy of topics inferred by newsgroups, or by analysing the temporal shift of articles for a given topic.

Notice also that, in principle, textual contents may contain further information sources, such as, for example, hyperlinks. Therefore a Web interface to a Usenet service may assign each article a unique URL address, thus allowing articles to link to each other directly by means of such URLs.

To summarise, an article can be represented by a feature vector **x = (y w)** in which the structured component (denoted by **y**) may comprise, for example, the features

Table 1. Structured Features of News Articles

feature	type	source header
Newsgroup hierarchy (e.g., comp.lang.c)	categorical	*Newsgroups:*
Follow-up newsgroup hierarchy	categorical	*Followup-To:*
Sender domain (e.g., yahoo.com)	categorical	*From:*
Weekday	categorical	*Date:*
Time period (e.g., early morning, afternoon, evening)	categorical	*Date:*
Expiration date	categorical	*Expires:*
Geographic distribution (e.g., world)	categorical	*Distribution:*
Article length	numeric	*Lines:*
Nr. of levels in newsgroup hierarchy	numeric	*Newsgroups:*

reported in Table 1, whereas unstructured information (denoted by **w**) is mainly obtained from the content and from the *Subject* header (or from the *Summary* and *Keywords* headers as well).

MINING CONTENT OF NEWS ARTICLES

A straightforward personalization strategy consists of providing searching capabilities within Usenet news. As a matter of fact, many Web interfaces to Usenet servers provide keyword-based querying capabilities and ranking mechanisms for the available articles. In general, queries involve relationships between terms and documents (such as, e.g., "find articles dealing with Java Native Interface"), and can be modelled as vectors in the vector-space model. Hence a typical ranking mechanism may consist of computing the score of each article in a collection as the *dot product* between its representative vector **w** and the vector **q** representing the query: $r_{q,w} = w \cdot q$. Articles with a high rank constitute the answer to the query.

A different approach to personalization is the identification of topics emerging from the articles, to be proposed to users in a more structured way: this can be accomplished by clustering articles on the basis of their contents. Clustering aims to identify homogeneous groups to be represented as semantically related in the re-organized news collection. Formally, a clustering problem can be stated as follows: given a set $M = \{m_1, ..., m_N\}$ of news articles, we aim to find a suitable partition $P = \{C_1, ..., C_k\}$ of M in k groups, such that each group contains a homogeneous subset of articles (or threads) with an associated label describing the main topics related to the group. The identification of homogeneous groups relies on the capability of: *(i)* defining matching criteria for articles according to their contents; *(ii)* detecting representative descriptions for each cluster; and *(iii)* exploiting suitable clustering schemas.

Homogeneity can be measured by exploiting the feature vectors defined above. A similarity measure $s(\mathbf{x}_i, \mathbf{x}_j)$ can be defined as $s(\mathbf{x}_i, \mathbf{x}_j) = \alpha s_1(\mathbf{y}_i, \mathbf{y}_j) + (1-\alpha) s_2(\mathbf{w}_i, \mathbf{w}_j)$, where s_1 and s_2 refer respectively to the similarity of the structured and unstructured components of the articles. In particular, s_1 can be defined by resorting to traditional similarity measures, such as *Dice, Euclidean* or *mismatch-count* distance (Huang, 1998). Mismatch-count distance can be exploited, for example, by taking into account the hierarchy of subgroups, as in principle, articles posted in newsgroups sharing many levels in the newsgroup hierarchy are more likely to be similar than articles posted in newsgroups sharing few levels. On the other hand, s_2 can be chosen among the similarity measures particularly suitable for documents (Baeza-Yates & Ribeiro-Neto, 1999; Strehl et al., 2000), such as the *cosine similarity*. Finally, $\alpha \leq 1$ represents the weight to be associated with the structured component.

Concerning labels, we have to find a suitable way of describing the main topics associated with a given group of semantically homogeneous articles. The structural part can easily be tackled by exploiting, for example, the *mode* vector (Huang, 1998) of the structured components *y*. The unstructured part requires some attention. In a sense, we are looking for a label reflecting the content of the articles within the cluster, and at the same time capable of differentiating two different clusters. To this purpose, a viable strategy can be to resort to *frequent itemsets discovery* techniques (Agrawal & Srikant,

1994; Beil et al., 2002), and associate the set of terms (or concepts) with each cluster that more frequently appear within the cluster.

Many different clustering algorithms can be exploited (Jain et al., 1999) to cluster articles according to the above mentioned matching criteria. Hierarchical methods are widely known as providing clusters with a better quality (Baeza-Yates & Ribeiro-Neto, 1999; Steinbach et al., 2000). In the context of newsgroup mining, such approaches are particularly attractive since they also allow the generation of cluster hierarchies (which ultimately represent topics and subtopics). However, hierarchical approaches suffer from serious efficiency drawbacks, since they require quadratic time complexity in the number of articles they deal with. By contrast, efficient centroid-based methods have been proposed in literature. In particular, Dhillon and Modha (2001) define a suitable partitional technique, namely *spherical k-Means,* which has the main advantage of requiring a linear number of comparisons while still guaranteeing good quality clusters. As stated above, feature vectors $\mathbf{w}_i$ are normalized. In such a case, the computation of the cosine similarity is reduced to the computation of the dot product among two vectors. The spherical k-Means algorithm aims to maintain such a property during the whole clustering phase. For each cluster C_j containing n_j documents, the algorithm computes the cluster center $\mu_j = 1/n_j \sum_{\mathbf{w} \in Cj} \mathbf{w}$. By normalizing μ_j, we obtain the concept vector c_j of C_j, which is the feature vector that is closest in cosine similarity to all the document vectors in the cluster C_j.

The main drawback of centroid-based techniques is that the quality of their results is strictly related to two main issues: the number of desired clusters, which has to be known a priori, and the choice of a set of suitable initial points. Combinations of hierarchical agglomeration with iterative relocations can be devised here (Manco et al., 2002), by first using a hierarchical agglomerative algorithm over a small arbitrary subset S of articles to seed the initial clusters for k-Means-based methods. Figure 2 shows an example of such an integration. Practically, by choosing a subset S of M, with a size $h \ll N$ as an input for a hierarchical clustering scheme, we avoid efficiency issues. The resulting partition provided by such an algorithm can be exploited within the k-Means algorithm, as it provides an optimal choice for both the desired number of clusters and the initial cluster centers (computed starting from the partition provided by the hierarchical approach).

Figure 2. Example of Integration of Hierarchical and Partitional Clustering

Input: a set $M = \{m_1, ..., m_N\}$ of news articles.

Output: a partition $P = \{C_1, ..., C_k\}$ of M.

Method:

– sample a small subset $S = \{m_1, ..., m_h\}$ of news articles randomly chosen from M;

– obtain the feature vectors $\{\mathbf{x}_1, ..., \mathbf{x}_h\}$ from S;

– apply hierarchical agglomerative algorithm on $\{\mathbf{x}_1, ..., \mathbf{x}_h\}$;

– let $c_1, ..., c_k$ be the concept vectors representing the clusters of the partition supplied from the hierarchical algorithm:

  • apply the k-Means algorithm on M exploiting $c_1, ..., c_k$ as initial centers;

  • answer $P = \{C_1, ..., C_k\}$ as the result of the k-Means algorithm.

MINING USAGE OF NEWS ARTICLES

This section is devoted to the problem of exploiting browsing patterns to learn user profiles. A profile is a synthetic description of information requirements, interests and preferences of a set of visitors. Earlier approaches to personalization required explicit user collaboration; that is, visitors had to fill in questionnaires concerning their navigation purposes. However, such an approach suffers from two main limitations. Firstly, questionnaires are subjective, and hence possibly unreliable. Secondly, profiles learned from questionnaires are static; that is, they depict the expectations of a group of users at a given point in time. This eventually requires new questionnaires to be periodically presented to visitors, thus making visitors reluctant to continuously provide information. By contrast, Web usage mining allows inferring user profiles by means of a silent analysis of visitors' browsing activities. Moreover, profiles learned from browsing patterns are both objective (they are deduced from exhibited navigational behaviours and therefore not affected by subjectiveness) and dynamic (they automatically reflect changes in using a Website).

A typical Web usage mining process can be divided into three phases (Srivastava et al., 2000): *data preprocessing,* the process of turning raw usage data into a meaningful data set (precisely, raw usage data are converted into high-level abstractions such as page views, sessions, transactions, users); *pattern discovery,* that is, the exploitation of a variety of techniques from different fields (such as machine learning, pattern discovery and statistics) to infer usage patterns potentially of interest; *pattern analysis,* the step in which the identified patterns are further inspected, aggregated and/or filtered to transform individual patterns into a deep understanding of the usage of the Website under investigation. In the following, data preprocessing and pattern discovery are taken into account.

Usage Data Preprocessing

A number of tasks must be accomplished in order to reconstruct a meaningful high-level view of users' browsing activities from the collection of their individual actions in a Web log. Typically, *data cleaning* is the first step. It is useful to remove irrelevant entries from Web logs, such as those denoting images or robot accesses. The intuition is that only entries explicitly requested by users should be retained for subsequent computations (Cooley et al., 1999); since Web usage mining aims at highlighting overall browsing patterns, it does not make sense to analyse entries that do not correspond to explicit visitor requests.

URI (Uniform Resource Identifier) normalization is conceived to identify as similar the URIs which, though syntactically distinct, refer to the same resource (such as, e.g., **www.mysite.com/index.htm** and **www.mysite.com**).

User identification is a crucial task for a variety of reasons such as caching policies, firewalls and proxy-servers. Many heuristics exist for identifying users, such as client-side tracking (i.e., the collection of usage data at client level through remote agents), cookies and embedded session IDs (also known as URL rewriting), chains of references and others (Pirolli et al., 1996). It is worth noticing that in spite of a considerable number of (more or less) accurate heuristics, user identification exhibits some intrinsic difficulties, like in the case of users with identical IP addresses, or in the case of an individual user who visits the same pages through two distinct Web browsers executing on a single machine.

For each user, *session identification* aims to divide the resulting set of requests into a number of subsets (i.e., sessions). The requests in each subset share a sort of temporal continuity. As an example, it is reasonable to consider two subsequent requests from a given user exceeding a prefixed amount of time as belonging to separate sessions (Catledge & Pitkow, 1995). Since Web logs track user behaviour for very long time periods, session identification is leveraged to distinguish between repeated visits of the same user.

The notion of page view indicates a set of page files (such as frames, graphics and scripts) that contribute to a single browser display. *Page view identification* is the step in which different session requests are collapsed into page views. At the end of this phase, sessions are turned into time-ordered sequences of page view accesses. *Support filtering* is typically leveraged in order to eliminate noise from usage data, by removing all those session page views characterized by either very low or extremely high support. These accesses cannot be profitably leveraged to characterize the behaviour of any group of users.

Transaction (or *episode*) *identification* is an optional preprocessing step that aims at extracting meaningful subsets of page view accesses from any user session. The notions of *auxiliary* page view (i.e., a page view mainly accessed for navigational purposes) and *media* page view (namely, an informative page view) contribute to identifying two main kinds of user transactions (Cooley, 2000): *auxiliary-content* and *media-only* transactions. Given a generic user session, for each media page view *P,* an auxiliary-content transaction is a time ordered subsequence consisting of all the auxiliary page views leading to *P* in the original user session. Browsing patterns emerging from auxiliary-content user transactions reveal the common navigation paths leading to a given media page view. Media-only transactions consist of all the media page views in a user session. They are useful to highlight the correlations among the media page views of a Website.

Pattern Discovery

A number of traditional data mining techniques can be applied to the preprocessed usage data in order to discover useful browsing patterns. Here these techniques are analysed in the context of personalization. In the following, the term *page* is used as a synonym for page view.

Association rules capture correlations among distinct items on the basis of their co-occurrence patterns across transactions. In the Web, association rule discovery can be profitably exploited to find relationships among groups of Web pages in a site (Mobasher et al., 2001). This can be accomplished through an analysis of those pages frequently visited together within user sessions. Association rules materialize the actual user judgment about the logical organization of the Web pages in a site: a group of (not necessarily inter-linked) pages often visited together implies some sort of thematic affinity among the pages themselves. *Sequential patterns* extend association rules by including the notion of time sequence. A sequential pattern indicates that a set of Web pages are chronologically accessed after another set of pages. These patterns allow Websites to be proactive, that is, to automatically predict the next request of the current visitors (Mobasher et al., 2002b). As a consequence, user navigation can be supported by suggestions to those Web pages that should best satisfy user browsing purposes.

Classification is a technique that assigns a given item to one of several predefined classes. Profiling is a typical application domain: in this case, the purpose of classification is to choose, for each visitor, a (pre-existing) user profile that best reflects his/her navigational behaviour (Dai et al., 2000). *Clustering* techniques can be used for grouping either pages or users exhibiting similar characteristics. Page clusters consist of Web pages thematically related according to user judgment. A technique (Mobasher et al., 2002a) for computing these clusters consists of exploiting the association rules behind the co-occurrence patterns of Web pages in such a way as to form a hypergraph. Hypergraph partitioning is then applied to find groups of strongly connected pages. Different approaches (either centroid-based (Giannotti et al., 2002) or hierarchical (Guha et al., 2000)) are aimed at clustering users' sessions. In general, page clusters summarize similar interests of visitors with different browsing behaviour. Session clusters, on the contrary, depict subsets of users who exhibit the same browsing behaviour.

Statistical techniques typically exploit data within user sessions to learn a probabilistic model of the dependencies among the specific variables under investigation. In the field of personalization, an approach consists of building a Markov model (from log data of a Website) that predicts the Web page(s) that users will most likely visit next (Deshpande & Karypis, 2001). Markov models can also be exploited in a probabilistic framework to clustering, based on the EM *(Expectation-Maximization)* algorithm (Cadez et al., 2000). The main idea here is essentially to learn a mixture of first-order Markov models capable of predicting users' browsing behaviour.

MINING STRUCTURE OF A NEWSGROUP

This section aims at investigating the basic intuitions behind some fundamental techniques in the field of structure mining. Though inspired by the same general principles, such techniques are however applied to a novel setting: the context of Usenet news articles. This allows us to deal with the main concepts of structure mining without considering the complexities that arise in a typical Web environment.

Differences and Similarities between the Web and Usenet Environments

The Web can be considered as a hyperlinked media with no logical organization (Gibson et al., 1998). Indeed, it results from a combination of three independent stochastic processes of content creation/deletion/update evolving at various scales (Dill et al., 2001). As a consequence, even if content creators impose order on an extremely local basis, the overall structure of the Web appears chaotic (Kleinberg, 1999). In such an environment, finding information inherent to a topic of interest often becomes a challenging task. Many research efforts in the field of structure mining are conceived to discover some sort of high-level structure to be exploited as a semantic glue for thematically related pages. The idea is that if pages with homogeneous contents exhibit some structure that does not depend on the nature of the content, then some effective strategy can be devised in order to address the chaotic nature of the Web. Such an intuition is supported by evidence that, from a geometric point of view, the Web can be considered as a fractal (Dill et al., 2001): highly-hyperlinked regions of the Web exhibit the same geometrical properties as the Web at large. This suggests exploiting structure mining to address relevant problems such as that of *topic distillation,* that is, the identification of a set of pages highly relevant to a given topic. The basic idea is qualitatively the following. Given a topic of interest, the focus of the approach is on the search for a known link structure surrounding the pages relevant to that topic: this requires exploiting only an extremely limited portion of the Web as a starting point. However, since hyperlinks encode a considerable amount of latent human judgment (Kleinberg, 1999), the structure among initial pages allows the collection of most of the remaining relevant pages: what the algorithm needs to do is, in a certain sense, choose and follow the structural connections (leading from the initial pages to unexplored regions of the Web) which are indicative of contents as prominent as those within the original pages.

By contrast, traditional approaches to information discovery on the Web are negatively affected by the chaotic nature of the Web itself. This characteristic seems to make every attempt at devising an endogenous measure (of the generic Web page) to assess the relevance of a given page to a certain subject fruitless.

Usenet benefits from a number of interesting features that contribute to make it an ideal application domain for structure mining techniques. Usenet's overall structure, in fact, appears as a network of news articles, semantically organized by topic. This is mainly due to the fact that users typically post news articles inherent to a specific (more or less broad) topic. Therefore, every single user is involved in playing a crucial role in the process of keeping the overall structure of any newsgroup ordered: the destination group of a news article is already established since the early stages of the inception of the article itself. Two more elements contribute to impose order over the entire structure of a newsgroup. Firstly, the evolution of any newsgroup is based on the sole process of news article posting: no content deletion and/or update is allowed. Secondly, in contrast with what happens on the Web, the process of content management is centralized: many users post their own articles to the same recipient entity, which is only responsible for their availability through the Web.

Usenet and the Web present many significant differences. However, some similarities can be highlighted. Newsgroups are available from the Web and this implies that every news article is a Web page, characterized by a proper content and its own structure. Users browse through the news articles within each group in order to find those that are mostly of interest; this is similar to what happens on the Web, though considerable differences characterize the search space in the two cases. Article browsing is made possible by a link topology that exists within each group and among the news articles belonging to distinct groups. Such a structure consists of three different kinds of links: *group links,* which belong to the hierarchy of newsgroups and connect a news article to its own group; *explicit links,* which correspond to links within the content of an article; and *implicit links,* which can be devised in order to model a number of distinct correlations among the news articles (for instance, implicit links can depict article dependencies such as the reply-to relationship).

The peculiarities of newsgroups as well as their affinities with the Web are the basis of the intuition of applying known structure mining techniques to Usenet. If approaches based on link analysis exhibit good performances on the Web, their behaviour should be at least as interesting if applied to a newsgroup environment.

HITS Algorithm

Kleinberg (1999) proposed an effective approach, namely *HITS*, for discovering Web pages relevant to a particular topic of interest. The algorithm aims to discover *authoritative* pages, that is, pages conveying prominent information, and *hub* pages, which consist of collections of links pointing to the authorities. The intuition is that if a page is an authority, then there should be a considerable number of hub pages (scattered on the Web) pointing to that authority. A mutually reinforcing relationship keeps authoritative and hub pages together: a good hub links to many good authorities, while a good authority is linked to by many good hubs. As a consequence, given a specific topic, hub pages play a crucial role in the process of identifying relevant information. Since they should point to nearly all the authorities on that topic, hubs can be considered as a sort of glue that keeps authorities together. The notions of hub and authority and the associated mutually reinforcing relationship materialize in a precise link structure, which is independent of the topic under investigation. Figure 3(a) illustrates the geometrical structure lying behind the notions of hub and authority.

HITS can be summarized as follows. The algorithm takes as input a focused subgraph G of the Web (in which nodes correspond to pages and edges to hyperlinks among pages), and computes hubs and authorities on the basis of the intuition discussed above. Precisely, authority and hub weights are assigned to each page p in G: respectively, x_p and y_p. A limited number of iterations are required before the algorithm converges. Each iteration consists of two steps. Firstly, authority and hub weights are updated for each page in G. Then, both kinds of weights are normalized. Formally, given a page p, its associated weights are updated on the basis of the operations below:

$$x_p = \sum_{q:(q,p)\in G} y_q \qquad y_p = \sum_{q:(p,q)\in G} x_q$$

At the end of the third phase, authorities (resp. hubs) correspond to the k pages with the highest authority (resp. hub) weight.

HITS is based on the assumption that all links within a given Web page have the same weight in the process of authority conferral. This inevitably causes both pages

Figure 3. Structural Patterns Behind Hubs and Authorities

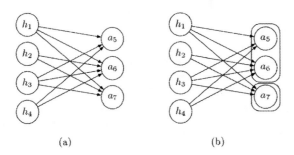

(a)   (b)

relevant to a certain topic and junk pages to receive the same amount of authority at each step. Different from the context of scientific literature, in which the process of blind review guarantees the quality of references, both Web pages and Usenet articles are generally neither critiqued nor revised. In the absence of any quality guarantee, HITS represents the simplest approach: news articles typically referred by a conspicuous number of distinct messages should be considered as authorities.

Bringing Hubs and Authorities to the Surface in the Usenet Environment

Since content homogeneity seems to depend mainly on topological properties, we claim that structure mining techniques can be profitably applied even in the restricted context of a newsgroup, provided that the latent structure among news articles is suitably reconstructed. A number of application scenarios are discussed next.

- *Finding authoritative articles.* The problem of locating articles relevant to a topic of interest can be addressed in a way that is slightly different from the original intuition behind HITS. A root set is formed by choosing (nearly) all those groups that are inherent to the specific topic. In such a scenario, both explicit and implicit links among news articles are exploited to model the conferral of authority from hubs to authorities. For instance, consider a discussion group on a generic topic *T*. A user u_i could post an article m_i containing questions about *T*. Another user u_j could reply to u_i by posting an article m_j with the required answers. m_i and m_j are tied by a reply-to relationship: (m_i, m_j) is an implicit directed link of the graph *G*, which in turn represents the overall network of dependencies among the news articles in the root set. Also, the content of m_j could include hyperlinks referring to other news articles. For any such link pointing to a destination article m_k, an explicit directed link (m_j, m_k) is added to *G*. An in-depth analysis of the resulting network of dependencies can highlight interesting (and often unexpected) structural patterns. Two interesting situations are discussed below. Firstly, a community dedicated to a given topic could include hubs from different groups, all referring to authorities in the same group. This could be due to that fraction of users who send their questioning articles to groups that are not strictly related to the article contents. Typically, replies from more experienced users could refer to the strongest authorities in the group that is the closest to the contents of the above news articles. Secondly, authorities in distinct groups could be pulled together by hubs in the same group. This could happen with topics having different meanings. If one of these meanings is overly popular with respect to the others, then its corresponding group is likely to collect even those articles concerning less popular facets of the general topic. Again, replies could show the proper authorities for such news articles.

- *Finding authoritative sites: articles as hubs.* This application aims to discover hybrid communities, that is, highly-cohesive sets of entities, where hubs correspond to news articles and authorities to Websites. Given a topic of interest, a root set is constructed as in the above case. However, only explicit links are taken into account during the process of reconstructing the link structure of the newsgroup region under investigation. The linkage patterns behind hybrid communities show strong correlations between the Usenet and the Web: precisely, contents on the latter either complement or detail information within the former. The geometrical characterization of the notion of hubs and authorities in terms of a bipartite graph structure in Figure 3(a) also applies to the Usenet environment, as far as the above two applications are concerned.

- *Authoritative people: articles as hubs.* The network of implicit links among articles is rich in information useful for finding authoritative people. Conceptually, since replies determine the introduction of implicit links into the network of news articles, any such link is indicative of an endorsement of the authority of the associated replying author. Precisely, an author who answers a considerable amount of user questions on a certain theme can be considered as an authority on that topic. Authoritative people emerge from an in-depth analysis of heterogeneous, bipartite graph structures that can be located within the overall article network. Heterogeneity depends on the intrinsic nature of these structures, where a hub is a questioning article, and an authority, instead, corresponds to a collection of replies grouped by their author (substantially, an authority is a set of nodes in the original article graph collapsed into a single entity). Figure 3(b) shows the geometrical characterization of the notion of hubs and authorities in this context. Authoritative people can be discovered at different extents: either for any subset of specified topics in the newsgroup, or taking into account all of the topics in the newsgroup itself. Both cases are useful in highlighting interesting structural patterns that are not obvious at first sight, such as those individuals who are authorities on a number of topics.

PERSONALIZATION IN USENET COMMUNITIES

Personalization can be defined as the process of tailoring the delivery of contents (or services) in a Website to address individual users' features such as their requirements, preferences, expectations, background and knowledge. It is a wide research and industrial area, which comprises notions such as *recommender systems* and *adaptive Websites.* Recommender systems are conceived to the automatic delivery of suggestions to visitors: suggested items can be information, commercial products or services. By contrast, adaptive Websites address visitors' features mainly by means of two adaptation methods (Brusilovsky, 1996): *adaptive presentation,* namely, adapting the contents in a Web page to the profile of a browsing visitor, and *adaptive navigation support,* that is, suggesting the right navigation path to each individual user on the basis of his/her browsing purposes.

From a functional point of view, Websites with personalization capabilities can be designed around the notions of *customization* and *optimization* (Perkowitz & Etzioni, 2000). Customization is adapting the content delivery of a Website to reflect the specific features of individual users; precisely, changes to the site organization (i.e., to both contents and structure) are brought about on the basis of the features of each single visitor. Optimization, on the contrary, is conceived to modify the site structure in order to improve usability.

Regarding the technologies behind personalization systems, four main categories can be identified (Mobasher et al., 2000): decision rules, content-based filtering, collaborative filtering and Web usage mining. Decision rules allow the explicit specification of how the process of content delivery can be affected by the profile of visitors. Such rules can either be inferred from user interactions with the Website or manually specified by a site administrator. Systems based on content-filtering (Lieberman, 1995) learn a model of user interests in the contents of the site by observing user navigation activities for a period of time. Then, they try to estimate visitors' interest in documents not yet viewed on the basis of some similarities between these documents and the profile to which visitors themselves belong to. Collaborative filtering systems explicitly ask for users' ratings or preferences. A correlation technique is then leveraged to match current users' data with the information already collected from previous users. A set of visitors with similar ratings is chosen and, finally, suggestions that are predicted to best adapt to current users' requirements (Konstan et al., 1997) are automatically returned.

Recently, an increasing focus has been addressed to techniques for pattern discovery from usage data. Not only does Web usage mining prove to be a fertile area for entirely new personalization techniques, but it also allows for the improvement of the overall performances of traditional approaches. For example, content-based personalization systems may fail at capturing latent correlations among distinct items in a Website. Such a limitation can be avoided by taking into account evidence from user browsing behaviour. Also, collaborative filtering can be revised in order to avoid the drawbacks due to the collection of static profiles.

PageGather Algorithm

In the following we discuss how Web usage mining techniques can be applied to the problem of providing a personalized access to Usenet communities. To this purpose, we analyse *PageGather* (Perkowitz & Etzioni, 2000), an optimization approach that achieves the goal of supporting user navigation through a given Website. PageGather is conceived to automatically create indexes for the pages in a Website. This allows visitors to directly access all the pages inherent to a given topic of interest, without having to locate them within the link structure of a Website. A visit-coherence assumption is the basis of the algorithm: the pages visited by an individual user during a navigation session tend to be conceptually related. The algorithm can be divided into three main steps.

- *Evaluation of similarities among Web pages.* For each pair of pages p_i and p_j in the Website, both the probabilities $\Pr(p_i \mid p_j)$ and $\Pr(p_j \mid p_i)$ of a user accessing a page p_i (resp. p_j), provided that he/she visited p_j (resp. p_i) in the same session, are computed. Then, the co-occurrence frequency between p_i and p_j is chosen to be the minimum of the two probabilities, in order to avoid mistaking asymmetrical relationships for true cases of similarity. A similarity matrix is finally formed, where the (i, j)-th entry is the co-occurrence frequency between p_i and p_j if there is no link between the two pages; otherwise the entry is 0. In order to reduce the effect of noise, all entries with values below a given threshold are set to 0.

- *Cluster mining.* A graph is formed from the similarity matrix. Here nodes correspond to Web pages and edges to the nonzero entries of the matrix. Two alternatives are now possible: finding either cliques or connected components. The former approach allows for the discovery of highly cohesive clusters of thematically related pages, whereas the latter is computationally faster and leads to the discovery of clusters made up of a higher number of pages.

- *Automatic creation of indexes for each group of related pages.* For each discovered cluster, an index consisting of links to each Web page in that cluster is generated. Indexes become preferred entry points for the Website: visitors only have to choose an index dealing with the topic of interest.

Usenet consists of a set of newsgroups hierarchically classified by topic. As a consequence, the process of finding interesting news articles necessarily implies a two-phase search. First, any newsgroup that deals with the required topic has to be identified. Second, trivial or uninteresting threads within each such newsgroup need to be filtered out. Such a laborious task may disorientate visitors, whose search activities may be biased by the huge number of both newsgroups and threads.

In such a context, PageGather can be profitably applied to optimize the access to Usenet news. The idea consists of providing users with a new logical organization of the threads, which captures their actual perception about the inter-thread correlations. Here, the visit-coherence assumption is made with respect to the threads. Statistical evidence, mediated on a huge number of browsing patterns, allows the finding of clusters of related threads according to the visitors' perception of logical correlations among the threads themselves. Each cluster deals with all the facets of a specific topic: it represents an overall view of the requirements, preferences and expectations of a subset of visitors. Finally, an index page could be associated to each individual cluster in order to summarize its contents and quickly access the specific facet of the corresponding topic.

Such an approach benefits from two main advantages. Firstly, a more effective categorization of Usenet contents is provided to visitors. Secondly, the technique is an optimization approach to the delivery of Usenet contents: it does not require that strategic changes are brought about to the original structure of Usenet newsgroups. Figure 4 depicts the revised version of PageGather.

Figure 4. Revised Version of PageGather for Usenet News Articles

Input: a set $S = \{s_1, ..., s_N\}$ of user sessions; a set $T = \{t_1, ..., t_M\}$ of threads; a threshold τ.

Output: a set $I = \{b_1, ..., b_K\}$ of newsgroup indexes.

Method:

– for each $s \in S$:

    • extract s_0, i.e. a chronologically ordered sequence of accesses to distinct threads;

– for each pair of threads $t_i, t_j \in T$:

    • compute the transition probabilities $\Pr(t_i \mid t_j)$ and $\Pr(t_j \mid t_i)$;

– compute a similarity matrix M such that $M(i, j) = min\{ \Pr(t_i \mid t_j), \Pr(t_j \mid t_i) \}$;

– form a graph G from all the entries of M whose value is greater than τ;

– let $C = \{c_1, ..., c_K\}$ be the set of either the cliques or the connected components found in G;

– for each index page $b \in I$:

    • for each thread $t \in c$ (where c is the cluster to which b is associated):

        ▪ add a new link referencing t to b;

CONCLUSIONS

We analysed three main lines of investigation that may contribute to providing personalized access to Usenet articles available via a Web-based interface. Current content mining techniques were applied on the management of news articles. To this purpose, we mainly studied the problem of classifying articles according to their contents. We provided an insight into techniques for tracking and profiling users in order to infer knowledge about their preferences and requirements. Our interest focused on techniques and tools for the analysis of application/server logs, comprising data cleaning and pre-processing techniques for log data and log mining techniques. Also, we modelled the events that typically happen in a Usenet scenario adopting a graph-based model, analysing the most prominent structure mining techniques, such as discovery of hubs and authorities and discovery of Web communities. We finally discussed personalization methodologies, mainly divided into optimization and customization approaches that can benefit from a synthesis of the above described techniques.

The devised Usenet scenario reveals a significant application of Web mining techniques. Also, it suggests devoting further attention and research efforts to the combination of the various Web mining techniques. Indeed, it is clear from the depicted context that the techniques proposed can influence each other, thus improving their effectiveness to the purpose of adaptive Websites.

REFERENCES

Agrawal, R., & Srikant, R. (1994). Fast algorithms for mining association rules. *Proceedings of 20th International Conference Very Large Data Bases (VLDB'94)*, 487-499.

Androutsopoulos, I., Koutsias, J., Chandrinos, K.V., & Spyropoulos, C.V. (2000). An experimental comparison of naive Bayesian and keyword-based anti-spam filtering with personal e-mail messages. *Proceedings of 23rd ACM International Conference on Research and Development in Information Retrieval* (SIGIR'00), 160-167.

Baeza-Yates, R., & Ribeiro-Neto, B. (1999). *Modern information retrieval.* ACM Press Books. Addison Wesley.

Beil, F., Ester, M., & Xu, X. (2002). Frequent term-based text clustering. *Proceedings of 8th ACM Conference on Knowledge Discovery and Data Mining* (KDD'02), 436-442.

Brusilovsky, P. (1996). Methods and techniques of adaptive hypermedia. *User Modeling and User Adapted Interaction, 6*(2-3), 87-129.

Cadez, I., Gaffney, S., & Smyth, P. (2000). A general probabilistic framework for clustering individuals and objects. *Proceedings of 6th ACM Conference on Knowledge Discovery and Data Mining* (KDD'00), 140-149.

Catledge, L., & Pitkow, J. (1995). Characterizing browsing behaviors on the World Wide Web. *Computer Networks and ISDN Systems, 27*(6), 1065-1073.

Chakrabarti, S. (2002). *Mining the Web: Discovering knowledge from hypertext data.* Morgan-Kaufmann.

Cooley, R. (2000). *Web usage mining: Discovery and application of interesting patterns from Web data.* Ph.D. thesis, University of Minnesota.

Cooley, R., Mobasher, B., & Srivastava, J. (1999). Data preparation for mining World Wide Web browsing patterns. *Knowledge and Information Systems, 1*(1), 5-32.

Dai, H., Luo, T., Mobasher, B., Sung, Y., & Zhu, J. (2000). Integrating Web usage and content mining for more effective personalization. *Proceedings of International Conference on E-Commerce and Web Technologies (ECWeb'00), 1875LNCS,* 165-176.

Deshpande, M., & Karypis, G. (2001). Selective Markov models for predicting Web-page accesses. *Proceedings of SIAM International Conference on Data Mining* (SDM'01).

Dhillon, I., & Modha, D. (2001). Concept decompositions for large sparse text data using clustering. *Machine Learning, 42*(1/2), 143-175.

Dhyani, D., Ng, W., & Bhowmick, S. (2002). A survey of Web metrics. *ACM Computing Surveys, 34*(4), 469-503.

Dill, S., Kumar, S., McCurley, K., Rajagopalan, S., Sivakumar, D., & Tomkins, A. (2001). Self-similarity in the Web. *The VLDB Journal,* 69-78.

Drucker, H., Wu, D., & Vapnik, V.N. (1999). Support vector machines for spam categorization. *IEEE Transactions on Neural Networks, 10*(5), 1048-1054.

Eirinaki, M., & Vazirgiannis, M. (2003). Web mining for personalization. *ACM Transactions on Internet Technology, 3*(1), 1-27.

Giannotti, F., Gozzi, C., & Manco, G. (2002). Clustering transactional data. *Proceedings of 6th European Conference on Principles and Practices of Knowledge Discovery in Databases* (PKDD'02), *2431LNCS,* 175–187.

Gibson, D., Kleinberg, J., & Raghavan, P. (1998). Inferring Web communities from link topology. *Proceedings of 9th ACM Conference on Hypertext and Hypermedia,* 225-234.

Guha, S., Rastogi, R., & Shim, K. (2000). ROCK: A robust clustering algorithm for categorical attributes. *Information Systems, 25*(5), 345-366.

Huang, Z. (1998). Extensions to the k-means algorithm for clustering large data sets with categorical values. *Data Mining and Knowledge Discovery, 2*(3), 283-304.

Jain, A., Murty, M., & Flynn, P. (1999). Data clustering: A review. *ACM Computing Surveys, 31*(3), 264-323.

Kleinberg, J. (1999). Authoritative sources in a hyperlinked environment. *Journal of the ACM, 46*(5), 604-632.

Konstan, J. et al. (1997). Grouplens: Applying collaborative filtering to usenet news. *Communications of the ACM, 40*(3), 77-87.

Kosala, R., & Blockeel, H. (2000). Web mining research: A survey. *SIGKDD Explorations, 2*(1), 1-15.

Lieberman, H. (1995). Letizia: An agent that assists Web browsing. *Proceedings of 14th International Joint Conference on Artificial Intelligence* (IJCAI'95), 924–929.

Manco, G., Masciari, E., & Tagarelli, A. (2002). A framework for adaptive mail classification. *Proceedings of 14th IEEE International Conference on Tools with Artificial Intelligence* (ICTAI'02), 387-392.

Mobasher, B., Cooley, R., & Srivastava, J. (2000). Automatic personalization based on Web usage mining. *Communications of the ACM, 43,* 142-151.

Mobasher, B., Dai, H., Luo, T., & Nakagawa, M. (2001). Effective personalization based on association rule discovery from Web usage data. *Proceedings of 3rd International Workshop on Web Information and Data Management* (WIDM'01), 9-15.

Mobasher, B., Dai, H., Luo, T., & Nakagawa, M. (2002a). Discovery and evaluation of aggregate usage profiles for Web personalization. *Data Mining and Knowledge Discovery, 6*(1), 61-82.

Mobasher, B., Dai, H., Luo, T., & Nakagawa, M. (2002b). Using sequential and nonsequential patterns for predictive Web usage mining tasks. *Proceedings of IEEE International Conference on Data Mining* (ICDM'02), 669-672.

Moens, M. (2000). *Automatic indexing and abstracting of document texts.* Kluwer Academic Publishers.

Perkowitz, M., & Etzioni, O. (2000). Towards adaptive Web sites: Conceptual framework and case study. *Artificial Intelligence, 118*(1-2), 245-275.

Pirolli, P., Pitkow, J., & Rao, R. (1996). Silk from a sow's ear: Extracting usable structures from the Web. *Proceedings of ACM Conference Human Factors in Computing Systems* (CHI'96), 118-125.

Srivastava, J., Cooley, R., Deshpande, M., & Tan, P. (2000). Web usage mining: Discovery and applications of Web usage patterns from Web data. *SIGKDD Explorations, 1*(2), 12-23.

Steinbach, M., Karypis, G., & Kumar, V. (2000). A comparison of document clustering techniques. *Proceedings of ACM SIGKDD Workshop on Text Mining.*

Strehl, A., Ghosh, J., & Mooney, R. (2000). Impact of similarity measures on Web-page clustering. *Proceedings of AAAI Workshop on Artificial Intelligence for Web Search,* 58-64.

About the Authors

Anthony Scime received the Doctor of Arts in 1997 from George Mason University with an interdisciplinary focus in Information Systems and Education. Currently, he is at the Computer Science Department of the State University of New York College at Brockport (USA), where he teaches courses in systems analysis and design, project management, and computer system organization. Prior to joining academia, he spent more than 20 years in industry and government applying information systems to solve large-scale problems. Dr. Scime is an internationally registered technology specialist (IR7) in the fields of information systems and knowledge management, and has been listed in the International Who's Who of Information Technology. His research interests include the World Wide Web as an information system and database, information retrieval, knowledge creation and management, decision making from information, and computing education.

*   *   *

Ricardo Baeza-Yates started his electrical engineering studies at the University of Chile in 1979, finishing with the BSc and MSc degrees and the award "Marcos Orrego Puelma" given by the Institute of Engineers of Chile to the best student each year. He finished his PhD studies at the University of Waterloo, Canada (1989). He held a post-doctoral fellowship for 6 months before returning to the Department of Computer Science at the University of Chile. He is a recipient of the Organization of American States (OAS) prize for young researchers in science; an award from the Institute of Engineers of Chile for the best 5-year engineering research trajectory; the Compaq Prize to the best Brazilian research article in basic CS with Eduardo Barbosa and Nivio Ziviani; and a grant from the Chilean government to launch the Center of Web Research. He has been president of the Chilean Computer Science Society (SCCC); chairman of the CS Department at the

University of Chile; in charge of the IEEE-CS chapter in Chile; and has been involved in the South American ACM Programming Contest; a member of the IEEE CS Board of Governors; president of CLEI, a Latin American association of CS departments, and coordinates the Iberoamerican cooperation program (CYTED) in Electronics and Informatics. His research interests include information retrieval, algorithms, and information visualization. He is co-author with Berthier Ribeiro-Neto of *Modern Information Retrieval* (1999, Addison-Wesley); co-author with Gaston Gonnet of the *Handbook of Algorithms and Data Structures* (second edition, 1991, Addison-Wesley); and co-editor with Bill Frakes of *Information Retrieval: Algorithms and Data Structures* (1992, Prentice-Hall), among other publications. He has been visiting professor or invited speaker at several conferences and universities, as well as referee of many journals, conferences, and for the NSF. He is member of the ACM, AMS, EATCS, IEEE-CS (senior member), SCCC and SIAM.

Juan A. Botía received a BEng in Computer Science and a PhD in Computer Science from the University of Murcia in Murcia, Spain (1996 and 2002, respectively). From 1996 to 1997, he was a senior engineer with Tecnatom, S.A., Madrid, Spain. From 1997 to 1999, he was also an associate professor at the University of Alcala, Alcala de Henares, Spain. In 1999, he joined the Department of Information Engineering and Communications, University of Murcia, where he is currently a full time assistant professor. His main research interests include multi-agent systems and ambient intelligence.

Zhixiang Chen received his PhD in Computer Science from Boston University (January 1996). He is currently an associate professor in the Department of Computer Science at the University of Texas – Pan American (USA). He taught at Southwest State University from fall of 1995 to September 1997. He also worked and studied at the University of Illinois and Huazhong University of Science and Technology. His research interests include intelligent Web search, machine learning, informational retrieval, data mining, Web mining, artificial intelligence, algorithms, and complexity theory. He has taught a wide range of computer science courses, and published about 80 papers in refereed journals and conference proceedings. He is the associate director for research at the Computing and Info Tech Center (CITec) at UTPA.

Honghua Dai is currently a software developer at Microsoft Corporation, working as part of the MSN Messenger team. She is also a PhD student at DePaul University, School of Computer Science, Telecommunication and Information Systems, and a researcher at the Center for Web Intelligence. Her research areas include Web data mining, Web personalization, semantic Web, and information retrieval. She has published several papers on integrating semantic knowledge and ontologies with Web usage mining for more effective personalization. Prior to joining DePaul, she received her BS in Computer Science from Shanghai JiaoTong University, and worked in the computer industry for 3 years as a software developer.

Richard H. Fowler is a professor in the Department of Computer Science at the University of Texas - Pan American (USA) and director of the University's Computing and Information Technology Center. He received a PhD in Psychology from the University of Houston and an MS in Computer Science from New Mexico State University. His primary research interests are in cognitive science and center on information visualization and interactive systems generally. Other projects are concerned with Internet-based hypertext systems and data mining.

Alex A. Freitas received a BSc in Computer Science from the Faculdade de Tecnologia de Sao Paulo, Brazil (1989); an MSc in Computer Science from the Universidade Federal de Sao Carlos, Brazil (1993); and a PhD in Computer Science from the University of Essex, UK (1997). He was a visiting lecturer at the Centro Federal de Educacao Tecnologica, in Curitiba, Brazil (1997-1998) and a lecturer at the Pontificia Universidade Catolica, also in Curitiba, Brazil (1999-2002). Since 2002, he has been a lecturer at the University of Kent, in Canterbury, UK. His publications include two books on data mining and more than 60 refereed research papers published in journals, books, conferences or workshops. He has organized two international workshops on data mining with evolutionary algorithms, and delivered tutorials on this theme in several international conferences. He is a member of the editorial board of *Intelligent Data Analysis* — an international journal. At present his main research interests are data mining and evolutionary algorithms.

Ada Wai-Chee Fu is an associate professor in the Department of Computer Science and Engineering, The Chinese University of Hong Kong, Hong Kong. She received her BSc in Computer Science from the Chinese University of Hong Kong (1983), and both MSc and PhD degrees in Computer Science from Simon Fraser University of Canada (1986 and 1990, respectively). She worked at Bell Northern Research in Ottawa, Canada (1989-1993) on a wide-area distributed database project, and joined the Chinese University of Hong Kong in 1993. Her research interests include distributed databases, replicated data, data mining, content-based retrieval in multimedia databases, and parallel and distributed systems.

Lixin Fu is an assistant professor at the Department of Mathematical Sciences, University of North Carolina at Greensboro (USA). He has been working there since 2001. Dr. Fu earned his PhD in Computer and Information Science at the University of Florida (2001). He got his master's degree in Electrical Engineering at Georgia Institute of Technology (1998) and his bachelor's degree in Mathematics at Wuhan University, China (1988). Dr. Fu's research interests include databases, data warehousing, data mining, and algorithms. Dr. Fu is an IEEE and ACM member. He is a program committee member for CIKM '03.

Katsuhiko Gondow is an associate professor in Tokyo Institute of Technology (Japan), where he received his BE, ME and PhD degrees (1989, 1991 and 1994, respectively). His research interest is in the field of software development environments.

Mohamed Salah Hamdi was born on April 1, 1967, in Sidi Bouzid, Tunisia. He received a Diploma degree ("Diplom-Informatiker Univ.") in Computer Science from the Technical University of Munich, Germany (1993) and a PhD (Dr. rer. nat.) in Computer Science from the University of Hamburg, Germany (1999). From 1994 to 1999, he was a lecturer in the Department of Computer Science of the University of Hamburg, Germany. In September 1999, he joined the National Institute of Applied Sciences and Technology of the University of Tunis, Tunisia, as an assistant professor. Since September 2001, he has been working as an assistant professor in the Department of Mathematics and Computer Science of the United Arab Emirates University in Al Ain. His research interests are focused on intelligent autonomous agents and machine learning and on artificial intelligence in general.

Juan M. Hernansáez received a BEng in Computer Science from the University of Murcia, Murcia, Spain (2002). Currently he is a PhD candidate at the Department of Information Engineering and Telecommunications of the University of Murcia. His main research interests include Web mining and multi-agent systems.

Ching-Chi Hsu received a BS in Physics from National Tsing Hua University, Hsinchu, Taiwan (1971), and both an MS and PhD in Computer Engineering from the Department of Electric Engineering, National Taiwan University, Taipei, Taiwan (1975 and 1982, respectively). In 1977, he joined the faculty of the Department of Computer Science and Information Engineering at National Taiwan University and became a professor in 1987. From 1984 to 1985, he was a visiting scholar of the Department of Computer Science, Stanford University. From 1997 to 2001, he was department head of his department. His research interests include distributed systems, distributed processing of data and knowledge, Internet, and intelligent systems.

Xiaodi Huang received his BSc in Physics in 1989, and his MPhil in Computer Applications in 1992. He is currently completing his PhD studies in the School of Information Technology at Swinburne University of Technology. He is also a lecturer in the Department of Mathematics and Computing, the University of Southern Queensland, Australia. His research areas include information visualization, information retrieval, software engineering, and multimedia applications. He has published numerous papers and book chapters.

Bernard J. Jansen is an assistant professor at the School of Information Sciences and Technology at the Pennsylvania State University (USA). Dr. Jansen has more than 40 publications in the area of information technology and systems. His articles appear in journals such as the *Communications of the ACM, IEEE Computer, ACM Transactions on Information Systems, Information Processing and Management,* and *Journal of the American Society of Information Science and Technology,* among others. Dr. Jansen's recently coauthored paper in *IEEE Computer,* analyzing a 4-year trend in how users search the Web, generated press coverage in over 100 news organizations worldwide, including wire services, cable and network television, radio, newspapers, and commercial Web sites. He has received several awards and honors, including an ACM Research Award, six application development awards, along with other writing, publishing, research, and leadership awards.

Takuya Katayama is a professor at Japan Advanced Institute of Science and Technology. He received his PhD from Tokyo Institute of Technology (TIT) (1971). He worked at the Department of Computer Science, TIT, as associate professor from 1974 to 1985, and professor beginning 1985. Professor Katayama joined Japan Advanced Institute of Science and Technology (JAIST) in 1991. He is working on formal aspects of software engineering.

Yasser Kotb received his PhD from Japan Advanced Institute of Science and Technology (JAIST) (2003). He received his BS and MS degrees in Computer Science from Ain Shams University (1991 and 1997, respectively). He has been working at the Department of Mathematics and Computer Science, Faculty of Science, Ain Shams University, as associate lecturer since 1991. He is now doing research on XML technologies, attribute grammars and semantics Web. He is a member of IEEE.

Wei Lai received a PhD in Computer Science from the University of Newcastle, Australia. His research areas include information visualization software engineering, software visualization image recognition and processing, and Internet and Web applications. He has authored or co-authored more than 50 papers in these areas. He serves on the program committees of several conferences

Gilbert W. Laware is an associate professor with Purdue University, School of Technology, in the South Bend, Indiana. With more than 30 years in IT, he brings a thorough understanding and breadth of experience in several industries, including project management, systems integration, systems development life cycle methodologies, enterprise architecture, data management and Web development. Gil's professional career included employment with IBM, Whirlpool, and DMR Consulting Group, where he specialized in software development, database, and data warehousing applications. He has served on the international board of directors for the Data Administration Management Association (DAMA), and is a member of the professional associations IRMA, IEEE, and Society for Information Technology Education (SITE).

Ee-Peng Lim is an associate professor at the School of Computer Engineering, Nanyang Technological University. He received his PhD from the University of Minnesota, Minneapolis (1994). He conducts research in Web warehousing, digital libraries, and database integration. His papers have appeared in *ACM Transactions on Information Systems* (TOIS), *IEEE Transactions on Knowledge and Data Engineering* (TKDE), *Decision Support Systems* (DSS), and other major journals. He is currently an associate editor of the *ACM Transactions on Information Systems* (TOIS). He is also a member of the editorial review board of the *Journal of Database Management* (JDM). He is a senior member of IEEE and a member of ACM.

Giuseppe Manco is currently senior researcher at the Institute for High Performance Computing and Networks (ICAR-CNR) of the National Research Council of Italy, and contract professor at University of Calabria, Italy. He holds a Laurea degree in Computer Science and a PhD in Computer Science from the University of Pisa. He has been contract researcher at the CNUCE Institute in Pisa, Italy, and visiting fellow at the CWI Institute in Amsterdam, Nederland. His current research interests include deductive databases, knowledge discovery and data mining, Web databases and semistructured data management.

Penelope Markellou has an MSc in Computer Science, in the area of designing and evaluating e-business systems. She is working in the Computer Engineering and Informatics Department of the University of Patras and as a researcher in the Internet and Multimedia Technologies Research Unit of the Research Academic Computer Technology Institute. Her research areas include personalization techniques in e-business and e-learning systems and the Web mining field. She has published several research papers and is co-author of the books *Multimedia and Networks, Usability Models for eCommerce Applications* and *eBusiness* (all available in Greek).

Xiannong Meng received his PhD in Computer Science from Worcester Polytechnic Institute (May 1990). He is currently an associate professor in the Department of Computer Science of Bucknell University (USA). He also taught and worked at University of Texas – Pan American, Worcester Polytechnic Institute and Nanjing Institute of Technology (now Southeast University). His research interests include intelligent Web search, information retrieval, distributed computer systems, computer networks and operating systems. He has taught a wide range of computer science courses, and published over 40 papers in refereed journals and conference proceedings.

Bamshad Mobasher is an associate professor of Computer Science and director of the Center for Web Intelligence at DePaul University in Chicago (USA). His research areas include Web data mining, intelligent Web agents, multi-agent systems, and reasoning with uncertainty in knowledge-based systems. He has published more than 50 papers and articles in these and other areas. As director of the Center for Web Intelligence, Dr. Mobasher is directing research in Web usage mining and automatic personalization, as well as overseeing several joint projects with the industry. He regularly conducts seminars and delivers presentations to a variety of companies and organizations involved with Web usage and e-commerce data analysis. Dr. Mobasher has served as an organizer and on the program committees of numerous conferences and workshops in the areas of Web data mining, artificial intelligence, and autonomous agents. Most recently, he has organized a series of workshops on intelligent techniques for Web personalization at the International Joint Conference on Artificial Intelligence, and two tutorials, "KDD for Personalization" and "Web Usage Mining for E-Business Applications" at the European Conference on Principles and Practice of Knowledge Discovery in Databases.

Roberto Navigli is a research fellow in the Department of Computer Science at the University of Rome, "La Sapienza", Italy. His research interests include natural language processing, ontology learning, knowledge representation and their applications to the semantic Web. He received his Laurea degree in Computer Science from "La Sapienza" (2001).

Wee-Keong Ng is an associate professor with the School of Computer Engineering at the Nanyang Technological University, Singapore. He is also director of the Centre of Advanced Information Systems that is affiliated with the School of Computer Engineering. He obtained his MSc and PhD degrees from the University of Michigan, Ann Arbor (1994 and 1996, respectively). He works and publishes widely in the areas of Web warehousing, information extraction, electronic commerce and data mining. He has organized and chaired international workshops, held tutorials, and has actively served in the program committees of numerous international conferences. He is a member of the ACM and IEEE Computer Society.

Riccardo Ortale holds a Laurea degree (University of Calabria, 2001) in Computer Engineering and a master's degree in Internet Software Design (Politecnico di Milano, Cefriel, Siemens SBS 2001). Currently, he is a PhD student at the University of Calabria. His research interests include knowledge discovery in databases and data mining; Web databases; adaptive Web sites and personalization/profiling Web systems.

Maria Rigou has an MSc in Computer Science, in the field of interactive systems evaluation. She is currently working as a researcher (PhD student) at the Computer Engineering and Informatics Department of the University of Patras, and also at the Internet and Multimedia Technologies Research Unit of the Research Academic Computer Technology Institute. She is currently working on personalization techniques and the use of Web usage mining in adapting Web site content and structure, and has several publications in the domain of Web mining and its applications in e-commerce, and e-learning, as well as the formation and behavior of online communities.

Neil C. Rowe is professor and associate chair of Computer Science at the US Naval Postgraduate School, where he has been since 1983. He has a PhD in Computer Science from Stanford University (1983), and EE (1978), SM (1978), and SB (1975) degrees from the Massachusetts Institute of Technology (MIT). His main research interest is intelligent access to multimedia databases. He has also done work on information security, image processing, robotic path planning, and intelligent tutoring systems.

Andrew Secker received a first class BSc with honors in Computer Science from the University of Kent, UK (2002). He is currently a PhD student at the University of Kent working under the supervision or Dr. Alex Freitas and Dr. Jon Timmis. Andrew's research interests are in population-based and biologically inspired systems. The working title for his PhD is "An Artificial Immune System for Web Mining".

Spiros Sirmakessis is an assistant professor in the Technological Education Institute of Messolongi and manager of the Internet and Multimedia Technologies Research Unit of the Research Academic Computer Technology Institute *(http://www.cti.gr)*. He is the coordinator of the NEMIS project *(http://nemis.cti.gr)*, a network of excellence in text mining and responsible for the Web mining working group. He is the editor of the book *Text Mining and Applications* (2003, Springer Verlag) and author of three books and several research papers published in international journals and conferences.

Antonio F.G. Skarmeta received an MS in Computer Science from the University of Granada and BS (Hons.) and the PhD degrees in Computer Science from the University of Murcia, Spain. Since 1993, he has been a professor in the same department and University. Dr. Skarmeta has worked on different research projects in the national environment either in the distributed artificial intelligence field or in tele-learning and computer support for collaborative work. In addition, he has also been involved in several R&D projects funded by the Spanish Research and Development programs. He was also coordinator of a Socrates CDA (European Master on Soft Computing) and a Leonardo project for Distance and Open Learning. He is currently collaborating in two IST projects related to tele-teaching and distance learning. Additionally, he is currently collaborating in two IST projects related to IPv6 Euro6IX and 6Power, in which several advanced services like multicast, multihoming, security and adaptive multimedia applications are being deployed in IPv6 networks. He has published over 50 international papers.

Amanda Spink is associate professor at the School of Information Sciences at the University of Pittsburgh (USA). She has a BA (Australian National University); Graduate Diploma of Librarianship (University of New South Wales); MBA (Fordham University), and PhD in Information Science (Rutgers University). Dr. Spink's research focuses on theoretical and applied studies of human information behavior and interactive information retrieval (IR), including Web and digital libraries studies. The National Science Foundation, Andrew R. Mellon Foundation, NEC, IBM, Excite, FAST and Lockheed Martin have sponsored her research. She has published over 180 journal articles and conference papers, with many in the *Journal of the American Society for Information Science and Technology, Information Processing and Management, Interacting with Computers, IEEE Computer, Internet Research,* the *ASIST* and *ISIC Conferences.*

Andrea Tagarelli is currently a PhD student in Computer Engineering at the Department of Electronics, Computer Science and Systems Science of the University of Calabria, Italy. He received a Laurea degree in Computer Engineering from the University of Calabria. His research activity is mainly concerned with knowledge discovery and data mining, Web databases and semistructured data management.

Mike Thelwall is head of the Statistical Cybermetrics Research Group in the School of Computing at the University of Wolverhampton, UK, and heads Wolverhampton's contribution to the European Union-funded WISER project *(http:// www.webindicators.org).* He obtained his PhD in Pure Math at the University of Lancaster, UK. His research interests are in the application of link analysis in a variety of contexts, from computer science to information science. He is on the editorial board of two journals and has published over 50 journal articles.

Jon Timmis is a lecturer in Computer Science at the University of Kent and is head of the Applied and Interdisciplinary Informatics Research Group. He received his PhD in Computer Science from the University of Wales, Aberystwyth, where he worked as a research associate investigating the use of immune system metaphors for machine learning. Dr. Timmis is principal investigator for a number of industrial and government funded research projects. He has served on several program committees for artificial immune systems at international conferences and has given a number of invited talks on artificial immune systems at UK and international universities. He has published over 35 papers on artificial immune system related research and is the co-author of the first book on artificial immune systems. He was the conference co-chair with Dr. Peter Bentley for the two International Conferences on Artificial Immune Systems (ICARIS) and continues to be the co-chair for the Third ICARIS in 2004. He is a member of the IEEE and a member of ISGEC (International Society of Genetic and Evolutionary Computation).

Chunyue Wang is a graduate student in the Department of Computer Science at the University of Texas – Pan American. Her research interests are data mining, Web mining, and Web-based database systems.

Yew-Kwong Woon received his BSc in Computer Engineering with first-class honors from the Nanyang Technological University (2001). He is currently pursuing a PhD in Computer Engineering at the Nanyang Technological University. His research interests include association rule mining, clustering, Web usage mining and bioinformatics. He has published papers in *IEEE Transactions on Knowledge and Data Engineering (TKDE)*, the *ACM Conference on Information and Knowledge Management (CIKM)*, the *International Conference on Web Information Systems Engineering (WISE)* and the *International Conference on Data Warehousing and Knowledge Discovery (DAWAK)*.

Fan Wu received his BSCS and MSCS from National Chiao Tung University and National Tsing Hua University, Hsinchu, Taiwan (1989 and 1991, respectively). In 1998, he received a PhD from the Department of Computer Science and Information Engineering, National Taiwan University, Taipei, Taiwan. Currently, he is an assistant professor in the Department of Management of Information Systems at National Chung Cheng University, Chia-Yi, Taiwan. His research interests include Internet, database systems and parallel architecture and processing.

Index